THE   INCONSTANT   SAVAGE

Medicine man of Roanoke, North Carolina, 1585. Watercolour by John White.
Reproduced by permission of the British Museum.

THE INCONSTANT SAVAGE

England and the North American Indian
1500-1660

H.C. Porter

Duckworth

First published in 1979 by
Gerald Duckworth & Co. Ltd.
43 Gloucester Crescent, London NW1.

Distributed in the USA by
Southwest Book Services Inc
4951 Top Line Drive
Dallas, Texas 75247

ISBN 0 7156 0968 8

Filmset by
Specialised Offset Services Ltd., Liverpool
and printed in Great Britain by
Redwood Burn Limited, Trowbridge and Esher

In Memory Of
Philip Seaman
1953–1978

Contents

Preface

The academic year 1956-7 I spent at Princeton as the Procter Visiting
Fellow from Cambridge. I was fortunate to come under the care of
Professor Wesley Frank Craven, and to attend his graduate seminar,
and audit his undergraduate lectures on American Colonial History.
At Professor Craven's suggestion, I prepared an essay springing from
my Cambridge PhD research on Elizabethan Cambridge, but
involving new (to me) colonial material. This essay, 'Alexander
Whitaker: Cambridge Apostle to Virginia', was published by the
William and Mary Quarterly in July 1957. Thereafter I taught at Toronto
for two years, and then for one year at the University of California at
Berkeley (where I first encountered Drake's Plate of Brass). I returned
to Cambridge in 1960, and became involved in other things. However,
in 1967 I was given a Visiting Fellowship by the Folger Shakespeare
Library, Washington DC, and spent the summer there. Here the
material for this book was basically prepared, under the eye of the
then Director, Louis B. Wright.

So in the United States I owe most to Frank Craven, and much to
Louis Wright.

In England, I am most grateful to Professor David Quinn of
Liverpool, who found time to read the whole of the manuscript;
making many corrections, improvements and suggestions; and
lending me books and offprints. I could not, of course, have had a
better adviser. I was fortunate enough to catch Professor J.H. Elliott
on a visit to Cambridge from Princeton in 1974; and he was persuaded
to read the three chapters with Spanish material, saving me from
many errors. For the two chapters on the Bible (and indeed
throughout) I needed informed theological advice. This has been
given by the Reverend John Sweet, Chaplain of Selwyn College,
Cambridge; who read those two chapters, and has for some time
patiently endured a stream of enquiries from an ill-informed and
sceptical layman.

So my thanks must be recorded to those three generous British
experts.

My manuscript was completed before the publication, late in 1974,
of the late S.E. Morison's *The Southern Voyages, 1492-1616* (Volume II of
his marvellous *The European Discovery of America*). Morison has material
on Drake in California (663-89) – he favours Drake's Bay as the site
and considers the Brass Plate a fake. (The Brass Plate, in the custody

of the University of California since 1937, was declared authentic after chemical study in 1938. More recent chemical analysis, described in a report by Helen V. Michel and Frank Asaro of Berkely, issued in July 1977, suggests that the Plate was probably manufactured in the late nineteenth or early twentieth century.)

Vespucci, Morison argues, was a member of a 1499 Spanish voyage, under Alonso de Ojeda, to Guiana and Venezuela; and of two Portuguese expeditions to Brazil (1501-2, 1503-4). Some members of the last expedition were left behind at Cape Frio, 100 miles east of Rio; as we shall see (below, p. 14) they included Raphael Hythloday. Thus, it is maintained, Vespucci's alleged voyage of 1497 (in which he landed on the mainland one year before Columbus) was a fabrication. (His account of it was based on the 1499 material.) Morison says (p. 306) that by 1515 people in England like Sebasian Cabot were suspicious of the 'first' Vespucci voyage. One reason, perhaps, why Thomas More tells us that Raphael had not been on the 1497 voyage, but only on the other three.

Five relevant books were published in the United States in the second half of 1975, and reached me after my manuscript had left my hands.

Honour, Hugh. *The New Golden Land: European Images of America from the Discoveries to the Present Time.*

Jennings, Francis. *The Invasion of America: Indians, Colonialism and the Cant of Conquest.*

Morgan, Edmund S. *American Slavery, American Freedom: The Ordeal of Colonial Virginia.*

Vaughan, Alden T. *American Genesis: Captain John Smith and the Founding of Virginia* (Library of American Biography).

Washburn, Wilcomb E. *The Indian in America* (New American Nation series).

My review of Francis Jennings' book appeared in the October 1977 number of *History*. Alden Vaughan published in the January 1978 *William and Mary Quarterly* an article on 'English Policy and the Virginia Massacre of 1622'. The English translation of essays by Mario Góngora, *Studies in the Colonial History of Spanish America* (1975) has relevant material; so does J.A. Fernández-Santamaria's *The State, War and Peace: Spanish Political Thought in the Renaissance, 1516-1559* (1977). Three volumes concerning Las Casas were published together in the United States in 1974: an English translation of Las Casas' *Defence of the Indians* (his reworking of his arguments at the 1550 Valladolid Disputation); a study of that disputation by Lewis Hanke (*All Mankind is One*); and a volume of essays, *Las Casas in History*, edited by J. Friede and B. Keen. *First Images of America: The Impact of the New World on the Old*, a collection of essays in two volumes, edited by Fredi Chiappelli, is the product of a conference in February 1975 at the University of California, Los Angeles.

Among the books I should have known about but didn't is John Parker's valuable *Books to Build an Empire: A Bibliographical History of*

English Overseas Interests to 1620 (1965.) The chapter on Richard Eden is a particularly welcome contribution to Tudor studies.

I have no pretensions to 'Ethnohistory' – for the development of which discipline see James Axtell's review essay 'The Ethnohistory of Early America' in the January 1978 *William and Mary Quarterly*. My subject is not Indian-European contact, but the reactions of Englishmen to that contact. My intention has been to present descriptions of the Indian and of Virginia by Tudor and Stuart observers, and to illustrate English thinking about Indians, and about the North American (particularly the Virginian) experience. This book, therefore, should be regarded as a contribution to the study of sixteenth- and seventeenth-century English thought, religion and literature.

In my footnotes, books and authors have usually been cited in the briefest form; for fuller details, the reader is referred to the Bibliography.

Faculty of History,   H.C.P.
West Road, Cambridge.
Spring 1978

Prologue

1611: 'The Tempest'

The Tempest, probably the last complete play Shakespeare wrote, was performed before the King and Court in the Banqueting House at Whitehall in November 1611. This may not have been the first performance; and it is possible that the text was later modified for masque presentation. In the First Folio of 1623 *The Tempest* came first, heading the 'Comedies'.[1]

The play was written for an audience eager to think, in the words of Antonio, that 'travellers ne'er did lie'. When 'we were boys', comments Gonzalo,

> Who would believe that there were mountaineers,
> Dew-lapp'd, like bulls, whose throats had hanging at 'em
> Wallets of flesh? or that there were such men
> Whose heads stood in their breasts?

Trinculo tells us that in England 'when they will not give a doit to relieve a lame beggar, they will lay out ten to see a dead Indian'.

'The Scene, an uninhabited Island': between Naples and Tunis. Prospero has been on the island for twelve years. He had been deprived of the Dukedom of Milan: by his brother Antonio, in collusion with Alonso, King of Naples, and Alonso's brother Sebastian. In Antonio, says Prospero, an 'evil nature' had awakened. Prospero's trust in him

> did beget of him
> A falsehood in its contrary, as great
> As my trust was.

Antonio later gives one of the advantages of Power:

[1] I follow the punctuation of the First Folio and the spelling of the Arden Shakespeare, edited by Frank Kermode, 1954. Kermode's introduction discusses the New World background, and the use of sources. For sources, see below Chapter 7, pp.144-45, and Chapter 14, pp.305-8. For Shakespeare and the travel literature: R.R. Cawley, *Publications Modern Language Association America*, September 1926, XLI, 3, 688-726; James, *Dream of Prospero*, 1967. A relevant and recommended essay is by Philip Brockbank, ' "The Tempest": Conventions of Art and Empire', in Brown and Harris, eds., *Later Shakespeare*, 1966.

I am very grateful to Charles Maude of Corpus Christi College Cambridge for his advice about this chapter.

>   my brother's servants
>   Were then my fellows, now they are my men.

Prospero was set adrift in a leaky boat. Fortunately Gonzalo, 'an honest old Councellor', provided food, water, 'rich garments, linens, stuffs and necessaries'; and books from the ducal library. Prospero's daughter Miranda went with him. She was then three; and is thus fifteen at the time of the play. By 'providence divine' the two reached the island. Prospero there found Ariel, an 'airy spirit', not human, confined in a 'cloven pine'. He had been in that 'torment' for twelve years; placed there by Sycorax, an exile from (apparently) Algiers, who was dead by the time of the landing of Prospero. Sycorax was a 'foul witch', pregnant by an incubus, banished to the island

>   For mischiefs manifold, and sorceries terrible
>   To enter human hearing.

Ariel became her 'servant'; but was

>   a spirit too delicate
>   To act her earthy, and abhorr'd commands.

Thus the imprisonment in the tree. Ariel becomes the 'slave' of Prospero. Prospero promised Ariel 'liberty': to 'bate me a full year' of service. That promise has not yet been performed: as Ariel reminds Prospero in Act I, scene 2.

Sycorax's child, Caliban, was presumably born soon after she was deposited on the island. So Caliban is now about 24.

A Neapolitan fleet approaches the island; and is battered by a tempest produced by Prospero, and directed by Ariel. Prospero is interested only in the royal flagship: bearing Antonio, Alonso and Sebastian; Gonzalo; Alonso's son Ferdinand; Stephano, a 'drunken butler'; and Trinculo, a 'jester'. The other vessels in the fleet escape from the storm, and head back to Naples. The royal ship, abandoned by the passengers (but not the crew) 'nigh shore', has been brought by Ariel safely to harbour:

>   in the deep nook, where once
>   Thou call'dst me up at midnight to fetch dew
>   From the still-vexed Bermoothes.

(That is, the Bermudas.) 'Not a hair perish'd': the mariners remain aboard, in a deep sleep; the passengers have been cast on shore.

The Tempest demonstrates variations on themes presented by a 'brave new world'. One theme is that of rightful title and possession. Both Prospero and Caliban have been deprived of territory they occupy; Prospero of his Dukedom, and Caliban of the island.

>   This island's mine by Sycorax my mother,
>   Whichthou tak'st from me.

Being born on the island, Caliban is technically a second-generation immigrant; and until Prospero came, was the island's sole human inhabitant. When Ferdinand appears, Prospero feigns to wonder whether the young man

> hast put thyself
> Upon this island, as a spy, to win it
> From me, the Lord on't.

'There's nothing ill can dwell in such a temple', comments Miranda. Could 'goodly' Ferdinand have an 'ill spirit'? (Can Caliban, 'capable of all ill', take 'any print of goodness'?)

Another theme is, the potentialities of settlement in a new world. Gonzalo outlines his proposed policy: 'Had I plantation of this isle.' (As we shall see in Chapter 7, Gonzalo is basing his programme on Montaigne, in the 1603 translation by John Florio.)

> I' th' commonwealth I would by contraries[2]
> Execute all things: For no kind of traffic
> Would I admit: No name of magistrate:
> Letters should not be known: Riches, poverty,
> Bourn, bound of land, tilth, vineyard none:
> No use of metal, corn, or wine, or oil:
> No occupation, all men idle, all:
> And women too, but innocent and pure:
> No sovereignty.[3]

A slight interruption. Then:

> All things in common Nature should produce
> Without sweat or endeavour: Treason, felony,
> Sword, pike, knife, gun, or need of any engine
> Would I not have: but Nature should bring forth
> Of it own kind, all foison, all abundance
> To feed my innocent people.[4]

Another interruption. The conclusion:

> I would with such perfection govern Sir:
> T' excel the Golden Age.

The island, we are told by Ariel, is 'most desolate'; 'bare', according to Prospero. When the group of shipwrecked Europeans enters, one of them – Adrian: a Lord – indulges in a verbal puzzle: 'Though this island seem to be desert': 'Uninhabitable, and almost inaccessible' – yet it 'must needs be of subtle, tender, and delicate temperance'. 'The

[2] Contrary to the usual custom.
[3] Traffic: business. Service: servants. Succession: inheritance of property. Bourn: limits of property. Tilth: tillage.
[4] Engine: weapon. Foison: abundance.

air breathes upon us here most sweetly,' says Adrian; like a rotten fen, retort Antonio (the usurper) and Sebastian. The philosophical Gonzalo: 'Here is every thing advantageous to life.' True, comments Antonio, 'save means to live'. The grass, says Gonzalo, is green, 'lush and lusty'. 'Tawny,' asserts Antonio. 'He misses not much,' says Antonio of Gonzalo: No, Sebastian comments, 'he doth but mistake the truth totally'. Later Gonzalo, seeing the 'strange shapes' he takes to be 'people of the island' bringing in a basket, dancing 'with gentle actions of salutations' and inviting the Europeans to eat, comments:

> Who though they are of monstrous shape, yet note
> Their manners are more gentle, kind, than of
> Our human generation you shall find
> Many, nay almost any.

Prospero, invisible, agrees:

> Honest Lord,
> Thou hast said well: for some of you there present;
> Are worse than devils.

Caliban is described in the 'names of the actors' as 'a salvage and deformed slave'.[5] On first seeing him, Stephano (the drunkard) says: 'Have we devils here? Do you put tricks upon's with salvages and men of Inde?' Although worried by the fact that Caliban speaks English, Stephano assumes he is 'some monster of the isle with four legs'. The clown Trinculo, in the same scene, wonders (because of the smell) whether Caliban is 'a man or a fish': but perceives that 'this is no fish, but an islander'. Prospero describes Caliban as, 'in his shape', 'disproportioned', 'mis-shapen'. He was a 'freckled whelp'. But Prospero makes clear that Caliban has a 'human shape'.[6]

The orphan Caliban, alone on the island, was about twelve when Prospero landed. At first the exiled European

> us'd thee
> (Filth as thou art) with human care, and lodg'd thee
> In mine own cell.

Caliban confirms this:

> When thou cam'st first,
> Thou strok'st me, and made much of me: wouldst give me

---

[5] For Caliban, J.E. Hankins, 'Caliban the Bestial Man', *Publications Modern Language Association America*, September 1947, LXII, 3, pp.793-801; R.H. Goldsmith, 'The Wild Men on the English Stage', *Modern Language Review*, October 1958, LIII, 4, pp.481-91; J.W. Draper, 'Monster Caliban', *Revue de Littérature Comparée*, 40, 1966. More generally, Earl Miner, 'The Wild Man Through the Looking Glass', in Dudley and Novak (eds), *Wild Man Within*, 1972.

[6] 'Then was this island/(Save for the son, that she did litter here,/A freckled whelp, hag-born) not honour'd with/A human shape.' (I, ii, 281-4.)

> Water with berries in't: and teach me how
> To name the bigger Light, and how the less
> That burn by day, and night: and then I lov'd thee
> And show'd thee all the qualities o' th' isle,
> The fresh springs, brine-pits; barren place and fertile.

Miranda taught him to speak English.

>   I pitied thee,
> Took pains to make thee speak, taught thee each hour
> One thing or other: when thou didst not (Savage)
> Know thine own meaning; but would gabble, like
> A thing most brutish, I endow'd thy purposes
> With words that made them known.

The harmony ended when Caliban (age 18?) tried to rape Miranda (age 8?):

>   thou didst seek to violate
> The honour of my child.

Thereafter Caliban has been confined to a 'hard rock', and forbidden to roam on the island. The sentence seems equitable to Miranda: Caliban's nature is 'vile' (or 'wild': First Folio, 'vild'):

>   thý vile race
> (Though thou didst learn) had that in't, which good natures
> Could not abide to be with; therefore wast thou
> Deservedly confin'd into this Rock, who hadst
> Deserv'd more than a prison.

Caliban, like Ariel, is a 'slave' of Prospero. Caliban

>   does make our fire,
> Fetch in our wood, and serves in offices
> That profit us.

'We cannot miss him,' says Prospero: we cannot do without him. Caliban regrets his contact with Civility:

> You taught me language, and my profit on't
> Is, I know how to curse: the red plague rid you
> For learning me your language.

Prospero tells his European guests that Caliban is

> A Devil, a born Devil, on whose nature
> Nurture can never stick: on whom my pains
> Humanely taken, all, all lost, quite lost,
> And, as with age, his body uglier grows,
> So his mind cankers.

Caliban is made drunk by the 'celestial liquor' of Stephano and Trinculo. He assumes they have 'dropped from heaven'; and promises to serve them. He will show them 'every fertile inch o' th' island'; fish for them, collect wood, pluck berries, dig earth nuts with his long nails; and help them to trap wild-fowl and monkeys. 'I'll swear myself thy subject': 'I prithee be my god.' Caliban has thus become both 'drunken monster' and 'servant monster'.

Stephano, the butler, plans to become ruler of the island, by killing Prospero and marrying Miranda. Trinculo and Caliban are to be 'viceroys'. Caliban had explained his grudge:

> I am subject to a Tyrant,
> A sorceror, that by his cunning hath cheated me
> Of the island.

Prospero assumes that the plot has its centre in Caliban:

> that foul conspiracy
> Of the beast Caliban, and his confederates
> Against my life.

Prospero, throughout the span of the action of the play (about four hours) is in control.

> At this hour
> Lies at my mercy all mine enemies.

At the resolution, he decides not to be vindictive.

> Though with their high wrongs I am struck to th' quick,
> Yet, with my nobler reason, gainst my fury
> Do I take part: the rarer action is
> In virtue, than in vengeance: they, being penitent,
> The sole drift of my purpose doth extend
> Not a frown further.

The three who had conspired to deprive Prospero of his Italian title are forgiven; and he reassumes his position as 'right Duke of Milan'. Ariel is given the promised 'liberty'. Caliban renounces his folly:

> I'll be wise hereafter,
> And seek for grace: what a thrice double ass
> Was I to take this drunkard for a god?
> And worship this dull fool?

The Europeans must 'know, and own' the drunken butler and the fool. Similarly Prospero will 'acknowledge' Caliban:

> this thing of darkness, I
> Acknowledge mine.

('Cauliban' was a Romany word for blackness.)[7]

The Europeans prepare to sail to Naples. Ariel remains on the island.

Presumably Caliban is also left behind. Unless Trinculo was granted his wish – to take Caliban to England and put him on exhibition: 'not a holiday-fool there but would give a piece of silver: there, would this monster, make a man: any strange beast there, makes a man.'

Kermode, xxxviii.

PART ONE

1

The Golden World

About mid-day on Friday 12 October 1492, Christopher Columbus stepped ashore onto an island in the Bahamas group. He named it San Salvador; today, Watling's Island. He went on to visit another four islands in the Bahamas; then Cuba; and then 'La Isla Española', Hispaniola. The homeward passage began on 4 January 1493. On Monday 4 March he anchored off Lisbon. His log-book (as edited later by Bartolomé de Las Casas) recorded his reception. Wednesday 6 March:[1]

When it was known today that the admiral came from the Indies, so many people came from the city of Lisbon to see him and to see the Indians, that it was a thing of wonder. They all marvelled, giving thanks to our Lord, and saying that it was owing to the great faith of the Sovereigns of Castile, and their desire to serve God, that the Divine Majesty had given them all this.

On 15 February, on his caravel off an island in the Azores, Columbus had dated a letter giving a short account of the islands discovered in the Indies.[2] (It seems that until his death – May 1506 – Columbus thought that he had reached the east coast of Asia.) The Spanish text of the letter was published at Barcelona in April. The only surviving copy of this four page black-letter folio is in the New York Public Library.

'Hispaniola is a wonder. The mountains and hills, the plains and meadow lands, are both fertile and beautiful.'

It has many large harbours finer than any I know in Christian lands, and many large rivers. All this is marvellous. The land is high and has many ranges of hills, and mountains incomparably finer than Tenerife. All are most beautiful and various in shape, and all are accessible.

The inhabitants of one of the Leeward Islands (Dominica?) to the south-east are said to be 'extremely fierce' and to 'eat human flesh':

---

[1] Cecil Jane, translator, L.A. Vigneras, editor, *Journal of Christopher Columbus*, 1968, 183-4.
[2] I have used the translation by J.M. Cohen in his Penguin Classics *Four Voyages of Christopher Columbus*, 1969, 115-23. Other translations are by Jane/Vigneras, 191-202; Morison, *Christopher Columbus:Mariner*, 1956, 212-23.

They have many canoes in which they travel throughout the islands of the Indies, robbing and taking all they can. They are no more ill-shaped than any other natives of the Indies, though they are in the habit of wearing their hair long like women. They have bows and arrows with the same canes as the others, tipped with splinters of wood, for lack of iron, which they do not possess. They behave most savagely to the other peoples.

But the natives of Hispaniola, and the other islands which 'I discovered or heard of', are much different. 'All have brought us something to eat and drink, which they have given with a great show of love.'

They were, we now know, Taino's; the Taino branch of the Arawak language group. They

go naked, as their mothers bore them, men and women alike. A few of the women, however, cover a single place with a leaf of a plant or piece of cotton which they weave for this purpose. They have no iron or steel or arms, and are not capable of using them not because they are not strong and well built, but because they are amazingly timid.

When they 'saw my men, all fled immediately, a father not even waiting for his son.' Not 'because we have harmed any of them.' Far from it:

Wherever I have gone and been able to have conversation with them, I have given them some of the various things I had, a cloth and other articles, and received nothing in exchange. But they have still remained incurably timid. True, when they have been reassured, and lost their fear, they are so ingenuous and liberal with all their possessions that no one who has not seen them would believe it. If one asks for anything they never say no. On the contrary, they offer a share to anyone, with demonstrations of heartfelt affection, and they are immediately content with any small thing, valuable or valueless, that is given them.

They think broken crockery, pieces of glass, and laces are 'the finest jewels in the world'; and especially value 'bits of broken hoops from wine barrels'. Some sailors received vast amounts of gold for trinkets. Columbus did not approve. 'This seemed to me to be wrong, and I forbade it.' Columbus, 'in order to gain their love and incline them to become Christians', made them gifts of 'a thousand pretty things that I had brought'.

Throughout the region, 'I saw no great difference in the looks of the people, their customs or their language'. The Indians are 'very well made'.

They are not Negroes as in Guinea, and their hair is straight, for where they live the sun's rays do not strike too harshly; but they are strong nevertheless.

Indian men 'are seemingly content with one woman'; except for the chiefs, who are allowed twenty or more. 'The women appear to work more than the men.' Columbus could not make out whether the Indians had a notion of private property:

I have not been able to find out if they have private property. As far as I could see, whatever a man had was shared among all the rest; and this particularly applies to food.

They do not have any religious creed; nor are they idolaters. But

all believe that power and goodness dwell in the sky, and they are firmly convinced that I have come from the sky with these ships and people. In this belief, they gave me a good reception everywhere, once they had overcome their fear; and this is not because they are stupid – far from it, they are men of great intelligence, for they navigate all those seas, and give a marvellously good account of everything – but because they have never before seen men clothed, or ships like these.

This 'brief account of the facts' ended with a tribute to 'the eternal God, our Lord'. He 'grants to all those who walk in His way victory over apparent impossibilities, and this voyage was pre-eminently a victory of this kind.' Thus

all Christendom will be delighted that our Redeemer has given victory to our most illustrious King and Queen and their renowned kingdoms, in this great matter. They should hold great celebrations and render solemn thanks to the Holy Trinity with many solemn prayers, for the great triumph which they will have, by the conversion of so many peoples to our holy faith, and for the temporal benefits which will follow, for not only Spain, but all Christendom, will receive encouragement and profit.

'I bring Indians as evidence,' Columbus says. *Indios*, the 'first appearance in print of this name that Columbus gave to the natives of America.'[3] Among the benefits of the Indies to Spain will be 'slaves': 'who will be taken from the idolaters' – if Christians are not the victims, the slave trade is righteous.

In April 1493 a Latin version of the Columbus Letter was printed in Rome. In all, the Letter was published nine times in 1493. One of the Latin editions, at Basle, had wood-cut illustrations. (These were probably existing woodcuts in the printer's shop, with no real relevance to Columbus.) There were nearly twenty editions by 1500; including translations into Catalan, French, German and Italian (this one was in rhyme).

When Columbus met Ferdinand and Isabella in Barcelona, he presented them with his log-book of the voyage (in Spanish). They kept it, and it has vanished. They sent to Columbus a transcript of the log book. Columbus died in 1506. The transcript (or, perhaps, a copy of it) passed to the library of Columbus' natural son, Fernando. On Fernando's death in 1539, his library was deposited in the Dominican

[3] Morison, *Christopher Columbus*, 221.

house of San Pablo in Seville. Here, in the 1550s, Las Casas made his version of the Columbus log (verbatim extracts, and abridgement) for his projected *Historia de las Indias*. The 1492/3 log survives only in the Las Casas version; the manuscript, in Las Casas' handwriting, was found in 1791, printed in 1825, and is now in the Biblioteca Nacional, Madrid.[4] There was an English translation in 1827. A more definitive edition of the Spanish text was published in 1892. An English translation by Cecil Jane was published by the Hakluyt Society in 1930.

The Cecil Jane translation was revised and edited by L.A. Vigneras (consulting the manuscript and the 1892 edition) for a volume first published in 1960: *The Journal of Christopher Columbus*, with an appendix by R.A. Skelton on cartography, and ninety illustrations. The illustrations include five of the 1493 Basle wood cuts: Ferdinand of Spain (p.5); Trading with the Indians (p.35); the islands discovered by Columbus (p.91: not unlike the frontispiece to the first edition of *Utopia*, 1516); the Spanish fort on Hispaniola (p.127); and the 'Santa Maria' (p.193). There is also (p.27) a wood cut from the Florence edition: Indians fleeing in terror of Columbus.

I have used the Jane/Vigneras text. J.M. Cohen translated the first quarter of the log-book for his Penguin Classics volume *The Four Voyages of Christopher Columbus*, 1969 (pp.37-76).

The Columbus/Las Casas log-book material can be legitimately used at this point; so long as it is remembered that until the nineteenth century hardly anyone knew of it.

The points made in the 1493 Letter are expanded in the log-book. There is more about the natives of the island of Caniba, or Carib. The Christians were warned of them on 23 November. Some were said to have 'the face of a dog',[5] and 'one eye in the forehead'. Others were said to be 'cannibals'. Columbus doubted this – the Indians had thought the Spanish were cannibals.[6] He thought these distant and feared Indians were 'under the dominion of the Great Khan' (of Cathay).[7] He also thought they were feared because they were 'more astute' and of 'greater intelligence' than the Indians he had personally met, who were 'very faint hearted'; and thus easy to capture (5 December).[8] On 13 January 1493 Columbus encountered an Indian whom he took to be from Carib. He was ugly; his face was stained with charcoal; and his long hair was 'drawn back and tied behind, and then gathered in meshes of parrot's feathers'. Seven of his sailors went ashore, to an island they presumed to be inhabited by Caribs. They met fifty Indians; who fled after a slight skirmish. In spite of the flight, Columbus judged them 'fearless' – other Indians were 'cowardly beyond reason'.[9]

Columbus first encountered Indians on Friday 12 October 1492.

[4] Wagner and Parish, *Bartolomé de las Casas*, 292.
[5] Jane/Vigneras, *Journal of Columbus*, 74. The subsequent page references are to this edition.
[6] 68-9.   [7] 74.   [8] 85.   [9] 146-9.

There are details of the San Salvador natives in the entries for the Friday and the Saturday.[10] All, men and woman, 'go naked as their mothers bore them'. They are 'very well built, with very handsome bodies and very good faces'; 'generally fairly tall, good looking and well proportioned'; 'very handsome', with 'very good figures' – 'no bellies'. Their legs are 'very straight', their heads and foreheads 'very broad', their eyes 'very lovely' and 'not small'. Their hair 'is not curly, but loose and coarse as the hair of a horse'. Their colour is that of 'the people of the Canaries, neither black nor white'. Some paint themselves: black, white, red, and other colours. The men seem young; Columbus saw none over forty. The Indians are good mimics. 'I see that they very soon say all that is said to them.' They are, then, 'of quick intelligence'. They would make 'good servants'.

Such was the initial impact of the American Indian on the European explorer.

During this first voyage, Columbus was most impressed by the natives of Hispaniola (Española). His sailors, too, found them 'fairer' than those they had previously encountered: some of the girls were 'as white as any that could be found in Spain' (13 December).[11] To Columbus they were 'stout and valiant, and not feeble like the others'; with 'very pleasant voices'[12] – 'soft voices, unlike the others, who seem to threaten when they talk.'[13] Not that the earlier Indians had been disappointing. By 16 October, having left San Salvador, Columbus had found Indians 'better disposed' than those of the 12th and the 13th: 'somewhat more domesticated and tractable, and more intelligent.' For one thing, the women wore a cover over their private parts.[14] They were 'mild and timorous', 'without arms',[15] 'unwarlike':[16] 'very gentle, and do not know what it is to be wicked, or to kill others, or to steal.'[17] On good days, they seemed 'very free from wickedness'.[18] On bad days, they seemed 'cowardly'.[19] But all the natives of the Indies seemed 'of a very generous disposition, so that they give whatever is asked of them with the greatest good-will in the world.'[20]

Everywhere in the Indies, Columbus (in the Las Casas paraphrase)

ordered all his men to be careful not to offend any one in any way, and to take nothing from them against their will, and so they paid them for everything which they received from them.[21]

Columbus – and these, Las Casas notes, are Columbus' 'actual words' – 'knew that they were a people to be delivered and converted to our holy faith rather by love than by force.'[22] On the other hand, on 14 October, after three days' experience of the Indian, Columbus had noted that the Indians could either all be taken to Spain, or held as

---

[10] 24-5.　[11] 96.　[12] 101.　[13] 119.　[14] 33.　[15] 52.　[16] 57.　[17] 58.　[18] 57.
[19] 74.　[20] 114.　[21] 111.　[22] 23.

slaves[23] – a passage by which Las Casas was much disconcerted.[24] Certainly Columbus felt that all Indians were 'fitted to be ruled, and to be set to work to cultivate the land'.[25] They should obviously be taught 'to go clothed, and adopt our customs'.[26]

The natives of Hispaniola were especially liberal. In the previous islands, 'all the men endeavoured to conceal the women from the Christians, owing to jealousy, but here they do not' (21 December). They are completely naked: no cover over the female privy parts.[27] The villages and houses are 'lovely'.[28] Earlier Indians had seemed 'without law'.[29] In Hispaniola 'there is government'; there is a 'judge or lord', whom 'all obey'. And the lords are 'men of few words, and excellent memories'.[30] The chief lord maintains 'a very marvellous state, of a style so orderly that it is a pleasure to see it'. They have, in brief, 'very good customs'.[31]

By 16 October 1492 (after five days) Columbus had noted of the Indians that

no creed is known to them, and I believe they would be speedily converted to Christianity, for they have a very good understanding.[32]

Thereafter, some Indians were carried in Columbus' caravel. He noted on 1 November[33] that these passengers had 'no creed that I know'; they do not 'offer any prayer'. But their gifts of mimicry are a sign of grace: they say, as they are shown, 'with their hands raised to heaven', the *Salve Regina* and the *Ave Maria*; and 'they make the sign of the cross'. On land, Columbus entered an Indian house on 3 December, saw shells and other ornaments hanging from the ceiling, and assumed it was a 'temple'. 'I asked them by signs if they offered prayer in it; they said, No.'[34] But on Hispaniola the Indians helped Columbus to erect 'a very mighty cross' in a village square. They 'offered prayer, and adored it'.[35]

It was the custom of Columbus to set up a cross wherever he landed: as 'an emblem of Christ Jesus our Lord, and to the honour of Christendom'[36]. He was an Italian of conservative maritime piety: noting the time in his log-book by the hour of terce and vespers;[37] naming a harbour 'San Nicolas' (St Nicholas Môte, Haiti) because he landed on the Feast of the Saint (6 December);[38] addicted to the custom of pilgrimages,[39] and the hope of the conquest of Jerusalem;[40] ready with a Biblical allusion; seeing his voyage as under Divine Protection, 'the predestined will of God';[41] not fond of Sunday travel – 'solely as a result of his piety, and not on account of any superstition'.[42] He was sure that none but 'Catholic Christians' should be allowed in the Indies:[43]

  [23] 28.

  [24] Cohen, Penguin Classics *Columbus*, inserts here a passage from Las Casas' *History of the Indies*, criticising these sentiments of Columbus: 59-60.

  [25] 101.   [26] 102.   [27] 111.   [28] 120.   [29] 52.   [30] 120.   [31] 124.   [32] 33.   [33] 50.

  [34] 84.   [35] 107.   [36] 94.   [37] 86, 182.   [38] 86.   [39] 166.   [40] 128.   [41] 128.

  [42] 114.   [43] 78.

This was the alpha and omega of the enterprise, that it should be for the increase and glory of the Christian religion, and that no one should come to these parts who was not a good Christian.

The Indians were ripe for Christianity. They

believe and know that there is a God in Heaven, and they are sure that we come from heaven, and they are very ready to repeat any prayer that we say to them, and they make the sign of the cross.

Ferdinand and Isabella

may believe that in all the world there cannot be a people better or more gentle. Your Highnesses should feel great joy, because they will presently become Christians, and will be educated in the good customs of your realm.[44]

What was needed in the Indies was 'devout religious persons, knowing their language'.[45]

Columbus did what he could. In a letter of 1500[46] he reported that he had told the Indians 'as much as I can about our Blessed Faith and the creed of Holy Mother Church'. He had stressed 'the civilisation and nobility of all Christians, and their faith in the Holy Trinity'.

There is no indication that there was a priest on the voyage of 1492/3. There is no mention of Columbus' carrying a Bible. Two points of similarity with the Portuguese Raphael Hythloday, who was to make his landfall on the island of Utopia about 1510.

Before his death in 1539, Fernando Columbus had completed a biography of his father. This was in Spanish. The original is lost; but an Italian translation was published at Venice in 1571. Fernando's quotations from his father (from the log-book transcript, and elsewhere) again amplify the Letter of 1493. I have used the translation by J.M. Cohen, who has 125 pages from the Biography in his 1969 Penguin Classics *The Four Voyages of Christopher Columbus*.

Concerning the 1492/3 voyage, the praise for the natives of Hispaniola is repeated. The land was 'very pleasant and rich in Indian foods', the natives 'fairer and handsomer than any they had seen so far on other islands': 'hospitable and well mannered'.[47] They are – and the section is quoted as Columbus' own words – 'affectionate' and 'in all ways so amenable': they have 'little greed'. 'They love their neighbours as themselves and their way of speaking is the sweetest in the world, always gentle and smiling.'[48]

The material about the second voyage (1493-96) – the members of which included Las Casas' father and uncle – includes a description of an exploration of Hispaniola. Here the 1493 theme of 'possessions in common' (not mentioned in the log book for the first voyage; or at least not in the Las Casas version) reappears.[49]

[44] 119. [45] 57. [46] Cohen, Penguin Classics *Columbus*, 225.
[47] *ibid.*, 86. [48] *ibid.*, 92. [49] *ibid.*, 161.

On his journey he passed many Indian villages with round houses thatched with straw. The doors are so low that you have to bend to get in. On entering these houses, the Indians whom the Admiral brought from Isabela[50] promptly seized anything that pleased them, and the owners showed no sign of resentment. They seemed to hold all possessions in common. Similarly, whenever any of the natives went up to a Christian, they took from him whatever they liked, in the belief that similar customs obtained among us. But they were quickly undeceived when they saw that this was not the case.

But there were the beginnings of trouble. At the landing on Jamaica (May 1494), the Indians appeared 'and hurled their spears'. The crews of the boats then 'fired such a volley from their crossbows that the natives were compelled to retire, with six or seven wounded'.[51] In March 1495 there was a battle on Hispaniola.[52] Columbus marched against the Indians with 200 men, twenty horses, and twenty hunting dogs. The indians began 'to break under the fire of muskets and crossbows'; and 'the cavalry and hunting dogs charged wildly upon them to prevent them re-forming'.

The Indians fled like cowards in all directions, and our men pursued them, killing so many and wrecking such havoc among them that, to be brief, by God's will victory was achieved, many Indians being killed and many others captured and executed.

(The rebel chief confessed to the murder of twenty Christians during the 1492/3 voyage.) The victory was the work of God.[53] The ill-armed and sick Christians would never have conquered the Indian multitude 'if the Lord had not wished to bring them beneath His hand'. The

marvellous victories and the conquest of these people were the work of His will and His mighty hand, and not the result of our strength and intelligence, and the cowardice of the Indians.

Fernando's material about the second voyage contains his father's 'own words' about Indian Religion;[54] based on a report prepared by a Spanish Friar, Ramón Pane, 'who made enquiries on my behalf'. There were thirteen priests on the second voyage. Apparently each India⌐ chief has a house outside the village containing 'wooden images carved in relief, and called by them *cemies*'. The Indians 'perform certain prayers and ceremonies here, as we do in church'. The main liturgical ingredient is a 'special powder', which, 'with certain rites' they place on the heads of the images. They then sniff the powder, by way of canes in the nostrils; this 'intoxicates them, and they babble like drunkards, but none of our men understand the words they use'. All the temples contain at least two images: some, more than ten. Each has a name: 'and I think that some represent the

[50] On the north coast of Hispaniola.   [51] Cohen, 172.
[52] *ibid.*, 189.   [53] *ibid.*, 191.   [54] *ibid.*, 192-4.

father, others the grandfather, and others both'. The Indians 'pay more devotion and respect to some than to others, as we do on the occasion of religious processions'. Christians are not allowed to enter the 'image house':

If they think that a Christian is coming they pick up the *cemies* and conceal them in the woods, fearing the Christians will take them from them, since they have the ridiculous custom of stealing one another's *cemies*.

On one occasion, some Christians did enter a temple; and found that the image was hollow, and contained a speaking tube, operated from a concealed part of the building by a servant. By this device the chief 'kept everyone obedient to him'; and begged the intruders not to give away the secret. The people believe that the *cemi* speaks; this is a 'superstitious belief', and so there is among the Indians 'some tinge of idolatry'. (We remember from Columbus' 1493 Letter that Idolators can be made Slaves.) The people also pay 'great devotion' to certain stones, in groups of three: one stone helps the harvest, another brings painless childbirth, the third brings needed rain or sun. (Columbus sent three such stones to Ferdinand and Isabella.)

The 'funeral rites' were of most interest to the Spaniards. When an Indian is on the point of death, he is carried out of the house – and sometimes placed on a hammock or string bed – and left there, with bread and water beside him. Except for the chiefs: who are strangled. (Some of the sick among ordinary Indians are also strangled, on the advice of the chief.) The dead are sometimes burnt in their houses, sometimes buried in a grave, sometimes decapitated and the head preserved. Except for the chiefs: they are prepared for the tomb 'by cutting open the body and drying it over a fire so as to preserve it entire'.

Pane was interested in 'what they know and believe about the place to which they go at death'. The chief king of Hispianola, Caonabo, told him that 'they go to a certain valley' (which each chief believes lies in his own region) where 'the dead meet their fathers and ancestors, eat, have wives, and take their pleasure and consolation with them'.

Of this Columbus material, the only item printed by 1503 was the 1493 Letter. In 1503 there were printed two editions of a brief Latin text: *Mundus Novus*, in one version; *De Novo Mundo*, in the other. The third printing was in Augsburg in 1504; and it was thereafter a much reprinted item. This was a Latin translation of a letter written in Italian in Lisbon in the spring of 1503, describing a voyage from March 1501 to September 1502 to America, under the auspices of the King of Portugal. Or one should say (without entering into the controversy) 'alleged voyage'. The author was Amerigo Vespucci.

Vespucci began his letter by announcing his 'return from the new countries':

It is lawful to call it a new world, because none of these countries were known to our ancestors, and to all who hear about them they will be entirely new.

The impact of this claim was such that Amerigo was to find his name given to the New World.

The letter included a section on the natives: of, presumably, Brazil.[55]

'As regards the people: we have found such a multitude in those countries that no one could enumerate them, as we read in the Apocalypse.' (The allusion is to Revelation 7:9: 'I beheld, and, lo, a great multitude, which no man could number, of all nations, and kindreds, and people, and tongues, stood before the throne, and before the Lamb, clothed in white robes.')

They are people gentle and tractable, and all of both sexes go naked, not covering any part of their bodies, just as they came from their mother's wombs, and so they go until their deaths. They have large, square-built bodies, and well proportioned. Their colour reddish, which I think is caused by their going naked and exposed to the sun. Their hair is plentiful and black. They are agile in walking, and of quick sight. They are of a free and good-looking expression of countenance.

Unfortunately they detract from their good looks by boring holes in their nostrils, lips, nose and ears (in the case of men: the women pierce the ears only), some of the perforations being the size of a plum, and inserting stones and bones. They have another custom 'beyond all human credibility':

Their women, being very libidinous, make the penis of their husbands swell to such a size as to appear deformed; and this is accomplished by a certain artifice, being the bite of some poisonous animal; and by reason of this many lose their virile organ and remain eunuchs.

They have no cloth: they do not need it. 'They have no commerce among each other, and they wage war without art or order.' The vanquished are eaten by the victors: 'for human flesh is an ordinary article of food among them.' Vespucci has seen a man eat his wife and children: and one Indian was said to have eaten 300 others.

I was once in a certain city, for twenty seven days, where human flesh was hung up near the houses, in the same way as we expose butcher's meat. I say further that they were surprised that we did not eat our enemies and use their flesh as food, for they say it is excellent.

The mariners 'did all we could to persuade them to desist from their evil habits, and they promised us to leave off'. They live for 150 years, and are seldom ill.

[55] Pp.45-7 of Markham, ed., *Letters of Vespucci*, Hakluyt Society, 1894. The Letter is pp.42-52.

They have no 'temples'. They are not 'idolaters'. They have 'no laws'.

They live amongst themselves without a king or ruler, each man being his own master, and having as many wives as they please. The children cohabit with the mothers, the brothers with the sisters, the male cousins with the female; and each one with the first he meets.

Nor have they 'any private property; everything being in common'.

'What more can I say! They live according to nature; and are more inclined to be Epicurean than Stoic'.

The 1501/2 voyage was Vespucci's third. (I shall assume here that the voyages were genuine; the issue does not affect the argument.) The first, under Spanish auspices, had left Cadiz in May 1497 and returned in October 1498. The second, also from Cadiz, left in May 1499 and was back in February 1500. The fourth was subsequent to the Letter, and was, like the third, Portuguese: leaving Lisbon in May 1503, returning on 18 June 1504. On 4 September 1504, Vespucci signed in Lisbon the Italian manuscript of his account of the four voyages. This was printed in Florence, possibly in 1505: *Lettera di Amerigo Vespucci delle isole nuovamente trovate in quattro suoi viaggi*. The text was 32 octavo pages. Not more than five copies survive; one in the British Museum. A Latin translation was published in April 1507 as part of *Cosmographiae Introductio*, by Martin Waldseemüller. The accompanying world map showed the new continent, a separate geographical entity, with the name 'America', the feminine form of Amerigo. Gerhard Mercator's world map of 1538 was to confirm the fact of the new, independent land mass.[56]

An English version (much abridged) of *Quatuor Americi Vesputii Navigationes* appeared in 1553; as part of *A treatyse of the newe India, with other new founde landes and ilandes*. The compiler and translator of this volume was Richard Eden.

Eden (1520-1576), a treasury official, scholar and man of science, was a Cambridge man. He later said that Thomas Smith, 'in my time the flower of the University of Cambridge' was 'sometime my tutor'. Smith was a Fellow of Queens' from 1530. A Richard Eden went up to Cambridge in 1535, and took his BA from Christ's in 1539, and his MA in 1544. He may have entered Queens', and then transferred; a not uncommon practice. (Unless Eden used the word 'tutor' in the sense of 'mentor'.) The 1553 volume was reprinted in 1885 by Edward Arber, in his *The First Three English Books on America*, from which my quotations from Eden are taken. The complete English translation I

[56] For the gradual realisation that the lands discovered were in fact a 'new' continent, see Marcel Bataillon, 'The Idea of the Discovery of America', in Highfield, ed., *Spain in the Fifteenth Century*, 1972. This is a translation of a 1953 review-article on a 1951 book by the Mexican philosopher-historian Edmundo O'Gorman, whose somewhat tortuous and scholastic publications on the meaning of the 'discovery' of America are best encountered in his book published, in English, in 1961: *The Invention of America: an inquiry into the historical nature of the New World and the meaning of its history*.

have basically used is that published in 1951 in Buenos Aires: *Americo Vespucio, El Nuevo Mundo*, a facsimile of the Italian edition, with translations into Spanish and English and a preliminary essay by Roberto Levillier. I have sometimes used the 1894 Hakluyt Society translation by Clements Markham, *Letters of Vespucci*, pp.1-56. And I have consulted the translation appended to the 1893 facsimile reprint of the Florence edition, London, Bernard Quaritch.

The first voyage (to Honduras, Yucatan and the Florida Channel?) has the interesting material. The other three are sketchy. In the second (to Guiana?) we read, in Eden's translation,[57] of 'a certain island in which was a beastly kind of people, and simple, yet very gentle'; of an 'Island of Giants' – five women and thirty five men of 'so great stature that they marvelled thereat' (Curacao?); and of four Indian youths 'having their privy members newly cut off' – 'they had been taken of the cannibals and should shortly have been eaten': castrated for fattening. The Indians encountered on the third voyage[58] (to Brazil?) were equally 'beastly': a young Spanish sailor was killed by a blow from behind with a stake by an Indian woman (while the other women 'stood gazing on him and feeling his apparel': the youth being 'very strong and quick'). The women then cut the body 'in pieces, even in the sight of the Spaniards, showing them the pieces, and roasting them at a great fire'. The fourth voyage was[59] a fiasco, during which one of the ships was wrecked, on 10 August 1503, and nothing achieved. The only noteworthy find was a 'rude and uninhabited island': nothing but birds, snakes, rats and lizards.

Vespucci had a noteworthy Portuguese ship-mate on the second, third and fourth voyages, Raphael Hythloday: who, Thomas More tells us in 1516, 'joined himself in company with Amerigo Vespucci, and in the three last voyages of those four that be now in print and abroad in every man's hands he continued still in his company, saving that in the last voyage he came not home again with him'.[60] Vespucci, in a passage not given by Eden, tells that his remaining five ships (after the shipwreck) reached a fine harbour about October 1503. The men stayed for five months and built a fort. The settlers included the crew of the lost vessel, all of whom had been saved. When Vespucci sailed for Lisbon at the beginning of April 1504, he left twenty-four colonists behind in the encampment, all of them members of the crew of the wrecked ship. The Indians had been pacified, and there were provisions for six months. More relates that Raphael was among those left behind, 'though it were sore against his will'.[61] Raphael soon left the colony, with five companions, presumably by September 1504, when the provisions ran out. The six 'travelled through and about many countries'. And Raphael and three others eventually reached

[57] Eden-Arber, 38.
[58] *ibid.*, 39.
[59] *ibid.*
[60] Everyman *Utopia* (Robinson translation), 15.
[61] *ibid.*, 16. See above, p.x.

the island of Utopia. A pleasant change, surely, after the islands he had encountered with Vespucci.

It seems a great pity that Raphael had not been on the first Vespucci voyage. Much of the experience would have been helpful to him on Utopia. One hopes that by the time he met More in Antwerp in 1515 he had found time to read about it.

In the following account of the first voyage I have, first, used the Eden version.[62] But as he gives less than half of Vespucci's text, I have mainly used, for the missing sections, the Buenos Aires translation.[63]

In the New World (Mexico?) the mariners found in 1497/98 'a nation of naked people': 'they go all as naked as they came forth of their mother's womb.' 'They suffer no hair on their body, saving only on their head, in so much that they pull off the hairs of their brows.' That sentence is all that Eden gives us of the passage:

They are of a medium stature, very well proportioned. Their skin is of a colour which inclines to red (*rosso*) like a lion's mane; and I believe that if they went clothed they would be white like ourselves. They have no hair at all on the body, except long and black hair on the head; especially the women, which makes them beautiful. They are not very fair of countenance, because they have broad faces, so that their appearance may be that of the Tartar (*al tartaro*). They do not let any hair grow in the eyebrows, nor in the eyelashes, nor in any other place, exception being made of the hair of the head; for they hold hair to be something ugly.

They are swift walkers and runners, and fine swimmers. (Eden tells us only about the swimmers.)

'They keep war against their borderers, which are of strange language' (Eden). Eden does not tell us that they take their women to war, as supply-carriers. The Vespucci text then notes that 'it is not their custom to have any captain, nor do they walk in orderly array; for each is master of himself'; and that they 'have neither king nor master, nor do they obey anybody; for they live in their individual liberty'. All that is crisply put by Eden: 'they have no magistrates.' Eden is fuller on the reason for their wars: 'They fight not for the enlarging of their dominion'; 'nor yet for the increase of riches (*cupidita*), because they are content with their own commodities; but only to revenge the death of their predecessors.' War is incited (Vespucci says: not Eden) by the 'eldest relative' of a slain man; who 'goes through the streets' exhorting vengeance.

Eden now omits two more passages. The first is about punishment:

They do not practice justice, nor punish the criminal, nor do father and mother punish their children; and, whether or not it was something unusual, we never saw disputing amongst them.

The second is about the language:

[62] Eden-Arber, 37.   [63] 311-15.

They speak little and with subdued voice. They use the same accents as ourselves, because they form the words either on the palate or the teeth or the lips; except that they use other words for things. Great are the varieties of dialects, for at every hundred leagues we found a change of tongues such that these were mutually unintelligible.

Eden is vicariously shocked by the Indian eating habits: 'At their meat, they use rude and barbarous fashions, lying on the ground without any table cloth or coverlet.' Vespucci went further: the fact that they 'do not eat at fixed times', but at any time they please, shows that 'the manner of their living is very barbarous': *el modo del lor vivere e molto barbaro.* 'Their bodies are very smooth and clean by reason of their often washing,' says Eden. 'They are in other things filthy and without shame.' This hides:

When they empty the stomach they do everything so as not to be seen, and in this they are clean and decent; but in making water they are dirty and without shame, for while talking with us they do such things without turning round.[64]

Eden has this about the marriage customs: 'They use no lawful conjunction of marriage, but everyone hath as many women as him listeth, and leaveth them again at his pleasure.' He neglects to add that 'in this the woman has as much liberty as the man'. And he omits Vespucci's observation that the Indians are lustful 'beyond measure, and the women far more than the men': 'I refrain out of decency from telling you the trick which they play to satisfy their immoderate lust.' (Presumably the practice already described in print in 1503.) The women also have a method of abortion, to spite their husbands: another piece omitted by Eden. Vespucci comments on female nudity: 'no one cares, for the same impression is made on them at seeing anything indecent as is made on us at seeing a nose or a mouth.'[65] Again, not translated. Eden does include the remark that the women do not have 'their bellies wrimpeled, or loose and hanging paps; by reason of their bearing many children'. He omits to say that the women 'shewed themselves very desirous of copulating with us Christians'. Nor is he interested in the religion: they do not offer any sacrifice, says Vespucci, nor do they have a 'house of prayer'. 'They can be termed neither Moors nor Jews; and they are worse than heathen (*gentili*).'
Eden is more interested in the housing.

Their houses and cabins are all in common. Their houses are fashioned like unto bells; are made of great trees fastened together, covered with the leaves of date-trees, and made very strong against wind and tempests. They are also in some places so great, that in one of them five hundred persons may lodge.

[64] Markham translation, 8.
[65] *ibid.*, 9.

They use every seventh or eighth year to remove and change their dwelling places, because that by their long continuance in one place the air should be infected.

(Vespucci meant that the whole village moves.) Eden also takes the point that they

use no kind of merchandise, or buying and selling, being content only with that which nature hath left them. As for gold, pearls, precious stones, jewels, and such other things which we in Europe esteem as pleasures and delicates, they set naught by.

He omits the balancing observation that

Their wealth consists of feathers of many hued birds, or of little rosaries which they make out of fish bones, or of white and green stones, which they stick through cheeks, lips and ears; and of many other things to which we attach no value.

A long section of Vespucci follows at this point which again we do not find in Eden. Vespucci begins with Indian liberality:

They are so liberal in giving that it is the exception when they deny you anything; and, on the other hand, they are free in begging, when they show themselves to be your friends. But the greatest token of friendship which they show you is that they give you their wives and daughters; and when a father or a mother brings you the daughter, although she be a virgin, and you sleep with her, they esteem themselves highly honoured. And in this way they practise the full extreme of hospitality.

Next there is material on burial customs.

When they die they use several kinds of burial. Some bury their dead with water and food, thinking they will want it. They have no ceremonies of lights, nor of weeping. In some other places they practise a most barbarous and inhuman kind of interment. This is, that when a sick or infirm person is almost in the throes of death, his relations carry him into a great wood, and fasten one of those nets in which they sleep to two trees. They put their dying relation into it, and dance round him the whole of one day. When night comes on they put water and food for four or six days at his head, and then leave him alone, returning to their village. If the sick man can help himself, and eats and lives so as to return to the village, they receive him with ceremony; but few are those who escape. Most of them die, and that is their sepulchre.

And thirdly a passage on medical habits. The bathing of a fevered patient in cold water, before placing him near a fire; the use of dieting (sometimes no food for three days) and blood-letting; the provoking of vomiting by herbs. 'They are much vitiated in the phlegm and in the blood because of their food': largely roots, herbs, fruit and fish.

Eden re-appears here: 'They have no kind of corn. Their common feeding is a certain root which they dry and beat and make flour or meal thereof', called *yuca*, Vespucci says. 'They eat no kind of flesh,' concludes Eden, 'except man's flesh; for they eat all such as they kill in their wars, or otherwise take by chance.' Vespucci was a little more copious: 'in this matter they are so inhuman that they exceed every custom of the beast.' How terrible to witness: 'as it was my fate to see it at very many times and in many places.'

Thus ends the section on the manners and customs of the Indians.

The reader of Richard Eden hardly received the full impact of Vespucci.[66] But some of the detail was there. And, indeed, from (say) 1505 much of Vespucci had become part of common European knowledge.

There has survived a German wood-cut print of the early sixteenth century, $13\frac{1}{2}''$ by $8\frac{1}{4}''$, once in the collection of Sir Thomas Phillipps, sold in 1919, which depicts American Indians: it is a shore scene – with two ships – showing five males, three females, a boy, and a child in arms. One of the men is eating a human arm; and a human head and shoulders are roasting over a fire. The Indians are adequately clothed in feathers and wear feather head-dresses. Below the picture is a caption in German, printed from metal type:[67]

The people are naked, handsome, brown, well shaped in body; their heads, necks, arms, private parts, feet of men and women are a little covered with feathers. The men also have many precious stones in their faces and breasts. No one has anything, but all things are in common (*Es hat auch nyemantz nichts sunder sind alle ding gemain*). And the men have as wives those who please them, be they mothers, sisters or friends, therein make they no distinction. They also fight with each other. They also eat each other, even those who are slain, and hang the flesh of them in the smoke. They become a hundred and fifty years old. And have no government (*regiment*).

The first English book printed about America (*c*.1510?) was *Of the newe landes and of ye people found by the messengers of the kynge of portyngale*. The first section refers to the voyage from Lisbon in 1497, and gives a précis of Vespucci:[68]

We at the last went a'land, but that land is not now known, for there have no masters written thereof, nor it knoweth, and it is named Armenica. There we saw many wonders of beasts and fowls that we have never seen before. The people of this land have no king nor lord, nor their god. But all things is common. This people goeth all naked; but the men and women have on their head, neck, arms, knees, and feet all with feathers bounden, for their beauty

[66] Compare Eden's 'softening' of Oviedo's Indian material: below, pp.162-66.

[67] Wilberforce Eames, 'Description of a Wood-Engraving illustrating the South American Indians', *Bulletin New York Public Library*, September 1922, vol.26, no.9, 755-60. The text and translation of the caption are on p.756. There is a full-scale facsimile of the wood-cut; which is also included (reduced) in the illustrations to the Jane-Vigneras *Journal of Columbus*, p.147.

[68] Arber, *First Three English Books on America*, xxvii.

and fairness. These folk liven like beasts, without any reasonableness; and the women be also as common. And the men hath conversation with the women, who that they be or who they first meet, is she his sister, his mother, his daughter, or any other kindred. And the women be very hot, and disposed to lecherdness. And they eat also one another. The man eateth his wife, his children, as we also have seen; and they hang also the bodies or person's flesh in the smoke, as men do with swine's flesh. And that land is right full of folk, for they live commonly 300 year and more, as with sickness they die not. They take much fish, for they can goen under the water, and fetch so the fishes out of the water. And they war also one upon another, for the old men bring the young men thereto, that they gather a great company thereto of two parties, and come the one agen the other to the field or battle, and flee one the other with great heaps. And who holdeth the field, they take the other prisoners. And they bring them to death, and eat them; and as the dead is eaten, then flee they the rest. And they had been then eaten also, or otherwise live they longer times and many years more than other people; for they have costly spices and roots, where they themselves recover with, and heal them as they be sick.

This book was printed at Antwerp by Jan van Doesborch, who was active there from 1508. Antwerp was the meeting place of Thomas More and Raphael Hythloday in 1515.

The 'first historian of America' was an Italian, who had been a court official in Spain from 1487: Peter Martyr – Pietro Martire of Anghiera (now Angera) sixty miles north-west of Milan; 1459-1526; not to be confused with the Florentine Peter Martyr, 1500-62, who became Regius Professor of Divinity at Oxford under Edward VI. Pietro's first book was published in Latin at Seville in 1511, when he was 52. This was the first part of a work eventually to run to eight parts: the 'Decades' *De Orbe Novo*. (Each 'Decade' was subdivided into ten sections.) My quotations are from the English translation by Richard Eden published in 1555.[69]

Pietro knew Amerigo Vespucci:[70]

My very familar friend, and a witty young man in whose company I take great pleasure, and therefore use him oftentimes for my geste. He hath also made many voyages into these coasts, and diligently noted such things as he hath seen.

But the importance of his 1511 book was that it made available to Europe fairly full accounts of the first three voyages of Columbus, 1492-1500. Indeed, Pietro gives us much information additional to the Columbus material already considered; sailor's tales, one supposes. (The edition contained a wood-cut of the West Indies.)[71] He was attractively modest about his own editing of the material concerning

[69] Reprinted by Arber (see note 64). Subsequent page references to this edition.
[70] 157-8. The date of Vespucci's birth is uncertain, but he was hardly a 'young man' at the time when this passage appears to have been written (*c*.1500.) The conventional birth date is 1451; this is probably at least ten years too early.
[71] Shown in Hoffman, *Cabot to Cartier*, 1961, 63.

the *Almirante del Mar Oceano*: 'The great, rich and plentiful ocean sea, heretofore unknown, and now found by Christopher Columbus' he presents 'like a golden chain'; but 'unworkmanly wrought'.[72]

Pietro's material about the first voyage, 1492-3, did not modify the impression created by Columbus' published Letter of 1493, although it supplied more detail.[73] We are given some Indian words: for 'heaven', 'house', 'gold', 'a good man', 'nothing'. We are told about the cannibals, a feature of the Indies which intrigued Europeans.

Such children as they take, they geld to make them fat, as we do cock chickens and young hogs, and eat them when they are well fed. Of such as they eat, they first eat the entrails and extreme parts, as hands, feet, arms, neck and head. The other most fleshy parts they powder for store, as we do pestles of pork and gammons of bacon. Yet do they abstain from eating of women, and count it idle. Therefore such young women as they take they keep for increase, as we do hens to lay eggs. The old women they make their drudges.

The non-cannibal Indians make bread from a plant 'much like unto wheat', but 'longer'; 'somewhat sharp towards the end, and as big as a man's arm in the brawn'; 'this kind of grain they call *Maizium*'. They are a 'meek and humane people'. 'Naked', 'humane', and 'religious', say the 1555 marginal notes. At dusk, 'when our men went to prayer and kneeled on their knees after the manner of the Christians, they did the like also'.

Columbus 'affirmeth these islands to be part of India'. This opinion, Pietro thought, 'doth not in all points agree with the judgement of the ancient writers, as touching the bigness of the sphere, and compass of the globe, as concerning the navigable portion of the same'. On the other hand, Aristotle and Seneca thought India was accessible from Spain; and the fauna of the new world 'savour somewhat of India, either being near unto it, or else of the same nature'.

The account of the third voyage (1498-1500) develops into a dirge about the vices of the Spanish mariners: convicts and rapists, addicted to 'idleness and sleep', whose idea of fun is to wager who can most cleanly, at one stroke, decapitate an Indian with the sword.[74] There are pleasanter touches. In the summer of 1498 Columbus landed on the mainland of Venezuela. Here the Indians

are white, even as our men are, saving such as are most conversant in the sun. They are also very gentle, and full of humanity toward strangers. They cover their privy parts with gossampine cotton[75] wrought with sundry colours; and are beside all naked. There was few or none that had not either a collar, a chain or a bracelet of gold and pearls; and many had all.

[72] Eden-Arber, 94.
[73] 66-7. [74] 91.
[75] A cotton-like fibre, from the shrub *bombax pentandrum*.

They 'entertained our men genteelly', with fruit and wine – the wine, 'both white and red', being made not 'of grapes, but of the liqueur of divers fruits, and very pleasant in drinking'.[76] Earlier, Columbus had landed in Trinidad. That 'he might allure the young men to him with gentleness', he offered 'looking glasses, fair and bright vessels of copper, hawks' bells and such other things unknown to them'. But the young men were nervous. So Columbus 'thought to prove what he could do with musical instruments; and therefore commanded that they which were in the greatest ships should play on their drums and shawms' (a kind of oboe). This was even less successful. The Indians thought the performance a 'token of battle'.[77]

The section of the 1511 book which made the most impact was that devoted to Columbus' second voyage: 1493-6. (Some of Pietro's documentation is dated 1494, the beginning of his life's work.)

Columbus sailed for home in March 1496, leaving his brother Bartolomeo as governor of the Indies. We are given some diverting details of life in Hispaniola under Columbus' regime. One Indian entertainment was especially memorable.[78]

There met them a company of thirty women, being all the king's wives and concubines, bearing in their hands branches of date-trees, singing and dancing. They were all naked, saving that their privy parts were covered with breeches of gossampine cotton. But the virgins, having their hair hanging down about their shoulders, tied about the forehead with a fillet, were utterly naked.

(The distinction, which we should bear in mind throughout, between 'naked' and 'utterly naked'.) The sailors were impressed:

They affirm that their faces, breasts, paps, hands, and other parts of their bodies, were exceeding smooth and well proportioned; but somewhat inclining to a lovely brown. They supposed that they had seen those beautiful Dryads, or the native nymphs or fairs of the fountains, whereof the Antiquites speak so much. The branches of date-trees which they bore in their right hands when they danced, they delivered to the Lieutenant with low curtsey and smiling countenance.

The Spaniards were then given a 'delicate supper' in the house of the chief. The next day they were taken to the 'common hall', in which the Indians gather 'as often as they make any notable games or triumphs'. There were 'many dancings, singings, masque-ings, runnings, wrestlings'. And then a mock battle between two groups of men. Not in fact very mock; within a hour four Indians had been killed, and many wounded, and the guests asked that the entertainment cease.

At the beginning of 1494 Columbus ('whom I usc familiarly as my very friend')[79] had decided to base his colony at Isabela, Hispaniola: 'A strong place where he may build a city, near unto a commodious harbour'. He soon built

[76] 89. [77] 88. [78] 83. [79] 72.

many houses, and a chapel in the which, as in a new world heretofore void of all religion, God is daily served with thirteen priests according to the manner of our churches.[80]

Columbus loved Hispaniola, 'which he affirmeth to be Ophir, whereof we read in the third book of the Kings'.[81]

The reference is in fact I Kings 9:26-8:

And king Solomon made a navy of ships in Ezion-geber, which is beside Eloth, on the shore of the Red sea, in the land of Edom. And Hiram sent in the navy his servants, shipmen that had knowledge of the sea, with the servants of Solomon. And they came to Ophir, and fetched from thence gold, four hundred and twenty talents, and brought it to king Solomon.

Hiram was the king of Tyre. The voyage to Ophir and back took about eighteen months. Ophir was in south-west Arabia; but, to Columbus, the fleet of Solomon sailed by way of the Persian gulf to the West Indies. Pietro was sceptical: 'Whether it be so or no, it lieth not in me to judge; but in my opinion it is far off.'[82] Francisco López de Gómara, in his *Historia General de las Indias*, 1552, was less respectful to the idea. Solomon sailed eastward: thus, in the English translation by Richard Eden published in 1555,[83] 'concerning the navigations of Solomon, it is not to be thought that his navies sailed to the west Indies, foreasmuch as to pass thither it was requisite for them to sail westward'. Moreover, the west Indies have no 'unicorns, elephants, diamonds, and such other things as they brought in the trade of their navigations'.

Ophir remained a potent 'myth'. In 1625 the reverend Samuel Purchas described the first chapter of his *Hakluytus Posthumus, or Purchas His Pilgrimes*, a chapter running to over 130 pages in the modern edition,[84] as:

A Large Treatise of King Solomon's Navy sent from Ezongeber to Ophir: Wherein besides the Typical Mysteries briefly unveiled, and many Moral Speculations observed, the voyage is largely discussed out of Divine, Ecclesiastical and Human Testimonies: Intended as an historical preface to the histories following.

Columbus landed in November 1493 at Guadeloupe (Santa Maria de Guadalupe). This was cannibal territory.[85]

At the entrance of one of their houses, they saw two images of wood like unto serpents, which they thought had been such idols as they honour. But they learned afterward that they were set there for comeliness only. For they know none other god than the Sun and Moon; although they make certain images of gossampine cotton to the similitude of such fantasies as they say appear to

[80] *ibid.* [81] 73. [82] 82. [83] 338.
[84] Glasgow edition, I, 1905, 1-135.
[85] Eden-Arber, 69.

them in the night. Our men found in their houses all kinds of earthern vessels, not much unlike unto ours. They found also in the kitchens man's flesh, duck's flesh, and goose flesh, all in one pot; and other on the spits ready to be laid to the fire. Entering into their inner lodgings, they found faggots of the bones of men's arms and legs, which they reserve to make heads for their arrows, because they lack iron. The other bones they cast away when they have eaten the flesh. They found likewise the head of a young man fastened to a post, and yet bleeding.

There is a 1555 Marginal Note: 'Fine cookery'. The natives fled. And in the 'common houses' (surrounding the 'great hall or palace') the Spaniards found 'about thirty children and women captives, which were reserved to be eaten; but our men took them away, to use them for interpreters'. Some of the cannibals were captured, and eventually brought back to Spain; Pietro has more than once been to see them.[86] They do

no more put off their fierceness and cruel countenances than do the lions of Libya when they perceive themselves to be bound in chains. There is no man able to behold them but he shall feel his bowels grate with a certain horror, nature hath endowed them with so terrible menacing and cruel aspect.

In July 1494 Columbus landed on Jamaica. There follows an episode given in 1555 the marginal note: 'The humanity of a reverend old governor'.[87]

As the Admiral heard mass on the shore, there came toward him a certain governor, a man of four score years of age, and of great gravity, though he were naked saving his privy parts. He had a great train of men waiting on him. All the while the priest was at mass, he showed himself very humble, and gave reverent attendance with grave and demure countenance. When the mass was ended, he presented to the Admiral a basket of fruits of his country, delivering the same with his own hands. When the Admiral had genteelly entertained him, desiring leave to speak, he made an oration in the presence of the interpreter.

Pietro gives the 'Oration of the naked governor':

I have been advertised, most mighty prince, that you have of late with great power subdued many lands and regions hitherto unknown to you; and have brought no little fear upon all the people and inhabitants of the same. The which your good fortune, you shall bear with less insolency if you remember that the souls of men have two journeys after they are departed from this body. The one foul and dark, prepared for such as are injurious and cruel to mankind. The other pleasant and delectable, ordained for them which in their lifetime loved peace and quietness. If, therefore, you acknowledge yourself to be mortal, and consider that every man shall receive condign reward or punishment for such things as he hath done in this life, you will wrongfully hurt no man.

[86] 70. [87] 78.

Columbus assured the Indian that 'the chief cause of his coming
thither was to instruct them in such godly knowledge and true
religion'. And to 'subdue and punish the cannibals and such other
mischievous people, and to defend innocents'. 'Comfortable words,'
comments Pietro.

Certain sections from Pietro's account of the second Columbus
voyage especially struck the imagination of Europeans from 1511. To
Pietro it is 'certain' that 'among them, the land is as common as the
sun and water'. He draws out the significance of the fact:[88]

Mine and Thine, the seeds of all mischief, have no place with them. They are
content with so little, that in so large a country they have rather superfluity
than scarceness. So that they seem to live in the Golden World, without toil,
living in open gardens, not entrenched with dykes, divided with hedges, or
defended with walls. They deal truly one with another, without laws, without
books, without judges. They take him for an evil and mischievous man which
taketh pleasure in doing hurt to others.

A lengthier passage on the same theme[89] has the 1555 marginal note:
'A happy kind of life.'

The inhabitants of these islands have been ever so used to live at liberty, in
play and pastime, that they can hardly away with the yoke of servitude,
which they attempt to shake off by all means they may. And surely if they
had received our religion, I would think their life the most happy of all men,
if they might therewith enjoy their ancient liberty. A few things content
them, having no delight in such superfluities for the which in other places
men take infinite pains and commit many unlawful acts, and yet are never
satisfied; whereas many have too much, and none enough. But among these
simple souls a few clothes serve the naked; weights and measures are not
needful to such as cannot skill of craft or deceit, and have not the use of
pestiferous money, the seed of innumerable mischiefs. So that if we shall not
be ashamed to confess the truth, they seem to live in that Golden World of
which the old writers speak so much: wherein men lived simply and
innocently, without enforcement of laws, without quarrelling, judges, and
libels, content only to satisfy nature, without further vexation for knowledge
of things to come. Yet these naked people also are tormented with ambition,
for the desire they have to enlarge their dominions, by reason whereof they
keep war and destroy one another. From the which plague I suppose the
Golden World was not free. For even then also *Cede, non cedam* (that is, give
place, and I will not give place) had entered among men.

The volume published in London in 1555, in the Richard Eden
translation, ran to nearly 800 pages. About half the book consisted of
Pietro's 'Decades' ('Decades' numbers 1, 2 and 3, published together
at Alcalá in 1516, shortly before *Utopia* was printed at Louvain). The
full Eden title is:

The Decades of the newe worlde or west India, conteynyng the navigations and conquests

[88] *ibid.*   [89] 70-1.

of the Spanyardes, with the particular description of the most ryche and large landes and Ilands lately founde in the west Ocean perteynyng to the inheritaunce of the kinges of Spayne. In the which the diligent reader may not only consyder what commoditie may hereby chaunce to the hole christian world in tyme to come, but also learne many secreates touchynge the lande, the sea, and the starres, very necessarie to be knowen to al such as shal attempte any navigations, or otherwise have delite to beholde the strange and woonderfull woorkes of God and nature. Wrytten in the Latine tounge by Peter Martyr, of Angleria, and translated into Englysshe by Rycharde Eden.

The publication of Richard Eden's tome in 1555 was an important moment in the story of pro-Spanish propaganda from London. Mary Tudor had come to the throne in July 1553. Mary was born in 1516, and her mother, Katharine of Aragon, was the daughter of Ferdinand and Isabella. (Ferdinand, heir to the throne of Aragon, had married Isabella, the heiress of Castile, in 1469.) In July 1554, in Winchester Cathedral, Mary married Philip, King of Naples and Jerusalem; who thereafter was styled King of England (although he was never crowned). Philip, born in 1527, was a great-grandson of Ferdinand and Isabella and was to become King of Spain in 1556. Eden had apparently been very impressed by the royal wedding procession through the City of London in August 1554. His book was published in September 1555; the first martyr had been burnt at Smithfield in February. Eden was cited for heresy in 1556, but merely lost his job.

In his long and effusive preface to *The Decades*, Eden recognised that there were those in 'unthankful England' who failed to appreciate the merits of 'our noble and gracious prince King Philip'. Eden has an extended and rhetorical section attacking the critics of Spain:[90]

Stop thine ears from vain fables, as from the enchanting mermaids. For as many speak of Robin Hood and of his bow that never shot therein, so do fools prate of such things as they know not.

The 'fables' included rumours that the Emperor Charles V was ill, or dead; that 'the Indies have rebelled', and have produced no gold; that Spain 'is a beggarly country'. Eden wishes to point out 'how England is in a few years decayed and impoverished, and how on the contrary part Spain is enriched' by the wealth of the Indies. England has gone to seed since the 1530s, and the dissolution of the Religious Houses: things are cheaper in Spain 'than ever they were in England since the sign of the steeple, the poor man's inn, was pulled down in all places'. English tourists have complained about the food and service in Spain; finding 'great fault that in travelling in Spain, men shall be served with half a hen, and go to the cooks for their meat, and to the tavern for their drink.' But is this not better than the profiteering caterers in London where the traveller sometimes has

to pay thrice for one thing; as the manner is to do in some of our inns and

[90] 53-4.

taverns, where all that eat roast meat are beaten with the spit. As were they that of late in Bartholomew Fair paid 40 pence for a pig, where the good man of the house was not ashamed to make his vaunt that he had made 4 shillings of a pig, and had in one day taken 4 pound for pigs.

There is a little essay in commendation of Spain, beginning with Pliny (born in Spain).

The hero figure is Ferdinand, who died in 1516.[91] If we look at his descendants we can but think of Genesis 17:4-6. 'God hath fulfilled in him also' writes Eden, 'the promises and blessings of Abraham, as to make him the father of many nations, and his seed to grow great upon the earth'. In a manner, 'Christ only excepted, there never lived man to whom God hath given greater benefits and showed more favours'. He was another Gideon, the warrior figure from the Book of Judges. He made conquests in France, Germany, Flanders, Africa and India. He drove out of Spain the Jews and the Moors, thus becoming a 'defence and brazen wall to all Christendom'. Indeed he surpassed the Heroes of the Old Testament. Solomon obtained great riches by the voyages to Ophir; but at that time there was 'no knowledge of Antipodes, neither did any of his ships sail about the whole world, pierce the ocean'. God gave grace to Noah: 'by whom He saved the remnant of mankind, being but few in number.' He gave greater grace to Ferdinand: 'by whose means He saved not only the bodies but also the souls of innumerable millions of men inhabiting a great part of the world heretofore unknown, and drowned in the deluge of error.' Ferdinand was the 'father of faith" to a 'spiritual Israel'; thus improving upon Abraham. Spain has 'planted a new Israel, much greater than that which Moses led through the Red Sea'. Throughout the ages, 'true commendation' has gone to men

which in building of cities, towns, fortresses, bridges, conduits, havens, ships, and such other, have so joined magnificence with profit that both may remain for an eternal testimony of absolute glory, whose perfection extendeth to the gratifying of universal mankind, as far as man's mortality will permit.[92]

Praise in the Old Testament went to 'excellent artificers': Solomon, who built the Temple, and Ezra who renewed it; Bezalel in the Book of Exodus, who engineered the construction of the tabernacle; Hiram King of Tyre, who (II Samuel) sent materials and craftsmen to David in Jerusalem. Cicero 'defineth true glory to be a fame of many and great deserts either toward our citizens, our country, or toward all mankind'. We look to the men 'whom the antiquity called Heroes'. Now, we look to the rulers of Spain: and 'the heroical acts of the Spaniards of these days'.[93]

Eden especially draws attention to 'their merciful wars against these naked people'.[94]

[91] 51-2. [92] 49. [93] 50. [94] *ibid.*

They have taken nothing from them but such as they themselves were well willing to depart with, and accounted as superfluities; as gold, precious stones, and such other. For the which they recompensed them with such things as they much more esteemed.

Critics have complained that the Europeans 'possess and inhabit their regions, and use them as bondsmen and tributaries; where before they were free'. Eden's reply:

They inhabit their regions indeed. Yet so, that by their diligence and better manuring the same, they may now better sustain both, than one before. Their bondage is such as is much rather to be desired than their former liberty: which was to the cruel cannibals rather a horrible licentiousness than a liberty; and to the innocent so terrible a bondage, that in the midst of their fearful idleness they were ever in danger to be prey to those man-hunting wolves.

The Indians have been converted; and 'those who could by no means be brought to civility' have been killed. Thus by the 'manhood and policy of the Spaniards' there has been fulfilled the prophecy of Isaiah: 'that the wolf and the lamb shall feed together' (Isaiah 65:25). Isaiah also prophecied: 'He shall bring forth judgement unto the Gentiles' (42:1). So

the Spaniards, as the ministers of grace and liberty, brought unto these new Gentiles the victory of Christ's death, whereby they, being subdued with the worldly sword, are now made free from the bondage of Satan's tyranny.

By the 'godly zeal' of the Kings of Spain 'this mighty portion of the world hath been added to the flock of Christ's congregation'. England should rejoice to see 'the kingdom of God to be so far enlarged upon the face of the earth, to the confusion of the devil and the Turkish Antichrist'.

There are those, Eden acknowledges, who 'hold opinion that none ought to be compelled to the faith'.[95] But

we see by experience that without disputing of opinions (lest the patients should die before the physicians agree of the remedy) these enterprises have taken good effect; to the great glory of God, who called men unto Him by divers means, and at divers ages of the declining world, otherwise now than in the time of Christ and His Apostles.

Israel took possession of the Land of Promise. If the old Israelites could

use all means and policies to build up the walls of earthly Jerusalem, how much more then ought the spiritual Israelites to use all possible means to build up the walls and temples of spiritual Jerusalem, whose foundation is

[95] 56.

Christ, willing all the nations of the world to be builded upon the same. It is the property of a wise builder to use such tools as the work requireth. And not in all times or in all works to use one tool.[96]

Others object that 'the desire of gold was the chief cause that moved the Spaniards and Portugals to search the new found lands'.[97] It is true that 'covetousness' must always be condemned. Many in England show 'little love, charity or liberality (if not rather cruelty, tyranny and oppression) to their poor neighbours and brothern dwelling even at home at their own elbow'; so naturally they will not 'depart with any of their goods, much less adventure their bodies, to the furtherance of Christ's religion in these regions, being so far from them'.[98] But though the 'desire of gold' may have been the 'chief cause' of the Spanish Conquest,[99]

yet doth it not follow that it was the only cause, forasmuch as nothing letteth but that a man may be a warrior or a merchant, and also a Christian. Therefore whatever our chief intent be, either to obtain worldly fame, or riches (although the zeal to increase Christian religion ought chiefly to move us) I would to God we would first attempt the matter.

Thus

may these barbarians by the only conversation with the Christians (although they were enforced thereto) be brought to such familiarity with civility and virtue, that not only we may take great commodity thereby, but they may also herewith imbibe true religion, as a thing accidental, although neither they nor we should seek the same. For like as they that go much in the sun are coloured therewith, although they go not for that purpose, so may the conversation of the Christians with the Gentiles induce them to our religion, where there is no greater cause of contrary to resist; as is in the Jews and Turks, who are already drowned in their confirmed error.

The American Indians are 'simple Gentiles living only after the law of nature'. They

may well be likened to a smooth and bare table unpainted, or a white paper unwritten, upon the which you may at the first paint or write what you list, as you cannot upon tables already painted, unless you raze or blot out the first forms. They may also the easier be allured to the Christian faith, for that it is more agreeable to the law of nature than either the ceremonious law of Moses, or portentious fables of Mohamet's Alcoran.

Not to support the American enterprise is 'the reproach of all Christendom'. It is an especial reproach to England. We are nearer the New World than are the Spaniards: 'within 25 days sailing, and less.'[100]
    Eden points out that[101]

---

[96] 56-7. [97] 57. [98] 59. [99] 57. [100] 55. [101] 55.

there yet remaineth another portion of that mainland, reaching toward the north-east, thought to be as large as the other, and yet not known but only by the sea coasts, neither inhabited by any Christian men.

One 'worthy old man yet living', as Pietro records, set out from England and landed 'in the north corner, and most barbarous part hereof; from whence he was repulsed with ice in the month of July'. (That was Sebastian Cabot; who had touched on Greenland, Newfoundland, and possibly Labrador, in 1508. He died in 1557.)[102] In this north part of America, as so far discovered (Mexico, mainly, and Florida)

there are many fair and fruitful regions, high mountains and fair rivers, with abundance of gold, and divers kinds of beasts. Also cities and towns so well builded, and people of such civility, that this part of the world seemeth little inferior to our Europe, if the inhabitants had received our religion. They are witty people, and refuse not bartering with strangers.

So here is the opportunity for England. England has had its Heroes. Eden mentions Sir Hugh Willoughby and Richard Chancellor, who had sailed in 1553,[103] inspired by the hopes of Sebastian Cabot and John Dee for a north-east passage. Chancellor got as far as Archangel, and established contact with the Czar of Moscow. If ever

since the beginning of the world any enterprise hath deserved great praise as a thing achieved by men of heroical virtue, doubtless there was never any more worthy consideration and admiration, than is that which our nation have attempted by the north seas, to discover the mighty and rich empire of Cathay.

For one thing, it might bring about the defeat of the Turk:[104]

There can nothing be imagined more effectual for the confusion of the Turk, if the great Cham of Cathay and the Sophy of Persia on the one side, and the Christian princes on the other side, should with one consent invade his dominions; as did Tamburlane the emperor of the Tartars.

But the missionary hope lay in north America.
   Here Eden brings to witness Erasmus.

What negligence and slackness hath hitherto been in Christian men in this kind of building of God's lively temple, the great clerk Erasmus hath declared in his book entitled *Ecclesiastes*.[105]

(*Ecclesiastae*, or *De Ratione Concionandi*, a work on Preaching, published in August 1535, and dedicated to the memory of John Fisher, who had been executed in June.)
   Eden gives an excerpt in Latin from this work. He goes on to tell us

[102] See below, p.33.   [103] Eden-Arber, 59.   [104] 60.   [105] 57.

that Erasmus had here been prompted by the Portuguese historian Damião de Goes; who also said that Erasmus 'was determined to write a just volume of this matter, if he had not been prevented by death'.[106] Erasmus died in 1536.

At the end of the 1555 volume, Eden permitted himself some verses:[107]

> I am not eloquent I know it right well.
> If I be not barbarous I desire no more,
> I have not for every word asked counsel
> Of eloquent Elyot or Sir Thomas More.
> Take it therefore as I have intended,
> The faults with favour may soon be amended.

Thomas More, with Mary's accession to the throne, had retrospectively become a Hero. A vast edition of his English works, edited in two volumes by his nephew William Rastell, was to be published in 1557. 1556 saw the publication of the second edition of the English translation of *Utopia*, by Ralph Robinson. In the first edition of 1551 Robinson had observed that

it is much to be lamented, and not only of us Englishmen, that a man of so incomparable wit, of so profound knowledge, of so absolute learning, and so fine eloquence was yet nevertheless so much blinded, rather with obstinacy than with ignorance, that he could not, or rather would not, see the shining light of God's holy truth in certain principal points of Christian religion; but did rather choose to persevere and continue in his wilful and stubborn obstinacy even to the very death.

But, wrote Robinson, 'letting this matter pass, I return again to Utopia'.[108] These observations were, of course, deleted in the edition of 1556.

Pietro Martire died in 1526. Decade I had been reprinted in Alcalá in 1516, and issued with II and III. The full eight Decades were published in 1533. The definitive Latin text (with a new index) appeared in Paris in 1587: *De orbe novo … decades*, dedicated to Sir Walter Raleigh. The editor, aged thirty-five, was an MA of Christ Church Oxford who had been chaplain and secretary to the English ambassador in Paris since 1583: the Reverend Richard Hakluyt.

---

[106] 58.   [107] 398.   [108] Everyman *Utopia*, 2-3.

2

The Utopia of the High Emperor of Inde

Thomas More crossed to Bruges in May 1515; sent as 'ambassador into Flanders' by Henry VIII, the 'most victorious and triumphant king', 'in all royal virtues a prince most peerless.'[1] He went on to Antwerp. And in August 1515, after he had heard mass in the collegiate church of Notre Dame, More saw his friend Peter Giles talking to a stranger, 'whom by his favour and apparel forthwith I judged to be a mariner'. This was Raphael Hythloday from Portugal. The three men returned to More's lodgings; 'and there in my garden, upon a bench covered with green turfs, we sat down talking together',[2] with More's boy, John Clement, in silent attendance.[3] During that summer day, Raphael 'rehearsed divers acts and constitutions' in the light of which Europeans 'may take example to amend their faults, enormities and errors'.[4]

Utopia, published at Louvain in December 1516, was in the same category as Tacitus' *On Germany*, a popular student text of the time (especially in Germany). Tacitus, writing in the year 98, held up the 'barbarian' Germans as an example to Rome. They gave an example of 'good morality'; better than the 'good laws in some places that we know'. Their sexual habits were refreshingly austere: 'there is no feature in their morality that deserves higher praise. They are almost unique among barbarians in being satisfied with one wife each.'

German women live in a chastity that is impregnable, uncorrupted by the temptations of public shows, or the excitements of banquets ... Adultery in that populous nation is rare in the extreme, and punishment is summary and left to the husband.

The husband shaves off the hair of his erring wife, strips her in the presence of her family, and flogs her through the village. 'No one in Germany finds vice amusing'.[5] The natives have valour, energy, and ability in battle.[6] They have 'holy places' – the 'woods and groves'.

[1] Everyman *Utopia* (R. Robinson translation), 13.
[2] *ibid.*, 14-16.
[3] *ibid.*, 8.
[4] *ibid.*, 18.
[5] *Tacitus on Britain and Germany*, Penguin Classics, tr. H. Mattingly, 1948, 115-17.
[6] *ibid.*, 106.

And 'they call by the name of God that hidden presence which is seen only by the eye of reverence'.[7] They are also extremely idle.[8]

Utopia was a familiar *type* of book. The type was made more cogent by the Christian context: the 'shame' expressed by a Spanish missionary friar in the 1590s:[9]

shame which we Christians should feel that pagans, of less talent than ourselves, should have been better ruled and ordered in matters of morality and behaviour during the time of their heathendom.

What makes *Utopia* individual and uniquely satisfying is the verisimilitude – careful, detailed, playful – of the fiction.

More's well-stocked imagination was alerted by the American experience. He had read the Columbus of 1493, the Vespucci of 1503 and 1507, the Pietro Martire of 1511. The 'oration of the naked governor' in Pietro is a good instance of the 'myth' of the Noble Barbarian, who goes so far as to admonish the Europeans.[10] Various details find their way onto the island of Utopia: Pietro on Indian 'wine'; the large, communal Halls described by Vespucci and Pietro; the Indian wars with their neighbours, mentioned by Vespucci; Pietro's information that the Indians had no judges; the fact that the Indians move their dwelling place every few years (Vespucci). Beyond the details, certain themes which tantalised the mind of More found echo in the travel literature. Columbus' 1493 belief that the Indians were ripe for Christianity; reinforced by Pietro's assumption that Christianity is 'agreeable to the Law of Nature'. The fact that the Indians set no store by gold or jewels (Vespucci); that they have no 'greed' (Columbus), *cupidita* (Vespucci), 'Mine and Thine', *Meum* and *Tuum* (Pietro). And, most important, the assumption – a possibility to Columbus, a hard fact to Vespucci and Pietro – that they have no private property. The Columbus/Pietro picture in 1511 of the Golden World in America was what More needed to spark his creative gift.

[7] *ibid.*, 108.

[8] *ibid.*, 113.

[9] Gerónimo de Mendieta. Quoted by Elliott, 'Discovery of America and Discovery of Man,' 24.

[10] On the earlier history of the idea of the 'noble savage', the best guide is George Boas. A.O. Lovejoy and G. Boas, *Primitivism and Related Ideas in Antiquity*, first published in 1935, has a long chapter, largely by Boas, on 'The Noble Savage in Antiquity', pp.287-367. Covers the fourth century B.C. to Tacitus; rather a card-index collection of extracts, but valuable. In 1948 Boas published *Essays on Primitivism and Related Ideas in the Middle Ages*: his chapter on 'The Noble Savage' ends with Columbus. (Two further volumes were to follow in this project, which was never realised.) Gonnard, *La Légende du bon sauvage*, 1946, goes from antiquity to the early nineteenth century; interesting and quite short, but uses mainly French material. Hoxie Neale Fairchild's *The Noble Savage: a Study in Romantic Naturalism*, 1928, is concerned with the eighteenth and early nineteenth centuries. Dr A.R. Sheldrake of Clare College, Cambridge, has pointed out to me the relatively recent concept in science fiction of *nasty* beings in a New World; dating from H.G. Wells' *War of the Worlds* – and condemned by the Soviets as 'anti-Utopian'!

From 1493 all thoughtful Europeans gave thanks (in the words of William Strachey in his *Historie of Travell into Virginia Britania*, written in 1612) to

> that mighty and merciful Providence, who in our times would vouchsafe to let us see those so many riches, wonders, and salvation of nations, the testimony of His great love unto us, which He had with strong bars, as it were, shut up from our forefathers.[11]

More heard travellers' tales in Bruges and Antwerp. He could also have heard them in London. John Cabot (Giovanni Cabota) had sailed from Bristol in 'The Matthew' in May 1497, and made his landfall on 24 June 1497, probably on the north-east tip of Newfoundland[12] – the 'New found land', as it was called by 1502. John left Bristol again in 1498, but was lost on the voyage.

During the year September 1501 to September 1502, noted the *Great Chronicle of London,* 'were brought unto the King three men taken in the New found Isle'. 'They were clothed in beasts' skins, and ate raw flesh, and spake such speech that no man could understand them, and their demeanour like to brute beasts.' Henry VII kept them at Court. The Chronicler saw two of them, wearing English clothes, at the Palace of Westminster in 1504.[13]

One of Giovanni's three sons was Sebastian, who in 1504 was chief navigator of an expedition to the 'Newe Found Iland'. In 1505 Sebastian was given an annuity of £10 by Henry VII for his work in 'the fyndinge of the newe founde landes'.[14] He made another expedition in 1508 (or at any rate during the years 1507-9), and reached Greenland (probably: or possibly Labrador).[15] This voyage was 'the first to have as its main objective the circumventing of North America', writes Professor Quinn,[16] who presents Sebastian as the inventor of the concept of the North-West passage – the precursor of the expeditions to Greenland, Baffin Island and Labrador by Martin Frobisher (1576-8) and John Davis (1585-7). Pietro Martire wrote of Sebastian's adventure in his *Decades* of 1516.

We have seen Richard Eden drawing attention to this section in his 1555 Preface.[17] In the text (in the Eden translation) Pietro called Sebastian 'my very friend, whom I use familiarly, and delight to have him sometimes keep me company in mine own house'.[18] His

[11] Ed. Wright and Freund, 1953, 138.

[12] Morison, *Northern Voyages*, 174. For John Cabot, see Morison Ch.6, 'John Cabot's Voyages 1497-98'.

[13] The passage is given in Williamson, *Cabot Voyages*, Hakluyt Society, 220.

[14] Alwyn A. Ruddock, 'The Reputation of Sebastian Cabot', *Bulletin Institute Historical Research*, May 1974, XLVII, 115, 95-9. Dr Ruddock announces her forthcoming book *Columbus, Cabot, and the English Discovery of America*.

[15] See Hoffman, *Cabot to Cartier*, Ch.4, 'The Voyage of Sebastian Cabot'; Quinn, *England and Discovery of America*, 139-43.

[16] Quinn, ed., *North American Discovery*, 211.

[17] Arber, ed., *First Three English Books on America*, 55.

[18] *ibid.*, 162.

description of the *c.*1508 voyage is as follows:[19] Sebastian

directed his course so far toward the north pole that even in the month of July
he found monstrous heaps of ice swimming in the sea, and in manner
continual daylight. Yet saw he the land in that tract, free from ice, which had
been molten by heat of the sun. Thus seeing such heaps of ice before him, he
was enforced to turn his sails and follow the west.

He coasted along a 'great land' which he called 'Baccallaos':

because that in the seas thereabout he found so great multitudes of certain
big fishes much like unto tunnies (which the inhabitants call *Baccallaos*) that
they sometimes stayed his ships. He found also the people of those regions
covered with beasts' skins; yet not without the use of reason.

He also saw

great plenty of bears in those regions, which use to eat fish. For plunging
themselves into the water where they perceive a multitude of these fishes to
lie, they fasten their claws in their scales, and so draw them to land and eat
them. So that (as he saith) the bears being thus satisfied with fish, are not
noisesome to men.

Sebastian brought some Indians home with him. But Henry VII had
died in April 1509; and Henry VIII did not have his father's
generosity towards Atlantic voyagers.

The conversation at More's house in the street called Bucklersbury,
in the City of London, could easily run to American matters. More's
sister Elizabeth had married a Coventry lawyer called John Rastell
(*c.*1475-1536): populariser of the law, M.P., editor of Chronicles, set-
designer and printer. During 1516 (*Utopia* was published in
December) John Rastell was making plans to lead an expedition to
the New Found lands.[20] He seems to have had in mind a 'colony': this
was to be more than a trading or exploring venture. A number of ships
departed in the spring of 1517, probably four or five. But the trip was
a failure: unruly mariners, bad leadership by the forty year old
Rastell. The fleet got no further than Ireland. Rastell himself
remained for a time at Waterford.

Rastell returned to England about 1519. About 1520 he printed a
play he had written: *A new interlude and a mery of the nature of the iiij
elements*. Only one copy survives, in the British Museum, containing
the first use in England of music printing from moveable type.[21] The
play was performed in Cambridge in 1971, as part of the 400th

[19] *ibid.*, 161. Morison thinks Sebastian was 'built up' by Pietro: *Northern Voyages*,
220-5.

[20] For the 1517 expedition, Quinn, *England and Discovery of America*, 162-9. For this,
and Rastell in general, Reed, *Early Tudor Drama*, 1-28, 187-233.

[21] A.H. King, 'The Significance of Early Music Printing', *The Library*, XXVI, 3,
September 1971.

anniversary celebrations of the establishment of the Cambridge University Press by John Siberch. The Interlude declares 'many proper points of Philosophy Natural', of 'divers strange Effects and Cures'; and 'of divers Strange Lands'. There is a long speech of 'Experience' to 'Studious Desire'. He refers to the world beyond Iceland:[22]

> so cold it is
> No man may there abide.
>
> This sea is called the great Ocean
> So great it is that never man
> Could tell it sith the world began
> Till now within this twenty year
> Westward be found new lands
> That we never heard tell of before this
> By writing nor other means
> Yet many now have been there.
>
> And that country is so large of room
> Much longer than all Christendom
> Without fable or guile.
> For divers mariners have it tried
> And sailed straight by the coast side
> About five thousand mile.
>
> But what commodities be within
> No man can tell nor well imagine
> But yet not long ago
> Some men of this country went
> By the King's noble consent
> It for to search to that intent
> And could not be brought thereto.
>
> But they that were there venturers
> Have cause to curse their mariners
> False of promise and dissemblers
> That falsely them betrayed
> Which would take no pain to sail farther
> Than their own list and pleasure
> Wherefore that voyage and divers other
> Such caitiffs have destroyed.
>
> O what thing a had be then
> If that they that be English men

[22] I have modernised the text printed in Arber in 1885: *First Three English Books on America*, xx-xxi. A modernised version of the whole play was printed in 1971: *Siberch Celebrations*, ed. Brooke Crutchley, London; the speech is 106-11. For Rastell's information about America, and knowledge (or lack of it) of geography and maps: G.B. Parks, 'The Geography of the *Interlude of the Four Elements*', *Philological Quarterly*, XVII, III, July 1938, 251-62; J. Parr, 'More Sources of Rastell's *Interlude*', *Publications Modern Language Association America*, vol.LX, no.1, part 1, March 1945, 48-58; J. Parr, 'Rastell's Geographical Knowledge of America', *Philological Quarterly*, XXVII, III, July 1948, 229-40.

Might have been the first of all
That there should have taken possession
And made first building and habitation
A memory perpetual
And also what an honorable thing
Both to the realm and to the King
To have had his dominion extending
There into so far a ground
Which the noble King of late memory
The most wise Prince the VII Henry
Caused first for to be found.

'Experience' now turns to the American Indian.

And what a great meritorious deed
It were to have the people instructed
To live more virtuously
And to learn to know of men the manner
And also to know God their maker
Which as yet live all beastly
For they nother know God nor the Devil
Nor never heard tell of heaven nor hell
Writing nor other scripture
But yet in the stead of God Almight
They honour the sun for his great light
For that doth them great pleasure.

Building nor house they have none at all
But woods, cotes,[23] and caves small.
No marvel though it be so
For they use no manner of iron
Nother in tool nor other weapon
That should help them thereto.

Copper they have which is found
In divers places above the ground
Yet they dig not therefore
For as I said they have none iron
Whereby they should in the earth mine
To search for any ore.

Great abundance of woods there be
Most part fir and pine apple tree
Great riches might come thereby
Both pitch and tar and soap ashes
As they make in the east lands
By brine-ing thereof only.

Fish they have so great plenty
That in havens take and slain they be
With stays[24] withouten sail.
Now Frenchmen and other have founden the trade

[23] As in 'dove cote'.   [24] 'Stay': a heavy rope.

> That yearly of fish there they laid
> Above an hundred sail.[25]

> But in the south part of that country
> The people there go naked alway
> The land is of so great heat
> And in the north part all the clothes
> That they wear is but beasts' skins
> They have no other feat.
> But how the people first began
> In what country or whence they came
> For clerks it is a question.
> Other things more I have in store
> That I could tell thereof, but now no more
> Till another season.

'Studious Desire', still awake, asks 'Experience' to continue:

> Then at your pleasure show some other thing;
> It liketh me so well your coming,
> Ye cannot talk amiss.

'Experience' mentions the Mediterannean, the Turk, Africa and India, the Khan of Cathay; and 'the land of prester John', in 'India major' (that is, modern India: middle or lesser India was Arabia and Ethiopia). But he reverts to the New Found Lands:

> But this new lands found lately
> Be called America, by cause only
> Americus did first them find.

He is doubtful whether America can be reached by 'the great East sea' (that is, the North-East Passage):

> But whether that sea go thither directly
> Or if any wilderness between them do lie
> No man knoweth for certain:
> But these new lands by all cosmography
> From the Khan of Cathay's land cannot lie
> Little past a thousand mile.
> But from these new lands men may sail plain
> Eastward and come to England again
> Where we began ere while.

At this point, 'Humanity' ·and 'Sensual Appetite' turn up, and the conversation switches to other merry matters.

We have noted the use of Vespucci material in 'the first English

---

[25] For rivalry in the Newfoundland fishery, see Cell, *English Enterprise in Newfoundland*, Chs. 1 and 2.

book on America': *Of the newe landes,* printed at Antwerp about 1510.[26]
The book made more than Vespucci available in English. The full title
was:[27]

*Of the newe landes and of ye people founde by the messengers of the kynge of portyngale
named Emanuel. Of the x dyvers nacyons crystened. Of pope John and his landes and of
the costely keyes and wonders molodyes that in that land is.*

The book begins with a reference to the voyage of Vasco da Gama
from Lisbon in 1497, under the patronage of King Manoel. According
to the editor, Da Gama reached 'Armenica': and here the Vespucci
paraphrase appears.[28] There are short sections on India, Arabia and
Africa; including a mention of the 'black moors' of Guinea,[29] who are
given a wood-cut illustration. (In 1555 Richard Eden wrote of 'the
black moors called Ethiopians or Negroes': as in Guinea.)[30] There
follows the (very brief) information about the 'ten divers christianed
nations':[31] Latin, Greek, Indian, Jacobite (Syria), Nestorian (Persia),
Maronite (Lebanon), Armenian, Syrian (India), Mororab, Georgian.
And then an item to which the second half of the book is devoted: a
letter, saluting the Roman Emperor and the King of France (and
asking the latter to recommend the author to 'the mighty King of
England') from 'I, Pope John, by the grace of God the mighty King,
above all Kings of the world:' ruling over greater and lesser India.[32]

John is 562 years old (at one point: 507 at another). His land is
divided from that of 'the great King of Israel' by a 'great river';
guarded on John's side by 42 castles, and 50,000 cavalry, with 6,000
cross bows and 15,000 long bows. There are 42 Kingdoms 'under us',
'and all good Christian people'. He writes to describe 'the manner of
our living', 'of our folk or people, and of our land'. The wild life
includes elephants, dromedaries, unicorns, bears, lions, serpents,
dragons, phoenixes, and oxes with seven horns; there are wood-cuts of
an elephant with a castle on its back, a flying gryphon carrying a man,
and a dragon guarding a tree. The natives include men and women
'the which have no more than one eye afore, and behind, they have
three, or four even'. They inhabit a 'great desert or forest'. There are
pigmies, the size of a child of seven, and giants thirty-three feet high.
Creatures like men from the waist up, like horses below; people with
round feet like horses, and four claws on their heels; and some who eat
human flesh (they are 'cursed of God'). There are wood-cuts of a man
with one eye in his forehead, of the round-footed people, of the
pigmies, and of a creature with the body of a man and the head of a
dog. There is an island populated entirely by warrior women, 'very
manly in fighting, and very hardy'; males are allowed there for only
nine days in the year, for 'conversation and fellowship'.

[26] Above, p.18.
[27] Arber, *First Three English Books on America,* xxvii.
[28] *ibid.*   [29] *ibid.,* xxviii.   [30] *ibid.,* 374.
[31] *ibid.,* xxx-i.   [32] *ibid.,* xxxii-vi.

The land is under the protection of the Apostle St Thomas; traditionally the founder of the 'Syrian' church in India. He 'doth more miracles than any saint in heaven': 'For he cometh bodily every year in his church, and doth a sermon.' The inhabitants 'believe in God the Father, in God the Son, and in God the Holy Ghost; the which be unpartable, and one very God, and is all things mighty.' Three wooden crosses are placed at the entrance of every city 'in worship of our Lord Jesus Christ'; and a cross is carried before John as he rides. The body of the prophet Daniel is also treasured in the empire. John is a priest-king: 'I myself say also Mass in the great Feasts of the year, and therefore I am called Pope John.' Christ sent an angel to John's father in a dream, commanding him to build a palace for 'your son coming': 'For he shall be the greatest king of the world, and he shall a long time live.' When the father awoke, he was 'very merry, and incontinent he began to make this palace'. (Incontinent: straightaway.) It is a Crystal Palace, and covered in precious stones; and the interior is 'wrought with stars, like if it were the heaven'. There are twenty four pillars of 'fine gold', 'of precious stones of all manner sorts' – and no windows. It contains a fountain, running with liquid 'like wine in drinking, so that who thereof drinketh he desired none other meat nor drink, and no man can tell from whence it cometh or whither it goeth'. There is another fountain in the empire, 'full of the grace of the Holy Ghost', in which if a man wash 'he shall become young of thirty year' (John has done so six times). Also,

there is another great marvel in this same palace. When we shall go to our dinner, so is there no manner of meat made ready for us, nor there is no manner of instruments to make ready withal; but there cometh before us all manner of delicious meat, that cometh there through the Holy Ghost.

On 'great feast days' John presides in his palace; and St Thomas obligingly 'preacheth' there to the people (in addition to his sermon in church).

'And it is not well possible to write all manner of goodness they have which yet be in our land. And ye shall understand that we write nothing to you but true is.' Certainly there was in the empire a regard for truth. A man telling a lie shall 'incontinent be slain'. The other capital offence is adultery:

There is also in our land no man so hardy that dare break his wedlock, but if he did he should incontinent be burned. For our Lord Himself hath ordained wedlock, therefore it should be kept, by reason if that we loved our Lord Jesu Christ. For it is one of the sacraments of the Holy Church.

This extraordinary pot-pourri borrows much from Pliny's description of Africa and the 'Ethiopians'. (Pliny was to appear in English in 1556.) Giants; anthropophagi, 'which we call cannibals'; men with no head (the mouth and eyes being in the breast); men with the head of a dog; men with one eye; men with no nose, upper lip or tongue.[33] The Greeks had coined the word 'Aethiopia' for north-east Africa. To the Israelites, it was the land of Cush, peopled by the tribe of Ham, son of Noah. It was traditionally a land of marvels and monsters. And it was traditionally confused with India.

In an article published in 1962,[34] J.D.M. Derrett drew attention to More's possible use of material from India proper; by way of an Indian Christian, Joseph, who from 1501 visited Portugal and Italy, giving details of Christian communities in India, as well as of native Indian religion (especially the Hindus of south-west India). This material was published in Italian translation in 1507. (The Portuguese captured Goa in 1510.)

The framework of the 1510 Antwerp version of the 'land of Prester John' is derived (rather carelessly) from the fourteenth-century *Travels* of Sir John Mandeville. Mandeville was an English physician who died at Liège in 1372, having left England thirty years earlier. His compilation was written in French about 1360.[35] The earliest known manuscript is French, 1371. There are three fifteenth-century English manuscripts. The best is in the British Museum (Egerton) Mss.: the translator worked from French and Latin versions. It was first printed in English, by Richard Pynson, about 1496; and was three times printed by Wynkyn de Worde between 1499 and 1503. Other published versions are: Dutch 1470; Italian 1480; French 1480; German 1481; Latin 1484.

Mandeville had spent a long time, he tells the reader, at the court of Prester John, 'emperor of India': called 'Prester' and 'John' because, while attending a Christian service in Egypt (he was not then Christian: many of his subjects were) he decided that 'he would no more be called King ne Emperor, but Priest'; and took the name of the first priest to leave the church – Priest John. In 'the land of Prester John' now 'are many good Christian men, and well living; and men of good faith, and of good law.'[36] There are 'noble cities', 'fair towns', and 'many isles great and large'.[37] The principal cities are Nise, a 'noble city and a rich', and Suse. The elaborate palace is at Suse; Mandeville gives more details of the precious fabric than we get in 1510.[38] And the emperor's bed is 'all of sapphire, well bound with gold, for to make him sleep well, and for to destroy lechery; for he will not lie by his wives but at four certain times in the year, and then all only for to get children'. The patriach 'is there as it were Pope'.[39] There are 'priests among them that say mass'; not exactly as in

[33] Jones, *Elizabethan Image of Africa* (Folger Booklet), 6-7.

[34] 'Thomas More and Joseph the Indian', *Journal Royal Asiatic Society*, April 1962.

[35] I have taken these 'facts' (which all attract controversy) from the Introduction by Malcolm Letts to his edition of *Mandeville's Travels* for the Hakluyt Society, 1953: two volumes, continuous paging. The article on Mandeville by Sir Henry Yule in the eleventh edition (1911) of *Encyclopaedia Britannica* is good.

[36] Letts (ed.), *Mandeville's Travels*, 210. Letts printed the Egerton MS.

[37] *ibid.*, 187-8.   [38] *ibid.*, 192-3.   [39] *ibid.*, 193.

Europe – they follow what 'St Thomas the Apostle taught them in old time'. For 'of the ordinances and additions of the Court of Rome which our priests use, ken they naught'.[40] The Emperor, who has the cross borne before him, is Christian, 'and the most part of his land also, if all it be so that they have not all the articles of our belief so clearly as we have'. They acknowledge God: Father, Son and Holy Ghost. And 'full devout men they are': without 'fraud or guile'.[41] The empire, which would appear to be in the area of Mongolia, is in in length four months' journey; and in breadth, without measure.[42] It has seventy-two provinces, each with a king.[43] There are some wild men with horns.[44]

'Trow all this, for sickerly I saw it with mine eyes, and mickle more than I have told you.'[45]

What Mandeville had seen with his own eyes was one of the many manuscripts in circulation of the *Epistola Presbyteri Johannis*, written in the mid-twelfth century. This is an insolent letter written to the Byzantine Emperor Manuel Comnenus (1143-80). The Emperor is addressed merely as 'governor': *gubernator*. The writer is *Presbyter Johannes: dominus dominantium* (Revelation 17:14, 'Lord of Lords and King of Kings' – a description of Christ); supreme ruler of the three Indies, with 72 liege provinces. The authorship is a mystery, and the language of the original is in doubt. Professor Karl Helleiner, in a brilliant paper given in Toronto in 1958,[46] thought the letter was written in Latin by someone with a smattering of Greek, and familiar with the pompus letter-writing style of the Constantinople Chancery. And

written, in part, as a piece of anti-Byzantine propaganda, perhaps by a man who served the political interest of the Norman princes of Sicily, or by a German (could it have been Wibald of Stablo by any chance?) who resented the monopolistic claims of the Greeks to the Imperial dignity.[47]

There are various points in the background which might be noted. The exotic wonders of the Indies had been a commonplace since Aristotle. St John the Apostle called himself 'presbyteros' in two of the three New Testament Epistles attributed to him. Eusebius mentioned, in the fourth century, a 'Presbyter Johannes'; presumably the Apostle. By tradition, the Apostle Thomas had been martyred in India; King Alfred had sent an embassy to his shrine. There were Christian communities in South India, and Christian monarchs in

[40] *ibid.*, 210.   [41] *ibid.*, 189.   [42] *ibid.*, 193.
[43] *ibid.*, 189.   [44] *ibid.*, 191.   [45] *ibid.*, 193.
[46] 'Prester John's Letter: A Medieval Utopia': printed in *The Phoenix* (Journal of the Classical Association of Canada), 1959, vol.13, no.2, 47-57. I was fortunate to hear this paper; and Professor Helleiner gave me an offprint, from which my material is shamelessly lifted. There is a translation of the letter, from a French version printed about 1500, in Vsevolod Slessarev, *Prester John: The Letter and the Legend*, 67-79.
[47] Helleiner, 'Prester John's Letter', 56.

Abyssinia. 'The Indies' covered south and east Asia, Indo-China, Arabia, and Ethiopia. The Christian church in Ethiopia dates from the fourth century; it was dependant on the Patriarch in Alexandria, who transferred to Cairo in the seventh century. In 1122 a professed dignitary of the Christian Church in India had visited first Constantinople, and then Rome, claiming to be the guardian of the shrine of St Thomas; Calixtus II had been impressed. It seems that in the early 1140s a Moslem force was routed in Turkestan, probably by a Buddhist Asian ruler; by 1145 in Western Europe this event had become the victory of a Christian Prince, Prester John, a descendant of the Magi. By 1147 the Second Crusade had failed. So the promise of *Presbyter Johannes* in the letter to lead his army to Jerusalem was not unwelcome. (He also promised to give the Byzantine Emperor a post as major-domo at his court.)

We are already familiar with the details of his realm. The absence of poverty and theft. The lack of discord: *nulla divisio est apud nos.* Liars are treated as if they are dead; sent to Coventry. We have the bed of sapphire, the three-monthly intervals between procreative intercourse, and so on. Mandeville for some reason omitted the magic mirror in which all the machinations against the Emperor could be observed[48] – apparently a theme in early Persian literature, and influenced by the light-house in the harbour at Alexandria. There is a combination of temporal and spiritual office: the high steward, the cup bearer and the chamberlain, all kings, are, respectively, a Primate, an Archbishop and a Bishop. We have the Phoenix, the Gryphon, the Elephant; the Cyclops, the Pigmy.

> The precious stones ennumerated in medieval lapidaries, all the exotic animals known to medieval man from his bestiaries, all the familiar monsters of ancient fable and fiction, are found in Prester John's kingdom.[49]

Malcolm Letts, who printed a translation of those parts of the Letter used by Mandeville,[50] writes:

> It seems to have had a wide circulation; it filled the early maps with monsters and fables, gave a new impulse to geographical discovery, brought fresh hope to Christendom, then thoroughly alarmed at the increasing power of the infidel, and provided story-tellers with material which must have lasted for centuries.[51]

The English story teller of 1510 has, even more than Mandeville, the spirit (and more of some detail) of the twelfth-century author.

According to Mandeville,[52] to the east of the lands of Prester John were 'wastes and wildernesses and great rocks and mountains and a murk land, where no man may see, night ne day'. Beyond the

[48] Letts (ed.), *Mandeville's Travels*, 192.
[49] Helleiner, 'Prester John's Letter', 48.
[50] Letts, 499-507.
[51] *ibid.*, 187. [52] *ibid.*, 214-16.

wilderness is 'Paradise terrestial'. Here 'Adam and Eve were put; but they were there but a little while'. In a rare attack of reticence Mandeville confesses: 'Of Paradise can I not speak properly, for I have not been there.' The site is so high that it escaped the flood. It is impossible to reach by land; and is enclosed by a wall, and by eternal fire – the flaming sword of God. So 'no man living may go to Paradise'.

Columbus considered the matter in his journal, as edited by Las Casas.[53] 'Holy Scripture testifies that our Lord made the earthly Paradise in which he placed the Tree of Life.' (God planted 'the tree of the knowledge of good and evil' in 'the garden of Eden', and placed Adam in the garden; Genesis 2:15,17.) Columbus continues:

I do not find, and have never found, any Greek or Latin writings which definitely state the worldly situation of the earthly Paradise, nor have I seen a world map which establishes its position except by deduction.

All 'learned theologians' agree that it is 'in the east': Isidore, Strabo, Ambrose, Duns Scotus and Petrus Comestor among them. Some 'heathens' thought it was in the Fortunate Islands: 'which are the Canaries.' 'At the end of the east': but, as Las Casas comments, Columbus thought that 'those lands which he had now discovered' were 'the end of the east'.[54] In August 1498 the hints became facts. Columbus landed in Venezuela and felt that he was coming close to the site of the earthly paradise, that the waters he saw flowed from it. 'I believe that the earthly paradise lies here, which no one can enter except by God's leave.'[55] Las Casas was to doubt this theological and geographical exegesis: Columbus was of humble birth, not learned – and a foreigner.[56] (We have already noted Pietro Martire's similar scepticism about Columbus' hypothesis that the Old Testament Kingdom of Ophir was in the West Indies.)[57] At any rate there was some scholarship and some observation behind Columbus' debates about the earthly Paradise.[58] It was not merely a poetical conceit, like Michael Drayton's salute in 1606 to

> Virginia,
> Earth's only paradise.[59]

William Strachey, in his *Historie of Travell into Virginia Britania*, written in 1612, wondered whether Columbus had read the *Timaeus* of

[53] Cohen, *Voyages of Columbus*, Penguin Classics, 220-1.
[54] Jane/Vigneras, *Journal of Columbus*, 176.
[55] Cohen, *Voyages of Columbus*, 221.
[56] Summarised from Las Casas' *Historia* by Cohen, *Voyages of Columbus*, 222.
[57] Above, p.22.
[58] 'Paradise' is Old Persian for an enclosed garden. Adam's garden was in the eastern part of 'Eden' (a plain). For traditions of thought about the location and character of the Earthly Paradise, see especially Duncan, *Milton's Earthly Paradise*.
[59] 'To the Virginian Voyage'. In Wright (ed.), *Elizabethans' America*, 161.

Plato, with its material on 'an ancient and superanuat history of an island in time of great antiquity called Atlantis (Athlantides), lying to the West'.[60] Plato, about 375 B.C., recounted a tradition told to Solon on a visit to Egypt about 594 B.C. of an island beyond the Straits of Gibraltar – civilised, literate, technological – which had disappeared some 9,000 years before. Was Atlantis in America? Or was there a sunken land mass in the Atlantic? Or does the story relate, as is now trendily thought, to the destruction of the volcanic island of Thera in the Aegean? Sir Mortimer Wheeler tells us that more than 2,000 works have been written on the subject. In his 1555 translations *The Decades of the newe worlde or west India*, Richard Eden included extracts from the *Historia General de las Indias* by Francisco López de Gómara (1512-1560), published in 1552.[61] Lopez de Gómara discussed 'the great Island which Plato called Atlantica or Atlantide': 'in the sea Atlantic, over against Africa', 'greater than Africa and Asia' – which sank. 'Some take this for a fable; and many for a true history' (Marsilio Ficino, for instance, the translator of Plato into Latin). López was convinced that 'the Indies are either the island and firmland of Plato, or the remnant of the same':

There is now no cause why we should any longer doubt or dispute of the island Atlantide, forasmuch as the discovering and conquest of the west Indies do plainly declare what Plato hath written of the said lands.

The Italian Girolamo Benzoni, who had been to Spanish America, was less certain in his *Historia del mondo nuovo*, Venice, 1565. Montaigne read a French translation of Benzoni, published in 1579; and used the Atlantis material in his essay 'Of Cannibals', published in 1580.[62]

But there is no great appearance, the said island should be the New World we have lately discovered; for, it well nigh touched Spain, and it were an incredible effect of inundation, to have removed the same more than twelve hundred leagues, as we see it is. Besides, our modern navigations have now almost discovered, that it is not an island, but rather firm land, and a continent.

Perhaps we should abide by the judgment of George Abbot, later Archbishop of Canterbury, in his *Briefe Description of the Whole Worlde*, published in 1599.[63]

Although some dispute out of Plato and the old writers that there was not

---

[60] Ed. Wright and Freund, 137.

[61] Arber, *First Three English Books on America*, 337-8.

[62] Florio translation, 1603: Dent edition, II, 217. For Montaigne's reliance on Benzoni in this passage, Chinard, *L'Exotisme Américain*, 197-200.

[63] Section 'De America sive Orbe Novo'. For the Atlantis and related myths, in their American context, Babcock, *Legendary Islands of the Atlantic*; Ashe, *Land to the West*; Ashe (ed.), *The Quest for America*.

only a guess but a kind of knowledge in ancient time that besides Europia, Asia and Africa there was another large country lying to the West, yet he that shall advisedly use the conjectures made thereupon may see that there is nothing of sufficiency to enforce any such knowledge; but that all antiquity was utterly ignorant of the new found countries toward the West.

What Antiquity *could* supply were ready made 'myths' which literate explorers could use as an allusive framework for the accounts of their exploits. When Giovanni da Verrazzano landed on the coast of North Carolina in 1524, he called the region 'Arcadia, owing to the beauty of the trees'. The Arcadians of Virgil, innocent folk in soft meadows, as re-told in the *quattrocento* novel *Arcadia* by Jacopo Sannazzaro.[64] There were the Greek myths of the Fortunate Islands and the Elysian Fields, the former definitely identified by Pietro Martire in 1516 as the Canaries.[65] By the seventeenth century the phrase 'Fortunate Islands' was used as a variant of 'the New World'.[66]

And so on.[67] There were other, even more fruitful, myths of antiquity: those without geographical associations. Of these, the most potent was the description by Ovid (43 B.C.–A.D. 17) of the Age of Gold, immediately following the creation of man, in Book One of *Metamorphoses*: an epic verse anthology of tales of transformations, collected from Greek and Latin myths, and beginning with the transition from chaos to an ordered cosmos. The following translation was published in 1621:[68]

> The Golden Age was first; which uncompelled
> And without rule, in faith and truth excelled.
> As then, there was nor punishment, nor fear;
> Nor threatening laws in brass prescribed were;
> Nor suppliant crouching pris'ners shook to see
> Their angry judge: but all was safe and free.
> To visit other worlds, no wounded pine
> Did yet from hills to faithless seas decline.
> Then, un-ambitious mortals knew no more,
> But their own country's nature-bounded shore.
> Nor swords, nor arms, were yet: no trenches round
> Beseiged towns, nor strifefull trumpets sound:
> The soldier, of no use. In firm content
> And harmless ease, their happy days were spent.
> The yet-free earth did of her own accord
> (Untorn with ploughs) all sorts of fruit afford.
> Content with nature's un-enforced food,

[64] Morison, *Northern Voyages*, 295.

[65] Arber, *First Three English Books on America*, 166.

[66] As by George Benson in 1609: *Sermon preached at Paules Crosse*, 57.

[67] Baudet has medieval and sixteenth-century material in *Paradise on Earth*. Also Cawley, *Unpathed Waters: studies in the influence of the voyagers on Elizabethan literature*, especially Part I, 'The Heritage of the Middle Ages'. And Hodgen, *Early Anthropology in the 16th and 17th Centuries*.

[68] See below, note 76.

They gather wildings, strawb'ries of the wood,
Sour cornels, what upon the bramble grows,
And acorns, which Jove's spreading oak bestows.
'Twas always spring: warm zephyrus sweetly blew
On smiling flowers, which without setting grew.
Forthwith the earth corn, unmanured, bears;
And every year renews her golden ears:
With milk and nectar were the rivers filled;
And honey from green holly-oaks distill'd.
   But, after Saturn was thrown down to hell,
Jove rul'd; and then the Silver Age befell:
More base than Gold ...

The Penguin Classics translation (1955), by Mary M. Innes, renders the passage thus:[69]

In the beginning was the Golden Age, when men of their own accord, without threat of punishment, without laws, maintained good faith and did what was right. There were no penalties to be afraid of, no bronze tablets were erected, carrying threats of legal action, no crowd of wrong-doers, anxious for mercy, trembled before the face of their judge: indeed there were no judges, men lived securely without them. Never yet had any pine tree, cut down from its home on the mountains, been launched on ocean's waves, to visit foreign lands: men knew only their own shores. Their cities were not yet surrounded by sheer moats, they had no straight brass trumpets, no coiling brass horns, no helmets and no swords. The peoples of the world, untroubled by any fears, enjoyed a leisurely and peaceful existence, and had no use for soldiers. The earth itself, without compulsion, untouched by the hoe, unfurrowed by any share, produced all things spontaneously, and men were content with foods that grew without cultivation. They gathered arbute berries and mountain strawberries, wild cherries and blackberries that cling to thorny bramble bushes: or acorns, fallen from Jupiter's spreading oak. It was season of everlasting spring, when peaceful zephyrs, with their warm breath, caressed the flowers that sprang up without having been planted. In time the earth, though untilled, produced corn too, and fields that never lay fallow whitened with heavy ears of grain. Then there flowed rivers of milk and rivers of nectar, and golden honey dripped from the green holm-oak. When Saturn was consigned to the darkness of Tartarus, and the world passed under the rule of Jove, the age of silver replaced that of gold, inferior to it.

Shakespeare (whose Gonzalo imagined a colony to 'excel the Golden Age') used the verse translation by Arthur Golding published in the 1560s. William Caxton had published his own translation in 1480; the manuscript is in Magdalene College Cambridge.

   Erasmus' Folly, whose oration was published in 1511 (dedicated to More: the title is a pun, *Moriae Encomium*) has a paragraph on the Golden Age (*saeculum, aetas*). The 'innocent folk of the Golden Age had

---

[69] Pages 31-2. For the Golden Age: Atkinson, *Nouveaux horizons de la Renaissance française*, 137-45, 346-50; Levin, *Myth of the Golden Age in the Renaissance*, 1969.

no sciences to provide for them, and lived under the guidance of nothing but natural instinct' (*solo naturae ductu instinctuque vivebat*). There was no grammar, dialectic, rhetoric, or jurisprudence (for there were no 'evil habits', *mores*). The natives were 'too pious in their beliefs to develop an irreverent curiosity for probing the secrets of nature' (*arcana Naturae*). But the *puritas* of the Golden Age 'gradually fell away'.[70]

Some sixteenth-century writers played with the assumption that the American Indian was living in the Golden Age, and Europe in baser times. Bishop Vasco de Quiroga, for example, a canon lawyer, who organised in Mexico from the 1530s Indian communities based (he specifically said) on the customs of the natives of Utopia.[71]

Quiroga founded two villages, both called Santa Fé, in which there was common ownership of property, a six hour working day, and other customs lifted from *Utopia*.[72] (The first bishop of Mexico, Fray Juan de Zumárraga, had in his library the 1518 Basle edition of *Utopia*.) Quiroga, bishop of Michoacán from 1537, wanted the Indians to be ruled by 'holy and good and catholic ordinances'.[73] For they recall the Golden Age:[74]

the same customs and manners, the same equality, simplicity, goodness, obedience, humility, festivities, games, pleasures, drinking, idling, pastimes, nudity, and lack of any but the poorest household goods and of any desire for better, the same clothing, footwear and food, all just as the fertility of the soil provided freely, and almost without any labour, care or seeking on their part. So that it seems now, in this New World, one may see these natives, with their disregard and scorn for anything superfluous, existing in the same freedom and liberty in their tranquil lives, seemingly immune from the hazards of fortune; pure and wise in their careful simplicity, marvelling rather at us and our pre-occupations, and the worries and restlessness which dog our footsteps, as some of them have at times already remarked to one of us with great astonishment. And almost the same customs, manners and conditions of life, not only in the matter of the servants, but even in the selection of the chiefs or head-men, whom they elect; as well as the same habit of being content with very little, satisfied to have sufficient for that day without care for the morrow, contemptuous or oblivious of all those other things so beloved, sought after and coveted in our turbulent world – scorned and discounted by them in this golden world of theirs – with all its greed, ambition, arrogance, ostentation, boasting, its toil and anxiety, which clearly find no place and play no part, nor are they known, in the life of these natives in this new, and to my way of thinking what is to them a golden, world: but with us already one of iron and steel and worse.

This is from a report he wrote in 1535: 'with much cause and reason is

[70] *Praise of Folly*, section 32. Translation by Betty Radice, Penguin Classics, 1971, 112-13; with a note by A.H.T. Levi on Erasmus' use of the myth (113).
[71] Silvio Zavala, 'Thomas More in New Spain: a Utopian Adventure of the Renaissance': a booklet published in 1955 in the Diamante series, Hispanic and Luso-Brazilian Councils, London.
[72] *ibid.*, 17-19.   [73] *ibid.*, 11.   [74] *ibid.*, 8.

this called the New World, not because it is newly found, but because in its people, and in almost everything, it is like as was the first and Golden Age'.[75]

The 1621 translation of Ovid, quoted above, has particular relevance to the story. It was by George Sandys, brother of Sir Edwin Sandys, London Treasurer of the Virginia Company from 1619. (Their father, Edwin Sandys, had been Master of St Catharine's College Cambridge under Edward VI, a Marian exile to Switzerland, and Elizabeth's bishop of Worcester, bishop of London, and archbishop of York.) A few weeks before the translation (Books I-V) was published, George had sailed to Jamestown; and he worked on Ovid during the voyage. He remained in Virginia for four years, overseeing the finances of the colony, and settling his own plantation. He returned in 1625, and in 1626 the remaining ten books of *Metamorphoses* were published. A revised edition of the whole came in 1632.[76] In the 1626 preface to Charles I, Sandys apologised for a work 'bred in the New-World, of the rudeness whereof it cannot but participate'[77] (and in an ode, hoped that the king might 'restore the Golden Age again').[78] In his commentaries, Sandys introduced information about hermaphrodites in Florida, cannibalism and human sacrifice in Spanish America, and Spanish Covetousness (in his note on the story of Midas in Book XI). He also tells us about the frogs and possums of Virginia.[79]

In his commentary on Book I, Sandys noted that the 'fiction of the four ages degenerating from better to worse' was derived from Hesiod, the Greek poet of the eighth century B.C.[80] The golden period of the rule of Saturn (son of Heaven and Earth) was described by Sandys thus:[81]

Then was there neither master nor servant: names merely brought in by ambition and injury. Unforced nature gave sufficient to all; who securely possessed her undivided bounty. A rich condition wherein no man was poor: avarice after introducing indigency: who by coveting a propriety, alienated all; and lost what it had, by seeking to enlarge it. But this happy estate abounding with all felicities, assuredly represented that which man enjoyed in his innocency: under the reign of Saturn – more truly of Adam.

It was a common belief, Douglas Bush tells us,[82] that pagan myths were a distorted version of Biblical truth. The four ages may owe much to Hesiod, but, said Sandys, they are also found in the Book of Daniel, in the prophet's interpretation of the 'great image' dreamed

[75] *ibid.*, 7.

[76] Reprinted in 1970, ed. K.K. Hulley and S.T. Vandersall, with preface by Douglas Bush, University of Nebraska Press. The Golden Age passage is pp.27-8. Subsequent page references are to this edition.

[77] 3.   [78] 4.

[79] R.B. Davis, 'America in Sandys' "Ovid" ', *William and Mary Quarterly,* July 1947, IV, 3, 297-304. Professor Davis later published a biography of Sandys (1955).

[80] 58.   [81] 59.   [82] xi.

by Nebuchadnezzar: of gold, silver, brass and iron (Chapter 2).[83] In 'tracing the almost worn-out steps of Antiquity,' wrote Sandys, 'the sacred stories afford the clearest direction.'[84] In conclusion, 'nothing can better ressemble those golden times, than a free commonwealth, ordered and maintained by well instituted laws'.[85]

From the start, it was natural to associate America with gold. Dürer's comment in 1520 on the Mexican treasures he saw in Brussels is well known.[86]

I saw the things which were brought to the King from the New Golden Land: a sun entirely of gold, a whole fathom broad; likewise a moon, entirely of silver, just as big ... I have never seen in all my days what so rejoiced my heart, as these things. For I saw among them amazing artistic objects, and I marvelled over the subtle ingenuity of the men in these distant lands.

And at the end of the sixteenth century, we have the vision of Sir Walter Raleigh: 'Many years since,' he wrote in 1596,[87]

I had knowledge, by relation, of that mighty, rich and beautiful Empire of Guiana, and of that great and golden city which the Spaniards call El Dorado.

'The Golden Man': the Indian king who covered his body in oil, rolled in gold dust, and stood before his subjects, the golden king in the golden city.

To all this must be added the medieval 'myths', especially those of chivalry. The first sight of Mexico City reminded the troops with Cortés of 'the enchanted things related in the book of Amadis'.[88] That is, the fourteenth-century Iberian prose epic *Amadis de Gaula*, printed in 1508, to be translated into English (the first part appearing in 1590) by Anthony Munday – *The ancient, famous and honourable history of Amadis de Gaule*.

In a lecture given in 1950 at Boston, Luis Weckmann of Mexico City College put forward the thesis that 'the Middle Ages found their last expression on this side of the Atlantic'.[89] Columbus, for instance, was 'the spiritual heir of Marco Polo', 'impelled by medieval quests'. The early Spanish explorers were 'lured' by traditional myths: the Fountain of Youth, El Dorado, and so on. The Conquest was an adventure in Chivalry. The lecture reads as a rather exhilarating attempt to emphasise a hitherto neglected theme in colonial studies; and Weckmann stressed that he was talking about Spanish America

[83] 58. [84] 8. [85] 59-60.

[86] Quoted in Hanke, *Aristotle and the American Indians*, 49.

[87] Epistle Dedicatory to *The Discoverie of the Large, Rich and Bewtiful Empyre of Guiana, with a relation of the great and Golden Citie of Manoa (which the Spanyards call El Dorado)*, 1596. Ed. V.T. Harlow, 1928, p.4.

[88] Elliott, *Imperial Spain*, Mentor edition, 63.

[89] 'The Middle Ages in the Conquest of America', *Speculum*, XXVI, 1, January 1951, 130-41.

(in particular Mexico) and about, primarily, the Spanish Middle Ages. Of late, the attempt to 'de-emphasise' the novelty of the discovery of the New World has become fashionable. The Cambridge medievalist Dr G.V. Scammell, in an article published in 1969,[90] argued, first, that the new experience was old experience writ large; that it was not in fact writ too large, the achievement being modest; and that the effect of the discoveries on European imagination and skills was slight. J.H. Elliott, in *The Old World and the New 1492-1650*, 1970, on occasion took a similar line. Europeans 'projected onto America their disappointed dreams'.[91] The slavish veneration of ancient myths was a 'closing of the mind' typical of the Renaissance.

It was perhaps to be expected that, having been deprived of the Industrial Revolution, and the Renaissance, we should next be deprived of what Francisco López de Gómara called in 1552 'the greatest event since the creation of the world, apart from the incarnation and death of Christ': 'the discovery of the Indies'.[92]

It might perhaps nervously be suggested that the myths of antiquity and the Middle Ages were influential only if they matched, in some degree, the actual experience of the explorers. Most of them would have read the 'True History' of Lucian (second century A.D.). (Lucian was a great favourite with the natives of the island of Utopia.) Lucian tells us that he sailed from the Straits of Gibraltar into the Atlantic, and found strange lands populated entirely by males. Eyes are detachable, there are no toes, cabbages grow above the buttocks, stomachs are used as handbags or lined with fur for use as prams in cold weather, and private parts are artificial (ivory for the rich, wood for the poor). Men marry each other; and have babies. They act the wifely role until they are 25, and the husbandly role thereafter. Thomas More as a young man wrote a dialogue on wife-sharing; in Lucian's New World there is merely boy-sharing.[93] It is doubtful whether the tradition of reports of sodomy among the Indians[94] owes more to Lucian than to the actual observation of the Spaniards.

The obvious, and expected, mingling of old and new in the minds of sixteenth-century Europeans is not to be regretted. It is part of the achievement and fascination of the period. A striking English instance is Sir Humphrey Gilbert.

In 1566, when we was twenty-nine, Gilbert – Eton; Oxford; Inns of Court; soldier-courtier – wrote *A Discourse Of a Discoverie for a new Passage to Cataia*, to be printed in 1576, and reprinted by Hakluyt in

---

[90] 'The New Worlds and Europe in the 16th Century', *Historical Journal*, XII, 3, 1969, 389-412. Included in the restrictive 'old familiar context' regretted by Dr Scammell are 'intimations of the end of the world, and the reign of God on earth'.

[91] p.26.

[92] Hanke, *Aristotle and the American Indians*, 124.

[93] The 'True History' is in the Penguin Classics *Lucian: Satirical Sketches*, tr. Paul Turner.

[94] See below, pp.130, 165-67.

the 1589 *Principall Navigations*.[95] Gilbert's intention was to prove 'a passage to be on the north side of America, to go to Cataia, China, and to the East India'.[96] He was in the tradition of Sebastian Cabot: the search for the North-West passage. As a point of the proof, Gilbert asserted that America is an island, with no land connection with Asia. There are two types of proof, says Gilbert. The 'simple', like 'brute beasts', judge 'by sense only': such a man 'gathereth no surety of anything that he hath not seen, felt, heard, tasted or smelled'. The 'wise' – truly 'men' – find 'the certainty of things by reason, before they happen to be tried'. Gilbert wishes to satisfy both types; so he has given 'proofs of both sorts'.[97]

He invokes 'the experience of painful travellers':[98] men he knew, like Anthony Jenkinson,[99] who had reached Russia in the late 1550s, and Sebastian Cabot.[100] Men whose travel narratives he had read: Jacques Cartier.[101] He has read the collections of travel literature by Pietro Martire[102] and López de Gómara.[103] He has used 'the authority of learned geographers',[104] pre-eminently the Ortelius world map of 1564.[105]

When I gave myself to the study of geography, after I had perused and diligently scanned the descriptions of Europe, Asia and Afrike, and conferred them with the maps and globes both antique and modern, I came in fine to the fourth part of the world, commonly called America: which by all descriptions I found to be an island environed round about with the sea.

To the south, the straits of Magellan; to the east, 'our west ocean'; to the west, 'Mare del Sur, which sea runneth towards the north, separating it from the east part of Asia, where the dominions of the Cataians are'; to the north, 'the sea that severeth it from Grondland, through which northern seas the passage lieth which I take now in hand to discover'.[106] If America were joined to Asia there would be 'civil men' in America as there are in Asia; but the Spaniards, Portuguese and French 'never saw so much as one token or sign that ever any man of the unknown part of the world had been there'. There are no American animals in Asia – and no Asian 'beasts' in America.[107] Gilbert thought it certain that America is 'in no part adjoining to Asia', and that the American Indians had no contact with the natives of Tartary, Cathay, or of 'any part of Asia'.[108]

---

[95] Facsimile reprint of the 1576 edition (from the copy in Trinity College Cambridge) in the series 'The English Experience', 1968, no.72 (Amsterdam and New York). Edited by Quinn, *Gilbert Voyages*, Hakluyt Society, 1940, I, 129-65. Subsequent page references are to Quinn.
[96] 135. [97] 147. [98] 134.
[99] 144. For Jenkinson, Rowse, *Expansion of Elizabethan England*, 169-72.
[100] 147.
[101] *ibid.*
[102] 139. [103] 146. [104] 134.
[105] Note by Quinn, 135.
[106] 137. [107] 142. [108] *ibid.*

Gilbert has had 'great conference' with 'such as I knew to be both wise, learned, and of great experience'.[109] He has also relied on 'the reasons of wise philosophers'.[110] Plato's material about Atlantis, the 'incomparable great island', supports the thesis.[111] So do Aristotle and 'other ancient philosophers'.[112] Alexander Nowell has translated into modern English a Saxon account of a voyage to Muscovy in the time of King Alfred: 871, the voyage of Ochther.[113] This narrative was confirmed by the voyages of Hugh Willoughby and Richard Chancellor in 1553: 'We in these our days find, by our own experiences, his former reports to be true.'[114]

Gilbert has 'devised' things to 'amend the errors of usual sea-cards': a 'spherical instrument, with a compass of variation, for the perfect knowing of the longtitude'; a 'precise order to prick the sea-card'; and 'certain infallible rules for the shortening of any discovery, to know at the first entering of any fret whether it lie open to the ocean'.[115]

Thus, in general, he has not 'taken in hand to discover Utopia, or any country feigned by imagination'.[116]

What men did get from the Ancients was the sense of the possibilities of a New World. In 1612, William Strachey, writing about Virginia, did an English version of 'the prophecy of Reverend Seneca':[117]

> That age shall come, albeit in latter times
> When as the sea shall ope her lock't up bounds,
> And mighty lands appear: new heavens, new climes
> Shall Typhis bring to knowledge, and new grounds
> New worlds display: then shall not Thule be
> The farthest Nor-west isle our eyes shall see.

The excitement of America could not have been so intense without the set of pre-fabricated myths which provided fore-play to the experience.

The localisation of the 'legends' by European explorers in the fifteenth and sixteenth centuries was sometimes a step towards the truth. Prester John is a case in point. For Mandeville, the empire of Prester John was (we have seen) in the area of Mongolia. Hakluyt, in the Index to the 1589 *Principall Navigations*, has: 'Presbiter John Emperor in Affrike.' To Richard Eden in 1555, he was 'Emperor of many Christian nations in Ethiope'.[118]

In 1493 the Portuguese Pedro de Covilhã, who had left Lisbon in 1487, reached the Court of the kingdom of Abyssinia; by way of Aden, Colombo, Kuwait and Mecca.[119] He remained there for some years.

---

[109] 134. [110] 134. [111] 137. [112] 139. [113] 140.
[114] 141. For Willoughby and Chancellor, Elton, *England under the Tudors*, 335.
[115] 164. [116] 134.
[117] *Travell into Virginia Britania*, ed. Wright and Freund, 138-9.
[118] Arber, *First Three English Books on America*, 51.
[119] Parry, *Age of Reconnaissance*, Mentor edition, 154.

In 1509 the Queen Regent, Helena (her son David II had succeeded in 1508 aged 11) wrote to the King of Portugal. The letter eventually reached Lisbon in 1513, brought by a legation from Abyssinia of two 'noble young men': one, Matthew, was *armenicus* ('Armenican born'); the other *abessinus*. Those details are from the Portuguese historian Damião de Goes, who was a page at the Court in Lisbon when the two men arrived in 1513; he was born in February 1502. Goes published a Latin account of the embassy and the letter in 1532 at Antwerp.

The account appeared in an English translation, running to fifty pages, in 1533: 'Printed by William Rastell in Fleet Street, in St Bride's Churchyard.'[120] William Rastell (1508-1565) was the son of John, our playwright and potential colonist in the New Found lands, who died in 1536. He was therefore Thomas More's nephew.

The translator was John More, son of Thomas, born in 1509. Confusingly, but understandably, Goes described the embassy as from 'the great emperour of Inde prester John': *Legatio Magni Indorum Imperatoris Presbyteri Joannis*.[121]

Helena's actual letter, as translated into Portuguese, did not come into the possession of Goes until the early 1520s. (Portuguese envoys had reached David's Court in 1518.) The letter, described by Goes in 1532 as *epistola* of *presbyter* John, 'hygh emperoure of Inde',[122] offered help to Portugal in the crusade against the Turks (whose power was a worry to Abyssinia); suggested marriage between the Portuguese and the Abyssinians; and reported the gift of a piece of the true cross from the Court of Abyssinia to the Court of Portugal.

More important is the material given by Goes which was based (or so he said) on the speeches of Matthew in Lisbon in 1513:[123]

Of the fayth of the Indyans, ceremonyes, relygyons, &c. Of the patryarche & his offyce. Of the realme, state, power, maiesty, and order of the courte of prester John.

Lisbon had learnt that 'the emperor's proper name is David'. His common name, prester John, king of the Ebbessins' (*Ebessinorum*). His titles (all held 'by the power of God and our redeemer Jesus Christ and by the power of our lady the virgin saint Mary') are 'King of Kings' (*rex regum*); 'King of Nilus flood' (*rex Nili*); and 'Judge' (*judex*) of 'the great Sodane' (*Sultani*), 'the country of Cayre' (*Cayri*) and 'the see of Alexandrine' (*cathedrae Alexandrinae*).[124] In 1513, as David was a minor, 'all the whole order and rule of the realm' had been committed to his mother Helena: 'a very holy woman, and one that showeth a great example of chastity.'[125] It is customary for an adult emperor to

---

[120] Elizabeth Brooke Blackburn, 'The Legacy of Prester John', *Moreana*, no.14, May 1967, 37-43; pp.44-98 are facsimile reprints, in parallel column, of the Latin and English editions. I am very grateful to Fr. Germain Marc'hadour, the editor of *Moreana*, for giving me a copy of this number, and discussing it, at the Folger Library in 1967. Subsequent page references are to the *Moreana* facsimile.

[121] 44.

[122] 54. Text of the 'Letter', 54-9.

[123] 1533 title page.   [124] 76.   [125] 79.

spend most of the time with his troops, in field exercises.[126] The 'estate and power' of the emperor are 'very great': 'he hath under his dominion three score christened kings, which be kings of great mighty kingdoms'; and also five Mohammedan kings.[127] There are princes (*regulos*), dukes (*duces*), marquesses (*marchiones*), earls (*comites*), and barons (*barones*). These 'observe and straitly keep whatsoever the emperor commandeth them'.[128] 'They keep very diligently in writing pedigrees, names and surnames of their ancestors, whereby every one may perfectly know his nation (*gens*) and stock (*genus*).'[129]

And they record 'the chronicles and noble acts of their princes'; 'whatsoever is worthy remembrance their secretary (*chronographos*) diligently registers'.[130] The nobles wear silk, cloth of gold, velvet, satin, and damask. 'The common people wear nothing but cloth.' The empire has mines of gold, silver, and other metals.[131] There are no coins; gold and silver are exchanged by weight.[132] The emperor sits in a council of twelve. There are judges: 'both to hear causes, and judge them.' The death penalty is inflicted for murder only.[133] Some soldiers 'ever go in white, with crosses on their coat armour, always ready to war for Christ's faith'. There are no Jews. Once there were many: but 'when the people could not suffer or bear their naughtiness, suddenly they set upon them, and utterly destroyed them'.[134]

Until recently, the only Europeans known were the French. But 'few years past' the 'noble acts' of the Portuguese (*Lusitani*) against the Turks, Persians, Arabs and Indians 'began to be well known, and had in much reverence and reputation amongst them'.[135] The subjects of Prester John would have reverenced the 'acts' of the Lusitanian Raphael Hythloday.

The Apostle Bartholomew 'preached first the gospel and Christ's faith' in the empire.[136] (Bartholomew, like Thomas, was associated with India by tradition.) Today, the people believe that God made heaven and earth 'of no subject matter at all, nor of nothing earthly, but by a marvellous means'. They acknowledge the Trinity: God as Father, Holy Ghost, and Son – Christ the Saviour, born at Bethlehem of a virgin, who died for our sins, rose from the dead, and ascended to heaven. They believe in the resurrection of the body; and the final 'universal judgement' of Christ the Judge. They accept, then, the Apostles' Creed; also the Lord's Prayer and the 'Hail Mary'. They have the Old and New Testaments; they know the Ten Commandments and the Seven Deadly Sins.[137] Their 'highest sacrament' is 'the blessed sacrament of the altar'; received in both kinds (bread and wine), as 'the undoubted body and blood' of Christ.[138] They have the sacrament of private confession to the priest, followed by penance.[139] They are baptised shortly after birth. And also circumcised – 'an old custom from their forefathers'. (This was in fact a Christian custom in Ethiopia.) Each year everyone is

[126] 77. [127] 73-4. [128] 74. [129] 78. [130] 74. [131] 72. [132] 73. [133] 74-5. [134] 75. [135] 79. [136] 68. [137] 60-2. [138] 63-4. [139] 64.

rebaptised, and makes a fresh profession of the faith.[140] Marriages are performed at the church door. No man has more than one wife.[141] Sundays and Holy Days are kept 'with all reverence', and there are Fasting Days.[142] There are 'many costly temples'. In these 'churches' they 'have and worship the images': of God, the Virgin, and 'other holy saints'. There is 'holy water'; and the garments in which mass is celebrated are 'consecrate'.[143] They 'burn tapers'; go on 'common processions'; observe an annual 'solemn dirge for Christian souls'; and use Lenten ashes.[144] Burials are conducted in church, with priests, crosses, prayers, 'and such other kind of ceremonies'.[145]

There is 'an infinite number of monasteries, as well of women as of men, living very straitly in great abstinence'. It is not unusual for a religious house to have over 700 inmates. The monks 'get their living by their handy labour': 'all manner of begging is utterly forbidden them.' Some monks and priests – the 'best learned' – preach to the people.[146] No one is admitted to 'the order of priesthood' before 'he shall be examined by a well learned company whether he be meet for it or no'. Priests can marry; but if their wife dies, they cannot marry again.[147] There are many 'hospitals', 'whereunto all poor folk be genteelly welcomed'.[148]

There is one 'chief priest or bishop': *Patriarcha Alexandrinum*. Of old, the Patriarch was chosen in Jerusalem 'by the voices of all good religious men of the empire of Prester John that there were at the same season dwelling'. The Patriarch (with the advice of his own council of 12) governs 'all spiritual matters'. 'He *only* hath power on spiritual matters; that is to say as well in ecclesiastical offices as dispensing with benefices; without the interruption of any temporal person.' The emperors 'have no power on the clergy' (*in clericos*): 'that is a thing belonging only to the patriarch.' If a 'spiritual man' (*ecclesiasticus*) commit 'abominable crime', the patriarch supervises his fasting to death. No cleric is put to death 'out of hand'; except for murder.[149] (In the churches, sanctuary is provided for malefactors; but to a murderer so little food is given that 'at the last he is compelled to die for hunger'.)[150] The patriarch receives the tithes of the whole empire, plus one third of the imperial revenue. This is given to the poor, orphans, and prisoners. When the patriarch dies, the emperor inherits all his wealth; the new patriarch starts afresh. The patriarch must be unmarried.[151]

When a man who has been dead for some time is found, after 'diligent search', to have been 'holy', of 'virtuous living' and 'good conversation', the people account him a 'saint', 'canonise him'.[152]

They 'acknowledge' the Pope. But they 'do not their obedience to him (as other Christians do)'. Why not? The journey: which is 'evil, difficult'.[153]

Goes presented a copy of the *Legatio* to Erasmus (who was in

---

[140] 63. [141] 67. [142] 64. [143] 67-8. [144] 65. [145] 67. [146] 65-6. [147] 71. [148] 66. [149] 69-71. [150] 66. [151] 69. [152] 67. [153] 68.

Freiburg) soon after its publication. The book was condemned by the Spanish Inquisition in 1540; and before his death in 1574 Goes had become acquainted with the inside of Portuguese prisons.[154]

John More, aged 23, said in the preface to the 1533 English version that the translation had been done 'through the help of a special familiar friend of mine'. John wished to publish it because 'every man naturally is desirous to hear new things and strange'; even if 'there were none other commodity thereof than the newelty'.[155] In fact, there is other 'commodity'. The empire of the *Legatio* may not be as extensive as 'the new founden lands that have been becomen christened within a few years of late'. But it should rejoice 'all good christian people' to read of the realm of Prester John:

> to perceive that, though there are divers things wherein they and we differ in rites laws customs and ceremonies, yet in all other things necessarily pertaining as well to the virtues of faith and religion as all other virtues moral, they so far accord and agree with these Christian nations of ours; and with the catholic doctrine of the Church.

Such 'full agreement and consent in so many things necessary to salvation' is the work of the Holy Spirit. And it is an argument against the 'new heretics';[156] it proves that for 1500 years, throughout Christendom (which includes the empire of Prester John) certain things have been 'continually believed and ever observed' (a major theme of the writings of John's father since 1523). Finally:[157]

> Since that we begin now we each to hear more of other, I pray God as there is in both many things very good, and some things that might be better, each people may learn and take of other those things that be good, and let the bad go by.

That sentiment was addressed to readers of the *legacye or embassate of the great emperour of Inde prester John*. It could have been addressed to readers of the embassy of Raphael Hythloday to the island of Utopia.

---

[154] 39 (essay by Blackburn).
[155] 45.   [156] 45-6.   [157] 47.

3

'Utopia': The Tale

The book universally known as *Utopia* was published in Latin at
Louvain in December 1516, when Thomas More was thirty-eight.[1]
The description in the title was: *Libellus vere aureus* (a truly golden little
book: the two parts ran to 91 pages) *nec minus salutaris quam festivus* (as
beneficial as it is merry) *de optimo reipublicae statu* (concerning the best
state of a 'respublica') *deque nova insula Utopia* (and the new island
Utopia). Sixteen pages of initial material, including a *praefatio* by
More, bring the length of the volume to 108 pages. The first English
version was by Ralph Robinson, born in 1521, Fellow of Corpus
Christi College Oxford from 1542, and was published in the reign of
Edward VI, in 1551, sixteen years after More's beheading. It was later
than the translations into German (1524), Italian (1548) and French
(1550). A revised second edition appeared in the reign of Mary: 1556.[2]

*A frutefull, pleasaunt, & wittie worke, of the beste state of a publique weale, and of the
newe yle, called Utopia: written in Latine, by the right worthie and famous Syr Thomas
More knyght.*

In my two chapters on *Utopia* I use the Robinson translation, as
printed in the Everyman Library, 1910, modernised spelling 1951. It
is exuberant rather than succinct, and sometimes runs to rhetorical
simplification. It is occasionally not very clear; and the (few)
misreadings and misprints in the Everyman text add to the confusion
at some points. But it has the Tudor flavour, and preserves the
Biblical echoes – qualities missing from J.P. Dolan's colourless version
(sometimes almost a paraphrase) in *The Essential Thomas More* (ed. J.J.
Greene and J.P. Dolan, 1967);[3] and from Paul Turner's rendering for
Penguin Classics (1965), which is lively but lacking in Tudor
precision. I refer to the Latin text as printed in 1965 in the 'Yale
Edition of the Complete Works of St Thomas More'.[4] The copy-text
here was the third printing of *Utopia*, Basle, March 1518. The English
translation in the Yale volume is that by G.C. Richards, 1923: with

[1] Facsimile edition by Scolar Press, 1966.
[2] Facsimile edition by Scolar Press, 1970.
[3] Mentor-Omega paperback. A very useful volume, nonetheless.
[4] Edited by Edward Surtz S.J. and J.H. Hexter, being volume 4 of the edition.

modifications. This version has grave weaknesses; as Quentin Skinner pointed out in his judicious and lengthy review in *Past and Present*, no.38, December 1967, pp.153-68. There are 320 pages of leisurely commentary; an essay of nearly 60 pages by the American Jesuit Surtz; and an essay of over 100 pages by J.H. Hexter, which he expanded and published again in 1974, in his *The Vision of Politics on the Eve of the Reformation*. The Yale volume is 823 pages. More's *Libellus* might appear to be somewhat submerged.

The 1516 title page – and the facing and following material – has the *figura* of the island; the Utopian alphabet, which, like Latin and Hebrew, has 22 letters (as against the modern English 26); a verse in the *vernacula Utopiensium lingua*; and six Latin lines of verses by the poet Anemolius, nephew of Raphael Hythloday. The 'Utopian' verse is translated into Latin; and subsequently into English by Robinson (Everyman, p.140). It is a speech by the island itself. *Utopus dux* ('King and conqueror') *ex non insula fecit insulam* ('hath made me an isle that erst no island was'): the inhabitants 'have shaped for man a Philosophical City' (*Civitas Philosophica*). The Anemolius verse is again a speech by the island: E140.[5] *Nunc civitatis aemula Platonicae*:

> Now I am like to Plato's city;
> Whose fame flieth the world thorough;
> Yea, like, or rather more likely
> Plato's plat to excel and pass.
> For what Plato's pen hath platted briefly
> In naked words, as in a glass,
> The same have I performed fully,
> With laws, with men, and treasure fitly.
> Wherefore not Utopie, but rather rightly
> My name is Eutopie: a place of felicity.

Ou-Topia: never land, nowhere land. In 1610 the London Council of the Virginia Company warned against the reports from Jamestown being received as 'partial falsehood, supposing them to be but Utopian, and legendary fables'.[6]

Thomas More took painstaking and skilful delight in working out the copious details of his island's story. The details are precise, and hang together. To be convinced of the quality of *Utopia*, one has only to read Francis Bacon's *New Atlantis*, 1627: the 'story' is inept, and can be skipped until the final Baconian speeches of the 'Father' of Solomon's House – a College for the Interpreting of Nature. Indeed, More's detail is more careful than that of Defoe in *Robinson Crusoe*. So the 'facts' about the island of Utopia, its natives and invaders, must be taken with pedantic seriousness if the skill of the author is fully to be savoured. One must (to adopt an imperative of D.H. Lawrence) trust the Tale.

---

[5] From henceforth, 'E' means Everyman edition, followed by the page number.
[6] *A True Declaration of the Estate of the Colonie in Virginia*: Force, *Tracts*, III, no.1, p.14.

There were three stages in the history of the island. The pre-Conquest era; the Conquest by Utopus in the third century B.C.; and the arrival of Raphael and his party about 1510.

The island was originally called Abraxa (E56). The word means something like 'island of the sun' (Yale 585). It is situated in 'the new world' (E14). The natives were by origin probably Greek: Raphael says, 'I think that this nation took their beginning of the Greeks' (E95). The language, though 'not much unlike the Persian tongue', retains 'divers signs and tokens of the Greek language' (E95).

Utopus and his army invaded the island about 245 B.C.; 1760 years ago, says Raphael (E61).

The Conquest and occupation were beneficial. The houses of Abraxa had been 'very low and like homely cottages or poor shepherd houses' (E61). All was improved. Utopus took care of the capital, Amaurate ('Darkling City': Y388).[7] He 'drew forth the platform of the city into the fashion and figure that it now hath' (E61). And throughout the island – which has 54 'large and fair cities' (E56: England had 53 shires plus London),

the houses be curiously builded after a gorgeous and gallant sort, with three storeys one over another. The outsides of the walls be made either of hard flint or of plaster, or else of brick, and the inner sides be well strengthened with timber work. The roofs be plain and flat, covered with a certain kind of plaster that is of no cost, and yet so temperered that no fire can hurt or perish it, and withstandeth the violence of the weather better than any lead. They keep the wind out of their windows with glass, for it is there much used, and somewhere also with fine linen cloth dipped in oil or amber, and that for two commodities, for by this means more light cometh in, and the wind is better kept out (E 61-2).

(Glass was not common in early Tudor houses.)

And Utopus 'brought the rude and wild people to that excellent perfection in all good fashions, humanity, and civil gentleness, wherein they now go beyond all the people of the world' (E56).

The Utopians have 'histories and Chronicles' (E53); which 'they keep written with all diligent circumspection' (E61). These tell the deeds of Utopus.

At the beginning of the fourth century A.D. (about 1200 years ago, says Raphael: E53) a ship containing Romans and Egyptians was driven to the island 'by tempest'; and some of the passengers settled there. This also was beneficial to the Utopians:

There was no craft nor science within the empire of Rome whereof any profit could rise, but they either learned it of these strangers, or else of them taking occasion to search for it, found it out (E53).

But, 'as their chronicles testify', the Utopians had no experience of

[7] From henceforth, 'Y' means Yale *Utopia*, followed by the page number.

modern European travellers: they called Raphael's party 'the ultra-equinoctials' (E53).

The Raphael group originally numbered six; but only four were left alive to reach the island. One, Tricius Apinatus, carried with him medical books by Hippocrates and Galen. Another had been baptised only recently – and was given to the excessive zeal of the new convert (E119). There was no priest: 'which I am right sorry for', said Raphael (E118).

Raphael (the Guardian Angel: the Healer)[8] was Portuguese. He was 'well stricken in age'; with a 'black sun-burned face', a 'long beard', and the bearing and garb of a 'mariner'. He was 'very well learned in the Latin tongue'. And, more important, 'profound and excellent in the Greek language'. Indeed, 'he knew that there is nothing extant in Latin to any purpose, saving a few of Seneca's and Cicero's doings' (E14-15). He had spent five months in England in 1497 (E21). And he had become

a man so perfect and expert in the laws and customs of every several country, as though unto what place soever he came guestwise, there he had led all his life. (E18).

Guestwise: a Tudor Americanism (both derived from the German). He had 'joined himself in company with Amerigo Vespucci'; and of the four Vespucci voyages 'that now be in print and abroad in every man's hand', he had been on the second, third and fourth (E15). But he had more permanent roving intentions:

When I was determined to enter into my fourth voyage,[9] I cast into the ship in the stead of merchandise a pretty fardel of books, because I intended to come again never rather than shortly. (E95)

And from the final Vespucci voyage he 'came not home'. Instead, he branched off with his party – and reached Utopia (E15). According to More, he was still alive in 1517, living in Portugal (Y253).

The quartet remained in Utopia 'five years and more' (E52).

His general experience as an explorer brought home to Raphael the image of the wilderness: *solitudo*. The first experience of a new world was

great and wide deserts and wildernesses, parched, burned, and dried up with continual and intolerable heat. All things be hideous, terrible, loathsome, and unpleasant to behold; all things out of fashion and comeliness, inhabited with wild beasts and serpents, or at the least wise with people that be no less savage, wild and noisome than the very beasts themselves be.

[8] Marc'hadour, *The Bible in the Works of St Thomas More*, Part V, 1972, 123-4: in Fr. Marc'hadour's essay on 'The Bible in *Utopia*', 119-26.

[9] Raphael means his separate voyage to Utopia, following upon his third voyage with Vespucci. See above, pp.x, 14.

The frontier. But there was hope – beyond the next horizon.

But a little farther beyond that, all things begin by little and little to wax pleasant; the air soft, temperate and gentle; the ground covered with green grass; less wildness in the beasts. At the last shall ye come again to people, cities and towns. (E17)

The passage reminds one of Columbus' hopes about Cuba, published in 1493:

Since there were no towns or villages on the coast, but only small groups of houses whose inhabitants fled as soon as we approached, I continued on my course, thinking that I should undoubtedly come to some great towns or cities.[10]

(Columbus thought Cuba was the mainland of Cathay.) Raphael acknowledged the Hope of America; definitively expressed in the final page of *The Great Gatsby*, as the narrator imagines the reactions of the first explorers 'in the presence of this continent', man 'face to face for the last time in history with something commensurate to his capacity for wonder'. Thomas Hariot succumbed to the lure in the 1580s.[11] The Englishmen in North Carolina clung to the coastline:

Yet sometimes as we made our journey further into the main and country, we found the soil to be fatter, the trees greater and to grow thinner, the ground more firm and deeper mould, more and larger champions, finer grass and as good as ever we saw any in England; in some places rocky and far more high and hilly ground, more plenty of their fruits, more abundance of beasts, the more habited with people, and of greater policy and larger dominions, with greater towns and houses.

'It eluded us then, but that's no matter – tomorrow we will run faster, stretch out our arms farther ... And one fine morning –'

As everyone knows, the inhabitants of the island of Utopia were worthy of European admiration. Not every region in that part of the new world was so favoured. Five hundred miles east of Utopia lived the 'wicked and cursed' Zapoletes (E111):

hideous, savage, and fierce, dwelling in wild woods and high mountains where they were bred and brought up. They be of an hard nature, able to abide and sustain heat, cold and labour, abhorring from all delicate dainties, occupying no husbandry nor tillage of the ground, homely and rude both in building of their houses and in their apparel, given unto no goodness, but only to the breeding and bringing up of cattle. The most part of their living is by hunting and stealing. They be born only to war.

---

[10] In Cohen, Penguin Classics, *Voyages of Columbus*, 115.

[11] Hariot, *A briefe and true report of the new found land of Virginia*, 1588, reprinted by Hakluyt 1589. Quoted section in Quinn, ed., *Roanoke Voyages*, 382; Quinn, ed., *Virginia Voyages from Hakluyt*, 74; Everyman Hakluyt, VI, 193-4.

The Utopians use them as mercenaries, paying them 'greater wages' than any other employer (E112). 'A people not unlike the Swiss', commented the Erasmian marginal note of 1516 (Y207): a comment tastefully deleted in the two Basle editions of 1518 (Y504). (The 1516 marginal notes were by Erasmus and Peter Giles: Y280-1. They are mainly little comments such as 'masterful', 'a striking simile', 'a choice tale', 'evidently this passage is satiric'.) The Utopians do not concern themselves about the number of the Zapoletes killed in their service: 'for they believe that they should do a very good deed for all mankind if they could rid out of the world all that foul stinking den of that most wicked and cursed people' (E112). They sound like the Caribs of Columbus' 1493 Letter.

The most wicked feature of the Zapoletes is their 'covetousness' (E112): *Avaritia* (Y208).

The Utopians, of course, are wholly other. Although

their soil be not very fruitful, nor their air very wholesome, yet against the air they so defend them with temperate diet, and so order and husband their ground with diligent travail, that in no country is greater increase and plenty of corn and cattle, nor men's bodies of longer life and subject or apt to fewer diseases. (E94)

In physique, they are

light and quick of body, full of activity and nimbleness, and of more strength than a man would judge them by their stature, which for all that is not too low. (E94)

In character, the Utopian is *facilis* ('gentle'), *facetus* ('merry'), *sollers* ('quick and fine witted'), and 'delighting in quietness': E94/Y178. They are not naked; but wear leather or skins for work, and woollen garments for leisure. (There is a slight difference of fashion for male and female, and for married and unmarried: E68.)

In general, 'there is in no place of the world neither a more excellent people, neither a more flourishing commonwealth' (E94). Marginal note: *Felicitas Utopiensium* (Y178).

The Utopians are good sailors, and explore 'the outlands on every side of them' (E97). They are also a colonial power. The population of the island is fixed and limited. If a town becomes over-populated, some of the inhabitants move to another. If the population of the island as a whole goes beyond the limit, the remedy is emigration. They 'choose out of every city certain citizens, and build up a town under their own laws in the next land where the inhabitants have much waste and unoccupied ground'. In the new territory, the settlers have 'bounds which they have limited and appointed out for themselves'. If the natives 'will not dwell with them to be ordered by their laws, then they drive them out'. And if they resist and rebel, then they make war against them. For they count this the most just cause of war, when any people holdeth a piece of ground void and vacant to no good nor profitable use, keeping others from the use and possession of it which notwithstanding by the Law of Nature ought thereof to be nourished and relieved. (E70)

(John Donne, Dean of St Paul's, was to make a similar point in a sermon to the Virginia Company in 1622.)[12] But when they make war, the Utopians do not 'despoil nor sack' a town they have captured: only those who opposed surrender are put to the sword; of the rest, the soldiers are put in 'bondage', and the 'weak multitude' is 'untouched' (E116).

If the natives will 'join and dwell' with the colonists, they are welcomed:

They thus joining and dwelling together do easily agree in one fashion of living, and that to the great wealth of both the peoples. For they so bring the matter about by their laws, that the ground which before was neither good nor profitable for the one nor for the other is now sufficient and fruitful enough for them both. (E70)

That is Utopian colonial policy. In foreign policy – relations with their 'borderers' (E104) – the Utopians prefer 'love and benevolence' to 'covenants of leagues' (E106). They have freed many of the neighbour peoples from 'tyranny'; the peoples thus delivered 'live free and under no subjection' (E104).

The island has a satisfactory export market. The Utopians export livestock; and grain, honey, wool, flax, wood, roots for dye, dyed skins, wax, and leather (E76). All at 'reasonable and mean prices'; and $14\frac{1}{2}\%$ of the produce is given to the poor (E77). Banking and credit is the concern of 'the whole city', with a 'common box' (E77). The only product the island lacks is iron (E77).

Life on Utopia has many features later to be associated with the American Frontier; features of an enclosed, semi-military community – sometimes rather unperceptively labelled 'puritan'. There is no 'liberty' to 'loiter'; no 'idleness'; no 'wicked councils or unlawful assemblies'; no brothels or taverns (E76). There are no spiritous liquors: 'They sow corn only for bread.' The natives drink 'clear water'. Or 'wine made of grapes, or else of apples and pears' (E58): grape juice, probably (though there are 'vineyards' on the island: E61). Erasmus tells us[13] that More (like his father) prefered to drink water, or very watered-down ale – which he drank from a pewter mug, to avoid embarrassing his guests. He would sip a little wine for hospitality's sake.

[12] Sermon of 13 November 1622. Number 10 in vol.4 (1959) of the California Edition of Donne's sermons, ed. Potter and Simpson. Relevant passage, 274-5.

[13] Letter of 1519 to Ulrich von Hutten. Translated by Barbara Flower in the 'Selected Letters' which form the Appendix to the Phaidon and Harper editions of Huizinga's *Erasmus*, 233.

Sancta Respublica, comments the 1516 marginal note against the section forbidding taverns and brothels: 'O Holy Commonwealth, and worthy of imitation even by Christians' (Y146-7).

The garments worn 'throughout all the island be of one fashion' (E63). And of one colour: the 'Natural colour of the wool' (E68). Thomas More himself, in a letter to Erasmus in December 1516, described the garb as 'Franciscan'.[14]

The Utopians rise at 4 a.m. and go to bed at 8 p.m. The actual working day is 6 hours: 9 a.m. to 12 noon; and 3 p.m. to 6 p.m. (E64).[15] Raphael argued that although six hours might to Europeans seem a 'small time', it is 'not only enough but also too much for the store and abundance of all things that be requisite for the necessity or commodity of life' (E66).[16] He develops the point into an Erasmus-style defence of 'profitable occupations'; as against the 'vain and superfluous' 'works' of priests and monks, gentry and nobility (E66). The Utopians shun 'unneedful labours' (E69). They avoid being 'wearied from early in the morning to late in the evening with continual work, like labouring and toiling beasts' (E64). In fact, fewer hours than 6 can be proclaimed at times when there is not sufficient profitable work to do (E69). All the natives are expert in 'husbandry'; learnt in theory at school, and in practice on the farms (E63). In addition, every man has a particular 'craft'. Usually, a boy is 'brought up in his father's craft'. If he not thus inclined, he is adopted by a family 'of that occupation which he doth most fantasy'. Or, he can learn an extra craft, in addition to the family tradition. Every man is to 'apply his own craft with earnest diligence' (E64). The crafts specifically named by Raphael (E63) are the making of wool and linen cloth (every family makes its own clothes); the mason, the smith, the carpenter, the woodcutter. The natives 'trim' and 'furnish' their gardens (E61). They keep their houses in good and constant repair (E68). They can 'abide and suffer much bodily labour' – 'when need requireth'. When need does not, 'they be not greatly desirous and fond of it; but in the exercise and study of the mind they be never weary' (E94). Before work begins at 9 a.m., there is a choice of lectures on 'science liberal'. Attendance is voluntary; except for 'the company of the learned' – those 'chosen and appointed to learning' (E65).

Dinner is at 12 noon: a 'very short' meal. Supper is longer; the prelude to 'sleep and natural rest', good for the digestion (E74). There are 'great and large halls' in every street on Utopia, holding thirty

[14] *More: Selected Letters*, ed. Rogers, 85.

[15] This is a passage where the Everyman reprint of Robinson is confusing (p.64). Everyman has Robinson writing 'six of those hours to work before noon': plus three hours later, making a 9 hour day. Robinson in fact had a comma: 'six of those hours to work, before noon … and after dinner' (1556, p.55).

[16] Compare the working day at Jamestown, pp.299, 300-1, 388-9. In great Tudor houses, the usual working day for servants was 6 a.m. to 10 p.m. (summer) and 7 a.m. to 9 p.m. (winter): with dinner at 11 a.m. and supper at 6 p.m. Rowse, *Elizabethan Renaissance: The Life of the Society*, 111.

families (each of at least thirty persons: E57), and providing 'good and fine fare'; 'though no man be prohibited to dine at home, yet no man doth it willingly' (except for 'cause reasonable') (E71-3). The frontiersmen, also, cannot dine in Hall; those who 'dwell alone far from any neighbours' (E75). The dinner and supper hour are announced from the Hall 'by the sound of a brazen trumpet' (E72). Before every meal, there is a reading in the Hall of 'something that pertaineth to good manners and virtue'⸱ (E74). In the seating arrangements, young and old are intermingled, 'that the sage gravity and reverence of the elders should keep the youngers from wanton licence of words and behaviour' (E74). There is a 'high table': for the head of the 'ward' and his wife, and the priests and their wives, among others (E73). The cooking is done by the women, on a rota system. They 'seethe' and dress the meat (E73). (Hunting, being unworthy of 'free men', is done by the butchers, who are bondsmen: E89.) Bondsmen are responsible for the 'vile service', 'labours and toil' and 'base business' of Hall and kitchen (E73). The food includes 'conceits' and 'junkets' (E74). There is music at supper. It is all very merry. At every table, says Raphael, the Utopians 'sit four at a mess' (E73). They would have been at home in the Inns of Court.

After dinner, there is a 'rest period' of two hours; after supper, an hour of 'play' – in summer, in the gardens, in winter in Hall, where there is music, games 'not much unlike the chess', and 'honest and wholesome communication' (E65). (We know from Erasmus that More loathed 'ball-games, cards and gambling'.)[17] But, in general, the eight 'free' hours of the day can be used 'every man as he liketh best himself' (E64).

Some natives of Utopia are in a condition of 'bondage'. There are the *famulus* (Y138) and the *servus* (Y184): Robinson translated both as 'bondsman'; the Yale translation renders both as 'slave'. (Dolan creditably has 'bondsman' for *famulus*, and 'slave' for *servus*.) Every household (of about forty members) has two *servi* (E57/Y114). They act, for instance, as wagon drivers. The status of 'bondage' (*servitus*, Y190) is usually a form of punishment for 'heinous offences' (E97): adultery (E101), or travelling without a permit (E75). Other types of *servus* were foreigners under sentence of death at home (E97), foreigners preferring bondage in Utopia to drudgery at home (E98), prisoners of war (E116), and zealots too vehement in religious debate (E119). The *servi* are kept in 'continual work and labour' (E97) – no leisure hours for them. They are also in bonds; 'great chains, fetters and gyves' – but made of gold and silver (E79). Thus the visiting Ambassadors with their golden chains were taken by the Utopians to be *servi* (E81) – and those with pearls and precious stones to be the ambassadors' Fools.

There is manumission. A 'bondsman' showing repentance can have his term of service shortened, or his conditions mitigated; or he can be

[17] Appendix to Huizinga, *Erasmus*, 234.

completely forgiven, 'sometimes by the prince's prerogative and sometimes by the voice and consent of the people' (E102).

The Utopians are admirably learned. In music, logic, arithmetic and geometry 'they have found out all in a manner that our ancient philosophers have taught' (E83). The study of medicine is held 'nowhere in greater honour' (E96). More impressive still, they are adept at searching out 'the secret mysteries of nature'. They assume that the 'Author and Maker' of Nature has 'set forth the marvellous and gorgeous frame of the world for men with great attention intentively to behold'. The Utopian is a 'curious and diligent beholder and viewer of His work, and marveller at the same'; any man having 'no regard to so great and wonderful a spectacle' they esteem as 'a very brute beast without wit and reason' (E96). In their speculations about the causes of natural phenomena and 'the original beginnings and nature of heaven and of the world' they 'hold partly the same opinions that our old philosophers hold' – though they disagree with some of the Europeans, as the Utopians have 'new reasons of things'; and like the Europeans, disagree among themselves (E83). Marginal note: *Physica Omnium Incertissima* (Y160). They are 'very expert and cunning' in plotting 'the course of the stars and the movings of the heavenly spheres'; and have

wittily excogitated and devised instruments of divers fashions, wherein is exactly comprehended and contained the movings and situations of the sun, the moon, and of all the other stars which appear in their horizon. (E83)

Their technology is quite advanced: they are 'marvellous quick in the invention of feats helping anything to the advantage and wealth of life' (E96).

Raphael was of help here. He displayed his collection of printed books, from the Venetian Press of Aldus Manutius (E96). He taught the natives how to make paper (previously they had written on skins, reeds, or tree bark) and how to print. They soon mastered these arts; and reprinted Raphael's library 'into many thousands of copies' (E97).[18] The books included 'the most part of Plato's works, more of Aristotle's'. Theophrastus' book 'of plants' had unfortunately been mangled on board by a monkey 'wantonly playing therewith' (E95). One is reminded of the large monkey which was allowed to run loose in More's garden, part of his large menagerie.[19]

Raphael's decisive contribution to Utopian culture was his knowledge of Greek. In Latin, 'there was nothing that I thought they would greatly allow, besides historians and poets' (E94). But they were allured by Greek 'literature' and 'learning', organised classes,

[18] For paper making, see McLean, *Humanism and the Rise of Science in Tudor England*, ch.1: 'The Impact of Printing'.

[19] Erasmus mentions the menagerie in his 1519 letter about More: Appendix to Huizinga, *Erasmus*, 235. More's monkey appears in Erasmus' 1531 Dialogue *Amicitia*: in *Colloquies of Erasmus*, tr. Thompson, 524.

and in three years learnt the language from Raphael (using the grammar of Constantine Lascaris, first printed in 1476 at Milan). They enjoy Plutarch; Aristophanes, Homer, Euripides and Sophocles; Thucydides, Herodotus and Herodian; the 'divers works' of Hippocrates and Galen's Greek 'Art of Medicine'; and the 'merry conceits and jests' of Lucian (some of whose dialogues More had translated into Latin, publishing a joint volume with Erasmus in 1506) (E95-6).[20]

In that part of *philosophia* concerning *mores* (Y160), 'manners and virtue' (E83), 'their reasons and opinions agree with ours' (E83). They discuss *virtus* and *voluptas*; and also *felicitas* (Y160). *Felicitas* rests in 'that pleasure which is good and honest' (E84). Marginal note: *Hoc iuxta Stoicis*, 'the definition of the Stoics' (Y162-3). Their hope is to live 'merrily'; for 'nature doth allure and provoke men to help one another to live merrily' (E86). They 'define virtue to be life according to nature'. To follow 'the course of nature' is to be 'ruled by reason'. And 'reason doth chiefly and principally kindle in men the love and veneration of the Divine Majesty' (E85).

Europeans were always fascinated by the *mores* concerning 'marriage' among the natives of the New World. Raphael is pleased that the Utopian men are content with 'one wife apiece'. Marriage can be terminated. But, in general, only by the adultery or 'intolerable wayward manners' of one party. In such a case, 'by licence of the Council' (a body of laity) the innocent party can take a new partner. The guilty party 'liveth ever after in infamy and out of wedlock' (E100). The 'breakers of wedlock' are condemned to bondage; or, for continual offences, death (E101). But 'now and then' (though they are 'loath' to do it) the Council, after they have 'diligently tried and examined the matter', can grant a divorce to a couple – both in 'full consent' – if the two have found that 'they cannot well agree between themselves, both of them finding other, with whom they hope to live more quietly and merrily' (E100-1).

In discussing *Felicitas* – 'True Felicity': 'Felicity or Blessedness' (E84) – the Utopians 'think reason (*ratio*) of itself weak (*mancus*) and unperfect (*imbecillus*)' (E84/Y160). To 'the reasons of philosophy' it is necessary to 'join' *principia ex religione deprompta*, 'certain principles taken out of religion' – principles 'pertaining to religion', although 'meet' to be 'believed and granted by proofs of reason' (E84/Y160). Raphael gives two such *principia*. He implies that there are others: 'these and suchlike' (E84).

The two are: first, 'that the soul is immortal, and by the bountiful goodness of God ordained to Felicity'; secondly, 'that to our virtues and good deeds rewards be appointed after this life, and to our evil deeds punishments' (E84). Marginal note: *Theologia Utopiensium* (Y160); and another note, 'The Immortality of Souls, about which not

---

[20] More's Latin versions of four works of Lucian, done in 1505 and 1506, appeared in 1974 in the Yale More: vol.3, part 1, ed. Thompson; with English translations.

a few, even Christians, have doubts nowadays' (Y162-3).[21] ('To the soul' the Utopians 'give intelligence and that delectation that cometh of the contemplation of truth': E90.) These 'principles' are never to be 'condemned' or 'disannulled'; otherwise it would be permissible to 'obtain pleasure by right or wrong' (E84).[22]

Utopus himself pronounced that there are certain regrettable ideas which imply 'a vile and base' 'opinion of the dignity of man's nature'. Two especially: that 'souls do die and perish with the body' (which occasioned one of the *principia ex religione*); and, secondly, that 'the world runneth at all adventures, governed by no divine providence'. And Utopus 'earnestly and straitly charged them that no man should conceive' such opinions (E120).

In post-Utopus Utopia, it was thought that a man holding the defined false opinions could not be considered a citizen, because he could 'nothing at all esteem' the 'common laws of his country' (E120-1). Nor could he be considered a man; being subject to 'madness' in degrading the 'high nature' of the soul 'to the vileness of brute beasts' bodies' (E120). Such a person was 'deprived of all honours, excluded from all offices, and reject from all common administrations in the weal-public'. He was also forbidden to discuss his *sententia* (Y222) among 'the common people'. He was, however, encouraged to do so 'among the priests and men of gravity': in the hope 'that at the last madness will give place to reason' (E121).

There are other ideological errors. These are less pernicious, because grounded 'upon some reason'. (One is, that the souls of animals are immortal.) Those preaching such ideas are 'no small number', and 'in their living neither evil nor vicious'. And they are not 'forbidden to speak their minds' (E121).

Erroneous opinion is *vitium* (Y222). The word means vice, flaw, fault. The 1967 Dolan translation has 'error'.[23] Robinson, interestingly, renders the word as 'heresy' (E121). Professor Douglas Thomson of the University of Toronto tells me that *vitium* 'could not, in my opinion, ever mean such a concept as heresy'. Robinson (as often) was here perceptive rather than pedantic.

Raphael thought that the religion of the Utopians is *gravis, severa, tristis, rigida* (Y160): 'grave, sharp, bitter and rigorous' (E84). Every inhabitant of Utopia agrees that 'there is one chief and principal god, the maker and ruler of the whole world' (E117). The god is commonly called Mithras; the Persian sun-god (Y517). But the precise incarnation of the chief god was a matter of varied opinion: some worship the sun, some the moon, some the planets, some a Utopian

---

[21] European explorers noted that all the native peoples they encountered in the sixteenth century believed in the immortality of the soul, with the possible exception of the natives of Java. Atkinson, *Nouveaux horizons*, 91-3.

[22] Quentin Skinner deals with this matter in pages 158-60 of his *Past and Present* review of the Yale *Utopia*: no.38, December 1967.

[23] *Essential Thomas More*, 88. The Penguin Classics version is too loose at this point to be considered.

alumnus. There is a 'variety of superstitions' (E118). But the wisest – and majority – opinion was this: there exists 'a certain godly power unknown, everlasting, incomprehensible, inexplicable, far above the capacity and reach of man's wit, dispersed throughout all the world in virtue and power', a power which is 'the father of all', responsible for 'the beginnings, the increasings, the proceedings, the changes, and the ends of all things' (E117). In church, every Utopian acknowledges *deus* 'to be his maker, his governor, and a principal cause of all other goodness, thanking Him for so many benefits received at His hand' (E130). All Utopians trust in immortality. Thus their hope is for a 'merry death'; they depart 'merrily and full of good hope'': *alacriter ac pleni bona spe* (Y222/E122). Or they should do. Some indeed are buried in 'sorrow and silence' – those who died 'in despair and vexed in conscience through some privy and secret foretelling of the punishment now at hand' (E121).

There is on the island an Order of 'men of religion, or religious men' (E124): *religiosi* (Y226), called by the Utopians 'Buthrescae'. Being 'so earnestly bent and affectioned to religion', they ignore Learning and give themselves to good works, and to 'unpleasant, hard and vile work'. They work harder than the *servi*. The 'wiser' of them (*prudentiores*) 'embrace matrimony, not despising the solace thereof'. For one thing, they have to 'their native country' the duty of 'procreation of children'. The 'holier' (*sanctiores*) are celibate: 'abstaining not only from the company of women but also from eating of flesh, and some of them from all manner of beasts.' They are 'wholly set upon the desire of the life to come by watching and sweating'. This celibate life, says Raphael, would be mocked if 'grounded upon reason': 'they be led to it by religion.' Raphael also points out that their communal life is 'merry and lusty'. (Y226/E123-4).

There is also an Order of priesthood: of 'dignity', and 'highly esteemed': 'to no office among the Utopians is more honour and pre-eminence given'. There are thirteen *sacerdotes* (Y226) in each city; 702, then, on the island. To Raphael, they are 'rare and few': 'they have priests of exceeding holiness, and therefore very few'. They are 'chosen of the people' by secret ballot; and are then 'consecrate of their own company'. The 'chief head of them all' is the 'bishop': *pontifex* (Y226). They instruct youth in 'good opinions and profitable for the conservation of their weal-public'. They rebuke 'dissolute and incontinent living'; and 'excommunicate' 'vicious livers' – if the excommunicated do not quickly repent, they are handed to the lay authority: 'taken and punished by the council, as wicked and irreligious.' In general, the priesthood exhorts and counsels: the magistrate corrects and punishes. The priests are 'the interpreters of God's will and pleasure': *Interpretum Dei* (Y186). A priest is 'dedicate and consecrate to God as a holy offering', 'hallowed and sanctified'. He is therefore not to be 'violently and unreverently touched'. Those who 'commit any offence' – criminous clerks – are 'under no common judgement, but be left only to God and themselves' (however vicious they may be). The Utopians 'think it not lawful to touch him with man's hand' (E124-6).

The clergy can marry. The priests 'take to their wives the chiefest women in all their country'. And there are female priests; but few only, and these widows and old women (E125).

The religious observances of the Utopians are partly private, partly communal. The 'private sacrifices and religions', the things 'peculiar to every several sect', are performed 'at home in their own houses'. Public worship is held in churches in the evening of the last day of the month, and the next morning; and the evening of the last day of the year and the next morning – twenty-six 'holy days' in all. This public worship does not affect the right of 'every man to conceive God by their religion after what likeness and similitude they will'; thus 'no image of God is seen in the Church'. Public prayers are 'such as every man may boldly pronounce without the offending of any sect'. Mithras is invoked; all 'agree together in one nature of the divine majesty, whatsoever it be'; but there is no 'peculiar word of God'. Church ceremonies 'agree indifferently' with all opinions: the 'kinds and fashions' can be 'sundry and manifold' – they are all 'going divers ways to one end': 'the honour of the divine nature' (E127).

The Utopians 'highly esteem and worship miracles that come by no help of nature, as works and witnesses of the present power of God' (E122); often obtained, in 'a sure hope and confidence and a steadfast belief', by 'common intercession and prayers' (E123). They remember the virtues of the dead; who are 'presently conversant among the quick as beholders and witnesses of their words and deeds' (E122).

The churches are large, 'very gorgeous', and 'somewhat dark'. The priests consider that 'overmuch light doth disperse men's cogitations, whereas in dim and doubtful light they be gathered together, and more earnestly fixed upon religion and devotion'' (E127). The worshippers use frankincense and other spices, and light candles: 'by these sweet savours and lights and other such ceremonies men feel themselves secretly lifted up and encouraged to devotion with more willing and fervent hearts'. This is an 'unhurtful and harmless kind of worship'. The Utopians do not suppose 'this gear' to be 'anything available to the divine nature' (E128).

The church service begins with the entry of the priests. At which all worshippers fall down 'everyone reverently to the ground': as though God 'were there personally present'. The garb of the priests is of 'changeable colours', wrought 'finely and cunningly with divers feathers of fowls'. They wear no gold or precious stones. The key is that the vestments 'in workmanship be excellent, but in stuff not very precious' (E129). There is music in the worship:

They sing praises unto God, which they intermix with instruments of music, for the most part of other fashions than these that we use in this part of the world. And like as some of ours be much sweeter than theirs, so some of theirs do far pass ours. But in one thing doubtless they go exceeding far beyond us. For all their music, both that they play upon instruments and that they sing with man's voice, doth so resemble and express natural affections, the sound and tune is so applied and made agreeable to the thing, that whether it be a prayer or else a ditty of gladness, of patience, of trouble, of mourning, or of anger, the fashion of the melody doth so represent the meaning of the thing, that it doth wonderfully move, stir, pierce, and inflame the hearers' minds. (E129)

At the end of the service:

The people and the priest together rehearse solemn prayers in words expressly pronounced, so made that every man may privately apply to himself that which is commonly spoken of all. In these prayers every man recogniseth and knowledgeth God to be his maker, his governor, and the principal cause of all other goodness, thanking Him for so many benefits received at His hand. But namely that through the favour of God he hath chanced into that public weal which is most happy and wealthy, and hath chosen that religion which he hopeth to be most true. In the which thing if he do anything err, or if there be any other better than either of them is, being more acceptable to God, he desireth Him that He will of his goodness let him have knowledge thereof, as one that is ready to follow what way soever He will lead him. But if this form and fashion of a commonwealth be best, and his own religion most true and perfect, then he desireth God to give him a constant steadfastness in the same, and to bring all other people to the same order of living, and to the same opinion of God, unless there be anything that in this diversity of religions doth delight His unsearchable pleasure. To be short, he prayeth Him that after his death he may come to Him; but how soon or late, that he dare not assign or determine. Howbeit, if it might stand with His Majesty's pleasure,[24] he would be much gladder to die a painful death and so to go to God, than by long living in worldly prosperity to be away from Him. (E129-30)

The prayer over, the congregation

fall down to the ground again, and a little after they rise up and go to dinner. And the residue of the day they pass over in plays[25] and exercise of chivalry. (E130)

Raphael tells us that in the period before the Conquest by Utopus, the natives of Abraxa were 'at continual dissension and strife among themselves for their religion': a condition of 'common dissension' (E119). This was Utopus' reason for invasion. He valued above all things 'the maintenance of peace, which he saw through continual contention and mortal hatred utterly extinguished'. Peace, he thought, produces 'the furtherance of religion' (E120). Thus he 'gave to every man free liberty and choice to believe what he would' (E120):

[24] More, of course, meant God; but Robinson, as usual, is suggestive.
[25] In the sense of 'games'.

'it should be lawful for every man to favour and follow what religion he would' (E119).

The freedom, as we have seen, was limited by the compulsion of three dogmas (at least): that the soul is immortal; that there are rewards and punishments after death; and that the cosmos is not capricious.

Those apart, every man has the right to 'do the best he could to bring other to his opinion' (E119). For God may deliberately 'inspire sundry men with sundry kinds of religion'. And even if there be 'one religion which alone is true, and all other vain and superstitious', Utopus believed that 'the truth, of its own power, would at the last issue out and come to light': if 'handled with reason and sober modesty'. To 'compel all other by violence and threatenings to agree to the same that thou believest to be true' seemed to Utopus 'very unmeet and foolish'; and 'a point of arrogant presumption'. Continual contention, in the Abraxa spirit, means that 'the best and holiest religion would be trodden underfoot, even as good corn is by thorn and weeds overgrown and choked': for it is 'the worst men' who are 'most obstinate and stubborn, and in their evil opinion most constant' (E120). So the man wishing 'to bring other to his opinion' must refrain, in the island newly named Utopia, from 'displeasant and seditious words'. He must use 'no kind of violence', but 'fair and gentle speech'; arguing 'peaceably, gently, quietly and soberly, without hasty and contentious rebuking and inveighing against others'. Those debating 'vehemently and fervently' were banished, or made *servi* (E119).

About 1510 the four Christian laymen arrived. The Utopians 'heard us talk of the name of Christ', 'of His doctrine, laws, miracles, and of the no less wonderful constancy of so many martyrs'. The impact was immediate: 'You will not believe with how glad minds they agreed unto the same' (E118). Raphael gives three reasons for this gratifying response (E118).

First: 'the secret inspiration of God'.

Secondly: they thought Christianity 'nighest unto that opinion which among them is counted the chiefest'.

Thirdly: 'they heard us say that Christ instituted among His all things common (*victus communis*: Y218) and that the same community doth yet remain among the rightest Christian companies' (*conventus*: Y218).

Victus (or *vita*) *communis* means life shared together. The details of how far Christ 'instituted' such a common sharing in other than a spiritual sense were presumably at the finger tips of the four mariners. A more precise source would have been the account of Christian communities in the second half of the first century given by Luke, Paul's fellow-traveller: 'The Acts of the Apostles', written between A.D. 60 and 90 (estimates vary).

And all that believed were together, and had all things common; And sold their possessions and goods, and parted them to all men, as every man had need. (2:44-5)

And the multitude of them that believed were of one heart and of one soul: neither said any of them that ought of the things which he possessed was his own; but they had all things common ... and distribution was made unto every man according as he had need. (4:32,35)

What Raphael related about the Christian *conventus* in the early 16th century also must be imagined; the word, of course, meant, or implied, 'religious house'.

Whatever the mariners said about Christian 'community' agreed with the *fundamentum*, the 'principal foundation', of the Utopian constitution. This was *victus communis*: 'the community of their life'.[26] Life 'without any occupying of money': *sine ullo pecuniae commercio.* (Y244/E135.)

Earlier in his relation about the island, Hythloday had said that Utopia was *velut una familia*: 'as it were one family or household' (Y148/E76). On Utopia 'there is nothing within the houses that is private or any man's own'; and the Utopians change houses by lot every ten years (E60-1). (Every man, however, can cultivate his own garden: E61.) Marginal note: 'These features smack of Plato's community' (Y121).

At the end of Book One – the dialogue between Raphael, Peter Giles, and the character called 'More' – Raphael had attacked the concept of *proprietas*: 'propriety', in the sense of 'ownership' (Y104/E51). *Prudentissima atque sanctissima instituta*, 'the wise and godly ordinances of the Utopians' (Y102/E5), result in 'all things being there in common': so 'every man hath abundance of everything' (E50). It is not possible 'that the weal public may justly be governed' when 'possessions be private' (E50); where 'every man's goods[27] be proper and peculiar to himself' (E51). Thus 'equality of all things should be brought in'; and *proprietas* 'exiled and banished' (E51/Y104).

Raphael's indignation in the Dialogue seems to arise in large degree from his persuasion that 'rich men be covetous' (E51). Earlier in the debate, in the long 'flashback' to his period in 1497 in the household of Archbishop Morton, he had attacked 'the unreasonable covetousness of a few': *cupiditas* (Y68/E28). By the end of Book II *cupiditas* had become 'unsatiable' (E133). 'Covetousness' is much the best translation of *cupiditas*, because it catches the New Testament tone. The operative passages are, first, St Paul: *Radix enim malorum est*

---

[26] As a translation of More's *victus communis*, Robinson's 'community of their life' is preferable to (or at any rate more Tudor than) Dolan's 'communistic life' and the Penguin 'communism'. Governor William Bradford of Plymouth Plantation was doubtful about the 'communality' practised in the first years of the settlement: *Of Plymouth Plantation*, ed. Morison, 133. See below, pp.487-8.

[27] 'gooddes' (1556, p.41) Everyman misprints this as 'good', in the singular (p.51).

cupiditas, in the Vulgate version: I Timothy 6:10. The Authorised Version and the New English Bible (1961) were to translate *cupiditas* as 'the love of money': 'the love of money is the root of all evil'. Tyndale, in 1525, had 'covetousness'. The second passage is the Epistle to the Hebrews 13:5, *Sint mores sine avaritia*. The Authorised Version has 'let your conversation be without covetousness'; here the AV was wise enough to adopt Tyndale. We have seen that the 'cursed' Zapoletes were governed by *avaritia*: 'covetousness' (Y208/E122). Robinson followed Tyndale. Perhaps, on just this one occasion, Thomas More might have approved of the Tyndale translation.

As a result of all this, 'many' Utopians were converted by the mariners. And the natives were 'washed in the holy water of baptism' (E118); a sacrament which in case of necessity could be administered by a layman. We remember that there was no priest with Raphael. The Utopians were deprived of 'those sacraments which here none but priests do minister'; but they 'understand and perceive' the sacraments, and are 'very desirous of the same' (E118). The Utopians discuss the Christian priesthood, as compared with their own; and wonder whether, with no Christian Bishop on the island, a Utopian 'may receive the order of priesthood'. They decided to choose a Utopian candidate for the Christian priesthood; but 'at my departure from them they had chosen none' (E119).

More's 1516 preface to *Utopia* included his joke about the 'professor of divinity' who desired to be consecrated Bishop of Utopia: 'to the intent he may further and increase our religion which is there already luckily begun' (E9).

The spirit of Utopus survived the advent of the Christians. The Utopians were accustomed to 'think he shall not be welcome to God which, when he is called, runneth not to him gladly, but is drawn by force and sore against his will' (E121). And the recently converted zealot among the mariners found himself disciplined. He

began against our wills, with more earnest affection than wisdom, to reason of Christ's religion, and began to wax so hot in this matter, that he did not only prefer our religion before all other, but also did utterly despise and condemn all other, calling them profane, and the followers of them wicked and devilish, and the children of everlasting damnation.

So he was expelled from Utopia as 'a seditious person, and a raiser up of dissension among the people' (E119). Just as Archbishop Morton, as recalled by Raphael in Book I, had silenced the Friar, 'a man of grisly and stern gravity', who had been shocked by the Jester's Erasmian humour about the similarity between friars and vagabonds, and invoked 'terrible threatenings out of Holy Scripture' (E37-8).

In his English sojourn in 1497, Raphael had also spoken to Morton about the Law and the Gospel (E31). Moses' Law was sometimes 'ungentle and sharp'. But, said the Portuguese sailor to the Cardinal Archbishop of Canterbury, God has given a 'new law of clemency and mercy, under the which He ruleth us with fatherly tenderness, as His dear children'.

After all, as one of the guests at the 'Godly Feast' (recorded by Erasmus in 1522)[28] was to argue, discussion of theology is 'permissible even for sailors, in my opinion, provided they're cautious about passing judgment'.

---

[28] Colloquy *Convivium religiosum*. Tr. Thompson, *Colloquies of Erasmus*, 57.

4

King Utopus and Chancellor More

'What marvel is it,' asked Bishop John Jewel of Thomas Harding in 1567, if the superstitious Indians invaded by the Spanish and the Portuguese were led into Popery – 'carrying such a show of apparel and holy ceremonies?'[1]

Raphael and his three mariners found the religious observances of the island of Utopia in many points not unlike those of Catholic Christendom. The 'dark' and 'gorgeous' churches (E128);[2] the candles and 'sweet savours' (E128); the colourful vestments of the priests (E127). It is true that the churches of Utopia have 'no image of any god' (E127). Perhaps this was a detail of the culture of the island which More later regretted committing to print.

In 1520 the French lawyer Guillaume Budé decided to publish some of the letters he had received from More. More asked him to postpone his plan until the letters could be revised:[3]

In my remarks upon peace and war, upon morality, marriage, the clergy, the people, etc, perhaps what I have written has not always been so cautious and guarded that it would be wise to expose it to captious critics.

After More joined the Privy Council, in the summer of 1517,[4] people noted his gift of diplomatic silence. And in the 1520s he developed a habit of revising and withholding; perhaps a lawyer's caution – Bacon was similar. More's *Reponsio ad Lutherum* was printed early in 1523; this version was withdrawn by More (only one copy now survives, at Durham), and a much revised and expanded text was published (under the pseudonym William Ross) later in the same year.[5] In 1532 More wrote to Erasmus (they had not met since 1521, at Bruges) suggesting that if the 'utter havoc' spread by the 'pestilential heresies' of the 1520s had been foreseen, Erasmus would surely have treated

[1] Jewel, *Works*, Parker Society, III, 197-9.

[2] As in the previous chapter, 'E' means the Everyman *Utopia* (Ralph Robinson translation): followed by the page number.

[3] *More: Selected Letters*, ed. Rogers, 145.

[4] For More's career, G.R. Elton, 'Thomas More, Councillor (1517-1529)', in *More: Action and Contemplation*, ed. Sylvester, 1972; reprinted in Elton, *Studies*, vol.1.

[5] *Responsio* was published in the Yale Edition of 'The Complete Works of St Thomas More' in 1972: being Vol.5 (in two parts), ed. Headley.

some 'points' in his early writings 'more gently and more delicately'.[6] This reserve may explain why More did not prepare a version of *Utopia* in English – after all, about 1513 he had written *Richard III* in both Latin and English.

Concerning images in churches, we know that More was in fact a great defender of their 'ordinate' use;[7] and in general a trenchant advocate of the traditional techniques of piety. On the other hand when John Colet, Dean of St Paul's, was suspended from preaching for four months in 1513 by the reactionary Bishop of London, one of the charges brought against him (according to Erasmus) was that he 'taught that images ought not to be worshipped'.[8]

The More of the late 1520s and early 1530s was grossly shocked by the anabaptists, and those who argued 'that no man should have anything proper of his own, but that all lands and all goods ought by God's law to be all men's in common; and that all women ought to be common to all men ... and every man husband to every woman, and every woman wife unto every man'.[9] Yet the youthful More, Erasmus tells us, wrote 'a dialogue in which he defended Plato's communism, even to the community of wives'.[10]

In the 1523 *Responsio* More took Luther as implying that 'we would do better to be without that law from which the ownership of goods arises, and would do better to live in a certain natural community' (*in communitate quadam naturali*). Well, suppose 'we could live in common (*in communi*) with far fewer laws'; we would need *some* laws – to prevent crime, to enforce 'the obligation to work' for 'certain classes'; and *res proprietas* 'could yet remain'. Possessions and property (*proprietas*) spring from a public agreement (*consensus*): and thus they are 'public law' (*lex publica*) – whether the law is expressed in custom, or in specific edict.[11]

In March 1518, in his preface to the Basle edition of *Utopia*, Budé praised the book for its portrayal of the *lex communionis*.[12] Budé, who had been attempting for two years to look after his country estate, was obsessed by the difficulties of being a property holder; and had come to the conclusion, in his legal dealings, that while actual law assumes the essence of happiness to be the accumulation of wealth, 'true

[6] *Selected Letters*, 175.
[7] As in 1528: *A dyaloge of syr T. More. Wherin be treatyd dyvers maters, as of the veneration & worship of ymagys.* Especially Book I.
[8] Erasmus' 1521 'essay' on Vitrier and Colet: in Olin, ed., *Christian Humanism and the Reformation: Erasmus*, 188 (J.H. Lupton translation.)
[9] *Confutacyon*, 1533, p.cclxix.
[10] Erasmus' 1519 'essay' on More (a letter to Ulrich von Hutten): in the 'Selected Letters' (tr. Barbara Flower) printed as Appendix to the Phaidon and Harper editions of Huizinga's *Erasmus*, 238.
[11] Yale *Responsio*, 276-7.
[12] Budé preface (a letter to Thomas Lupset) in Yale *Utopia*, 4-15 (Latin text and English translation). This reference, p.8. The page references in the text are to this edition.

equity' does not. True Equity is based on the Principle of Christ and the *ritus* (usage) of His followers (p.6). Actual laws should be seen in the light of *norma veritatis*, the standard of truth; and of the *simplicitas* commanded by the Gospel (p.6). Christ came to abolish (*abrogare*) things as they legally are – 'among His own at least'. And in His *lex communionis* Christ 'left among His followers a Pythagorean communion (*communio*) and charity' (p.8). 'Communion' as in Holy Communion. Budé was thinking in moral and spiritual terms. Christ, further, is the *conditor* and *moderator* of *possessio*: 'the founder and supervisor of possessions' (p.8). On the island of Utopia are enforced three 'divine principles' (*divina instituta*): the contempt of money; the love of *pax* and *tranquillitas*; and *aequalitas* among fellow citizens (*inter cives*). The dominant vice in Christendom is *avaritia*. If rooted out, there would return 'the golden age of Saturn': *aureum saeculum Saturnium* (p.10). On Utopia there is no *avaritia*, no *cupiditas*. There is no pride (*superbia*); and no *contentio* (p.10). The natives of Utopia have 'adopted the customs (*ritus*) and true wisdom (*germana sapientia*) of Christianity' (p.10).

Budé reminds one of Colet. In his Oxford lectures of the late 1490s on Paul's Epistle to the Romans, Colet had condemned the *jus gentium* as an imperfect law, which 'brought in ideas of *meum* and *tuum*; of property, that is to say, and deprivation' (*proprietas, privatio*), 'ideas contrary to a good and simple Nature, for that would have a community in all things'.[13] The root of all evil is avarice and greed of money.[14] Covetousness (especially among the clergy and ecclesiastical lawyers) was an obsessive theme with Dean Colet. It is ironical that among the charges made against the London merchant Richard Hunne in heresy proceedings during 1514 (when More was Under-Sheriff – chief magistrate – of the City of London) was that Hunne has condemned tithes as being ordained only by 'the covetousness of priests'.[15]

Budé concluded that the natives of Utopia were in a condition of *beata innocentia*: indeed, of a 'heavenly life' (*vita caelestis*). This 'island of the New World' is 'undoubtedly one of the Fortunate Isles; perhaps close to the Elysian Fields' (p.12).

Captain Gabriel Archer, in his description of the Indians of the James River area in 1607, noted that there is 'no respect of profit, neither is there scarce that we call *meum* and *tuum* among them' (except in their 'several gardens').[16] To European colonists, this was criticism, not praise. The Vice-Regent of Peru in the 1560s declared:

> it is not surprising that these poor Indians should be idle and take no trouble to work, because up to now they have had no private property, but everything in common.

[13] Colet, *Creation, etc*, ed. Lupton, 134.

[14] Colet, *Lectures on Romans*, ed. Lupton, 118.

[15] Quoted in my essay 'The Gloomy Dean and the Law: Colet', in Bennett and Walsh, eds., *Essays in Modern English Church History*, 23.

[16] Barbour, ed., *Jamestown Voyages*, 101.

The civilised Polity demanded a wage economy.[17]

Raphael, one of the earliest European colonists, embellished his description of the religious practices of the natives with further material which would have struck John Jewel as Popish. On Utopia, there is worship of miracles, and remembrance of the dead (E122). Celibacy is a holy state (E124). In his eloquent passage on church music (E129) – which looks forward to a familiar section of Hooker[18] – Raphael was critical of the over-elaborate liturgical music dominant in early sixteenth century Europe. Erasmus would have agreed.[19] Erasmus wrote in 1519 that More 'delights in every kind of music' (although 'he seems to have no natural gift for vocal music'). More had induced his second wife to play 'the cithern, the lute, the monochord and the recorders'.[20]

Particularly striking is Utopian veneration for the priests, *sacerdotes* (Y226).[21]

The priesthood is in control of education (E125). This provision would not have pleased Colet. He had entrusted the governing of his new St Paul's School (founded about 1509) to a City Company. According to Erasmus, he found 'least corruption' in the London lay mercantile community.[22]

Colet, however, would have approved of the Utopian conception of the priesthood as 'interpreters of God's will': *Interpretum Dei* (E98/Y186). The Oxford lectures tell us that the priesthood know 'the grounds of what is sacred'; and are 'guardians' of the 'hidden treasures of God'.[23] Colet's favourite text on this theme was from the Sermon on the Mount: 'Give not that which is holy unto the dogs, neither cast ye your pearls before swine' (Matthew 7:6). More refered in 1528[24] to the fact that Moses had ascended Mount Sinai alone to commune with God and receive the Ten Commandments (p.201). God said to Moses and the elders:

Moses alone shall come near the Lord: but they shall not come nigh; neither shall the people go up with him. And Moses came and told the people all the words of the Lord, and all the judgements; and the people answered with one voice, and said, All the words which the Lord hath said will we do. (Exodus 24:2-3, Authorised Version)

The fact of the people 'tarrying beneath', wrote More,

signified that the people be forbidden to meddle with the high mysteries of

[17] Elliott, 'The Discovery of America and the Discovery of Man', 19.
[18] *Laws of Ecclesiastical Polity*, V. xxxviii. 1.
[19] Bainton, *Erasmus of Christendom*, 280-5.
[10] Appendix to Huizinga, *Erasmus*, 233, 236.
[21] As in the previous chapter, 'Y' means Yale *Utopia*, followed by the page number.
[22] Lupton translation of 1521 letter, Olin, *Christian Humanism*, 180.
[23] *Lectures on Corinthians*, ed. Lupton, 150.
[24] 1528. *Dialogue*. Page references are to the section printed in 1967 in *The Essential Thomas More*.

Holy Scripture, but ought to be content to tarry beneath, and meddle none higher than is meet for them. (p.201)

The people are not to 'dispute' the scripture; but to 'fulfil' it (p.201). And Paul wrote, in 'divers of his epistles', that in the Church God 'will have some readers, and some hearers, some teachers and some learners – we do plainly pervert and turn upside down the right order of Christ's Church when the one part meddleth with the other's office' (p.202).

The Readers and Teachers are 'the wisest and best learned, and he that therein hath by many years bestowed his whole mind' (p.203). To expound scripture 'is the preacher's part, and theirs that after long study are admitted to read and expound it' (p.204). They alone can approach the 'great doubts and high questions of Holy Scripture, and of God's great and secret mysteries' (p.203). The Bible has its 'high secret mysteries' and 'hard texts' (p.201). And 'inordinate is the appetite when men unlearned' are 'busy to ensearch and dispute the great secret mysteries of Scripture, which, though they hear, they be not able to perceive' (p.201). There is danger of 'newfangleness' (p.205) among the 'common people':

when the wine were in and the wit out, would they take upon them with foolish words and blasphemy to handle Holy Scripture in more homely manner than a song of Robin Hood. And some would, as I said, solemnly take upon them, like as they were ordinary readers, to interpret the text at their pleasure. (p.203)

Similar points had been made in the 1523 *Responsio*. In 1523 More argued that Scripture has its obscure and ambiguous places;[25] and that Luther relied 'on his own interpretation', measuring the Bible by 'feeling' (*adfectus*) and 'fancy' (*libido*). 'Here he clearly opens the windows by which the people may plunge into perdition.'[26] So much for Erasmus' 1516 vision of the scripture recited by the farmer at the plough and the weaver at the loom.[27] There was no such 'newfangleness' on the island of Utopia. In support of his thesis, More in 1528 noted that it was 'provided by the emperor, in the law civil, that the common people should never be so bold to keep dispicions upon the faith or Holy Scripture, nor that any such thing should be used among them or before them' (p.202).

The reader will be reminded, ironically, of the account by Raphael of Law on Utopia (E103-4). Raphael argues that laws in Europe have become 'too blind and intricate', needing 'great wits and long arguing'; and unfortunately beyond the 'judgement' of the 'vulgar sort of the people' (who are the 'most in number'). Erasmus' weavers and farmers? Things are different in the New World. On Utopia there is

---

[25] Yale *Responsio*, 127.
[26] *Ibid.*, 283.
[27] *Paraclesis*. Olin, 87.

no 'crafty and subtle interpretation'. For there is 'open to every man' the 'simple, the plain and gross meaning of the laws'; the 'plainer' the interpretation, the better. Thus there are no barristers and solicitors on Utopia. There are Judges; before whom the natives 'think it most meet that every man should plead his own matter'.

More's opponents of the 1520s argued that 'every man' had a similar right in matters of Scripture, and the 'mysteries' of God.

It is difficult to decide how much to make of the fact that Raphael does not appear to have carried a Bible in his library. Perhaps, like Columbus, he was so soaked in Holy Writ (or parts of it) that it was unnecessary to mention the Bible specifically. Perhaps he was so enamoured of Greek that only Erasmus' Greek New Testament would have pleased him, and that was not printed until 1516, a few months before *Utopia*; the first Greek text of the New Testament to be published. However, the Latin version of the Old and New Testaments, the Vulgate, was readily available in compact Venetian editions.[28]

Raphael noted that on Utopia the priests are venerated as though in them god were 'personally present' (E129): 'hallowed and sanctified' (E126); 'dedicate and consecrate to God as a holy offering' (E125). Colet would have approved of this point also. In his sermon in St Paul's cathedral in 1512 to the Convocation of Canterbury, Colet had reminded the assembled priesthood that they were 'the light of the world'.[29] The dignity of the priesthood, said the Dean, is 'greater than either the King's or Emperor's; it is equal with the dignity of angels'.[30] During the sermon, he also defended the right of clerics 'not to be drawn before secular judges'.[31] Part of 'the church's liberty'.

In February 1515, three months before More left London for his five months in Flanders, an indictment of murder was preferred by a grand jury of the City against (among others) the chancellor of the Bishop of London; he was a cleric, *clericus*, though in minor orders only (below the grade of deacon).[32] Late in 1512 a Parliamentary statute had declared that those in minor orders accused of murder were not to allowed *privilegium clericale*; they were to be tried not in the bishop's court, but 'by the course of the common law'. But a papal bull of May 1514 re-affirmed that all clerks, whether in major or minor

[28] See M.H. Black, 'The Printed Bible', in *Cambridge History of the Bible: the West from the Reformation*, ed. Greenslade, 1963; especially p.417.

[29] English text of sermon in Williams, ed., *English Historical Documents, V, 1485-1558*. Relevant passage, 653.

[30] *ibid.*, 655.

[31] *ibid.*, 659.

[32] A stage in the Richard Hunne case, which agitated London from 1511. See my 1966 essay on Colet (note 15). The best brief account of the affair is in Dickens, *English Reformation*, 1964. R.J. Schoeck has discussed More's concern with the case in two papers: 'Common Law and Canon Law in the Writings of More: the affair of Hunne', *Monumenta Juris Canonici*: Series C, Subsidia, vol.4 (Vatican City, 1971); and 'Common Law and Canon Law in their relation to More', *More: Action and Contemplation*, ed. Sylvester, 1972.

orders were immune from proceedings in secular courts. In the autumn of 1515 there was a conference in London of lawyers, clerics and legislators to discuss the problem. So this topic was much in the London air at the time More was thinking about *Utopia*. His sympathies lay with the 'high clerical' party; with Colet. Raphael tells us this about the priests of the island: if 'they commit any offence, they be under no common judgement, but be left only to God and themselves' (E125).

Bishop Jewel would certainly have considered the natives of Utopia ripe for Popery.

Abraxa, before the Conquest, had been in a condition of 'continual contention' and 'mutual hatred' (E120); of 'continual dissension and strife for their religions', a 'common dissension' of 'every several sect' (E119). Would England in the 1520s come to resemble Abraxa?

The 1523 *Responsio*[33] was a defence of 'the public faith of the whole church' (p.53); and of 'law and order' (p.141), of 'fixed and definite laws' as against 'indefinite whims' (p.277). The Lutherans 'would have all human laws abolished' (p.271). This is an inevitable product of heresy. (Raphael had said that 'you may be sure' that the heretic would either mock or violently break 'the common laws of his country': E121). The zealot in Raphael's party was expelled from the island because he was 'a seditious person'; a 'raiser up of dissension among the people' (E119). The 'common people' of the island are protected from controversial *sententia* (Y222). Such opinions are to be discussed only with the priests and 'men of gravity' (E121).

To More, as he explained in 1528, it was the heretic who *first* used violence: 'the violent cruelty first used by the heretics themselves against good Catholic folk'. Thus the lay magistrate was 'driven' himself to use 'force and violence', 'for preservation, not of the faith only, but also of the peace among their people'.[34]

The 1523 *Responsio* attacked Luther as the initiator of chaos; with his 'brawling', 'wrangling', 'raving', 'vomiting out such continuous and senseless abuse'.[35] The danger was the seducing of 'good and simple men'.[36] Luther invoked the *'populus*: the 'whole people' – which is to say, 'anyone whatsoever'.[37] (One remembers the important place of the 'consent of the people' in many matters on Utopia; in 1520, in his letter to Budé, More listed 'the people' among the themes about which he had not been sufficiently 'cautious and guarded'.)[38] How (this is 1523 again) can things be 'left wholly to each individual to approve, disapprove, change, condemn, reject, wherever, whensoever, as often as he pleases'?[39] Lutheranism was 'an ocean of nonsense', a

[33] All page references to Yale *Responsio*.
[34] 1528 *Dialogue: The Essential Thomas More*, 209.
[35] Yale *Responsio*, 11.
[36] *ibid.*, 19.
[37] *ibid.*, 613.
[38] *Selected Letters*, 145.
[39] Yale *Responsio*, 319.

'bottomless pit of madness',[40] 'an abyss of violent passion'.[41] And Luther was a hypocrite, 'in fact being led on by foolish conceit and a greedy desire for renown'.[42]

Thomas More was like Joseph Conrad as characterised by Bertrand Russell:[43]

He thought of civilised and morally tolerable life as a dangerous walk on a thin crust of barely cooled lava which at any moment might break and let the unwary sink into fiery depths. He was very conscious of the various forms of passionate madness to which men are prone, and it was this that gave him such a profound belief in the importance of discipline.

King Utopus invaded Abraxa for 'the furtherance of religion' and 'the maintenance of peace' (E120); the exact motives of the 'good princes' who use force against heretics, in the 1528 *Dialogue*.[44] He decreed that any inhabitants of the island who 'strive and contend' in their 'cause' 'vehemently and fervently' were to become exiles or bondsmen (E119). (The Heretic, wrote More in 1528, has 'indiscreet zeal', an 'over-fervent mind', and 'an angry and cruel heart'.[45]) Utopus also laid down certain compulsory 'opinions'. These affirmed 'the dignity of man's nature' (E120).

The first was, that the soul does not 'die and perish with the body' (E120). The Utopians thereafter held to this notion of the 'high nature' of the soul (E120). It was one of the Utopian *principia ex religione deprompta*: 'principles taken out of religion' (Y160/E84). To deny it – for a man to lower 'the high nature of his soul to the vileness of brute beasts' bodies' (E120) – was *vitium*: 'heresy', in the Tudor translation (Y222/E121).

In 1646 the General Court of Massachusetts, while affirming that 'no human power' could be 'lord over the faith and consciences of men', or could 'constrain them to believe or profess against their conscience', listed certain 'heresies' of 'such nature and degree' that they are 'damnable', 'tending to the subversion of the Christian faith and destruction of the souls of men'. First on the list was 'denying the immortality of the soul'. (In Massachusetts, advocates of the opinion were 'restrained'; this meant a fine.)[46]

The natives of Utopia were not Vespucci's 'simple Gentiles living only after the law of nature'.

The second dogma of Utopus was that the universe does not run 'at all adventures, governed by no divine providence' (E120). The cosmos is not capricious: God is not a tyrant. The Utopians believed that God welcomes the man who runs to Him 'gladly': *Libens*, willingly, with pleasure. Not the man 'drawn by force and sore against his will':

[40] *ibid.*, 9. [41] *ibid.*, 15. [42] *ibid.*, 3.
[43] *Autobiography of Bertrand Russell*, I, 1967, 208.
[44] *The Essential Thomas More*, 209.
[45] *ibid.*, 212.
[46] Shurtleff, ed., *Records of Massachusetts*, II, 1853, 177.

detractus, dragged, forced; *invitus*, reluctant (Y222/E121). Thomas More argued in 1534:[47]

It is not the custom of God by force to make men good, whether they will or no; nor in His election He chooseth not folks by violence, but by good advice and monition.

The Lutherans, he had earlier written, 'give the whole glory to God': assuming that men should use

none endeavour at all, nor do anything, nor say anything, nor think nothing; but even sit still, sadly, and gape up by day against the sun, by night against the moon, till either some blind beetle or some holy bumble bee come fly in at the their mouths and buzz into their breasts.

Such argument is 'as full of reason as an egg full of mustard'.[48] The will of man works 'not as a dead vessel'; but 'as a quick instrument'. Man 'wittingly and willingly" receives the 'liberal offer' of God.[49] He is a worker with God, working with God. He has an 'inclination of reason'; which God 'helpeth unto the assent and obedience of faith".[50] Reason is 'servant to Faith, and not enemy'.[51] God, in Hamlet's words (iv:4), did not give us 'godlike reason' to 'fust in us unus'd'. Thomas More, like King Utopus, wished to strike a blow for 'the dignity of man's nature' (E120). That dignity, on Utopia as in Christendom, was protected by dogma. Those denying the dogma, in England as on Utopia, were to be penalised.

During his thirty months as Lord Chancellor (October 1529 to May 1532) More was vigorous in proceedings against heresy. He had no power to try heretics; but he could arrest, imprison, and investigate. About thirty heretics were imprisoned at his instigation or with his approval. On this point, the portrait of More given by John Foxe has been decisively confirmed by Dr G.R. Elton.[52] On Utopia, it was the 'office' of the Spiritualty to 'give good exhortations and counsel': it was 'the duty of the prince and other magistrates to correct and punish' (E124). In England, More pointed out in 1528, the 'order of the spiritual law' demands penance from the heretic; if that is not forthcoming, excommunication.[53] The ultimate punishment in England for the heretic was death by burning. This was 'lawful': the provision of a statute of 1401. It was also 'necessary and well done'.[54] England is 'a good catholic realm',[55] demanding 'bodily punishment'

---

[47] *The answere* (to 'The Supper of the Lord'): *Works*, 1557, 1075.

[48] *Confutacyon*, 1533, p.cxviii.

[49] *ibid.*, cxvi.

[50] *ibid.*, ccclxxv.

[51]. 1528 *Dyaloge*. Table of contents summary of ch.23.

[52] G.R. Elton, 'More and the Opposition to Henry VIII', *Bulletin Institute Historical Research*, May 1968, XLI, 103. Reprinted 1974 in Elton's *Studies*, vol.1.

[53] *The Essential Thomas Moore*, 212.

[54] *ibid.*, 208. [55] *ibid.*, 211.

of the unrepentant heretic. But the Spiritualty, so More argued, neither 'doth' nor 'commandeth' death: 'the clergy doth not procure it, but only the good and politic provision of the Temporalty.'[56] It is 'not the clergy that laboureth to have them punished by death'.[57] It was the lay magistrate, symbolised by the Lord Chancellor. On Utopia the maintainer of 'heresy' was deprived of all honours, excluded from all public office, and 'despised as of an unprofitable and of a base and vile nature' (E121). The Utopians were denied the benefits of English statute law. Perhaps, like the killing of beasts on Utopia, the killing of heretics in England was 'only for necessity' (E89).

The inscription More wrote for his tomb at Chelsea includes the phrase 'he was a source of trouble to thieves, murderers and heretics'.[58] 'I wrote that with deep feeling,' More explained to Erasmus in June 1533:[59]

I find that breed of men absolutely loathsome, so much so that, unless they regain their senses, I want to be as hateful to them as anyone can possibly be; for my increasing experience with those men frightens me with the thought of what the world will suffer at their hands.

'Increasing experience': he had had not a little experience by 1516. We are 'nowadays grieved of heretics, men mad with marvellous foolishness', said Colet in his Convocation Sermon of 1512.[60] In December 1514 there was a heresy trial in the Lady Chapel of St Paul's Cathedral. This was an ecclesiastical court, presided over by the Bishop of London; those present included three bishops, 25 clerics; but also, as observors, the Lord Mayor, some aldermen, and the Under-Sheriff, Thomas More. A verdict of guilty was returned. The trial was of a corpse: Richard Hunne had been found dead a week earlier. His body was burnt at Smithfield on 20 December 1514.[61]

In 1528 More made clear that 'heretics' and 'heathen men' are 'two divers cases'.[62] Heretics are men 'rising among ourselves and springing of ourselves'. By 'any covenant with them Christendom can nothing win'. They are 'in no wise to be suffered, but to be oppressed and overwhelmed in the beginning'. But the 'heathen men' are outside the covenant of Christendom: Gentiles, 'Turks, Saracens and Pagans'. And if pagans would 'suffer the faith of Christ to be peaceably preached among them', and 'we Christian men should therefore suffer in like all their sects to be preached among us, and violence taken

---

[56] *ibid.*, 208.
[57] *ibid.*, 211.
[58] *Selected Letters*, 181.
[59] *ibid.*, 180.
[60] Williams, 656 (see note 29).
[61] See note 32. John Rastell was given the wardship of Hunne's two daughters, and a grant from the estate: Reed, *Early Tudor Drama*, 9, 14-16.
[62] *The Essential Thomas More*, 210.

away by assent on both the sides, I nothing mistrust that the faith of Christ should more increase than decay.' Christendom would 'seem to dishonour God if we mistrusted that His faith preached among other indifferently without disturbance should not be able to prosper.' If Raphael were still alive in 1528, he could have confirmed the point.

King Utopus, Raphael and Thomas More were akin: in spirit, highly conservative Christians of Latin Christendom.

Essentially there is no contradiction between the More who wrote *Utopia*, More the controversialist from 1523, and More the Lord Chancellor from 1529. It must, however, be granted that the manner of the controversial writing often seems alien to the *tone* of *Utopia*. Utopus had appealed to 'sober modesty', 'fair and gentle speech', and urged his subjects to discuss 'peaceably, gently, quietly and soberly, without hasty and contentious rebuking and inveighing against others'. To Utopus, 'threatenings' in debate were 'unmeet and foolish'; a fruit of 'arrogant presumption' (E119-20). The zealous mariner had debated with 'more earnest affection than wisdom', being inclined to 'wax so hot' that he came to 'despise and condemn' religious opinions not his own, calling them 'profane, and the followers of them wicked and devilish' (E119). Utopus and the Utopians might have been disconcerted by More's attack on Luther in 1523: 'with his filth and dung, shitting and beshitted' (*cum suis merdis et stercoribus, cacantem cacatumque*);[63] a 'lousy friarlet' (*pediculosus fraterculus*);[64] an 'abuser, this cashiered friarlet, this Hussite, this Satanist from hell' (*abusor, ex authoritas fraterculus, Hussiasta, Satanista, ex tartaro.*)[65] The mariner-zealot had called his opponents 'the children of everlasting damnation' (E119), and so was expelled.

More's defence would be that Luther had initiated the violence, both of opinion, and language. One has to acknowledge More's 'savage indignation'. And also his obsession with sex. In 1523 this emerged in the discussion of the sacrament of marriage. Lutheranism was 'the religion of the Bohemian backcountry (*ruris Bohemici*) where religion means nothing but to increase and multiply and to mate in church like a pack of dogs'.[66] Luther married in 1525. He had both broken his vows and succumbed to 'lechery': the 'fond frantic friar' had wedded a 'naughty nun'.[67] Much of the *Confutation* is great fun, in the manner of Lucian. It also calls for commentary by a psychiatrist. One has to remember that More himself had been tempted by the Religious Life: according to Erasmus, he resisted the temptation because of his 'inability to shake off his longing for a wife'.[68] More had recognised his nature – and chosen the second best: Luther had elected to assume the privilege of the tonsure, and had subsequently betrayed his vocation.

In 1519 Erasmus wrote that More 'diligently cultivates true piety,

[63] Yale *Responsio*, 683. Translator, Sister Scholastica Mandeville.
[64] *ibid.*, 79.   [65] *ibid.*, 212.   [66] *ibid.*, 221.
[67] *Confutacyon*, 1533, p.cccccxii.
[68] Appendix to Huizinga, 235.

while being remote from all superstitious observance'.[69] It should be noted, however, that Erasmus later wrote (1532) that More preferred superstition to impiety.[70]

Utopia is a serious book: *salutaris*, says the title, 'fruitful'. It would be difficult, in view of More's future, not to be moved by the Utopian Prayer (E129-30): the acceptance of 'that religion which he hopeth to be most true' unless God reveal 'any other better'; the rejoicing that 'he hath chanced into that public weal which is most happy and wealthy'; the desiring 'God to give him a constant steadfastness' in religion and to 'bring all other people to the same order of living and to the same opinion of God'; the recognition that even an inhabitant of a happy island might 'die a painful death and so go to God'.

But *Utopia* is also *festivus*, 'pleasant and wittie'. Raphael assumes that 'nature doth allure and provoke men one to help another to live merrily' (E86). Monks on Utopia are 'merry' (E123). Raphael was instinctively suspicious of any 'man of grisly and stern gravity' (E37). The Utopians (like Archbishop Morton in the English 'flashback') 'have singular delight and pleasure in Fools' (E102). They also appreciated the 'merry conceits and jests' of Lucian (E95); an author to be firmly condemned by the Protestant Reformers. Erasmus wrote in 1519 that More's character and expression were 'better suited to merriment than to seriousness or solemnity'. As a boy, he had written, and acted in, comedies; and always delighted in 'joking', 'clever sallies of ingenious flavour', and 'paradoxical themes'.[71]

In a letter to Erasmus in the month of the publication of the book (December 1516) More imagined himself as a new Utopus,[72] having been chosen as prince by the natives (the king of Utopia was elected for life: E62).

I can see myself now, marching along, crowned with a diadem of wheat, very striking in my Franciscan frock, carrying a handful of wheat as my sacred sceptre, thronged by a distinguished retinue of Amaurotians, and, with this huge entourage, giving audience to foreign ambassadors and sovereigns; wretched creatures they are, in comparison with us, as they stupidly pride themselves on appearing in childish garb and feminine finery, laced with that despicable gold, and ludicrous in their purple and jewels and other empty baubles.

The prince of Utopia wore no 'princely apparel' or 'robe of state' or 'crown or diadem royal'; he was distinguished from his subjects only by 'a little sheaf of corn carried before him' (E103). (Erasmus wrote in 1519 that More 'likes to dress simply, and does not wear silk or purple, or gold chains, excepting where it would not be decent not to wear them'.)[73] More was referring in his letter to the episode of the

[69] *ibid.*, 238.
[70] P.S. Allen, ed., *Erasmi Epistolae*, X, p.137 (no.2750).
[71] Huizinga Appendix, 232, 234, 238.
[72] *Selected Letters*, 85.
[73] Huizinga Appendix, 233.

visit of the ambassadors from Anemolia (E79-81). They arrive in attire very unlike the 'homely and simple array' prized by the Utopians. The Utopians assume from the golden chains and precious stones that they are bondsmen or fools. On Utopia, precious stones were given to children (E79). Gold was imported, as payment for exports. But 'none of them doth more esteem it than the very nature of the thing deserveth'; the contrary estimate in Europe is a product of 'folly' (E78). The Utopians have 'gold and silver among them in reproach and infamy'. Gold and silver are used for rings, chains, and headbands for criminals, for the chains of bondsmen – and for chamber pots. These details stuck in the popular memory. In George Chapman's *Eastward Ho*, acted in London in the spring of 1605, Sir Petronel Flash, organiser of a topical 'Virginian venture' (the charter of the Virginia Company was granted in 1606) tells his associates some facts about Virginia.[74] Rubies and diamonds, gathered by the sea shore, are used to embellish the coats and hats of Indian children, 'as commonly as our children wear saffron gilt broaches, and groats with holes in them'. Street chains are made of gold, as are prisoners' fetters. And the 'dripping pans' and 'chamber pots' are 'pure gold'.

Much of the humour of *Utopia* is in a vein which reminds the reader of Erasmus. More presumably 'highlighted' the story of the Ambassadors because he felt the episode particularly 'Erasmian'. It is doubtful whether much, beyond similarities in some details of wit, united More and Erasmus. Erasmus, for example, could never be a Hammer of Heretics: he was too aware of the Christ who does not snap off the broken reed or snuff out the smouldering wick;[75] and too conscious of the accusations of heresy made against himself by his enemies! He wrote to the Pope from Basle about heresy in 1523: saying that in Brabant he himself had been proclaimed a heretic, in both private and public; and advising Adrian VI not to combat Lutheranism by 'prisons, whips, confiscations, banishments, censures and deaths'.[76] In a letter of 1519 (in which he used the reed/wick image) he had warned that a man 'who accuses another person of heresy should exhibit in his own life a demeanour worthy of a Christian, charity in admonishing, mildness in correcting, open mindedness in judging, and deliberation in pronouncing sentence'. In 1519, he felt, 'men are inventing new fundamentals': 'new criteria by which they proclaim as heretical anything they do not like'. 'The most excellent part of Christianity is a life worthy of Christ': if that be present, it is difficult to bring a charge of heresy.[77] 'The most excellent part of Christianity is a life worthy of Christ.' If the essential Christian is the man displaying the spirit of Christ, irrespective of his specific allegiance, it is implied that dogma is ultimately irrelevant: a matter

---

[74] *Eastward Ho*, III, 2. See below, ch.13.
[75] See below, p.122.
[76] *Erasmus and His Age: Selected Letters of Erasmus*, ed. Hillerbrand, 73.
[77] *ibid.*, 135.

of the 'letter', the 'flesh'. This was a basic and consistent assumption in the thinking of Erasmus. He wrote in 1516:[78]

Do not think that Christ is found in ceremonies, in doctrines kept after a fashion, and in constitutions of the Church. Who is truly Christian? Not he who is baptised or anointed or who attends Church. It is rather the man who has embraced Christ in the innermost feelings of his heart, and also emulates Him by his pious deeds.

Such an emphasis was not natural to More. Certainly, More might have agreed with Erasmus that 'those whom we call Turks are to a great extent half-Christian, and probably nearer true Christianity than most of our own people'.[79] Turks were pagans, heathens: gentiles, like the natives of Utopia. But Erasmus – although he was naturally nervous of stressing the point – thought that the 'nearer true Christianity' tribute might extend also to dissenters within Christendom itself.

More, in addition, was remarkably insular. His arguments against scripture in the vernacular surely seemed dated to many Catholics in Europe. Erasmus wrote that when he himself was a boy (that is, the 1470s), the Bible had been read in French and German.[80] The Bible had been printed in German in 1466, and in Dutch in 1477; the New Testament in French in 1476. More in 1516 would have appreciated the thanksgiving of the man of Utopia that 'he hath chanced into that public weal which is most happy' (E130). There was always in More a touch of the famous headline in the London *Times*: 'Fog in Channel: Continent Cut Off.'

In a dialogue published in 1524, 'The well-to-do beggars', Erasmus tried his hand at incorporating the American experience. There is a discussion about clothes.[81]

I think this whole matter of dress depends upon human custom ... Not long ago I had guests here who affirmed that they had travelled through various lands recently discovered, and missing in the maps of the old cosmographers. They told of having reached an island with an extremely mild climate, where covering the body was considered the height of indecency.

Perhaps, comments the other character, 'those people lived like beasts'. Not at all:

According to the travellers, they lived a most civilised life. They lived under a king. Him they joined in the morning's work, which lasted no longer than an hour on any single day ... They picked up a kind of root they used in place of wheat. After doing this, each returns to his own affairs and does what he

[78] *Education of a Christian Prince*, tr. Born, 153.
[79] 1515, *Dulce Bellum Inexpertis*: tr. Phillips, *Adages of Erasmus*, 346.
[80] In a letter to his Sorbonne adversary Noel Beda, 15 June 1525: Allen, ed. *Erasmi Epistolae*, VI, no.1581.
[81] *Colloquies of Erasmus*, tr. Thompson, 213-14.

pleases. They rear their children conscientiously. They shun vices and punish them, but none more severely than adultery.

The adultress is pardoned, 'allowance being made for her sex'. The male has to wear for the rest of his life, when he is in public, a cloth over his private parts. 'A hard punishment.' Indeed: 'But custom has convinced them that this is the worst possible punishment.'

In the 1523 *Responsio* More discussed Luther's conception of the 'spiritual church'. A notion, thought More, 'somehow imperceptible and mathematical, like Platonic Ideas, which is both in some place and in no place'.[82] In the margin of one of the paragraphs criticising Luther's Ideal Church there was printed a note: 'Perhaps he has seen it in Utopia' (*Eam fortasse vidit in Utopia*).[83]

It is, unfortunately, not known whether this note was written by More or by the printer.

---

[82] Yale *Responsio*, 167.
[83] *ibid.*, 118-19.

5

The Old Testament: A Book Sealed and Closed

Christ advised the Jews who persecuted Him to read more attentively the Old Testament (John, 5:39, 46-7):

Search the scriptures; for in them ye think ye have eternal life: and they are they which testify of me ... For had ye believed Moses, ye would have believed me: for he wrote of me. But if ye believe not his writings, how can ye believe my words?

Moses, wrote Alderman Robert Johnson in 1612 in *The New Life of Virginea*, was 'the first historian that ever wrote'.[1] William Whitaker, appointed Regius Professor of Divinity in Cambridge in 1580, published in 1588 at Cambridge his lectures on the Bible, 'as they were taken down by some of my constant and attentive auditors', 'afterwards reviewed by myself': *Disputatio de Sacra Scriptura*, published in an English translation by the Parker Society in 1849.[2] (In 1588 Whitaker had been Master of St John's College for one year; and his son Alexander Whitaker was three years old.) Whitaker hardly needed to inform his audience that 'the books of Moses are more ancient than the writings of any other men, and contain the oldest of all histories, deduced from the very creation of the world'.[3] The 'books of Moses' were the first five books of the Old Testament: Genesis, Exodus, Leviticus, Numbers, Deuteronomy. The books are not only the first History: they contain a 'full and perfect body of doctrine',[4] 'the whole of the Gospel', 'the sum of its teaching' – illustrated and accomplished by the rest of the Old Testament, and the New Testament. There is 'illustrious proof' in the five books of every article in the Christian creed.[5] A 'testament' is something declaring 'the perfect will' of the maker of the testament; in this case, God – the Old and New Testaments 'contain the full and perfect will of God and Christ.' They tell of a 'covenant unfolded': which Christ 'confirmed and established in His own blood'.[6]

[1] Force, *Tracts*, I, no.7, p.7.
[2] *Disputation on Scripture*, tr. William Fitzgerald.
[3] 293-4. [4] 616. [5] 618-19. [6] 651.

It was, naturally, a dogma to the first English settlers in North America that all men derive from the first act of Creation. The Indians are descendants of Adam. The settlers also knew, from Genesis Chapter 3, that Adam 'was afraid, because I was naked' (v.10). Adam and Eve made themselves 'aprons' of fig leaves (v.7); and then God made them 'coats of skins' (v.21). Men knew, from Chapter 20 of Isaiah, that the Egyptian prisoners of the Kings of Assyria were 'afraid and ashamed' because they had been made 'naked and barefoot', with 'their buttocks uncovered' (vv.4-5). (It was true, however, that Isaiah himself had at the command of God walked for three years 'naked and barefoot': 'for a sign and wonder upon Egypt and upon Ethiopia' (v.4).) Those who are naked 'flee away' (Amos, 21:16). Thus the 'young man' who discarded his 'linen cloth' in Mark's Gospel (14:52) 'fled from them naked'. The 'nakedness' of the Indians of South and North America was constantly to affront European observers; although by 'naked' the English meant 'not dressed in European fashion'. The Indians of Virginia and New England were seldom naked in the full, or full frontal, sense.

Sir George Peckham, in his *True Report* of the discovery of 'the Newfound Landes' by Sir Humphrey Gilbert, published in 1583,[7] pointed out 'how that after Noah's flood was ceased, restoration of mankind began only of those few of Noah's children and family as were by God pre-elected to be saved in the ark with him'. God had made a promise to Noah when He ordered the building of the ark: 'with thee will I establish my covenant' (Genesis 6:18). This was confirmed with Noah and his three sons after the flood: 'I establish my covenant with you, and with your seed after you' (9:9). So, said Peckham (in a chapter proving that 'it is lawful and necessary to trade and traffic with the savages, and to plant in their countries'), 'God chose out of the multitude a peculiar people to Himself'.[8]

Noah had three sons at the time of the flood: Japheth, Shem and Ham. Ham observed Noah when the patriarch was both drunk and naked. This occasioned Noah's curse on the line of Ham, one of Ham's sons being Canaan: 'Cursed be Canaan; a servant of servants shall he be unto his brethren' (Genesis 9:25). The European mind in the sixteenth and seventeenth centuries was much intrigued by the sons of Noah.[9]

The legend had developed that Noah took his three sons on a tour of the known world for ten years. He then retired to his capital in Armenia, produced numerous other sons, and sent them out as colonists. Japhet was upright and moral: the obvious founder of

---

[7] *A True Reporte, Of the late discoveries, and possession, taken in the right of the Crowne of Englande, of the Newfound Landes: By that valiaunt and worthye Gentleman, Sir Humfrey Gilbert Knight.* In Quinn, ed., *Gilbert Voyages*, 435-80.

[8] 453-4.

[9] The following paragraphs owe most to Allen, *Legend of Noah*, ch.6: 'The Migrations of Men and the Plantation of America'.

Britain. The family of Shem were to retain most of the religion taught them by Noah: Hamon L'Estrange, in a book published in London in 1652, thought that Shem had colonised America – so did John Eliot, the Apostle to the Indians of New England. (Others thought that Noah himself had crossed to Brazil.) But the most obvious Founding Father of America was Ham. Ham (sometimes spelt 'Cham') had originally settled in Africa. (The 'Hamitic' language group is of African languages, including ancient Egyptian and Berber.) He then usurped the crown in Italy, until Noah arrived and deposed him – Noah died in Italy. Ham then continued his wanderings. William Strachey had a chapter on 'The Origin of Peoples' in his *The Historie of Travell into Virginia Britania*, written in 1612.[10] The Indians, of course, are 'descended from the people of the first creation'. How, then, can they 'maintain so general and gross a defection from the true knowledge of God, with one kind, as it were, of rude and savage life, customs, manners and religion?' We must look to the 'universal deluge': the 'scattering of Noah, his children and nephews, with their families, as little colonies, some to one, some to other borders of the earth to dwell'. And 'Ham and his family were the only far travellers and stragglers into divers and unknown countries' (starting with Arabia): the 'vagabond race of Ham'. From Ham sprang 'the first universal confusion and diversity, which ensued afterwards throughout the whole world, especially in divine and sacred matters'. Wherever the descendants of Ham settled, 'there began both the ignorance of true godliness, and a kind of bondage and slavery to be taxed one upon another.' The Ham line was 'instructed in the forms of profane worship and of an unknown deity'; ignorant of 'the true worship of God', addicted to 'the inventions of heathenism', 'adoration of false gods' and 'bloody ceremonies of will and act'.

Sir John Mandeville, in his *Travels*, completed about 1360, tells us that Ham 'was he that saw his father's privy members naked as he slept'. (That is the phrasing in the best surviving English manuscript, of the fifteenth century; the text printed by Wynkyn de Worde in 1499 had 'his faders balockes'.) He 'went tell his brethren, and shewed them them in scorn'. Hence the 'malison'. The three sons travelled. Shem took Asia, and is thus the founder of the Saracens. Japhet took Europe, and initiated the Europeans and the Israelites. Ham took Africa; and of his kindred came also 'the paynims and divers manner of men of the isles of India'. Many 'fiends' took to copulating with the women of the tribe of Ham; the result was 'giants and other monsters of horrible figure, some without heads, some with hounds' heads, and many other disfigured and misshapen men'. The 'folk of Tartary' also came 'of the kindred' of Ham. Ham was very rich, and very mighty, and called himself 'God's son and lord of all the world'. The emperor of Tartary, says Mandeville, 'occupies the same land' as Ham

[10] Ed. Wright and Freud, 1953. Quotations, pp.53-5.

(Cham); and thus, some say, is called Cham, or Khan (Mandeville discounts this as the reason for the name).[11]

William Strachey thought it 'very probable' that America was 'peopled' by the tribe of Ham.

There were difficulties. How account for the apparently unique American livestock: for 'after the general flood were not anew created'. Strachey merely raised the point. Others in the seventeenth century were to attempt to puzzle it out. Were American animals in the ark? if so, how did they get to America? – did they swim, were they transported, or did they use the land bridge of Atlantis? Or was America not completely touched by the flood? In which case, American fauna and flora were those of the first Creation.

It was a Jewish tradition that the descendants of Ham were dark-skinned. The assumption arose that the African Negro was of the 'cursed' tribe of Ham, by way of his son Cush.[12] By 1580 it was orthodoxy that Cush had been made black by the curse on his father; or, at least, that he had negroid genes (perhaps because the mind of Ham's wife was dominated by thoughts of blackness at the time of the conception of Cush). An English writer in 1578 spoke of the 'loathsome' 'black moors' as the 'black and cursed tribe'.[13] So the idea of the Negro as the cursed posterity of Ham, both blackness and bondage being part of the curse, became commonplace in the seventeenth and eighteenth centuries (although Cotton Mather in Boston in 1706 thought it 'not so very certain').[14] There was also an enticing idea in the eighteenth century that while Adam was a White Anglo-Saxon Protestant, Eve was a Negress.[15]

From 1619, when the first Negroes arrived in Jamestown, the weight of Genesis Chapter 9 was turned on the blacks. The Indian benefited from the assumption of the darker and more cursed nature of the Negro.

In the early 1650s the theory of the Jewish or Hebrew origin of the American Indian received fresh stimulus. The text was not Genesis, but the second book of Esdras in the 'Apocrypha': a pessimistic series of visions, supposedly by the prophet Ezra, written at the end of the first century A.D., and reflecting the misery of the Jews after the destruction of Jerusalem in A.D. 70. In the sixth vision (Chapter 13) the Messiah destroys his enemies and gathers together His tribes:

They are the ten tribes which were taken off into exile in the time of King Hoshea, whom Shalmaneser king of Assyria took prisoner. He deported them beyond the River, and they were taken away into a strange country.

The Jewish tribes decided to leave this country, 'populated by the Gentiles'; and 'go to a distant land never yet inhabited by man'. They

[11] *Mandeville's Travels*, ed. Letts, Hakluyt Society, 1953, 154-5.
[12] Allen, 119. See Jordan, *White Over Black*, 17-20, 35-7, 41, 60, 62, 111, 245.
[13] Jordan, 41. [14] Jordan, 200. [15] Jordan, 525.

crossed the Euphrates to the region of Arzareth. (Verses 40-45: New English Bible translation. II Kings, Chapter 17, had told the story of the defeat of Hoshea by Shalmaneser, and the deportation of the 'children of Israel'). From the 1580s the theory that Arzareth was America had been accepted by some Spanish writers. In 1650 Manasseh Ben Israel (1604-57), a Portuguese Jew then chief rabbi of the Amsterdam synagogue, published his *Spes Israelis*; in which he argued that the tribes eventually arrived in Labrador, by way of Greenland. The Indians had many customs in common with the Jews; including the detestation of sodomites. The book appeared in English translation in 1650: *The Hope of Israel*. England in the 1650s was fertile ground for the thesis. The more apocalyptic English prophets expected in that decade the final climax of the power of Antichrist; to be followed, about 1700, by the Millennium – the thousand year reign of Christ and His resurrected saints: Revelation 20:4. The conversion of the Jews must precede the fall of Antichrist; this conversion was also expected in the 1650s.[16] The Jews had been expelled from England in 1290: Oliver Cromwell readmitted them in 1656. Manasseh was in England from 1655, and published in 1655 a 'Humble Address' to His Highness' the Lord Protector 'on behalf of the Jewish Nation'. In 1650 Thomas Thorowgood published his *Jewes in America, or probabilities that the Americans are of that race*. (Some of his information came from Roger Williams.) The Indians of course were *degenerate* Jews. They practised cannibalism: this was foretold in Leviticus 26:29, 'ye shall eat the flesh of your sons, and the flesh of your daughters shall ye eat'. Thorowgood's book was intended to promote missionary activities among the American Indians. He quoted George Herbert:[17]

> Religion stands on tip-toe in our land,
> Readie to passe to the *American* strand.

(A passage which had upset Archbishop Laud.) Thorowgood was also arguing against New Englanders such as John Cotton, who thought it undoctrinal to expect the conversion of the Indian before the 'calling' and conversion of the Jews. (They used as a proof text Revelation 15:8 – 'no man was able to enter into the temple, till the seven plagues of the seven angels were fulfilled'.) John Eliot was a friend of Thorowgood. And by 1658 Thorowgood had prepared his 'Jews in America, or probabilities that those Indians are Judaical, made more probable by some Additionals to the former conjectures': this included an essay by Eliot. The manuscript was submitted to the 'Society for the Propagation of the Gospel in New England', founded

---

[16] C. Hill, *Antichrist in Seventeenth-Century England*, 108, 111, 114.
[17] 'The Church Militant', published 1633: World's Classics edition of Herbert's poems, 187.

by Act of the House of Commons in 1649.[18] The Society did not
sponsor the book: it was eventually published in 1660. Thorowgood
was concerned to refute such as Sir Hamon L'Estrange, who had
published in 1652 his *Americans no Jewes, or Improbabilities that the
Americans are of that race.*

John Eliot wrote a letter from Roxbury, Massachusetts, in May
1649 concerning the opinions of Rabbi Ben Israel (opinions well
known, therefore, before the actual publication of the *Spes Israelis*).
Eliot thought it most probable that the Indians were descendants of
Shem, and the English, children of Japhet. (The point here is
probably a negative one: Eliot wished the Indians *not* to be
descendants of Ham.) The letter was published in London in 1651 in
a volume edited by Henry Whitfield, a Cambridge BD who had
founded Guilford, Connecticut, in 1639, and returned to England in
1650 to help with the organisation of the Society for the Propagation
of the Gospel.[19] Whitfield was looking for proof that 'at least some of
the ten tribes are in America'. Proof was to hand. A Captain
Cromwell, who had died at Boston in the late 1640s, had told
Governor Thomas Dudley that he had seen 'many Indians to the
southward circumcised': 'he was often conversant among them, and
saw it with his own eyes, and was undoubtedly certain of it'. Whitfield
commented that this 'seemeth to me to be one of the most probable
arguments that ever I yet heard of'.[20] The point for Eliot was that if
the Indians were 'lost and scattered Israelites' (whatever the exact
details of descent) then they were under 'Covenant and Promise'.

The thesis of the Jewish tribes had been attacked in 1642 by Hugo
Grotius in his *De Origine Gentium Americanarum*. Grotius thought the
North American Indians were probably Scandinavians, by way of
Greenland; those of South America were from Africa and China. By
1600 there were, as one could expect, numerous theories about the
First Americans: Greeks, Romans, Phoenicians, Chinese, Egyptians,
Africans, Scyths, Frisians, French – and, as we shall see in Chapter
11, Welsh. Edward Brerewood, in *Enquiries touching the diversity of
languages and religions through the chief parts of the world*, first edition 1614,
thought the Indians came from Asia: 'they resemble the old and rude
Tartars' – not civilised enough to be from India or China. The Tartar
theory was supported by Thomas Gage in 1645, and Nicholas Fuller
in 1650. Humphrey Gilbert, writing in the 1560s, had however been
certain that the American Indians did *not* come from Asia.[21]

[18] Kellaway, *New England Company*, 5, 24. See, for the 'Jewish' origin of the Indians,
Huddleston, *Origins of the American Indians*, especially pp.33-47, 114-35.
[19] *The Light appearing more and more towards the perfect Day*. Reprinted in 1834 in
Collections of the Massachusetts Historical Society, 3rd series, vol.4: *Tracts relating to the
attempts to convert to Christianity the Indians of New England*. (Seven tracts.) Eliot's letter is
pp.119-20.
[20] 128.
[21] Quinn, ed., *Gilbert Voyages*, 142. In the summer of 1974, a team of Soviet and
American archaeologists discovered tool blades on an Aleutian island (Anangula)
which matched blades discovered earlier in Siberia, 9000 years old. The head of the

Another possibility, hardly to be countenanced by the men of our period, was this: perhaps all men were not descended from Adam; perhaps there were men before Adam, and creations apart from Adam. Paracelsus appears to have thought this in the sixteenth century. The Bordeaux Huguenot Isaac de La Peyrère (1594-1676) put the thought to print in 1656 in his 'Preadamites' (*Praeadamitae*), which took Romans 5:14 as proving that there were men before Adam: 'Death reigned from Adam to Moses, even over them that had not sinned after the similitude of Adam's transgression.' The book appeared in the same year in English translation (*Men before Adam*). Adam was the first *Jew*, the first of the favoured. But there were other 'first men'; from one of whom the Americans were descended. Moreover, the flood was a little local difficulty in Palestine. Genesis Chapter 9 was irrelevant to discussion of the American Indian.

We may note here that Columbus was devoted to the prophet Esdras. Esdras said to the Lord (II Esdras 6:42):

Upon the third day thou didst command that the waters should be gathered in the seventh part of the earth: six parts hast thou dried up, and kept them, to the intent that of these some being planted of God and tilled might serve thee.

The fact that the ocean sea covered only one seventh of the globe gave him confidence, in the Atlantic, that land was ahead; and that the land would be large. Columbus probably owed the reference to one of his favourite books, *Ymago Mundi* by Cardinal Pierre d'Ailly, written about 1410, in which the Esdras passage was used.[22] But such pre-occupations have been taken to lend support to the theory that the Columbus' family were Spanish Jews settled in Genoa. Salvador de Madariaga, in a biography published in 1939, presented Columbus as a 'Jewish missionary visionary'.[23] A more recent work, Simon Wiesenthal's *The Secret Mission of Christopher Columbus*, argues that Columbus was searching for the lost tribes; and perhaps also for a new land to which Jews could emigrate.

We return to Genesis. Chapter 11: the story of the Tower of Babel. The inhabitants of the earth spoke one language. (Hebrew, said William Whitaker: the language of Adam.) But they were proud, building a 'city and a tower' (v.4). The Deity disliked the ziggurat and 'scattered them abroad from thence upon the face of all the earth' (v.8). God also decided to 'confound their language, that they may not understand one another's speech' (v.7). (Pure language and pure religion, according to Whitaker,[24] were 'propogated in the family of

American team said that this was the first direct proof that the Aleuts came over the Bering land bridge then connecting Siberia and Alaska. London *Times*, 24 August 1974.

[22] The d'Ailly passage is in Quinn, ed., *North American Discovery*, 23-5.
[23] *Christopher Columbus*, 100-1.
[24] *Disputation*, 112-13.

Abraham'; the other languages were all derived from Hebrew, 'dialects and varieties' of it.) *A True Declaration of the estate of the Colonie in Virginia*, a pamphlet published in London in 1610 'by advice and direction of the Council of Virginia', pointed out the virtues of the people being 'cloven': they were divided into 'colonies'. God had acted in the project of plantation. A disaster had become a blessing. And 'God's actions are our instructions'. The 'divine' action of Genesis 11 is confirmed by many 'human, external and domestical examples' – the Romans, who 'deduced 53 colonies out of the City of Rome into the womb of Italy'; the French in Florida in the 1560s.[25]

Robert Johnson, in *The New Life of Virginea* (1612), also took up the action of the 'scattering'.[26] It occasioned a 'dispersed crew', with 'innumerable languages', of 'inhumane behaviour and brutish conditions', guilty of the conspiracy 'to climb the celestial throne', 'strangers from the commonwealth of Israel', Gentiles. But from these Old Testament gentiles, saints arose: the Old Testament traces the development of the 'family of saints and sons of Gods'. The new 'scattered Gentiles' are the American Indians. The Ammonites, 'heathens', sacrificed their children to Moloch. The Indians 'sacrifice their children to serve the Devil'. God, through Moses, ordered the death by stoning of those offering a child to Moloch (Leviticus 20:2).[27] Josiah, boy King of Judah (Edward VI had been the 'new Josiah') destroyed the 'high places' of Moloch (II Kings 23:13). Also, the Indians 'consist of infinite confused tongues and people'. Just as the God of the Old Testament, in His 'secret counsel', extended Grace to the 'scattered Gentiles', God now may have among the Indians 'His special numbers, from whose necks He will now remove that heavy yoke': the yoke of bondage to the Devil. The Indians are 'our kindred and younger brethren'.

In April 1609 William Symonds, literary collaborator of John Smith, preached at Whitechapel to members of the Virginia Company.[28] He emphasised – we are making textual progress – Genesis Chapter 12, the first three verses.

Now the Lord had said unto Abraham, Get thee out of thy country, and from thy kindred, and from thy father's house, unto a land that I will show thee: And I will make of thee a great nation, and I will bless thee, and make thy name great; and thou shalt be a blessing: And I will bless them that bless thee, and curse him that curseth thee.

Naturally, Symonds stressed that this text was a directive to the English: an imperative for the Virginia enterprise.

When Abraham's wife Sarah died, Abraham bought, from Ephron son of Zohar, the 'cave of Machpelah' as a burial place (Genesis 23).

[25] Force, *Tracts*, III, no.1, p.4.

[26] *ibid.*, I, no.7, p.7-8.

[27] Other Old Testament references to child sacrifice: Psalm 106:38; Jeremiah 7:31, 19:4-5; Ezekiel 16:21, 23:27; II Chronicles 28:3; II Kings 17:17, 21:6.

[28] Published 1609: *Virginia: a sermon preached at Whitechapel ...*

The 'field of Ephron' was 'made sure unto Abraham' as his 'possession' (v.20). The 1610 *True Declaration of the estate of the Colonie in Virginia*[29] took this episode as an archetype of the 'lawful possession' of the English in Virginia. The English had bought land from the Indians for copper; Abraham had bought his property for 400 shekels weight of silver (v.16).

The 'nation' of Israel (the 'children', the 'tribes' of Israel) spent 430 years in exile in Egypt. The Israelites lived, by grant of Pharaoh, in the East Nile Delta, in the territory of Goshen: 'the land of Goshen', said God, 'in which my people dwell' (Exodus – the second book of Moses – 8:22). Israel, said the 1610 *True Declaration*, had 'lawful possession of Goshen': similarly, the English have 'lawful possession' of Virginia.[30]

In due time, God spoke to the young Moses about 'my people which are in Egypt'. This is related in Exodus Chapter 3:

I am come down to deliver them out of the hand of the Egyptians, and to bring them up out of that land unto a good land and a large, unto a land flowing with milk and honey; unto the place of the Canaanites. (v.8)

The Promised Land. This is the most frequent Old Testament image in the literature of Virginia. Hakluyt used it in 1587.[31] A letter from Jamestown on 22 June 1607, five weeks after the settlement there, hoped that Virginia would 'flow with milk and honey'.[32]

Virginia in fact might exceed the Land of Canaan. In August 1607 a London executive in the Virginia Company wrote to Robert Cecil, Earl of Salisbury: 'We are fallen upon a land that promises more than the Land of Promise; instead of milk, we find pearl; and gold instead of honey.'[33] The gold was already a false hope; the minerals sent from Jamestown had been tested, and were not satisfactory. 'Our new discovery,' admitted the same executive, 'is more like to prove the Land of Canaan than the land of Ophir.'[34] Ophir was the territory from which gold was imported to Judah: II Chronicles 8:18. It was also, some said, the name by which the ancients knew America.[35]

But to possess the Land of Canaan was adequate enough.

The Old Testament presented God's call to Moses as a stage in the development of the Covenant. God, hearing the Israelites 'groaning' in Egypt, 'remembered His covenant with Abraham, with Isaac and with Jacob' (Exodus 2:24): the tribes of Israel sprang from the twelve sons of Jacob. God's covenant with Abraham was: 'Unto thy seed have I given this land, from the river of Egypt unto the great river, the river Euphrates' (Genesis 15:18): 'the land of Canaan' (Exodus 6:4).

[29] Force, *Tracts*, III, no.1, p.7.

[30] *ibid.*

[31] Dedication to Raleigh of the edition of Peter Martyr. Quinn, ed., *Roanoke Voyages*, 514-15.

[32] Barbour, ed., *Jamestown Voyages*, 79. [33] *ibid.*, 108. [34] *ibid.*, 111. [35] See above, p.22.

The covenant was in operation; with Moses it was ratified, and the promise made effective.

The period between Moses and Christ, Whitaker said, was 'the second age of the Church'.[36]

Peckham employed Mosaic material in 1583. God chose from the posterity of Noah 'a peculiar people to Himself'. Under Moses, God 'made a grant to inherit the Land of Canaan, called the Land of Promise, with all the other rich and fertile countries adjoining thereunto'.[37] From 1583, English writers were concerned to emphasise that the occupation of Virginia presented less difficulties than that of the Land of Canaan. The natives were not so powerful or terrifying as the 'sons of Anak' (Numbers 13:33) – the Anakim tribe. William Symonds wrote to Captain John Smith in 1612:[38]

There is no cities, so no sons of Anak: all is open for labour of a good and wise inhabitant; and my prayer shall ever be, that so fair a land may be inhabited by those that profess and love the Gospel.

The Exodus from Egypt (about 1300 B.C.) marked the birth of Israel as a nation. Before the crossing of the Jordan, there were forty years of wandering in the 'wilderness'. Exodus 7:14-16:

And the Lord said unto Moses ... Get thee unto Pharoah ... And thou shalt say unto him, the Lord God of the Hebrews hath sent me unto thee, saying, Let my people go, that they may serve me in the wilderness.

The Vulgate translation, *solitudo*, occurs twenty-seven times in the Old Testament.

The writers of the Old Testament (like the seventeeth-century New Englanders) were concerned to emphasise the barrenness of the wilderness, thus pointing the miracle of survival. The Hebrew word for 'wilderness' means grazing land, as well as desert: but the later meaning was more evocative – the 'desert land', the 'waste, howling wilderness', in which the peculiar people are kept 'as the apple of His eye' (Deuteronomy 32:10); living on God-given manna, bread from heaven (Exodus 16). Psalm 107:4-7:

They wandered in the wilderness in a solitary way; they found no city to dwell in. Hungry and thirsty, their soul fainted in them. Then they cried unto the Lord in their trouble, and He delivered them out of their distresses. And He led them forth by the right way, that they might go to a city of habitation.

The wilderness image is most sustained in the Book of Isaiah. The wilderness is trackless, dry and solitary; crooked, confused, rough. But 'the glory of the Lord shall be revealed'. The wilderness can have

---

[36] *Disputation*, 517.
[37] *True Reporte*. Quinn, ed., *Gilbert Voyages*, 454.
[38] Barbour, ed., *Jamestown Voyages*, 464.

pathways, can be watered, can blossom. Chapter 35: 'the wilderness and the solitary place shall be glad for them; and the desert shall rejoice, and blossom as the rose' (v.1); 'in the wilderness shall waters break out, and streams in the desert' (v.6). Chapter 40: 'Comfort ye my people, saith your God' (v.1):

The voice of him that crieth in the wilderness, Prepare ye the way of the Lord, make straight in the desert a highway for our God. Every valley shall be exalted, and every mountain and hill shall be made low: and the crooked shall be made straight, and the rough places plain: And the glory of the Lord shall be revealed. (vv.3-5)

Chapter 43: 'Behold, I will do a new thing: I will even make a way in the wilderness, and rivers in the desert' (v.19).

Mark's gospel took up the imagery of Isaiah, in Chapter 1:

As it is written in the prophets, Behold, I send my messenger before thy face, which shall prepare thy way before thee. The voice of one crying in the wilderness, Prepare ye the way of the Lord, make his paths straight. (vv.2-3)

Thus John the Baptist 'did baptise in the wilderness, and preach the baptism of repentance for the remission of sins' (v.4). The Dominican friar Antonio de Montesinos used this text in a sermon preached in Santo Domingo, Hispaniola, in December 1511:[39]

In order to make your sins against the Indians known unto you, I have come up on this pulpit, I who am a voice of Christ crying in the wilderness of this island.

Montesinos's theme was 'the cruelty and tyranny you use in dealing with these innocent people'. 'On what authority have you waged a detestable war against these people, who dwelt quietly and peacefully on their own land?': 'Have they not rational souls?' Montesinos was supported by the Dominican prior in Hispaniola. He preached a similar sermon on the next Sunday, taking as his text Job 36:3 'I will search far and wide to support my conclusions, as I defend the justice of my maker' (New English Bible).[40] The colonists sent a Franciscan friar back to Spain to complain to Ferdinand. Montesinos himself also returned; and the result was the Laws of Burgos in 1512 – the first public recognition of the status of the Indian.

St Mark relates that Jesus was 'baptised of John in Jordan, and thereafter driven by 'the spirit' into the 'wilderness' (1:12). 'And He was there in the wilderness forty days, tempted of Satan; and was with the wild beasts; and the angels ministered unto Him' (v.13). The 'wilderness' theme was elaborated by the author of the final book of the New Testament, the Book of Revelation (Greek, *apocalypsis* – an

[39] Hanke, *Spanish Struggle for Justice*, 17-18.
[40] MacNutt, *Las Casas*, 54-5.

uncovering, a revelation). This was written at a time when Christian communities were being persecuted; probably under the Emperor Domitian (81-96). (Erasmus thought the Book of Revelation poisonous.) In Chapter 12 various wonders in heaven are thought of. A woman, after bearing 'a man child, who was to rule all nations with a rod of iron' (v.5), fled 'into the wilderness, where she hath a place prepared of God, that they should feed her there' (v.6). She remained for 1260 days. There had been 'war in heaven' (v.7); and the 'dragon' and his 'angels' were 'cast unto the earth' (v.9). The woman was secure from Satan: for 'to the woman were given two wings of a great eagle, that she might fly into the wilderness, where she is nourished ... from the face of the serpent' (v.14).

The image of the 'great and fearful wilderness' was effectively used by Tyndale.[41] And the 'errand into the wilderness' theme was especially used (over-used, indeed) by New England writers.

William Bradford, Governor of Plymouth Colony, wrote in 1630 of the feelings of the passengers on board the 'Mayflower' at anchor in Cape Cod Bay in November 1620.[42] They were 'Englishmen which came over this great ocean, and were ready to perish in this wilderness': what could they see before them but 'a hideous and desolate wilderness, full of wild beasts and wild men'. (The prospect was too much for Bradford's wife Dorothy, from Wisbech, Cambridgeshire; she fell overboard and was drowned – perhaps a suicide.) Bradford referred to verse 4 of Psalm 107, 'they wandered in the desert wilderness in a solitary way; they found no city to dwell in'. But who wandered in the wilderness? Verse 2 tells us: 'the redeemed of the Lord', those 'whom He hath redeemed from the hand of the enemy'. The wilderness is for God's 'poor people',[43] his 'poor persecuted church':[44] the godly remnant. Thomas Shepard, who graduated from Emmanuel College Cambridge in 1624, and became minister at Cambridge Massachusetts in 1635, wrote that New Englanders had a 'liberty' allowed to 'God's Saints in all ages': 'to fly into the wilderness from the face of the Dragon'.[45]

The wilderness is remote, barren, wild. That is one aspect of the theme. In the 1640s and 1650s the New Englanders, sensitive to the possible reproach from Old England that they were living in ease, while their brethren at home were bearing the heat and burden of the day, made much in their writings (published in London) of the trials and sorrows of the wilderness.[46] What sacrifices they had made by crossing the Atlantic! But the theme of course had another aspect: the

[41] Parker Society Tyndale, I (*Doctrinal Treatises*) 140: from *Obedience of a Christian Man*, 1528.

[42] *Of Plymouth Plantation*, ed. Morison, 62-3.

[43] *ibid.*, 215.

[44] *ibid.*, 324.

[45] Extract in *The Puritans*, ed. Miller and Johnson, Harper Torchbook, 119.

[46] I owe this point to William Breitenbach of Harvard, later of Clare College Cambridge.

wilderness could blossom as the rose – if tended by the godly.[47] It could become *New England Canaan* – the title of a book by Thomas Morton of Merry Mount, Massachusetts, published in the 1630s. Nathaniel Morton wrote his *New Englands Memoriall*, published at Cambridge, Mass., in 1669, to show 'God's great work' in the planting of New England; especially His 'making this howling wilderness a chamber of rest safety and pleasantness'. God 'brought a vine into this wilderness'. Morton referred here to Psalm 80:8-9. 'Thou hast brought a vine out of Egypt: Thou hast cast out the heathen and planted it. Thou preparedst room before it, and did cause it to take deep root, and it filled the land.' (The God who 'cast out the heathen' had relevance to the fate of the Indian.) Morton also invoked Exodus: 'Thou in Thy mercy hast led the people which Thou hast redeemed: Thou hast guided them in Thy strength unto Thy holy habitation' (15:13).[48]

One remembers the persuasion of Richard Hooker in 1593 that the puritans would be tolerable 'if they did not live amongst men, but in some wilderness by themselves'.[49]

The Book of Numbers (the fourth book of Moses) tells of Trouble in the Wilderness. The Hebrews 'murmured' against the leadership of Moses.

Would God that we had died in the land of Egypt! or would God we had died in this wilderness! And wherefore hath the Lord brought us into this land, to fall by the sword, that our wives and our children should be a prey? were it not better for us to return into Egypt? (14:2-3)

Reports from the Land of Promise had been taken as depressing. Moses had sent spies, including Caleb and Joshua: Chapter 13. Their instructions were to report on whether the land is 'good or bad', 'whether it be fat or lean, whether there be wood therein or not'; whether the natives be 'strong or weak, few or many', 'what cities they be that they dwell in, whether in tents or in strong holds' (vv.18-20). The spies returned after forty days. They praised the land – 'surely it floweth with milk and honey' (v.27). But some were less enthusiastic about the inhabitants. They seem 'stronger than we'; they live in cities which are 'walled and very great'; and they include the 'children of Anak' – 'giants'. So the Hebrews were discontented. Opposition was quelled by the young Joshua, and his senior, Caleb: 'Caleb stilled the people before Moses, and said, Let us go up at once, and possess it; for we are well able to overcome it' (13:30). Caleb and Joshua

---

[47] Carroll is very good on the Wilderness/Canaan tension in New England: *Puritanism and the Wilderness*. The early part (pp.1-43) of Nash, *Wilderness and the American Mind* has some material on the colonial period. In general, Williams, *Wilderness and Paradise in Christian Thought*, 3-137.

[48] Everyman Library *Chronicles of the Pilgrim Fathers*, 1910, 4-5.

[49] *Laws of Ecclesiastical Polity*, I, xvi.6 (Everyman ed., I, p.229).

rent their clothes: And they spake unto all the company of the children of Israel, saying, The land, which we passed through to search it, is an exceeding good land. If the Lord delight in us, then He will bring us into this land, and give it us; a land which floweth with milk and honey. Only rebel not ye against the Lord, neither fear ye the people of the land. (14:6-9)

In 1615 Ralph Hamor, in *A true discourse of the present estate of Virginia*,[50] urged Englishmen nervous of the Virginia enterprise to

hearken unto Caleb and Joshua, who stilled the people's mourning, saying, Let us go up at once and possess it, for undoubtedly we shall overcome.

He printed Jamestown letters from 'some Calebs and Joshuas': Thomas Dale, Alexander Whitaker (son of William), and John Rolfe. Rolfe himself, writing in 1616, paid this tribute to his patron, William Herbert, Earl of Pembroke:[51]

As Caleb and Joshua in the very heat of the grudgings, murmurs and assemblies of the children of Israel stood stoutly for the Lord's cause, commending the goodness of the land they discovered to the faces of their opposers, and the easiness to obtain it, even to the peril of their lives: so many right honourable and worthy personages both here and in Virginia, amongst whom yourself not the least protector, when generally the greatest part withdrew themselves, that this action was almost sunk down in forgetfulness, have mightily upheld this Christian cause; and God, even our own God, did help them.

Moses reminded Israel (Deuteronomy 7:6):

Thou art an holy people unto the Lord thy God: the Lord thy God hath chosen thee to be a special people unto Himself, above all people that are upon the face of the earth.

The Elect Nation. The 'special people' were a minority among the people on the face of the earth. This fact was developed into the image of the 'godly remnant': a basic imperative of Protestantism and Puritanism. Isaiah 1:9:

Except the Lord of Hosts had left unto us a very small remnant, we should have been as Sodom, and we should have been like unto Gomorrah.

Christ refered to his followers as a 'little flock': 'Fear not, little flock; for it is your father's good pleasure to give you the kingdom' (Luke 12:32). The theme was stressed by Peter: 'ye are a chosen generation, a royal priesthood, an holy nation, a peculiar people' (I Peter 2:9). And it was definitively developed by Paul. Among the Jews, 'at this present time also there is a remnant according to the election of grace'

[50] P.48.
[51] Rolfe, *True Relation of the State of Virginia*, ed. Taylor, p.41.

(Romans 11:5). There are 'the saints', the 'faithful in Christ': 'He hath chosen us in Him before the foundation of the world', 'predestinated us unto the adoption of children by Jesus Christ to Himself, according to the good pleasure of His will' (Ephesians 1:1,4,5). The 'elect of God' (Colossians 3:12): 'whom He did foreknow, He also did predestinate to be conformed to the image of His son' (Romans 8:29). These 'sons of God' shine 'as lights in the world' among 'a crooked and perverse nation' (Philippians 2:15). 'Ye are all the children of light, and the children of the day: we are not of the night, nor of darkness' (I Thessalonians 5:5). Paul's use of the phrases 'saints' and 'brethren' (II Corinthians 9) was to be irresistible to the puritans.

To William Whitaker there was a 'whole multitude of those who profess the christian religion and the external worship of God'. There were also, within the multitude, those who have 'union with Christ': the 'elect and faithful'.[52]

The author of the Book of Revelation supplied his own cadenzas to the theme. He wrote at a time of oppression by 'the Gentiles' (11:2): a period of 'tribulation', 'labour', 'poverty', 'liars', 'prison' and 'martyrs' (2:2,9,10,13). He wrote for the 'wretched, and miserable and poor, and blind, and naked' (3:17). The hope was for the 'saints': 'they that keep the commandments of God, and the faith of Jesus' (14:12); 'brethren that have the testimony of Jesus' (19:10). These have 'the seal of the living God' (7:2). 'And I heard the number of them which were sealed': 144,000–12,000 from each of the twelve tribes of Israel (7:4-8). (A pocket calculator is helpful in reading Revelation.) No one can learn the song of angels except the 144,000 'which were redeemed from the earth' (14:3). They have 'gotten the victory over the beast, and over his image, and over his mark': 'they sing the song of Moses the servant of God, and the song of the Lamb' (15:2-3). And they 'lived and reigned with Christ a thousand years' (20:4). At the Day of Judgment 'whosoever was not found written in the Book of Life was cast into the lake of fire' (20:15). Those men, that is, 'which have not the seal of God on their foreheads' (9:4), who 'worship the beast and his image, and receive his mark' (14:9). Those 'whose names were not written in the Book of Life from the foundation of the world' (17:8).

In 1616 John Rolfe wrote from Jamestown of the 'zealous work' of the colonisation of Virginia by the English: 'What need we then to fear, but to go up at once as a peculiar people, marked and chosen by the finger of God to possess it.'[53]

The occupation of the Land of Canaan – Palestine – was the work of Moses' minister and successor: Joshua. And the Book of Joshua – the sixth Book of the Old Testament – was favourite reading for European experts on the colonisation of America.

[52] *Disputation*, 613.
[53] *True Relation*, ed. Taylor, 41.

After the death of Moses, God said to Joshua (1:2-6): 'Arise, go over this Jordan, thou and all this people, unto the land which I do give to them.' 'I will be with thee: I will not fail thee, nor forsake thee. Be strong and of a good courage': 'From the wilderness and this Lebanon even unto the great river, the river Euphrates, all the land of the Hittites, and unto the great sea toward the going down of the sun, shall be your coast.' Richard Hakluyt invoked Joshua in a letter to Walter Raleigh in May 1587:[54]

I conceive great comfort of the success of this your action, hoping that the Lord, whose power is wont to be perfected in weakness, will bless the feeble foundations of your building. Only be you of a valiant courage and faint not, as the Lord said unto Joshua, exhorting him to proceed on forward in the conquest of the Land of Promise.

From the wilderness, Joshua sent two spies to Jericho in the Land of Canaan. They were protected by the harlot Rahab; who said to them: 'I know that the Lord hath given you the land, and that your terror is fallen upon us, and that all the inhabitants of the land faint because of you' (2:9). On the eve of invasion, Joshua addressed the Israelites (Chapter 3). The 'living God is among you':

He will without fail drive out from before you the Canaanites, and the Hittites, and the Hivites, and the Perizzites, and the Girgashites, and the Amorites, and the Jebusites. (v.10)

The key to the treatment of the native population had been given by Moses (Deuteronomy 7:2): when God 'shall deliver them before thee, thou shalt smite them, and utterly destroy them; thou shalt make no convenant with them, nor show mercy unto them'.

The waters of the river dried up. And the 40,000 Israelites 'passed clean over Jordan' (Joshua 3:17).

The decisive event in the conquest of Canaan was the destruction of Jericho: described in the Book of Joshua, Chapter 6. God said to Joshua: 'I have given into thine hand Jericho' (v.2). During the seige Joshua decided: 'the city shall be accursed, even it, and all that are therein' – except Rahab and her kindred (v.17). After extra-mural musical activity, the city fell. And the Israelites

utterly destroyed all that was in the city, both man and woman, young and old, and ox, and sheep, and ass, with the edge of the sword ... And they burnt the city with fire, and all that was therein ... So the Lord was with Joshua; and his fame was noised throughout all the country. (vv.21,24,27)

(Rahab and her household were spared: because she had concealed the spies, v.25.)
Chapters 10 and 11 relate how Joshua 'took the whole land,

[54] Taylor, ed., *Writings of the Hakluyts*, 376.

according to all that the Lord said unto Moses' (11:23): cities 'utterly destroyed' with 'the edge of the sword'. Joshua 'left none remaining, but utterly destroyed all that breathed, as the Lord God of Israel commanded' (10:40).

Naturally, the tribal chiefs in the Promised Land were apprehensive: because 'God commanded His servant Moses to give you all the land, and to destroy all the inhabitants' (9:24). Some came to Joshua, saying 'We are your servants: therefore now make ye a league with us' (9:11). With them Joshua made peace: 'and made a league with them, to let them live' (9:15). They became 'hewers of wood and drawers of water' (9:27).

In 1513 the colonist Martin Fernández de Enciso used this material to defend the royal rights over the Indies.[55]

Joshua conquered all the Land of Canaan by force of arms, and many were killed, and those who were captured were given as slaves, and served the people of Israel. And all this was done by the will of God, because they were idolators.

In 1560 Las Casas petitioned the Pope to excommunicate anyone asserting that idolatry in itself justified war.[56] War against the Canaanites in particular was not, for Las Casas, an example to be followed against idolators in general.[57]

'If the Indians would not do this, he might justly wage war against them', Enciso said. He had in mind Deuteronomy 20:10-14:

When you advance on a city to attack it, make an offer of peace. If the city accepts the offer and opens its gates to you, then all the people in it shall be put to forced labour and shall serve you. If it does not make peace with you but offers battle, you shall beseige it, and the Lord your God will deliver it into your hands. You shall put all its males to the sword, but you may take the women, the dependants, and the cattle for yourselves, and plunder everything else in the city. You may enjoy the use of the spoil of your enemies which the Lord your God gives you. (New English Bible)

Such was the Biblical fibre of the Spanish document to be read to the Indians: the 'Requirement'.[58]

From the 1580s, the English found inspiration in such precepts.

Peckham, in his *True Reporte* of 1583, devoted three paragraphs to Joshua: 'this valiant captain his conquest'.[59] In the wilderness

Joshua their leader, replenished with the spirit of God, being assured of the justness of his quarrel, gathered the chief strength of the children of Israel together, to the number of 40,000, with whom he safely passed the huge river Jordan.

[55] Hanke, *Spanish Struggle for Justice*, 32. [56] *ibid.*, 184.
[57] Wagner and Parish, *Las Casas*, 179.
[58] See below, p.157.
[59] Quinn, (ed.), *Gilbert Voyages*, 454-55.

Before Jericho,

perceiving none of the Gentiles disposed to yield or call for mercy,[60] he then commanded (as God before had appointed) that both the city Jericho should be burned, yea, and all the inhabitants, as well old as young, with all their cattle, should be destroyed, only excepted Rahab, her kindred and family.

Peckham tells the story of the burning and massacre of the city of Ai (Joshua Chapter 8). And tells of those Gibeonites who 'sent ambassadors unto Joshua, to entreat for grace, favour and peace', occasioning the order of Joshua that 'all their lives should be spared, and that they should be admitted to the company of the children of Israel' – as 'drudges to hew wood and to carry water and other necessaries for his people'. Them apart, Joshua continued his Conquest:

which he pursued and never left till he had subdued all the Hethites, Amorites, Cananites, Pheresites, Hevites and Jebusites, with all their princes and kings, being thirty and one in number, and divers other strange nations besides, whose lands and dominions he wholly divided among God's people.

One of the leaders in the Exodus and Conquest was Judah. The book of Judges, the seventh Book of the Old Testament, tells how after the death of Joshua God appointed Judah (a personification of the tribe) as captain, and 'delivered the land into his hand' (1:2). The subsequent campaign was summarised by Peckham:[61]

Judah was constituted lord over the army, who, receiving like charge from God, pursued the proceedings of the holy captain Joshua, and utterly vanquished many gentiles, idolators, and adversaries to the children of Israel, with all such rulers or kings as withstood him: and namely Adoni-Bezek the most cruel tyrant, whose thumbs and great toes he caused to be cut off, forasmuch as he had done the like before unto seventy kings, whom, being his prisoners, he forced to gather up their victuals underneath his table.

Adoni-Bezek, king of the Canaanites in the town of Bezek, had cut off the thumbs and great toes of seventy kings, who then 'gathered their meat under my table' (1:7). Thus the mutilation by Judah was a just punishment: 'as I have done, so God hath requited me' (v.7). Peckham commented: 'In this, God showed His justice to revenge tyranny.' A marginal note (1583) stressed another point: 'A good note for all conquerors to be merciful.'
   The successor to Joshua and Judah was Gideon: a 'most puissant and noble warrior', wrote Peckham, who continued their 'worthy

---

[60] In fact, the Book of Joshua gives no indication that the inhabitants of Jericho were given the choice of surrender.
[61] Quinn, (ed.), *Gilbert Voyages*, 455.   [62] *ibid.*

acts'.[62] The story of Gideon, who saved the Israelites from the Midianites (a Bedouin people who controlled the central area of the Promised Land) is told in Judges, Chapters 6, 7 and 8. Peckham summarised the material:

In short time he not only delivered the children of Israel from the hands of the multitude of the fierce Midianites, but also subdued them and their Tyrants, whose lands he caused God's people to possess and inherit.

At this point in his discussion of how Christian colonists can behave if the natives 'practice violence' in 'repelling' or 'withstanding' them, Peckham ended his foray into the Old Testament. 'I could recite divers other places out of the scripture which aptly may be applied hereunto; were it not I endeavour myself by all means to be brief.'

The 1610 *True Declaration of the estate of the Colonie in Virginia* made play with an episode in the reign of King David.[63] It concerns Hanun, King of the Ammonites, on the borders of Israel. The story is in the second Book of Samuel. David said: 'I will show kindness unto Hanun' (10:2). He sent ambassadors from Jerusalem to the Ammonite capital, Rabbah. Unfortunately, they were taken to be spies; and Hanun 'shaved off the one half of their beards, and cut off their garments in the middle, even to their buttocks, and sent them away' (10:4). This meant war. The Israelites 'destroyed the children of Ammon, and beseiged Rabbah' (11:1). (This was the campaign to which David sent Bathsheba's husband Uriah.) Joab, the Israelite general, captured Rabbah, and David 'brought forth the spoil of the city in great abundance' (12:30-1):

And he brought forth the people that were therein, and put them under saws, and under harrows of iron, and under axes of iron, and made them pass through the brick-kiln: and thus did he unto all the cities of the children of Ammon.

The 1610 pamphlet (approved by the London Council of the Virginia Company) explained that Hanun and the Ammonites had 'violated the law of nations' by their treatment of David's envoys: thus David had 'just cause to war'. In Virginia, the Indians have responded to the English in Ammonite fashion. Therefore war 'is lawful in us, to secure ourselves against the infidels'.

An issue naturally raised in the English colonisation of North America was that of intermarriage with the Indians. Here again, settlers such as John Rolfe consulted their Old Testament. Moses had spoken to 'all Israel' about God's command concerning the natives of the Land of Promise (Deuteronomy 7:3-4):

Neither shalt thou make marriages with them; thy daughter thou shalt not

---

[63] Force, *Tracts*, III, no.1, p.6.

give unto his son, nor his daughter shalt thou take unto thy son. For they will turn away thy son from following me, that they may serve other gods.

Also when the Israelites were in the 'wilderness', before the crossing of the Jordan, it was decreed that daughters should marry only within 'the tribe of their fathers' (Numbers 36:6-7):

So shall not the inheritance of the children of Israel remove from tribe to tribe: for everyone of the children of Israel shall keep himself to the inheritance of the tribe of his fathers.

(William Whitaker explained that the directive applied only to heiresses, and was to prevent confusion of estates between tribes: in fact, he said, 'many examples occur in scripture of marriages contracted between persons of different tribes'.)[64] The main authority on the matter of intermarriage was the Book of Ezra, the fifteenth book of the Old Testament.

The task of Ezra, a 'ready scribe in the law of Moses' (7:6) – 'the law of the God of Heaven' (7:21) – was to enforce the observance of the Jewish Law in the fourth century B.C. He went from Babylon (where many Jews were exiled) to Jerusalem, 'to seek the law of the Lord, and to do it, and to teach in Israel statutes and judgements' (7:10).

Ezra was much approved of by William Whitaker:[65] he was 'skilful in the law' not merely because he knew the literal text, but because 'he explained the sense and meaning of the law, so as to enable the people to understand it'.

The problem of mixed marriages was central to Ezra. God said that the Promised Land had become

an unclean land with the filthiness of the people of the lands, with their abominations, which have filled it from one end to another with their uncleanness. Now therefore give not your daughters unto their sons, neither take their daughters unto your sons, nor seek their peace or their wealth. (9:11-12)

Ezra heard of such 'transgression': and was 'astonied' (9:4).

The people of Israel, and the priests, and the Levites, have not separated themselves from the people of the lands, doing according to their abominations, even of the Canaanites, the Hittites, the Perizzites, the Jebusites, the Ammonites, the Moabites, the Egyptians and the Amorites. For they have taken of their daughters for themselves, and for their sons: so that the holy seed have mingled themselves with the people of those lands. (9:1-2)

---

[64] *Disputation*, 169. It may be noted that the Welsh had been forbidden to intermarry with the English after the Owen Glendower rebellion (1403). Rowse, *Expansion of Elizabethan England*, 45.
[65] *ibid.*, 213.

The struggle of the Unique Nation against contamination. Ezra said: 'Ye have transgressed, and have taken strange wives, to increase the trespass of Israel' (10:10). The Israelites decided to

make a covenant with our God to put away all the wives, and such as are born to them, according to the counsel of my Lord, and of those that tremble at the commandment of our God; and let it be done according to the law. (10:3)

Ezra ordered the transgressors to

make confession unto the Lord God of your fathers, and do His pleasure: and separate yourselves from the people of the land, and from the strange wives. (10:11)

The 'strange wives' were put away. Thus was turned from Israel 'the fierce wrath of our God' (10:14)

John Rolfe in Jamestown wrote early in 1614 to the Governor of the colony, Sir Thomas Dale, about 'a matter of no small moment'; 'which toucheth me so nearly as the tenderness of my salvation.'[66] He was 'in love' with Pocahontas, the daughter of the Indian emperor Powhatan. To her

my heart and best thoughts are and have been a long time so intangled and inthralled in so intricate a labyrinth that I was even awearied to unwind myself thereout.

Pocahontas was 'discrepant in all nutriture from myself'. Her 'education hath been rude, her manners barbarous'. Also, her 'generation' has been 'cursed': an allusion to Genesis 9:25, and the tribe of Ham.

Rolfe was versed in the Book of Ezra:

Nor am I ignorant of the heavy displeasure which Almighty God conceived against the sons of Levi and Israel for marriage of strange wives; nor of the inconveniences which may thereby arise.

And – although he does not specifically refer to it in the letter to Dale – Rolfe would be equally exercised by the advice of Paul to the Christians at Corinth (II Corinthians 6:14-15):

Be ye not unequally yoked together with unbelievers: for what fellowship hath righteousness with unrighteousness? And what communion hath light

---

[66] Printed from Ashmole MS. in the Bodleian by Barbour, *Pocahontas and her World*, 1971, Appendix III:247-52. For the literature on mixed marriages, Gary B. Nash, 'The Image of the Indian in the Southern Colonial Mind', in Dudley and Novak (eds.), *Wild Man Within*: p.85. Professor Nash is an expert on the history of American race relations, and his essay (pp.55-86) is a very good brief survey of the 16th and 17th century material.

with darkness? And what concord hath Christ with Belial? Or what part
hath he that believeth with an infidel?

A passage much favoured by Calvinist puritans such as Rolfe, some of
whom went on to follow the directive in verse 17: 'Wherefore come out
from among them, and be ye separate, saith the Lord.' So Rolfe was
fighting the feeling that his affections were 'wicked instigations
hatched by him who seeketh and delighteth in man's destruction'.

His affections won the day. Pocahontas had 'capableness of
understanding', 'aptness and willingness to receive any good
impression', 'desire to be taught and instructed in the knowledge of
God' – and 'great appearance of love to me'. And it is surely the 'duty
of a good christian', the 'converting to the true knowledge of God and
Jesus Christ an unbelieving creature'. Rolfe invoked St Paul: 'for the
lawfulness of marriage, I hope I do not far err from the meaning of the
Holy Apostle.' He quoted I Corinthians 7:14: 'For the unbelieving
husband is sanctified by the wife, and the unbelieving wife is
sanctified by the husband.' (New English Bible: 'The heathen
husband now belongs to God through his Christian wife, and the
heathen wife through her Christian husband.') Rolfe erred a little, at
any rate, for Paul, it appears, was writing about couples already
married, one of whom was Christian, the other heathen; some in
Corinth had urged that the Christian partner should separate. Paul
would appear to have encouraged future marriage only 'in the Lord':
to another Christian. Rolfe buttressed his Pauline quotation with a
passage from Calvin's *Institutions* (to hand at Jamestown), book 4,
chapter 16, section 6:

Even as the children of the Jews were called a holy seed, because being made
heirs of the same Covenant which the Lord made with Abraham, they were
different from the children of the ungodly: for the same reason even yet also
the children of the Christian are accompted holy, yea, although they be the
issue of but one parent faithful; and (as the prophet witnesseth) they differ
from the unclean seed of idolatry.

(Calvin was discussing the validity of the outward sacrament of
baptism as a confirmation of the covenant.)

Paul concluded this section of his advice to the Christians at
Corinth with 'Think of it': 'as a husband you may be your wife's
salvation' (v.16: New English Bible).

It is worth noting that there was no question of 'colour' in Rolfe's
hesitations. The stumbling block was the 'unclean seed of idolatory'.

From his 'reading, and conference with honest and religious
persons', Rolfe had 'received no small encouragement'. In addition,
'*serena mea conscientia*: the clearness of my conscience'. In April 1614
Rolfe married Pocahontas at Jamestown, the princess having been
instructed and baptised by Alexander Whitaker, son of Dr William
Whitaker.

Tudor and Stuart Englishmen had a defective sense of time. It was perhaps understandable that Peter Wentworth, speaking to the House of Commons in 1576, should have thought of Christ as an honorary Elizabethan MP: for 'God saith: "Where two or three are gathered together in His name, there am I in the midst among them".'[67] But it is sometimes disconcerting to sense that, just as Shakespeare's Roman plays were acted in Elizabethan and Stuart dress, the heroes of the Old Testament were regarded as contemporary figures. Joshua in the 1580s was an honorary adventurer to Virginia, and was from 1606 an honorary member of the Virginia Company.

But what was the intention of the Old Testament stories? It was assumed, as William Whitaker said, that 'all the books of the Old and New Testaments were written not merely by the will and command, but under the very dictation, of Christ': 'with the deliberate purpose of serving the Church in all ages.'[68] Both Testaments are 'as it were a letter sent to us from God'.[69] But there arose, of course, questions of 'strict' and 'metaphorical' interpretation. It is a 'general rule', said Whitaker, that 'we ought not to imitate everything that is related, or even praised, in the scriptures'.[70] Here he mentioned St Augustine's influential book on scripture interpretation, *De Doctrina Christiana*. Augustine taught that the 'transactions' recorded in the Old Testament 'are to be taken not literally only, but figuratively':[71] the actions of the characters cannot 'be transfered to the present time as a habit of life'.[72] The Old Testament must be interpreted 'not only in its historical and literal, but also in its figurative and prophetic sense'.[73] The interpretation of an Old Testament 'precept' must be 'referred to the love of God' and 'the love of one's neighbour':[74] the 'end' of the Old Testament is 'love towards God or our neighbour'.[75] The 'rule', in reading, must be to 'meditate upon what we read till an interpretation be found that tends to establish the reign of love'. Thus, if a 'sentence' of the Old Testament 'seems to enjoin a crime', then 'it is figurative'.[76]

Such matters of hermeneutics (the science of interpretation) had their importance for the future of the American Indian.

The 1610 *True Declaration of the estate of the colonie in Virginia* discussed the *praecepta* of the Old Testament:

That which Origen said of Christ's actions in virtues moral, holdeth proportion with God's actions in government political: *Dei facta sunt nostra praecepta*, God's actions are our instructions.[77]

In a sermon of 1609, Robert Gray, discussing Joshua, had argued that every 'example' in the Old Testament is a 'precept'.[78] Others were more sophisticated. William Whitaker cautioned that 'some precepts

---

[67] Speech in Porter, ed., *Puritanism in Tudor England*, 167.
[68] *Disputation*, 528.
[69] 445. [70] 494.
[71] *On Christian Doctrine*: tr. J.F. Shaw, *Works of Augustine*, ed. Dods, vol.9, 1873, 100.
[72] 96. [73] 93. [74] 94. [75] 93. [76] 95.
[77] Force, *Tracts*, III, no.1, p.4.
[78] *Good Speed to Virginia*, B.3.r.

are proposed to all in common, some privately to special persons'.[79] And there was a traditional distinction between a 'precept' and a 'counsel': a 'precept' being a commandment, an obligation; a 'counsel' being not necessarily binding on all men at all times. William Crashaw in 1610 recognised that the Israelites had a 'commandment' to possess Canaan and to kill the heathen. But 'we have no such commandment touching the Virginians'. The English have 'leave' to dwell in Virginia. They are 'forbidden' to kill; and 'commanded to convert'.[80] Ralph Hamor, who had been in Jamestown from 1609 to 1614, also acknowledged the force of the precedent of the occupation of Canaan; but the English must possess Virginia by 'gentleness, love, amity and religion'.[81]

Robert Cushman, a London man of business who preached to the planters at Plymouth Planatation during a short visit there in December 1621, published in 1622 an essay 'touching the lawfulness of removing out of England into the parts of America'.[82] He dealt with the precedent of the Jewish possession of Canaan. That possession was 'legally holy, and appropriated unto a holy people, the seed of Abraham': and it was a 'Type' of eternal rest in Heaven. So the precedent cannot be exact. Today there is 'no land of that sanctimony, no land so appropriated; none Typical; much less any that can be said to be given of God to any nation, as was Canaan.' Today 'we are in all places strangers and pilgrims, travellers and sojourners' (a paraphrase of Hebrews 11:13 – a favourite text in Plymouth). But we can use the Biblical stories, 'rightly understood': 'the ordinary example and precepts of the scriptures, reasonably and rightly understood and applied, must be the voice and word that must call us, press us, and direct us in every action.'

In 1523 Erasmus added a passage to his Cambridge essay 'War is sweet to those who do not know it' (*Dulce bellum inexpertis*, first published 1515). God chose Solomon to build the Temple. His father David 'otherwise distinguished by many excellent virtues, was cut off from the building of the Temple because he was a man of blood'.[83]

The reference is to I Chronicles 22:7-8:

David said to Solomon, My son, as for me, it was in my mind to build an house unto the name of the Lord my God: But the word of the Lord came to me, saying, Thou hast shed blood abundantly, and hast made great wars: thou shalt not build an house unto my name, because thou hast shed much blood upon the earth in my sight.

[79] *Disputation*, 494.

[80] *New-yeeres Gift to Virginia*, F.3.r-v.

[81] *True Discourse of the Present Estate of Virginia*, 1615, 48.

[82] Printed in *A Relation or Iournall of the beginning and proceedings of the English Plantation setled in New England*. Ed. Cheever, 1848, 101-8. Quotations in this paragraph, 102.

[83] M.M. Phillips, '*Adages' of Erasmus*, 328.

It is true, wrote Erasmus, that David 'made war by the commandment of God'. But his wars were 'against the wicked'. And they were 'in an age which had not yet been taught, by Him who came to complete the Mosaic law, that we must love our enemies'. This addition was to the 1515 point: 'When Christ was born, the angels sang not of wars or triumphs, but of peace.' Similar points were made by Las Casas.[84] William Whitaker said that 'the knowledge of Christians is now much clearer than was formerly that of the Jews'. The Old Testament is 'like a book sealed and closed': the New Testament, 'like a book opened'.[85] Christ Himself, according to Matthew (5:17) said that that He was come to 'fulfil' the Old Testament (Tyndale and Authorised Version; Vulgate, *adimplere*; New English Bible, 'complete').

To John Milton 'the Gospel enjoins no new morality; save only the infinite enlargement of Charity'.[86]

---

[84] Hanke, *Spanish Struggle for Justice*, 32, 125.

[85] *Disputation*, 389.

[86] *Doctrine and Discipline of Divorce*, Bk.II, Ch.17 (1643). Everyman *Milton's Prose Writings*, 299.

6

The New Testament: A Book Opened

I

Christopher Columbus, Admiral of the Indies, wrote in 1500 of 'the new heaven and the new earth which our Lord made, as St John writes in Revelations'.[1] The allusion was to Revelation 21:1: 'And I saw a new heaven and a new earth.' The author, as the pious Italian knew, was 'following the words given to Isaiah'. Isaiah 65:17, 'Behold, I create new heavens and new earth'; and 66:22, 'The new heavens and the new earth, which I shall make, shall remain before me, saith the Lord.' Isaiah, continued Columbus, was the 'messenger' of God. The Admiral was thinking of 6:8:

I heard the voice of the Lord, saying, Whom shall I send, and who will go for us? Then said I, Here am I; send me.

The prophet of the Old Testament spoke again in the final book of the New Testament.

Concerning the 'new heaven and the new earth' of John, as of Isaiah, observed Columbus, 'all men were incredulous'. So had they been of his own plan for the enterprise of the Indies. But 'hope in my Creator sustains me, since His aid has always been very swift'. God gave to Isabella 'the spirit of understanding and great courage, and He made her His dear and much beloved daughter, heiress to it all'. Thus Columbus 'took possession of all these lands in her royal name'. The Biblical vision of 'a new earth' had found a local habitation in the New World.

In that New World, Columbus wished to win the love of the Indians; and – the phrase is from his Letter of 1493 – 'incline them to become Christians'.[2]

This was an imperative of the New Testament.

In Matthew's Gospel, Chapter 24, the twelve disciples came to Christ 'privately' on the Mount of Olives, overlooking Jerusalem, and asked: 'What shall be the sign of Thy coming, and of the end of the world?' (v.3). Christ's prophecy of the future included: 'This gospel of the kingdom shall be preached in all the world for a witness unto all

[1] Penguin Classics *Four Voyages of Columbus*, tr. Cohen, 265.
[2] *ibid.*, 118.

nations; and then shall the end come' (v.14). This was naturally a favourite text for the advocates of colonisation in North America. It was printed on the title page of Roger Green's *Virginias Cure* in 1662.[3] In 1610 the author of *A True Declaration of the estate of the Colonie in Virginia* (commissioned by the London Council of the Virginia Company) noted the 'determined truth, that the Gospel should be preached to all the world before the end of the world'.[4]

The prophecy on the Mount of Olives can be considered together with Christ's directive to the disciples after His resurrection: 'Go ye therefore, and teach all nations, baptising them in the name of the Father, and of the Son, and of the Holy Ghost.' That is the version given by Matthew: 28:19. Mark has: 'Go ye into all the world, and preach the Gospel to every creature' (16:15). And Luke: 'Repentance and remission of sins should be preached in His name among all nations' (24:47). The Gospel of the Kingdom of Christ – repentance: remission of sins – must be preached to all nations, all the world, and the nations baptised.

The saying of Christ was quoted by Pope Paul III in the crucial Bull *Sublimis Deus*, 4 June 1537:[5]

Christ, who is the Truth itself, that has never failed and can never fail, said to the preachers of the faith whom He chose for that office, 'Go ye and teach all nations: *Euntes, Docete Omnes Gentes'*. He said all, without exception, for all are capable of receiving the doctrines of the faith.

The Devil has inspired his *satelites* to argue that

The Indians of the West and the South (*occidentales et meridionales Indos*) and other people of whom We have recent knowledge should be treated as dumb brutes (*muta animalia*) created for our service, pretending that they are incapable of receiving the catholic faith.

All men possess 'the nature and faculties' which make them capable of receiving the faith: *necesse est, hominem talis conditionis et naturae esse, ut Fidem Christi recipere possit.* The Indians can be 'converted to the faith of Jesus Christ by preaching the word of God and by the example of good and holy living'. They are 'truly men' (*veri homines*): 'They are not only capable of understanding the catholic faith, but, according to our information, they desire exceedingly to receive it.'

The sublime God so loved the human race that He created man in such wise that he might participate, not only in the good that other creatures enjoy, but endowed with capacity to attain to the inaccessible and invisible *Summum Bonum* and behold it face to face.

The 'Go thee and teach all nations' text was also, predictably, a

[3] Force, *Tracts*, III, no.15. See below, p.532.
[4] Force, *Tracts*, III, no.1, p.5.
[5] English translation and Latin text in MacNutt, *Las Casas*, 426-31.

favourite with Las Casas. He made effective use of it in his most
famous tract, *Brevissima relacion de la destruycion de las Indias*, published
at Seville in 1552, and translated into English in 1583 as *The Spanish
Colonie, or Briefe Chronicle of the Acts and gestes of the Spaniardes in the West
Indies, called the newe World.*[6]

George Abbot, Master of University College Oxford (to be
Archbishop of Canterbury from 1611 to 1633) wrote in 1599[7] that God
raised up Columbus and 'set his mind to the discovery of a new world'
because He remembered 'the prophecy of His Son, that the Gospel of
the Kingdom should before the Day of Judgement be preached in all
coasts and quarters of the world'. God looked over America, 'in his
mercy intending to free the people – or at least some few of them –
from the bondage of Satan': a nice Calvinist touch.

Another relevant text was a saying of Christ after the resurrection,
reported by the author of the Acts of the Apostles:

Ye shall receive power, after that the Holy Ghost is come upon you: and ye
shall be witnesses unto me both in Jerusalem, and in all Judaea, and in
Samaria, and unto the uttermost part of the earth.

John Donne used this passage (Acts 1:8) as the text for his sermon to
members of the Virginia Company in London in November 1622.[8]

Hakluyt pointed out in 1584 that the English monarch was
Defender of the Faith.[9] He must not only 'maintain and patronise'
that Faith; but also 'enlarge and advance' it. This latter should indeed
be his 'principal and chief' work: 'according to the commandment of
our Saviour Christ'. Matthew 6:33 (part of the Sermon on the
Mount): 'But seek ye first the kingdom of God and His righteousness;
and all these things shall be added unto you.' ('These things' being
food, drink and clothing.)

Chapter 25 of Matthew gives Christ's vision of the day of
Judgement, 'when the Son of man shall come in His glory':

before Him shall be gathered all nations: and He shall separate them one
from another, as a shepherd divideth his sheep from the goats: And He shall
set the sheep on His right hand, but the goats on the left. (31-3)

The 'righteous' on the right hand go 'into life eternal' (46).

For I was an hungred, and ye gave me meat: I was thirsty, and ye gave me
drink: I was a stranger, and ye took me in: Naked, and ye clothed me. (35-6)

They 'inherit the Kingdom prepared for you from the foundation of
the world' (34). Those on the left 'go away into everlasting
punishment' (46):

[6] 1583, C.1.v.
[7] *Briefe Description of the whole Worlde*: section 'De America sive orbe novo'.
[8] Number 10 in vol.4 of the California ed. of Donne's Sermons.
[9] Taylor, *Writings and Correspondence of the Hakluyts*, 214-15.

Depart from me, ye cursed, unto everlasting fire, prepared for the devil and his angels: For I was an hungred, and ye gave me no meat: I was thirsty, and ye gave me no drink: I was a stranger, and ye took me not in; naked, and ye clothed me not. (41-3)

So the Indian, spiritually hungry and thirsty, must be given meat and drink. He must also be clothed.

'I am the way, the truth, and the life: no man cometh unto the Father, but by me' (John 14:6). And the punishment awaiting those without allegiance to Christ was painted in terms of terror which impelled conscientious Englishmen to save the Indian from a fate worse than death. St Paul:

The Lord Jesus shall be revealed from heaven with His mighty angels, in flaming fire taking vengeance on them that know not God, and that obey not the gospel of our Lord Jesus Christ: who shall be punished with everlasting destruction from the presence of the Lord, and from the glory of His power. (II Thessalonians 1:7-9)

This text was used in 1622 by the schoolmaster John Brinsley to emphasise the danger of allowing the Indian – and the Irish and the Welsh – to remain in a state of idolatry.

Woeful is the case of all those amongst whom Satan reigns and who worship him instead of Christ, as all do who know Him not; and much more those poor Indians, among whom he (as is reported) is visibly adored and sacrificed unto as their god.

Brinsley had been a member of Christ's College Cambridge from 1581 to 1588, when William Perkins was a Fellow. In 1622 (*A Consolation for our Grammar Schooles*)[10] he argued for the building of schools in 'ruder countries and places': Ireland, Wales, Virginia. The Indian must be warned, and instructed – with the Virginia Company as foster-father.

In 1610 there was published in London *A True and Sincere Declaration of the purpose and ends of the Plantation begun in Virginia*; the hope of the London Virginia Council being that the Colony should continue *untill by the mercies of God it shall retribute a fruitful harvest to the Kingdome of heaven, and this Common-Wealth*. The title page carried two Biblical quotations, neither from the New Testament.[11] From the Book of Proverbs, the twentieth Book of the Old Testament ('The proverbs of Solomon the son of David'): 'A word spoken in due season, is like apples of God, and pictures of silver' (25:11 – in the forthcoming Authorised Version, 'A word fitly spoken is like apples of gold in pictures of silver'). And secondly, from the Apocrypha (Wisdom of Solomon 17:11): 'Fear is nothing else but a betraying of the succours

[10] Quotations from the Epistle Dedicatory: to the Lord Deputy of Ireland, the Lord President of Wales, the Governors of Guernsey and Jersey, and the Treasurer, Council and Company of Virginia and the Sommers Islands (Bermuda).

[11] Brown, *Genesis*, I, 338.

which reason offereth.' (William Whitaker thought that Wisdom, like Ecclesiasticus, was rightly excluded from the Old Testament canon, while 'replete with very beautiful admonitions, precepts and sentiments'.)[12] But the Biblical allusions in the 1610 text as a whole are to the New Testament.

The 'principal and main ends' of 'the hopeful plantations began in Virginia' are

to preach and baptise into Christian religion, and, by propagation of the Gospel, to recover out of the arms of the Devil a number of poor and miserable souls wrapped up unto death in almost invincible ignorance; to endeavour the fulfilling and accomplishment of the number of the elect, which shall be gathered from out all corners of the earth; and to add our mite to the treasury of heaven, that, as we pray for the coming of the Kingdom of Glory, so to express in our actions the same desire, if God have pleased to use so weak instruments to the ripening and consummation thereof.[13]

No Englishman can 'flatter himself, that it concerns not him'.[14] For one thing, there must be 'a virtuous emulation between us and the Church of Rome'. Both churches have a common enemy: the Devil.

How far hath she sent out her apostles, and through how glorious dangers? How is it become a mark of honour to her faith, to have converted nations, and an obloquy cast upon us, that we, having the better vine, should have worse dressers and husbanders of it?

The English should be stirred in this matter: by 'piety', 'honour', 'conscience' – and 'profit'. If they are not:

Then let us turn from hearts of stone and iron, and pray unto that merciful and tender God, who is both easy and glad to be entreated, that it would please Him to bless and water these feeble beginnings; and that, as He is wonderful in all His works, so to nourish this grain of seed, that it may spread till all people of the earth admire the greatness and seek the shades and fruit thereof. That by so faint and weak endeavours His great councils may be brought forth, and His secret purposes to light, to our endless comfort and the infinite glory of His sacred name.

The 'grain of seed' allusion is to a parable of Christ. Matthew 13:31-2:

The kingdom of heaven is like to a grain of mustard seed, which a man took, and sowed in his field: Which indeed is the least of all seeds; but when it is grown, it is the greatest among herbs, and becometh a tree, so that the birds of the air come and lodge in the branches thereof.

Another version in Mark 4:30-2, Luke 13:18-19. (The image gave William Perkins a title for a 1597 book: *A Graine of musterde-seede, or the*

[12] *Disputation*, 86.
[13] Brown, *Genesis*, I, 339.
[14] Subsequent quotations, *ibid.*, 351-2.

least measure of grace that is or can be effectual to salvation.) So, the London
Council of the Virginia Company directed:

Let every man look inward, and disperse that cloud of avarice which
darkeneth his spiritual sight, and he will find there that when he shall appear
before the tribunal of heaven it shall be questioned him what he hath done.
Hath he fed and clothed the hungry and naked? It shall be required, what he
hath done for the advancement of that Gospel which hath saved him; and for
the relief of his Maker's image, whom he was bound to save.·

II

In Luke's Gospel, Christ tells a story (Chapter 14) about a 'certain
man' who invited many guests to a feast. All made excuses, and did
not arrive. The man ordered that there should be summoned the poor,
maimed, crippled and blind. They came; but there were still vacant
places. So the man issued a directive to his servant (v.23): 'Go out into
the highways and hedges, and compel them to come in, that my house
may be filled.' This was a favourite text for those advocating a 'hard'
line against the Indian: conversion by compulsion. Juan Ginés de
Sepúlveda so used it in the 1540s, and in 1550 during the Disputation
at Valladolid.[15] His opponent, Las Casas, argued that the directive
was to be interpreted as internal, not external, compulsion: the
inspiration of God.[16]

There was other material in the New Testament which the 'hard
liners' could appropriate. They could invoke the Christ who cursed
the fig tree (Matthew 21:19; Mark 11:14) or the Christ who cast out
the money changers from the Temple (Matthew 21:12; Mark 11:15;
John 2:15). They could take as model the figure in Chapter 19 of the
Book of Revelation who sat on a white horse: 'He was clothed with a
vesture dipped in blood' (v.13), 'and in righteousness he doth judge
and make war' (v.11); 'his name is called the Word of God' (v.13),
and 'he hath on his vesture and on his thigh a name written, King of
Kings and Lord of Lords' (v.16);

and out of his mouth goeth a sharp sword, that with it he should smite the
nations: and he shall rule them with a rod of iron: and he treadeth the
winepress of the fierceness and wrath of Almighty God. (v.15)

Christ said: 'Suppose ye that I am come to give peace on earth? I tell
you, Nay; but rather division' (Luke 12:51); 'Think not that I am
come to send peace on earth: I came not to send peace, but a sword'
(Matthew 10:34).

But Christ also said: 'All they that take the sword shall perish with
the sword' (Matthew 26:52). (Compare Revelation 13:10: 'He that
killeth with the sword must be killed with the sword.') Isaiah wrote a

[15] Parry *Age of Reconnaissance*, Mentor ed., 330.
[16] Hanke, *Spanish Struggle for Justice*, 120-121.

prophecy about the 'servant' who 'shall bring forth judgement to the Gentiles' (42:1-4):

He shall not cry, nor lift up, nor cause his voice to be heard in the street. A bruised reed shall he not break, and the smoking flax shall he not quench; he shall bring forth judgement unto truth. He shall not fail nor be discouraged, till he have set judgement in the earth; and the isles shall wait for his law.

When Christ urged discretion on His followers ('charged them that they should not make Him known') Matthew set this in context:

That it might be fulfilled which was spoken by Esaias the prophet, saying, Behold my servant, whom I have chosen; my beloved, in whom my soul is well pleased: I will put my spirit upon him, and he shall shew judgement to the Gentiles. He shall not strive, nor cry; neither shall any man hear his voice in the streets. A bruised reed shall he not break, and smoking flax shall he not quench, till he send forth judgement unto victory. And in his name shall the Gentiles trust. (12:16-21)

The Christ who 'will not snap off the broken reed, nor stuff out the smouldering wick' (New English Bible) was the Christ of Erasmus; following Paul's tribute to 'the meekness and gentleness of Christ' (II Corinthians 10:1), 'the simplicity that is in Christ' (II Corinthians 11:3).

Erasmus quoted the flax/reed passage in his forty-five page essay on the adage 'War is sweet to those who do not know it': *Dulce bellum inexpertis*, probably written at Cambridge in the autumn of 1513 (he was based in Cambridge from the summer of 1511 until the beginning of 1514), first published in 1515, and printed in English in 1534.[17] The image means, said Erasmus, that Christ 'cherished and bore with the imperfect until it could grow better'.[18] And yet:

We are getting ready to annihilate all Asia and Africa with the sword, though most of the population there are either Christians or half-Christians.

(As we have seen, to Erasmus 'the most excellent part of Christianity is a life worthy of Christ'.)[19] What should Christian policy be to the natives of Asia and Africa? 1513 was slightly early for Erasmus, in East Anglia, to mention America: we may mentally make the addition.

Why do we not rather acknowledge them, give them encouragement and gently try to reform them? If we have designs of political expansion, if we are hankering after their wealth, why do we cover up such a worldly thing with the name of Christ?[20]

[17] New translation by M.M. Phillips, 1964: *The 'Adages' of Erasmus*, 308-53.
[18] *ibid.*, 346.
[19] Letter of 14 April 1519 (no.939 in Allen): tr. in Hillerbrand, ed., *Erasmus and His Age: Selected Letters*, 135. See above, p.88.
[20] Phillips, 347.

Erasmus' Christ, quoted in this Cambridge essay, was He who said, 'I am meek and lowly in heart' (Matthew 11:29); who said, 'Put up again thy sword into his place: for all they that take the sword shall perish with the sword' (Matthew 26:52); who promised, 'Peace I leave with you, my peace I give unto you' (John 14:27). And yet Christians fight wars, including colonial wars, in His name: 'we make Christ the witness and authority for so criminal a thing'.[21] 'Christ who is Love, and who taught nothing, handed down nothing, that is not love and peace':[22] 'Examine the whole of His teaching: you will find nothing anywhere which does not breath the spirit of peace, which does not savour of love.'[23] The same is true of Erasmus' Paul: 'What else rings through all Paul's letters, but peace, gentleness and love?'[24]

Erasmus had been decisively impressed by lectures he had heard at Oxford in his brief stay there in 1499. The subject was St Paul: the lecturer, John Colet, M.A. One of Colet's themes in his attempt to follow 'the mind of Paul'[25] was that the work of the Holy Spirit is 'to make mild';[26] that Christ acted 'abjectly, gently, quietly, and in an acceptable way'.[27]

In 1533 Erasmus published *Symbolum sive Catechismus* (also known as the *Explanatio*) dedicated to Thomas Boleyn, Viscount Rochford, Earl of Wiltshire, and father of Anne Boleyn, who had married Henry VIII in January. An English translation (by William Marshall?) was printed at Easter 1534: *A playne and godly exposytion or declaration of the commune Creede*, by 'the famous clarke Mayster Erasmus of Roterdame'. It came to be used as a 'catechism' in many schools, including Winchester. The work takes the form of a dialogue between Master and Disciple. The Disciple asks about the Church. Part of the Master's reply is this:[28]

It is sufficient to believe that in the earth there is such a certain society and fellowship of them that are predestinated to life, which company Christ hath glued or joined together with His spirit (*Christus suo Spiritu conglutinavit*) whether they be among the Indians (*apud Indos*), or else among the Gaditans (*apud Gaditanos*), or else among the Hyperboreans (*apud Hyperboreos*), or else among the peoples of Affryke (*apud Afros*). And it may be so, that in the world there are some lands, other islands, or else dry lands (*aliquae terrae, vel insulae vel continentes*), which are not yet found of mariners or geographers: in which for all that the Christian faith is strong and quick.

Did Erasmus mean communities like the kingdom of Prester John? Or was 'the spirit of Christ' among the heathen Indians, the law of nature, sufficient to glue them into the society of the Church? Was Erasmus thinking of the *insula* called Utopia?

---

[21] *ibid.*, 322.   [22] *ibid.*, 352.   [23] *ibid.*, 328.   [24] *ibid.*, 329.
[25] *Lectures on Corinthians*, ed. Lupton, 119.
[26] Romans commentary, in *Mosaic Account of the Creation*, ed. Lupton, 86.
[27] *Lectures on Romans*, ed. Lupton, 115.
[28] 1534, folio 115, verso. Latin text; Leiden *Opera Omnia*, V, 1704, 1175A.

III

Of central importance to thinking about the American Indian was Paul's teaching about the 'Gentiles': those not of *us* – the 'heathen'.[29] Paul was a Hebrew, an Israelite, of the seed of Abraham (II Corinthians 11:22); and also of the tribe of Benjamin (Romans 11:1). In the Old Testament the Gentile was the non-Jew; although a Jew could live 'after the manner of Gentiles, and not as do the Jews' (Galatians 2:14). It was assumed in Christian thought, however, that in the Old Testament period there were among the Gentiles (the words are William Whitaker's)[30] 'some pious persons really zealous for true religion'.

Paul became a minister of Christ: Christ who, as a young infant, had been saluted in the Temple by Simeon as 'A light to lighten the Gentiles' (Luke 2:32). And Paul was moved to preach the Gospel both to Jew and Gentile: 'To the Jew first, and also to the Greek' (Romans 1:16). The minds of the Jews were 'blinded' (II Corinthians 3:14); they 'have a zeal of God, but not according to knowledge' (Romans 10:2). Paul was 'the apostle of the Gentiles' (Romans 11:13), 'the minister of Jesus Christ to the Gentiles' (Romans 15:16), 'a teacher of the Gentiles in faith and verity' (I Timothy 2:7). His vocation was to 'preach among the Gentiles the unsearchable riches of Christ' (Ephesians 3:8). Both Jews and Gentiles are 'under sin' (Romans 3:9). But God 'hath called, not of the Jews only, but also of the Gentiles' (Romans 9:24).

So the word 'Gentile' comes to mean in the New Testament those

without Christ, being aliens from the commonwealth of Israel, and strangers from the covenants of promise, having no hope, and without God in the world. (Ephesians 2:12)

But among those 'baptised into Christ':

There is neither Jew nor Greek, there is neither bond nor free, there is neither male nor female: for ye are all one in Christ Jesus. (Galatians 3:27-8)

Again:

There is no difference between the Jew and the Greek: for the same Lord over all is rich unto all that call upon him. For whosoever shall call upon the name of the Lord shall be saved. How then shall they call on him in whom they have not believed? And how shall they believe in Him of whom they have not

---

[29] In 'Recessional' (1897) Kipling had. 'Such boastings as the Gentiles use,/Or lesser breeds without the Law.' The Gentiles were probably non-British Europeans; the lesser breeds, colonial natives.

[30] *Disputation*, 518.

heard? And how shall they hear without a preacher? And how shall they preach, except they be sent? (Romans 10:12-15)

Hakluyt quoted the Romans passage in 1584.[31] Who would be the English apostle to the new Gentiles, the American Indians?

To Paul, all non-Jews were 'gentiles' (*ethne*: literally, 'people'). And, once in contact with the Gospel, 'the offering up of the Gentiles might be acceptable, being sanctified by the Holy Ghost' (I Corinthians 14:10).

To those fluent in Greek, men ignorant of Greek, being unintelligible, were 'barbarians': 'If I know not the meaning of the voice, I shall be unto him that speaketh a barbarian, and he that that speaketh shall be a barbarian unto me' (I Corinthians 14:11). The barbarian voice had of course its own validity: there are 'so many kinds of voices in the world, and none of them is without signification' (I Corinthians 14:10). The notion of the 'barbarian' was a general Greek concept. Discovery of the Indies occasioned Spanish debate about 'barbarians' which owed as much to Aristotle as to St Paul. For Las Casas in the 1550s the word 'barbarian' could be used to mean four things. A beast devoid of reason: that is of the 'essence' – and does *not* apply to the Indian. In the other three, the 'barbarism' is matter of 'accident', those who have never heard the Christian message; those without law or political arrangement; and those who speak a strange language (and here, of course, he quoted Paul).[32]

On the other hand, the friar Tomás de Mercado wrote in the 1560s that Negroes and Indians are 'barbarians' because 'they are never moved by reason, but only by passion'.[33] The Spanish jurist and colonial administrator Juan de Matienzo, in a book on Peru published in 1567, thought of the Indians as 'animals who do not even feel reason, but are ruled by their passions'. They were of the 'type' of Melancholic Humour: and men 'of this type or complexion are, according to Aristotle, very fearful, weak and stupid'. That they are of this 'complexion' is clear 'from the colour of their faces'.[34] Not all Spanish experts on the Indies accepted this equation of 'colour' and Aristotelian 'slavery by nature'. López de Gómara, in his *Historia General de las Indias*, published in 1552, wrote – in a passage translated into English by Richard Eden in 1555[35] – that 'colour' is 'one of the marvellous things that God useth in the composition of man'. A marvel which

[31] Taylor, *Writings of the Hakluyts*, 214-15.
[32] Elliott, *Old World and the New*, 49.
[33] *ibid.*, 44.
[34] Eliott, 'Discovery of America and Discovery of Man', Raleigh Lecture, 1972, 10-11.
[35] Part of *Decades of the newe worlde or west India*. Ed. Arber, *First Three English Books on America*, 338.

cannot be considered without great admiration in beholding one to be white
and another black, being colours utterly contrary. Some likewise to be
yellow, which is between black and white; and other of other colours, as it
were of divers livers (living creatures). And as these colours are to be
marvelled at, even so it is to be considered how they differ one from another,
as it were by degrees; forasmuch as some men are white after divers sorts of
whiteness, yellow after divers manners of yellow, and black after divers sorts
of blackness. And how from white they go to yellow, by discolouring, to
brown and red; and to black, by ash colour, and murrey (mulberry)
somewhat lighter than black, and tawney like unto the west Indians, which
are altogether in general either purple, or tawney like unto sodden quinces,
or of the colour of chestnuts or olives – which colour is to them natural, and
not by their going naked, as many have thought: albeit their nakedness have
somewhat helped thereunto.

It is difficult to see the cause of the diversity: 'We be all born of Adam
and Eve.' We can only

consider that His Divine Majesty hath done this, as infinite other, to declare
His omnipotency and wisdom in such diversities of colours; as appear not in
the nature of man, but the like also in beasts, birds and flowers.

'All which things may give further occasion to philosophers to search
the secrets of nature, and complexions of men, with the novelties of the
New World.'

The debate on 'barbarism' could be broadened into considerations
of 'civility' and 'civilisation'. Las Casas praised the architecture of
Mexico.[36] Francisco de Vitoria in the 1530s emphasised certain
aspects of Indian culture 'which call for the use of reason': orderly
politics and laws, the institution of marriage, the workshops, the
system of exchange, and 'a kind of religion'; Indian defects were the
result of upbringing.[37] Alonso de Zorita, probably in the 1560s,
concluded that a 'barbarian' (for the Greeks and Romans for
instance) was merely someone *different*. He went on to extol the 'great
simplicity and great innocence' of the Indian – easily cheated by the
Spanish.[38]

In the Preface to his English translation, published in 1555, of the
first part of the 'Decades' *De Orbe Novo* by Pietro Martire, Richard
Eden reminded the English that St Paul was 'the doctor of the
Gentiles', 'to whose Apostleship these new Gentiles do pertain'.[39] The
Indians are a 'tractable people and pure Gentiles, not being hitherto
corrupted with any other false religion, and therefore the easier to be
allured to embrace ours'. Not 'corrupted' as were the Jew and the
Turk. Eden related the missionary adventures of Paul, and
reproached the laggard English:

[36] Eliott, *Old World and the New*, 45.
[37] *ibid.*
[38] *ibid.*, 46.
[39] Arber, *First Three English Books on America*, 55-6.

What then think you he would do if he were now alive? Is it to be thought that he would not adventure twenty-five days sailing, to come to such a mart of souls, in such readiness to be easily obtained?

Paul trusted in the God who had spoken to Isaiah (66:19). God will send some 'unto the nations'; to Tarshish, Put, Lud, Meshek, Rosh, Tubal and Javan (to Africa, Libya, Italy and Greece, says Eden); 'to the isles afar off, that have not heard my fame, neither have seen my glory; and they shall declare my glory among the Gentiles.'

The Gentiles, said St Paul, are 'alienated from the life of God'. Paul noted their 'ignorance', 'the vanity of their mind', the 'blindness of their heart'; 'having the understanding darkened', 'being past feeling', they 'have given themselves over unto lasciviousness' (Ephesians 4:17-19). Some do worse: they 'sacrifice to devils' – 'I would not that ye should have fellowship with devils' (I Corinthians 10:20). Alderman Robert Johnson picked on these passages in his discussion of the American Indian in 1612.[40] The 'poor Indians' may seem 'intolerable wicked and rooted in mischief': but

be not discouraged, they are no worse than the nature of Gentiles, and even of those Gentiles so heinously deciphered by St Paul to be full of wickedness, haters of God, doers of wrong such as could never be appeased.

Paul, Johnson insisted, lived to see many such become 'true believing Christians'.

One had to remember always the Comfortable Words of Paul: God 'will have all men to be saved, and to come to the knowledge of the truth' (I Timothy 2:4).

The most influential passage in Paul's writing about the Gentiles was Romans 2:14-16:

When the Gentiles, which have not the law, do by nature the things contained in the law, these, having not the law, are a law unto themselves: Which show the work of the law written in their hearts, their conscience also bearing witness, and their thoughts the mean while accusing or else excusing one another: In the day when God shall judge the secrets of men by Jesus Christ according to my gospel.

New English Bible (1961):

When Gentiles who do not possess the law carry out its precepts by the light of nature, then, although they have no law, they are their own law, for they display the effect of the law inscribed on their hearts. Their conscience is called as witness, and their own thoughts argue the case on either side, against them or even for them, on the day when God judges the secrets of human hearts through Christ Jesus. So my gospel declares.

The possible offering of the heathen by nature, by the light of nature:

[40] *The New Life of Virginia.* Force, *Tracts*, I, no.7, p.18.

in conscience and in heart (*kardia*: mind, intellect).

The passage was commented upon by Richard Hooker in 1593, in Book I of *The Laws of Ecclesiastical Polity*:[41]

His meaning is, that by force of the light of reason, wherewith God illuminateth everyone which cometh into the world, men being inabled to know truth from falsehood, and good from evil, do thereby learn in many things what the will of God is; which will Himself not revealing by any extraordinary means unto them, but they by natural discourse attaining the knowledge thereof, seem the makers of those laws which indeed are His, and they but only the finders of them out.

'Wherewith God illuminateth every one which cometh into the world': the allusion was to Chapter 1 of John's Gospel. In God, said John, 'was life; and the life was the light of men' (v.4). John the Baptist 'was sent to bear witness of that Light. That was the true Light, which lighteth every man that cometh into the world' (vv.8-9).

In a specific comment on John Chapter 1, Hooker wrote: 'The light of natural understanding, wit and reason is from God, He it is which thereby doth illuminate every man entering into the world.' God is

the author of all that we think or do by virtue of that light, which Himself hath given. And therefore the laws which the very heathens did gather to direct their actions by, so far forth as they proceeded from the light of nature, God Himself doth acknowledge to have proceeded even from Himself and that He was the writer of them in the tables of their hearts.[42]

In Romans 2, wrote Hooker,[43] Paul teaches that

those men who have no written law of God to show what is good or evil, carry written in their hearts the universal law of mankind, the law of reason, whereby they judge as by a rule which God hath given unto all men for that purpose.

The 'Law of Reason': Hooker preferred this phrase to the more usual 'Law of Nature'. And, for Hooker, 'the minds, even of mere natural men, have attained to know, not only that there is a God, but also what power, force, wisdom, and other properties that God hath, and how all things depend on Him'.[44] To anyone who had read Thomas Hariot's *Brief and True Report of the New-Found Land of Virginia*, 1588, or the Roanoke narratives printed by Hakluyt in 1589, Hooker was not theorising, but describing.

The puritan country parson Richard Bernard – a product of the Christ's College Cambridge of William Perkins – published in 1631 a treatise on Conscience.[45] He clarified and extended a tradition in England of interpretation of Romans Chapter 2. Natural man has

---

[41] I: viii:3.   [42] III: ix:3.   [43] I: xvi:5.   [44] I: viii:7.

[45] *Christian see to thy conscience: or a treatise of the nature, the kinds, and manifold differences of conscience.* Quotations in this paragraph: pps. 43-7, 118, 140, 238-41, 244-6, 256.

certain 'common principles of truth', in the understanding: God exists, is all powerful, and must be worshipped; the soul is immortal; men must love one another; adultery and murder are wrong; private property is necessary. There are also 'common natural notions of right and wrong' – discussed by Bernard in terms of the 'moral conscience'. All 'pagans and heathen people' have this 'light of nature'. And at the Day of Judgment, they will be judged by that. For nature can be abused. And there was a tradition which stressed that those 'lacking the light of God's word' could be punished for their 'abuse of natural reason' – punished not by God only: they could be disciplined by man.[46] Some heathen, said Bernard, have 'lost' the 'light of nature'. They are 'savages', 'gross vulgars': 'little better than brute beasts; through their sottish ignorance, savage qualities, unruly passions, and beastly sensuality doing many things against common reason and the light of nature itself.' Bernard did not mention the Indian. But William Strachey, a graduate of Emmanuel College, who had lived in Jamestown, wrote in 1612 that if the Indians were of the tribe of Ham, one could think of them as a people 'abhorring the inbred notions of Nature itself'.[47]

Hooker had written in 1593 that 'lewed and wicked custom' can 'smother the light of natural understanding'; and that sometimes the 'natural understanding even of sundry whole nations hath been darkened'.[48]

A reasonably balanced estimate of Light and Dark in Indian America was given in *A briefe Description of the whole Worlde*, first published in 1599. The author was George Abbot. Discussing the first reports to Spain from the New World, Abbot wrote that the conquerors found

nothing showing traffic or knowledge of any other nation, but the people naked, uncivil, some of them devourers of man's flesh, ignorant of shipping, without all kind of learning, having no remembrance of history, or writing, among them; never having heard of any such religion as in other places of the world is known, but being utterly ignorant of scripture, or Christ, or Moses, or any God; neither having among them any token of cross, church, temple, or devotion agreeing with other nations.

They were 'naked, without clothes or armour'. At the same time, the Spaniards found them 'most simple, without fraud, giving them kind entertainment according to their best manner'.[49] Later, in Peru, the Indians were found

for the most part very barbarous, and without God. Men of great stature, yea, some of them far higher than the ordinary sort of man in Europe; using

[46] This sentence is from a sermon preached in 1550 by Thomas Lever, Master of St John's College Cambridge: *Sermons* (1550), ed. Arber, 124.

[47] *Virginia Britania*, ed. Wright and Freund, 55.

[48] I, viii:11. I: xii:2.

[49] *Briefe Description of the whole worlde*: section 'De America sive orbe novo'.

to shoot strongly with bows made of fish bones; most cruel people to their enemies.

The Portuguese in Brazil were only marginally more fortunate. They found

men also utterly unlearned, but men more ingenious than the common sort of the Americans: goodly of body and straight of proportion, going always naked, reasonable good warriors after their country fashion; using to fat such enemies as they take in the wars, that afterwards they may devour them, which they do with great pleasure.[50]

In the 1605 edition of *Briefe description of the whole worlde*, 'newly augmented'. Abbot enlarged the section 'De America sive orbe novo'. The Oxford High Calvinist considered the question, why the Indians are not 'coal black, and very Negroes', but of 'reasonable and fair complexion'. The answer – it is due 'only unto God's peculiar will'.[51] The Spanish found among the Indians 'adoration of devils; sodomy; incest and all kind of adultery; ambition in very high measure; a deadly hatred each to other'. Also 'blind witchcraft', 'acquaintance and intercourse with foul spirits'.[52] Yet the Indians had 'reason, and the shape of men'. Why were they 'so brutishly ignorant of all kind of true religion, and understanding devotion'? Because they were 'blockish': the victims of 'ignorance'. 'In all ages it hath appeared that Satan had used ignorance as one of the chiefest means whereby to increase idolatry, and consequently to enlarge his kingdom.'[53] But Abbot introduced the 'light of nature':[54]

It is certain that by the very light of nature, and by the ordinary course of human shape, there were among this people very many good things, as affability, in their kind; hospitality towards strangers which had not offended them, according to their ability, and open and plain behaviour.

Romans Chapter 2 was invoked in Boston, Massachusetts. Increase Mather, Secretary of the General Court, quoted St Paul in his preface in 1648 to *The book of the general laws and liberties concerning the inhabitants of the Massachusets*.[55] The theme of the preface is the importance of Law to God's 'own people', his 'peculiar people'; once in Israel, now in Boston. Mather considered the question whether 'other nations' had and have 'something of God's presence amongst them'. He cited Romans 2:14: 'They did by nature the things contained in the law of God.' It is true that the 'light and law of nature' exist, said Mather. The trouble is that the 'other nations' did not in fact follow it. 'If they had walked according to that light and law of nature they might have been preserved' from 'moral evils' and 'might have enjoyed a common

[50] Section 'De Peru & Brasilia'.
[51] 1605 edition, R.2.r.
[52] R.2.v.   [53] Q.4.r.   [54] R.2.r-v.
[55] Printed at Cambridge, Mass.: A.2.r-v. 1929 reprint, ed. Farrand.

blessing in all their natural and civil ordinances'. But they were 'given up to abominable lusts': and 'God withdrew His presence from them proportionably'. Here Mather gave a reference to Romans again: this time, Chapter 1.

Paul ('debtor both to the Greeks, and to the Barbarians; both to the wise, and to the unwise': v.14) was concerned with 'the wrath of God' against the 'ungodliness and unrighteousness of men' (v.18). Such men

became fools, and changed the glory of the uncorruptible God into an image made like to corruptible man, and to birds, and fourfooted beasts, and creeping things. Wherefore God also gave them up to uncleanness through the lusts of their own hearts, to dishonour their own bodies between themselves: ... God gave them up unto vile affections: for even the women did change the natural use into that which is against nature: And likewise also the men, leaving the natural use of the woman, burned in their lust one toward another; men with men working that which is unseemly. (vv.22-7)

(The 'cause' why God 'gave them up' to such 'shameful passions' – New English Bible – was that they had 'changed the truth of God into a lie, and worshipped and served the creature more than the Creator': v.25.) So God 'withdrew His presence' from some nations, said Mather. He was thinking of Laudian England. How the Indian might fit into the model is again a matter for guesswork. It would presumably ultimately depend on experience of the habits of the Indian: was he seemly or unseemly? On the other hand, observation was more often than not conditioned by pre-conception; in this case, Biblical preconception.

It may be remarked in passing that there are in accounts by English colonists few (if any) references to homosexual practices among the Indians. Perhaps the colonists were not anxious to advertise competition in the English vice. The eighth of the fifteen capital offences in the 1648 Massachusetts 'Laws and Liberties' was: 'If any man lieth with man kind as he lieth with a woman.' Marginal note: 'Sodomy: Genesis 19:5'[56] – in which text the 'men of Sodom' ask Lot to produce his male guests 'so that we can have intercourse with them' (New English Bible). Both parties 'shall surely be put to death'; unless one party was 'forced', or under fourteen – in which case that party 'shall be severely punished' (Leviticus 20:13). (The 'destestable and abominable vice of buggery committed with mankind or beast'

---

[56] *ibid.*, 1929, 5. In Leviticus (18:22) it is 'abomination' to 'lie with a man as with a women': both parties 'shall be put to death' (20:13). Paul regarded 'perverts' as ungodly, offenders against the Law; and thought that those indulging in 'homosexual perversion' cannot 'possess the kingdom of God' (I Corinthians 6:9). The sole New Testament reference to the popularity of 'unnatural' relations is Romans Chapter 1. The Old Testament references are Genesis 19:5, and Judges 19:22. The existence of 'male prostitutes attached to the House of the Lord' is condemned in Deuteronomy 23:17; I Kings 14:24, 15:12, 22:46; and II Kings 23:7. All translations from the New English Bible.

was punishable by death in England by an Act of 1533, revived in 1563.)[57] However, it must be noted that in Massachusetts 'no man shall be put to death without the testimony of two or three witnesses; or that which is equivalent thereunto.'[58]

There was a scandal in 1642 at Duxbury, in the Colony of New Plymouth, when a youth 'made some sodomitical attempts upon another' (the account is by Governor William Bradford).[59] The youth explained that 'he had long used it in Old England'. Worse, a boy of 17 was indicted for buggery with a mare, a cow, two goats, five sheep, two calves and a turkey – 'he was taught it by another that had heard of such things from some in England when he was there; and they kept cattle together.' The legal questions arose of witnesses; of how far the magistrate could exact a confession (self-accusation) in a capital case, seeing 'no man is required to incriminate himself'; and also of 'whether contact and friction leading to the effusion of semen, without penetration, are acts of sodomy punishable by death'. Three clerics submitted written remarks on these points:[60] Ralph Partridge (Trinity College Cambridge), pastor of Duxbury; John Rayner (Magdalene College Cambridge), teacher at Plymouth; and the pastor at Plymouth, Charles Chauncey, sometime Fellow of Trinity College Cambridge, and a future President of Harvard. It was not *quite* certain that homosexual acts other than intercourse *cum penetratione corporis* incurred the death penalty. Rayner alone was adamant that *all* homosexual acts are 'against the light of nature', 'utterly extinguishing all light of nature'. The youth who made 'attempts' was not killed. The cowboy was; after the slaughter of the cattle 'before his face, according to the Law, Leviticus 20:15'. The episode occasioned William Bradford (a Pilgrim Father) to write gloomy thoughts about the newer settlers. He consoled himself with Exodus 12:38. The children of Israel journeyed from Ramesis to Succoth: but 'a mixed multitude went up also with them'.

IV

Richard Hooker's patron and hero was John Jewel: 'The worthiest divine that Christendom hath bred for the space of some hundreds of years'.[61] Jewel was Bishop of Salisbury from 1559 until his death in 1571. In the 1560s he had a literary controversy with the English Catholic Thomas Harding (both were former Oxford dons). In this debate occured the first specific discussion, in English theology, of the nature of the American Indian.

Jewel's concern was the defence of the Church of England against the Church of Rome. In 1559 he preached his 'challenge' sermon,

[57] 25 Henry VIII, cap. 6. 5 Elizabeth, cap. 17.
[58] *Laws and Liberties*, 1929, p.54.
[59] Bradford, *Plymouth Plantation*, ed. Morison, 320-1.
[60] *ibid.*, 404-13.
[61] II: vi:4.

printed in 1560.[62] In 1564 Thomas Harding, formerly of Winchester and New College, published at Louvain an *Answere to Maister Iuelles Chalenge*. Jewel's *Replie unto M. Hardinges Answeare* came in 1565, Harding's *Reioindre to M. Jewels Replie* in 1566 (Antwerp: revised version, Louvain, 1567). Parallel with this debate about the Sermon went controversy about Jewel's *Apology*. Jewel's *Apologia Ecclesiae Anglicanae* was published early in 1562; an English translation by Lady Anne Bacon was printed in 1564 (Anne was the mother of Francis, born in 1561). Harding's *Confutation* appeared in Antwerp in 1565. There followed Jewel's *Defence of the Apologie*, 1567, Harding's *Detection of Sundrie Foule Errors*, Louvain, 1568, and Jewel's second edition of the *Defence*, 1570.

Thus the sweep of the controversy embraces five works by Jewel, all in English save the original Latin *Apologia*; and four English works by Harding. It was the most sustained debate in print between Englishmen (both Devonshire men) since More versus Tyndale in the late 1520s and early 1530s. The Elizabethans compared the two to Athenian orators. To Gabriel Harvey in the early 1590s

Harding and Jewel were our Aeschines and Demosthenes: and scarcely any language in the Christian world hath afforded a pair of adversaries equivalent to Harding and Jewel, two thundering and lightening Orators in Divinity.[63]

In the 1565 *Confutation*, Harding made much of the missionary successes of the Church of Rome. Jewel took up this point in the *Defence* of 1567.[64] Harding, said the Bishop, brings us 'many of news' from 'strange, and far countries': Peru, south-east Africa (Monomotapa), the island of Ormuz in the Persian gulf, Ceylon, the kingdom of Cambay near Bombay, the Malay Archipelago (Macassar), China and Japan. In all such regions, according to Harding, 'the faith professed in the holy Roman church is now preached'; and members of the Society of Jesus have converted many countries, kings and princes. Jewel: 'I marvel, he saith not, the man in the moon was likewise newly christened, to make up the muster.'

Jewel argues, citing Amerigo Vespucci, that in 'the East India' there had been 'sundry whole countries converted and christened', and 'many godly bishops', before the arrival of the Portuguese and the Jesuits. He then considers 'the West Spanish Indies'; relying here on the 'Decades' of Pietro Martire.

The people there lived not only without all manner knowledge of God, but also wild, and naked, without any civil government, offering up men's bodies

[62] *A Sermon pronounced by the Byshop of Salisburie at Paules Crosse*. First preached November 1559; repeated March 1560. Jewel's *Works* were printed in four volumes by the Parker Society, 1845-50: ed. J. Ayre.

[63] *Pierces Supererogation*, 1593, p.13.

[64] 1567 edition, 37-8. Parker Society, III, 197-9.

in sacrifice, drinking men's blood, and eating men's flesh. Some of them worshipped the sun, and the moon: some, an ancient old tree: some, whatsoever they saw first in the morning, they thought the same for that day to be their God. Some worshipped certain familiar devils, and unto them sacrificed young boys, and girls.

Such was obviously a 'miserable state'. But man is by nature a religious animal. After all,

the great King of Tartary of late, finding himself and his people without any manner religion, was contented to borrow some religion of the Turks. For men would rather clothe themselves with leaves, and barks, than to go quite naked: and rather eat acorns, than die for hunger.

Similarly, the Indians of Spanish America were in a condition of 'abhorring and loathing their own blindness'. They did so 'naturally by the sense, and judgement of common reason'.

Thus we are led to Pauline territory: the Gentiles showing the 'work of the law' 'by nature', 'in their hearts' and 'their conscience'.

Unfortunately, Jewel's 1567 argument continues, these instincts of nature made the Indians of South and Central America easy prey for the wiles of popery: 'What marvel is it, if they were easy to be led into any religion, especially carrying such a shew of apparel, and holy ceremonies.' God was using the Spanish successes as an interim measure; a stepping stone to the acceptance by the American Indian of the perfections of Protestantism.

And what if God would use this mean for the time, afterward the better to lead the said nations to the clear light of the gospel; as St Augustine saith the shoemaker useth his bristle, not to sew withal, but to draw in his thread? No doubt, M. Harding, if your doctrine and ours were laid together, the very Indians themselves, be they never so rude, would be able to see a great difference.

In his reply, the *Detection* of 1568, Harding was horrified that the Bishop had attributed 'the glorious conversion of the Indians' to 'the leading of natural reason'. This was 'heathenish'.[65]

Jewel expanded his position in 1570, in the enlarged edition of the *Defence*. In 1570 Jewel specifically quoted St Paul.[66] Romans 2:14-15:

The heathen, that have not the law of God, yet by nature do the things that pertain to the law; and, having no law, they are a law to themselves, and shew forth the work or effect of the law written within (by nature) in their hearts.

The point was buttressed by Romans 1:19-20:

[65] Quoted by Jewel in the 1570 edition of the *Defence*: p.32. Parker Society, III, 198.
[66] 1570 edition, 42-3. Parker Society, III, 198-9.

That thing that may be known of God is opened unto them: the invisible things of God are known (naturally) by the creatures of the world; even the everlasting power power of God and His divinity.

The Authorised Version was to have:

that which may be known of God is manifest in them; for God hath shewed it unto them. For the invisible things of Him from the creation of the world are clearly seen, being understood by the things that are made,. even His eternal power and Godhead.

The Pauline perceptions about 'natural men, and of the light of nature', were confirmed by St Ambrose (one quotation) and St Jerome (three quotations). Certainly, said Jewel, 'nature alone' cannot 'lead us into the perfection of faith', 'the secrecies and mysteries of Christ's gospel'; or 'endue our hearts with the Spirit of God'. But (and two quotations from Cicero support him) 'nature of herself is oftentimes able to discern between truth and falsehood'. Further, 'the heart of man is naturally inclined to religion'. This remains true, even if man, 'blinded with original sin', in choosing a religion 'oftentimes falleth into horrible errors'.

The points of 1567 were repeated and expanded in 1570. The 'poor Indians',

living by man's flesh, and going naked, having no manner sense, nor knowledge of God, but falling down either before an old tree, or before the sun, and the moon, or whatsoever thing they saw first in the morning, when they saw the religion of Rome, with so many ceremonies, and shews of holiness, very nature taught them, to think the same far better, than their own.

They remain 'blind'. But

if they might see both your, and our religion set open before them, I doubt not, but nature herself would lead to judge, that ours is the Light, and yours Darkness.

Jewel always had an attractive pastoral sense; expressed most eloquently in his fine Salisbury sermons (whose poised style some may prefer to that of his protégé Richard Hooker). His feel for the 'poor simple people'[67] of Christendom, 'the ignorant and unlearned sort of people, that offend of simplicity and have a zeal of God, although it be not according to knowledge'[68] (an echo of Paul on the Jews: Romans 10:2), coloured his theories about the American Indian. He concluded his 1570 discussion of the topic by quoting Christ's words to the Pharisees, Matthew 23:15. In the Authorised version:

[67] Parker Society, II, 675 (1565 *Replie*).
[68] Parker Society, II, 997. A Salisbury sermon.

Woe unto you, scribes and Pharisees, hypocrites! For ye compass sea and land to make one proselyte, and when he is made, ye make him twofold more the child of hell than yourselves.

For Jewel, this was a warning to the missionaries of the Church of Rome:

Ye seek about by sea, and by land, to find one Novice: and, when ye have gotten him, ye make him the child of hell, double worse, than yourselves.

The American Indians were by nature not Angels but Anglicans.

7
John Florio and Montaigne's 'Bon Sauvage'

The *Essais* of Michel, seigneur of the domain of Montaigne – over 100 in all – were published in the 1580s: the first group in 1580, at Bordeaux (thirty miles west of Montaigne); the second group at Paris in 1588, when Montaigne was 55. The note to the reader, 1 March 1580, declared that 'it is myself I portray', 'my self am the groundwork of my book': *je suis moy-mesmes la matière de mon livre*. And an American note was introduced:

If my fortune had been to have lived among those nations, which yet are said to live under the sweet liberty of Nature's first and uncorrupted laws (*la douce liberté des premières loix de nature*), I assure thee, I would most willingly have portrayed myself fully and naked (*tout entier, et tout nud*).

I use the English version by John Florio, published in 1603.[1]

Material relating to the New World frequently served Montaigne's purpose. The final essay, 1588, 'Of Experience', commended the wise provision of King Ferdinand that no lawyers or law students should be sent to the Indies, 'lest controversies, suits or processes should people that new found world'. Law is (Montaigne was a lawyer) 'a science that of her own nature engendereth altercation and division'. Ferdinand, like Plato, judged that 'lawyers and physicians are an ill provision for any country'. The magistrate Montaigne claimed the most desirable laws to be 'the simplest and most general':

And yet I believe, it were better to have none at all, than so infinite a number as we have. Nature gives them ever more happy, than those we give ourselves. Witness the image of the golden age that Poets fain; and the state wherein we see divers nations to live, which have no other.[2]

In one of the 1580 essays ('Of Couriers') he mentioned the postal deliveries of Peru, where

they went post upon men's backs, who took their masters upon their

---

[1] Page references to the three volume edition published by Dent in 1928, with an introduction by Desmond MacCarthy. Quotes from the Preface; I, 15.
[2] III, 323-4.

shoulders, sitting upon certain bears[3] or chairs, with such agility, that in full running speed the first porters, without any stay, cast their load upon other who upon the way waited for them, and so they to others.[4]

In another, he cited as an instance of the tyranny of custom the fact that in 'the new-found world of the Indians' some natives eat spiders.[5] ('I am of opinion, that no fantasy so mad can fall into human imagination, that meets not with the example of some public custom.')[6] In 'Of the use of apparel' (1580) Montaigne considered the challenge of nudity.

I was devising in this chill-cold season, whether the fashion of these late discovered nations to go naked, be a custom forced by the hot temperature of the air, as we say of the Indians and Moors, or whether it be an original manner of mankind.[7]

In the same *essai* he noted that

the king of Mexico was wont to change and shift his clothes four times a day, and never wore them again, employing his leavings and cast-suits for his continual liberalities and rewards; as also neither pot nor dish, nor any implement of his kitchen or table were twice brought before him.[8]

The longest essay of the 1580 collection was the 'Apology'. In this we learn, in a passage on fashion, that 'we hide ourselves when we will enjoy our wives: the Indians do it in open view of all men'.[9] It was also argued – the theme here being the virtue of ignorance – that 'incivility, ignorance, simplicity and rudeness are commonly joined with innocency':[10] *L'incivilité, l'ignorance, la simplesse, la rudesse s'accompaignent volontiers de l'innocence.* In the 'Apology' – 'the fullest expression of his reasons for doubt'[11] – Montaigne asserted that 'the simple and the ignorant (saith St Paul) raise themselves up to heaven'.[12] This curious allusion may be based on I Corinthians Chapter 1: 'The foolishness of God is wiser than men.' (v.25); 'God hath chosen the foolish things of the world to confound the wise' (v.27). Matthew (11:25) and Luke (10:21) report Christ's remark that God 'has hid these things from the wise and prudent, and hast revealed them unto babes'. Montaigne's phrase resembles St Paul in neither expression nor thought; it is a garbled memory of the New Testament in general.[13] Another passage of the 'Apology' presented those 'vain shadows of our religion' found in 'infidel' and 'barbarous' nations; a confirmation (probably

[3] Rough mats. [4] II, 408. [5] I, 105. [6] *ibid.*, 108-9. [7] I, 239.
[8] *ibid.*, 242. [9] II, 300. [10] *ibid.*, 199.
[11] Frame, *Montaigne's Discovery of Man*, 1955, 60. Frame also wrote *Montaigne: A Biography*, 1965. Also recommended is Sayce, *The Essays of Montaigne*. On the New World background: Chinard, *L'Exotisme américain dans la littérature française au XVIe siècle*, 1; Atkinson, *Les Nouveaux horizons de la renaissance française*.
[12] II, 198.
[13] Information provided by Rev. John Sweet, Selwyn College, Cambridge.

ironical) of 'the dignity and divinity' of Christianity. These traces include belief in one God, in a resurrection and a Day of Judgement and a kind of purgatory, the use of charms and religious ornaments, the belief in miracles, the celibacy and private language of priests; and the fact that in the New World Christian crosses were 'in great esteem'.[14] We are also reminded that the Indians are 'without magistrates or law'; and thus 'live much more regularly and formally than we, who have amongst us more officers and laws, than men of other professions.'[15] Jean de Léry, in his *Histoire* of his voyage to Brazil, published in 1578, had claimed that the Indians live till a very advanced age; and commended the 'peu de soin et de souci qu'ils ont des choses de ce monde'. Léry, a protestant pastor, went on to compare this with the European mind, dominated and tormented by avarice, envy, and ambition. Montaigne repeated the information about longevity: and attributed it not to 'the clearness and calmness of their air' but to

the calmness and clearness of their minds, void and free from all passions, cares, toiling and unpleasant labours, as a people that pass their life in a wonderful kind of simplicity and ignorance, without letters, or laws, and without kings, or any religion (*sans religion quelconque*).[16]

A further 1580 essay, 'Of Moderation', used a passage from López de Gómara relating an Indian oration on the occasion of the bringing of three kinds of gifts to Hernán Cortés:[17]

If thou be a fierce God (*un dieu fier*) that loveth to feed on flesh and blood, here are five slaves, eat them, and we will bring thee more: if thou be a gently mild God (*un dieu débonnaire*) here is incense and feathers; but it thou be a man, take these birds and fruits, that here we present and offer unto thee.

This passage was effectively used by John Dryden in his play *The Indian Emperour, or, the Conquest of Mexico by the Spaniards*, performed in London in 1665, and printed in 1667. In Act One, scene two, Montezuma kneels to Cortez, and makes the following speech (lines 235-45):

> Thy actions shewe thee borne of Heav'nly Race.
> If then thou art that cruell God, whose Eyes
> Delight in bloud, and humane sacrifice,
> Thy dreadful Altars I with slaves will store,
> And feed thy nostrills with hot reeking gore;
> Or if that mild and gentle God thou be,
> Who dost mankind below with pitty see,

[14] II, 289-91.
[15] *ibid.*, 198.
[16] *ibid.*, 190 Chinard, *L'Exotisme américain*, prints the Léry and Montaigne passages in parallel column: 196-7.
[17] I, 215.

With breath of Incense I will glad thy heart,
But if like Us, of Mortal seed thou art,
Presents of rarest fowles and fruites I'll bring,
And in my Realmes thou shalt be more then King.

The essay 'Of Moderation' is Chapter 29 of Book One. Chapter 30 is an extensive treatment of Indian material: *Des Cannibales*.

Montaigne mentioned in this essay that he had been introduced to three Indians from Brazil at Rouen (the centre of French trade with America). That was in September 1562, when Montaigne was 29. Through an interpreter, he had talked with one of them.[18] Two of the things the chief said remained in his memory when he was preparing the essay in the late 1570s. The chief was amazed that the royal Swiss guard should submit to a 'beardless child' (Charles IX was twelve) and not 'choose one among them to command the rest'. And he was surprised that

there were men amongst us full gorged with all sorts of commodities, and others which, hunger-starved, and bare with need and poverty, begged at their gates: and found it strange, these moyities so needy could endure such an injustice, and that they took not the others by the throat, or set fire on their houses.

(They 'have a manner of phrase whereby they call men but a moitie one of another'.)[19]

Montaigne was in turn surprised that the Indians had 'quit the calmness of their climate, to come and see ours'. Montaigne's library included some transcriptions of Indian songs: a 'warlike song' – defiant verses 'made by a prisoner'; and an 'amorous canzonet'.[20] He had eaten Indian bread; and found it too sweet.[21] By the late 1570s he had employed for 'long time' a servant, 'a simple and rough hewn fellow', 'fit to yield a true testimony', who had lived in Brazil for 'ten or twelve years'. He had introduced Montaigne to 'divers mariners, and merchants, whom he had known in that voyage'. He had lived 'in these parts where Villegagnon first landed, and surnamed Antartike France'.[22]

Nicolas Durand de Villegagnon had established a fort on an island in the Bay of Rio de Janeiro in November 1555. The patron of the enterprise was Coligny; and one of the aims was to establish a haven for French protestants. In 1556 Villegagnon wrote to Calvin asking for pastors from the seminary at Geneva. Calvin, secure in Geneva from 1555, was turning his attention to missionary work: two pastors had been sent to Piedmont, and one to Poitiers, in 1555, and one to Bourges in 1556. Two pastors were sent to Brazil: Pierre Richier and Guillaume Chartier. They arrived with the second contingent of colonists in March 1557. The colony was rather a disaster: there was

[18] I, 228-9.
[19] Moiety: an equal part.
[20] 227-8. [21] 221. [22] 216, 218.

much *odium theologicum*; and soon the settlement was destroyed by the Portuguese. In 1565 there was published a *Bref Recueil de l'affliction* ... *au Pays du Brésil*, with the running title *Les Martyrs de Nostre Temps* (those who defended the principles of Geneva in a strange land). But the main authorities were the colonists André Thevet (1502-1590) and Jean de Léry (1534-1611). In 1556, shortly after his return, Thévet published in Paris *Singularités de la France antarctique, autremont nommée Amerique* (second edition, Antwerp 1558). Léry, a theological student at Geneva, published his version in 1578 at La Rochelle: *Histoire d'un voyage fait en la terre du Brésil*. We have already encountered Léry as a source for Montaigne.[23]

The idea of a Huguenot colony in the New World survived into the 1560s. In 1562 Jean Ribault established a settlement in 'Florida': Charlesfort, on Parris Island, Port Royal Sound, in the deep south of South Carolina (just north of Savannah, Georgia). The garrison revolted, and the survivors returned. Ribault went to London in 1563 and there published, also in 1563, *The whole and true discoverye of Terra Florida*. This was reprinted by Hakluyt in 1582 in *Divers voyages touching the discoverie of America*. In 1564 René de Laudonnière founded a fort in the very north of the present state of Florida: Fort Caroline, at the mouth of the St John's River, nearly forty miles north of St Augustine. The colonists were attacked by the Spaniards in 1565; among the survivors was the painter Jacques Le Moyne de Morgues.[24] Laudonnière wrote *L'histoire notable de Floride*, the manuscript of which Hakluyt acquired from Thévet in Paris in the mid-1580s; he published it in Paris, and prepared an English translation, published in London in 1587, with a dedication to Sir Walter Raleigh – *A notable historie containing foure voyages made by certayne French captaynes unto Florida*.

Montaigne relied heavily on Léry. Another of his sources in the late 1570s was the 1579 French translation (by Urbain Chauveton, published at Geneva) of *La Historia del mondo nuovo*, Venice 1565, of the Milanese Girolamo Benzoni, born in 1519, who went to Spanish America in 1541 and returned in 1554: his book was largely a compilation of earlier material, including passages from Columbus and Pietro Martire.

In some ways, the essay 'Of the Cannibals' notes, 'in respect of us, these are very savage men'. For one thing, the men have many wives, who procure for their husbands as many other females as they can.[25]

Our women would count it a wonder, but it is not so: It is virtue properly matrimonial; but of the highest kind. And in the Bible, Leah, Rachel, Sarah, and Jacob's wives, brought their fairest maiden servants unto their husbands' beds.

[23] Chinard, *L'Exotisme américain*: Ch. 4, 'Les Français au Brésil: l'expédition de Villegagnon et le Cosmographe André Thévet'; Ch. 6, 'Un Moraliste Voyageur: Léry.' Also Atkinson, *Nouveaux Horizons*.

[24] For all this, see Quinn, ed., *North American Discovery*, 140-62: 'French Florida 1562-1580'.

[25] II, 228.

Sarah, the principal wife of Abraham, indeed gave her handmaiden to her husband as his concubine. Leah and Rachel, wives of Jacob, both gave their maids to him. But Montaigne's venture into the Book of Genesis is rather confusingly phrased.

The cannibalism was of course the fascinating 'savage' feature. Léry had not been terribly indignant about cannibalism: it was the result of superstition, and the desire to be rid of enemies – and the Indians, the pastor remarked, would be horrified by the Massacre of St Bartholomew and subsequent horrors in France.[26] Montaigne adopted this approach. The Indians kill a prisoner, with ceremony: 'They roast, and then eat him in common, and send some slices of him to such of their friends as are absent.' This is 'an extreme, and inexpiable revenge'. But Europeans 'mangle by tortures and torments', set dogs and swine on a prisoner 'to gnaw and tear him'; and 'roast him in pieces'. This is, symbolically, to eat a live man: and 'I think there is more barbarism in eating men alive, than to feed upon them being dead'. The more so as Europeans do such things 'under pretence of piety and religion'. The Indians have seen the Portuguese bury prisoners to the waist, shoot at them with arrows, and then hang them. We should note the 'barbarous horror' of cannibalism; but Montaigne is 'grieved, that prying so narrowly into their faults we are so blinded in ours'.[27]

Montaigne much admired the 'invincible courage' of the Indian, his glory and valour.[28] 'Their wars are noble and generous, and have as much excuse and beauty, as this human infirmity may admit.'[29] And: 'It is an admirable thing to see the constant resolution of their combats, which never end but by effusion of blood and murder: for they know not what fear or routs are.' The victors bring home the heads of the slain, and fix them to the entrance of their dwellings.[30] All this is from the section on cannibalism.

The Indian language is 'a kind of pleasant speech, and hath a pleasing sound, and some affinity with the Greek terminations'.[31] Their food is fish and flesh with 'no resemblance at all with ours'; eaten 'without any sauces, or skill of cookery, but plain boiled or broiled'. They eat one meal a day, at rising. At the meal they do not drink; but thereafter 'drink many times a day, and are much given to pledge carouses'. The drink

is made of a certain root, and of the colour of our claret wines, which lasteth but two or three days; they drink it warm: it hath somewhat a sharp taste, wholesome for the stomach, nothing heady, but laxative for such as are not used unto it, yet very pleasing to such as are accustomed unto it.

The warming of the drink is the 'chiefest office' of the women. The

---

[26] Chinard, *L'Exotisme américain*, 136-7. Las Casas made a similar point: Wagner and Parish, *Las Casas*, 179.

[27] II, 223-24.

[28] 225.   [29] 224.   [30] 223.   [31] 228.

elders 'never miss' to remind men 'that it is their wives which keep their drink luke-warm and well seasoned'. There are two moral obligations: 'First, valour against their enemies, then lovingness unto their wives.' The women, however, spent the night apart from their husbands; 'every one hath his several couch' (their beds being 'of a kind of cotton cloth, fastened to the house-roof, as our ship cabins'.) Their houses are like European barns; very long, with a capacity of two or three hundred persons, and 'covered with barks of great trees, fastened in the ground at one end, interlaced and joined close together by the tops, after the manner of some of our granges; the covering whereof hangs down to the ground, and steadeth them as a flank.' From their hard wood they make swords, knives, and 'grid-irons to broil their meat with'. They also make razors from wood or stone: and 'are shaven all over, much more close and cleaner than we are'. Examples of their hammocks, ropes, swords, knives, wooden bracelets and 'great canes open at one end, by the sound of which they keep time and cadence in their dancing' are 'in many places to be seen', 'and namely in my own house'.[32]

There is material about religious beliefs and ceremonies.[33]

They believe their souls to be eternal, and those that have deserved well of their gods, to be placed in that part of heaven where the sun riseth, and the cursed toward the west in opposition. They have certain prophets and priests, which commonly abide in the mountains, and very seldom show themselves unto the people; but when they come down, there is a great feast prepared, and a solemn assembly of many townships together.

The 'Prophet' addresses the people,

exhorting them to embrace virtue and follow their duty. All their moral discipline containeth but these two articles; first an undismayed resolution to war, then an inviolable affection to their wives. He doth also prognosticate of things to come, and what success they shall hope for in their enterprises: he either persuadeth or dissuadeth them from war.

What Montaigne approved of was that 'if he chance to miss of his divination, and that it succeed otherwise than he foretold them, if he be taken, he is hewn in a thousand pieces, and condemned for a false prophet'. In Europe, there are too many false prophets 'that gull and conycatch us with the assurance of an extraordinary faculty'. ('Conycatch' means a cheat; one who traps a cony – a dupe, a sucker.) 'Divination,' Montaigne argued, 'is the gift of God; the abusing whereof should be a punishable imposture.'

America is a country of 'exceeding pleasant and temperate situation'. Indeed,

as my testimonies have told me, it is very rare to see a sick body amongst

[32] 220-2.   [33] 222.

them; and they have further assured me, they never saw any man there, either shaking with the palsy, toothless, with eyes dropping, or crooked and stooping through age.[34]

Those of similar age 'do generally inter-call one another brethren, and such as are younger, they call children, and the aged are esteemed as fathers to all the rest'. They have 'all necessary things'; and consider things other than 'natural necessities' to be 'superfluous'. Thus they 'contend not for the gaining of new lands'. Goods are bequeathed *en commun* to all a man's heirs: 'without other claim or title, but that which nature doth plainly impart unto all creatures, even as she brings them into the world.'[35] They know 'how to enjoy their condition happily, and are contented with what nature affordeth them'.[36]

The New World is under the 'command' of 'the laws of nature': *les loix naturelles leur commandent encores*. What a pity, observed Montaigne, that Plato did not know of this 'purity'.[37] Europe has neglected 'our great and puissant mother Nature':[38]

We have so much by our inventions surcharged the beauties and riches of her works, that we have altogether overchoked her: yet wherever her purity shineth, she makes our vain and frivolous enterprises wonderfully ashamed.

(The 'ordinary faults' of Europeans are: treason; treachery; disloyalty; tyranny; cruelty.)[39] The Indians 'have received very little fashion from human wit', and are still 'near their original naturality'.[40] Thus they seem 'barbarous' to us – just as the Greeks were 'wont to call all strange nations' 'barbarous'.[41] 'We may then well call them barbarous, in regard of reason's rules, but not in respect of us that exceed them in all kinds of barbarism.'[42]

This point developed into a particularly fine passage:[43]

I find (as far as I have been informed) that there is nothing in that nation, that is either barbarous or savage, unless men call that barbarism which is not common to them (*il n'y a rien de barbare et de sauvage en cette nation, à ce qu'on m'en a rapporté, sinon que chacun appelle barbare ce qui n'est pas de son usage*). As indeed, we have no other aim of truth and reason, than the example and Idea of the opinions and customs of the country we live in. There is ever perfect religion, perfect policy, perfect and complete use of all things. They are even savage, as we call those fruits wild, which nature of herself, and of her ordinary progress hath produced: whereas indeed they are those which ourselves have altered by our artificial devices (*artifice*), and diverted from their common order, we should rather term savage.

The most familiar passage in the 'Cannibals' essay is that which Shakespeare used, in the Florio version, for the speech of Gonzalo in *The Tempest* about his ideal commonwealth. Gonzalo's plantation, as we have seen, was based on Nature, and would 'excel the Golden

[34] 220. [35] 224-5. [36] 225. [37] 220. [38] 219. [39] 224. [40] 220. [41] 215. [42] 224. [43] 219.

Age'. There were 'all things in common'. And a list of things lacking: sovereignty and 'name of magistrate'; 'occupation' ('all men idle'); 'use of service'; riches and poverty; 'traffic' and contracts; cultivated and reserved land; private inheritance ('succession'); vineyards, wine, corn and oil; metal; weapons; treason and felony; letters. Montaigne/Florio wrote thus about the Indian 'nation':[44] it

hath no kind of traffic, no knowledge of letters, no intelligence of numbers, no name of magistrate, nor of politic superiority; no use of service, of riches or of poverty; no contracts, no successions, no partitions, no occupation but idle; no respect of kindred, but common, no apparel but natural, no manuring of lands, no use of wine, corn or metal. The very words that import lying, falsehood, treason, dissimulations, covetousness, envy, detraction, and pardon, were never heard of amongst them.

Here is the French text:

Il n'y a aucune espèce de trafique; nulle cognoissance de lettres; nulle science de nombres; nul nom de magistrat, n'y de superiorité politique; nuls usage de service, de richesse ou de pauvreté; nuls contrats; nulles successions; nuls partages; nulles occupations qu'oysives; nul respect de parenté que commun; nuls vestemens; nulle agriculture; nul metal; nul usage de vin ou de bled. Les paroles mesmes qui signifient la mensonge, la trahison, la dissimulation, l'avarice, l'envie, la detraction, le pardon, inouïes.[45]

The passage was a criticism of the republic of Plato: 'How dissonant would he find his imaginary commonwealth from this perfection!' For the experience of the New World

doth not only exceed all the pictures wherewith licentious Poesie hath proudly embellished the Golden Age, and all her quaint inventions to fain a happy condition of man, but also the conception and desire of Philosophy. They could not imagine a genuity[46] (*naïveté*) so pure and simple, as we see it by experience; nor ever believe our society might be maintained with so little art and human combination.

Dryden also used passages from 'Of Cannibals' in *The Indian Emperour*. The first scene of the play is set in 'a pleasant Indian Country' in Mexico. And the play opens with dialogue between Cortez and his subordinate, Vasquez.

Cortez.   On what new happy Climate are wee throwne,
        Soe long kept secret, and soe lately knowne;

---

[44] 220.

[45] The translation by J.M. Cohen (*Montaigne: Essays*, Penguin Classics, 1958) runs: 'There is no kind of commerce, no knowledge of letters, no science of numbers, no title of magistrate or of political superior, no habit of service, riches or poverty, no contracts, no inheritance, no divisions of property, only leisurely occupations, no respect for any kinship but the common ties, no clothes, no agriculture, no metals, no use of corn or wine' (p.110). The 'use' of corn presumably refers to liquor.

[46] Genuity: simplicity.

	As if our old world modestly withdrew,
	And heere, in private, had brought forth a new!
Vasquez.	Corne, Wine and Oyle are wanting to this ground,
	In which our Countryes fruitfully abound:
	As if this infant world, yet unarray'd,
	Naked and bare, in Nature's lapp were layd.
	Noe usefull Arts have yet found footeing here;
	But all untaught, and Salvage, does appeare.
Cortez.	Wild and untaught are termes which wee alone
	Invent, for fashions diffring from our owne:
	For all their Customes are by Nature wrought,
	But wee by Art, unteach what Nature taught.

Montaigne ends the essay nicely:[47] 'All that is not very ill; but what of that? They wear no kind of breeches nor hosen.' (*Tout cela ne va pas trop mal: mais quoy, ils ne portent point de haut de chausses!*)

Implicit in this essay of 1580 is the theme which Montaigne was to develop in 1588. Once, indeed, it is explicit:[48] the Indians are

ignorant how dear the knowledge of our corruptions will one day cost their repose, security, and happiness, and how their ruin shall proceed from this commerce, which I imagine is already well advanced (miserable as they are to have suffered themselves to be so cozened by a desire of newfangled novelties).

Book Three of the *Essais*, published in 1588, contained *Des Coches*, 'Of Coaches'. In 1584 there had appeared in French translation (by Martin Fumée) the *Historia General de las Indias*, of Francisco López de Gómara (1512-1560), the Spanish original of which was published at Saragossa in 1552. This had appeared in Latin and Italian before Montaigne prepared the 1580 essays; and indeed the imaginary commonwealth passage, among others, in 'Of Cannibals' incorporated material found in Gómara.[49] But the impact of the Gómara material about Mexico and Peru was revealed only in *Des Coches*.

The 1588 essay took up a theme of·1580. 'Our world hath of late discovered another':[50]

no less-large, fully-peopled, all-things-yielding, and mighty in strength, than ours: nevertheless so new and infantine, that he is yet to learn his A.B.C. It is not yet full fifty years that he knew neither letters, nor weight, nor measures, nor apparel, nor corn, nor vines. But all was naked, simply-pure, in Nature's lap, and lived but with such means and food as his mother-nurse afforded him (*ny lettres, ny pois, ny mesure, ny vestements, ny bleds, ny vignes. Il estoit encore tout nud au giron, et ne vivoit que des moyens de sa mère nourrice*).

But Montaigne was now concerned with the nature of the Spanish

47 229.   48 228.
49 Sayce, *Essays of Montaigne*, 193.
50 III, 141.

claim to America. The Spanish appeared on behalf of the King of Castile, 'the greatest king of the habitable earth, unto whom the Pope, representing God on earth, had given the principality of all the Indies'. The conquerors declared that if the Indians would become 'tributaries' to the king, 'they should be most kindly used and courteously entreated'. And they pressed the Indians to embrace Spanish Christianity, 'adding thereto some minatory threats'. The Indian reply was that the Pope had given 'unto a third man, a thing which was not his own'; that 'they would by no means change their religion, under which they had for so long time lived so happily'; that 'they were not accustomed to take any counsel, but of their friends and acquaintance'; and that their only concern was to live their lives 'happily and pleasantly'.[51]

The Spanish had an easy opportunity 'profitably to reform, and christianly to instruct, minds yet so pure and new, so willing to be taught, being for the most part endowed with so docile, so apt and so yielding natural beginnings'. They could have presented the Indian with 'examples, demeanours and policies' which would have 'allured those uncorrupted nations, to the admiration and imitation of virtue' and 'established between them and us a brotherly society and mutual correspondency'. If only the Conquest had been by Alexander, or the 'ancient Greeks and Romans', or by

such hands as would gently have polished, reformed and incivilised, what in them they deemed to be barbarous and rude: or would have nourished and fostered those good seeds, which nature had there brought forth: adding not only to the manuring of their grounds and ornaments of their cities, such arts as we had; and that no further than had been necessary for them, but therewithal joining unto the original virtues of the country, those of the ancient Grecians and Romans.

Instead, the Europeans made use of the Indians' 'ignorance and inexperience, to draw them more easily unto treason, fraud, luxury, avarice, and all manner of inhumanity and cruelty, by the example of our life and pattern of our customs''.[52]

Montaigne dwelt on the 'proud pomp and glorious magnificence' of Mexico and Peru: 'Nor Greece, nor Rome, nor Egypt can (be it in profit, or difficulty or nobility) equal or compare sundry and divers of the works.'[53]

The wonderful, or as I may call it, amazement-breeding magnificence of the never-like seen cities of Cuzco and Mexico, and amongst infinite such like things, the admirable garden of that king, where all the trees, the fruits, the herbs and plants, according to the order and greatness they have in a garden, were most artificially framed in gold: as also in his cabinet, all the living creatures that his country or his seas produced, were cast in gold; and the exquisite beauty of their works, in precious stones, in feathers, in cotton and

[51] 145. [52] 144. [53] 150.

in painting: show that they yielded as little unto us in cunning and industry.[54]

Think also of the walled highway in Peru, with its streams of running water, from Quito to Cuzco.[55] Equally striking was their 'excellency of natural wit, or perspicuity'. The Indians out-do the Europeans in 'unfeigned devotion, awful observance of laws, unspotted integrity, bounteous liberality, due loyalty and free liberty'. As also in 'hardiness and undaunted courage', in 'matchless constancy, unmoved assuredness, undismayed resolution against pain, smarting, famine and death itself': indeed here they rival 'the most famous ancient examples we may with all our industry discover in all the annals and memories of our known old world'.[56]

The Indians were 'for the most altogether unarmed, except some bows, stones, staves and wooden bucklers'. They were 'unsuspecting poor people', 'silly naked people, saving where the invention of weaving of cotton cloth was known and used'. But they had 'curiosity to see strange and unknown things' – such as the invaders, 'mounted on great and unknown monsters'.[57] Thus the invaders could use the 'wiles, the policies and stratagems' to 'cozen, to conycatch, and to circumvent them'; 'under colour of amity and well-meaning faith'.[58] We 'sold him our opinions, our new-fangles, and our arts'. 'I fear, that by our contagion, we shall directly have furthered his declination and hastened his ruin.'[59] Worse, the Conquest was

so bloody a butchery, as upon savage beasts; and so universal as fire or sword could ever attain unto; having purposely preserved no more than so many miserable bond-slaves, as they deemed might suffice for the digging, working and service of their mines.

A matter of 'great pillages, and ill gotten goods'. The Spanish might have considered that Christianity is not to be propagated 'by possession of lands, but of men': they might have been 'satisfied with such slaughters, as the necessity of war bringeth'.[60] Instead:

So many goodly cities ransacked and razed; so many nations destroyed and made desolate; so infinite millions of harmless people of all sexes, states and ages, massacred, ravaged and put to the sword; and the richest, the fairest and the best part of the world topsiturvied, ruined and defaced for the traffic of pearls and pepper.

O mechaniques victoires: in Florio's version, 'Oh mechanical victories, oh base conquest.'[61]

Montaigne gave details of the conquest of Mexico by Cortés from 1520. Montezuma, the Aztec king, of 'unmatched constancy', treated with 'inhumane cruelty': the 'cruellest tortures and horriblest torments' of 'barbarous minds'.[62] There was a section on the murder

[54] 142. [55] 150. [56] 142. [57] 143. [58] 142-3. [59] 142. [60] 148. [61] 144. [62] 147-8.

in 1533 of Atahualpa, the Inca king of Peru: deposed, baptised, publicly hanged and strangled, before his 'silly unsuspecting people, amazed and astonished at so strange a spectacle': 'A horrible and the like never heard of accident.' Atahualpa had shown himself to be of a 'free, liberal, undaunted and constant courage', a 'pure, noble, and well composed understanding': he endured his death 'with an unmoved manner, and truly-royal gravity, without ever contradicting himself either in countenance or speech'.[63] 'These narrations we have out of their own books.'[64] In sum:[65]

It was an unpolluted, harmless, infant world; yet have we not whipped and submitted the same unto our discipline, or schooled him by the advantage of our valour or natural forces, nor have we instructed him by our justice and integrity; nor subdued by our magnanimity.

The English translation of *The Essais of Michell lord of Montaigne* appeared in 1603; and again in 1613 and 1632. John Florio, a well-connected language tutor, was 50.[66] His parents were Italian Protestants, who had come to England; John was born in London in 1553. The father had been a Franciscan friar; converted to Protestantism in the early 1540s, he arrived in England in 1550, and became pastor of the London congregation of Italian protestants. He married in London. He also taught Italian to Lady Jane Grey (daughter of Henry Grey, Duke of Suffolk; wife of John Dudley, Northumberland's son). And he was to write an Italian biography of Lady Jane, published in Venice in 1607. The family left England in 1554, when John was scarcely one year old, and went to Strasbourg: Marian Exiles by adoption, so to speak. John was probably educated at Tübingen: he appears never to have visited Italy. He came to England, unable to speak English, about 1570, and settled in London. In 1578 he published *First Fruits*, a series of dialogues for the teaching of Italian, in the Erasmus tradition. And in 1578, when he was about 25, he went to teach Italian at Oxford. In 1581 he was registered at Magdalen as a 'poor scholar'.

At Florio's Oxford the Reverend Richard Hakluyt – three years his senior – was an M.A. of Christ Church.[67] In the Epistle Dedicatory to the *Principall Navigations* of 1589 Hakluyt gave memorable snatches of autobiography. As a schoolboy at Westminster in the mid-1560s (his father was a member of the Skinners' Company) Hakluyt visited his elder cousin at the Middle Temple, saw his 'universal map' and 'certain books of cosmography', and was reminded of the words of Psalm 107: 'They which go down to the sea in ships, and occupy the great waters, they see the works of the Lord, and his wonders in the deep.' He resolved to pursue such studies at Oxford. He went up to

---

[63] 146-7.   [64] 148.   [65] 142.

[66] Yates, *John Florio*, 1934.

[67] Details of Hakluyt's career from D.B. and A.M. Quinn, 'A Hakluyt Chronology', in D.B. Quinn, ed., *The Hakluyt Handbook*, vol.1, (Hakluyt Society 1974).

Christ Church in the autumn of 1570, when he was about $18\frac{1}{2}$ – rather elderly for a Tudor freshman: 15 or 16 was more usual. He had an allowance of £2.13.4 each year from the Skinners' Company. He took his B.A. in 1574, when he was 22. Apart from the regular academic curriculum, he read all the available travel literature: Greek, Latin; Spanish, Portuguese, Italian, French; and English. He was an M.A. in 1577; and began the graduate course in Theology. As a young resident M.A. he had the duty of lecturing in the University: and

in my public lectures I was the first that produced and showed both the old, imperfectly composed, and the new, lately reformed, maps, globes, spheres, and other instruments of this art for demonstration, in the Common Schools; to the singular pleasure and general contentment of the auditory.

(The Common Schools: University, rather than College, lectures.) Hakluyt, then, did the sort of thing John Dee had wished to do at Cambridge in the reign of Edward VI, when he was a Fellow of Trinity: he did it in Louvain and Paris instead. In 1582 Hakluyt suggested that a lectureship in navigation should be endowed in London or Oxford, worth at least £40 a year:[68] slightly more than the salary (exactly £40) of the Regius Professors. The average don got less than £10 a year. (In 1571 Dee had appealed for new Readers in Mathematics at Cambridge and Oxford, to have £65 a year.)[69] Hakluyt's Oxford audience probably included Thomas Hariot, who was at St Mary's Hall from 1577 to 1580; Hariot's home was in Oxford.

Hakluyt was ordained priest in the late 1570s, and did his stint of preaching, both in Oxford and in London. He remained basically resident at Christ Church until the summer of 1583; when, after over twelve years at Oxford, he was given leave of absence to go to Paris as chaplain and secretary to the English ambassador. He vacated his Fellowship in 1586.

Florio's Italian was an indispensable gift to the Hakluyt circle. And Hakluyt was soon providing Florio with financial support, to work on the literature. The first result was published in 1580: *A Shorte and briefe narration of the two Navigations and Discoveries to the North weast partes called Newe Fraunce.*

This was a 'narration' of the two voyages of Jacques Cartier: 1534, and 1535-36. Florio translated the Italian version by Giovanni Ramusio, published in 1556 in his *Delle Navigationi et Viaggi.* Cartier's own account of the first voyage (or an edited version thereof) was rediscovered only in the nineteenth century: so Ramusio was definitive for this expedition of 1534 – to Newfoundland, Labrador, the Magdalen Islands, Prince Edward Island, and Gaspé Bay. An edited version of Cartier's account of the second voyage was printed in Paris in 1545:

[68] Hakluyt, *Divers Voyages*, ed. Jones, 16-17.
[69] Dee, 'Mathematical Preface', a.iiii.r.

Brief recit, & succincte narration, de la navigation faicte esysles de Canada, Hochelage & Saguenay & autres, avec particulieres meurs, langaige, & cerimonies des habitans d'icelles: fort delectable a veoir.

In 1535-36 Cartier had gone down the St Lawrence to Quebec and Montreal.[70] The Ramusio/Florio book was incorporated by Hakluyt into the 1600 volume of *Principal Navigations*. Cartier made a third voyage in 1541. When Hakluyt was in Paris in the 1580s, he acquired an account of this expedition from a crew member; and translated this himself for his 1600 volume.

Florio wrote a preface, dated 25 June, for the 1580 *Shorte and briefe narration*. He pointed out that the Indians, 'though simple and rude in manners, and destitute of the knowledge of God or any good laws' are 'of nature gentle and tractable, and most apt to receive the Christian religion, and to subject themselves to some good government'. The opportunity was taken to prod the laggardly English. The opportunities of America 'might suffice to induce our Englishmen, not only to fall to some traffic with the inhabitants, but also to plant a colony in some convenient place'.[71] The guiding hand of Hakluyt is apparent.

The poet Samuel Daniel (1562-1619) was at Magdalen from 1579 to 1582. (There is a tradition that Florio married Daniel's sister.) In 1602 Daniel published a poem in defence of learning, *Musophilus*. A passage at the end of this, in praise of Eloquence, may be taken as enthusiastically expressing the hopes of the Oxford group of 1580.[72]

> And who, in time, knows whither we may vent
> The treasure of our tongue, to what strange shores
> This gain of our best glory shall be sent,
> T'inrich unknowing Nations with our stores?
> What worlds in th'yet unformed Occident
> May come refin'd with th'accents that are ours?
> Or, who can tell for what great work in hand
> The greatness of our style is now ordain'd?

It should also be noted that by 1594, Florio was Italian tutor to Henry Wriothesley, the young Earl of Southampton (born in 1573), a future patron of Virginia.

Florio, who taught Italian to Queen Anne, and possibly to Prince Henry (1594-1612), died in London in 1625. By then, some at least of his hopes of 1580 had been realised:[73]

Thus beseeching God that this my travail may take that effect for the which it is meant, I commend the diligent consideration to all such gentlemen,

---

[70] For the Cartier voyages, Morison, *Northern Voyages*, chs. 11 and 12.
[71] 'To all Gentlemen, Merchants and Pilots': B.i.r.-B.ii.v. Facsimile reprint 1967 in Quinn, *Richard Hakluyt, Editor*.
[72] Daniel, *Complete Works*, ed. Grosart, 1885, I, 255.
[73] Florio, preface to *Shorte and briefe narration*, B.ii.v.

merchants and pilots as seek God's glory, the advancement of their country; and the happy success to the providence of the Almighty, who in my opinion hath not in vain stirred up the minds of so many honourable and worshipful persons to the furtherance of these commendable and worthy discoveries. *In Oxford, J.F.*

8

Las Casas in English

In 1583 there was printed in London a book *written in the Castilian tongue by the reverend Bishop Bartholomew de las Casas or Casaus, a Friar of the order of S. Dominicke. And now first translated into english, by M.M.S.* The English title was *The Spanish Colonie, or Briefe Chronicle of the Acts and gestes of the Spaniardes in the West Indies, called the newe World, for the space of xl yeeres*; or, as the title in the body of the text has it (A.1.r) *A brief narration of the destruction of the Indies by the Spaniards.* The running title was *The Spanish Cruelties.* The 'space of forty years': Fray Bartolomé de Las Casas completed the manuscript, he tells us, at Valencia on 8 December 1542 (M.3.r). It was published in 1552 at Seville as *Brevissima relacion de la destruycion de las Indias.* (In modern Spanish: *Brevísima relación de la destruición de las Indias.*) The English text of the work ran to 104 pages, printed in black letter. It had previously been translated into Flemish (1578) and French (1579); a German translation was to come in 1597, and Latin versions in 1592 and 1598. The latter had engravings of atrocities, done by Theodore de Bry from drawings by Jodocus a Winghe.

M.M.S appears to have worked from the Flemish edition. Or, at any rate, he translated its Preface, 'To the Reader' – which pointed out that the Low Countries should know their enemy, and the policy which there 'had not God stopped their course, they had long since put in execution'; and praising Las Casas, who 'durst oppose himself to his cruel and barbarous nation'.

In the prologue, Las Casas characterised his book as a 'brief summary of a most large history that might and ought to be written of such slaughter and sports as they have made and perpetrated'. Casas left in manuscript such a history when he died in 1566 at the age of 92. Or rather, two histories: *Historia de las Indias*, in 1,199 folios, first printed in the 1870s; and *Apologética historia sumaria ... de las gentes destas Indias occidentales y meridionales*, first printed in part in 1876, and in full in 1909.[1]

[1] The definitive text of the *Historia* is that of 1951, three volumes, over 1500 pages (Mexico); and of the *Apologética Historia*, that edited in 1967 by Edmundo O'Gorman, two volumes, over 1350 pages (Mexico). My material about Las Casas' works is from the 'Narrative and Critical Catalogue' in Wagner and Parish, *Life and Writings of Bartolomé de las Casas*, 1967, 253-98. The biography published in 1909 by Macnutt is

Las Casas was concerned, he wrote in the 'Prologue' to Prince Philip, with 'this so large new world of the Indies, which God and holy Church have committed and commended unto the King of Castile'. Let Charles I (the Emperor Charles) 'take some order for this New World that God hath given him'. Las Casas feared 'the utter ruin and perdition of this new world'. He was

come into this Court of Spain to see that the hell might be withdrawn from the Indies, and that these innumerable souls, redeemed by the blood of Jesus Christ, should not perish for evermore without remedy, but that they might know their Creator and be saved. Also for the care and compassion that I have of my country, which is Castile, to the end that God destroy it not for the great sins thereof, committed against the faith and His honour, and against our neighbours. (M.3.r-v.)

Las Casas thought that by his 'relation' 'a man may see, in what estimation the Spaniards have the Indians; and how they accomplish the commandment of God touching the love of their neighbour, of the which dependeth the law and the prophets' (H.4.r). The allusion is to the account in Matthew's Gospel (22:35-40) of the lawyer among the Pharisees who tested Christ with the question 'which is the greatest commandment in the Law?'

Jesus said unto him, Thou shalt love the Lord thy God with all thy heart, and with all thy soul, and with all thy mind. This is the first and great commandment. And the second is like unto it, Thou shalt love thy neighbour as thyself. On these two commandments hang all the law and the prophets.

Las Casas had been ordained priest in Hispaniola in 1510, when he was 36, by the Dominican Prior Pedro de Córdoba, who had arrived earlier in the year (one of the first four Dominican friars in the Indies), and who had a papal faculty to administer ordination. Las Casas was a 'plantation owner', an *encomendero*, who had been in Hispaniola since 1502: his father, who had been on the second Columbus voyage (1493-6) had remained in the Indies – and sent back an Indian youth for his son; the youth was returned to the Indies in 1500, with other transported Indians, by order of an indignant Queen Isabella.[2]

'Plantation owner' is not an accurate rendering of *encomendero*. The dictionary definition of *encomienda* is concession, holding; it was a

---

still useful, and well written: *Bartholomew De Las Casas: His Life, His Apostolate, and His Writings.* MacNutt printed his own complete translation of the *Brevissima Relacion*: 311-424. Hanke is the doyen of present day Las Casas scholars: of his many books, the most comprehensive are *The Spanish Struggle for Justice in the Conquest of America*, 1949; and *Aristotle and the American Indians: A Study in Race Prejudice in the Modern World*, 1959. Among English scholars, Elliott: *Imperial Spain*, 1963; *The Old World and the New 1492-1650*, 1970; *The Discovery of America and the Discovery of Man*, Raleigh Lecture, 1972. Parry, *The Age of Reconnaissance*, 1963, is extremely useful: especially the final chapter, 'Rights of Conquerors and Conquered'. See also Part I, 'Theoretical Assumptions', of Washburn, *Red Man's Land-White Man's Law*.

  [2] MacNutt, 6-7.

conferring of lordship over Indians (not a grant of land). The holder of such a concession was an *encomendero*: commissioner, the dictionary says. Professor J.H. Elliott tells me that the words are not translatable. So hereafter they will be given in Spanish.

In 1511, Las Casas took part in the conquest of Cuba. In preparing a sermon in Cuba in 1514, he was struck by a passage from the Book of Ecclesiasticus, in the Apocrypha, which occasioned his 'change of heart'. Chapter 34, verses 18-22:[3]

> A sacrifice derived from ill-gotten gains is contaminated,
> a lawless mockery that cannot win approval.
> The Most High is not pleased with the offering of the godless,
> nor do endless sacrifices win his forgiveness.
> To offer a sacrifice from the possessions of the poor
> is like killing a son before his father's eyes.
> Bread is life to the destitute,
> and it is murder to deprive them of it.
> To rob your neighbour of his livelihood is to kill him,
> and the man who cheats a worker of his wages sheds blood.

Las Casas renounced his *encomienda*. He was then forty. In 1515 he returned to Spain, and was interviewed by the dying Ferdinand. He returned in 1516, having been given the title 'Protector of the Indians'. His periods in the Indies were: 1502-15; 1516-17; 1520-40; 1545-7. In 1523 he became a Dominican. In 1544, at Seville, he was consecrated Bishop of Chiapa, Mexico. His programme as Bishop insisted that the Indians should be freed from slavery, extortion, and being worked like beasts – and from all other tyrannies of the plantation owners, hindering preaching by the friars.[4] His period in the diocese, of less than one year, was unhappy and controversial.

His first book was written in Latin during his period in Mexico in the late 1530s. Only a part of the manuscript survives; this was printed in 1942. It concerned 'the only way of attracting all peoples to the true faith': *De unico vocationis modo omnium gentium ad veram religionem*. Las Casas maintained in the book that the Indians are 'ingenious, and even more so than other peoples, in the government of human life'. They have 'common sense, imagination, fantasy, memory'; temperance, continence, indifference to wordly goods, and great artistic skill. They have – all people have – a capacity to understand the Gospel. They have never harmed the Christians: to make war on them would be 'unjust, perverse and tyrannical'.

One and only is the method that Divine Providence instituted in all the world and at all times to teach men the true religion; namely that which persuades the understanding with reason, and gently attracts the will; and this is common to all men without any difference.

[3] New English Bible translation.
[4] Wagner and Parish, 145.

'Corruption of customs' is not relevant to the point.[5]

After his return in 1547, Las Casas remained in Spain until his death in 1566. His will (July 1566) was permeated by the themes of his life, as most influentially expressed in the *Brevísima relación*. In the will,[6] Las Casas acknowledged that God 'saw fit to choose me as his minister' to 'plead for all those people of the Indies': 'rational men, peaceful, humble, most amenable and simple beings, well fitted to receive our holy Catholic faith.' From the Spaniards, the Indian had received only 'unheard of and unimagined oppressions and evils and injuries.' The Indians had been robbed, enslaved and killed. Their lands had been reduced to 'universal desolations'. Their 'primitive liberty' had been 'unjustly taken from them'. The Spaniards had committed 'sins' and 'injustices'; contrary to both 'natural reason' and the gospel of Christ. They obscured the Faith, and made infamous the name of Christ by their 'impious and ignominious works, so unjustly and tyranically and barbarously committed'. 'God will pour His fury and anger upon Spain if she does not perform a great penance.' Such penitence was unlikely; because of Spanish 'blindness' and 'denseness of understanding'.

The English reader learnt in 1583 that the Indians are 'poor innocent people' (Prologue); 'harmless' and 'silly' (D.4.v); 'peaceable' (I.2.v); 'amiable', 'meek as lambs' (I.1.v) – 'those so sweet lambs' (M.1.v). They are 'as free born as I am' (D.1.r).

God created all these innumerable multitudes in every sort very simple, without subtlety or craft, without malice, very obedient and faithful to their natural liege lords, and to the Spaniards whom they served, very humble, very patient, very desirous of peacemaking, and peaceful, without brawls and strugglings, without quarrels, without strife, without rancour or hatred, by no means desirous of revengement.

They are 'very gentle, and very tender, and of an easy complexion'. 'They are also very poor folk, which possess little, neither yet do so much as desire to have much wordly goods, therefore neither are they proud, ambitious, nor covetous.' Their food resembles that of the 'holy fathers in the desert' (A.1.r).

Most important, they are amenable to the Faith. 'Undoubtedly these folks should be the happiest in the world, if only they knew God.'

They have their understanding very pure and quick, being teachable and capable of all good learning, very apt to receive our holy Catholic faith, and to be instructed in good and virtuous manners, having less encumbrances and disturbances to the attaining thereto than all the folk of the world besides; and are so inflamed, ardent and importune to know and understand the matters of the faith after they have but begun to taste them, as likewise the exercise of the sacraments of the Church, and the divine service. (A.1.r)

[5] *ibid.*, 101-2.
[6] *ibid.*, 239-40.

Fundamentally, Las Casas thought of the Indian as of a child of ten or twelve years old (B.2.v).

The Spanish laity in the Indies had been a hindrance to the Faith. They

have had no more care to procure that unto those people should be preached the faith of Jesus Christ than as if they had been cur dogs, or other beasts: but in lien thereof, which is much worse, they have forbidden by express means the Religious men to do it.

In 1542 'there is no more knowledge of God throughout the Indies, to wit whether He be of timber, of the air, or the earth, than there was an hundred years ago'; except where 'the Religious men have gone, which is but a little corner of the Indies'. Thus the Indians 'perish all without faith, and without sacraments' (M.2.v).

As a model, Las Casas tells of five Franciscans who arrived in Yucatan after there had been seven years of lay colonisation: to 'pacify' and 'preach to' and 'to win unto Jesus Christ' those Indians 'which might be remaining' (F.4.v). The Gospel had not yet been heard there. The friars 'persuaded and induced':

After the end of forty days that they had preached unto them, the lords of the country brought unto them and put into their hands their idols, to the end that they should burn them. After also, they brought unto them their young children, that they should catechise them, whom they love as the apple of their eye. They made for them also churches and temples and houses. (G.1.r)

In all places, Indians received friars

as angels comen from heaven; and heard with great affection, attention and willingness such words as the Religious at that time were able to give them to understand, more by signs than otherwise, for they knew not the tongue. (H.2.r)

(Las Casas himself never achieved fluency in the Indian tongues: he was not 'Apostle to the Indians', but their *Procurador* in Spain.)

The pernicious thing was the *Requerimiento*, the 'requirement'. This document, to be read to the Indians by the Spaniards, was first taken to the Indies in 1514.[7] The Indians were to acknowledge the authority of the Pope and of the rulers of Castile over the Indies (by Alexander VI's Bull of May 1493), and agree to accept the Faith; if they refused, the Spaniards could legimately proceed by fire and sword, take slaves, and seize land and goods. The first recorded use was in 1514 by Oviedo; he made fun of it by reading it aloud in a deserted village. (Las Casas said of the *Requerimiento* that he was unable to decide

---

[7] Material here from Hanke, *Spanish Struggle for Justice*, ch.3: 'The Requirement – A Most Remarkable Document'.

whether to laugh or cry.) The so-called 'first letter' of Cortés described its use in Yucatan in 1519:[8]

After having read the *requerimiento* to them three times, and having asked Your Royal Highness' notary to witness that he did not want war; but seeing that the Indians were most resolutely determined to prevent him from landing, and indeed had already begun to shoot arrows at us, he had ordered us to fire the guns and attack.

Las Casas wrote in 1552/1583 of these 'orders' to 'receive the faith, and render themselves unto the obedience of the King of Castile, or otherwise to bid them battle with fire and sword, and to slay them or make them slaves':

As if the Son of God which died for every one of them had commanded in His law, where He saith Go teach all nations, that there should be ordinances set down unto infidels, being peaceful and quiet and in possession of their proper land, if so be they received it not forthwith, without any preaching or teaching first had, and if they submitted not themselves to the dominion of a King whom they never saw, and whom they never heard speak of, and namely such a one whose messengers and men were so cruel, and so debarred from all pity, and such horrible tyrants, that they should for that lose their goods and lands, their liberty, their wives and children, with their lives. Which is a thing too absurd and fond, worthy of all reproach and mockery, yea worthy of hell. (C.1.v)

The Spaniards have been the initial offenders.

I know for certain and infallible, that the Indians had evermore most just cause of war against the Spaniards; but the Spaniards never had any just cause of war against the Indians, but they were all diabolical and most unrighteous, more than can be spoken of any tyrant that is on the whole earth.

The Indians 'never committed against the Spaniards any one mortal offence punishable by the law of man' (B.2.v). They 'never wrought any displeasure unto the Spaniards; but rather that they reputed them as come from heaven' (A.3.r). They 'never did harm unto the Spanish in any place wheresoever, until such time that they first received wrongs' (M.2.v). They

never gave no more occasion or cause, than might a convent of good religious persons well ordered, why they should be robbed and slain, and why they that escaped the death should be retained in a perpetual captivity and bondage. (B.2.v)

The bulk of the 'brief narration' was devoted to atrocity stories: in Hispaniola, Jamaica, Cuba, and Trinidad; Florida (from 1528) and

---

[8] *Cortés: Letters from Mexico*, tr. Pagden, 20.

Peru (which Casas never visited); and (modern) Mexico, Guatemala, Nicaragua, Colombia, and Venezuela. We have Montezuma (D.3-D.4); and Atahualpa (K.4.r) – here Las Casas based his account on the report of a Franciscan eye-witness (who considered the Incas 'the most kind hearted that ever hath been seen among all the Indians'). The theme, of course, is the 'most pernicious blindness which hath always possessed those who have governed the Indians, instead of the care which they should have for the conversion and salvation of those people, which they have always neglected' (C.1.v). Because of the wars and massacres 'there are dead more than fifteen millions of souls' (A.2.v). (Elsewhere he had 12 million, and 20 million: the population of Central Mexico on the eve of the Conquest was possibly 25 million.) Las Casas' statistics passed into the European consciousness:[9] the famous assertion that the population of Hispaniola had been reduced from three million to 200, for instance (A.2.r). Without 'the present succour of his Majesty to stay these unnatural devilish tyrannies, there will not remain as much as one man alive' (M.1.r). The Spaniards 'tear them in pieces, kill them, afflict them, torment them, and destroy them by strange sorts of cruelties' (A.1.r); using, for instance, hounds specially trained to tear Indians apart (M.2.r). Las Casas himself saw in Cuba 'so great cruelties, that never any man living either have or shall see the like' (B.4.v). In Hispaniola, where the Indians are 'the best made and most beautiful' (B.1.v), Casas saw 'infinite' horrors (A.4.r); including the roasting alive of five Indian chiefs on a grid-iron. (A.3.v). 'I have seen all the aforesaid things'; and he knew the perpetrators – 'I know his name, and friends in Seville' (A.4.r). There is for the reader, unfortunately perhaps, a law of diminishing returns in an incessant parade of atrocities. One passage can suffice. An Indian youth of Yucatan in the 1530s had refused to leave his home. A Spaniard

drawing out his dagger cut off first one then the other ear. The young man abiding by it still that he would not leave his country, he mangled off also his nose, with the uppermost of his lips, making no more scrupulosity of the matter, than if he had given him but a fillip. This damnable wretch magnified himself, and vaunted him of his doings villainously unto a reverend religious person, saying that he took as much pains as he could, to beget the Indian women in great numbers with child, to the end he might receive the more money for them in selling them great with child for slaves; ... a certain Spaniard went one day with his dogs on hunting of venison, or else conies, and, not finding game, he minded his dogs that they should be hungry, and took a little sweet baby, which he bereaved the mother of, and cutting off from him the arms and the legs, chopped them in small gobbets, giving to every dog his livery or part thereof; by and by, after

[9] On Mexico statistics, Elliott, *Imperial Spain*, Mentor ed., 288. Cook and Simpson, *Population of Mexico in the 16th Century*. It appears that the Indian population of Central Mexico was 11 million in 1520, $6\frac{1}{2}$ million by 1540 and $2\frac{1}{2}$ million by 1600. See also Parry, *Spanish Seaborne Empire*, Ch.11. Modern scholars point out the importance of epidemics and so on, rather than extermination as a sole factor.

these morsels thus dispatched, he cast also the rest of the body or the carcass to all the kennel together. (F.4.r-v)

For those not slain, there was 'bondage and calamity' (B.3.v): 'the most cruel, dreadful and heinous thraldom that ever hath been laid upon men or beasts" (A.2.v).

What was the cause of these hard hearts? The 'Prologue' pin-pointed the Biblical words: 'Avarice'; 'ambition'. The diagnosis is insisted upon in the text. The 'perverse, wilfully blind and obstinate greediness and insatiable wretchedness of these most covetous tyrants' (I.4.r). The Spaniards are 'blinded with the covetousness of the riches' of the Indies (F.4.v). They are like Jeroboam, King of Israel, in the first Book of Kings, who built calves of gold to rival the Temple at Jerusalem (Chapter 12): as Las Casas has it, 'made Israel to sin by making two golden calves for the people to fall down before'. They are also like Judas (G.2.r). Although 'bearing the name of Christians', they are 'cursed' (H.3.r). By their treatment of a people 'created after the image of God, and redeemed with the blood of His Christ' they show that 'God hath delivered them up into a reprobate sense' (F.4.v). Of a certain 'tyrant' in Florida, Casas wrote:

We need not to doubt but that he lieth buried in hell; if algates [nevertheless] God of His infinite mercy secretly dispensed in His hidden wisdom hath not prevented him; not dealing with him after his demerits. (K.1.v)

In 1512 two friars from the Indies had appeared before Ferdinand. The Dominican, Antonio Montesinos, had preached in Hispaniola in December 1511 against the Spanish treatment of the Indian,[10] and reports of his sentiments had alarmed the Dominicans in Spain: Montesinos was said to have denied the right of Spain to conquer the Indies. The other friar, a Franciscan, was sent by the colonists to present a defence of Spanish activities. Ferdinand was impressed by Montesinos, and appointed a committee of lawyers and theologians to consider the matter.[11] The Dominican Bernardo de Mesa stressed the incapacity of the Indian. The Indians are a prey to idleness; they are inconstant; they have no natural inclination to the Faith; by nature they have a lack of understanding, and no capacity for goodness; by astrological influence they are servile. Thus the King of Castile can take charge of them for their own good, by entrusting them to faithful colonists; for their own sake they must be regulated in some sort of servitude. (Las Casas later said his fellow Dominican – who had never been to the Indies – regarded the Indians as savages to be divided up like cattle.) The committee did not disallow the system which had developed in Spanish America during the past decade: the *encomienda*. The Indian, though free, and able to possess his own land and property, must be obliged to work – and receive wages in kind; they

---

[10] See above, p.101.
[11] Material here from Wagner and Parish, 8-11.

must be useful to the King under whose lordship they were. Only one member of the commission struck at the notion of Indian servitude: a Dominican ally of Montesinos, Matías de Paz. His Latin manuscript *De dominio regum Hispaniae super Indos*, not published until 1933, argued that the plantations were despotic, and that the Spaniards were obliged to render restitution – a point which in 1514 was accepted by Las Casas. The result of the commission was the Laws of Burgos of December 1512; confirming the *encomienda* and the custom of Indian forced labour.

One of Las Casas' enemies (or so Las Casas thought) was the planter and colonial official Oviedo. Gonzalo Fernández de Oviedo (1478-1577): best known, surely, as Oviedo, though sometimes placed by index-makers and library cataloguers under 'F'. A courtier-soldier, Oviedo went to the Caribbean in 1514 as an overseer of the mining and smelting of gold on the mainland. He eventually became well established in Colombia, in the town of Santa María del Antigua del Darién; with a house

of such sort that I may well entertain and commodiously lodge any Lord or nobleman, reserving also a part for myself and family. For in this may many households be kept, both above and beneath. It hath also a fair garden with many orange trees both sweet and sour; cedars also, and lemonds, of the which there is now great plenty in the houses of the Christians. On one side of the garden there runneth a fair river. The situation is very pleasant, with a good and wholesome air, and a fair prospect about the river.

(Translation by Richard Eden, 1555.)[12]

Oviedo and Las Casas clashed in Barcelona in 1519.[13] Las Casas was soliciting a land grant on the mainland; and proposing to convert the Indians. Oviedo was among those opposing the concession; and eventually Las Casas was allowed a more modest grant in Venezuela. Las Casas was to write of Oviedo:[14]

He was one of the greatest enemies the Indians have had and has done them the worst harm, for he was blinder than others in not knowing the truth, perhaps because of his greater cupidity and ambition, qualities and customs which have destroyed the Indies.

Oviedo was an *encomendero*. He was also a naturalist and a reporter: his idol was Pliny (another Spaniard). He began work on a 'natural' and 'general' history of the Indies, being commissioned to write it by Charles. The *Natural hystoria de las Indias* was published at Toledo in 1526: 'a brilliant account of the flora, fauna, geography, folk-lore and customs of the natives of the Caribbean area.'[15] It appeared in Italian

[12] Arber (ed.), *First Three English Books on America*, 238.
[13] Wagner and Parish, 53-9.
[14] *ibid.*, 53-4.
[15] Stoudemire, Introduction to his translation: *Natural History of the West Indies*, 1959, ix. In 1969 the University of North Carolina Press published, in honour of Stoudemire, a facsimile of the 1526 edition.

in 1534, and in French in 1545. And in 1555 Richard Eden published his extracted, re-arranged and often cavalier translation as the second part of *The Decades of the newe worlde of west India*; Gonzalus Ferdinandus Oviedus being the best authority after Pietro Martire.[16]

The 1555 *Decades of the newe worlde* has been considered in Chapter 4, in relation to Pietro Martire. We now discuss the translation of Oviedo's material on the Indian – remembering that Oviedo was primarily a naturalist in the 1526 book, and the Indian material was not his prime concern.[17]

Of the Indians of Hispaniola, we read:[18]

The people of this island are commonly of somewhat less stature than are the Spaniards, and of shining or clear brown colour. They have wives of their own, and abstain from their daughters, sisters and mothers. They have large foreheads, long black hair, and no beards or hair in any other parts of their body, as well men as women, except very few, as perhaps scarcely one among a thousand. They go as naked as they were born; except that on the parts which may not with honesty be seen, they wear a certain leaf as broad as a man's hand, which nevertheless is not kept close with such diligence but that sometimes a man may see that they think sufficiently hid.

On the mainland, one chief

had a great part of his body painted with a black colour which never fadeth; and is much like unto that wherewith the Moors paint themselves in Barbary, in token of nobility. But the Moors are painted specially on their visage and throat, and certain other parts. Likewise the principal Indians use these paintings on their arms and breasts, but not on their visages, because among them the slaves are so marked.

The Indians of the mainland 'give great honour and reverence' to their chiefs.[19] In many places, when the chief dies, his servants kill themselves, being taught by the Devil 'that they which kill themselves when the king dieth go with him to heaven and serve him in the same place and office'. Of those that refuse, it is thought that when they die their soul dies with the body, and is 'dissolved into air and become nothing, as do the souls of hogs, birds or fishes or other brute beasts'. The suicides have buried with them a 'portion of the grain of *Maizium*'; for possible use in heaven. Oviedo has seen this, having had two graves opened.[20]

The devil rules the Indian mind, in all regions:[21]

The devil, being so ancient an astronomer, knoweth the times of things and seeth how they are naturally directed and inclined. And maketh them believe

---

[16] Arber, 207.

[17] The Oviedo translation is pp.210-42 of Arber (ed.), *First Three English Books on America*. I give a page reference to Arber (A): followed by the relevant reference to Stoudemire (S).

[18] A:240-41. S:13.   [19] A:237. S:44.   [20] A:216. S:37.   [21] A:215. S:33-4.

that they come so to pass by his ordinance, as though he were the lord and mover of all that is and shall be. And that he giveth the day-light and rain; causeth tempest and ruleth the stations of times, giving life or taking away life at his pleasure. By reason whereof, the Indians being deceived of him, and seeing also such effects to come certainly to pass as he hath told them before, believe him in all other things and honour him in many places with sacrifices of the blood and lives of men, and odiferous spices. And when God disposeth the contrary to that which the devil hath spoken in oracle whereby he is proved a liar, he causeth the *Tequinas*[22] to persuade the people that he hath changed his mind and sentence for some of their sins, or deviseth some such lie as liketh him best, being a skilful master in such subtle and crafty devices to deceive the simple and ignorant people, which hath small defence against so mighty and crafty an adversary. And as they call the devil *Tuyra*, so do they in many places call the Christians by the same name, thinking that they greatly honour them thereby, as indeed it is a name very sweet and agreeable to many of them, having laid apart all honesty and virtue, living more like dragons than men among these simple people.

However, the coming of Christianity has meant a decline in devilish practices. It is to be noted that the 'great tempests' caused by the devil, 'so vehement that they overthrow many houses and great trees', have become lessened in force where the Holy Sacrament is reserved.[23]

Oviedo is very aware that 'the manners and customs of the Indians are diverse in divers provinces'. To a certain extent at any rate:[24]

Some of them take as many wives as them list, and other live with one wife whom they forsake not without consent of both parties, which chanceth especially when they have no children. The nobility, as well men as women, repute it infamous to join with any of base parentage, or strangers, except Christians, whom they count noble men by reason of their valiantness, although they put a difference between the common sort and the other to whom they show obedience, counting it for a great matter and an honourable thing if they be beloved of any of them. Insomuch that if they know any Christian man carnally, they keep their faith to him, so that he be not long absent far from them. For their intent is not to be widows, or to live chaste like religious women. Many of them have this custom, that when they perceive that they are with child, they take an herb wherewith they destroy that is conceived. For they say that only well aged women should bear children, and that they will not forbear their pleasures and deform their bodies with bearing of children, whereby their teats become loose and hanging, which thing they greatly dispraise. When they are delivered of their children, they go to the river and wash them. Which done, their blood and purgation ceaseth immediately. And when after this they have a few days abstained from the company of men, they become so straight, as they say which have had carnal familiarity with them, that such as use them cannot without much difficulty satisfy their appetite. They also which never had children are ever as virgins. In some parts they wear certain little apernes (aprons) round about them before and behind, as low as to their knees and hams, wherewith they cover their privy parts, and are naked all their body beside. The principal men bear their privities in a hollow pipe of gold; but

[22] The Priests: *Tequinas*.   [23] A:216. S:37.   [24] A:237. S:31-2.

the common sort have them enclosed in the shells of certain great welks, and are beside utterly naked. For they think it no more shame to have their cods seen, than any other part of their bodies. And in many provinces both the men and women go utterly naked, without any such coverture at all.

In a section on Jewels and Ornaments we read:[25]

The principal women when their teats fall or become loose bear them up with bars of gold of the length of a span and a half, well wrought, and of such bigness that some of them weigh more than 200 castilians or ducats of gold.

Oviedo also mentions 'a thing which I have oftentimes noted in these Indians' (of the mainland).[26] They

have the bones of the skulls of their heads four times thicker and much stronger than ours. So that in coming to hand strokes with them, it shall be requisite not to strike them on the heads with swords; so have many swords been broken on their heads with little harm done.

Eden's version of Oviedo was not presented as a full translation:[27]

As touching other things of this island whereof Peter Martyr hath more largely entreated in his Decades, I have thought it superfluous to repeat the same again out of this History of Gonzalus Ferdinandus; but have here gathered only such things as either are not touched of Peter Martyr, or not so largely declared; as I have done the same in all other notable things which I have collected out of this Summary of Gonzalus.

Eden seemed most fascinated by Indian devil-worship: even to the extent of incorporating a long passage about the séances of the hermits of Hispaniola[28] which is not from the 1526 *Natural hystoria*. This replaced a passage with took a rather Las Casas line about the Spaniards. Eden has, as we have quoted, a line about the Spaniards 'living more like dragons than men among these simple people'. The 1526 text continued (in the translation by Stoudemire published in 1959):[29]

Maliciously they have caused the death of many Indians who could have been converted and saved. Even if those who died could not have been converted, they would have been useful to your Majesty and helpful to the Christians. And no part of the island would have been completely depopulated, for from the above cause it is almost uninhabited. Those who have perpetrated those crimes call the uninhabited places 'peaceful'. I feel they are more than peaceful; they are destroyed.

(An allusion to Tacitus' text of the speech of a leader of the Britons, in

[25] A:238. S:43.   [26] A:238. S:43.   [27] A:241.
[28] A:215-16. Stoudemire noted that the Eden text contained 'translations of similar works from the same period' (v).
[29] S:34.

Agricola: 'Robbery, butchery, rapine, the liars call Empire; they create a desolation and call it peace.')[30] But Oviedo was sure that 'God is satisfied, and so is the world, with the sacred purpose and work of your Majesty'. Charles' Council for the Indies (*El Consejo Real y Supremo de las Indias*), established in 1524, is 'made up of prelates, professional and learned men, priests, lawyers, all great in ability, and men of conscience'. Charles has 'provided and remedied' everything with his 'justice'; with the 'advice of many· theologians, jurists and men of high intelligence'.

Eden, writing in the England of Philip and Mary, made Oviedo less critical of the Spanish conquerors than he was in the original text. But also – and less predictably – the Indian is a gentler person in 1555 than he was in 1526. Eden deleted the 1526 material about syphilis:[31] 'Your Majesty may rest assured that this horrible disease came from the Indies.' It was brought to Spain by members of Columbus' first and second voyages; carried to Italy by Spanish soldiers in 1495; and from there spread over Christendom, and into Africa. 'Very few Christians who associate and lie with the Indian women have escaped the malady.' Although it 'can also be caught by eating from the same plates and drinking from the same glasses and cups used by those who have the disease, and especially by sleeping on the same sheets and bedclothes which they have used'. Many Indians are cured by drinking water boiled with splinters of wood from the tree called by the Indians 'guayacan'; best obtained on the island of Beata, off the south coast of Hispaniola.

In Eden/Oviedo the Indians honour the devil 'with sacrifices of the blood and lives of men'. There had been more material on this point in 1526. Also, Oviedo wrote, in another passage omitted in 1555, that (as well as the Caribs) the inhabitants of the Colombia coast practice cannibalism.[32]

They eat all the men that they kill, and use the women they capture; and the children that they bear – should any Carib couple with them – are also eaten. The boys that they take from foreigners are castrated, fattened, and eaten.

The Indians of the northern coastal area of Brazil also 'eat human flesh'; they are 'filthy' and 'cruel'; 'and they are also sodomites.'[33] A letter written from Mexico in July 1519 to the Spanish Court contained: 'We have been informed, and are most certain it is true, that they are all sodomites, and practise that abominable vice.' That letter was not printed until 1842.[34] But the picture of the 'unnatural' Indian was common even by 1519. Pietro Martire in the 'Third Decade' published in 1516, had recounted the experience of Vasco Núñez governor of Darien. Eden translated this for the 1555 *Decades*:[35]

[30] Penguin Classics, *Tacitus on Britain and Germany*, tr. Mattingley, 80.
[31] S:88-90.   [32] S:33.   [33] S:26.
[34] The so-called 'First Letter of Cortés'. *Cortéz: Letters from Mexico*, tr. Pagden, 37.
[35] A:138.

with the marginal note, 'unnatural lechery'. Núñez 'found the king's
brother and many other young men in women's apparel, smooth and
effemiṇately decked'; and these the king ('by the report of such as
dwelt ʾabout him') 'abused with preposterous Venus'. There were
about forty offenders; and Núñez set the Spaniards' dogs on them,
who tore them to pieces. Oviedo in 1526 had a longer section:[36]

In many places the Indians are sodomites. The Indian chiefs and lords
publicly have boys with whom they commit this damnable sin. As soon as
these boys begin this practice, they put on the short cotton skirt of the Indian
women, which extends from the waist to the knees. They also wear bead
bracelets and necklaces, and other adornments usually worn by women.
These boys do not go to war, nor do they occupy themselves with other
labours of men. Rather they work in the house, sweeping, cleaning, and
other customary duties of the women. The boys are hated most violently by
the women. The women, however, are very submissive to their husbands,
and do not dare speak of this often, except to the Christians. These boys are
called in the Cueba language *camayoa*. And when one Indian wishes to insult
another, or say he is effeminate, he calls him *camoyoa*.

This passage was omitted by Eden in 1555. Perhaps, having printed
earlier in the volume the Pietro Martire material, he feared repetition.
   The Dominican Tomàs Ortiz argued before the Council of the
Indies in 1525 that the Indians 'are more given to sodomy than any
other nation'.[37]
   Although the theme of Indian vice and uncivility was not Oviedo's
main concern, there was a notable absence in his book of any material
which might confirm Las Casas' presentation of the Indian as a gentle
child. The Eden version is not so 'black' as the real text. In 1535
Oviedo published in Seville the first part of his longer work, *Historia
General y Natural*; the second part did not appear until 1557
(Valladolid). There has never been an English translation of the
General History. However, in 1949 Lewis Hanke compiled a brief
'estimate' of Oviedo's general portrait of the Indian,[38] as

naturally lazy and vicious, melancholic, cowardly, and in general a lying,
shiftless people. Their marriages are not a sacrament but a sacrilege. They
are idolatrous, libidinous, and commit sodomy. Their chief desire is to eat,
drink, worship heathen idols, and commit bestial oscenities. What could one
expect from a people whose skulls are so thick and hard that the Spaniards
had to take care in fighting not to strike on the head lest their swords be
blunted?

   The 1583 *Briefe Chronicle of the Acts and gestes of the Spaniardes in the
West Indies* contained further Las Casas material in addition to the

---

[36] S:104-5. To the Elizabethans, sodomy was the Spanish, as well as the Indian,
Vice: Maltby, *Black Legend in England*, 30, 85, 94.
[37] Quoted Washburn, *Red Man's Land – White Man's Law*, 9.
[38] *Spanish Struggle for Justice*, 11; see *ibid.*, 182, note 29.

translation of the *Brevísima Relación*. An appendix, printed in roman type, contained eight pages devoted to 'The sum of the disputation between Friar Bartholomew de las Casas' and the Emperor's 'chronographer', Doctor Sepúlveda.

Juan Ginés de Sepúlveda (indexed sometimes under 'G' and sometimes under 'S': surely 'S' is more helpful) was born in 1490, studied at the new university of Alcalá, and then, from 1515, spent twenty years in Italy.[39] In 1526 at Rome he published a confutation of Luther's treatise on free will (thinking that Erasmus' 1524 Reply had been too timid). And at Rome in 1535 he published a Dialogue on the theme of the Just War: called *Democrates*, the name of one of the debaters. His main field of study was Aristotle: his Latin translation of the *Politics* was published in Paris in 1548. The theme of the Just War had obvious relevance to Spanish policy towards the Indian. And by 1542 Sepúlveda had completed a sequel, concerning the Indies: *Democrates alter o secundus, sive de justis belli causis apud Indos*. In the event, this remained unpublished until 1750.[40]

The 1583 'sum of the disputation' gives the 'two principal conclusions' of *Democrates alter*: that 'the Spaniards' wars against the Indians were, as concerning the cause and equity that moved them thereto, very just' and 'may and ought to be continued'; and that 'the Indians are bound to submit themselves to the Spaniards' government, as the foolish to the wise: if they will not yield' the Spaniards may wage war (Q.3.r).

We may give here a fuller account. Democrates argues for the justice of war against the Indian. His adversary, Leopoldus, who thinks the Conquest unjust, is characterised as 'a German considerably tainted with Lutheran errors'.[41]

Democrates relates Oviedo-type material about the Indian State of Nature:[42] their cannibalism, human sacrifice, sodomy and unnatural acts, their tribal wars, and their cowardice. They are merely *homunculi*: sorry creatures. They do not 'entirely lack reason': but in them

you will scarcely find even vestiges of humanity, who not only possess no science, but who also lack letters, and preserve no monument of their history ... Neither do they have written laws, but barbaric institutions and customs. They do not even have private property.

Homunculus had an implied association with 'monster'. Paracelsus had written a book *De Homunculis et Monstris*; the homunculus being a child produced by a sort of artificial insemination.[43]

In Sepúlveda's conception of the Law of Nature, what is 'natural' is

---

[39] See the brief monograph by Bell, *Sepulneda*, 1925.

[40] Edition of the Latin text, with a Spanish translation, Madrid, 1951: editor, A. Losada.

[41] Hanke, *Aristotle and the American Indians*, 40.

[42] *ibid.*, 46-7.

[43] T.S. Healy, note on p.112 of his edition of Donne's *Ignatius His Conclave*.

what conforms to reason and civility. The Law of Nature, crystallised in the *Jus Gentium*, is found only among civilised peoples, 'the wisest and most prudent men of the higher races'. Thus the Indian is living in defiance of Natural Law.[44] (Sepúlveda was of course a theorist entirely: he had never been to the Indies.) In sum, the Indian by nature is *servus*:[45] which in Spanish at that time could be rendered *siervo* (serf) or *esclavo* (slave) – the words were used interchangeably.

Sepúlveda took this notion of the 'slave by nature' from Aristotle; in particular, *Politics*, Book I, Chapter 5:[46]

There can be no objection in principle to the mere fact that one should command and another obey; that is both necessary and expedient. Indeed some things are so divided right from birth, some to rule, some to be ruled.

The condition 'where body rules over mind', 'found to exist in bad men or in men in bad condition', is 'in itself a bad thing and contrary to nature'. A man who 'participates in the reasoning faculty so far as to understand, but not so as to possess it' is a 'slave by nature'. (Just as 'between male and female the former is by nature superior and ruler, the latter inferior and subject'.)

It is clear then that by nature some are free, others slaves, and that for these it is both right and expedient that they should serve as slaves.

Thus, says Democrates, the Indian is inferior, 'as women are to men': 'as children are to adults.' They are a 'cruel people'. The Spaniards are a 'mild people': an 'humane nation', a people of 'prudence, genius, magnanimity, temperance, humanity and religion'.[47] (Perhaps Sepúlveda was conscious that his long Italian sojourn had made him appear to some a foreigner in Spain.) Thus the Indians can be justly conquered.

The Conquest must be 'just, moderate and humane': not cruel, or inspired by greed. First the Indians must be invited – 'perhaps without using arms' – to accept the dominion and religion of Spain. They can even be given time to discuss the matter. Some will accept the offer; they can be apportioned to 'honourable, just and prudent Spaniards' who will 'train their Indians into virtuous and humane conditions, and teach them the Christian religion' by precept and example. But most will refuse the offer; the majority will not renounce their religion and customs. There are the objects of a 'just war'; they can be vanquished, dispossessed and enslaved.[48]

Democrates of course is outlining the 'Requirement'. He also quotes Christ's words in Luke 14:23: 'Go out into the highways and

[44] Parry, *Age of Reconnaissance*, Mentor ed., 329.
[45] Hanke, *Aristotle and the American Indians*, 59.
[46] Penguin Classics translation by T.A. Sinclair, 1962, 32-4.
[47] Hanke, *Aristotle and the American Indians*, 47.
[48] *ibid.*, 60-3.

hedges, and compel them to come in.' *Compelle eos intrare.*[49]

The benefits of Conquest follow: livestock, crops, metals; and religion.[50]

Las Casas thought that preachers could be sent among the Indians if there was no danger. If there was danger, forts should be built, dominated by ecclesiastics, and the Indians won over by example – rather like the later Spanish missions in California, New Mexico and Texas. Sepúlveda, aware of the massacre of friars, thought this irresponsible and dangerous.[51]

It certainly could be dangerous. In 1549, for example, we are told by López de Gómara, five Dominican friars landed in Florida, accompanied only by unarmed sailors; three of the friars were killed and eaten.[52]

The fate of the second *Democrates* dialogue was told to the English in the 1583 *Briefe Chronicle*. Neither the Council of the Indies nor the Council of Castile would authorise publication. In 1548 (the year after Las Casas returned finally from the Indies) it was declared doctrinally unsound by the Universities of Alcalá and Salamanca. In 1550 there met at Valladolid, at Charles' request, a committee of fourteen theologians, jurists, and officials to consider the question of the justice of making war on the Indians.[53]

The committee met in August 1550. On the first day Sepúlveda made a statement, three hours long. On the second day (Sepúlveda did not appear again) Las Casas began to read his 'Apology', which took five 'days; the manuscript of nearly 600 pages has not yet appeared in print. A member of the committee prepared a summary of the issues. There was then a gap of eight months. The committee met again in April 1551 to consider its report.

The 1583 *Briefe Chronicle* gave but little space to 'Doctor Sepulveda his drifts and devices' (Q.3.v). The Las Casas material was alone of importance. The figure of those slain in the Indies was now 20 million (R.2.v). And, concerning the Indian human sacrifices, the Spaniards 'have yearly sacrificed to their so dearly beloved and reverend goddess Covetousness more people than the Indians have done in 100 years' (R.2.r). The motivation of Spanish expansion in the Indies is clear: covetousness and ambition.

The Spaniards have not entered into India for any desire to exalt God, honour, or for zeal to the Christian religion, either to savour and procure the salvation of their neighbours, no neither for their Prince's service, whereof they do so vainly brag: but covetousness hath brought them, and ambition hath allured them, to the perpetual dominion over the Indies. (R.2.v)

[49] Parry, *Age of Reconnaisance*, Mentor, ed., 330.
[40] Hanke, *Aristotle and the American Indians*, 52-3.
[51] *ibid.*, 66.
[52] Passage in Quinn (ed.), *North American Discovery*, 90-1.
[53] For the Valladolid Disputation, Hanke, *Spanish Struggle for Justice*, ch.8; *Aristotle and the American Indians*, Chs. 4, 5, 6. Wagner and Parish, 176-82.

The Valladolid Committee never published a formal decision. *Democrates secundus* remained unpublished; although Sepúlveda wrote a defence of it, which was published at Rome in 1550 – *Apologia pro libro de justis belli causis*. Las Casas published no less than eight books at Seville in 1552;[54] including *Brevísima Relación*, and the account of the Valladolid disputation from which the 1583 appendix material was taken. So even if, as with Dr Geoffrey Scammell,[55] the Valladolid Disputation is taken to be a 'rather academic and inconclusive encounter' on 'well-worn medieval themes' – the legality of slavery: the nature of a just war – the Las Casas publications following thereupon did have their effect on the modern world. A translation of the *Brevissima Relacion* was printed in New York in 1898 as propaganda for the war with Spain (April–August 1898).[56]

Las Casas did not accept that the American Indian fell within Aristotle's category of 'a slave by nature': 'he who participates in reason enough to apprehend, but not to have, reason.'[57] The point at issue in the sixteenth century was the capacity of the Indian to apprehend the Gospel. Aristotle was thus irrelevant. Las Casas had described Aristotle in 1519 as 'a gentile burning in hell, whose doctrine we do not need to follow except insofar as it conforms with Christian truth'.[58] This was in argument with a New World Bishop, Juan Quevedo, who had discussed the Indian within the Aristotelian framework. (The first person to do so in a published work, of 1520, was John Major, a Cambridge man.) The Papal Bull *Sublimis Deus* of 1537[59] had insisted that 'all' are qualified for the Faith: *omnes capaces*. The Bible makes clear, said Paul III, that the whole human race has the 'nature' (*natura*) and 'faculties' (*conditio*) to receive the Faith. All have the *natura hominis*. Man is well adapted (*habilis*) to accept the Faith. The Indians are not 'dumb brutes' (*muta animalia*) but 'truly men' (*veri homines*). They

are by no means to be deprived of their liberty, or the possession of their property (*dominium*), even though they be outside (*extra*) the faith of Jesus Christ; and they may and should, freely and legitimately, enjoy their liberty and the possession of their property; nor should they be any way enslaved. Should the contrary happen, it shall be void and of no effect.

In his *Apologética Historia* of *las gentes destas Indias*, Las Casas wrote:[60]

Mankind is one, and all men are alike in that which concerns their creation

---

[54] In the 'Narrative and Critical Catalogue' in Wagner and Parish, nos. 18, 19, 23, 41, 43, 44, 48, 49.
[55] G.V. Scammell, 'The New Worlds and Europe in the sixteenth Century', *Historial Journal*, XII, 3, 1969, 390.
[56] Hanke, *Las Casas: Bookman, Scholar and Propagandist*, 1952, 59.
[57] *Politics*, I, 5: in the Benjamin Jowett translation, ed. H.W.C. Davis, 1905, 34.
[58] Hanke, *Aristotle and the American Indians*, 16.
[59] Text and translation in MacNutt, *Las Casas*, 426-31.
[60] Hanke, *Aristotle and the American Indians*, 112.

and all natural things, and no one is *born* enlightened. From this it follows that all of us must be guided and aided at first by those who were born before us. And the savage peoples of the earth may be compared to uncultivated soil that readily brings forth weeds and useless thorns, but has within itself such natural virtue that by labour and cultivation it may be made to yield sound and beneficial fruits.

English readers of Las Casas from 1583 would be aware of the argument that 'title and right' to the Indies

is not founded upon the entry into those countries, and against those people to rob, slay and tyrannously to rule over them under pretence of preaching the faith; as those tyrants entered and have done, who by an universal massacre and slaughter have massacred a multitude of innocents. But it consisteth of a peaceable, loving and gentle preaching of the Gospel. (R.1.v)

In October 1584 the reverend Richard Hakluyt presented to the Queen his manuscript *Discourse* 'concerninge the greate necessitie and manifolde commodytes that are like to growe to this Realme of Englande by the Western discoveries lately attempted'.[61] The intention of the argument was 'to induce her Majesty and the state to take in hand the western voyage, and the planting there'.[62] One of the inducements was the possible alliance with the Indians:[63]

The Spaniards have executed most outrageous and more than Turkish cruelties in all the west Indies, whereby they are everywhere there become most odious unto them, who would join with us or any other most willingly, to shake off their intolerable yoke.

On the cruelties imposed upon the 'lowly, mild and gentle' Indian the authority of course is Bartholomew de las Casas, 'a Bishop in Nova Spania': 'it seemeth best unto me to bring him in' – there follow four pages of extracts from *The Spanish Colonie, or Briefe Chronicle*.[64] The Indians must in time rebel; indeed, 'in many places they have already begun to do of themselves, without the help of any Christian Prince'. The next sentence was deleted by Hakluyt in the manuscript:[65]

I leave it to the deep consideration of the wise, what great matters may be brought about by our nation if her Majesty, being a mighty prince at sea, would put a foot into that enterprise, and assist the revolted Indians.

Hakluyt's reward was the promise of a well-paid position at Bristol Cathedral. He began his career as a prebendary there in 1586: stipend, £20 a year.

---

[61] Usually known as the 'Discourse of Western Planting'. Printed in 1935, from the manuscript in the New York Public Library, by Taylor, *Original Writings of the two Richard Hakluyts*.
[62] Taylor, 213.
[63] 257. [64] 258-61. [65] 258.

Hakluyt was in fact able to take a more balanced view than Las Casas. In the Dedicatory Epistle to Sir Walter Raleigh in his 1587 Latin edition of the *Decades* of Pietro Martire,[66] Hakluyt (*Oxoniensis Anglus*: 'of Oxford, Englishman') commended the Italian because 'he hunts out with the utmost perseverance' crimes committed by the Spanish: 'I am ashamed', he says in one place, 'to recount these matters, but it is essential to set down the truth.' He

records their avarice, ambition, butchery, rapine, debauchery, their cruelty towards defenceless and harmless people; and occasionally the disaster suffered by their warriors and the slaughter of their armies at the hands of uncivilised races, and those too unarmed.

At the same time, 'he praises the constancy of the Spaniards, and their stubborn spirit, and with the warmest approbation he recounts their endurance in thirst, hunger, dangers, toils, watches, and in their frequent troubles'. Pietro was a true historian.

Hakluyt died in 1616. His editorial work was continued by the reverend Samuel Purchas, Bachelor of Divinity, who had taken his M.A. in 1600 from St John's College, Cambridge, which he had entered in 1594. In 1625 he published in four volumes his massive collection *Hakluytus Posthumus*: the modern edition of which runs to 20 volumes (Glasgow, 1905-7).

Hakluytus Posthumus or Purchas His Pilgrimes, contayning a History of the World, in Sea voyages & lande Travells, by Englishmen & others. Wherein Gods Wonders in Nature & Providence, the Actes, Arts, Varieties & Vanities of Men, with a world of the Worlds Rarities, are by a world of Eywitnesse-Authors, Related to the World. Some left written by Mr Hakluyt at his death. More since added. His also perused & perfected. All examined, abreviated. Illustrated with notes. Enlarged with Discourses. Adorned with pictures, and expressed in Mapps.

Purchas reprinted the 1583 Las Casas translation; including the appendix material (with its summary of the Las Casas/Sepúlveda disputation).[67]

This book is extant in Spanish, Latin, Dutch, and in English also printed 1583, whenas peace was yet betwixt England and Spain; which English copy I have followed.

Or rather, he condensed it; 'above a third part is left out:'

yet more than enough left to testify that man's heart, given over to covetousness or other vice, is a bottomless hell, wicked and deceitful above all: who can search it? The colours which the Spaniards pretended for such executions were the man-eatings, sodomies, idolatries, and other vices of Americans; perhaps made worse in the telling.

[66] Taylor, *Writings of the Hakluyts*, 364.
[67] Glasgow ed., XVIII, 1906, 83-180.

The over-zealous 'telling' was one reason for the abridgement:

I have left out many, many invectives and bitter epithets of this author, abridging him after my wont, and lopping off such superfluities which rather were the fruit of his zeal than the flower of his history.

Las Casas' 'zeal flings forth fiery terms, and paints out their acts in the blackest ink, and most hyperbolical phrases'. However, his story is not 'incredible'; and his 'zeal of reformation' is worthy of honour,

his godly zeal of converting souls to Jesus Christ from the power of ethnic darkness; which was hindered by a worse darkness in those which professed themselves children of light, and had the name and sacraments of Christians ... For my part, I honour virtue in a Spaniard, in a Friar, in a Jesuit.[68]

Purchas even attempted to make some sense from Las Casas' statistics. Against the figure of 3 million dead in Hispaniola, he had a marginal note that Oviedo gave a figure of 1,600,000.[69] At various points Las Casas put the number of the slain in the Indies as 12 million, 15 million, and 20 million. In none of these cases, said Purchas, was Las Casas referring to the entire Indies. A figure for the Indies as a whole would be higher, including the 'innumerable multitudes' in areas not mentioned by Las Casas.[70]

Purchas also pointed out that the zeal of Las Casas occasioned 'the alteration of government in the Indies, by the gentleness of the King of Spain, which freed them from slavery, and took better order both for their bodily and spiritual estate'. A reference to the 'New Laws' of 20 November 1542 (the year of the composition of the *Brevísima Relación*).[71]

The theme of the tyranny of Spain, and its consequences for the Indian, was of course no novelty in England in 1583. Las Casas supplied figures, and details which gave an air of verisimilitude, and a new impetus, to the legend. George Abbot, Master of University College Oxford (and later Archbishop of Canterbury) wrote about Spanish America in his *Briefe description of the whole worlde*, 1599:[72]

The tyranny and covetousness of the Spaniards was such, in taking from them their goods, in deflowering their wives and daughters, but especially in forcing them to labour in their gold mines without measure, as if they had been beasts, that the people, detesting them and the name of Christians for their sakes, did some of them kill themselves, and the mothers destroyed their children in their bellies, that they might not be born to serve so hateful a nation; and some of them did in war conspire against them; so that by slaughter and otherwise, the people of the country are almost all wasted now,

---

[68] *ibid.*, 80-2.   [69] *ibid.*, 87.   [70] *ibid.*, 180.

[71] *ibid.*, 81. On the 'Leyes Nuevas', and their actual effect, see Hanke, *Spanish Struggle for Justice*, 91-105; Elliott, *Imperial Spain*, Mentor ed., 71-4.

[72] Section 'De America sive orbe novo'.

within one hundred years, being before many millions: those which remain are as slaves.

Francis Bacon said in the House of Commons in 1592 that 'whereas the Christian religion generally brought enfranchisement of slaves in all places where it came', in the 'poor Indies' the natives 'in a contrary course are brought from freemen to be slaves, and slaves of most miserable condition'.[73] In 1597, again in the House of Commons, Bacon condemned Spain's 'great and barbarous tyrannies which they have committed upon the poor Indians'.[74] John Donne published in 1611 his Erasmus-type dialogue *Ignatius His Conclave*, a series of speeches by 'new fangled' men claiming the right of admission to Hell. One of the claimants was Columbus; who 'having found all ways in the earth and sea open to him, did not fear any difficulty in Hell'. He is however brushed aside by the prime claimant: the Jesuit Ignatius Loyola.[75]

You must remember, sir, that if this kingdom have got any thing by the discovery of the West Indies, all that must be attributed to our Order: for if the opinion of the Dominicans had prevailed, That the inhabitants should be reduced, only by preaching and without violence, certainly their 200,000 of men would scarce in so many ages have been brought to a 150 which by our means was so soon performed. And if the law, made by Ferdinando, only against Cannibals: That all which would not be Christians should be bond-slaves, had not been extended into other Provinces, we should have lacked men, to dig us out that benefit, which their countries afford. Except we when we took away their old Idolatry, had recompensed them with a new one of ours; except we had obtruded to those ignorant and barbarous people sometimes natural things, sometimes artificial, and counterfeit, instead of Miracles; and except we had then been always ready to convey, and to apply this medicine made of this precious American drug, unto the Princes of Europe, and their Lords, and Councillors, the profit by the only discovery of these places (which must of necessity be referred to fortune) would have been very little.

(Donne had been interested in the possibility of a post in London with the Virginia Company.)

Sir Walter Raleigh wrote an attack on Spain in the early 1590s, in the form of an account of the surrender of the *Revenge* and the death of Sir Richard Grenville in 1591: *A report of the truth of the fight about the Isles of Azores the last of August 1591 betwixt the Revenge, one of her Majesty's ships, and an armada of the King of Spain.* Raleigh did not lose the opportunity to invoke the testimony of Las Casas:

In one only island called Hispaniola they have wasted 3,000,000 of the natural people, besides many millions else in other places of the Indies. A

[73] *Life and Letters*, ed. Spedding, I, 137.
[74] *ibid.*, II, 88.
[75] *Ignatius His Conclave*, ed. Healy, 69.

poor and harmless people, created of God, and might have been won to his knowledge; as many of them were.

The story is 'at large': 'written by a Bishop of their own nation called Bartholomew de las Casas, and translated into English and many other languages, entitled The Spanish Cruelties.' The *Report* was printed by Hakluyt in the second edition of *Principal Navigations*, 1600.[76] Raleigh was obsessed by the Spanish theme in the 1590s.

I have therefore laboured all my life, both according to my small power, and persuasion, to advance all those attempts that might either promise return of profit to ourselves, or at least be a let and impeachment to the quiet course and plentiful trades of the Spanish nation.

The quotation is from his book published in 1596: *The Discoverie of the Large, Rich and Bewtiful Empyre of Guiana*.[77] 'Guiana' meant the interior of the area between the Orinoco and the Amazon: Venezuela, Guiana, northern Brazil. In 1595 Raleigh had been on an expedition to the region, sailing along the Orinoco: the first time Englishmen had been to the interior of South America. Raleigh wanted government support for a settlement there. There survives in the British Museum a manuscript, 'Of the Voyage for Guiana', which has been attributed to Raleigh.[78] Professor Quinn believes it is almost certainly by Laurence Keymis; or, 'just barely possibly', Thomas Hariot.[79] The manuscript is shot through with Las Casas material.

The desired aim was to attack Spain in the Indies: and in particular 'to have the Empire of Guiana subdued, and united to the Crown of England'.[80] This could be accomplished by landing about 500 men elsewhere in the Indies (Peru, Mexico, Florida): Captains, gunners, armourers, casters of ordnance, with 'armour and munition to furnish the people, with instruction to set them to war against the Spaniards'.[81] The Indians were to expel the Spaniards, armed and instructed by the English.

The Spaniards are 'mere usurpers' in America; they possess their territories by 'violent intrusion'. Their conquest is notoriously unjust:[82]

The matter being called into question in Spain, between the Lord Bishop of Chiapa and Dr Sepulveda, the two universities of Salamanca and Alcala, and also (if I mistake not mine author) the lords of the assembly who were appointed to hear the controversy debated, did resolve that such kind of invasive wars upon infidels could not be justified.

[76] Everyman edition, V, 1-15: quotation on p.13.
[77] Ed. Harlow, 1928, 10.
[78] Sloane MSS 1133. Printed by Harlow as Appendix C to his edition of *The Discoverie of Guiana*: pp.138-49.
[79] D.B. Quinn, in a private note, 1974.
[80] Harlow, 140. The subsequent page references are to this edition.
[81] 148.   [82] 143.

The Spaniards assert that it is legitimate to deprive idolators of their territory and property; and of their lives. In fact in the Old Testament God often gave land to 'idolators': to 'wicked' Ishmael; to Nebuchadnezzar. By 'the gift of God, idolaters, pagans and godless persons be entitled to the possession, and have a capacity to take and an ability to hold, a property in lands and goods'. Judges Chapter 11 tells of a dispute about Amorite territory, possessed by Israel, but claimed by the King of Ammon. Jephthah, the Israelite commander, vanquished the Ammonites: but not under 'pretence of their idolatry or gentile-ism', commented the author, but because God had given the territory to Israel. The text is Judges 11:23-4. Jephthah: 'The Lord God of Israel drove out the Amorites for the benefit of his people Israel. And do you now propose to take their place?'; 'All that the Lord our God gave us as we advanced is ours' (New English Bible). What mattered was the gift of God, not the defects of the enemy. But, the writer continues (in a singularly dusky passage of exegesis) the 'good' rulers of the Old Testament invaded territory only 'upon just cause of wrongs from the idolaters received'. And although when Jephthah invaded the land occupied by the Ammonites he did so from the correctest motives, such Old Testament precedent does not now apply. 'God hath given no Christians any such warrant, therefore they may not do the like':

Christians are commanded to do good unto all men, and to have peace with all men; to do as they would be done unto; to give none offence to one or other. And lastly Christ willed the disciples to pay tribute to Caesar, an infidel; He refused a worldly kingdom, as not appertaining unto Him; he reproved His apostles when they desired that fire might come from heaven to destroy the Samaritans who refused to entertain Him, saying, You know not what spirit you are of, the Son of Man is not come to destroy men's lives but to save them. Therefore no Christian prince under pretence of Christianity only, and of forcing of men to receive the Gospel or to renounce their impieties, may attempt the invasion of any free people not under their vassalage. For Christ gave not that power to Christians as Christians, which He Himself, as Sovereign of all Christians, neither had, nor would take.[83]

The author had in mind (among other possible passages) words of St Paul: 'Let us do good unto all men' (Galatians 6:10); 'Live peaceably with all men' (Romans 12:18); 'that no man put a stumblingblock or an occasion to fall in his brother's way.' And sayings of Christ: 'Blessed are the peacemakers' (Matthew 5:9); 'All things whatsoever ye would that men should do to you, do ye even so to them' (Matthew 6:12); 'A new commandment I give unto you, That ye love one another' (John 13:34 and 15:12). 'Render unto Caesar the things that are Caesar's' is reported in Matthew 22:21, Mark 12:17, and Luke 20:25. 'My kingdom is not of this world' is

[83] 142.

John 18:36. The Samaritan episode is told in Luke 9:52-6. Christ sent messengers

unto a village of the Samaritans, to make ready for him. And they did not receive him, because his face was as though he would go to Jerusalem. And when his disciples James and John saw this, they said, Lord, wilt thou that we command fire to come down from heaven, and consume them, even as Elias did? But he turned, and rebuked them, and said, Ye know not what manner of spirit ye are of. For the Son of man is not come to destroy men's lives, but to save them. And they went to another village.

Thus, argued the author, 'Christians may not warrantably conquer infidels upon pretence only of their infidelity.'[84] The 'rules of justice' give 'to every man his own': it is against those rules to deprive men of 'goods, lands, liberties or lives, without just title thereunto'.[85]

In short, 'no Christians may lawfully invade with hostility any heathenish people not under their allegiance, to kill, spoil and conquer them' on the 'pretence' of their Infidelity.

The author wishes to 'lay this down as a maxim': 'which yet, upon better advice, I am ready to retract.'(!)[86]

Because of their 'oppressions and usurpations' in the Indies, the Spaniards are 'detested and feared' by the Indians.[87] Let it

be remembered how the Spaniards have without just title, or any wrong at all done to them by the harmless Indians, forcibly invaded and wrongfully detained their countries about 100 years, committing barbarous and exquisite massacres to the destruction of whole nations of people (arising, by estimation of some of accompt among them, and acquainted with their proceedings, in some few years to the number of 20 millions of reasonable creatures made to the image of God, and less harmful than the Spaniards themselves) whereby more fruitful land was laid waste and depopulated than is in all Europe and some parts of Asia; in revenge whereof their own religious men to make accompt that the just God in judgement will one day horribly chasten, and peradventure wholly subvert and root out the Spanish nation from the world.

God the Judge has now

heard the sighs, groans, lamentations, tears and blood of so many millions of innocent men, women and children, afflicted, robbed, reviled, branded with hot irons, roasted, dismembered, mangled, stabbed, whipped, racked, scalded with hot oil, suet and hogsgrease, put to the strapado, ripped alive, beheaded in sport, drowned, dashed against the rocks, famished, devoured by mastiffs, burned, and by infinite cruelties consumed.

And God intends 'to scourge and plague that cursed nation, and to take the yoke of servitude from that distressed people, as free by

---

[84] 143. [85] 142. [86] 141. [87] 139.

nature as any Christian'. So the English can 'proceed in this voyage'; having 'a most just cause'.[88]

It will be necessary in the enterprise to make 'league' with the Indians of the territories near Guiana. The question arises: can a Christian nation make an alliance with idolators? The Old Testament answer would appear to be, No.[89] It is true that Asa, king of Judah, successfully appealed to Syria for help against Israel ('There is a league between men and thee': I Kings 15:19); but Asa, although victorious, was reproved 'because thou hast relied on the king of Syria, and not relied on the Lord thy God' (II Chronicles 16:9). The like reproof, comments the author, 'is to be answered for Hernando Cortes and others, who conquered by the help of some Indian idolators'. Another king of Judah, Jehoshaphat, made alliance with Ahaziah, king of Israel, who was wicked and served Baal; and Jehoshaphat was reproved by God (II Chronicles Chapter 20). A third king of Judah, Amaziah, recruited mercenaries from Israel in his campaign against Edom, and was told: 'Let not the army of Israel go with thee; for the Lord is not with Israel' (II Chronicles 25:7) – so he dismissed the idolatrous mercenaries. Thus the Indians ought to be converted before they become allies.

On the other hand, it might, 'after deliberation' be found 'agreeable' to join with them before their conversion; in which case the Biblical objections 'need less to trouble us'.

The Indians, both outside Guiana and, eventually, within Guiana, must be instructed in the use of arms. ('Always provided that this policy of arming the inhabitants, as a special secret, be discreetly carried and concealed until it be ripened, and brought into open action.')[90] We must be careful to arm and instruct only 'such of them as we find must trusty, and most prone to Christianity'.[91]

As propaganda to discredit the Spaniards, there must be distributed throughout the Indies

Bartol: de las Casas' book of the Spanish cruelties, with fair pictures; or at least a large table of pictures expressing the particularities of the cruelties there specified, neatly wrought, for the better credit of our workmanship, and their easier understanding.[92]

When the 'easy and compendious way of possessing Guiana' has been successful, the English must be sure not to treat the Indians with 'the Spaniards' cruelties'. The Spaniards incurred the anger of God, and the hatred of the Indians: 'as Barth: de las Casas expressly certified the Emperor Charles V in his suit unto him for redress of the horrible outrages perpetrated by his Spaniards against the Indians.'[93] The offer to the Indians of Guiana must be[94]

1. First that we will defend them, their wives, children and countries against the Spaniards and all other intruders. 2. Then that we will help them to

88 140.   89 144-5.   90 149.   91 148.   92 143.   93 148.   94 146.

recover their country of Peru. 3. That we will instruct them in liberal arts of civility behoveful for them, that they may be comparable to any Christian people. 4. And lastly that we will teach them the use of weapons, how to pitch their battles, how to make armour and ordnance, and how to manage horses for service in the wars.

As colonists, there must be sent 'well governed soldiers and artisans that will not wrong the Indians in their persons, women and possessions'. Justice must be seen to be done. Among the settlers

severity of martial discipline is to be used in the open presence of the Guianians (being made acquainted with the cause of the punishment) with full satisfaction for all injuries which by the ruder sort shall be offered, This will be a singular mean to work their conversion, to procure their loving affections, and to oblige them in assured loyalty to her Majesty.[95]

Some Indians must be brought to England: 'which, being civilised and converted here, upon their return, and receiving of others in their rooms, they may be matched in marriage with English women.'[96] Preachers 'of good discretion and behaviour'[97] must be sent; this is 'reasonable and charitable'. The preachers, 'safely guarded if need be', will 'offer infidels the glad tidings of the Gospel'. The Indians may refuse this offer; they may give 'hard measure to the preachers'. But 'this can ground no sufficient quarrel to overrun their countries'.[98] So much for Dr Sepúlveda and the 'Requirement'.

The colonists must, through the Indian chief, 'persuade the people to abandon their idols, and to surcease their bloody sacrifices'. And 'experience in other places giveth great hope that little persuasion will serve to effect this'. In China the natives 'were readily persuaded to relinquish their sodomitry and idolatry'. And

the Lord Bishop of Chiapa, who lived many years among the Indies, avoucheth that they were teachable, and capable of all good learning, very apt to receive the catholic faith, and to be instructed in good manners.[99]

When the Indians have 'conceived a good opinion' of the Europeans they show 'great love and faithfulness'.

The Indians for the most part are a people very faithful, humble, patient, peaceable, simple; without subtlety, malice, quarrels, strife, rancour, or desire of revengement; as meek as lambs, as harmless as children of ten or twelve years. As the Bishop of Chiapa (a man as seemeth of good credit) of his own experience doth witness; and we ourselves in part have had the like proof of them.[100]

The 'voyage for Guiana' is necessary and profitable. It is also honourable.[101]

[95] 148. [96] 146. [97] 148. [98] 143. [99] 145. [100] 147. [101] 138.

It is honourable, both for that by this means infinite numbers of souls may be brought from their idolatry, bloody sacrifices, ignorance and incivility, to the worshipping of the true God aright, to civil conversation; and also their bodies freed from the intolerable tyranny of the Spaniards, whereunto they are already, or likely in short space to be, subjected: unless her excellent Majesty, or some other Christian Prince, do speedily assist and afterwards protect them in their just defensive wars against the violence of usurpers.

The Virginia Company was founded in 1606; and the Spanish claim to America was one of the things much discussed by its leading spokesmen. There survives a short manuscript of about 1606, in the Bodleian Library, Oxford, 'A Justification for Planting Virginia'. To the English, the Spanish scholastic gymnastics in the debate on 'the struggle for justice' were alien and null:

When at first discovery of those parts the Spaniard did subject the consideration of it to casuists and confessors, it became so interminable that he was forced to resolve roundly upon the worst way lest he should have none: to prosecute the Indians as barbars, and therefore naturally slaves.

After fifty years 'his friars declined him from that severe and unjust course, and he laboured by men of all learning to provide himself of a more acceptable title'. The 'men of discourse' spoke of the Indians 'transgressing the law of nature'; the civil lawyers discussed the Indians 'denying commerce'; the canon lawyers emphasised the Bull of Alexander VI; the divines spoke of 'preparation of religion'. All these arguments of the Schools were 'incoherent, and resisted by one another'.[102]

A pamphlet published in 1610 'by advice and direction of the Council of Virginia', was also satirical about the Spanish tradition – 'to preach the Gospel to a nation conquered, and to set their souls at liberty when we have brought their bodies to slavery'.[103] The Spaniards set 'the gloss of religion' upon 'mere ambition'. There is a point at issue: 'how the possessor of the west Indies first destroyed; and then instructed.' 'Let the divines of Salamanca discuss that question'!

[102] Kingsbury, *Records*, III, 2-3.
[103] *A True Declaration of the estate of the Colonie in Virginia*. Force, *Tracts*, III, no.1, p.6.

PART TWO

9

Drake in New Albion, 1579

On 17 June 1579, during his voyage round the world, Francis Drake (probably returning from north of Vancouver Island) anchored his damaged flagship – the 'Golden Hind' – in a 'convenient and fit harbour': a 'fair and good bay', at about 38° 30′ N. This was in the San Francisco region. (There are those who maintain that San Francisco means 'Sir Francis'; against the more orthodox theory that the Bay was named after St Francis of Assisi in the late 1760s.) It is now usually thought that the 'bay' was Drake's Bay, on the coast north of San Francisco. Some are in favour of Bodega Bay, further north (where Alfred Hitchcock filmed *The Birds*). Other candidates are Tomales Bay, south of Bodega Bay, and Bolinas Bay, south of Drake's Bay. Others believe that Drake anchored within San Francisco Bay itself, to the north-west, near the present San Quentin Bridge. The approach of the four hundredth anniversary, 1979, makes these issues lively in California.[1] The inset sketch of *Portus Novae Albionis* in the 1589 map of Jodocus Hondius (Josse De Hont) of *Vera Totius Expeditionis Nauticae* certainly looks very like San Francisco Bay. (In that 1589 map, the east coast of North America is divided between 'Florida' and 'Nova Francia'.)

Whichever specific bay it was, Drake's vessel remained there for five weeks: until 23 July.

Drake's log-book, presented to Elizabeth I, has not survived. But a crew member, Francis Fletcher, preacher, took full notes of the voyage. These were used by Richard Hakluyt in the account of the voyage he printed in 1589: the California section is in volume 6 of the Everyman Library Hakluyt, pages 240-5. A fuller version, incorporating other material, and edited by Drake's nephew (also called Francis) was printed in London in 1628.

The World Encompassed by Sir Francis Drake, being his next voyage to that to Nombre de Dios formerly imprinted; carefully collected out of the notes of Master Francis Fletcher Preacher in this imployment, and divers others his followers in the same: Offered now at

[1] Robert H. Power, 'Drake's Landing in California: A Case for San Francisco Bay', *California Historical Quarterly*, Summer 1973 (LII, 2). Rear Admiral Morison supports Drake's Bay: *Southern Voyages*, Ch.10. There are heretics who think the bay was not in the San Francisco area, but much further north.

last to publique view, both for the honour of the actor, but especially for the stirring up of heroick spirits, to benefit their Countrie, and eternize their names by like noble attempts.

A facsimile edition of this appeared in 1969, as Number 103 of 'The English Experience' (Amsterdam and New York). The relevant pages are 64 to 81. *The World Encompassed* was edited for the Hakluyt Society in 1854, by W.S.W. Vaux; and is most recently available in a collection of narratives edited in 1972 by John Hampden, *Francis Drake Privateer*. Fletcher, like most Elizabethans, was insatiably curious, and his California detail is precise and valid. His account is also, when interpreted, highly comic, in its unintentionally ironic presentation of the uncomprehending clash between two 'Culture Patterns'. My 'interpretation' is from Robert F. Heizer, *Francis Drake and the California Indians*, University of California Press, 1947; supplemented on occasion by Henry R. Wagner, *Drake's Voyage Around the World*, San Francisco, 1926.

My text is from 1628, with occasional interpolations from 1589.

On 18 June 'the people of the country showed themselves; sending off a man with great expedition to us in a canoe'. The Indians were the Miwok, of the coastal area of central California (a tribe surviving until the 1920s). The canoeist 'spake to us continually as he came rowing on', then stopped, made a 'long and tedious oration' (the puritan Fletcher would recognise the idiom), and returned to shore 'with great show of reverence and submission'. He paddled out again with a 'bunch of feathers, much like the feathers of a black crow, very neatly and artificially gathered upon a string, and drawn together into a round bundle' – such as 'they that guard their king's person wear on their heads': the ceremonial black feather bundle associated with the Kutsu cult of central California. He also brought 'a little basket made of rushes, and filled with an herb which they called Tabacco (1589)/Tabah (1628)'. It is uncertain what the herb was, but it was almost certainly not tobacco (first brought to England in 1565 by John Hawkins from Florida, and grown in England by the 1570s). The canoeist, refusing to accept any gifts from the English, again set out for the shore. Thereafter, the pinnace 'could row no way, but, wondering at us as at gods, they would follow after the same with admiration'.

On 21 June a landing party from the 'Golden Hind' began 'to build tents and make a fort'. The Indians approached from the hills:

with no hostile meaning, or intent to hurt us; standing, when they drew near, as men ravished in their minds with the sight of such things as they never had seen or heard of before that time: their errand being rather with submission and fear to worship us as gods, than to have any war with us as with mortal men.

The sailors motioned the Indians to lay down their bows and arrows, which they did; and the crowd grew to 'a great number, both of men and women'. Drake, a man of 'natural and accustomed humanity' (1589),

used all means possible gently to entreat them, bestowing upon each of them liberally, good and necessary things to cover their nakedness, withal signifying unto them we were no gods, but men, and had need of such things to cover our own shame; teaching them to use them to the same ends, for which cause also we did eat and drink in their presence, giving them to understand that without that we could not live, and therefore were but men as well as they.

Gifts were now exchanged: shirts and linen clothes, for feathers, net caps, quivers made of fawn skins. The Indians then returned to their houses, less than a mile from the shore. Whereupon they

began amongst themselves a kind of most lamentable weeping and crying out, the women especially extending their voices in a most miserable and doleful manner of shrieking.

The English, most probably, had been taken for spirits come back from the dead: the associations were ghost-like. Moaning was apparently a cultural feature of central California, associated with the return of spirits.

Drake and his party then as quickly as possible 'set up our tents and entrenched ourselves with walls of stone'. For 'we thought it no wisdom too far to trust them (our experience of former infidels dealing with us before, made us careful to provide against an alteration of their affections, or breach of peace)'.

On 23 June Indian men, women and children drew near to the camp. Another tedious oration. The men presented gifts. The women were more dramatic: and

as if they had been desperate, used unnatural violence against themselves, crying and shrieking piteously, tearing their flesh with their nails from their cheeks in a monstrous manner, the blood streaming down along their breasts; besides despoiling the upper parts of their bodies of those single coverings they formerly had; and, holding their hands above their heads that they might not rescue their breasts from harm, they would with fury cast themselves upon the ground, never respecting whether it were clean or soft, but dashed themselves in this manner on hard stones, knobbly hillocks, stocks of wood, and pricking bushes, or whatever else lay in their way, iterating the same course again and again. Yea women great with child, some nine or ten times each, and others holding out till fifteen or sixteen times (till their strengths failed them) exercised this cruelty against themselves.

(Self-laceration was another cultural feature of the Miwok attitude to ghosts.)

Drake and his men were naturally alarmed by the 'bloody sacrifice'. So they 'fell to prayers', and by signs in lifting up our eyes and hands to heaven, signified unto them that that God whom we did serve, and whom they ought to worship, was above; beseeching God, if it were His good pleasure, to open by some means their blinded eyes; that they might in due time be called to the knowledge of Him, the true and everliving God, and of Jesus Christ whom he hath sent, the salvation of the Gentiles. In the time of which prayers, singing of the Psalms, and reading of certain chapters in the Bible, they sat very attentively, and observing the end at every pause, with one voice still cried Oh; greatly rejoicing in our exercises. Yea they took such pleasure in our singing of Psalms, that whensoever they resorted to us their first request was commonly this, Gnaah, by which they entreated that we would sing.

(The Coast Miwok word for 'sing' was 'koya'.)

Such evangelical nautical piety was natural to Drake (whose father, late in life, had become a parson). We know that he was in the habit of reading the psalms and preaching to his crew. And when he on one occasion entertained some Spanish prisoners to dinner in his cabin, he read to them from Foxe's 'Book of Martyrs'; then knelt on a cushion in silent prayer for fifteen minutes; after which, four violinists having appeared, he and the officers sang psalms – and finally (and perhaps unexpectedly) a cabin boy came in, and danced.

We also know, from a Portuguese pilot, that Drake

kept a book in which he entered his navigation, and in which he delineated birds, trees and sea-lions. He is adept in painting, and has with him a boy, a relative of his, who is a great painter. When they both shut themselves up in his cabin, they are always painting.[2]

One would love to know whether Drake sketched the California Indians, anticipating by six years the water-colours done in Carolina by John White.

On 26 June there gathered the largest crowd of Indians the English had thus far seen. The King was there, 'a man of goodly stature and comely personage'; with an élite guard of 'about 100 tall and warlike men', who approached the camp intoning

continually, after a singing manner, with a lusty courage. And as they drew nearer and nearer towards us, so did they more and more strive to behave themselves with a certain comeliness and gravity in all their actions.

They had a 'sceptre or royal mace, made of a certain kind of black wood and in length about a yard and a half', tied to which were two ceremonial net caps with feather decorations, and chains of linked clam shells, from Bodega Bay most likely. The King wore a head-dress and a coat of woven rabbit-skin blankets; his guard wore feather caps and beaver coats. After them, 'in their order, did follow the naked sort of common people, whose hair, being long, was gathered into a bunch behind, in which stuck plumes of feathers': with a single

---

[2] Nuttall (ed.), *New Light on Drake* (Hakluyt Society, 1914), 303.

feather at the front. All the Indians had painted their faces; white, black and other colours (was this in fact a description of tattooing?). The women were still scarred (ornamental?). Everyone bore gifts in feather decorated bowls embellished with pearl shells: roots, fish and plants. The English tried to look military; the Indian men, including the King, sang and danced; then they all were invited into the fort.

In the fort, Drake was ceremonially crowned. A unique honour it was thought: interpreted as a gesture of 'resigning and receiving the Kingdom'. The ceremony was interpreted in England as the Indian King's 'yielding himself to the subjection of the Queen of England'.[3]

The Indians indicated that Drake should 'take the province and kingdom into his hand, and become their king and patron'. The king set the royal head-dress on Drake's head. And there was 'a song and dance of triumph'. Drake (then in his late thirties) rose to the occasion:

In the name and to the use of her most excellent majesty he took the sceptre, crown and dignity of the said country into his hand; wishing nothing more than that it had lain so fitly for her majesty to enjoy, as it was now her proper own.

He declared himself especially gratified

that so tractable and loving a people as they showed themselves to be might have means to have manifested their most willing obedience the more unto her, and by her means, as a mother and nurse of the Church of Christ, might by the preaching of the Gospel be brought to the right knowledge and obedience of the true and everliving God.

The Indians, men and women, now went through what we now know to be traditional mourning ceremonies: 'taking a diligent view or survey of every man, and finding such as pleased their fancies (which was commonly the youngest of us)' – young men back from the beyond,

they, presently enclosing them about, offered their sacrifices unto them, crying out with lamentable shrieks and moans, weeping and scratching and tearing their very flesh off their faces with their nails. Neither were it the women alone which did this, but even old men, roaring and crying out, were as violent as the women were.

Drake's men were again appalled to witness 'the power of Satan so far prevail in seducing these so harmless souls'. They tried physical restraint. They demonstrated the lifting of eyes and hands to heaven. Neither ploy was successful; and the younger sailors were sent away. The Indians then displayed their physical deformities, their wounds

---

[3] Abbot, *Briefe description of the whole worlde*, 1599, section 'De Partibus Americae'. In 1599 Theodore de Bry published an engraving of the offering of the crown to Drake, in Part VIII of his *America* (Frankfurt).

and ulcers and sores, 'making signs that if we did but blow upon their griefs or but touched the diseased places they would be whole'. The English could cope with this. They brought their medical chests, their ointments and plasters, and set to work, continuing medical treatment for the remainder of their stay in the Bay. They also found it necessary to feed some of the Indians, who presumably had come from regions beyond the bay; perhaps Pomo Indians, from Russian river.

Fletcher gave some details of Indian domestic life. Their houses were circular, semi-subterranean constructions, roofed with poles (redwood bark?) and covered in earth: they were

digged round within the earth, and have from the uppermost brim of the circle clefts of wood set up, and joined close together at the top, like our spires on the steeple of a church; which, being covered with earth, suffer no water to enter and are very warm. The door in the most part of them performs the office also of a chimney, to let out the smoke; it's made in bigness and fashion like to an ordinary scuttle in a ship, and standing slopewise. Their beds are the hard ground; only with rushes strewn upon it, and lying round the house, have their fire in the midst, by which reason that the house is but low vaulted, round and close, giveth a marvellous reflection to their bodies to heat the same.

Indian attire was also described. The males 'for the most part go naked'. The females wore was what general to central California – skirts of shredded bulrushes, and shoulder capes of deer skin. The women

take a kind of bulrushes, and combing it after the manner of hemp, make themselves thereof a loose garment, which being knit about their middles, hangs down about their hips and so affords them a covering of that which nature teaches should be hidden. About their shoulders they wear also the skin of a deer, with the hair upon it. They are very obedient to their husbands.

The Indians impressed Fletcher as very strong – able to carry up and down hill a load appropriate to three men. They ran quickly, and for a long time. They fished in an interesting way: surf fishing, with a round hand-net. They used their bows and arrows skilfully; but in comparison with the longbow it seemed 'more fit for children than for men'.

They may have been naked, subject to madness, and spiritually blind; but 'they are people of a tractable, free and loving nature, without guile or treachery'.

The 'Golden Hind' repaired, and the men rested and in good heart, the time came to venture onto the Pacific. The day of departure was memorable. The Indians lit fires, in which they burnt shell beads; a tribal custom in memory and honour of the dead. Fletcher described their melancholy:

They did not only lose on a sudden all mirth, joy, glad countenance, pleasant speeches, agility of body, familiar rejoicing one with another, and all pleasure what ever flesh and blood might be delighted in, but with sighs and sorrowing, with heavy hearts and grieved minds; they poured out woeful complaints and moans, with bitter tears and wringing of their hands, tormenting themselves. And as men refusing all comfort, they only accounted themselves as castaways, and those whom the gods were about to forsake.

The English response to the pyres was predictable:

Prayers and singing of Psalms; whereby they were allured immediately to forget their folly, and leave their sacrifice unconsumed, suffering the fire to go out. And imitating us in all our actions, they fell a-lifting of their eyes and hands to heaven, as they saw us do.

Thus, like all the best stories from California, it seemed to have a happy ending.

Before embarking, Drake had fashioned a metal plate, probably from a gun carriage, a notice was chiselled on it, and it was fixed to a post. The drift of the words was given by Hakluyt in 1589: the name of the Queen; the date of the English arrival; 'the free giving up of the province and people into her majesty's hands.' A sixpenny piece was inset 'under the plate': the Queen's likeness, and arms, 'whereunder was also written the name of our General'.

Fletcher tells us that Drake named the region Nova Albion. Albion was the ancient name of the British Isles, probably Celtic in origin; used by Ptolemy, and taken over by the Romans as suggesting 'white', *albus* – and often translated 'white land'. John Bale, in the 1540s, published details of Albion, a giant, son of Neptune, who conquered the island of England and Scotland, ruling it for 44 years; this story was ridiculed by Milton.[4] (The island of Albion, inhabited only by giants, was conquered by Brutus, great-grandson of Aeneas of Troy, who called it – with reference to his own name – Britain.) The name 'Nova Albion' was applied to California in 1579 so that the region 'might have some affinity with our country in name, which sometime was so called'. And because of the white cliffs and white sand dunes of the California coast life.

Drake returned to Plymouth in September 1580, was knighted by the Queen on the deck of the 'Golden Hind'; and became a hero of Old Albion. In an essay on 'the honour of England' published in 1621, the puritan country parson Richard Bernard (who had earlier been a minister in the Scrooby/Gainsborough/Worksop area: the cradle of Massachusetts) gave his list of England's especial worthies, the prophets of the Honour of England.[5] They were twelve in number. The first was Joseph of Arimathaea: the rich disciple of Jesus, councillor of the city of Arimathaea, who had asked Pilate for the body of Jesus, and laid it in his private new stone tomb in a garden

[4] Milton, *The History of Britain* (1671), ed. French Fogle, Yale, 1971, 6.
[5] *Seaven Golden Candlesticks*, E.6.r.

near the site of the crucifixion – and who, according to William of Malmesbury in the twelfth century, had come to England with the Holy Grail and built a church at Glastonbury in Somerset. The second was King Lucius, ruler of Britain in the second half of the second century: a Briton (as distinct from a Roman), who received instruction and baptism from delegates of the Bishop of Rome, and under whose rule Christianity was confirmed in Britain (authorities: John Foxe,[6] and Foxe's basic source, Geoffrey of Monmouth, *c.*1140[7]). Then the following. Constantine, 288-337, whose mother was a Briton, and who was born, and proclaimed Emperor, in England. Bede, 673-735. Alexander of Hales (in Gloucestershire), 1170-1245; Duns Scotus, 1264-1308; and Thomas Bradwardine, 1290-1349 (Archbishop of Canterbury and exponent of a rigid predestinarianism which appealed to Elizabethan High Calvinists such as William Perkins). John Wyclif, 1329-1384 (in matters of Reformation, as Milton was to say,[8] God revealed Himself, 'as His manner is, first to His Englishmen'). Three Tudor monarchs: Henry VIII; Edward VI, the new Josiah – Josiah being a youthful King of Israel in the seventh century B.C. who 'made a covenant with the Lord' and purged the realm of idolatry (rather like Lucius); and Elizabeth, 'successor to the saints'. That makes eleven indigenous worthies. The twelfth was less predictable: Sir Francis Drake.

In 1933 a chauffeur employed on a ranch in Marin County found an old plate of brass half a mile inland from Drake's Bay. He later threw it out of his car window. In the summer of 1936, in Marin County, near San Quentin, a travelling salesman rediscovered the (presumably) same plate: eight inches long, five inches wide, and one eighth of an inch thick. He cleaned it, and crudely chiselled letters emerged, which read as follows:

Be it known unto all men by these presents. June 17, 1579. By the grace of God and in the name of Her Majesty Queen Elizabeth of England and her successors for ever, I take possession of this kingdom; whose king and people freely resign their right and title in the whole land unto Her Majesty's keeping: now named by me and to be known unto all men as Nova Albion. G. Francis Drake.

There was a crude hole at the bottom of the plate into which a sixpence could have fitted. The plate was intensively examined by the Professor of Electrochemistry at Columbia, helped by a consulting metallurgical engineer, who published a report in 1938 declaring that the plate was genuine. It was bought for the University of California and is now in the Bancroft Library at Berkeley: Drake's Plate of Brass.[9]

[6] *Acts and Monuments*, ed. Townsend, I, 308-11.

[7] *History of the Kings of Britain*, Everyman edition, 86-8.

[8] *Areopagitica* (1644).

[9] California Historical Society: Special Publication No.13, 'Drake's Plate of Brass', with essays by H.E. Bolton and D.S. Watson, 1937; Special Publication No.14, 'Drake's Plate of Brass Authenticated', by C.G. Fink and E.P. Polushkin, 1938.

John White's water colour of the Indian chief Wingina (Carolina, 1585) shows him wearing, from a string around his neck, a copper plate about six inches square. An Indian ruler in the San Francisco area may well have similarly sported the Drake plate.

A further episode in the saga came in the spring of 1974, when an archaeologist discovered a sixpenny piece, dated 1567, on the site of the Indian village of Olompali, near Novato, thirty miles north of San Francisco. This, of course, has been taken by some to be the missing coin from the plate of brass; and to give support to the San Francisco Bay lobby.

It must be recorded, however, that there were, and are, those who doubt the authenticity of the discovered brass plate!

10

The Lure of Norumbega, 1578-1582

In May 1582 there was published in London a documentary compilation by the reverend Richard Hakluyt, a don at Christ Church, Oxford, who was then thirty-one: *Divers voyages touching the discoverie of America and the ilands adjacent to the same, made first of all by our Englishmen and afterwards by the Frenchmen and Bretons.*[1] The volume included material about the Cabot voyages under Henry VII; and in the dedicatory epistle to Sir Philip Sidney, Hakluyt pointed out that exactly ninety years had passed since the discovery of America, and the English had hardly been conspicuous in the story. But 'there is a time for all men': and 'I conceive great hope that the time approacheth, and now is'.[2]

François I had employed as an explorer the Italian Giovanni da Verrazzano, born in Tuscany about 1485. In 1524, in 'La Dauphine', he had toured the American coastline from South Carolina to Newfoundland.[3] His experiences he described in an Italian letter to François in July 1524, which G.B. Ramusio printed in 1556. Hakluyt included a translation of this in the 1582 *Divers Voyages*: 'The Relation of John Verazanus'[4] – later included in the second edition of *Principal Navigations* (1600).

Verrazzano had anchored at the beginning of March 1524 near Cape Fear, midway down the coast of North Carolina.[5] The 'great fires that we saw by the sea coast' proved that the land was inhabited. After a reconnoitre in 'La Dauphine' southwards – as far as Charleston, South Carolina – Verrazzano anchored again near Cape Fear, and a boat was sent ashore. On the shore

we saw great store of people, which came to the seaside, and seeing us to approach they fled away, and sometimes would stand still and look back,

[1] Ed. Jones, Hakluyt Society, 1850.
[2] Jones, 8.
[3] For the reaction in England to Verrazzano's voyage, Quinn, *England and the Discovery of America*, 172-4.
[4] Jones, 55-71. Interpretation from Morison, *Northern Voyages*, 277-325: ch.9, 'The Voyages of Verrazzano'. There is a transcription of the MS in the Pierpont Morgan Library, and a translation by Susan Tarrow, in Wroth, *The Voyages of Verrazzano*, Yale, 1970.
[5] Jones, 56-7.

beholding us with great admiration. But afterwards, being animated and assured with signs that we made them, some of them came hard to the seaside, seeming to rejoice very much in the sight of us, and marvelling greatly at our apparel, shape and whiteness.

The Indians also offered food to the explorers. These Indians of North Carolina, recorded Verrazzano,

go altogether naked, except only that they cover their privy parts with certain skins of beasts like unto martens, which they fasten unto a narrow girdle made of grass, very artificially wrought, hanged about with tails of divers other beasts, which round about their bodies hang dangling down to their knees. Some of them wear garlands of birds' feathers. The people are of colour russet, and not much unlike the saracens. Their hair black, thick, and not very long; which they tie together in a knot behind, and wear it like a tail. They are well featured in their limbs, of mean stature, and commonly somewhat bigger than we; broad breasted, strong arms, their legs and other parts of their bodies well fashioned; and they are disfigured in nothing, saving that they have somewhat broad visages, and yet not all of them, for we saw many of them well favoured, having black and great eyes, with a cheerful and steady look; not strong of body, yet sharp witted, nimble, and great runners, as far as we could learn by experience.

As nimble, apparently, as the inhabitants of 'the uttermost parts of China'. The European party stayed only briefly on the shore, so could not record 'their manner of living, nor their particular customs'.

At the end of March Verrazzano landed on the Carolina outer Banks; less than fifty miles south of Roanoke. The Indians of that region (Pamlico Sound) were found to be 'very courteous and gentle'.[6] A young sailor was equipped with a packet of sheets of paper, mirrors and bells, and sent swimming to the shore from a boat. When he was three or four yards offshore, he tossed the packet to the Indians (not trusting them) and turned back to the ship. But the waves were too much for him, and he was forced back towards the shore. He was

so bruised that he lay there almost dead, which the Indians perceiving ran to catch him, and drawing him out, they carried him a little way off from the sea. The young man, perceiving they carried him, being at the first dismayed, began then greatly to fear, and cried out piteously. Likewise did the Indians which did accompany him, going about to cheer him and give him courage; and then, setting him on the ground at the foot of a little hill, against the sun, began to behold him with great admiration, marvelling at the whiteness of his flesh. And putting off his clothes, they made him warm at a great fire; not without our great fear which remained in the boat that they would have roasted him at that fire and have eaten him.

The young sailor revived, and after a while indicated his desire to return to the ship.

[6] 59-60.

And they with great love clapping him fast about with many embracings, accompanying him unto the sea, and, to put him in more assurance, leaving him alone, they went unto a high ground, and stood there beholding him until he was entered into the boat.

The Europeans noted that the Indians were

of colour inclining to black, as the other were; with their flesh very shining, of mean stature, handsome visage, and delicate limbs; and of very little strength, but prompt wit.

The next stop, about 10 April, was at Kitty Hawk, part of the Carolina outer Banks: off Albermarle Sound, north of Roanoke. Twenty men landed, and remained for three days; and christened the area Arcadia.[7] The Indians 'fled to the woods for fear'. But the Europeans encountered an old woman, with a child of eight years old on her back, and two infants on her shoulders; and, with her, a maiden aged 18 or 20, also carrying infants. They 'hid themselves in the grass for fear'.

To quiet them and to win their favour, our men gave them such victuals as they had with them to eat, which the old woman received thankfully. But the young woman disdained them all, and threw them disdainfully on the ground. And going about to take the young woman, which was very beautiful and of tall stature, they could not possibly (for the great outcries that she made) bring her to the sea. And especially having great woods to pass through, and being far from the ship, we purposed to leave her behind, bearing away the child only.

The Indians of the Albemarle Sound area were 'more white than those that we found before'. They were clad in 'certain leaves that hang on boughs of trees, which they sew together with threads of wild hemp'. They live by fishing and fowling. And their basic food is leguminous – beans, peas, lentils: 'Whereof they have great store, differing in colour and taste from ours: of good and pleasant taste.' The Europeans saw Indian canoes, made from trees, with an aperture burnt out. Verrazzano – born in Chianti country – was impressed by the vines:

If by husbandmen they were dressed in good order, without all doubt they would yield excellent wines. For we having oftentimes seen the fruit thereof dried; which was sweet and pleasant, and not differing from ours.

European investigation was limited:

We knew not their dwellings, because they were far up in the land: and we judge by many signs that we saw, that they are of wood, and of trees framed together. We do believe also, by many conjectures and signs, that many of them, sleeping in the fields, have no other cover than the open sky. Further

[7] 61-2.

knowledge have we not of them. We think that all the rest whose countries we passed live after one manner.

On 17 April 'La Dauphine' reached New York Bay; and the Europeans saw the mouth of the Hudson. The Indians seemed like those of North Carolina.[8] And they 'came towards us very cheerfully, making great shouts of admiration, showing us where we might come to land most safely with our boat'.

They sailed on to Narragansett Bay: and sheltered for two weeks in the harbour of Newport, Rhode Island.[9] Indeed, they gave Rhode Island its name. They 'discovered an island in the form of a triangle, distant from the mainland three leagues, about the bigness of the island of the Rhodes'. This was Block Island, off the coast of Connecticut, beyond Long Island. Roger Williams in the 1640s was to misinterpret Verrazzano, thinking he meant Aquidneck, the seat of Newport. In Narragansett Bay, the explorers encountered the Wampanoag Indians of Rhode Island and Massachusetts – the tribe which from 1621 was to be the ally of Plymouth Plantation. They had conquered the area recently (from the Narragansetts): and were in need of allies. Indians came out in two boats to greet the visitors:

They all made a loud shout together, declaring that they rejoiced. When we had something animated them, using their gestes, they came so near us that we cast them certain bells and glasses and many toys, which when they had received they looked on them with laughing, and came without fear aboard our ship.

The Indian party included two 'kings': of 'goodly stature and shape'. One was about forty, the other about twenty. The elder

had upon his naked body a hart's skin, wrought artificially with divers branches like damask. His head was bare, with the hair tied up behind with divers knots. About his neck he had a large chain, garnished with divers stones of sundry colours.

The young chief was similarly clad. The Wampanoag tribe especially impressed the explorers.

This is the goodliest people, and of the fairest conditions, that we have found in this our voyage. They exceed us in bigness. They are of the colour of brass; some of them incline more to whiteness, others are of yellow colour. Of comely visage, with long and black hair, which they are very careful to trim and deck up. They are black and quick eyed. I write not to your majesty of the other part of their body, having all such proportion as appertaineth to any handsome man. The women are of the like conformity and beauty, very handsome and well favoured; they are as well mannered and continent as any women of good education; they are all naked, save their privy parts, which they cover with a deer's skin, branched or embroidered, as the men use; there are also of them which wear on their arms very rich skins.

[8] 63. [9] 64-8.

Skins of leopards, said Verrazzano: in fact, of wildcats or lynxes. Some
of the women

adorn their heads with divers ornaments made of their own hair, which hang
before on both sides their breasts. Others use other kind of dressing
themselves, like unto the women of Egypt and Syria. These are of the elder
sort.

When married, both men and women adorn themselves with trinkets:
'according to the usage of the people of the East.' They wear 'plates of
wrought copper' which 'they esteem more than gold'. (These may
have come from the Indians of the Great Lakes or they may have been
European.) Of the European gifts, they preferred the tiny bells, the
Venetian crystal beads, and various trinkets which they could wear.
They fancied neither iron nor steel, cloth of silk nor cloth of gold. As a
sign of joy they sometimes have 'their faces all bepainted with various
colours'.

In their fortnight in the Bay, the explorers found the Indians 'very
liberal, for they give that which they have: we became great friends'.
The Indians were anxious to please. One day one of the two chiefs
'drawing his bow, and running up and down with his gentlemen,
made much sport to gratify our men'. Every day Indians rowed to 'La
Dauphine': 'bringing their wives with them, whereof they are very
jealous' (the wives were not allowed to board the vessel, but waited in
the canoes).

Verrazzano made comparatively extensive notes. The Indian
houses were

made in circular or round form, ten or twelve feet in compass, made with half
circles of timber, separate one from another, without any order of building,
covered with mats of straw wrought cunningly together, which save them
from the wind and rain. And if they had the order of building and perfect
skill of workmanship as we have, there were no doubt but that they would
also make eftsoons great and stately buildings.

The straw covers were taken off when the Indians moved, and fitted
onto the wooden structures they had built elsewhere: the migration
depended on the season. In each house dwelt the 'father' and 'the
whole family': 25 or 30 persons, sometimes. The basic food, as in
Carolina, was leguminous: though in the Narragansett Bay region the
vegetables were grown 'with better order of husbandry' than in the
South. In their sowing they observe 'the course of the moon, and the
rising of certain stars, and divers other customs spoken of by
Antiquity'. They live by hunting and fishing. Moreover, they

live long, and are seldom sick; and if they chance to fall sick at any time they
heal themselves with fire, without any physician, and they say that they die
for very age.

They are a compassionate people, 'very pitiful and charitable towards their neighbours'. In adversity, they make 'great lamentations': in misery, they 'reckon up all their felicity'. Death is marked by 'mourning, mixed with singing, which continueth for a long space'.

'La Dauphine' left Narragansett Bay on 5 May; sailed through Nantucket Sound, rounded Cape Cod, and anchored off the coast of Maine, near Portland. The Indians here – the Abnaki – were not at all pleasant.[10] When twenty-five men from the vessel landed, the Indians 'shot at us with their bows, making great outcries, and afterwards fled into the woods'. The Europeans did exchange goods with the Indians: but the Indians took no account of European 'courtesy' – and delivered their offerings by ropes from the crags!

The people differ much from the other, and look how much the former seemed to be courteous and gentle, so much were these full of rudeness and ill manners, and so barbarous that by no signs that ever we could make we could have any kind of traffic with them. They clothe themselves with bears' skins, and leopards and seals, and other beasts' skins. Their food, as far as we could perceive, repairing often unto their dwellings, we suppose to be by hunting and fishing, and of certain fruits (which are a kind of roots which the earth yieldeth of her own accord). They have no grain, neither saw we any kind or sign of tillage. Neither is the land, for the barrenness thereof, apt to bear fruit or seed.

'La Dauphine' sailed along the east coast of Newfoundland: and then set out east for home.

Verrazzano committed himself about the religion – or lack of it – of the American Indian in general: similar, he assumed, from South Carolina to Maine.[11]

Touching the religion of this people which we have found. For want of their language we could not understand, neither by signs nor gesture, that they had any religion or law at all; or that they did acknowledge any first cause or mover; neither that they worship the heaven or stars, the sun or moon or other planets, and much less whether they be idolators. Neither could we learn whether that they used any kind of sacrifices or other adorations. Neither in their villages have they any temples or houses of prayer. We suppose that they have no religion at all, and that they live at their own liberty. And that all this proceedeth of ignorance. For that they are very easy to be persuaded; and all that they see us Christians do in our divine service, they did the same, with the like imitation as they saw us do it.

Giovanni da Verrazzano was to be murdered and eaten by cannibals on the island of Guadeloupe in 1528.

When Ramusio printed this letter in 1556, he gave it the running title 'Della Terra de Norumbega' – in the 1582 Hakluyt edition, 'The Discovery of Norumbega'. Giovanni's brother Girolamo had prepared a map to accompany the letter, on which Maine was marked as

[10] 70.   [11] 71.

'Oranbega'. In the Abnaki dialect, this meant a stretch of quiet water between two rapids; and was probably a descruption of Penobscot Bay, Bangor, Maine.[12] By the 1540s French writers had extended the name to the whole region.[13] Norumbega (Norambega, Norembega, Norembegge, Norembeque, Norimbega, Norombega, Norumberg, Norunnbedge) usually meant the area later to be called New England: the 'north part' of Virginia. On occasion it was used as an alternative to 'Virginia'. But there was a 'northern' ring to it. Nomenclature was often vague. The term 'New England' (suggested by Drake's 'Nova Albion') was given currency by John Smith's *A Description of New England*, 1616. But in 1615 the historian William Camden could still write of 'the north part of America, which we call New-found-land'.[14] And a marginal note in the 1582 *Divers Voyages* noted of Verrazzano's section on Narragansett Bay: 'The country of Sir Humphrey Gilbert's voyage'[15] (his intended voyage, that is).

In September 1583 Hakluyt left Oxford to go to Paris as chaplain and secretary to the English ambassador; and compiler of information about French activity in North America. He also edited the Latin text of Pietro Martire's *De Orbe Novo Decades*, which he published in Paris in February 1587, dedicated to Sir Walter Raleigh. Hakluyt was based in Paris for five years (1583-8). After a year, he had completed his short *A Discourse of Western Planting*, written at the request of Raleigh, and presented to the Queen in manuscript in October 1584. It was not printed until 1877.[16] The correct title is: 'A particuler discourse concerninge the greate necessitie and mainfolde commodyties that are like to growe to this Realme of England by the Westerne discoveries lately attempted' – attempted, that is, by Humphrey Gilbert and Walter Raleigh.

One of the 'commodities' likely to benefit England by American colonisation, Hakluyt argued, was the relief of over-population and idleness. The kingdom, because of 'long peace and seldom sickness', has 'grown more populous than ever heretofore'.[17] In particular, it is 'swarming with lusty youths that be turned to no profitable use'.[18] This was quite an obsession with Hakluyt. In the 1582 letter to Philip Sidney he had mentioned the crowded prisons, and the incessant hangings – all because of 'superfluous people'. He drew an analogy with bees: 'We read that the bees when they grow to be too many in their own hives at home are wont to be led out by their captains to swarm abroad.'[19] George Peckham, associate of Humphrey Gilbert, in

[12] Morison, *Northern Voyages*, 311.
[13] *ibid.*, 464-70.
[14] Quoted Quinn, *Gilbert Voyages*, 427.
[15] Jones, 64.
[16] In Cambridge, Mass. The manuscript is in the New York Public Library. Printed 1935 in Taylor, *The Writings of the Hakluyts*, 211-326.
[17] Taylor, 234.
[18] *ibid.*, 249.
[19] Jones, 9.

an essay published in 1583, had similarly suggested that 'great numbers' might find it attractive to become emigrants, living 'in such penury and want, as they could be contented to hazard their lives, and to serve one year for meat, drink and apparel only, without wages, in hope thereby to amend their estates'. For Peckham, success in America could mean 'all odious idleness from this our realm utterly banished, divers decayed towns repaired, and many poor and needy persons relieved, and estates of such as now live in want shall be embettered'. For one thing, children could be set to work making trinkets for the Indians;[20] Gilbert had made the same suggestion in 1566.[21] Hakluyt, Gilbert and Peckham certainly had the 'convict' theory of colonisation: export the dregs of the population. But Hakluyt in 1584 also had a feel for America as 'a safe and a sure place to receive people from all parts of the world that are forced to flee for the truth of God's word'[22] – not merely English people, note. Asylum America: Crèvecoeur, writing about 1770, wrote of British North America as 'the asylum of freedom', the 'refuge of distressed Europeans', and of Englishmen who 'when convulsed by factions, afflicted by a variety of miseries and wants, restless and impatient, took refuge here'.[23] Perhaps America has always been the home of Elizabethan lost causes. Peckham, who belonged to a Catholic gentry family, may have been thinking of America as a possible refuge for the adherents of Rome.[24] Hakluyt, a conventional Elizabethan cleric, thought of it more as a depository for the troublesome Puritans, who cause 'inconveniences and strifes amongst ourselves at home in matters of Ceremonies'. Contention would end if the Puritans would cross the Atlantic:

Those of the clergy which by reason of idleness here at home are now always coining of new opinions, having by this voyage to set themselves on work, in reducing of the savages to the chief principles of our faith, will become less contentious, and be contented with the truth in religion already established by authority.[25]

Hakluyt did not live to hear of the Pilgrim Fathers – he died in 1616. Richard Hooker, the most wide ranging and stylish defender of the Elizabeth Church, thought that Puritan Ideals might be more acceptable if the Puritans 'did not live among men, but in some wilderness by themselves'.[26] Hakluyt's thesis that the 'Errand into the Wilderness' might basically be attributed to Idleness has, at any rate, an agreeable simplicity about it.

[20] Quinn, *Gilbert Voyages*, 469, 476, 462.
[21] *ibid.*, 161.
[22] Taylor, 318.
[23] Crèvecoeur, *Letters from an American Farmer*, Everyman, 5, 39.
[24] See Quinn, *England and Discovery of America*, ch.14: 'English Catholics and America, 1581-1633.'
[25] Taylor, 217.
[26] *Laws of Ecclesiastical Polity*, I, xvi, 6.

Hakluyt invoked Las Casas in 1584, repeating the story of the fifteen million exterminated Indians; one of the objectives of the English would be to liberate the Indians still oppressed by Spain. And the English would treat the Indian with 'humanity, courtesy and freedom'.[27] The Indians, of course, were idolators. Hakluyt lifted from Oviedo the story that in 1524 some Indians 'from the coast of Norembega' were taken to Spain; where all saw that they 'worshipped the sun, the moon and the stars, and used other idolatry'. He also quoted Jacques Cartier, who asserted that the Indians 'believe not at all in God, but in one whom they call Cudruaigny: they say that often he speaketh with them, and telleth them what weather shall follow, whether good or bad, etc.'. But Cartier (and Verrazzano) had made clear that the Indians are

very easy to be persuaded, and do all that they saw the Christians do in their divine service, with like imitation and devotion, and were very desirous to become Christians, and would fain have been baptised.

All the Indians need is godly preachers, to rise to the challenge of 'reducing of infinite multitudes of these simple people that are in error, into the right and perfect way of their salvation.' And the reducing should not be by force. The preachers and the settlers must learn the Indian language; and

by little and little acquaint themselves with their manner, and so with discretion and mildness distil into their purged minds the sweet and lively liquor of the gospel.[28]

Hakluyt's editorial activity in the early 1580s was intended as support for the American enterprises of Sir Humphrey Gilbert. On 11 June 1578 – almost exactly one year before Drake's adventures in California – the Queen had granted Letters Patent to Gilbert:[29] 'Our trusty and well beloved servant Sir Humphrey Gilbert of Compton in our county of Devon, knight, and to his heirs and assigns.' Gilbert was given 'free liberty and license' to 'discover, search, find out and view such remote heathen and barbarous lands, countries and territories not actually possessed of any Christian prince or people': these he could 'have, hold, occupy and enjoy', having authority to 'inhabit or remain there, to build and fortify'. He had 'full power' to dispose of the territory 'according to the order of the laws of England, as near as the same conveniently may be' to any person within the allegiance of the crown: at his 'will' and 'pleasure'. (Elizabeth merely required homage – and 20% of any gold and silver mined there.) Those settlers born in England, Ireland, or 'any place within our allegiance', were to 'have and enjoy all the privileges of free denizens and persons native of

[27] Taylor, 318.
[28] *ibid.*, 214-15.
[29] Quinn, *Gilbert Voyages*, 188-94.

England and within our allegiance, in such like ample manner and form as if they were born and personally resident within our said realm of England'. Gilbert had 'full and mere power and authority to correct, punish, pardon, govern and rule' in all capital, civil, criminal and marine cases: providing that his colonial 'statutes, laws and ordinances' were 'as near as conveniently may be, agreeable to the form of the laws and policies of England'; and also 'not against the true Christian faith or religion now professed in the Church of England'. All this was for 'uniting in more perfect league and amity, of such countries, lands or territories so to be possessed and inhabited as aforesaid, with our realms of England and Ireland'. The 'territory' was taken to cover six hundred miles in all directions from the place of initial settlement.

Gilbert was much concerned with his 'full power and authority' in America. In 1571, when he was 34, he had sat in the House of Commons as member for Plymouth. On 14 April, after craving 'patience and toleration of the House', he made a speech – which was to be very unpopular – in defence of the 'Prerogative Imperial', asserting that 'it is not good to sport or venture too much with Princes': her Majesty might 'use her power any way', as the French monarchy had done – and he pointed out that 'other kings had absolute power, as Denmark and Portugal'.[30] Gilbert was thinking of the absolute authority of the Crown of Castile; of the untrammelled authority of the Queen to give him authority in America, and of the nature of his own power when he arrived there – one of the occasions on which Elizabethan constitutional points are fully comprehensible only in an American context. The speech is noteworthy – if for no other reason – because it occasioned, on 20 April, the maiden speech of Peter Wentworth, who attacked Gilbert's 'disposition to flatter and fawn on the Prince, comparing him to the chameleon, which can change himself into all colours, saving white'.[31]

Gilbert would have approved of the 'Maryland' Charter of 1632, in which the Baron of Baltimore in Ireland and his heirs were made 'true and absolute lords and proprietaries of the region', having the same 'rights, jurisdictions, privileges, prerogatives, royalties, liberties, immunities, and royal rights, and temporal franchises' as the Bishop of Durham 'within the bishopric or county palatinate of Durham'.[32]

Gilbert was conscious of the fact that the English monarch was 'King' of Ireland: a title assumed by Henry VIII in 1540 – the previous style had been 'Lord' of Ireland. Gilbert had been a soldier in Ireland from 1566 to 1570; and had been knighted at Drogheda in January 1570, when he was 32. In the late 1560s the Lord Deputy of Ireland, the highly efficient Sir Henry Sidney, had pursued a comparatively effective policy, both by destroying the power of the savage Shane O'Neill in the province of Ulster, and by encouraging

[30] D'Ewes, *Journals*, 1693, 168.
[31] *ibid.*, 175.
[32] Jensen, *American Colonial Documents*, 86.

English colonising, or 'planting' in the provinces of Munster and Leinster. West Country gentry – the Gilberts, the Raleighs, the Grenvilles – were especially interested in the planting of Ireland; and much of this seems a rehearsal for the American story. The Indians and the Irish were often compared. To the Elizabethans, Ireland was in a primitive (and popish) state of nature. The country was beautiful, the Irish were brave and comely – but they were also unclean, promiscuous, beastly, and unfit to have care of land. A character in John Webster's play *The White Devil* (1612) remarks (IV,1):

> Like the wild Irish, I'll ne'er think thee dead
> Till I can play at football with thy head.

Only an English conquest could ensure Civility; and there was no certainty of this until 1603. Gilbert wrote a paper on the plantation of Munster in 1569. One of the points he made was that the laws of the settlers should be 'agreeable to the laws of this realm';[33] by that time Gilbert was a member of the Dublin House of Commons.

Elizabeth always tried, in Ireland, to do things on the cheap. More was hoped for under James I. Francis Bacon, writing to the King in 1606 about the new schemes for Irish plantation,[34] pointed out the virtues of the organisation of the Virginia Company, formed earlier in 1606: a 'Council of Plantation' in London, and a council in the colony. Bacon professed to think the American enterprise a poor thing compared with the 'plantation of great and noble parts of the island of Ireland'. Ireland lacked the spurious appeal of novelty: 'there is no warm winters, nor orange trees, nor strange beasts, or birds, or any other points of curiosity or pleasure, as there are in the Indies and the like.' But in Ireland, James could colonise without 'the effusion of blood'. For another – and here Bacon in writing of Ulster was referring by implication to Virginia – James could 'join the harp of David, in casting out the evil spirit of superstition, with the harp of Orpheus, in casting out desolation and barbarism'. Orpheus

> by the virtue and sweetness of his harp, did call and assemble the beasts and birds, of their nature wild and savage, to stand about him, as in a theatre, forgetting their affections and fierceness, of lust and of prey; and listening to the tunes and harmonies of the harp. And soon after called likewise the stones and the woods to remove and stand in order about him.

A fable, said Bacon, traditionally applied to colonisation

---

[33] Quinn, *Gilbert Voyages*, 123. Pages 118-28 cover Irish colonisation schemes 1567-72. See also Quinn, *The Elizabethans and the Irish*, 1966, Ch. 9, 'Ireland and America Intertwined'; and, for the pattern of referring Indian practices to those of the Irish, 23-27; and Nicholas P. Canny, 'The Ideology of English Colonisation: From Ireland to America', *William and Mary Quarterly*, ser.3, vol.30, no.4, Oct. 1973, pp.575-98.

[34] Bacon, *Life and Letters*, ed. Spedding, IV, 116-26.

when people of barbarous manners are brought to give over and discontinue their customs of revenge and blood, and of dissolute life, and of theft and rapine, and to give ear to the wisdom of laws and governments.

Over ten years later, in 1617, Bacon felt entitled to pay tribute to the decade's work in Ireland – the last country in Europe to be 'reclaimed from desolation; and a desert (in many parts) to population and plantation; and from savage and barbarous customs, to humanity and civility'.[35] And in 1621, speaking in the House of Lords,[36] Bacon (Baron Verulam, Viscount St Alban) linked the 'reduction to civility' of Ireland with the fact that the United Kingdom had 'gotten a lot or portion in the New World, by the plantation of Virginia and the Summer Islands'. A grain of mustard seed – on earth, as in the Kingdom of Heaven – could become a great tree.

Bacon in fact was accustomed to equating the Wild Irish (with their liquor) and the Wild Indians (with their tobacco).[37] The equation became a commonplace. Hugh Peter in 1646 asserted that 'the wild Irish and the Indian do not much differ'; and should therefore be similarly handled.[38] After all, Las Casas, speaking of the Indian, had drawn attention to the fact that in ancient Ireland cannibalism was rife.[39]

The Elizabethans' plans for settlement in America lacked effective royal supervision; and – more important – royal financial aid. George Peckham, writing of the Gilbert enterprise in 1583, was aware that some critics condemned the American dream to failure for that very reason. Not so, said Peckham: look at the private noblemen who conquered Ireland in the reign of Henry II 'at their own proper charges'.[40] Especially Strongbow: Richard Fitz Gilbert, second Earl of Pembroke, who captured Waterford and Dublin in 1170, and became King of Leinster in 1171. Hakluyt encouraged Raleigh with the same example in 1587;[41] reminding Raleigh of John Hooker's dedication to him of the 'Irish History' by Giraldus Cambrensis (Gerald of Wales) in the second edition of Holinshed's *Chronicles*, published earlier that year. Strongbow, said Hakluyt, 'accompanied only with certain of his private friends', was so successful that he opened the way for Henry II to proceed to 'the speedy subjection of all that warlike nation to this crown of England: which so continueth to this present day'. Thus 'mean and private men' were the best colonisers. Peckham and Hakluyt neglected to point out that for Henry II Ireland was a personal possession of which he was feudal landlord: he crossed to Ireland in 1171 to keep the Strongbows in their place, and to accept homage. Hakluyt in fact knew quite well that (as William Camden was to comment, in discussing Gilbert's 1583

---

[35] *ibid.*, VI, 205.   [36] *ibid.*, VII, 175.   [37] *ibid.*, VI, 306.
[38] Quoted Stearns, *Strenuous Puritan*, 288.
[39] Elliott, *Old World and the New*, 34.
[40] Quinn, *Gilbert Voyages*, 471.
[41] Taylor, 376.

expedition) 'it is a difficulter thing to carry over colonies into remote countries upon private purses, than he and others in an erroneous credulity had persuaded themselves, to their own cost and detriment'.[42] Hakluyt's 1584 'Discourse' was really a plea for government support – which is probably why the work was not at the time printed.

For Gilbert, the plans for English plantation in Ireland in the late 1560s may have been an alternative to his dream of Cathay. He was fascinated by the prospect of a north west passage to Asia; and petitioned the Queen about it in 1565. He might reasonably have expected Elizabeth to be sympathetic. Gilbert had entered her service at Hatfield in 1554, when he was 17 (a product of Eton and Oxford). In 1566 he wrote *A New Passage to Cataia*, which we have already discussed. And Gilbert from his boyhood (according to John Hooker of Exeter, uncle of Richard) had taken 'great delight in the study of cosmography, and especially in navigations'.[43] Not until 1578 was Gilbert to have opportunity to search across the Atlantic for his unimaginary Utopia.

The Letters Patent of 1578 were valid for six years: until June 1584. In November 1578 – after a false start in September – seven ships left Dartmouth for what in the event was a six month cruise. Gilbert himself was on board, and his half-brother Walter Raleigh. (Walter's father was the second husband of Humphrey's widowed mother: Humphrey was born in 1539, Walter in 1552.) With them were nearly 400 'gentlemen, soldiers and mariners'; including three surgeons, one physician, six 'musicians', two trumpeters and a drummer.[44] The account of this adventure published in Holinshed's *Chronicles* in 1587 (a section probably written by John Hooker) said the aim was to discover 'the country of Norembega': 'with intention to settle an English colony there'.[45] This may have been true. But there was no settlement, and no discovery. Gilbert himself got no further than Ireland.

The next year, 1579-80, two vessels of reconnaissance were sent by Gilbert to Norumbega; and they apparently reached the Penobscot Bay, 'the river of Norembega'.[46] But Gilbert stayed at home. And Nothing effective happened until 1582.

In July 1582 Sir George Peckham, of Denham, Bucks, went to Mortlake to consult John Dee about the English claim to Norumbega – in view of possible Spanish and Portuguese oppoisition to the theory of the claim.[47] Dee, alchemical philosopher, mystical mathematician, antiquarian, scientific and technical experimenter (or dabbler), and amateur of the occult, had prepared about 1580 a map of North America.[48] Dee was also interested in the use of mathematics in

---

[42] Quinn, *Gilbert Voyages*, 428.
[43] *ibid.*, 434. [44] *ibid.*, 210-12. [45] *ibid.*, 237.
[46] Morison, *Northern Voyages*, 468.
[47] Quinn, *Gilbert Voyages*, 280.
[48] *ibid.*, pocket at end of Vol. II.

navigation. 'John Dee His Mathematical Preface', published in 1570 (Preface to an English translation of Euclid) contained a section on the practical application of geometry in the preparation of maps, charts and globes,[49] and a later passage on navigation as one of the 'Arts Mathematical'. Here Dee said that English pilots should be especially skilful; because of the 'privilege God had endued this land with, by reason of situation, most commodious for navigation to places most famous and rich'. He also mentioned Gilbert:[50] 'a young gentleman, a courageous captain', who in 1567 had been 'in great readiness, with good hope and great causes of persuasion, to have ventured for a Discovery' either to the east or to the west. But he was called instead to Ireland. In 1582 Dee was reassuring about the English claim to Norumbega.

Slightly later in 1582 – August and September – a small committee in London interviewed various people who might have useful information for the Norumbega enterprise; the committee included Gilbert, Peckham, Sir Francis Walsingham (Secretary of State) and (probably) Hakluyt. The main witness was David Ingram: who claimed that in 1568 he had walked, with others, the three thousand miles from the Gulf of Mexico to Cape Breton – which took them twelve months. The story was open to many doubts; but there seemed to be something in it, and Hakluyt printed the material in 1589[51] (though he deleted it later). Ingram had much to say about the Indians of Norumbega.

The people commonly are of good favour, feature and shape of body, of growth above five feet high, somewhat thick, with their faces and skins of colour like an olive, and towards the north somewhat tawney, but some of them are painted with divers colours; they are very swift of foot; the hair of their head is shaven in sundry spots, and the rest of their head is traced.

In the southern regions, 'they all go naked: saving that the noblemen's privities are covered with the neck of a gourd, and the women's privities with the hair or leaf of the palm tree'. In the north, they are 'clothed with beasts' skins, the hair side being next to their bodies in winter'. In some ways they are very improper; being 'so brutish and beastly that they will not forbear the use of their wives in open presence'. But at the same time they have severe penalties for adultery – both the man and the woman have their throats cut, the man by the woman, and then the woman by her family. So that was all right. They are 'naturally very courteous, if you do not abuse them, either in their persons or goods, but use them courteously'. They are not cannibals. They honour

for their god a devil, which they call Colluchio, who speaketh unto them

[49] Dee, 'Mathematical Preface', A.iiii.r.
[50] A.i.r.
[51] Quinn, *Gilbert Voyages*, 281-310.

sometimes in the likeness of a black dog, and sometimes in the likeness of a black calf. And some do honour the sun. the moon and the stars.

Black, by a 1589, was coming to mean Bad: a writer on witchcraft in 1584 described a devilish apparition in England as having 'a skin like a Niger'.[52] Two of Ingram's party, Richard Brown and Richard Twide, visited the dwelling of a humble Indian, and there saw the 'Colluchio or devil, with very great eyes like a black cat'. Brown called on Father, Son and Holy Ghost; Twide said, I defy thee and all thy works. And 'presently the Colluchio shrank away in a stealing manner forth of the doors, and was seen no more unto them'. Ingram gave Indian words for Good Day, King, Lord, Bread, Sun, and Private Parts. And related that all the Indians wear bracelets of gold and silver; that the nobles carry feathers in their hair; and that the Kings wear 'painted or coloured garments', rubies four inches long and two inches broad, and are carried in chairs of silver or crystal.

Perhaps Hakluyt was wise to omit this material in his second edition. Admiral Morison, however – although suspicious of the yarns – accepts that Ingram was not at base a liar.[53]

We should remember that Ingram, like all Sinbads, had to tell marvels in order to live, and that not all he says is pure imagination. But he so mixes things up – penguins next to flamingoes, tropical plants next northern pines – that it is difficult to sift out his Norumbega data from those about Florida and the country between.

[52] Quoted Thomas, *Religion and the Decline of Magic*, 475: from Reginald Scot, *Discoverie of Witchcraft* (1584).

[53] Morison, *Northern Voyages*, 489. See also the essay on Ingram by Quinn and Thomas Dunbabin in *Dictionary of Canadian Biography*, I (1000-1700), 1966: 'The framework of the story has some degree of plausibility, even if the details have little coherence.'

11

Humphrey Gilbert and the Newfound Lands, 1583

A fleet of five ships left Plymouth on 11 June 1583, headed by the 'Delight' (120 tuns) in which Gilbert sailed.[1] One of the five, the 'Raleigh' (200 tuns), financed by Sir Walter, turned back after two days because of disease. The 'Swallow' was 40 tuns; the 'Squirrel' a pinnace of 10 tuns. And Edward Hayes was 'captain and owner' of the 'Golden Hind', 40 tuns, named in honour of Drake. Hayes' account of the expedition, printed by Hakluyt in 1589, is the eye witness narrative.[2] The first account to be printed, late in 1583, was by Sir George Peckham, who was not a member of the expedition: he relied on what Hayes told him.[3]

Hayes matriculated from King's College Cambridge as a Fellow Commoner in 1571. His was a Liverpool family, of gentry status; his father had traded from Liverpool to Ireland and London. After leaving King's, Hayes had lived with the family of the Hobys, at Bisham Abbey, Berkshire: Elizabeth Hoby, *née* Cooke, was a sister in law of both Nicholas Bacon and William Cecil, Lord Burghley. Edward was tutor to her young son. He had subscribed to the Gilbert expedition in 1578, and may have been a member of that abortive venture.[4]

Hayes tells us that there were 260 men on the 1583 fleet: including shipwrights, carpenters, masons, smiths, and a German expert on minerals and metals. Also Stephen Parmenius (István Paizsos), an Hungarian poet who had been a 'bed-fellow' of Hakluyt at Christ Church in 1581 (Hakluyt was to print one of his letters and one of his poems).[5] Parmenius had been commissioned to compose an account of the expedition in Latin verse. Also,

---

[1] Morison, *Northern Voyages*, 572.

[2] Quinn, *Gilbert Voyages*, 385-423. Everyman Hakluyt, VI, 1-38. Quinn's two volumes (continuous paging) are hereafter cited as *GV*. *Dictionary of Canadian Biography*, I (1000-1700), 1966, has an essay on Gilbert by Quinn.

[3] *GV*, 435-80. Everyman Hakluyt, VI, 42-78.

[4] For Hayes, Quinn, *England and the Discovery of America*, Ch.8, 'Hayes and the Americas'. There is also an essay on Hayes by Quinn in *Dictionary of Canadian Biography*, I.

[5] *The New-Found Land of Stephen Parmenius*: translations by N.M. Cheshire, commentaries by D.B. Quinn. Quinn wrote the essay on Parmenius in *Dictionary of Canadian Biography*, I.

for solace of our people, and allurement of the savages, we were provided of music in good variety; not omitting the least toys, as morris dancers, hobby horses, and Maylike conceits to delight the savage people, whom we intended to win by all fair means possible. And to that end we were indifferently furnished of all petty haberdashery wares, to barter with those simple people.[6]

One wonders if any clerics were aboard; none is mentioned.

It had been intended to take a surveyor and painter: to

draw to life all strange birds, beasts, fishes, plants, herbs, trees and fruits, and bring home of each root, as near as you may. Also draw the figures and shapes of men and women in their apparel, as also of their manner of weapons in every place as you shall find them differing.[7]

But this intention was not apparently realised.

Gilbert was thinking in terms of the north, Norumbega, rather than the south: 'the north parts of America about the river of Canada', said Hayes: possibly as a challenge to the French. If there were 'good success in the North parts', it would 'greatly advance the hope of the South' (which appears not to have been thought of with much optimism). The fleet could either have gone to Florida and worked north: or, maybe, have gone 'from the north southward'. In the event, the captains decided 'to take the Newfoundland in our way'. The north-south tension was not too important, for the coastline of America from Florida 'infinitely into the North' was available to the English. Gilbert's general intention, in his 'western discovery of America', was to 'plant Christian inhabitants in place convenient upon those large and ample countries extended northward from the cape of Florida'.[8]

On 3 August 1583 the four ships reached St John's Newfoundland. In the harbour, they found nearly forty fishing vessels: English – and also Spanish, Portuguese and French.

The cod of the Grand Bank Fisheries had attracted Europeans since the first years of the sixteenth century. The French were there by 1504; and Newfoundland Indians (Beothucks) were taken to Rouen as early as 1507.[9] Cartier made a landfall in 1534 on the east coast of Newfoundland, at Cape Bonavista; but this was already 'a favourite landfall of French fishermen'.[10] We have seen that Verrazzano skirted the east coast, on behalf of François I, in 1524. Admiral Morison thinks it 'beyond reasonable doubt' that the northern tip of Newfoundland was the site of 'Vinland', the colony of Leif Ericsson in the early eleventh century.[11] British fishing fleets from the West

[6] *GV*, 396.

[7] *American Drawings of White*, I, 34-5.

[8] Hayes, *GV*, 385, 390-2.

[9] Morison, *Northern Voyages*, 254.

[10] *ibid.*, 346.

[11] *ibid.*, 38. Ch.3: 'The Norsemen and Vinland 800-1400'.

Country were visiting the Fisheries by 1480s. And Henry VII, following the discoveries of Cabot (1497) and his Bristol successors (and predecessors?), referred in 1502 to 'th'isle': 'the new found land.'[12] In 1502 there were Beothuck Indians at his court. The fact that they died their skins with scarlet vegetable juice is said to have occasioned the description 'Red Indian'.[13]

An Act of Parliament in 1542[14] complained that English fishermen, instead of catching the cod themselves, are in the habit of buying it: from 'Picards, Flemings, Normans and Frenchmen' – sometimes 'half the seas over': an occasion of carousing – hence the subsequent expression. But by the late 1570s the English seemed to have wrested the supremacy in the Fisheries from the French (and the Portuguese). So the time was perhaps ripe for a 'colony'.[15]

Gilbert wrote to Hakluyt on 8 August 1583.[16] The land was 'very good and full of all sorts of victual': deer, pheasant, partridge, swans, and 'divers fowl else' (and of course the fish). And on 5 August Gilbert had 'entered here in the right of the Crown of England; and have engraven the arms of England, divers Spaniards, Portugals, and other strangers, witnessing the same'. (This was on lead fixed to a post: shades of Drake four years earlier!) Gilbert had initially introduced himself as 'her Majesty's lieutenant'. On 5 August the principal officers of all the ships in the harbour were summoned to his tent.[17] The Letters Patent were read (and interpreted to the non-English) making clear Gilbert's purpose 'to take possession of those lands to the behalf of the crown of England, and the advancement of Christian religion in those paganish regions'. Gilbert dug a piece of turf; and 'took possession' in 'the right of the crown of England' of St John's and the territories within six hundred miles 'everyway', now 'appertaining to the Queen of England, and himself authorised under her Majesty to possess and enjoy it'. Gilbert was 'absolute governor there, by virtue of her Majesty's patents'. Later, he 'ordained and established laws'; one of them, that 'religion publicly exercised should be such, and none other, than is used in the Church of England'. And all laws, of course, to be 'in all points, as near as might be, agreeable to the laws of England'.

Exactly four weeks after the landing, on 31 August, Gilbert decided to return to England, with the intention of coming back in the spring of 1584. Gilbert had become definitely a man of the north. He had decided that in 1584 there would be two parties. One fleet, including Hayes and the 'Golden Hind', could go to the area near Florida. But 'he reserved unto himself the North, affirming that the voyage had

---

[12] *ibid.*, 219.

[13] Carrington, *British Overseas*, 575.

[14] Morison, *Northern Voyages*, 471.

[15] See Cell, *English Enterprise in Newfoundland*, Ch.2: 'The Fishery: A Time of Expansion, 1577-1604'.

[16] *GV*, 383.

[17] This account combines Peckham (*GV*, 401-3) and Hayes (*GV*, 444-5).

won his heart from the South, and that he was now become a Northern man altogether'.[18]

The return trip was a disaster. On 9 September 1583 Gilbert was 'swallowed by the ocean' (in the phrase of Camden): Hayes reports his saying, 'We are as near to heaven by sea as by land'. He was 46: 'Drowned', as an inscription on a portrait has it, 'in the Discovery of Virginia'.[19] Had the term been then current, a more accurate halo would have been, 'drowned in the discovery of New England'.

Sir George Peckham, late in 1583, decided to give both an account of the expedition, and a general defence of 'trade, traffic and planting in America', between Florida and Labrador against 'detractors and hinderers of this journey''. Peckham thought carefully and impressively about the issues involved:

I drew myself into a more deeper consideration of this late undertaken voyage, whether it were as well pleasing to Almighty God as profitable to men; as lawful as it seemed honorable; as well grateful to the savages, as gainful to the Christians.

His book (running to nearly fifty pages in the reprint by Professor Quinn) was published in November 1583, ten weeks after the death of Gilbert:

A True Reporte, Of the late discoveries, and possession, taken in the right of the Crowne of Englande, of the Newfound Landes: By that valiaunt and worthye Gentleman, Sir Humfrey Gilbert Knight. Wherein is also breefely sette downe, her highnesse lawfull Tytle thereunto, and the great and manifolde Commodities, that is likely to grow thereby, to the whole Realme in generall, and to the Adventurers in particular. Together with the easines and shortnes of the Voyage.

Concerning the title of the English Crown to North America, the Elizabethan assumption was that here was a restoration, not an innovation, a claim similar to the parallel argument that the reformed Church of England was a return to early purity (Saxon, or, if this seemed unconvincing, earlier). In 1571 Archbishop Matthew Parker published an Anglo-Saxon translation of the gospels, from one of the manuscripts he was engaged in collecting from the dispersed monastic libraries (an enterprise in which John Dee was actively interested). This Saxon text (with an Elizabethan translation), had a preface by John Foxe, to show

how the religion presently taught and professed in the Church at this present, is no new Reformation of things lately begun, which were not before, but rather a reduction of the Church to the pristine state of old conformity which once it had, and almost lost by discontinuance of a few later years.[20]

[18] Hayes. *GV*, 418.
[19] Camden, *GV*, 427. Hayes, *GV*, 420. *GV* portrait frontispiece.
[20] Foxe: preface to *The Gospels of the fower Evangelistes translated in the olde Saxons tyme*

Hakluyt and his circle had a similar approach to the history of the Tudor claim to America. John Foxe's *Ecclesiasticall history, contayning the actes and monuments of things passed* (known from the eighteenth century as the 'Book of Martyrs'), and Richard Hakluyt's *The principall navigations, voiages and discoveries of the English nation* are key and twin revelations of the Elizabethan mind. The apostles in this thesis of pure British tradition thwarted were Prince Madoc, the Columbus brothers, and the Cabots. Peckham discussed all three stories.

Madoc, Peckham explained, was the son of Owen Gwyneth, Prince of Wales in the reign of Henry II. Madoc,

departing from the coast of England, about the year of our Lord God 1170, arrived and there planted himself and his colonies (i.e., in the New Found Lands) and afterward returned himself into England, leaving certain of his people there, as appeareth in an ancient Welsh chronicle, where he gave to certain islands, beasts and fowls, sundry Welsh names, as the Isle of Penguin, which yet to this day beareth the same.[21]

The Indians of Newfoundland called the Great Auk (or the gare-fowl) a 'penguin'. Thus the Indians of North America were descendants of the twelth century Welsh. (There are other Welsh words in use, said Peckham). Moreover, David Ingram had seen bearded Indians: 'which cannot be natural countrymen, for that the Americans are void of beards.' (John White and Thomas Hariot later noted the 'thin' beards of the Carolina Indians.)

So Madoc appeared for the first time in print. The legend was already established. John Dee had written on the back of his map of North America that Madoc 'led a colony, and inhabited in Terra Florida, or thereabouts'.[22] Peckham's 'ancient Welsh chronicle' was a fifteenth century continuation, by Gutyn Owen, of the work ascribed to Caradoc of Llancarfan, who died in 1156. This chronicle was printed in 1584, in the first history of Wales ever published, originally compiled by Humphrey Lloyd (Lhuyd), and edited and expanded after Lloyd's death in 1568 by the Welsh antiquary Dr David Powell, Fellow of All Souls:

The historie of Cambria, now called Wales: A part of the most famous Yland of Brytaine, written in the Brytish language above two hundreth yeares past: translated into English by H. Lhoyd Gentleman; Corrected, augmented and continued out of Records and best approoved Authors, by David Powel, Doctor in divinitie.

This history gave the Madoc story in more detail. The Prince

prepared certain ships with men and munition, and sought adventures by

---

out of Latin into the vulgare toung of the Saxons, newly collected out of auncient monumentes of the sayd Saxons, John Day, 1571, B.ii.r.

[21] *GV*, 459. There is an essay on Madoc by Quinn in *Dictionary Canadian Biography*, I.

[22] Williamson, *Cabot Voyages under Henry VII*, 201.

seas, sailing West, and leaving the coast of Ireland so far north, that he came to a land unknown, where he saw many strange things. This land must needs be some part of that country of which the Spaniards affirm themselves to be the first finders since Hanno's time (about 800 B.C.) for by reason and order of cosmography this land to which Madoc came must needs be some part of Nova Hispania or Florida. Whereupon it is manifest that that country was long before by Britons discovered, afore either Columbus or Americus Vespatius led any Spaniards thither.[23]

Madoc returned home; and then made a second voyage, after which 'he and his people inhabited part of those countries'. Thus there were Christians in America before the Spanish, which explains why some Indians are reported to have honour for the Cross. Powell thought Mexico the most likely site of the Madoc settlement.

Hakluyt incorporated this section of the *Historie of Cambria* into his 1589 *Principall Navigations*. And he had made reference to the Madoc story in his 'Discourse of Western Planting', completed in 1584 after the publication of the *Historie*. The Prince, 'weary of the civil wars and domestical dissensions' in Wales, made two voyages, 'and discovered and planted large countries which he found in the main ocean south-westward of Ireland in the year of our Lord 1170'. This fact is

confirmed by the language of some of those people that dwell upon the continent between the Bay of Mexico and the grand Bay of Newfoundland, whose language is said to agree with the Welsh in divers words and names of places, by experience of some of our nation that have been in those parts.[24]

Thereafter the story was repeated by most writers on America. The fact that the Tudors had Welsh blood, through Edmund Tudor, father of Henry VII, of course made it especially relevant. William Strachey (ancestor of Lytton Strachey), writing in 1612, had Madoc settling in the West Indies. Strachey gave more details of the Indians honouring the Cross. These came from López de Gómara's *Historia General de las Indias*, 1552, translated in 1578 as *The Pleasant Historie of the Conquest of the Weast India, now called newe Spayne*. Strachey repeated Gómara's account of Indians who, when the Spanish arrived, already 'had their crosses in their chapels, and in dedicated groves, in gardens, by woods, springs and foundations, which they did honour and fall down before'. Strachey, writing about the Jamestown settlement (he had been there) stressed that the Indian language has 'much and many words, both of places, and names of many creatures, which have the accents and Welsh significations'.[25] In 1608 a Welsh colonist at Jamestown, Captain Peter Wynne, had gone on an exploring trip outside the tribes owing allegiance to Powhatan, to 'a

[23] 228-9. See McKisack, *Medieval History in the Tudor Age*, 1971, 56-8. Hanno, Prince of Carthage, was mentioned by John Smith in the 1624 *General History*: Smith-Arber, 304.
   [24] Taylor, *Writings of the Hakluyts*, 290.
   [25] Strachey, *Virginia Britania*, 11-12.

country called Monacan' (the Monacan group of tribes along the upper James): 'the Indians there (he wrote to Sir John Egerton) speak a far differing language from the subjects of Powhatan, their pronunciation being very like Welsh' – so Wynne was used as interpreter.[26] (They spoke in fact either Siouan or 'a highly divergent and extremely old dialect of the basic Algonkian language stock'.)[27]

There is no similarity to Welsh in any Indian dialect today. But, the argument runs, in the past there may have been. Those interested in this fascinating piece of American folk-lore can be referred to Richard Deacon's *Madoc and the Discovery of America*, published in 1967, which is a discursive but enthusiastic survey (one of the proofs of the Welsh Indians in the 1820s was that Indian women talk while copulating; apparently a Welsh trait). The Madoc cult flourished in the late eighteenth and early nineteenth centuries: Robert Southey's poem 'Madoc' appeared in 1805. Welsh Indians have been located at various times in at least fourteen states of the Union – and in Mexico and Peru. It is current orthodoxy that Madoc landed near Mobile, Alabama. In 1953 the Virginia Chapter of the Daughters of the American Revolution erected a memorial at Fort Morgan, Alabama: 'In memory of Prince Madoc, a Welsh Explorer, who landed on the shores of Mobile Bay in 1170, and left behind, with the Indians, the Welsh language' – the authorities cited are The Encyclopedia Americana, copyright 1918; Webster's Encyclopedia; Hakluyt, 'Welsh historian and geographer' (in truth his family came from Herefordshire); Redpath's History of the World; and the fact that primitive forts in Tennessee resemble early medieval Welsh forts – and also the forts of the 'pale Indians' of the Tennessee and Missouri rivers. (Shortly after the publication of Deacon's book, there was discovered in Arizona a likeness of Madoc carved on a rock, his helmet decorated with the feathers of the Prince of Wales, and letters in Celtic inscribed on his forehead.)[28]

Next, the Columbus brothers; Christoforo, born about 1451, and Bartolomeo, born in 1460. According to Peckham, Christopher informed Henry VII of 'his intended voyage for the Western discoveries'. But the enterprise was 'derided and mocked generally, even here in England' – the Spanish had made fun of Christopher's loutish garments, his 'simple and silly looks': 'consideration of the inward man' was lacking (a marginal note in 1583 commented that 'God doth not always begin his greatest works by the greatest persons'.)[29]

Peckham's version of the story was very abrupt. Hakluyt was more scholarly. The date, he wrote in 1584, was 1488: an 'offer of the West

[26] Barbour, *Jamestown Voyages*, 245-6.
[27] Nancy O. Lurie, in Smith (ed.), *Seventeenth Century America*, 43.
[28] 'Times Literary Supplement', 2 March 1967. See Morison on Welsh Indians, *Northern Voyages*, 84-7, 106.
[29] *GV*, 448-9. Christopher was in England in 1477: he may have made contact with Edward IV. Quinn, *England and the Discovery of America*, 71-2.

Indies' to Henry VII, delivered in person by Bartolomeo. Or rather, 1488 was the date of Christopher's idea; in the event Bartolomeo was delayed, his maps were stolen by pirates, and so on, and so by the time Henry accepted the offer 'with a cheerful countenance', Christopher had already won support from Ferdinand and Isabella. The authority here was Christopher's natural son, Fernando (1488-1539), who wrote a biography of his father in Spanish, which was published, in Italian translation, at Venice in 1571: *Historie del S.Don Fernando Colombo*. This biography was not fully translated into English until 1704, but in the *Principall Navigations* of 1589 Hakluyt gave the Italian text and a translation of the Henry VII passage.[30] Bartolomeo was 'a man of experience, and skilful in sea causes, and could very well make sea cards' (charts, that is) 'and globes, and other instruments belonging to that profession'. It seems (it is difficult to work out the timing) that he came to England in the late 1480s, showed Henry his maps, and explained Christopher's hopes. Henry was impressed; 'with joyful countenance' (*con allegro volto*) he asked Bartolomeo to invite his brother to England – but, comments Fernando, 'God had reserved the said offer for Castile'. There seem various possibilities: that Henry was sympathetic but too slow; or that he turned the offer down (this now seems the more likely). (We may note that Christopher had docked in England in a Genoese ship in 1477, when he was about twenty-six.)[31]

The somewhat frail story had been launched. George Abbot repeated it in 1599, in his *Briefe Description of the whole Worlde*.[32] And by 1609, the year of the second charter of the Virginia Company, it could trenchantly be utilised as a warning to the laggardly English not to make a similar mistake again. Three versions of the story were printed in 1609; by alderman Robert Johnson, and the clerics Daniel Price and Robert Gray.[33]

According to Johnson, when Christopher 'was to make his proffer where he liked best, he chose Henry VII of England, as in those days the most worthy and best furnished for navigations of all the Kings in Christendom'. But Christopher (who Johnson apparently thought saw Henry VII) had 'poor apparel and simple looks', and his offer was spurned – proof of 'the blind diffidence of our English natures'. Price and Gray also had harsh words about the English character. Price preached that 'some idle, dull and unworthy sceptics moved the King not to entertain the notion'. Gray, at more length, portrayed the English as thinking about Columbus as an 'idle novelist'; an attitude illustrating

[30] *Principall Navigations*, 507-8. In Williamson, *Cabot Voyages under Henry VII*, 199-200; Taylor, *Hakluyts*, 282-3. 1704 translation of complete biography: *A Collection of Voyages and Travels*, ed. A. and J. Churchill, Vol.2 (Henry VII section, 575-77). New translation of biography 1960, by Benjamin-Keen (Folio Society).

[31] *Journal of Columbus*, tr. Jane, ed. Vigneras, 110.

[32] Section 'De America sive orbe novo'.

[33] Johnson, *Nova Britania*, B.3.r. Price, *Sauls Prohibition Stayed*, F.2.r. Gray, *Good Speed to Virginia*, B.1.r.

the improvidency and imprudency of our nation, which hath always bred such diffidence in us, that we conceit no new report, be it never so likely, nor believe anything be it never so probable, before we see the effects. This hath always been reported of the English.

William Strachey, in 1612, also had Henry VII as the obvious patron, with 'the goodliest navy of any king in Christendom'. He discussed the story twice in his book. At first, Henry accepts the offer, and 'entered into capitulations' with Bartolomeo, in 1489. Later we read that Henry 'much repented him for rejecting the first profer of Columbus', who could have made him 'lord and king of those golden islands'.[34] Presumably Henry withdrew his initial refusal; but by then it was too late.

Thus, in the words of a Virginia Company pamphlet in 1610, 'Henry VII by overwariness lost the riches of the golden Indies'.[35]

Thirdly, still in the reign of Henry VII, there is the claim of the Cabots. The Cabot family probably arrived in Bristol about 1494. Giovanni Caboto (*c*.1451-1499) was a Venetian by citizenship but not by birth – he was probably born in Chioggia. His three sons were Sebastiano, born in Venice about 1484, dying in 1557; Luigi; and Santo. In 1496 Henry VII issued Letters Patent to the four Cabots. They were given 'full and free authority, leave and power to sail to all parts, countries and seas of the East, of the West, and of the North' – at 'their own proper cost and charges', be it noted – to 'seek out, discover and find' 'isles, countries, regions or provinces of the heathen and infidels whatsoever they be, and in what part of the world soever they be, which before this time have been unknown to all Christians'. They could 'set up our banners'; and 'subdue, occupy and possess' as 'our vassals and lieutenants, getting unto us the rule, title and jurisdiction'. The enterprise was to be undertaken from Bristol. The Cabots were to be exempted from customs duty on any produce they brought back – and Henry was to get 20% of the net profits.

It is instructive to compare the Cabot Letters Patent with those to Humphrey Gilbert eighty-two years later. The 1578 commission is three times as long; there is hope that the voyagers will 'inhabit and remain'; there is new material on the rights, laws, and religion of the English; and less emphasis on the rights of the crown – Gilbert had more potential power than the Cabots.

On 20 May 1497 John Cabot left Bristol in 'The Mathew'.[36] The

---

[34] *Virginia Britania*, 10-11, 139. Quinn discusses the Bartholomew/Henry VII episode in *England and Discovery of America*, 75-81.

[35] *True Declaration*. Force, *Tracts*, III, no.1: p.24.

[36] Morison, *Northern Voyages*, Ch.6, 'John Cabot's Voyages 1497-98': on the landfall, 174, 192-209. Quinn, *England and Discovery of America*, 93-103, 133-37; and Ch.5 (Sebastian Cabot). For the possibility of Bristol discovery west of Iceland as early as 1481, see Ch.1 of Quinn, 'The Argument for the English Discovery of America 1480-94'. Professor Quinn's former pupil Dr Alwyn Ruddock is sceptical about the pre-1497 voyages: *Bulletin of the Institute of Historical Research*, May 1974, XLVII, 115, 95-9.

landfall was on 24 June: in 'the land of America', or, more precisely, 'Newfoundland'. There are many suggestions about the place of landing. Admiral Morison argues for Griquet Harbour, on the northeast tip of Newfoundland. Professor Quinn favours Cape Breton, Nova Scotia. Others (less convincingly) have suggested Maine. Giovanni apparently set up three banners – of Henry VII, the Pope, and St Mark of Venice. He then cruised for four weeks, certainly reaching the north of Newfoundland. He was back in Bristol by 10 August.

Hakluyt discovered the Cabot Letters Patent in the royal archives, and printed them in 1582 in *Divers Voyages*, with a translation (which I have used above). He also printed material concerning Sebastian Cabot (he thought). This, unfortunately, is confusing. We are given the story of the first American Indians to be brought to England: 'three men taken in the new found Island':

They were clothed in beasts' skins, and ate raw flesh, and spake such speech that no man could understand them, and their demeanour like to brute beasts: whom the King kept a while after. Of the which upon two years passed I saw two apparelled after the manner of Englishmen, in Westminster Palace, which at that time I could not discern from Englishmen, till it was learned what they were. But as for speech, I heard none of them utter one word.

The author of that account was Alderman Robert Fabyon, chronicler, who died about 1513. Hakluyt took it from 'an old Chronicle' written by Fabyon, now 'in the custody' of John Stow. (Not from Fabyon's *New Chronicles of England and France*, first published in 1516, and in an expanded version, including the reign of Henry VII, by William Rastell in 1533.) So far, so good. But Hakluyt described the Fabyon material as 'a note of Sebastian Cabot's voyage of discovery'; and gave the date of the arrival of the three Indians as 1502.[37] The date is probably correct; but Sebastian Cabot may not have been a member of the 1502 voyage from Bristol to the 'New Found Ile'.[38] Professor Quinn thinks it 'not improbable' that Sebastian was 'associated in some way' with the syndicate of Bristol merchants who organised a series of voyages from 1501 and 1505. Miss Ruddock suggests that he may have been chief navigator on the voyage of 1504.[39] Sebastian is, at any rate, frustratingly elusive.

For George Peckham, the grant of 1496 and the voyage of 1497 meant that the whole coastline from Florida to Baffin Island was under the control of the English crown. Edward Hayes made the same point: 'all that great tract of land stretching from the Cape of Florida unto those islands which we now call the Newfoundland' was, by the

---

[37] *Divers Voyages*, ed. Jones, 23-4. Letters Patent, 19-22. The most likely dates for the arrival of the Indians are autumn 1501, or summer 1502.

[38] Quinn, *England and Discovery of America*, 117-18.

[39] Quinn, 137-8; Ruddock, 98.

venture of John Cabot, 'annexed unto the Crown of England'. (Hayes added a new twist: Henry VII had financed the voyage!)[40]

William Strachey, in 1612, quoted Hayes (without acknowledgement); emphasised that the Cabots were the equivalent of Columbus; and said that the Cabots' map could be seen in the monarch's privy gallery in the Palace of Westminster. Gilbert had mentioned this, and other charts of Sebastiano, in 1566.[41] (That section of the Palace of Westminster was burnt in 1698.)

The 1610 *A True Declaration of the estate of the Colonie in Virginia*, published by the London Council of the Virginia Company, confirmed that Cabot 'discovered the North parts of America'; 'and so it was annexed to the Crown of England'.[42]

Strachey summed up the theme of the continuity of the English claim to America from Madoc, through Columbus and the Cabots, to James I.[43] Henry VIII had been unable to follow up the initiative of his father: being 'full of many impatient and personal, as well as domestic, troubles'. Edward VI was rightminded, and had subsidised Sebastiano Caboto (who was in England again from 1549): but Edward was 'unhappily cut off' (at the age of 15.10: he could have been a freshman). What Edward had encouraged, Mary, 'the too too affecting Rome, the otherwise faultless, Queen', neglected, 'though perhaps not without some princely and economic colour of reason, being contracted to the Spanish Philip'. The American enterprise awaited Elizabeth to 'anew, revive, and give a fresh birth and spirit unto'. This she did in the 1580s.

We can now continue the argument of Peckham's *True Report* of 1583. David Ingram was put forward as witness to the fact that the Indians 'generally for the most part are at continual wars with their next adjoining neighbours, and especially the cannibals'. If the Indian quarrels are just, the English should be 'ready with force of arms to assist and defend them'; and any aid given against the cannibals is just and lawful.[44]

Less trivially, Peckham discussed the problem of Indian land tenure.[45] The Indians, of course, have 'great abundance' of land. But God created land 'to the end that it should by culture and husbandry yield things necessary for man's life'. The Indians make 'small account' of their land, 'taking no other fruits thereby than such as the ground itself doth naturally yield'. The Indians can be taught how 'to till and dress their grounds', for one thing, and in general made to 'understand how the tenth part of their land may be so manured and employed, as it may yield more commodities to the necessary use of man's life than the whole now doth'. When the Indians have assimilated 'the knowledge to put their land to some use', they will be

[40] *GV*, 386, 388.
[41] Strachey, *Virginia Britania*, 12-13; Gilbert, *GV*, 147.
[42] Force, *Tracts*, III, no.1:p.8.
[43] *Virginia Britania*, 140-1.
[44] *GV*, 452.   [45] *GV*, 452-3, 468-9.

on the way from 'brutish ignorance to civility and knowledge'.

Naturally, there was more to Civility than that. It meant that the Indians must be 'reduced' from

unseemly customs to honest manners; from disordered riotous routs and companies, to a well governed commonwealth; and withal shall be taught mechanical occupations, arts and liberal sciences.[46]

Other benefits of Civility, if superficial, are tangible:

It is well known that all savages, as well those that dwell in the south as those that dwell in the north, so soon as they shall begin but a little to taste of civility, will take marvellous delight in any garment, be it never so simple: as a shirt, a blue yellow red or green cotton cassock, a cap or such like, and will take incredible pains for such a trifle. For I myself have heard this report made sundry times by divers of our countrymen who have dwelt in the southerly parts, of the West Indies, some twelve years together, and some of less time: that the people in those parts are easily reduced to civility both in manners and garments.[47]

It is also much reported that the Indians are 'thirsting after Christianity (as may appear by the relation of such as have travelled in those parts)'.[48] Hayes was especially to commend the intention in the Gilbert expedition of 'planting Christian people and religion in those remote and barbarous nations of America'; the chief intention of any right thinking American enterprise is the sowing among the pagans of 'the seed of Christian religion', with the hope of 'a most plentiful harvest and copious congregation of Christians'.[49] Peckham concluded his *True Reporte* in similar vein:[50]

By Christian duty we stand bound chiefly to further all such acts as do tend to the increasing the true flock of Christ, by reducing into the right way those lost sheep which are yet astray. And that we shall therein follow the example of our right vertuous predecessors of renowned memory, and leave unto our posterity a divine memorial of so godly an enterprise.

There are two sorts of Christian 'planting', explained Peckham[51] (this section was to be approvingly quoted by William Strachey in 1612).[52] The first, 'when Christians by the good liking and willing assent of the savages are admitted by them to quiet possession'; the second, 'when Christians, being unjustly repulsed, do seek to attain and maintain the right for which they do come'. Both those methods are lawful and just. But the first method must be tried before recourse is had to the second. The Indian is 'fearful by nature, and fond otherwise'; he will be suspicious of strange armour and weapons and clothes. So the Christians must approach the Indians with 'quiet, peaceable conversation', being 'defensive and not offensive' – adopting

---

[46] *GV*, 468.   [47] *GV*, 448.   [48] *GV*, 448.   [49] *GV*, 390, 386 (Hayes).   [50] *GV*, 476.
[51] *GV*, 451-2.   [52] *Virginia Britania*, 26.

a 'measure of blameless defence'. It is 'a principle taught us by natural reason' that 'courtesy and mildness' are to be preferred to 'cruelty and roughness'. The Indians will understand that the English are settlers

not to their hurt, for for their good; and to no other end but to dwell peaceably amongst them, and to trade and traffic with them for their own commodity, without molesting or grieving them any way: which must not be done by words only, but also by deeds.

The deeds can include gifts, to 'induce their barbarous natures to a liking and a mutual society with us' – mirrors, bells, beads; bracelets, chains and necklaces of amber, jet or glass. By such 'friendly signs and courteous tokens' the Indians

may easily perceive (were their senses never so gross) as an assured friendship to be offered them, and that they are encountered with such a nation as brings them benefit, commodity, peace, tranquillity and safety.

But suppose the Indians do not respond to these 'good and fair means'? Suppose they prevent the settlers' enjoying 'the rights for which both painfully and lawfully they have adventured themselves thither'? Suppose the settlers are attacked? The settlers are entitled to security and 'reasonable quietness'. They may 'do whatever is necessary for the attaining of their safety'; and they may 'resist violence with violence' – they may 'by strong hand pursue their enemies, subdue them, take possession of their towns, cities or villages', invoking 'the law of arms, as in like case among all nations at this day is used'. All this would be within 'the bonds of equity and civility': neither has been breached.[53] Here Peckham brings in Old Testament precedent – Noah, Moses, Joshua, Jericho – in a lengthy passage which has already been considered.[54] He also uses the example of Constantine;[55] advising us to read Eusebius (died 340), and Socrates 'Scholasticus' and Sozomen, both of Constantinople, who continued Eusebius' history to the 420s and 430s. Eusebius' *Ecclesiastical History*, with some of the continuations, had been published in an English translation from the Greek in 1577. Eusebius

in precise terms and in divers places maketh mention how Constantine the Great not only enlarged his empire by the subduing of his next neighbours, but also endeavoured by all means to subject all such remote barbarous and heathen nations as then inhabited the four quarters of the world.

He conquered the 'remote Ethiopians, that are now the people of Presbyter John, who yet till this day continue and bear the name of Christians'. He also, with his Christian army,

in proper person himself came even unto this our native country of England,

---

[53] *GV*, 453.   [54] Part I, Ch.5, pp.92, 100, 107-9.   [55] *GV*, 457-8.

then called the Island of Brittaines, bending from him full west, which he wholly conquered, made tributary, and settled therein Christian faith, and left behind him such rulers thereof as to his wisdom seemed best.

When faced with the Gentiles, Constantine 'overcame and vanquished'. Yet there are those in England in 1583, writes Peckham, who think that such planting of the faith by force is 'scarce lawful'. These objectors include 'such as do take upon them to be more than meanly learned'. A hint – and there are others later: in 1609, for example[56] – that objection came from Oxford and Cambridge. Obviously too clever by half.

So the American enterprise is basically 'for Conquest'.[57] And England has her precedence of teaching nations how to live. England is 'reserved' to accomplish in America the preaching of God's word.[58] A small sign of this is 'the peculiar benefit of archers which God hath blessed this land withal, before all other nations', which 'will stand us in great stead amongst those naked people'.[59] And Peckham was concerned to emphasise to his countrymen that the time is Now: 'It hath pleased Almighty God, of His infinite mercy, at the length to awake some of our worthy countrymen out of that drowsy dream wherein we have all so long slumbered.'[60] Another point, this, which the American enterprise shared with the Reformation: the apocalyptic warnings of William Tyndale and John Frith in the late 1520s that the light has now dawned – the light of God's word in scripture – and failure to follow the light will be wilful and without excuse.

Edward Hayes was also to stress the theme of England as the Elect Nation; and was here more eloquent than Peckham.[61] God has not thus far permitted His grace to be revealed to the Indian because God has an 'appointed time'. True, on occasion he has allowed there to be revealed in America 'a certain obscure and misty knowledge', by way of preperation for the 'due time ordained' of 'effectual and complete discovery'. In the 1580s we can 'confidently repose in the preordinance of God' that now 'the time is complete of receiving also these Gentiles into His mercy'. We are in the 'last age of the world': there are 'infallible arguments of the world's end approaching'. And it is no less certain that 'the countries lying north of Florida, God hath reserved the same to be reduced unto Christian civility by the English nation'.

As Hakluyt had written to Sir Philip Sidney in 1582, 'the time approacheth, and now is'. Hakluyt was the chronicler of how in the event it nearly was. The Epistle Dedicatory to the *Principall Navigations* (to Sir Francis Walsingham) is dated 17 November 1589. Hakluyt had frequently visited London from Oxford (his family lived in the City) from about 1580. In London he took pleasure (he tells us in the Epistle Dedicatory) in meeting mariners and merchants, from whom he

---

[56] See above, Ch.17, p.350.
[57] *GV*, 470.   [58] *GV*, 476.   [59] *GV*, 469.   [60] *GV*, 449.   [61] *GV*, 386-8.

obtained 'somewhat more than common knowledge' (a course of practical study which Milton was to propose in his scheme for private academies in 1644). Then, as we have seen, he went to Paris in September 1583 and remained there, basically, until the early summer of 1588. In the excitements of Paris he became more than ever aware of the 'continual neglect' and 'sluggish security' of the English in the matters which most interested him. His editorial work was spurred on: and the 'Principal Navigations', a folio of nearly 850 pages, was published at the end of 1589:

The Principall Navigations, Voiages and Discoveries of the English Nation, made by sea or over Land, to the most remote and farthest distant quarters of the earth at any time within the compasse of these 1500 yeeres.

The first voyager of the English Nation was Helena, only child of Coelus King of Britain, wife of the emperor Constantius Chlorus, who died at York – and mother of Constantine. Helena 'went to Jerusalem and visited all the places there which Christ had frequented'.[62] The second voyager was Constantine:[63] 'King of the Britaines after his father, and Emperor of the Romans, born in Britanie of Helena his mother, and there created Emperor' and 'made his native country partaker of his singular glory and renown'. He was 'the first that appointed an Imperial Diadem or Crown to the Kings of Britaine' – 'this realm of England', the Act in restraint of appeals had confirmed in 1533, 'is an empire'. Constantine (Hakluyt relies on Eusebius) was a 'notable preacher of Christian discipline'; teaching for instance that 'godliness was to be preferred before riches'. He was careful of churches, and of 'poor, sick persons, widows and orphans'. He was a patron of 'those that spent their time in the study of Divinity, which he called Christian Philosophy': *Philosophia Christiana*. But he was also the overthrower of 'the false gods of the heathens', the abrogator within the Empire and also in Greece, Egypt, Persia and Asia, of 'the worshipping of images':

commanding Christ only, by his edicts, to be worshipped, the sacred gospel to be preached, the ministers thereof to be honored and relieved, and the temples of idols everywhere to be destroyed.

(No wonder the English Reformers had wanted Edward VI to be another Constantine.) And he was also a conqueror: of the Spanish, the French and the Italians – and as far as Asia. A lively exemplar for right thinking Elizabethans.

The third section of the 'Principal Navigations' (pages 506 to 825) was of material concerning 'the English valiant attempts in searching almost all the corners of the vast and new world of America, from 73 degrees of northerly latitude' (that is, to Baffin Bay) 'southward to

---

[62] *Principall Navigations*, 1589, p.1. (facsimile ed. 1965).
[63] *ibid.*, 2-3.

Meta Incognita, Newfoundland, the main of Virginia, the point of Florida'; to the bay of Mexico, Nova Hispania, Brazil, South America; and 'the gulf of California, Nova Albion, upon the backside of Canada'. Included, of course, was the Drake and Gilbert material. But more extensive was Hakluyt's editing of the material concerning the expeditions from 1584 to the coast of what is now the State of North Carolina.

To these expeditions we now turn.

12

'That Part of America called Ossomocomuck, alias Wingandacoia, alias Virginia': 1584-1590

The death of 'your half-brother Humphrey Gilbert', wrote the Devonshire historian John Hooker from Exeter to Walter Raleigh in 1586, made a 'hard beginning' to the story of Elizabethan Englishmen in North America.[1] But Raleigh, to Hooker's delight, had not been discouraged in his 'derogation of the glory of the Spaniards' and 'impeach to their vaunts'. Hooker dwelt on the inhumanity of the Spanish conquests:

With all cruel immanity, contrary to all natural humanity, they subdued a naked and a yielding people, whom they sought for gain, and not for any religion or plantation of a commonwealth, over whom, to satisfy their most greedy and insatiable covetousness, did most cruelly tyrannise, and most tyranically and again the course of all human nature did so scorch and roast them to death, as by their histories doth appear.

He implicitly compared Raleigh to Columbus, by referring to a eulogy of the Italian published in London during 1585: the *Columbeidos*, by Guilio Cesare Stella, edited by Giacopo Castelvetro, with a dedicatory epistle to Sir Walter. Raleigh 'did not give over, until you had recovered a land, and made a plantation of your own English nation in Virginia, the first English colony that ever was there planted'.

That was on Roanoke Island, off the coast of North Carolina. English exploration there dates from 1584; the first colony was in 1585. Raleigh was patron and director of these voyages of the 1580s – he himself was never a passenger (the Queen refused to let him go).

Much of the documentation of the 1580s enterprise was printed by Hakluyt in the 1589 *Principall Navigations*, second edition 1600, and is conveniently available in volume 6 of the Everyman's Library Hakluyt (no.339), first printed 1907. But the indispensable collection of source

---

[1] Part of Hooker's dedication to Raleigh of the 'Irish History' by Giraldus Cambrensis, in 1587 ed. of Holinshed's Chronicles. Quinn, *Roanoke Voyages*, 490-1. For this chapter, Morison, *Northern Voyages*, chs 19-20 (617-84): for topography. For the 'story', Quinn, *Raleigh and the British Empire*, is concise and clear. In the notes to this chapter, Quinn's two volumes *The Roanoke Voyages 1584-1590* (continuous paging) will be cited as *RV*.

material is Professor Quinn's impeccable and imaginative *The Roanoke Voyages 1584-1590*, Hakluyt Society, 1955, two volumes, published by the Cambridge University Press. Professor Quinn's textual editing, his copious (but always precise) and wide ranging annotation, and his knowledge of the terrain, make these 1040 pages an achievement of the first order. Fifteen items, including material by Arthur Barlow, Ralph Lane, Thomas Hariot and John White, are also to be found in the volume edited by Professor and Mrs Quinn for the 'Oxford English Memoirs and Travels' series, published by Oxford University Press in 1973: *Virginia Voyages from Hakluyt*.

A list of the 1580s expeditions may be found useful:

1584   First Voyage. Arthur Barlow.
1585   Second Voyage. Richard Grenville.
       1585/86: *First Colony* (Ralph Lane, Thomas Hariot, John White)
1586   Third Voyage (Grenville relief voyage).
       1586/87: *Second Colony* (Grenville's holding party)
1587   Fourth Voyage. John White.
       Third Colony (the 'Lost Colony')
1590   Fifth Voyage. White: search for the 'Lost Colony'

On 25 March 1584 Elizabeth signed Letters Patent to Raleigh (aged about thirty) 'for the discovering and planting of new lands and countries'.[2] They were almost identical with the 1578 Gilbert Letters Patent; due to expire in June 1584. (The main difference was that Raleigh had no rights over the Newfoundland fishery.)[3] And two vessels left the West of England (probably Plymouth) on 27 April 1584, at the 'charge and direction' of Raleigh. On 2 July they reached the Georgia coast; and from 4 July to 13 July they sailed north, following the long series of narrow islands which screen the mainland of North Carolina, the Outer Banks. The two captains were Arthur Barlow (who had served with Raleigh in Ireland) and Philip Amadas, a Plymouth man; and the expedition may have included the painter John White, and also Thomas Hariot.[4] Barlow described the Carolina Outer Banks as 'a tract of islands, two hundred miles in length', with occasional inlet entrances to the 'enclosed sea' between the Banks and the mainland: in which sea – Pamlico Sound, Albemarle Sound – are 'about a hundred islands of divers bigness' (including Roanoke). On 13 July they found an inlet, and landed on the barrier island of Hatarask – or Hatteras – part of 'that land which lieth between Norembega, and Florida in the West Indies'.[5] They 'took possession' of the country 'in the right of the Queen's most excellent Majesty as

[2] *RV*, 82-9.
[3] Quinn, *Raleigh and British Empire*, 50.
[4] Quinn, 'Thomas Harriot and the New World', in Shirley, ed., *Thomas Harriot: Renaissance Scientist*, 1974.
[5] *RV*, 91 (Holinshed 1587).

rightful Queen and Princess of the same'; and then 'delivered' it to the 'use' of Raleigh.[6] The vessels remained in the area for six weeks; leaving on 23 August 1584, with two Indians – Wanchese, and Manteo, a native of the barrier island of Croatoan, to the south.[7]

Arthur Barlow wrote an account of the expedition, running to about a dozen pages, which was edited by Hakluyt in 1589.[8] To him, and to other Englishmen in 1584, the Roanoke country was known as Wingandacoia (the King was Wingina); understood to be the Carolina Algonquian name for the territory (there are at least sixteen alternative spellings). Raleigh thought the word meant the wearing of 'gay clothes';[9] apparently it is more likely to mean 'fine evergreens'. (Later in the 1580s 'Ossomocomuck' emerged as the Algonquian name for the mainland.) Barlow's picture of the land and the people remains attractive, even though the reader is aware of its propaganda intent (at least in the edition by Hakluyt). 'The soil is the most plentiful, sweet, fruitful and wholesome of all the world.'[10] And – a sentence which for some reason (theological?) the Reverend Richard Hakluyt deleted in 1600 – 'the earth bringeth forth all things in abundance, as in the first creation, without toil or labour'.[11] The islands are 'replenished with deer, conies, hares and divers beasts, and about them the goodliest and best fish in the world, and in greatest abundance';[12] Among the trees are 'the highest and reddest cedars of the world', the woods not 'barren and fruitless' as in Bohemia or the Caucasus – in fact the experienced Barlow, faced with the Red Cedar, thought 'in all the world the like abundance is not to be found: and myself having seen those parts of Europe that most abound, find such difference as were incredible to be written".[13]

After landing on Hatarask Island, the English saw no Indians for two days. Then, while the English were on board, three natives approached in a canoe.[14] One came ashore; and, 'never making any show of fear or doubt' was invited aboard, presented with a shirt and a hat, and taught to 'taste of our wine and our meat, which he liked very well'. He inspected both the flagship and the pinnace, then went fishing for a time and returned with his catch: a gift for the English. The following day the Indians appeared in some numbers: Granganimeo, the brother of Wingina (who had been wounded in battle) 'accompanied with forty or fifty men, very handsome and goodly people, and their behaviour as mannerly and civil as any in Europe'. Granganimeo 'never mistrusted any harm to be offered from us, but sitting still, he beckoned us to come and sit by him, which we

[6] *RV*, 94.

[7] For the geography, see map in *RV*: on which are based the maps in *Virginia Voyages from Hakluyt*, and in Morison, *Northern Voyages*, 680. There is a more basic, but attractive, map in Lacey, *Sir Walter Ralegh*, 67. See also *RV* Appendix I: 841-72.

[8] Barlow, 'Discourse': *RV*, 91-116; Everyman Hakluyt, VI, 121-32; *Virginia Voyages*, 1-12.

[9] *RV*, 116-17 (Raleigh, *History of the World*).

[10] *RV*, 106. [11] *RV*, 108. [12] *RV*, 115. [13] *RV*, 95-7.

[14] This paragraph, *RV*, 98-9.

performed; and being set, he made all signs of joy and welcome, striking on his head and his breast, and afterwards on ours, to show we were all one, smiling and making show the best he could of all love and familiarity'.

A day or two later 'we fell to trading with them'; exchanging trinkets for skins.[15] Granganimeo most fancied a 'bright tin dish', bartered for twenty skins worth £7. He bored a hole in it, and hung it round his neck, 'making signs that it would defend him against his enemies' arrows' – one is reminded of the square copper-coloured plate worn by the 'chief Werowans' in John White's water colour drawing.[16] A copper kettle, worth less than three shillings in England, fetched £18 worth of skins. But the English declined to part with their axes, knives and swords.

On one occasion Granganimeo brought along his wife and children. The wife

was very well favoured, of mean stature, and very bashful. She had on her back a long cloak of leather, with the fur side next to her body; and before her a piece of the same. About her forehead she had a band of white coral, and so had her husband, many times. In her ears she had bracelets of pearls hanging down to her middle.

(One such bracelet was to be sent home for Raleigh.) Granganimeo wore on his head 'a broad plate of gold or copper'. Otherwise, the men and the women dressed alike: except that 'the women wear their hair long on both sides, and the men but on one.' Their hair is black, 'for the most part' (though some of the children have auburn or chesnut coloured hair).

Barlow described the Indian colour as 'yellowish'.[17] John White was to paint them in his water colours as a yellowy brown. In Richard Eden's 1555 translation of Pietro Martire's first *Decade* of 1511 – in a passage summarising the observations of Columbus in 1498 – the Indians are described as 'of yellow colour'. But they are 'white'; that is, not 'black', like the 'Ethiopians'.[18] Benjamin Franklin in the 1750s categorised the American Indian as 'tawny'; Saxons were 'white', Europeans 'swarthy', the natives of Africa 'black or tawny', and the Asians 'chiefly tawny'. Elsewhere, Franklin described the Indian as of 'reddish-brown skin'. To Thomas Jefferson the Indians of Virginia were a 'race' of 'red men': 'in body and mind equal to the white man' – they were, after all, 'Americans'. (Winthrop D. Jordan comments that for Jefferson the Indian was 'a degraded but basically noble brand of white man'.)[19]

[15] *RV*, 99-101.
[16] Plate 45 in *American Drawings of White*.
[17] *RV*, 101-2.
[18] Arber, ed, *First Three English Books on America*, 88.
[19] *White Over Black*, 477. Franklin, 254, 277; Jefferson, 439, 453, 480. See also Craven, *White, Red, and Black*, 39-41.

Barlow gives a description of the Indian cultivation of maize, 'their country corn, which is very white, fair and well tasted, and groweth three times in five months.' And the English

proved the soil, and put some of our peas into the ground, and in ten days they were of fourteen inches high. They also have beans very fair, of divers colours and wonderful plenty, some growing naturally and some in their gardens.

Granganimeo gave the English a lot of Indian corn; he also sent them 'divers kinds of fruits, melons, walnuts, cucumbers, gourds, peas and divers roots and fruits very excellent good'. And there was for a time a daily delivery of 'a brace or two of fat bucks, conies, hares, fish, the best of the world'.[20]

One day a small English party sailed along the Sound and 'came to an island which they call Roanoake'. At the north end of the island was 'a village of nine houses, built of cedar, and fortified round about with sharp trees'. An enclosed village, then. This was where Granganimeo lived. He was away at the time; but his wife invited them into her house, partitioned by reed screens into five rooms (or so Barlow said).[21] She

caused us to sit down by a great fire; and after, took off our clothes and washed them, and dried them again. Some of the women pulled off our stockings, and washed them. Some washed our feet in warm water.

A buffet was laid out, on wooden platters and in large white earth pots. There was Indian corn, boiled in water and seasoned with herbs. This native American plant (to be known as maize) was assumed by the English in the 1580s to be an African or Asian grain: 'Guinea' wheat or 'Turkey' wheat. There was fish: boiled, roasted or marinated. There were pumpkins, both raw and boiled; and fruit. Barlow noted, as, later, did William Strachey, that the Indian drink was water – 'as the Turks', said Strachey.[22] The water was 'sodden, with ginger in it and black cinnamon, and sometimes sassafras and divers other wholesome and medicinal herbs'. Not unlike Coca Cola! ('Sodden' is the past participle of 'seethe': boiled; or steeped, marinated.) Barlow thought that the Indians drink wine 'while the grape lasteth', but lacked casks to store it. This would appear to be wrong. Strachey tells us that 'albeit they have grapes, and these good store, yet they have not fallen upon the use of them, nor advised how to press them into wine'. Barlow found the Indian meat well cooked; and the broth 'very sweet and savoury'.

A basic weakness of the English in Virginia was their reliance upon the Indians for food: corn and fish, especially. This reliance developed as a cause of friction.

[20] *RV*, 105-6.
[21] This paragraph, *RV*, 106-9.
[22] Strachey, *Virginia Britania*, 81.

The Indians, during the whole six week period, seemed especially impressed by the English boats and firearms. They themselves had bows, and arrows like small canes 'headed with a sharp shell or tooth of a fish, sufficient to kill a naked man'. They had a type of sword and breastplate, fashioned of wood. The Indians were also fascinated by the colour of the English:[23] 'they wondered marvellously when we were amongst them at the whiteness of our skins, ever coveting to touch our breasts, and to view the same.'

In the Granganimeo house was 'their idol, which they worship, of whom they speak incredible things'.[24] And Barlow tells of a festival at the village of Secoton, at which the Indians 'were altogether merry, and praying before their idol, which is nothing else, but a mere illusion of the devil'.[25] He also says (and it was, so modern experts say, unusual) that the Indians carried the idol to war:[26]

When they go to wars they carry about with them their idol, of whom they ask counsel, as the Romans were wont of the oracle of Apollo.

Barlow was a practical man. He knew that Granganimeo's people 'maintain a deadly and terrible war with the people and king adjoining'.[27] He noted that the Indians 'sing songs as they march towards the battle, instead of drums and trumpets';[28] and comments that

their wars are very cruel and bloody, by reason whereof, and of their civil dissensions which have happened of late years amongst them, the people are marvellously wasted, and in some places the country left desolate.

He gave stories of the 'mortal malice' shown by some tribes. Indeed, the local Indians had recommended that the English raid a particular village which had 'great store of commodities'; whether the advice was 'to the end they may be revenged of their enemies, or for the love they bear to us, we leave that to the trial hereafter'.

The Roanoke Indians were tribes of the south-eastern Algonquian linguistic group. To the north lived Powhatan, who in 1584 was in his mid-thirties. By 1607, when the English arrived at Jamestown, Powhatan had built up, in a region of 9000 square miles, his 'Confederacy' (Thomas Jefferson was the first so to call it). The nucleus was six tribes he had inherited, in the region of the James and the York. His influence spread over 30 Algonquian speaking tribes (controlled by his kinsmen) along the coast of the modern State of Virginia, the Nansemond and Chesapeake tribes being the most southerly of the bloc. The Indians of the Roanoke area were similar culturally, as well as lingustically, to those of the Confederacy.[29]

The Roanoke Indians had some knowledge of the white man before

[23] *RV*, 112.   [24] *RV*, 109.   [25] *RV*, 131.   [26] *RV*, 112.   [27] *RV*, 101.
[28] For the rest of this paragraph, *RV*, 112-13.
[29] Nancy O. Lurie, in Smith (ed.), *17th Century America*, 40-44.

1584. Barlow tells us that about 1558 there was a shipwreck four day's journey south from Roanoke: 'Whereof some of the people were saved, and those were white people, whom the country people preserved.'[30] The Indians had some tools also 'out of a wreck which happened on their coast of some Christian ship';[31] this was about 1564, and there had been no survivors.

Manteo and Wanchese were the first Indians of the area to be taken to England. An observer commented in October 1584, seeing them in Raleigh's household:

They were in countenance and stature like white moors. Their usual habit was a mantle of rudely tanned skins of wild animals, no shirts, and a pelt before their privy parts. No one was able to understand them, and they made a most childish and silly figure.[32]

That was before Thomas Hariot had instructed them in English, and they him in Algonkian.

Yet when Barlow, the practical colonist, generalised about the Indian he was usually (at least in the Hakluyt text) rapturous. Of the day *chez* Granganimeo he wrote:[33]

We were entertained with all love and kindness, and with as much bounty, after their manner, as they could possibly devise. We found the people most gentle, loving and faithful, void of all guile and treason, and such as live after the manner of the golden age.

Of course, the entertainment had been largely by the women; and in spite of an invitation to sleep in the village, Barlow and his party cautiously spent the night in their boat. But they left the island of Roanoke feeling that 'a more kind and loving people there cannot be found in the world, as far as we have hitherto had trial'.[34]

Barlow also noted that 'no people in the world carry more respect to their king, nobility and governors than these do'.[35] The only specific hint in his 'Discourse' of the Indian as a reproving mirror for England.

The Second Voyage: The First Colony, 1585/6

The planning of a second expedition was under way by the winter of 1584. In December there was the somewhat curious story of the House of Commons Bill to confirm the Raleigh Letters Patent.[36] Raleigh was among the new MPs in November 1584 – together with Drake, Robert Cecil, Fulke Greville and Francis Bacon. Apparently he was himself responsible for drafting the Bill. If it had gone through, his possessions

---

[30] *RV*, 111.   [31] *RV*, 104.
[32] Lupold von Wedel: quoted *RV*, 116.
[33] *RV*, 108.   [34] *RV*, 110.   [35] *RV*, 103.
[36] *RV*, 122-9. J.E. Neale did not mention this bill in *Elizabeth I and her Parliaments 1584-1601*, 1957.

in North America would have been held by authority of the Parliament, for ever – which might have made constitutional thought in Colonial America (especially in the 1760s and 1770s) rather different. Raleigh may have prepared the bill for publicity purposes. The Commons' Committee dealing with it included Greville, Drake, Sir Philip Sidney and Sir Francis Walsingham. The bill was read twice in the Commons on 14 December, and a third time on the 18th. It was dropped, following the Christmas recess, after a first reading in the Lords on 19 December. Why? Probably by order of the Queen, whose authority thus far in the reign had been, in her eyes, overmuch defined by 'authority of Parliament' and 'by virtue of this act'. Why include north America in 'the winning of the initiative by the House of Commons'?

On Sunday 6 January 1585 Walter Raleigh was knighted at Greenwich. He had already hit on the name 'Virginia' for the American territory; and early in 1585 (before the end of March) he received his seal as *Dominus et Gubernator Virginiae*.[37] The name was of course in tribute to the Virgin Queen. According to Robert Beverley of Virginia, in his *The History and Present State of Virginia* (1705),[38] it was appropriate also because the country

did seem to retain the virgin purity and plenty of the first creation, and the people their primitive innocence. For they seemed not debauched nor corrupted with those pomps and vanities, which had depraved and enslaved the rest of mankind; neither were their hands hardened by labour, nor their minds corrupted by the desire of hoarding up treasure. They were without boundaries to their land, and without property in cattle, and seemed to have escaped, or rather not to have been concerned in, the first curse: Of getting their bread by the sweat of their brows. For by their pleasure alone, they supplied all their necessities; namely by fishing, fowling and hunting.

Throughout the 1580s people still wrote of Wingandacoia, and late in the 1580s of Ossomocomuck: the 'Ossomocomuck alias Wingandacoia alias Virginia' phrase, chosen as a title for this chapter, was still in use by Raleigh in 1589.[39] Norumbega still had its fans, too. As late as 1597 John Gerard the herbalist wrote of 'Virginia, or Norembega'; though even for him the tide was turning – Norumbega 'now called Virginia'.[40]

By the end of the 1580s, as Hakluyt shows, the 'country of Virginia' was taken to mean essentially the area between Charleston, South Carolina and Philadelphia: the present States of South and North Carolina, Virginia, Delaware, Maryland, and (in part) Pennsylvania and New Jersey.

There survives in the Essex County Record Office a set of notes – fully made public by Professor Quinn[41] – 'for Master Rawley's voyage': dating from late 1584, the time of the planning of the second expedition. It was recommended that the Planters should include

[37] *RV*, 147. [38] Wright ed., 17. [39] *RV*, 573. [40] *RV*, 445-6. [41] *RV*, 130-9.

masons, carpenters, mud-wall makers, Cornish miners, and farmers; a physician, a surgeon and an apothecary; an 'alcamist', to 'try the metals'; an expert in gems and stones; a 'good geographer' and an 'excellent painter' (functions fulfilled in 1585 by Thomas Hariot and John White). The General in charge in America should 'command absolutely' in matters of a military nature, in appointments, and in punishments (though the death penalty must be 'by order of law'). It was all a very military style exercise. And the suggestions for the treatment of the Indian were in line with the conventional military code of conduct. No Indian should be forced to work against his will: a settler so forcing him would be liable to three months' imprisonment. No one was to 'strike or misuse any Indian': penalty, twenty blows with a club in the presence of that Indian. No one was to enter any Indian dwelling without the leave of the owner: if he did, he was liable to six month's imprisonment or to 'slavery' for a period.

It may be noted that there was no mention of a cleric in the Essex Record Office notes. Civility was far too serious a matter to be left to the clergy.

The fleet, of which Grenville, Raleigh's 'cousin', was General, sailed from Plymouth on 9 April 1585: five ships and two pinnaces. (One of the ships was supplied by the Queen, who may also have invested money.) There were about five hundred men on board: 250 sailors, 140 soldiers, and 108 Colonists; Amadas and Barlow, Hariot and White; Manteo and Wanchese; and a mineral expert born in Prague (Joachim Ganz). There does not appear to have been a chaplain. Hariot was to be the effective missionary – a lay mathematician and scientist. The second-in-command, and Governor of the prospective Colony, was the experienced soldier and disciplinarian Ralph Lane, who had served in Ireland, becoming Sheriff of Kerry, and who brought some Irish personel with him – including an Irish boy who was later to shoot Wingina in the buttocks with a cavalry pistol.[42] Later Lane, complaining about the settlers, said the soldiers were interested in treasure, but not in agriculture or trade.[43] On 20 June the mainland of North America was sighted (Georgia). And on the 29th the Roanoke region was approached. Hariot described the arrival at Roanoke Island (ten miles long and two miles broad) thus:[44]

We came unto a good big island, the inhabitants thereof as soon as they saw us began to make a great and horrible cry, as people which never before had seen men apparelled like us, and came a way making out cries like wild beasts or men out of their wits. But being gently called back, we offered them of our wares, as glasses, knives, dolls and other trifles, which we thought they delighted in. So they stood still, and perceiving our good will and courtesy, came fawning upon us, and bade us welcome.

[42] *RV*, 287. [43] *RV*, 272.
[44] *RV*, 414. One of Hariot's Latin notes for the 1590 edition of White's drawings; English translation by Hakluyt.

(In White's water-colour of the wife and daughter of a Werowans of the village of Pomeiooc, the daughter, aged eight or ten, is carrying an English doll.)

A majority of the English, including Grenville, sailed back to England on 25 August. But about 108 remained, including Lane as General or Governor. We know the names of 105.[45] They remained until June 1586. The base was Roanoke Island. Here defences were completed; a fort (excavated and restored between 1947 and 1953); and cottages, maybe of timber, and of two storeys, with brick chimneys and reed thatch; a jail, a granary and a treasury. Most of the settlement was outside the 'fort'. There were also expeditions of discovery: to the north, the Chesapeake Bay area (perhaps led by Hariot); to the south, the Pamlico river; to the west, the Roanoke river; and to the north-west, the Chowan river. The English travelled about 100 miles in each of these directions.

The 'first colony' ended untidily. There was real danger from the frightened Indians. Lane, sensing an Indian conspiracy in June 1586, attacked a village on the mainland; and Wingina was beheaded. There was a food shortage, in spite of the corn stolen from the Indians. The company was small and weak. Relief was expected in April 1586; the relief ship, in the event, did not arrive until the end of June. Grenville was hoped for; but his three ships did not leave England till the end of April. Early in June 1586 Drake arrived in the area, sailing from the West Indies. His twenty-three ships were sighted about the 8th. To Lane this seemed 'the very hand of God':[46] stretched out to take us from thence.' The 103 surviving colonists decided to return with Drake; who sailed on 19 June, reaching Portsmouth thirty-nine days later, 27 July 1586. The final days had been chaotic in Roanoke: tempests and assorted mishaps. Three Englishmen were left behind, up country. Drake had on board some three hundred Indians and nearly 200 (liberated) Negroes for the colony. No one knows what happened to the Indians, the Negroes, or the three Englishmen.[47]

The first 'letters from America' were written by Ralph Lane on 12 August 1585. He wrote two to Sir Francis Walsingham. The first was very short.[48] The second[49] ended with a reference to Habakkuk; and was an

assurance of her Majesty's greatness hereby to grow by the addition of such a Kingdom as this is to the rest of her dominions, by means whereof likewise the Church of Christ throughout Christendom may by the mercy of God in short time find a relief and freedom from the servitude and tyranny that by Spain (being the sword of that Antichrist of Rome and his sect) the same hath of long time been most miserably oppressed with.

[45] List (from Lane), edited in *RV*, 194-7; *Virginia Voyages*, 20-1.
[46] *RV*, 292.
[47] See Quinn, *England and Discovery of America*, 433-4.
[48] *RV*, 197-8.
[49] *RV*, 199-204.

(One of the intentions behind the founding of a colony in Virginia was to provide a base for privateering against the Spanish). Lane also thought the new kingdom 'a vast country yet unmanured, though most apt for it'. The third letter, to Philip Sidney, was also brief.[50]

Hakluyt printed in 1589 a Roanoke letter of Lane's, written on 3 September 1585 to Richard Hakluyt of the Middle Temple (elder cousin of the Editor).[51] This 'main', Lane wrote, is 'the goodliest soil under the cope of heaven'; with its grapes, drugs, flax, silk, and Indian corn (which he thought to be an African grain, Guinea Wheat – Hakluyt, as editor, added the word 'maize').

Besides that, it is the goodliest and most pleasing territory of the world; for the soil is of an huge and unknown greatness, and very well peopled and towned, though savagely, and the climate so wholesome that we have not had one sick since we touched land here.

What Virginia lacked was horses and cattle. The colonists had collected in the West Indies, Grenville was to explain, 'cattle and beasts as are fit and necessary for manuring the country'.[52] If there were such beasts, 'I dare assure myself, being inhabited with English, no realm in Christendom were comparable to it'. The land is rich. But 'being savages that possess the land, they know no use of the same'. Not that the Indian is ignoble:

The people naturally most courteous, and very desirous to have clothes, but especially of coarse cloth rather than silk; coarse canvas they also like well of: but copper carrieth the price of all, so it be made red.

Five days later, on 8 September, Lane wrote to Walsingham: a letter not printed by Hakluyt.[53] He assured the Secretary of State that there are

fertile and pleasant provinces in the main, fit to be civilly and Christianly inhabited, as at the present it is inhabited only with savages, but most populously, specially towards the west, where there are towns of their fashion.

Lane also gave some details of the Indian green corn festival in August, 'one of their holy days': it had attracted a crowd of 700. Such a festival was sketched by White.

But the most famous document of Lane's is his narrative and account of the colony written for Raleigh in England, and printed by Hakluyt: his 'Discourse' – 'an account of the particularities of the employments of the Englishmen left in Virginia': 17 August 1585 to 18 June 1586.[54]

[50] *RV*, 204-6.
[51] *RV*, 207-10; Everyman Hakluyt, VI, 140; *Virginia Voyages*, 22-3.
[52] *RV*, 219. [53] *RV*, 210-14.
[54] *RV*, 255-94; Everyman Hakluyt, VI, 141-62; *Virginia Voyages*, 24-45.

Like Barlow in 1584, Lane was obviously a tough military man of martial/evangelical piety. This was the dominant tone of English settlement in America: more important to remember than generalisations like 'puritan-ism'. The frontier was here: in the 16th century, as in the 19th (all that happened in American history was that the frontier moved always further west).

The theme of Indian betrayal – or potential betrayal – runs through Lane's narration. But treachery was never allowed to pervert his feeling for the Indian. On the expedition to the Chowan river in March 1586, Lane took a chief prisoner. He was 'for a savage, a very grave and wise man, and of very singular good discourse': in two days 'he gave me more understanding and light of the country than I had received by all the searches and savages that, before, I or any of my company had conference with'.[55] This chief (of the Chowanoac tribe) gave Lane a rope of black pearls – to be lost in the chaos of the June 1586 departure. Lane felt that he had had 'traffic with white men that had clothes as we have'.[56] There were in Lane's discourse various descriptions of skirmishes with the Indians. One such involved Manteo, still loyal to the English (unlike Wanchese, who had fled to his tribe). One day about three p.m.,

we heard certain savages call, as we thought, Manteo, who was also at that time with me in the boat. Whereof we all being very glad, hoping of some friendly conference with them, and making him to answer them, they presently began a song: as we thought, in token of our welcome to them. But Manteo presently betook him to his piece and told me that they meant to fight with us.

And before the English could lower the light boat they carried with them, 'there lighted a volley of arrows'.[57]

One old Indian had told his people that the colonists were 'the servants of God', not susceptible to extermination by the Indian. In fact, he said, if the English were killed they could harm the Indian more than if they were alive. One is reminded of Drake in California. Many Carolina Indians 'hold opinion, that we be dead men returned into the world again, and that we do not remain dead but for a certain time, and that then we return again'.[58]

Lane's lay efforts as a practical missionary were not too successful.[59] At first, the Indians had 'reverend opinion, in show, of the Almighty God of heaven, and Jesus Christ, whom we serve and worship': this God 'they would acknowledge and confess the only God'. But later they grew 'into contempt of us'; and said 'that our Lord God was not God, since he suffered us to sustain much hunger, and also to be killed'.

So much for Ralph Lane, whose main concern was a week-by-week narrative (not in fact always very lucid), not a display of emotion recollected in tranquillity. It was Thomas Hariot who, from his

---

[55] *RV*, 259. [56] *RV*, 261. [57] *RV*, 271. [58] *RV*, 278. [59] *RV*, 277.

experiences as a colonist in 1585/6 (when he was twenty-five), produced an essay, written in 1586/7, which was of more than transitory importance. *A briefe and true report of the new found land of Virginia* was first published, in London, in 1588, with a preface by Ralph Lane. The 1588 text is printed by Professor Quinn;[60] and a facsimile edition appeared in 1971 as number 384 of the series 'The English Experience' (Amsterdam and New York). Hakluyt edited the text for the 1589 *Principall Navigations* and revised it for the edition of 1600.[61] The work runs to about thirty pages in the Everyman reprint. At Frankfurt-am-Main in 1590 Hakluyt's printer friend Theodor de Bry published it as part of one of his volumes called *America*. This appeared in separate Latin, English, French and German versions; and the volume contained engravings based on some of John White's water-colour drawings of 1585/6, for which engravings Hariot wrote commentaries in Latin, translated by Hakluyt for the English version. Thus the Virginia of Hariot and White became definitive for the imagination of Europe.

Hakluyt referred to Hariot in 1587, in a letter dedicating to Raleigh his Paris edition of Peter Martyr.[62] The 'chief ornament of an island kingdom', wrote Hakluyt (echoing John Dee) is 'skill in the navigator's art', 'if the aid of the mathematical sciences were enlisted.' Raleigh perceived this in the early 1580s, and from that time, at Durham House, London,

maintained in your household Thomas Hariot, a young man pre-eminent in those studies, at a most liberal salary, in order that by his aid you might acquire those noble sciences in your leisure hours, and that your sea captains, of whom there are not a few, might link theory with practice.

(We have seen Hakluyt himself making a similar suggestion in 1582.) Raleigh (after a period of military service) had been at Oriel College, Oxford, probably from 1572 to 1574.[63] Hakluyt, we have seen, was a resident member of Christ Church from 1570 to 1583. Hariot, who was born in Oxford about 1560, went up to the university in 1577, the year in which Hakluyt became an M.A. and began his university lectures on cosmography and navigation. Hariot was at St Mary Hall, in effect an annexe of Oriel, and took his B.A. in 1580. So the Oxford/Hakluyt/Raleigh/Hariot link is quite clear, and, to use Hakluyt's phrase in 1587, 'not without almost incredible results'.

We learn from the *Briefe and true report* of some of the instruments which Hariot took to Virginia in 1585.[64] Compasses; a lodestone (magnetic iron ore, showing polar magnetism); burning glasses;

[60] *RV*, 317-387; *Virginia Voyages*, 46-76 (1589 Hakluyt text). For the date of composition see Quinn in Shirley (ed.), *Thomas Harriot*, 83.
[61] Everyman Hakluyt, VI, 164-96 (1600 text).
[62] *RV*, 513.
[63] C.S. Emden, *Oriel Papers*, 1948, Ch.2, 'Raleigh: His Friends at Oriel'.
[64] *RV*, 375-6. Everyman Hakluyt, VI, 189.

spring clocks; decorative fireworks and rockets (very popular at
Elizabeth's court: what amused courtiers might impress Indians).
And 'a perspective glass, whereby was shewed many strange sights'.
This was almost certainly not a telescope, of the sort which Galileo
was to write about twenty-five years later, which Dee had appealed for
fourteen years earlier – and which Hariot was to use in London from
1609. It could have been some sort of magnifying glass, or a type of
mirror.[65] At all events, it was enough to persuade Henry Stevens of
Vermont, writing in the 1880s, that Hariot was 'undoubtedly as great
a mathematician and astronomer as Galileo'.[66] Hariot died in 1621,
and his will shows that he had a collection of mirrors and 'perspective
trunks' (with which he looked at sun spots and at Venus, especially).[67]
One thinks of Dee's Elizabethan laboratory at Mortlake. Hariot also
corresponded from 1606 with Johann Kepler, then living in Prague,
about optics and the refraction of light. By the 1590s Hariot, Dee (and
Thomas Digges) were usually grouped together as 'profound'
mathematicians. So scholars have confirmed the assessment of Henry
Stevens: in the United States, Majorie Hope Nicolson (in her 1935
essay 'The "New Astronomy" and English Imagination', reprinted in
her *Science and Imagination*, 1956) and Hiram Haydn (*The Counter-
Renaissance*, 1950); in England, Christopher Hill (*Intellectual Origins of
the English Revolution*, 1965). The unsatisfactory state of Hariot's
surviving papers (at the British Museum, and Petworth House,
Sussex) – and the fact that much, including some Roanoke material,
appears lost – make a definitive assessment for the moment
impossible. An edition of Hariot's works is under consideration.[68] And
in the summer of 1974 the Clarendon Press published a collection of
seven essays, edited by J.W. Shirley, Research Professor in the
History of Science at the University of Delaware: *Thomas Harriot,
Renaissance Scientist*. To contemporaries, Hariot's claims to fame were
less technical. For William Strachey in 1612 he was 'that great lover of
virtue, and very learned professor of all arts and knowledge'.[69]

In 1588 Hariot was concerned with the fact that the Virginia
enterprise had been 'slandered'.[70] There had been 'divers and variable
reports', and 'slanderous and shameful speeches' by 'many that
returned from thence'. Mainly rootless young layabouts from the
gentry, one supposes – there were no married settlers before 1587.
Pampered men, said Hariot, with 'little understanding, less
discretion, and more tongue than was needful or requisite'. Too many

[65] J. North, 'Harriott and the First Telescope Observations of Sunspots', in Shirley
(ed.), *Thomas Harriot*, 143. For Harriot's use, from 1609, of a telescope: 141-4.

[66] Henry Stevens, *Thomas Hariot*, 1900; Stevens died in 1886, and his son edited the
text. See R.C.H. Tanner, 'Henry Stevens and the Associates of Harriott', in Shirley
(ed.), *Thomas Harriot*.

[67] Stevens, 194.

[68] See D.B. Quinn and J.W. Shirley, 'A Contemporary List of Hariot References',
Renaissance Quarterly, Spring 1969, XXII, 1, 9-25.

[69] Strachey, *Virginia Britania*, 21.

[70] *RV*, 320-3.

of them had been 'of a nice bringing up, only in cities and towns'. And thus in Virginia, because

there were not to be found any English cities, nor such fair houses, nor at their own wish any of their old accustomed dainty food, nor any soft beds of down or feathers, the country was to them miserable, and their reports thereof according.

There had indeed been obvious disadvantages in 1585/6.[71] The explorers slept on the ground, in the open; there was a shortage of clothes; food was difficult – only with Indian help could the English procure beasts, birds and fowl: mainly they lived as best they could, with only water to drink. But the health of the settlers had been good: only four members of the first colony had died (and they had been in bad health anyway). Hariot praised the climate of Virginia: 'the excellent temperature there at all seasons, much warmer than in England', and never as 'violently hot' as the tropics; like Persia, or the south of Greece, Italy and Spain.[72]

There is material about the produce of the region: the products of the pine trees (North Carolina was to be dubbed 'the Turpentine State'); sassafras, 'a kind of wood of most pleasant and sweet smell, and of most rare virtues in physic'[73] (used in the treatment of syphilis); cedar, for making chests-of-drawers, bedsteads, tables, desks, lutes and virginals; iron, copper, and a metal thought to be silver. Hariot included silk worms and alum, though it is doubtful whether in fact they existed there. Fruits; two types of grape (small and sour, large and sweet); chestnuts, walnuts, medlars, strawberries.

The Indians made good use of their beans. They boiled them into broth, or cooked them by boiling. Or, when completely 'sodden', 'they bruise or pound them in a mortar, and thereof make loaves or lumps of doughish bread'. Also, they make 'a thick broth or pottage' from beet, *genus atriplex*. The cobs of Indian corn are made edible 'either by parching them, or seething them whole until they be broken, or boiling the flour with water into a pap'. The basic Indian 'meat' is 'maize sodden, of very good taste' ('maize' was an editorial addition by Hakluyt); venison, or flesh 'of some other beast'; and fish. The fish they 'broil' over a fire. They 'fill the vessel with water, and then put they in fruit, flesh and fish, and let all boil together like a gallimaufry, which the Spaniards call Olla Podrida': a ragout.[74] (Nowadays a popular dish among large families in Northern Italy is finely ground Indian corn (*Polenta*) stirred into boiling salted water and cooked until it is a thick purée; then poured onto a wooden board in a layer a quarter of an inch thick, and covered in meat sauce – what is left over is trimmed into squares and grilled.)[75]

Hariot gives quite full descriptions of the Indian method of setting and sowing the corn; but, like Lane, laments the fact that 'the ground

[71] *RV*, 383-4.   [72] *RV*, 383, 325.   [73] *RV*, 329.   [74] *RV*, 337-40.
[75] Elizabeth David, *Mediterranean Food*, 100.

they never fatten with muck, dung, or any other thing, neither plough nor dig it, as we in England'.[76]

The wild life is also catalogued. The Virginia white-tailed deer; elks; grey squirrels and black bears (both of which the settlers shot and ate – some of the settlers ate dogs, including English bull mastiffs). There were cocks, hens, partridges, cranes, geese and swans; and some unusual fowl – we 'have the pictures as they were there drawn'.[77] The fish include sturgeon, herring, trout, porpoise, mullet, plaice, mussels, crabs and oysters: there are pictures of some of these – and of the tortoise as well. (Clams and oysters were staple Indian diet: some from what H.L. Mencken of Baltimore was to call 'the immense protein factory of Chesapeake Bay'.)

And then was the herb *nicotiana rustica*:[78] 'the Spaniards generally call it tobacco'. This the Indians suck through clay pipes 'into their stomach and head, from whence it purgeth superfluous phlegm and other gross humours, openeth all the pores and passages of the body'. Thus their 'bodies are notably preserved in health, and know not many grievous diseases wherewithal we in England are oftentimes afflicted'. The colonists of the 1580s introduced to England not tobacco itself, but the pipe, and the habit of 'drinking tobacco': an Indian pipe of red clay, four inches long, is among the relics preserved in the museum at Roanoke. Hariot says that the English learned 'to suck it after their manner, as also since our return; and have found many rare and wonderful experiments of the virtues thereof' – it was recommended by learned physicians. Hariot was a heavy smoker; he died of cancer of the nose.[79] Tobacco for the Indian had a ritual significance: being

of so precious estimation amongst them that they think their gods are marvellously delighted therewith. Whereupon sometime they make hallowed fires, and cast some of the powder therein for a sacrifice. Being in a storm upon the waters, to pacify their gods they cast some up into the air and into the water. So a weir for fish being newly set up, they cast some therein, and into the air. Also after an escape of danger, they cast some into the air likewise. But all done with strange gestures, stamping, sometimes dancing, clapping of hands, holding up of hands, and staring into the heavens, uttering therewithal, and chattering strange words and noises.

We are told also about Indian dies: black and red, used for the staining of hair and faces, and the tinting of deer skins, and rushes used for mats and baskets. The English made malt from Indian corn, and brewed 'as good ale as was to be desired'. If hops were added, it made good beer.[80]

About a quarter of Hariot's little book was devoted to 'the nature and manners of the people'.[81]

[76] *RV*, 341. [77] *RV*, 358. [78] *RV*, 344-6.
[79] R.C.H. Tanner, in Shirley (ed.), *Thomas Harriot*, 93-4.
[80] *RV*, 335, 338.
[81] *RV*, 368-87; Everyman Hakluyt, VI, 186-93.

The stature of the Indians was similar to that of the English. (In 1590, in the De Bry notes, Hariot stated that the women were 'of reasonable good proportion', with 'small eyes, plain and flat noses, narrow foreheads, and broad mouths'.)[82] White showed that the basic Indian dress, for both sexes, was the apron-skirt of deer skin. Hariot says they were 'clothed with loose mantles made of deer skins, and aprons of the same round about their middles, all else naked'. From White's water colours we can add details of Indian decoration: the bracelets, beads and ear rings; the painted designs, and the tattooes; the ornamental feather (turkey?) worn by the men at the back of the head. The men had bows made of witch-hazel, arrows of reed, wooden clubs about three feet long, and a sort of armour of laced wood. The Indian villages, said Hariot, are few, and small – with ten or twelve houses: the largest seen by the English had thirty houses. The villages are protected with 'barks of trees made fast to stakes; or else with poles only, fixed upright, and close one by another'. To the engraving of White's drawing of the mainland village of Pomeiooc, twenty miles from Roanoke, with its eighteen houses (and a dog) Hariot wrote the caption that it shows the 'true form of their houses, covered and enclosed some with mats, and some with barks of trees; all compassed about with small poles stuck thick together instead of a wall'.[83] In 1588 he wrote that the houses were

made of small poles, made fast at the tops in round form, after the manner as is used in many arbours in our gardens of England; in most towns covered with barks, and in some with artificial mats made of long rushes, from the tops of the houses down to the ground. The length of them is commonly double to the breadth: in some places they are but twelve and sixteen yards long, and in some other we have seen, of four and twenty.[84]

In 1590, Hariot permitted himself some reflections on eating habits. White had a drawing of fish, grilling on a frame: 'the boiling of their fish over the flame of fire' (in Florida, the Indians smoked the fish, and preserve it for winter). White also showed Indians cooking in a pot over a fire. Indian women, says Hariot, 'know how to make earthern vessels with special cunning, and that so large and fine that our potters with their wheels can make no better'. The Indians

are moderate in their eating, whereby they avoid sickness. I would to God we would follow their example. For we should be free from many kinds of diseases which we fall into by sumptuous and unseasonable banquets, continually devising new sauces and provocation of gluttony to satisfy our unsatiable appetite.

There is also a White drawing of an Indian man and woman eating boiled maize from a circular wooden dish (in the engraving, De Bry –

[82] RV, 423-4.
[83] RV, 415.
[84] For this paragraph, RV, 368-70.

presumably with the consent of White – added a tobacco pipe).
Hariot commented:

> They are very sober in their eating and drinking, and consequently very long
> lived, because they do not oppress nature.[85]

There was a slight discussion of Indian government. The word for
the chief or leading man in a tribe was 'werowans' or 'werowance'.
(Lane had taught the Indians to acknowledge Elizabeth as 'the great
Werowans of England';[86] it was apparently possible among the
Algonkians of the region for a women to hold high office.) Most chiefs,
said Hariot, rule only one village.[87] But one chief had sway over
eighteen villages, with a fighting force of eight hundred men. In 1590
Hariot added the touch that the chief men of the village 'fold their
arms together as they walk, or as they talk with one another, in sign of
wisdom':[88] as shown in White's drawing of a 'chief werowans'.

Hariot had taught himself (with the help of Manteo and Wanchese)
to be at home in the Algonquian language. He gave thirty-three Indian
words in the *Briefe and true report*; while recognising that the dialect of
every 'government' was different.[89] There were dialect differences
among the Carolina Algonkians; and the English in 1585/86 also met
Iroquoian and Siouan speaking peoples.

The danger, for Hariot as for Lane, was the Indian surprise attack,
or ambush, or other 'subtle devices'. In a set battle the English of
course had the advantage of firearms: and 'the turning up of their
heels against us in running away was their best defence'.[90] But on the
whole the English should not be suspicious of the Indian: 'they, in
respect of troubling our inhabiting and planting, are not to be feared'
– 'they shall have cause both to fear and love us, that shall inhabit
with them'.[91]

The disadvantages of the Indian State of Nature are obvious. 'In
respect of us, they are a poor people.' They have 'no letters or other
such means as we to keep records of the particularities of times past,
but only tradition from father to son'. They have 'no such tools, nor
any such crafts, sciences and arts as we'. They 'esteem our trifles
before things of greater value': and display 'want of skill and
judgement' in the 'knowledge and use' of English implements. But in
their own way, 'in their proper manner', they 'seem very ingenious':
'in those things they do, they show excellency of wit.' When they come
to realise how much the skill of the English exceeds that of the Indian,
'the more is it probable that they should desire our friendship and
love, and have the greater respect for pleasing and obeying us'. So

---

[85] Hariot 1590, tr. Hakluyt: *RV*, 435, 437-8, 430.
[86] *RV*, 279. [87] *RV*, 370. [88] *RV*, 439.
[89] *RV*, 371. For Hariot's knowledge of Algonquian, see Quinn, in Shirley (ed.),
Thomas Harriot, 39-40, 48, 53. 'Algonquian': the language group. 'Algonkian': the
people.
[90] *RV*, 371. [91] *RV*, 368.

there is great hope. If 'means of good government' are used, the Indian 'may in short time be brought to Civility, and embracing the true religion'.[92]

The most relevant section of the 1588 report is that devoted to 'the sum of their religion; which I learned by having special familiarity with some of their priests'.[93]

To the Indian, 'all the gods are of human shape'. Thus, in houses or temples, they have 'images': *Kewas* (singular), *Kewasowak* (plural). The temples have from one to three images, and 'the common sort think them to be gods'. In such temples 'they worship, pray, sing, and make many times offering unto them'.[94] One of De Bry's engravings in 1590 was of 'the idol Kiwasa'. No actual White drawing of such an idol survives, as such – it is probably a 'blow up' of the idol shown, for instance, in the drawing of the Ossuary Temple. Hariot's note on the engraving is as follows:[95]

The people of this country have an idol, which they call Kiwasa. It is carved of wood, in length four foot, whose head is like the heads of the people of Florida. The face is of a flesh colour; the breast white; the rest is all black; the thighs are also spotted with white. He hath a chain about his neck of white beads, between which are other round beads of copper, which they esteem more than gold or silver. This idol is placed in the temple of the town of Secoton, as the keeper of the King's dead corpses. Sometimes they have two of these idols in their churches, and sometime three, but never above, which they place in a dark corner, where they show terrible.

The temple of the dead is shown in White's drawing, with his own caption:

The tomb of their werowans or chief personages; their flesh clean taken off from the bones, save the skin and hair of their heads, which flesh is dried and enfolded in mats laid at their feet; their bones also being made dry or covered with deer skins, not altering their form or proportion. With their idol Kywash, which is an image of wood, keeping the dead.

The idol is a curious, clothed, crouching figure, with a hat. There was a priest attached to such a temple, shown in the engraving, but not in the drawing (which shows merely two skins laid for the priest to sleep on). Here, says Hariot, the priest 'hath his lodging, which mumbleth his prayers night and day, and hath charge of the corpses'.[96] Such mummification was only for the chief men: ordinary mortals were buried. 'These poor souls,' comments Hariot, 'are thus instructed by nature to reverence their princes even after their death'.

White's fine drawing of the village of Secoton showed, explained Hariot, 'the place of solemn prayer'. It also showed, in a dancing

[92] *RV*, 371-3.
[93] *RV*, 372-81; Everyman Hakluyt, VI, 187-93.
[94] *RV*, 373. [95] *RV*, 424-5. [96] *RV*, 427.

group, 'a ceremony in their prayers, with strange gestures and songs, dancing about posts carved on the tops like men's faces'. At Secoton there were 'solemn feasts'; after sunset, to avoid the heat. They 'solemnise their feasts in the night, and therefore they keep very great fires, to avoid darkness, and to testify their love'.[97] White also drew a ritual harvest festival, with a circle of posts, 'carved with heads', says Hariot, 'like to the faces of nuns covered with their veils'. At this neighbourhood festivity, 'they sing, dance and use the strangest gestures they can possibly devise'.[98] Hariot and White also saw Indians who, as thanks for escape from danger, sat round a fire with gourds as rattles, singing and making merry: 'a strange custom, and worth the observation.'[99]

There is a White drawing of one of, as he says, the 'religious men' of Secoton (Hariot prefers to use 'priests'). They were the *magi*, 'notable enchanters'; elders, 'well striken in years, and it seemth of more experience than the common sort'. Their hair style was odd: the head shaven, except for a coxcomb crest reaching from the forehead to the nape of the neck, and a fringe over the forehead, being stiffened with grease to stand firm – 'in manner of a periwig', says Hariot.[100] (The werowans had a not dissimilar hair style.) The priest is shown wearing a thigh-length cloak of woven rabbit skins. White also painted a *praestigiator*, in Hariot's description, a 'conjurer' or 'juggler' (White called him a 'flyer'). This was a class distinct from the priests; medicine men, or soothsayers, wearing a breech cloth and a skin pouch, having a shaven head with a crest – and above one ear, as 'a badge of their office', a small black bird. These men, said Hariot. 'use strange gestures, and often contrary to nature, in their enchantments. For they be very familiar with devils, of whom they enquire what their enemies do, or other such things'. The people 'give great credit unto their speech, which oftentimes they find to be true'.[101]

Hariot's general thesis was this: 'Some religion they have already; which although it be far from the truth, yet, being as it is, there is hope that it may be the easier and sooner reformed.' (A more charitable verdict than he would have made on mediaeval popery; but then the Indians were not heretics but gentiles – this was as valid a distinction for an evangelical Calvinist such as Hariot as it had been for Thomas More.) The Indians believe in 'one only chief and great God, which hath been from all eternity'. But, inferior to this Supreme Being (but not subordinate to it) are other gods, 'of different sorts and degrees'. The plural word for gods was 'Montoac': this might mean a snake, for instance (though the missionaries preferred it to mean 'spirit' or 'divinity'). The Supreme Being 'when he purposed to make the world, made first other gods of a principal order, to be as means and instruments to be used in the creation'. The waters were created first, 'out of which by the gods was made all diversity of creatures that are visible or invisible'. The sun, moon and stars rank as 'petty gods'.[102]

[97] *RV*, 421-3. [98] *RV*, 428. [99] *RV*, 429. [100] *RV*, 431. [101] *RV*, 442-3. [102] *RV*, 372.

As regards the creation of mankind, 'a woman was made first, which by the working of one of the gods conceived and brought forth children'.[103]

The Indians (like the Utopians) believe in the Immortality of the Soul:

As soon as the soul is departed from the body, according to the works it hath done, it is either carried to heaven, the habitacle of gods, there to enjoy perpetual bliss and happiness, or else to a great pit or hole, which they think to be in the furthest parts of their world, toward the sun-set, there to burn continually: the place they call Popogusso.[104]

(Does this reflect the influence of Spanish missionaries in the Chesapeake Bay area?) The Indians demonstrated the verity of this opinion by two stories which Hariot noted.[105] First, that of a bad man who died and was buried. The next day the earth of his grave was seen to move, and he re-appeared, saying that his soul had nearly reached Popogusso when 'one of the gods saved him, and gave him leave to return again, and teach his friends what they should do to avoid that terrible place of torment'. This event was recent. The other story concerned an event in 1585, in a village six miles from Roanoke. Another body had risen from the grave, saying that his soul had lived

and had travelled far in a long broad way, on both sides whereof grew most delicate and pleasant trees, bearing more rare and excellent fruits than ever he had seen before, or was able to express. And at length came to most brave and fair houses, near which he met his father that had been dead before, who gave him great charge to go back again, and show his friends what good they were to do to enjoy the pleasures of that place, which when he had done he should after come again.

This dogma of the Immortality of the Soul had beneficial effects.[106] Among the 'common and simple sort of people' the 'opinion' makes them have 'great respect to their governors, and also great care what they do to avoid torment after death, and to enjoy bliss'. Although of course the Indian did not reserve punishment solely to the after-life. Thieves, whoremongers, 'and other sorts of wicked doers' are punished here and now; with death, or forfeiture, or beating, 'according to the greatness of the facts'.

Such is the Hariot sketch of the Indian religion. As a proselytiser, he was appropriately convinced that the Indians were not in their beliefs 'so sure grounded, nor gave such credit to their traditions and stories' that

through conversing with us they were brought into great doubts of their own, and no small admiration of ours: with earnest desire in many to learn more than we had means, for want of perfect utterance in their language to express.[107]

[103] *RV*, 373.　[104] *RV*, 373.　[105] *RV*, 374.　[106] *RV*, 374-5.　[107] *RV*, 375.

In 1590, in the caption to De Bry's 'Image', Hariot wrote:[108]

These poor souls have none other knowledge of God, although I think them
very desirous to know the truth. For when as we kneeled down on our knees to
make our prayers unto God, they went about to imitate us, and when they saw
we moved our lips, they also did the like. Wherefore it is very like that they
might easily be brought to the knowledge of the Gospel.

They need (1588 again) 'discreet dealing and government'; that
ensured, they will embrace the truth – and consequently 'honour,
obey, fear and love us'.[109]

The Indians already held the English in 'wonderful admiration'.
When they saw Hariot's scientific instruments and technological
effects

they thought they were rather the works of gods than of men, or at the
leastwise they had been given and taught us of the gods. Which made many
of them to have such opinion of us, as that if they knew not the truth of God
and religion already, it was rather to be had from us, whom God so specially
loved.[110]

England the Elect Nation once again. When there was a drought,
'many would come to us and desire us to pray to our God of England
that He would preserve the corn'.[111] Our God of England – a phrase
first used by Hugh Latimer in 1537, on the occasion of the birth of
Edward VI.[112]

There were rather mysterious outbreaks of disease among the
Indians during the English sojourn in the Roanoke area. After the
English had visited a village, on occasion 'the people began to die very
fast, and many in short space': 'this happened in no place that we
could learn, but where we had been', and the Indian medicine men
'neither knew what it was, nor how to cure it', as it had 'never
happened before, time out of mind'.[113] (Measles? Smallpox? Malaria?
The common cold?) At any rate, the Indians tended to attribute their
misfortunes to the fact that they had offended the English. One
werowance was ill on two occasions: and

doubting of any help by his own priests, and thinking he was in such danger
for offending us, and thereby our God, sent for some of us to pray, and be a
means to our God that it would please Him either that he might live, or after
death dwell with Him in bliss; so likewise were the requests of many others in
the like case.[114]

Disease seemed to the Indian 'the special work of God, for our sakes'.
And the English had 'cause in some sort' to think so too – though

---

[108] *RV*, 425. [109] *RV*, 381. [110] *RV*, 376. [111] *RV*, 377.
[112] Latimer, *Remains*, Parker Society, 385.
[113] *RV*, 378. [114] *RV*, 377.

Hariot was not sure about this. After all, a comet had appeared in October 1585, and on the Atlantic voyage in April, there had been an eclipse of the sun. Kepler, aged 14, at school in Adelberg, Germany, recorded the comet: Hariot noted it at Roanoke. Were they the cause of the plague? Hariot thought not – but for thinking so he had 'further reasons than I think fit at this present to be alleged'.[115]

The Indians were dying, but no Englishman was ill. Were the English supernatural beings, or souls returned from the dead? The Indians were thinking along those lines. And

they noted also that we had no women amongst us, neither that we did care for any of theirs. Some therefore were of opinion that we were not born of women, and therefore not mortal; but that we were men of an old generation many years past, then risen again to immortality. Some would likewise seem to prophesy that there were more of our generation yet to come, to kill theirs, and take their places, as some thought the purpose was by that which was already done. Those that were immediately to come after us they imagined to be in the air, yet invisible and without bodies, and that they by our entreaty and for the love of us, did make the people to die in that sort as they did, by shooting invisible bullets into them.

Their medicine men, bewildered, encouraged this belief, sucking 'strings of blood' from the sick bodies – 'the strings wherewithal the invisible bullets were tied and cast'.[116]

The Indians also asked the English to ensure that enemy Indian tribes would die. This appeared 'ungodly': the English argued that

Our God would not subject himself to any such prayers and requests of men; that indeed all things have been and were to be done according to His good will and pleasure, as He had ordained.

The Pauline phrases were favourite Calvinist texts: and Hariot referred all things 'to be done according to His divine will and pleasure, and as by His wisdom He had ordained to be best'.[117] One is reminded that in 1621, Hariot, in his will, doubted not that he was partaker of the merits of Christ, 'to the end that I may enjoy the kingdom of heaven prepared for the elect'.[118]

Hariot tried to persuade the Indians that they should desire their enemies to live: 'that they with them might live together with us, be made partakers of His truth and serve Him in righteousness.'[119] This was part of his missionary activity, a central theme in Hariot's stay in Roanoke.

Many times, and in every town where I came, according as I was able, I made declaration of the contents of the Bible; that therein was set forth the true and only God and His mighty works; that therein was contained the

---

[115] *RV*, 380. [116] *RV*, 379-80. [117] *RV*, 379. [118] Stevens, *Hariot*, 194. [119] *RV*, 379.

true doctrine of salvation through Christ; with many particularities of
miracles, and chief points of religion, as I was able then to utter and thought fit
for the time.[120]

Archbishop Thomas Cranmer in 1540, in his preface to the complete
Bible in English (which had been ordered to be placed in every
English parish church by Easter 1539) warned against the danger of
excessive stress on the Bible: it should not become an Idol, as the sun
and the moon and the stars had once been Idols.[121] Hariot had a
similar fear:[122]

Although I told them the book materially and of itself was not of any such
virtue as I thought they did conceive, but only the doctrine therein contained,
yet would many be glad to touch it, to embrace it, to kiss it, to hold it to their
breasts and heads and stroke over all their body with it, to show their hungry
desire of that knowledge which was spoken of.

The chief of the Roanoke Indians, Wingina,

and many of his people would be glad many times to be with us at our
prayers, and many times call upon us, both in his own town and also in
others whither he sometimes accompanied us, to pray and sing psalms:
hoping thereby to be partaker of the same effects which we by that means
also expected.

In general, said Hariot, 'we sought by all means possible to win
them by gentleness'.[123] For (a passage from 1590) the Indians by
nature 'live cheerfully and at their hearts' ease'. They are – another
Pauline phrase, which echoes *Utopia* – 'void of all covetousness'.[124]

1586: The Grenville relief voyage. 1586/87: the Second Colony

The 1585 colonists, as we have seen, departed from Roanoke on 19
June 1586. The Grenville fleet – two large vessels, and some smaller,
with four hundred men-left England at the end of April, and probably
arrived at Roanoke in the third week of July 1586. Grenville returned;
leaving at Roanoke, with provisions for two years, a group of men:
certainly fifteen, probably eighteen. Two, we know, were killed. The
rest were never found. So this was the first 'lost colony'.

An expedition arrived at Roanoke in July 1587, with John White as
its captain and chronicler. They of course hoped to find the
Englishmen left a year earlier. They landed at Roanoke:[125] 'but we
found none of them, nor any sign that they had been there, saving only
we found the bones of one of those fifteen, which the savages had slain
long before.' White 'walked to the north end of the island, where
Master Ralph Lane had his fort, with sundry necessary and decent

[120] *RV*, 376.
[121] Cranmer, *Miscellaneous Writings and Letters*, Parker Society, 122.
[122] *RV*, 377. [123] *RV*, 378. [124] *RV*, 423. [125] *RV*, 523-4.

dwelling houses made by his men about it'. The earth works of the fort area had been razed; but the party found 'all the houses standing unhurt, saving the nether rooms of them, and also of the fort, were overgrown with melons of divers sorts, and deer within them, feeding on these melons'.

Later White heard some of the story from the Indians.[126] About thirty Indians had attacked the English settlement, and there was a battle for about an hour. The houses were set on fire, and two of the English were killed (one by a blow on the head, the other by an arrow in the mouth). Four Englishmen were away oyster fishing at the time, so that left about a dozen on Roanoke after the attack. (The attacking Indians included Wanchese.) The dozen made a getaway by boat, picking up the fishers and landing on another island, 'but afterward departed, whither as yet we know not.'

And that is the end of the story of the Second Colony. There is a postscript.[127] In 1586 Grenville had taken back an Indian to his home in Bideford. He was christened in Bideford Parish Church in March 1588: 'Raleigh, a Wynganditoian.' He died in April 1589, and was buried in the churchyard: 'Rawly, a man of Wynganditoia.'

1587: The Fourth Voyage. The Third Colony (the 'Lost Colony'). John White

On 7 January 1587 there was issued a Grant of Arms for a city of 'Raleigh' in Virginia:[128] 'there hath been and now is a barbarous and heathen land or country found out and discovered, called or now termed Ossomocomuck alias Wyngandacoia alias Virginia.' John White of London, gentleman, has been nominated 'chief governor' there (Deputy Governor, that is, under Raleigh in England). And he and twelve 'assistants', as a Council, have been incorporated into 'one body politic by the name, title and authority of the Governor and Assistants of the City of Raleigh in Virginia' – and are now granted a coat of arms. This was a group of London merchants, including Thomas Smythe.

Hayluyt was in Paris, seeing to the printing of his edition of Peter Martyr, which he dedicated to Raleigh. The dedication was written on 28 February 1587.[129] 'Continue to adorn the Sparta that you have won'. This was an adage upon which Erasmus had written an essay: *Spartam nactus est, hanc orna* (you have obtained Sparta, adorn it). 'There yet remain for you new lands, ample realms, unknown peoples.' Hakluyt was well aware of the discontent propagated by some survivors of the 1585/6 colony:

Let them go where they deserve, foolish drones, mindful only of their bellies and gullets, who fresh from that place like those whom Moses sent to spy out the promised land flowing with milk and honey, have treacherously published ill reports about it.

---

[126] *RV*, 528-9.   [127] *RV*, 495.   [128] *RV*, 507-9.   [129] *RV*, 514-15

In 1587 Hakluyt also published his own translation from the French of the chronicles of voyages to Florida in the 1560s by René de Laudonnière: *A notable historie containing foure voyages made by certayne French captaynes unto Florida*. That was also dedicated to Raleigh, the dedicatory essay being ready by November, and reprinted in 1589 in *Principall Navigations*.[130] Here Hakluyt took occasion to meditate on the Virginia enterprise at some length.

I affirm, that if the same may speedily and effectually be pursued, it will prove far more beneficial in divers respects unto this our realm than the world, yea many of the wiser sort, have hitherto imagined.[131]

(The universities again?) The mainland of Virginia

is replenished with many thousands of Indians, which are of better wits than those of Mexico and Peru, as hath been found by those that have had some trial of them. Whereby it may be gathered that they will easily embrace the gospel, forsaking their idolatry, wherein at this present, for the most part, they are wrapped and entangled.

Of course, different colonisers have different motives. There may be one meadow: but an ox will eat the grass, a stork will seek snakes, a hound will hunt hares. We must acknowledge 'sundry desires of divers men': some seek power, some experience, some profit (usually by 'dishonest and unlawful means'). The 'fewest number' seek 'the glory of God and the saving of the souls of the poor and blinded infidels'. Raleigh was among the few: he intended 'hereafter' to send 'good churchmen' to Virginia.[132]
    Raleigh was Joshua.[133]

Be you of a valiant courage and faint not, as the Lord said unto Joshua, exhorting him to proceed on forward in the conquest of the land of promise.

Private men can succeed in such enterprises; here Hakluyt cited Strongbow, in a passage we have already noted.[134] Virginia is a big country, with possibilities of expansion, 'especially to the west'; though perhaps 'the land on the back part of Virginia extendeth nothing so far westward as is put down in the maps of those parts'. And – a favourite Hakluyt grouse – experience since 1585 has shown that England can 'spare 10,000 able men without any miss'.[135]

Seeing therefore we are so far from want of people, that, retiring daily home back out of the Low Countries, they go idle up and down in swarms, for lack of honest employment, I see no fitter place to employ some part of the better sort of them, trained up thus long in service, than in the inward parts of the

---

[130] Everyman Hakluyt, VI, 227-32. *RV* (545-52) has only extracts from the letter. Full text also in *Virginia Voyages*, 87-92. I cite the Everyman paging.
    [131] Everyman, 228.   [132] Everyman, 230.   [133] Everyman, 231.   [134] Above, p.203.
    [135] Everyman, 231.

firm of Virginia, against such stubborn savages as shall refuse obedience to her Majesty.[136]

(In December 1585 Robert Dudley, Earl of Leicester, had sailed for the Netherlands with a force of 6,000 foot and 1,000 horse. The campaign was a failure; Sir Philip Sidney died; and Leicester returned in November 1586.)

John White and his three ships left Plymouth on 8 May 1587.[137] Two Indians were on board, including Manteo; the idea was for him to be the 'chief' of the region. The expedition included seventeen women, the most significant indication of the colonising hopes of 1587. Ten of the seventeen were travelling with their husbands; and two were pregnant (including White's daughter, Eleanor Dare). There were three children, also: and three apparently unattached boys. The Gilbert-Raleigh clan had made the English presence in North America a 'family affair' in one sense. Now it was a 'family affair' in another sense.

They landed at Roanoke on 22 July. Raleigh had in mind the Chesapeake Bay, it seems;[138] but the pilot may have blundered. Once landed on the island, the English repaired the houses and built 'other new cottages'.[139] With the help of Manteo, fairly friendly relations were established with the Indians. The English insisted that 'our coming was only to renew the old love that was between us and them at the first, and to live with them as brethren and friends'. This 'seemed to please them well'. The English pressed on: 'if they would accept our friendship we would willingly receive them again' and 'all unfriendly dealings past on both parts should be utterly forgiven and forgotten'.[140] Manteo throughout behaved 'as a most faithful Englishman',[141] though he had been upset when he shot a friendly Indian by error one dark night.

On 13 August 1587 Manteo was 'christened in Roanoke, and called Lord thereof'.[142] The Book of Common Prayer allows baptism by a layman in case of necessity; and although many (including James I) disliked lay baptism, it was traditional. There is no record of a cleric in Virginia in 1587. (There may, true, have been a ship's chaplain.) On Sunday 24 August there was another baptism; of the daughter of Eleanor and Ananias Dare, born on the 18th, 'the first Christian born in Virginia',[143] and christened Virginia Dare. White himself, as governor, probably baptised both Manteo and his own grand-daughter.

We note that, with the name Ananias ('Yahweh has dealt graciously') White's son-in-law was clearly of a puritan family.

After five weeks – at the end of August – White returned to

---

[136] Everyman, 232.

[137] *RV*, 515-38 (1589 Hakluyt text of White's account of 1587 voyage); Everyman Hakluyt, VI, 196-211; *Virginia Voyages*, 93-106.

[138] Quinn, *England and Discovery of America*, 435-70.

[139] *RV*, 524.   [140] *RV*, 526-7.   [141] *RV*, 530.   [142] *RV*, 531.   [143] *RV*, 532.

England. He had not at first wished to leave. But the colonists needed supplies, and thought White the best person to argue their case in London.[144] 'Starvation was the arch-enemy of the early colonists.'[145] White left his goods behind in three chests: armour, books, maps and drawings.[146] He left about 114 colonists on Roanoke:[147] eighty-two men; the two Indians; and the women and children and boys.

A pinnace was left for the colonists. And the intention presumably was that in time they would move north into the Chesapeake Bay area (partially explored by Lane early in 1586) to find a site for the 'city' and 'fort' of Raleigh. (They may indeed have reached the Chesapeake Bay by October 1587.)[148]

White agreed on a 'secret token' with the planters: 'they should not fail to write or carve on the trees, or posts of doors, the name of the place where they should be seated.' It was also agreed that 'if they should happen to be distressed' they 'should carve, over the letters or name, a cross'.[149]

As things turned out, White was away for three whole years.

He reached Southampton on 8 November 1587, and saw Raleigh on the 20th. He wrote to Roanoke; comforting the settlers by promising that 'with all convenient speed' (ominous phrase!) 'he would prepare a good supply of shipping and men, with sufficience of all things needful; which he intended, God willing, should be with them the summer following.'[150]

The summer of 1588. A fleet was prepared at Bideford, under the direction of Grenville – seven or eight ships and pinnaces. But by the end of March 1588 the English needed all the ships they could muster to face the Spanish Armada. And on 31 March Grenville received a letter from the Privy Council ordering him to 'forbear to go his intended voyage, and to have the ships so by him prepared to be in a readiness to join with her Majesty's navy' – her Majesty 'doth receive daily advertisement of the preparations of the King of Spain to increase, whereupon it is also thought necessary her navies on the seas should be reinforced and strengthened'.[151] In spite of that directive, two pinnaces, with fifteen planters, and provisions, left Bideford, with White on board, in April 1588. The expedition was a disaster; and, as White wrote, 'by casualty took no effect'.[152]

And thereafter nothing happened until March 1590.

1590: The Fifth Voyage. John White: the search for the 'Lost Colony'

John White left Plymouth with three ships on 20 March 1590. On 12

[144] *RV*, 534.
[145] Andrews, *Earliest Colonial Settlements*, 19.
[146] *RV*, 615.
[147] List edited *RV*, 539-43; *Virginia Voyages*, 107-9.
[148] Quinn, *England and Discovery of America*, 438-9.
[149] *RV*, 613-14. [150] *RV*, 563. [151] *RV*, 560-1. [152] *RV*, 562.

August he anchored near the island of Croatoan, south of Roanoke. He had last left the region three years before, in August 1587. He later sent an account of the voyage, 'my fifth and last voyage to Virginia', to Hakluyt,[153] who printed it in 1600, in the new edition of *Principal Navigations*. The original intention had been to take new colonists, but the ship owners apparently forbade this.

On 15 August the ships approached Roanoke. And

we saw a great smoke rise in the Isle Roanoke, near the place where I left our colony in the year 1587: which smoke put us in good hope that some of the colony were there expecting my return out of England.

This was probably dried vegetation, set on fire by the sun. White ordered shots to be fired at intervals, 'to the end that their reports might be heard to the place where we hoped to find some of our people.'[154] The conditions in the sound were very bad, and there were many misadventures, 'evils and unfortunate events', during this approach to Roanoke. Eventually

we espied towards the north end of the island the light of a great fire through the woods, to which we presently rowed. When we came right over against it, we let fall our grapnel near the shore, and sounded with a trumpet and call, and afterwards many familiar English tunes of songs, and called to them friendly. But we had no answer. We therefore landed at daybreak; and coming to the fire we found the grass and sundry rotten trees burning about the place.

The land was on a small creek at the north-east end of the island. Eventually 'we came to the place where I left our colony'.

In all this way we saw in the sand the print of savages' feet, of two or three sorts, trodden the night. And as we entered up the sandy bank, upon a tree in the very brow thereof were curiously carved these fair Roman letters: C R O. Which letters presently we knew to signify the place where I should find the planters seated.[155]

(As late as the 1770s such a tree was shown to tourists!) There was no distress signal; the sign of the Cross. The cottages had been 'taken down'; and the site 'very strongly enclosed with a high palisado of great trees', very 'fort like'. And

one of the chief trees or posts at the right side of the entrance had the bark taken off; and five feet from the ground, in fair capital letters, was graven C R O A T O A N: without any cross, or sign of distress.

[153] White's Journal: *RV*, 598-622; Everyman Hakluyt, VI, 213-27; *Virginia Voyages*, 117-30. 1593 Letter: *RV*, 712-16; Everyman, 211-13; *Virginia Voyages*, 115-16. It is uncertain whether White would have regarded the abortive 1588 expedition as a 'voyage'.
[154] *RV*, 610. [155] *RV*, 613.

we found many bars of iron, two pigs of lead, four iron fowlers, iron sacker-shot, and such like heavy things, thrown here and there, almost overgrown with grass and weeds.[156]

There was no sign of the boats or the pinnace; and no pieces of ordnance. The departure must have been organised. But White found

where divers chests had been hidden, and long since digged up again and broken up, and much of the goods in them spoiled, and scattered about. But nothing left – of such things as the savages knew any use of – undefaced.

In a trench originally dug in 1585 were discovered

five chests that had been carefully hidden of the planters. And of the same chests three were my own; and about the place many of my things spoiled and broken, and my books torn from the covers, the frames of some of my pictures and maps rotten and spoiled with rain, and my armour almost eaten through with rust.[157]

Poor John White. But

I greatly joyed that I had safely found a certain token of their safe being at Croatoan, which is the place where Manteo was born, and the savages of the island our friends.[158]

The weather continued foul. There was little food, and no fresh water. So there was no hope of exploring. The ships sailed south to the West Indies, and back across the Atlantic, reaching Plymouth on 24 October 1590.

Under the Letters Patent of 1584, Raleigh had a first claim to North America if he had established a colony there by 1591. The continued existence of the 1587 colony was therefore an article of faith for any claim Raleigh had on Virginia.[159]

Professor Quinn, in his essay 'The Lost Colony in Myth and Reality, 1586-1625', printed in 1974 as Chapter 17 of his *England and the Discovery of America, 1481-1620* (pp.432-81), thinks it most likely that the colony as a whole moved north to the Chesapeake shortly after August 1587. However, a holding party was left behind, to await White's planned return in 1588. When he did not arrive, the party went south, to the protection of Manteo at Croatoan; expecting White to make contact with Manteo when he eventually arrived (pp.441-2). The Croatoan tribe migrated to the interior of North Carolina in the mid-seventeenth century. The tribe has a tradition that the colonists

---

[156] *RV*, 614. [157] *RV*, 615. [158] *RV*, 616.
[159] The briefest and most measured assessment of Raleigh and America is in the lectures published by Charles M. Andrews in 1933: *Our Earliest Colonial Settlements*, ch.2, 'Raleigh and Roanoke'.

amalgamated with them. Most of the Chesapeake colonists may have been slaughtered by Powhatan about 1606. The fate of the survivors is not known.

In 1937 a stone was found in North Carolina inscribed by Eleanor Dare. Others were found in South Carolina and Georgia; presumably dropped as a trail by the colonists. However, all this was revealed as a hoax.[160]

John White, in a letter to Hakluyt of 4 February 1593 (written at Newton, County Cork) assumed that the colonists were still alive.[161] His grand-daughter Virginia would then have been 5.5. In 1603 Bartholomew Gilbert (no relation of Humphrey) voyaged to Virginia; one of his aims was 'to seek after the people for Sir Walter Raleigh, left near these parts'.[162] He landed in July, and was killed by the Indians. In George Chapman's play *Eastward Ho*, early in 1605, there is a Virginia promoter, Captain Seagull, who discourses in a tavern on the attractions of the country:[163] 'Virginia longs till we share the rest of her maidenhead.' Someone asks him whether Virginia is 'inhabited already with any English?' 'A whole country of English is there,' replies Seagull, 'bred of those that were left':

They have married with the Indians, and make them bring forth as beautiful faces as any we have in England; and therefore the Indians are so in love with 'em, that all the treasure they have, they lay at their feet.

Jamestown was founded in 1607. A map of Virginia drawn in 1608 marked Peccarecanick, North Carolina, as the place where 'remain the four men clothed that came from Roanoke'.[164] In 1608 John Smith wrote from Jamestown to the London Virginia Council hoping to find 'any of them sent by Sir Walter Raleigh'.[165] Search parties were sent out from Jamestown in 1608, and again early in 1609: one reported that they 'found little hope and less certainty of them that were left by Sir W.R.'; the other, that 'nothing could we learn, but they were all dead'.[166] In May 1609 the London Virginia Council gave instructions to the new governor, Sir Thomas Gates.[167] These stated that there had been a 'slaughter of Powhatan of Roanoke upon the first arrival of our colony' – that is, 1607; but at Peccarecanick 'you shall find four of the English alive, left by Sir Walter Raleigh', living 'under the protection of a wereowance called Chepanoc, enemy to Powhatan' – 'one of them were worth much labour', said the Council: and suggested that south of Jamestown was 'more probable than towards the north'. A pamphlet printed in London early in 1610 by authority of the Virginia

---

[160] L.B. Wright, in *American Drawings of White*, I, 59-60; Morison, *Northern Voyages*, 684.

[161] *RV*, 716.

[162] Purchas, Glasgow ed., XVIII, 329-35.

[163] Act III, Scene 2: ed. J.H. Harris, 45.

[164] Barbour, *Jamestown Voyages* (cited as *JV*) 240.

[165] *JV*, 242. [166] *JV*, 449. [167] *JV*, 265.

Council mentioned 'some of our nation planted by Sir Walter Raleigh, yet alive, within fifty miles of our fort'.[168] A Dutch writer later in 1610 repeated this hope: 'they have had word, and found crosses carved in trees.'[169] William Strachey, who arrived at Jamestown in May 1610, reported that 'the men, women and children of the first plantation at Roanoke were by practice and commandment of Powhatan, he himself persuaded thereunto by his priests, miserably slaughtered'[170] – all but seven, who escaped: four men, two boys and one girl.[171]

And that is the last we hear of the 'lost colony', which now passed into folk lore. Today a community in Hanock County, north Tennessee, claims descent from the colonists (with a touch of Prince Madoc thrown in for good measure).

White may have been optimistic in 1593. But to most Englishmen the Virginia enterprise seemed a failure, unlikely to be undertaken again. George Abbot, Master of University College, Oxford, wrote of it in 1599:[172]

the possession of this Virginia is now discontinued, and the country at this present left to the old inhabitants.

There were those, of course, who attributed failure to reasons less earthy than the lack of effective government support. Hakluyt, writing of the failure of the first colony, 1585/6, thought that in 'this paradise of the world' the colonists had betrayed their trust: 'the hand of God came upon them for the cruelty and outrages committed by some of them against the native inhabitants of that country.'[173] White certainly thought in 1587 that there had been 'unfriendly dealings past on both parts'.[174] And Hariot in 1588 wrote that some of the English 'showed themselves too fierce in slaying some of the people in some towns, upon causes that on our part might easily enough have been borne withal'.[175]

The real monument of the Virginia enterprise of the 1580s is the 1590 volume published at Frankfurt-am-Main by Theodore de Bry (born at Liège in 1528) containing the text of Hariot's *Briefe and True Report*, and engravings of some of John White's water-colour drawings, with notes by Hariot (facsimile reproduction from the Library of Congress copy, New York, 1972, Dover Publications, Inc.; with an introduction by Paul Hulton).

De Bry visited England in the early part of 1588, and met Hakluyt, who was on leave from Paris. Hakluyt introduced him to White, and De Bry saw the water-colours. White probably sold him a set, which

---

[168] *True and Sincere Declaration*: Brown, *Genesis*, I, 349.

[169] *JV*, 279.

[170] *Virginia Britania*, 91.

[171] *ibid.*, 34.

[172] *Briefe Description of the Whole Worlde*. See below, p.259.

[173] *RV*, 478.   [174] *RV*, 527.   [175] *RV*, 381.

was sent to Frankfort. This set consisted of copies by White of his own drawings, maybe enlarged and modified. (There probably was a number of such 'sets' of copies, done by White.) De Bry, with some help from his firm of engravers, designed the Virginia plates for his book: twenty-one pictures in all, plus two maps. De Bry advertised these as 'the true pictures and fashions of the people in that part of America now called Virginia', 'diligently collected and drawn by John White, who was sent there specially', 'now cut in copper, and first published by Theodore de Bry'.[176]

The British Museum acquired 75 of the White drawings in 1866; a portfolio which had been bought in 1788 from a London bookseller by the first Earl of Charlemont, for fourteen guineas. These were White's copies of the Virginia originals (which have vanished). The portfolio contains other drawings than the Virginia ones: Florida Indians, copied from Le Moyne; Eskimoes, drawn in England in the late 1570s; ancient Picts and Britons. There is also a group, five in number, of Turkish, Levantine and Tartar men and women, which may not be by White.

The De Bry set of copies has never been found. It is possible that in the eighteenth century it was in England, at the manor house of Scadbury Park, in Chislehurst, Kent.[177]

Thirteen of the drawings in the British Museum Collection are Indian 'portraits'. The soothsayer or medicine man, and the priest; a werowance; an Indian in body paint; four Indian women (one with a baby, one with a young girl); an old man; a man and woman eating; Indians fishing, dancing, and seated round a fire. There is also the ossuary temple, and the villages of Secoton and Pomeiooc. We also have the cooking of fish; and cooking in a pot. All these were engraved by De Bry, who also gave an Idol, and Indians making canoes – probably based on White originals which have disappeared. White also drew the flora and fauna of Virginia – the iguana, the gadfly, the loon, the sturgeon, the tortoise, the turtle. These are in fact neater than the Indian portraits, which are rather crudely drawn, though of course they do have a simplicity and immediacy. Experts say that White in his water-colours slightly Europeanised the features of the Indians; how the experts know this is not clear. De Bry certainly did: indeed he 'Romanised' some of them. (De Bry adapted fairly freely, showing rear and reverse views, for instance, of White's frontal drawings; but he probably worked with the advice of White and Hariot.)

The first paintings of the American Indian had been done in Florida in the early 1560s by Jacques Le Moyne de Morgues. Earlier, there had been woodcuts, done from pen and ink drawings; those of Oviedo, for instance, from the 1520s. Drake, as we have seen, was a

---

[176] *RV*, 399. Quinn on White's drawings: *RV*, 390-464.

[177] Virginia F. Stern, 'A Second Set of John White Drawings', *Renaissance Quarterly*, Spring 1968, XXI, 1.

painter. Le Moyne survived a Spanish attack of 1565 on the French settlement at Fort Carolina, and in the early 1570s joined Raleigh's household in London, dying in 1588. His oil paintings were obtained from his widow by De Bry, who engraved some of them in 1591. Only one of Le Moyne's originals now survives, in the New York Public Library. White, we have seen, copied some of them. (A Le Moyne sold at Sotheby's in 1967 for £5,000, and again offered for sale in 1969 by another dealer for £45,000, was probably a copy from a De Bry engraving.) Hakluyt mentioned Le Moyne in 1587, as the artist who had done some Florida paintings in the 1580s at the request of Raleigh, and published some of them in 1586 (hand coloured illustrations, 'lively drawn in colours at your no small charges by the skilful painter James Morgues, yet living in the Blackfriars in London').[178]

But the De Bry-White pictures were the best known representations of the American Indian until the paintings reproduced in 1841 by the Pennsylvania lawyer George Catlin (1796-1872), *The Manners, Customs and Conditions of the North American Indians*. Catlin's paintings were done from the 1830s, and exhibited from 1837; he came to London with his exhibition in 1839 – 'Catlin's Indian Gallery'. His collection – of the Plains Indians, west of the Mississippi – is now in the Smithsonian Institution, Washington D.C.

De Bry wrote in English a preface to his 1590 volume:

Although, friendly reader, man by his disobedience were deprived of those good gifts wherewith he was indued in his creation, yet he was not bereft of wit to provide for himself, not discretion to devise things necessary for his use, except such as appertain to his soul's health, as may be gathered by this savage nations, of whom this present work entreateth. For although they have no true knowledge of God nor of his holy word, and are destituted of all learning, yet they pass us in many things, as in sober feeding, and dexterity of wit in making, without any instrument of metal, things so neat and so fine, as a man would scarcely believe the same, unless the Englishmen had made proof thereof by their travels into the country.[179]

De Bry also engraved five of White's water colours of Ancient Britons, 'Some pictures of the Picts which in the old time did habit one part of the Great Britain'. This to demonstrate that 'the inhabitants of the Great Britanny have been in times past as savage as those of Virginia'. White did drawings (now in the British Museum collection) of three 'British' warriors and two 'British' women. They are shown as painted and decorated, rather in the Indian manner; of a very fearsome general air, but with surprisingly coy features. The effect is very 'camp'. De Bry captioned three of the people as Picts, and two as British, 'neighbour unto the Picts'. His engravings are very free adaptations.

The theme of the resemblance of the Indian to the ancient Briton

[178] *RV*, 546. [179] *RV*, 399-400.

was to be much emphasised in the early seventeenth century. We were once 'poor and naked Britons', said alderman Robert Johnson in 1609:[180] let us therefore be humane to the Indian. The reverend Richard Eburne wrote in 1624[181] that 'we ought to consider, that time was the old Britons, the ancient inhabitants of this land, were as rude and barbarous as some of those of foreign parts with whom we have to do.' We are their 'offspring': therefore

we ought not to despise even such poor and barbarous people, but pity them, and hope that as we are become now by God's unspeakable mercy to usward to a far better condition, so in time may they.

Since 1947 work was in progress to publish facsimiles of the British Museum White collection. The project came to fruition in 1964, with the publication of *The American Drawings of John White 1577-1590: with drawings of European and Oriental subjects*, 2 volumes, 70 guineas. The publishers were in London the Trustees of the British Museum, and in the USA the University of North Carolina Press, Chapel Hill. The editors were Professor Quinn, and Paul Hulton, Assistant Keeper of Prints and Drawings at the British Museum. The printers were the Cambridge University Press. The first volume is the introduction; the second, reproductions of the drawings, done in Paris, with colour printed collotype as basis, thereafter colour brushed through stencils, by hand. The De Bry engravings are also reproduced.[182] In April and May 1964 there were John White exhibitions both at the British Museum and at the United States Embassy, Grosvenor Square. William Gaunt, in the London *Times*, wrote that White 'made an appeal to the world's imagination, and established a permanent image of North America and its indigenous inhabitants', showing 'a realistic approach for which there seems little parallel in the English art of his time'; 'though manner was necessarily subordinate to subject matter, he has touches of that exquisite quality which makes his contemporary, Nicholas Hilliard, exceptional in Elizabeth art.'

So the Virginia enterprise at least contributed to the history of the English water-colour. The tantalising thing is that, apart from the material used in this chapter, nothing is known about John White. One point can be cleared up. We know that White the artist was the same man as the White who commanded the 1587 and 1590 voyages. John Gerard, in *The herball, or generall historie of plantes*, 1597, wrote of 'Master White, an excellent painter, who carried very many people into Virginia (or after some, Norembega) there to inhabit'.[183] White had discussed with Gerard the flora of Virginia.

[180] *Nova Britannia*, C.2.r.

[181] *Plain Pathway*, ed. Wright, 56.

[182] There are reproductions in colour (reduced) of nearly 40 White water-colours in *The Discovery of North America*, by W.P. Cumming, R.A. Skelton and D.B. Quinn, 1971; which also has Le Moyne reproductions.

[183] Quoted by Edmund S. Morgan, 'John White and the Sarsaparilla', *William and Mary Quarterly*, July 1957, XIV, 3, 417.

There survive at Roanoke various relics of the 1585/86 colony.[184] A wrought iron sickle; the top of a glazed earthern ware jar; a stone axe; spikes; fragments of jars; a brass buckle; pieces of copper; pendants; a fragment of brick – and the Indian tobacco pipe of red clay.

And by 1590 there was ample evidence for what was to be the basic English deduction about the American Indian: 'at first very fair and friendly, though afterwards they gave great proofs of their deceitfulness.'[185]

---

[184] *RV*, 907-9: Appendix II, 'The Archaeology of the Roanoke Settlements'. For the 'Roanoke Colony Memorial Association', Powell, *Paradise Preserved.*
[185] Beverley, *History and Present State of Virginia*, 1705, ed. Wright, 29.

13

The North Part of Virginia, 1590-1612

Writing in 1599, George Abbot observed this about the settlements of the 1580s: 'being enterprised on the charge of private men, and not thoroughly being followed by the state, the possession of this Virginia is now discontinued.'[1]

Raleigh had the rights over Virginia until his conviction for high treason in November 1603. His overall patent had not been affected by his delegation in 1587 of powers over the projected city of Raleigh to a group of London merchants. William Strachey was to write of Raleigh that until 1603 no one could 'make intrusion' in Virginia 'without his leave', 'the title being only in him'.[2] Raleigh claimed that he had intended personally to visit Virginia in 1595, during his expedition to Guiana. And he may have sent more than one expedition to North America in the final years of Elizabeth's reign. We know of one, in 1602; a commercial venture, of two vessels, under Captain Samuel Mace, landing halfway down the coast of North Carolina (south of the Roanoke area), remaining for one month, and bringing back sassafras and sarsaparilla to Weymouth.[3]

To the far north: in March 1597 a group of puritans wishing to separate from the corruptions of England – 'strangers and pilgrims', as Henry Ainsworth had called them in 1596, following Hebrews 11:13 – were allowed permission by the Privy Council to plant a colony in 'The Province of Canada', in the Magdalen group of islands in the Gulf of St Lawrence; on the island of Ramea, now Amherst Island. Their leader was Francis Johnson, former Fellow of Christ's College Cambridge. An advance party (including Francis and his brother George) went out in 1597. Their expedition failed, largely because of French opposition.[4] The French were becoming active in the St Lawrence in the late 1590s; Samuel de Champlain was to sail to New France in 1603. So the pilgrims went instead to Amsterdam.

[1] *Briefe description of the whole worlde*, 1599: section 'De Partibus Americae versus Septentrionem'.

[2] *Virginia Britania*, 15.

[3] For the voyages of 1602 and 1603, Quinn, ' "Virginians" on the Thames in 1603', being Ch.16 of *England and Discovery of America*.

[4] *ibid.*, Ch.12, 'England and the St Lawrence 1577-1602'; Ch.13, 'The First Pilgrims'. For the Johnsons, see my *Reformation and Reaction in Tudor Cambridge*.

Raleigh would have had more than a passing interest in the 'Brownist' colonial plan. In a House of Commons debate in 1593 on the treatment of separatists (those who believed, to use the title of a tract published by Robert Browne in 1582, in 'Reformation without tarrying for any') Raleigh argued that 'the Brownists are worthy to be rooted out of a commonwealth'; but was worried about the expense, and the question of 'whither will you send them?'[5]

In the 1590s, with the editions of Hakluyt and the publications of De Bry, Virginia was at any rate secure in and fertile for the imagination of both England and Europe. But effective English activity across the Atlantic was concentrated on the Newfoundland fishery, where, after the late 1580s, English fishermen achieved supremacy over their Spanish, Portuguese and French rivals. There were also those, in the tradition of Humphrey Gilbert, who thought in terms of colonisation rather than merely of cod. In 1610 a party of settlers crossed to Newfoundland under John Guy of Bristol, who established what is now the oldest surviving British colony. A charter had been given in 1610 to 'The Treasurer and Company of Adventurers and Planters of the City of London and Bristol for the Colony or Plantation in Newfoundland'.[6] (The members of the Company, headed by Henry Howard, Earl of Northampton, included the Solicitor General, Francis Bacon.) There was a desire to 'make plantation to inhabit and establish a colony or colonies in the southern and eastern parts of the country and island commonly called Newfoundland' – an island to which Englishmen 'have for the space of fifty years and upwards yearly used to resort in no small numbers to fish'. The intention of the plantation was not only 'to secure and make safe the trade of fishing to our subjects for ever'; but also 'the conversion of the people in those parts, if any be there inhabiting, unto the true worship of God and Christian religion' – although it was recognised that Newfoundland was 'so desolate of inhabitants that scarce any one savage person hath in many years been seen in the most parts thereof'. Professor Quinn writes[7] that the 1610 enterprise

was not a bid to take over the fishery but an experiment to discover whether it was possible for one or two small permanent colonies (in sample Newfoundland ports) to support themselves agriculturally and also to gain some advantages over the seasonal fisherman by starting to catch fish early in the year before ships could come from Europe.

John Guy, once sheriff of Bristol, and later mayor, was the governor of the colony. In the winter of 1612 he explored his domain, having crossed to Newfoundland for the second time earlier in that

---

[5] D'Ewes, *Journals*, 1693, 517.

[6] Prowse, *History of Newfoundland*, 122-5. The standard work is now Cell, *English Enterprise in Newfoundland 1577-1660*. Ch.7 of Rowse, *Elizabethans and America*, 'Newfoundland, Nova Scotia and the North-West Passage', covers 1480-1630.

[7] Quinn (ed.), *North American Discovery circa 1000-1612*, 1971, xxxix.

year. He took with him a cleric of puritanical leanings, Erasmus Stourton: probably the brother of Edward Stourton of Leicestershire, whose son Erasmus, born in 1601, was to go up to St John's College Cambridge in 1619. Guy's account of the meetings of his party with the Beothuck Indians was first printed, from the manuscript in Lambeth Palace, in 1957.[8]

A party of nineteen left Harbour Grace on 17 October 1612 in two vessels. On the 26th they saw two fires; one on an island in a lake, the other on the lake shore. They also saw two Indians rowing a canoe. Guy and fourteen others ventured to the shore fire, but the Indians had gone to the island. The English 'found no savages, but three of their houses, whereof two had been lately used, in one of which the hearth was hot' – and where they found 'a copper kettle kept very bright, a fur gown, some seal skins, an old sail and a fishing reel'. The explorers tidied the effects, and left 'some biscuit and three or four amber beads': 'This was done to begin to win them by fair means'. The 'houses' were

nothing but poles set in a round form, meeting all together aloft, which they cover with deer skins. They are about ten foot broad, and in the middle they make their fire. One of them was covered with a sail, which they had gotten from some Christian.

The party then stole away, in the moonlight. They did not meet any Indians until 6 November; when

two canoes appeared, and one man alone coming towards us with a flag in his hand of a wolf skin, shaking it, and making a loud noise, which we took to be for a parley; whereupon a white flag was put out and the bark and shallop rowed towards them, which the savages did not like of, and so took them to their canoes again, and were going away.

Guy ordered the bark to be anchored, 'which pleased them, and then they stayed'. One of the Englishmen landed, and two Indians approached, one of whom 'made a loud speech'. The ice was broken; and the two came towards the English, 'dancing, leaping and singing', and presenting a leather chain embossed with periwinkle shells, a knife, a head feather, and an arrow. In return, the two were given a linen cap and a hand towel by the Englishman: 'And after, hand in hand, they all three did sing and dance.' A second Englishman went ashore; and 'all four together danced, laughing and making signs of joy and gladness'. The occupants of the shallop went ashore, including Guy, with a shirt, two table napkins, a towel, bread, butter and raisins, and spirits to drink: one of the Indians, 'blowing in the aquavitae bottle, it made a sound which they all fell into a laughing

---

[8] As Appendix I (52-64) of 'The New World: a catalogue of an Exhibition at Lambeth Palace Library 1957'; published by the Church Information Board, for the Library.

at'. More Indians appeared, behaving themselves 'civilly'; and deer's flesh was shared with the English. There were eight Indians in all.

They are of a reasonable stature, of an ordinary middle size; they go bareheaded, wearing their hair somewhat long, but rounded; they have no beards. Behind they have a great lock of hair platted with feathers, like a hawk's lure, with a feather in it standing upright by the crown of the head, and a small lock platted before. A short gown or cassock made of stag skins, the fur innermost, that came down to the middle of their leg, with sleeves to the middle of their arm, and a beaver skin about their neck, was all their apparel; save that one of them had shows and mittens; so that all went bare legged, and most barefoot. They are full dyed of a black colour. The colour of their hair was diverse, some black, some brown and some yellow; their faces something flat and broad, red with ochre, as all their apparel is, and the rest of their body. They are broad-breasted and stand very upright.

The regrettable fact is that the subsequent relations between the English and the Beothucks were rarely good. In the early nineteenth century there was trouble and warfare, and the tribe was extinct by the late 1820s.

English interest in the mainland of 'the north part of Virginia' had been continuous (even if fitful) since the early 1580s, and the fascination with Norumbega. Edward Hayes, whom we last saw as a chronicler of the 1583 Gilbert expedition, maintained his concern for 'the north-west regions of America', the area north of New York City. There survives in the Cambridge University Library the manuscript of a tract written by Hayes in the 1590s, running to eighteen pages, divided into seven chapters: 'A discourse concerning a voyage intended for the planting of Christian religion and people in the north-west regions of America, in place most apt for constitution of our bodies and the speedy advancement of a state.'[9] A version of this was printed in 1602,[10] the final year of the reign of Elizabeth I, by which time Hayes had been for over three years involved with military organisation in Ireland.

Hayes was uncertain about the fate of the Roanoke planters: 'how it fareth with our colony in Virginia we know not.' One thing Hayes was sure of – hopes for the colony would have been higher had it been planted further north, 'near unto this trade of Newfoundland, and in convenient harbour'. It would then have been easy to send supplies to the settlers; and advantage could have been taken of 'the trade unto the Newfoundland', established for many years, a 'concourse' which could be 'easily and speedily removed unto our habitations, planted so near unto them', bringing 'the benefit of an exceeding great trade and concourse of merchants which frequent the same coasts yearly with

[9] MS.Dd.III.85, no.4. Quinn drew attention to this item in his 1959 essay on Hayes in Vol.111 of *Transactions of the Historic Society of Lancashire and Cheshire*; now reprinted as Ch.8 of *England and Discovery of America*, 'Edward Hayes and the Americas'.
[10] As appendix to John Brereton, *Brief and True Relation*.

three or four hundred sails of ships at the least'. So Hayes' ideal was a settlement on the mainland 'near adjoining' Newfoundland, on the coast of the Northern Part of Virginia. This would be more 'secure and gainful' to England than the existing fishery – more continuous, less a prey to rivals and pirates. The region was temperate in climate – not too cold, as some thought; it was known to be fruitful, in fish at any rate; and English merchants could without difficulty supply bread, cattle and cloth. Hayes was especially keen on the necessity of trade: 'it is trade that enricheth countries and causeth the same to abound in wealth and prosperity.' 'No prince with his proper treasure hath at any time, nor can, erect a new commonwealth or state to make the same flourish unless the place be endued with needful and vendible commodities, and aptly situated for trade.' That being acknowledged, the enterprise could flourish on what Abbot had seen fit to criticise – 'the charge of private men'. One doesn't necessarily need 'a prince of wealth and power'. The initial expenses would indeed be high for 'private men'. But success breeds success, and by the third voyage the enterprise would be safe: 'the Englishman by nature is slow to begin a matter wherein appeareth difficulty and doubt; but is vehement in prosecuting and following.' For the first year, £2000 would be needed; and this would best be organised through 'a body politic and incorporate'. Hayes is the bridge between the Gilbert and Raleigh ventures, and the Virginia Company of 1606.

England is a 'most happy and puissant kingdom'. The English have special and relevant virtues: 'the valour of the inhabitants and people in conquering; their art and industry in raising of commodities and drawing traffic unto them; and their policy in governing'. We have 'enjoyed so long peace'; which has occasioned the problem that 'our people are increased exceedingly, and fail of employments'. England, to Hayes, was 'overburdened and, as it were, pestered with people', having 'a multitude of distressed people, both of men, women and children, which the realm may happily spare' – 20,000 such, he estimated. Thus the English 'may be thought very remiss in so long neglecting the benefits which God hath offered unto us, by means of our long and happy peace, and multitude of spare people to plant and possess those ample and most fertile countries'.

After all, by way of John Cabot Elizabeth was 'the successor and rightful inheritor unto all the ample dominions of America' from Chesapeake Bay to Labrador. The French have no 'settled possession of government' in North America. The Portuguese and Spanish both lack 'peace and people'. And although the Spanish are 'prosperous' in the south, they have been 'unfortunate in all their northerly attempts': a sign that 'God hath appointed their limits not to exceed north of Florida'. 'As if God had defended the right of England against both the Spaniards and French; and had reserved the countries to be by us converted unto the faith at His appointed time.'

Chapter Two of the manuscript has the title: 'That our church and faith shall receive great advancement and propagation by performance of this action.' North America, again, 'seemeth to be reserved for us' (because 'God did first discover the same unto us'). The Spanish and Portuguese prosper 'because they preach Christ' – albeit in a 'mixture of superstition and error'. And 'our adversaries have noted this to be a very great defect in our church, that we have not converted infidels unto the faith'. But now 'in this later age' the English

are to travail in sowing the seed of pure religion in these exceeding large and populous nations lying to the northwest of America, and to set them free from the captivity of the devil, who holdeth them under miserable idolatry and paganism, being nevertheless found a people docible, and very capable of Christianity.

Hayes drew a (rather strained) 'probable conjecture' from 'the revolution of God's word: which hitherto hath moved circularly'.

For like as the same began in the East in Paradise, and moved westward into Palestine and at length into Europe, there beginning in the east also, proceeded by south unto the west, and spread afterwards north, even so from Europe it hath continued his revolution west into America. Notice it began east, proceeded south and west, and may happily more purely be preached also in the north by us. Unto which time (this being the last of the last age of the world) we are now arrived; and therefore may hope by so much the more of our good success in this action now, seeing the last days are come upon us, and that now or never their conversion is to be expected.

In 'older times' many 'holy men' were 'stirred up to the converting of us in these north, and then obscure, regions of Europe'; without them 'we also had continued barbarians unto this day'. Similarly 'very many zealous men are moved by the same charitable spirit towards those paganish Americans' – and by the desire 'to supply that defect in our church before noted'. We wish to 'establish religion' in America. And this cannot be done 'without a habitation of Christians first settled there, and continued'.

The Indians are known to be teachable:

The natural inhabitants are savage, simple, naked and unarmed people, destitute of edge-tools and weapon, whereby they shall be unable to defend themselves or to offend us. Neither is our intent to provoke; but to cherish and win them into Christianity by all fair means, to provide yet against occurrences and not unadvisedly to trust. Notwithstanding, both the Frenchmen and our nation in Virginia have found the people kind and tractable; in so much as some, both French and English, have gone up into land unto their habitations, and remained with the people in great security, without pledges given for the same. And at what time have we ever heard that any colony hath been distressed or overthrown by those silly people?: unless among the Spaniards, whose tyranny hath exceeded toward them; yet could those unarmed wretches never prevail.

Thus to Hayes the colonial imperatives of the 1580s were still valid in the 1590s: 'We have intent, by God's assistance, to plant Christian inhabitants and true religion in a remote and heathen land.' But the future seemed to him to lie in the north, rather than in Raleigh's 'Virginia'. And the north, with its rivers and bays, might prove more navigable than Chesapeake Bay as a passage to the Back Sea of America, a gateway to the riches of the East – even though North America would appear to be bigger than Europe.

In March 1602 a 'small bark', the *Concord*, left Falmouth with thirty two men on board, landed in mid-May on the Maine coast, explored the Massachusetts Bay area until 18 June, and returned to Exmouth by the end of July. This expedition would appear to have infringed the rights still belonging to Raleigh, although the organisers claimed to have his permission. Raleigh was half angry, half glad: as he wrote in a letter of 21 August 1602, he still had hopes of Virginia – 'it were pity to overthrow the enterprise; for I shall yet live to see it an English nation'.[11] The twenty four gentlemen on the expedition (in addition to eight sailors) included Bartholomew Gosnold, Gabriel Archer, John Brereton and Bartholomew Gilbert. Captain Gilbert was the commissary officer, responsible for food supplies. He was apparently no relation of the half-brothers Humphrey Gilbert and Walter Raleigh. Archer and Gosnold were Cambridge men. Archer had gone up to St John's in 1591, the year in which William Crashaw took his B.A. from the college. The Master was William Whitaker. When Archer entered the college, one of the inhabitants of the Master's Lodge was Alexander Whitaker, aged six. Archer remained in Cambridge for about two years, and then went on to Gray's Inn: standard procedure for the gentry. Gosnold matriculated in 1587 from Jesus, not at that time a particularly prominent college. He was of a Suffolk gentry family, and also left Cambridge for the Inns of Court. A John Brereton went up to Caius from Norwich Grammar School in 1589 taking his B.A. in 1593 and his M.A. in 1596, and becoming, after his ordination in 1598, a parson in Suffolk. It is possible, though not certain, that this was the Brereton of the 1602 expedition. Brereton it was who wrote the account of the voyage: *A Brief and True Relation of the Discovery of the North Part of Virginia*, twice printed in London in 1602/3, sponsored by Hakluyt, with a dedication to Raleigh, and including an abridged version of Hayes' Cambridge University Library 'Discourse'. Gosnold was the leader of the expedition and he used Hayes' essay as a prospectus. Indeed, it is possible that the voyage was planned by Hayes, with the help of Hakluyt – who from 1590 had been rector of Wetheringsett in East Suffolk, twenty five miles from Gosnold's home, Bury St Edmunds. (The cousin of Gosnold's wife was Sir Thomas Smythe, knighted in

[11] Letter printed in Gookin-Barbour, *Gosnold*, 168-9. (Rev. Warner F. Gookin left at his death in 1953 an incomplete study of Gosnold; this was completed and edited by Philip L. Barbour for the Dukes County Historical Society, and published in 1963 at Hamden, Connecticut.)

1603.) So the thesis runs that Gosnold was carrying out the ideas of Hayes. Hariot was probably involved also.[12]

Gosnold gave a name to 'Cape Cod'; to the 'Elizabeth Islands' – after the Queen, and also after his sister; and to the island of 'Martha's Vineyard' (Martha being the name both of his mother-in-law and of his first child, who had died in 1598 before reaching her first birthday).

The expedition returned after deciding that their resources were too small for a settlement. Back in England, Gosnold, like Hayes, was concerned to stress the healthiness of the terrain, and the attractiveness of the Indians: 'being of tall stature, comely proportion, strong, active, and some of good years, and as it should seem very healthful' – this in a letter to his father, September 1602.[13] But the definitive account of the expedition was that by Brereton.[14] (Archer's day-by-day journal was to be printed in 1625 by Samuel Purchas in *Purchas his Pilgrimes*.)

The landfall was on Friday 14 May 1602, 'early in the morning', at Cape Neddick, on the very south of the Maine coast, within twenty miles of Portsmouth, New Hampshire. They anchored about noon; and six Indians approached in a Basque shallop – Brereton understood that Basques, or 'of Saint-Jean-de-Luz' (between Biarritz and the Spanish frontier) had 'fished or traded' there – the longtitude was similar. One of the Indians wore a waistcoat and black serge breeches; another had breeches of blue cloth; the rest were 'naked'. They were 'of a black, swart complexion', with eyebrows painted white, 'of tall stature, broad and grim visage'.

They were almost certainly of the Massachuset tribe.

The harbour seemed unsatisfactory, so the English weighed anchor at 3 p.m. that day, and sailed south, reaching Cape Cod on the morning of the 16th. Brereton, Gosnold and three others went ashore and explored for six hours, meeting one Indian, 'a young man of proper stature and of a pleasing countenance', with whom they had 'some familiarity'. Brereton saw that 'there is upon this coast better fishing and in as great plenty as in Newfoundland': cod, mackerel, herring. They sailed round the 'headland', through Nantucket Sound, and reached the island they called Martha's Vineyard. They saw no Indians there. But on the adjacent islands (Elizabeth Islands, to the north)

we saw many Indians, which are tall, big-boned men, all naked, saving they cover their privy parts with a black, tawed skin, much like a blacksmith's apron, tied about their middle and between their legs behind. They gave us of their fish, ready boiled (which they carried in a basket made of twigs not unlike our osier), whereof we did eat, and judged them to be freshwater fish.

[12] Quinn, *England and Discovery of America*, Ch.15, 'Harriot and the Virginia Voyages of 1602'.

[13] Gookin-Barbour, Appendix B.

[14] My text is from Wright, *Elizabethans' America*, 137-44.

They gave us also of their tobacco, which they drink green, but dried into powder, very strong and pleasant, and much better than any I have tasted in England. The necks of their pipes are made of clay, hard-dried (whereof in that island is great store, both red and white); the other part is a piece of hollow copper very finely closed and cemented together. We gave unto them certain trifles, as knives, points and such-like, which they much esteemed.

('Points' are tools.)

Considering the things which 'God and Nature hath bestowed' on the islands (Pemkese, Cuttyhunk, Nashawena, Pasque, Naushon and Nonomesset, grouped as the Elizabeth Islands, Massachusetts; plus Martha's Vineyard) 'the most fertile part of all England' seemed 'but barren'. A landing party in a light boat then crossed to the mainland. Coming ashore (presumably in the neighbourhood of New Bedford, Massachusetts) 'we stood awhile like men ravished at the beauty and delicacy of this sweet soil'. They saw seven Indians, and approached them: 'At first they expressed some fear, but, being emboldened by our courteous usage, and some trifles which we gave them, they followed us to a neck of land' – where they saw a possible harbour, but, being dusk, they sailed back to Cuttyhunk. A day or two later nine canoes, with fifty Indians, landed from the mainland. They

all sat down upon the stones, calling aloud to us (as we rightly guessed) to do the like a little distance from them. Having sat a while in this order, Captain Gosnold willed me to go unto them; one of them, to whom I had given a knife two days before in the main, knew me (whom I also very well remembered) and, smiling upon me, spake somewhat unto their lord or captain, which sat in the midst of them, who presently rose up and took a large beaver-skin from one that stood about him and gave it unto me, which I requited for that time the best I could. But I, pointing towards Captain Gosnold, made signs unto him that he was our Captain, and desirous to be his friend and enter league with him, which (as I perceived) he understood, and made signs of joy. Whereupon Captain Gosnold with the rest of his company, being twenty in all, came up unto them, and after many signs of gratulations, Captain Gosnold presenting their lord with certain trifles which they wondered at and highly esteemed, we became very great friends, and sent for meat aboard our shallop, and gave them such meats as we had then ready dressed, whereof they misliked nothing but our mustard, whereat they made many a sour face.

So everyone was very 'merry'; and 'the rest of the day we spent in trading with them for furs'. Brereton also noted their 'great store of copper' – used for their chains, ear-rings, collars, arrow heads, and drinking cups. The Indians remained for three days; after which all but half a dozen returned to the mainland. From their canoes 'they made huge cries and shouts of joy unto us; and we, with our trumpet and cornet, and casting up our caps into the air, made them the best farewell we could'. The six who remained helped the English in the forest, cutting and carrying sassafras; and 'some of them lay aboard our ship'.

Brereton had now seen about sixty Indians from Massachusetts (including three women), and was in a position to generalise.

These people, as they are exceeding courteous, gentle of disposition, and well-conditioned, excelling all others that we have seen, so for shape of body and lovely favour I think they excel all the people of America: of stature much higher than we; of complexion or colour much like a dark olive; their eyebrows and hair black, which they wear long, tied up behind in knots, whereon they prick feathers of fowls in fashion of a crownet. Some of them are black, thin bearded. They make beards of the hair of beasts; and one of them offered a beard of their making to one of our sailors for his that grew on his face, which, because it was of a red colour, they judged to be none of his own. They are quick-eyed and steadfast in their looks; fearless of others' harms, as intending none of themselves; some of the meaner sort given to filching, which the very name of savages (not weighing their ignorance in good or evil) may easily excuse –

one of the Indians on the 'merry' day had stolen a shield. They were clothed in deerskins, and some wore fur scarves. Brereton was especially impressed by their adroit mimicry.

They pronounce our language with great facility; for one of them one day sitting by me, upon occasion I spake smiling to him these words: 'How now, sirrah, are you so saucy with my tobacco?' Which words (without any further repetition) he suddenly spoke so clear and distinctly as if he had been a long scholar in the language.

The women were 'but low of stature; their eyebrows, hair, apparel and manner of wearing like to the men; fat and very well favoured; and much delighted in our company.' The men were very 'dutiful' to the women.

Brereton was concerned to stress the wholesomeness of the climate. That is what made the Indians agreeable, and 'of a perfect constitution of body, active, strong, healthful, and very witty, as the sundry toys of theirs, cunningly wrought, may easily witness'. Early summer in off shore Massachusetts suited the English also:

We found our health and strength all the while we remained there so to renew and increase as, notwithstanding our diet and lodging was none of the best, yet not one of our company (God be thanked) felt the least grudging, or inclination to any disease or sickness, but were much fatter and in better health than when we went out of England.

The 'Concord' was loaded with sassafras, cedar, furs and skins. And on Friday 18 June, exactly five weeks after the landfall in Maine, the English weighed anchor. Raleigh was distressed by the import of twenty two hundredweight of sassafras; it lowered the price in England.

Captain John Smith (who was in Transylvania in 1602) was later to salute the Brereton-Gosnold expedition: 'all hopes of Virginia thus

abandoned, it lay dead and obscured from 1590 till this year 1602';
'twelve years it lay dead'.[15]

In 1603, shortly before the death of Elizabeth I, a voyage 'set out
from the City of Bristol at the charge of the chiefest merchants of the
said City, with a small ship and a bark, for the discovery of the North
Part of Virginia', under the command of Martin Pring, whose
narrative was to be printed in 1625 by Purchas.[16] Hakluyt and Robert
Salterne (later ordained) had obtained leave, 'under his hand and
seal', from Raleigh, 'which had a most ample patent of all those parts
from Queen Elizabeth'. The ship had thirty men and boys, the bark
thirteen men and one boy; they were victualled for eight months; and
they carried 'slight merchandises' for the Indian – coloured hats,
clothing, stockings, and shoes; saws, axes and pick axes, spades,
shovels, hatchets, hooks, knives, scissors, hammers, nails, chisels, fish
hooks; bells, bugles, beads, mirrors; thimbles and pins, needles and
thread. Elizabeth died on 24 March: the voyagers did not hear the
news until 10 April, when they were off Milford Haven,
Pembrokeshire.

Pring's two vessels arrived off the coast of New Hampshire, sailed
south, reaching the future sites of Boston and Plymouth, and
eventually landed and spent seven weeks, probably south of
Plymouth, in Cape Cod Bay, Massachusetts. They built a 'small
barricado', which the men left to cut down sassafras trees, sassafras
being 'a plant of sovereign virtue for the French pox' (and the plague).
Pring was superciliously suspicious of the Indian – 'we sent them
back, and would have none of their entertainment', he wrote on one
occasion. But there was method in it: he sensed that the Indians were
'given to treachery'. (All the same, it was surely hardly necessary,
'when we would be rid of the savages' company' to let loose the two
mastiffs he had brought: 'suddenly with great outcries they would flee
away.') The Indians were curious, and friendly, paying visits (a group
of 120 on one occasion) and eating the English peas and beans ('Their
own victuals were most of fish'). Pring described the Indian bows (of
witch hazel, six feet long, painted black and yellow), arrows (with
three black eagle or vulture feathers bound on) and quivers (a yard
long, and decorated). The Indian men were 'of stature somewhat
taller than our ordinary people, strong, swift, well-proportioned': they
were 'inclined to a swart, tawney or chestnut colour, not by nature, but
accidentally'. One English youth had brought his cithern – a kind of
zither:

in whose homely music they took great delight, and would give him many
things, as tobacco, tobacco pipes, snakes' skins of six feet long (which they
use for girdles), fawns' skins and such like, and danced twenty in a ring, and
the gittern in the midst of them, using many savage gestures, singing Jo, Ja,

---

[15] Smith-Arber, 332 (*General History*, Book I).
[16] *Purchas His Pilgrimes*, Glasgow ed., XVIII, 322-9.

Jo, Ja, Ja, Jo: him that first broke the ring, the rest would knock, and cry out
upon.

The bark was loaded with sassafras and sent on ahead. The rest
stayed for another two weeks; and observed that the wheat, barley,
oats and peas they had sowed six week before came up well.

On 10 May 1603 – nearly seven weeks after the accession of James I
– one ship, the 'Elizabeth', left Plymouth bound for Chesapeake Bay.
The small party was under the command of Bartholomew Gilbert.
Purchas printed the account of the voyage by Thomas Canner of
Barnard's Inn (one of the minor Inns of Court).[17] The landfall was on
23 July 1603, probably in northern New Jersey. Gilbert 'thirsted' to
'seek out the people for Sir Walter Raleigh left near those parts in the
year 1587'. There was bad weather, and 'extremity for water and
wood, victuals and beer'. There was a landing party on 29 July, and
Gilbert and four others were killed by Indians, leaving only eleven
men in the expedition. They arrived back in London at the end of
September, 'finding the City most grievously infected with a terrible
plague'. Finding also that Raleigh was in the Tower under a charge of
high treason.

Raleigh's patent reverted to the Crown, and the first subsequent
expedition was in 1605. The patrons were Henry, Earl of
Southampton, and his brother-in-law Thomas Arundell, papist, newly
created Baron Arundell of Wardour. The intention may have been to
find a site for a Catholic colony. The commander was Captain George
Weymouth; the one ship, with less than thirty adventurers and
sailors, sailed from the Thames in March 1605, and was back in
Dartmouth, Devon, on 18 July. An account of the voyage was
published in London later in 1605; and again in 1625 by Purchas, who
used a longer text. I have followed the 1605 version. The author was
James Rosier, a member of the expedition; the title, *A True Relation of the
Most Prosperous Voyage Made in this Present Year 1605 by Captain George
Weymouth in the Discovery of the Land of Virginia*; and the running title, 'the
last discovery of the north part of Virginia'.

(Robert Beverley, in *The History and Present State of Virginia*, published
in 1705, said that the 1605 expedition intended to land in the region of
Delaware Bay, but in fact made landfall 'upon the eastward parts of
Long Island'; later the company 'ranged forty miles up Connecticut
River, and called the harbour where they rid Pentecost Harbour,
because of their arrival there on Whitsunday'.)[18]

Rosier gave quite detailed descriptions of the Indians of the Maine
and Massachusetts shore line.

The shape of their body is very proportionable. They are well countenanced,
not very tall nor big, but in stature like to us. They paint their bodies with
black; their faces, some with red, some with black, and some with blue. Their

[17] *ibid.*, 329-35.
[18] Ed. Wright, 24.

clothing is beavers' skins or deers' skins, cast over them like mantles, and hanging down to their knees, made fast upon the shoulder with leather. Some of them had sleeves, most had none. Some had buskins of leather tied. They have besides a piece of beaver's skin between their legs, made fast about their waist, to cover their privities. They suffer no hair to grow upon their faces, but on their head very long and black, which those that have wives bind up behind with a leather string, on a long round knot. They seemed all very civil and very merry, showing tokens of much thankfulness for those things we gave them. We found them then (as after) a people of exceeding good invention, quick understanding and ready capacity.[19]

Rosier found the women very shy: perhaps because of 'the commanding jealousy of their husbands'. But they were 'very well favoured in proportion of countenance, though black; low of stature, and exceeding fat'. The 1605 text[20] described the women as 'covered only, as the men, with the foresaid beaver's skins'; in the Purchas version, this description would be reduced to: 'naked'.

Rosier, with the help of information from a crew mate called Owen Griffin, reported on 'the ceremonies of their idolatry':

One among them (the eldest of the company as he judged) riseth right up, the other sitting still, and, looking about, suddenly cried with a loud voice: Baugh Waugh.

A passage which scholars say was noted by Shakespeare; Ariel's song 'Come into these yellow sands' in *The Tempest* (1611) includes the refrain (in the spelling of the First Folio), 'Hark, hark, bowgh wawgh: the watch dogs bark, bowgh-wawgh.' (Unless of course both Shakespeare and Rosier were independently rendering the noise of canine barking; however, the Owen Griffin contribution to English Literature is a nice thought.) Upon this barking,

the women fall down and lie upon the ground, and the men – all together answering the same – fall a'stamping round about the fire with both feet as hard as they can, making the ground shake, with sundry outcries and change of voice and sound. Many take the fire sticks, and thrust them into the earth, and then rest silent a while. Of a sudden beginning as before, they continue so stamping till the younger sort fetched from the shore those many stones, of which every man takes one, and first beat upon them with their fire sticks, then with the stones beat the earth with all their strength. And in this manner (as he reported) they continued above two hours. After this ended, they which have wives take them apart, and withdraw themselves severally into the woods all night.[21]

The English were certainly well aware, realistically, of the possibility of treachery. These Indians could well be like 'other savages who have been by all travellers in most discoveries found very treacherous'.[22] But these suspicions were kept in check; if only

[19] B.3.r-B.3.v.   [20] C.2.r.   [21] C.2.v.   [22] C.2.v.

because of the model behaviour of the Indians whom the English took into custody:

After perceiving, by their kind usage, we intended them no harm, they have never since seemed discontented with us, but very tractable, loving, and willing by their best means to satisfy us in any thing we demand of them, by words or signs, for their understanding. Neither have they at any time been at the least discord among themselves, insomuch as we have not seen them angry, but merry; and so kind, as if you give anything to one of them, he will distribute part to every one of the rest. We have brought them to understand some English; and we understand much of their language, so as we are able to ask them many things.[23]

The English brought five such Indians back home with them, probably of the Abenaki tribe. One chief, said Rosier, three gentlemen, and one servant.[24] Two were taken to London for the Lord Chief Justice, Sir John Popham. The Indians 'show great reverence to their king, and are in great subjection to their governors; and they will show a great respect to any we tell them are our commanders'.[25] Three were kept at Plymouth Fort for Sir Ferdinando Gorges (a Somerset man, like Popham).

After Gorges had had his three Indians for a time, he 'observed in them an inclination to follow the example of the better sort, and in all their carriages manifest shows of a great civility, far from the rudeness of our common people':[26]

And the longer I conversed with them the better hope they gave me of those parts where they did inhabit, as proper for our uses, especially when I found what goodly rivers, stately islands and safe harbours those parts abounded with, being the special marks I levelled at as the only want our nation met with in all their navigations along the coast. And having kept them full three years, I made them able to set me down what great rivers ran up into the land, what men of note were seated on them, what power they were of, how allied, what enemies they had.

'Full three years': summer 1608.

There is a deal of evidence for popular English interest in North America in 1605. In March (probably) – the time of the departure of the Weymouth expedition – the play *Eastward Ho* was acted in the City of London at the Blackfriars Playhouse; published in September, and then twice more before the end of the year.[27] The title page described the play as 'made' by George Chapman, Ben Jonson and John Marston. The experts tell us that most of it was by Chapman, with contributions by Marston, Jonson being over-all planner. Sir Petronel Flash is an improverished adventurer-gallant, with an eye to the gold of the New World. He is the organiser of a 'Virginian venture' (IV,1): 'All

[23] E.2.r.   [24] E.4.r.   [25] E.2.r.
[26] Quoted Rowse, *Elizabethans and America*, 96.
[27] Ed. J.H. Harris, Yale University Press, 1926.

he could any way get, is bestowed on a ship now bound for Virginia'
(II,1). His associates in the projected voyage are Captain Seagull and
his cronies Scapethrift and Spendall. The latter three have a scene in a
tavern, written by Chapman (III,2).

Seagull	Come boys, Virginia longs till we share the rest of her maidenhead.
Spendall	Why, is she inhabited already with any English?
Seagull	A whole country of English is there, man, bred of those that were left in 79. They have married with the Indians, and make 'hem bring forth as beautiful faces as any we have in England: and therefore the Indians are so in love with 'em, that all the treasure they have they lay at their feet.
Scapethrift	But is there such treasure there, captain, as I have heard?
Seagull	I tell thee, gold is more plentiful there than copper is with us; and for as much red copper as I can bring, I'll have thrice the weight in gold. Why man, all their dripping pans and their chamber pots are pure gold; and all the chains with which they chain up their streets are massy gold; all the prisoners they take, are fettered in gold; and as for rubies and diamonds, they go forth on holidays and gather 'hem by the sea shore to hang on their childrens' coats and stick in their caps, as commonly as our children wear saffron gilt brooches and groats with holes in them.
Scapethrift	And is it a pleasant country withall?
Seagull	As ever the sun shined on; temperate and full of all sorts of excellent viands; wild boar is as common there as our tamest bacon is here; venison, as mutton. And then you shall live freely there, without serjeants or courtiers or lawyers or intelligencers.

There follows a passage in Seagull's speech which led to the
imprisonment of all three authors, although it was probably an
addition by Marston. No lawyers or intelligencers (spies):

Only a few industrious Scots perhaps, who indeed are dispersed over the face
of the whole earth. But as for them, there are no greater friends to
Englishmen and England, when they are out an't, in the world than they are.
And for my part I would a hundred thousand of them were there, for we are
all one countrymen now, ye know; and we should find then times more
comfort of them there, than we do here.

Too strong for James Stuart! The speech concludes:

Then for your means to advancement, there it is simply, and not
preposterously mixed. You may be an alderman there, and never be
scavenger; you may be a nobleman, and never be a slave; you may come to
preferment enough, and never be a pandar; to riches and fortune enough,

and have never the more villainy, nor the less wit. Besides, there we shall have no more law than conscience, and not too much of cither; serve God enough, eat and drink enough, and enough is as good as a feast.

The episode ends with Captain Seagull assuring Spendall that the voyage is short: 'Some six weeks' sail, no more, with an indifferent good wind.'

In November 1604 *Westward Ho*, by Thomas Dekker and John Webster, had been acted in London, entered in the Stationers' Register in March 1605, and finally printed in 1607. Dekker and Webster's *Northward Ho* was also published in 1607.[28] The titles are deceptive, for the pieces contain nothing about over-seas expansion (the titles were cries of Thames bargemen); they are sex comedies set among the citizens of London, trenchant, calculatingly obscene, and rather funny.

Nine years after *Eastward Ho*, in 1614, George Chapman was to provide the text for the Middle Temple and Lincoln's Inn Masque performed at Whitehall on Shrove Tuesday to celebrate the marriage of the King's daughter Elizabeth. The Masque usually known as 'The Virginian Princess':[29] 'supplied, applied, digested and written', the printed text tells us, by Chapman; and 'invented and fashioned, with the ground and special structure of the whole work, by our kingdom's most artful and ingenious architect, Inigo Jones'. The splendours included two triumphal chariots, each containing six musicians (in all six singers and six lutanists) 'attired like Virginian priests, by whom the sun is there adored': the costume was 'strange hoods of feathers, and scallops about their necks, and on their heads turbants, stuck with several coloured feathers, spotted with wings of flies, of extraordinary bigness, like those of their country'.[30] The main performers, on horseback, represented 'the noblest Virgineans': and were dressed[31]

in Indian habits, all of a ressemblance. The ground cloth of silver, richly embroidered with golden suns; and about every sun ran a trail of gold, imitating Indian work. Their bases of the same stuff and work; but betwixt every pane of embroidery went a row of white ostrich feathers, mingled with sprigs of gold plate. Under their breasts they wore bawdricks[32] of gold, embroidered high with pearl; and about their necks, ruffs of feathers, spangled with pearl and silver. On their heads, high sprigged feathers compact in coronets, like the Virginian princes they represented. Betwixt every set of feathers, and about their brows, in the underpart of their coronets, shined suns of gold plate, springled with pearl, from whence sprung rays of the like plate, that, mixing with the motion of the feathers, showed exceedingly delightful and gracious. Their legs were adorned with close long white silk stockings, curiously embroidered with gold to the middle leg. And

---

[28] Both plays in F. Bowers (ed.), *Dramatic Works of Dekker*, 1955.
[29] *The Memorable Maske ... of 15 of February 1613* (i.e. 1614).
[30] A.1.v.   [31] A.2.r-v.
[32] 'Bawdrick': baldric – belt or strap.

over these, being on horse back, they drew greaves³³ or buskins embroidered with gold, and interlaced with rows of feathers. Altogether estrangeful, and Indian-like.

Each horse was flanked by two 'moors' 'attired like Indian slaves', and with the player, on each horse, sat a torchbearer in costume 'likewise of the Indian garb, but more stravagant'.³⁴ Chapman's words were rather secondary, in this context! But some of the text (which runs to only two dozen pages) is interesting.³⁵

> Virginian Princes, ye must now renounce
> Your superstitious worship of these suns,
> Subject to cloudy darknings and descents,
> And of your sweet devotions, turn the events
> To this our Britan Phoebus, whose bright sky
> (Enlightened with a Christian piety)
> Is never subject to black error's night,
> And hath already offered Heaven's true light
> To your dark region; which acknowledge now;
> Descend, and to him all your homage vow.

After the homage to James, a dance.

Back to 1605. London merchants were obviously interested in Virginia. But Bristol and the West Country ports were anxious not to be overshadowed. They had been behind the Brereton-Gosnold and Weymouth expeditions; their patron was John Popham; their advisers included Hakluyt, who was a prebendary of Bristol Cathedral from 1586 until his death in 1616. The voyages of 1602 and 1605 had hardly been earth-shaking. But Gosnold was active, thinking of a permanent settlement in North America; Hayes and Hakluyt were in his circle; and in the spring of 1605 Gosnold met John Smith, who had achieved the military rank of captain in the army of the Emperor Rudolph II, and had to his credit a string of wonderful adventures in Hungary, Transylvania, Russia and Morocco.³⁶ In March 1606 the Spanish Ambassador in London wrote to Philip III that plans were afoot to send five or six hundred men to settle in Virginia.³⁷

But how was such an expedition to be organised and financed, in view of the lessons of the last quarter of a century? By 1606 Edward Hayes had lost his assurance of the infallibility of private enterprise. In that year he wrote to Robert Cecil, Lord Salisbury, about the American 'project':³⁸

So great a business for planting of Christianity amongst heathens can never

³³ 'Greaves': armour for the leg below the knee.
³⁴ A.3.v.   ³⁵ D.4.v.
³⁶ The best book on Smith is by Barbour: *The Three Worlds of John Smith*, 1964.
³⁷ Barbour, *Jamestown Voyages*, 66.
³⁸ Historical Manuscripts Commission, Calendar, Marquis of Salisbury, Hatfield House, Part XVIII, 1940, 407-8.

be duly effected by private means, in which course some of us have many years past ventured both life and substance without fruit; who have devised another way without offence to public or private, whereby the cause may be completely set forward, supported and seconded, until it be grown to such perfection as it may stand up itself, and yield large recompense to all co-assistants. Which means require the consent of Parliament; whereunto a motion is drawn by us, and a brief discourse of inducement also, for satisfaction of sundry objections made heretofore, seeming fit to leave as little scruple as may be in men's minds and consciences; whose furtherance must be required in the House, some copies whereof we intend to deliver amongst divers our friends, members of the same. Nevertheless we thought it our duties first to acquaint your lordship therewith.

The Parliament was in session from 21 January to 26 May 1606. The MPs included Sir Thomas Smythe and Sir Edwin Sandys. And Hayes had been impressed by some of the work of the first session of James' first Parliament, in 1604. He wrote in 1605 that 'the state has wisely in Parliament sought redress' for one of his bugbears: 'Our country is strangely annoyed with idle, loose and vagrant people.'[39] (Presumably a reference to the motion of 12 May 1604 for 'the continuance, explanation and enlarging of the Statute of rogues, vagabonds and sturdy beggars'.)[40]

Among the papers preserved in the Lansdowne manuscripts in the British Museum is a document from the Admiralty papers of Sir Julius Caesar, endorsed 'Reasons to move the High Court of Parliament to raise a stock for the maintaining of a Colony in Virginia'. This was printed in 1890 by Alexander Brown of Virginia;[41] who thought it was probably written early in 1606 by Sir John Popham. The theme of these six pages is the disadvantage of private enterprise:

Private purses are cold comfort to Adventurers, and have ever been found fatal to all enterprises hitherto undertaken by the English, by reason of delays, jealousies, and unwillingness to back that project which succeeded not at the first attempt.

In Virginia there was danger from France – and from Denmark. The author invoked the example of the Dutch East India Company of 1602, which has 'effected marvellous matters in trade and navigation'. What mattered was the 'whole state': public service, public consent. 'It is honorable for a state rather to back an exploit by a public consent than by a private monopoly.'

As in 1584, ideas of bringing the House of Commons into the American colonial story were dropped. But that had been one possibility: a trading company under both royal and private control,

[39] *ibid.*, Part XVII, 1938, 412 (Hayes to Salisbury, 4 September 1605).
[40] *Journal of the House of Commons*, I, 1742, 207.
[41] Brown, *Genesis*, I, 37-42. For Alexander Brown, see Craven, *Dissolution of Virginia Company*, 12-21.

with Parliamentary consent. Another, more traditional, possibility was
to confine the American enterprise to private monopoly, a sort of
feudal domain. Another possibility, favoured by Popham, was to
organise a royal colony, administered by the central government in
London. Amid these notions, a definite move: in the autumn of 1605,
as Robert Beverley put it,[42] merchants from London (including Sir
Thomas Gates, Sir George Somers and Edward Maria Wingfield),
from Plymouth (including George Popham and Raleigh Gilbert – son
of Sir Humphrey), from Bristol and from Exeter,

joined together in a petition to King James I, showing forth that it would be
too much for any single person to attempt the settling of colonies, and to
carry on so considerable a trade. They therefore prayed His Majesty to
incorporate them, and enable them to raise a joint stock for that purpose.

The Charter of the Virginia Company (technically a Letter Patent:
the first in our story since 1584) was issued on 10 April 1606.[43]
    The adventurers (eight of them named, including Hakluyt) had
'licence to make habitation, plantation, and to deduce a colony of
sundry of our people into that part of America commonly called
Virginia'. In fact the Company, although its administrative centre was
London, was divided into two: the London Company, with authority
south of the Potomac, and the Plymouth Company, with authority
north of New York City (the intermediate region was available to
both, so long as London and Plymouth did not there settle within one
hundred miles of each other). Thus the 'northern part of Virginia'
was, in the words of John Smith, 'appropriated to the Cities of Bristol,
Exeter and Plymouth, etc, and the West parts of England'.[44] The 'two
several colonies and plantations' were under the control of a Council
in London, appointed by the King: 'The King's Council of Virginia'
(fourteen members, as it turned out, including Thomas Smythe,
Gorges, a merchant of Bristol and a merchant of Plymouth, and Sir
Thomas West, Lord De La Warr since 1602). Thus 'policy' was
ultimately supervised by the King. Each of the two colonial
settlements in America was to be governed on the spot by a council,
nominated by the Council of Virginia in London, with a President, to
be chosen annually by the members of the local council.
    In the April 1606 Charter, all colonists were to have 'all liberties,
franchises and immunities to all intents and purposes as if they had
been abiding within this our realm of England'. And the intention was
naturally stressed of 'propagating of Christian religion to such people
as yet live in darkness and miserable ignorance of the true knowledge

[42] *History and Present State of Virginia*, ed. Wright, 26.
[43] In Bemiss (ed.), *Three Charters of the Virginia Company*. An analysis of the investors
in Virginia from the 1580s to the 1620s (with interesting material on the use of
computers in this type of technical historical research) forms part of the work by
Rabb, *Enterprise and Empire*.
[44] Smith-Arber, 695.

and worship of God'; bringing 'infidels and savages living in those parts to humane civility, and to a settled and quiet government'.

Further royal instructions came in November 1606.[45] It was made clear that in America laws enacted by the local authority were to be 'for the substance thereof, as near to the common laws of England, and the equity thereof, as may be'. Also that

the true word and service of God and Christian faith be preached, planted and used, not only within every of the said several colonies and plantations, but also, as much as they may,• among the savage people which do or shall adjoin unto them or border upon them, according to the doctrine, rites and religion now professed and established within our realm of England.

(The authorities in America also had power 'to punish all manner of excess, through drunkenness or otherwise, and all idle, loitering and vagrant persons'.) The colonists were firmly instructed to 'well entreat those savages in those parts, and use all good means to draw the savages and heathen people' to 'the true service and knowledge of God'; and 'that all just, kind and charitable courses shall be holden with such of them as shall conform themselves to any good and sociable traffic and dealing with the subjects of us, our heirs and successors'.

The Instructions of the London Council itself followed early in December 1606.[46] The 'captains and company which are sent at this present to plant there' were ordered to 'have great care not to offend the naturals, if you can eschew it; and employ some few of your company to trade with them for corn, and all other lasting victuals'. But never be unsuspicious: 'how weary soever your soldiers be, let them never trust the country people with the carriage of their weapons, for if they run from you with your shot, which they only fear, they will easily kill them all with their arrows.' If any English are killed, conceal the fact, or the Indians will conclude that the colonists are but 'common men': 'you shall do well also not to let them see or know of your sick men.' These Instructions (now in the Library of Congress) were practical, sensible, pithy; worth a dozen sermons.

The voyagers under the auspices of the Virginia Company of Plymouth (120 of them, all male) settled in August 1607 a quarter of the way up the coast of Maine (twenty-five miles north-east of Portland) on the river then called Sagadahoc (now, Kennebec). They arrived in two vessels, one controlled by the aged George Popham, who became President of the colony, the other by Raleigh Gilbert. The vessels had left Plymouth within four weeks of each other, in May and June. (In August 1606 the Plymouth Company had sent out an exploring ship, captured by the Spanish; and in October 1606 another vessel, with Martin Pring on board, which had reached Maine successfully, and returned with good reports.)

[45] Barbour, *Jamestown Voyages*, 34-44.
[46] *ibid.*, 49-54.

This 'northern colony on the river Sagadahoc' barely lasted a year. It was abandoned in the summer of 1608. A 'fort' had been constructed, Fort St George. The painstaking Reverend Richard Seymour (not, it seems, a Cambridge man) had preached the first sermon heard in New England: August 1607. But the two ships returned to England late in 1607, leaving only forty-four settlers to face a harsh winter – but no colder, William Strachey was critically to comment, than winter in Scotland.[47] There were quarrels and factions, and a devastating fire. Sir John Popham died in England; George Popham died in the Fort; and the impetuous Raleigh Gilbert decided, for family reasons, to return to England. Thus the plantation, wrote John Smith, was 'begun and ended in one year, and the country esteemed as a cold, barren, mountainous, rocky desert'.[48]

The New England coast was left for the moment to the fishing vessels.

As we know now, the London branch of the Virginia Company stole the limelight. Their three ships set sail down the Thames on 20 December 1606: the 'Susan Constant', under Christopher Newport, the 'Discovery', under John Ratcliffe, and the 'Godspeed' – under Bartholomew Gosnold.

[47] *Virginia Britania*, 35.
[48] Smith-Arber, 696. For the Sagahadoc colony: Andrews, I, 90-7; Rowse, *Elizabethans and America*, 98-101.

14

Trouble in Paradise:
Jamestown 1607-1610

The 145 colonists aboard the three vessels which set sail during the night of 19/20 December 1606 were under the leadership of Christopher Newport, aged 46, highly experienced in Atlantic waters,[1] with Bartholomew Gosnold as his second-in-command. The weather worsened; and the little fleet was delayed for some six weeks in the Channel. The Reverend Robert Hunt, chaplain, became very ill when the 'Susan Constant' was stranded off the Sussex Downs – a dozen miles from his old parish of Heathfield, Sussex.

Edward Wingfield, who was among the colonists, had during 1606 concerned himself with 'a right choice of a spiritual pastor'; he consulted Archbishop Bancroft; and finally settled upon Hunt, 'truly in my opinion a man not any way to be touched with the rebellious humours of a popish spirit, nor blemished with the least suspicion of a factious schismatic, whereof I had a special care'.[2] Hunt was nearly forty: rather elderly, one might think. He may have been the Robert Hunt who went up to Magdalen, Oxford, in 1589. At all events, our Hunt became Vicar of Reculver, on the coast of northern Kent, in 1594, and stayed there eight years: one of his neighbour clerics had been Richard Hooker, friend and former Oxford tutor of Edwin Sandys; rector of Bishopsbourne, near Canterbury, from 1595 until his death in 1600. Hunt moved in 1602 to Heathfield, in mid-Sussex. On 24 November 1606 two clerics were given dispensation to go to Virginia, and be absent from their English cure of souls, while retaining the stipend.[3] One was Robert Hunt, M.A. The other was Richard Hakluyt,

clerk prebendary both in the collegiate church of St Peter, Westminster, and in the cathedral church of the Holy and Undivided Trinity, Bristol, as well as rector of the parish church of Wetheringsett in our county of Suffolk, diocese of Norwich, and one of the perpetual chaplains of our hospital of le Savoy in our county of Middlesex.

[1] K.R. Andrews, 'Christopher Newport of Limehouse, Mariner', *William and Mary Quarterly*, January 1954 (3rd series, vol.XI, no.1).
[2] Philip L. Barbour, ed., *The Jamestown Voyages under the First Charter 1606-1609*, Hakluyt Society, 1969, 2 vols., continuous paging, 233. Mr Barbour's meticulously researched volumes, carefully noted and presented, are the basis for this chapter. Hereafter cited as *JV*. [3] *JV*, 62.

Perhaps Hakluyt had intended to go. At any rate he had the prior right. But Hunt had signed his will four days earlier, on 20 November. From the will we deduce that his motives for leaving Sussex were perhaps more personal than evangelical: Hunt decreed that his wife 'shall be excluded from being my executor' should she 'commit the act of incontinency' or co-habit with John Taylor of the parish.[4] (Hunt had a son and a small daughter.) The very generous stipend, £50 a year, was no deterrent.

By 1608 Edward Wingfield was rejoicing that 'my travels and dangers have done somewhat for the behoof of Jerusalem in Virginia'.[5]

The image of Zion in America was not invented by the settlers at New Plymouth in 1620, or the emigrants to New England in the 1630s. 'Ye are the light of the world. A city that is set on a hill cannot be hid' – the words of Christ in the sermon on the mount, as given by Matthew (5:14); and the more thoughtful of the Jamestown settlers were quite aware of the relevance. Sir Thomas Dale, Governor at Jamestown in 1614, referred to 'the hope to have builded up this heavenly new Jerusalem'; and mourned 'the great captain of our Israel', Prince Henry, who had died in November 1612 at the age of 18.[6] Ralph Hamor in 1615 commended the settlements on the James River as a 'Sanctum Sanctorum, an holy house, a sanctuary to Him, the God of the Spirits, of all flesh, amongst such poor and innocent seducted savages'.[7] A broadsheet of 1615 depicted two (engraved) Indians, addressing the English:[8]

> Once, in one State, as of one Stem,
> Mere strangers from Jerusalem,
> As We, were Ye; till others Pity
> Sought, and brought You to that City.
>
> Dear Britons, now, be You as kind;
> Bring Light and Sight to Us yet blind:
> Lead Us, by doctrine and Behaviour,
> Into one Sion, to one Saviour.

Hakluyt in the 1580s had thought of America as an asylum – and as a region to which puritans might reasonably be exported. More positively, he used of Virginia in 1589 the phrase 'this paradise of the world'.[9] Michael Drayton's Ode 'To the Virginian Voyage', published in 1606,[10] held out the hope that the English settlers, 'brave heroic minds' that 'honour still pursue', enflamed to seek fame by reading of 'industrious Hakluyt', might (in addition to getting 'the pearl and gold')

[4] *JV*, 60-2.   [5] *JV*, 233-4.
[6] Quoted in Hamor, *True Discourse*, 1615, 51.
[7] *ibid.*, 'Letter to the Reader'.
[8] Brown, *Genesis*, II, 761.
[9] Quinn (ed.), *Roanoke Voyages*, 479.
[10] Conveniently found in Wright (ed.), *Elizabethans' America*, 160-2.

                              ... hold
                            Virginia,
                            Earth's only Paradise:

Drayton was in the tradition of 'the golden age', 'nature's laws' –
phrases from the ode. But evangelical military martinets (under
instruction, as we have seen, to punish idleness and drunkenness)
could give to the concepts an intellectual stiffening which owes as
much to the conditions of the frontier as to any 'puritan' temper.

So the Reverend Robert Hunt, on his sick bed in the channel, had
an unnerving responsibility. He at least tried to calm the 'envy and
dissension' that had already sprung up in the fleet;[11] springing, we
read in 1612,[12] from those colonists 'little better than atheists', with
'scandalous imputations' and 'disastrous designs' – those colonists 'of
the greatest rank amongst us': who could that be save Wingfield, and
George Percy, younger brother of the Earl of Northumberland?

It was February (1607) before the three ships lost sight of England.

Coming north from the West Indies (where John Smith, on the
orders of Wingfield, had been restrained as a prisoner) the colonists
eventually 'descried the land of Virginia'[13] on 26 April 1607, eighteen
weeks after leaving London. They drew into the Chesapeake Bay area,
and a sealed box, containing the names of the colonists' council,
appointed by the London Council, was opened. There were seven
names, including Gosnold, Wingfield, Newport, Ratcliffe – and John
Smith: who was still in disgrace, and not admitted until later. A party
went ashore, at Cape Henry, and met their first Indians, 'creeping
upon all fours from the hills, like bears, with their bows in their
mouths'. Gabriel Archer and a sailor were wounded. The English
fired back; and the Indians 'returned into the woods with a great
noise'.

The account is by George Percy, whose 'Discourse' was first printed
in 1625 by Samuel Purchas in his *Pilgrimes*.[14] Percy was about twenty-
six, with a military career in the Netherlands behind him. He was a
good observer, with a deal of common sense.

For eighteen days the colonists reconnoitred the Bay (using the
ship's boat). Percy tells us of the visit to the coastal village of
Kecoughtan (later Elizabeth City, now Hampton).[15] Newport saw five
Indians on the shore, who at first were very 'timorsome'. Newport laid
his hand on his heart, and 'upon that they laid down their bows and
arrows, and came very boldly to us, making signs to come ashore to
their town'. So the party landed; and the Indians 'made a doleful
noise, laying their faces to the ground, scratching the earth with their
nails. We did think they had been at their idolatry'. But then the

---

[11] *JV*, 70.   [12] *JV*, 378.
[13] *JV*, 133 (George Percy).
[14] Vol.4, pp. 1685-90. Glasgow ed., XVIII, 403-19. *JV*, 129-46. My quotations, *JV*,
134.
[15] *JV*, 135-6.

Indians brought out seating mats, and gave the explorers 'their bread, which they make of their maize or guinea wheat'. Later, Percy describes the Indian method of baking bread:[16]

After they pound their wheat into flour with hot water, they make it into paste, and work it into round balls and cakes. Then they put it into a pot of seething water. When it is sod thoroughly they lay it on a smooth stone; then they harden it – as well as in an oven.

At Kecoughtan Percy noted the 'fine and beautiful strawberries, four times bigger and better than ours in England', and the large oysters, delicate to the taste when roasted over a fire – mussels and oysters lay on the ground 'as thick as stones': the English opened some oysters, and found many pearls. After the food, the Indians distributed tobacco, which they smoked 'in a pipe made artificially of earth, as ours are, but far bigger, with the bowl fashioned together with a piece of fine copper'. There was then Indian dancing.

One of the savages standing in the midst singing, beating one hand against another, all the rest dancing round him, shouting, howling and stamping against the ground, with many antic tricks and faces, making noise like so many wolves or devils. One thing of them I observed. When they were in their dance, they kept stroke with their feet just one with another; but with their hands, heads, faces and bodies, every one of them had a several gesture. So they continued for the space of half an hour.

The dancing over, Newport distributed beads and trinkets. Percy made notes on Indian appearance:

They hang through their ears fowls' legs. They shave the right side of their heads with a shell, the left side they wear of an ell[17] long, tied up with an artificial knot, with a many of fowls' feathers sticking in it. They go altogether naked, but their privities are covered with beasts' skins, beset commonly with little stones or beasts' teeth. Some paint their bodies black, some red; with artificial knots of sundry lively colours, very beautiful and pleasing to the eye, in a braver fashion than they in the West Indies.

In this period of early May 1607, while exploring for a settlement site, the English met various Indian chiefs.[18] One was the werowance of Paspahegh, at the mouth of the Chickahominy River. Another was the werowance of Quiyoughcohannock. He entertained the English in his house 'in good humanity': behaving 'in so modest a proud fashion as though he had been a prince of civil government, holding his countenance without laughter, or any such ill behaviour'. His body was painted 'crimson', his face painted blue, and tattooed. He wore a head-dress of deers' hair, and two long feathers; and a copper plate

[16] *JV*, 142.
[17] Ell: a measure of length, about 45 inches.
[18] *JV*, 137-8.

was attached to the shaven side of his head. He played a reed flute.

On 8 May a party landed near the village of Appomattoc. The Indians were at first hostile:

At our landing there came many stout and able savages to resist us with their bows and arrows, in a most warlike manner, with the swords at their backs beset with sharp stones and pieces of iron able to cleave a man insunder. Amongst the rest, one of the chiefest, standing before them cross-legged, with his arrow ready in his bow in one hand and taking a pipe of tobacco in the other, with a bold uttering of his speech demanded of us our being there, willing of us to be gone.

But the English managed to communicate their peaceable intentions, and they were allowed to land quietly.

A settlement site was chosen, thirty miles down the Powhatan river from the sea. And on 14 May 1607 – eighteen days after Virginia had been sighted – 'we landed all our men, which were set to work about the fortification, and others, some to watch and ward, as it was convenient.'[19] The site was an isthmus or peninsula two miles long and one mile broad, attached to the shore by a narrow sand bar; once a camping site for the Paspahegh tribe (and still regarded by the Indians as tribal hunting ground). It was a low and swampy position; but it was a good control point on the broad river, the anchorage was good, and the pasture. The name chosen for it was Jamestown; and the great river was called the James.

Trees were felled to make room for tents; wood was collected to repair the three vessels; 'some make gardens, others nets'.[20] And so the fort took shape. One tent became a beer house, or tavern (although at first liquid refreshment was supplied from the ships): by 1608 this was known as the 'old tavern'.[21]

Provision had to be made for the ministrations of Rev. Robert Hunt. John Smith tells us about this in 1630:[22]

When I first went to Virginia, I well remember we did hang an awning (which is an old sail) to three or four trees to shadow us from the sun. Our walls were rails of wood, our seats unhewed trees till we cut planks, our pulpit a bar of wood nailed to two neighbouring trees. In foul weather we shifted into an old rotten tent; for we had few better, and this came by the way of adventure for new. This was our church; till we built a homely thing like a barn, set upon cratchets, covered with rafts, sedge and earth.

The first communion service for which there is evidence was on Sunday 21 June 1607. The evidence is the 'narrative' of Gabriel Archer.[23] But it seems probable that Hunt would have previously said

[19] *JV*, 138 (Percy).
[20] *JV*, 380.
[21] *JV*, 417; cf.384.
[22] Smith-Arber, 957 (*Advertisements for the unexperienced Planters of New England*).
[23] *JV*, 98.

the communion service on Whit-Sunday, 24 May.

Hunt died in the spring of 1608. His Jamestown ministry was thus for no more than one year. In that year, recalled Smith, the colonists had daily morning and evening prayer: 'every Sunday two sermons; and every three months the holy communion'. Smith approved of Hunt: 'an honest, religious and courageous divine', by whom factions were 'oft qualified' and extremities 'comforted'. Smith himself approved of the Book of Common Prayer, preaching, the observation of the Sabbath, and diligent catechising – 'strict and careful exercise'. Such 'commendable good orders' lead planters 'into a Christian conversation, to live well, to fear God, serve the King, and love the country'.[24] A Church of England man, of evangelical tastes and military piety; very typical, like Drake. He approved of settlers being 'good Catholic Protestants according to the reformed Church of England; if not, it is well they are gone'. Again, this was an opinion expressed late in life, in 1630, after his experience with the potential emigrants to New England: some of whom he thought 'more precise' than necessary (precise: puritan). He disliked 'discontented Brownists, Anabaptists, Papists, Puritans, Separatists and such factious humorists',[25] and disapproved of some of those preparing in the 1620s to make their errand into the wilderness: he called them 'this absolute crew, only of the elect, holding all but such as themselves reprobates and castaways' and hating 'the name of a bishop', the sight of a cross or surplice, the Book of Common Prayer.[26] We may take it that the average Jamestown settler in 1607 would have endorsed the traditional requirement that religious exercises in America should be according to the provisions of the Church of England. The more literate would have taken Francis Bacon's point that just as 'the general law by which they must be governed and guided must be the common law of England', so 'for the discipline of the church in those parts, it will be necessary that it agree with that which is settled in England: else it will make a seam and rent in Christ's coat, which must be seamless'.[27] (A reference to the tunic of Christ, taken by the soldiers after the crucifixion: 'the coat was without seam, woven from the top throughout', John 19:23.)

The first President of the Colony, chosen by the colonial councillors, was Edward Wingfield; a poor choice, as things turned out, for he was a rather negative leader, and was deposed and replaced by John Ratcliffe after four months. We have seen him accused of atheism by some of his fellow colonists during the voyage. The change lingered in Jamestown. In 1608 he wrote that it had been said that 'I am an atheist, because I carried not a bible with me, and because I did forbid the preacher to preach'. His Bible had been lost in England, in a mislaid piece of luggage. He had once advised Hunt not to give his sermon, when there had been an Indian attack, and 'our men were

[24] Smith-Arber, 958.
[25] *ibid.*, 926.
[26] *ibid.*, 954.
[27] Spedding (ed.), *Life and Letters of Bacon*, VI, 50-1, (1616).

weary and hungry'. Wingfield maintained that 'I never failed to take such notes by writing out of his doctrine as my capacity could comprehend; unless some rainy day hindered my endeavour'.[28] Poor Mr President.

On 21 May 1607, a week after the landing at Jamestown, a party of two dozen left in a boat to explore. There were eighteen mariners and sailors, and half a dozen gentlemen, including Newport, Percy, Archer and Smith (who was now back in comparative favour). They were away for six nights, and went about eighty miles down the James River, towards the modern site of Richmond.

There are two authorities for this trip, Archer and Smith. Archer's *Relatyon* is in the Colonial State Papers in the Public Record Office, and was not printed until 1860. It was definitively edited in 1969 by Philip L. Barbour.[29] Archer's account is brief – practical working notes, unpolished and haphazardly arranged. He had no eye to posterity; but there are trenchant touches. Smith's account was published in London in the autumn of 1608, in his first book: *A true relation of such occurences and accidents of note as have happened in Virginia synce the first plantinge of that Colonye which is nowe resident in the south parte of Virginia.*[30] For his 1969 text Barbour used a British Museum copy with helpful early-seventeenth-century annotations.[31] In 1607 Smith was twenty-seven; his unnerving capacity for involvement in bizarre adventures was not to be discouraged in the Virginia colony, where he remained until October 1609.

Smith gave a mere sketch,[32] mainly praising the generosity of Newport, who distributed to the Indians bells, pins, beads and mirrors; which 'liberality made them follow us from place to place, and ever kindly to respect us' – and to provide strawberries, mulberries, bread and fish. Smith also noted the fame of the 'great emperor', Powhatan.

Powhatan, the 'Overlord of Tidewater Virginia',[33] was probably born about 1550. His name was Wahunsonacock. He inherited six tribes in the region of the James and the York (Pamunkey). The tribes were the Powhatan, Arrohattoc, Pamunkey, Youghtanund, Appomattoc and Mattaponi. That was the nucleus of his empire, which by 1607 extended over 30 tribes: maybe 11,000 Indians in all, a unified bloc of the Indians of Tidewater Virginia. In 1607 Powhatan lived at Werowocomoco on the York River, some fifteen miles from both Jamestown and West Point. It is important to realise, first, that Powhatan saw the English settlers as potential allies in his task of consolidating, extending and protecting his Empire. The English could be *used*. (Also, they had copper, which he needed.) Secondly, that the Indians, though conventionally denounced as wandering

[28] *JV*, 229-30.
[29] *JV*, 80-98. See 465-6 for editorial notes on geography and names.
[30] *JV*, 165-208. Smith-Arber, 1-40.
[31] *JV*, 477-82.   [32] *JV*, 170-71.
[33] Barbour, *Three Worlds of Smith*, 140.

herds, were 'urban', compared with the English settlers: living, Nancy Oestreich Lurie writes in an excellent essay, 'according to a well-ordered and impressively complex system of government. They dwelled in secure villages, had substantial houses, and extensive gardens.'[34] The tribes of the 'Confederacy' (to use Jefferson's misnomer) were of the Algonquian language family. Powhatan did not die until 1618. One of his sons, Parahunt, was called 'little Powhatan' – a source of confusion to the English in 1607.

Archer gave the details of the expedition of May 1607.[35] The English throughout 'were used kindly by the people'. Twenty miles up river Archer gave an Indian some paper and a pen, 'showing first the use'; and the native 'laid out the whole river from the Chesapeake Bay to the end of it, so far as passage was made for boats'. Indian guides were taken on the boat, one of whom intructed Archer in the language, so that after a week he was 'excellently ingenious' in understanding it.

The Indians provided food: oysters, mulberries, acorns, 'sod wheat and beans', roasted deer ('which according to their custom they seethed again'), maize bread. The Algonquian word for 'bread' was *apoan*: hence 'pone'. Strawberries were shaken off the trees, 'dropping on our heads as we sat.' In return the English gave out pieces of pork 'sod' with peas; the trinkets mentioned by Smith; and beer, sack and spirits – one of the Indian chiefs was made ill by the strong drink: 'hot drinks', firewater.

The English met the werowance of the village and tribe of Arrohattoc, a 'goodly man', who was frightened when someone, at his request, fired a musket: he 'started, stopped his ears, and expressed much fear, so likewise all about him; some of his people, being in our boat, lept overboard at the wonder hereof.' Newport gave him a red waistcoat to placate him.

They also met 'little Powhatan', the son – at the time the English thought him to be the emperor. Archer 'certified him that we were friends with all his people and kingdoms, neither had any of them offered us ill, or used us unkindly'. The son 'moved of his own accord a league of friendship with us, which our Captain gladly embraced'. A cross was set up, with the inscription 'Jacobus Rex 1607'; and Newport explained that the two arms of the cross symbolised Newport and Powhatan: 'the fastening of it in the midst was their united league'.

Opechancanough, the younger 'brother' of the emperor, was also

---

[34] For Powhatan and the Confederacy, Nancy O. Lurie, in Smith (ed.), *Seventeenth-Century America*, 40-4: my quotation, 44. Also 'Powhatan' in *Dictionary of American Biography*; McCary, *Indians in Seventeenth-Century Virginia*; Barbour, *Three Worlds of Smith*; Barbour, *Pocahontas*; C.F. Feest, 'Powhatan: A Study in Political Organisation', *Weiner Volkerkundliche Mitteilungen* XIII, viii, 1966, pp.69-83; James Mooney, 'The Powhatan Confederacy', *American Anthropologist*, new series, vol.9, 1907, 129-52.

[35] *JV*, 82-94.

encountered, making a bad impression: he 'so set his countenance, striving to be stately, as to our seeming he became fool'. He was to seem less of a fool to the English along the James in 1622, when he master-minded a crucial and traumatic massacre.

Nearly forty miles along the river from Jamestown, on the north bank, the party met an Indian Queen. She held court on a mat under a mulberry tree. Sitting 'with a staid countenance', she would permit none to stand or sit near her. She was

a fat, lusty, manly woman. She had much copper about her neck, a crownet of copper upon her head. She had long black hair which hanged loose down her back to her middle, which only part was covered with a deer's skin, and else all naked. She had her women attending on her adorned much like herself, save that they wanted the copper.

John White would have enjoyed doing a drawing of her. She relaxed her 'we are not amused' pose when Newport presented his gifts. She then asked to hear a musket, and, unlike Arrohattoc, took the noise calmly. She seemed to Archer to be 'of as great authority' as any male chief in the region. Newport dubbed her settlement 'Queen Appomattoc's Bower'.

Archer's observations give a general impression of 'great joy and gladness'. Dancing, eating, fishing, and friendly welcomes: 'We sat merry, banqueting with them, seeing their dances and taking tobacco'; 'we were entertained with great joy and gladness, the people falling to dance, the women to preparing victuals, some boys were sent to dive for mussels: they gave us tobacco, and very kindly saluted us'.

Things were not so happy at Jamestown itself. When the boat returned, the explorers found that two settlers, one of them a boy, had been killed, and more than a dozen hurt, in a sixty minute Indian attack on the settlement; Wingfield had received an arrow through his beard. Archer commented that the Indians must be 'a very valiant people'.[36]

On 22 June 1607 the 'Susan Constant' and the 'Godspeed' sailed back to England, with Newport, leaving the 'Discovery', a pinnace, at Jamestown, and provisions calculated to last until the end of September. By the time of departure, the palisading of the settlement, and the fortification, had been completed, and the triangular Fort of Jamestown stood firm. There were frequent Indian attacks: 'Alarums by ambuscadoes', as Smith said.[37] Archer remarked that the English had been unwise enough to have long grass and reeds uncut near the fort; one colonist had gone into the grass 'to do natural necessity', and was wounded.[38] There were positive things. Percy tells us that the settlers had 'sown most of our corn on two mountains, it sprang a man's height from the ground'.[39] A collection of material from the

---

[36] *JV*, 95. [37] *JV*, 172. [38] *JV*, 96. [39] *JV*, 142.

original planters published in London in 1612 (edited by the Reverend William Symonds)[40] is less bland:

What toil we had with so small a power to guard our workmen a'days, watch all night, resist our enemies, and effect our business; to reload the ships, cut down trees, and prepare the ground to plant our corn.

There were quarrels, with Hunt again as the reconciler. And not much to eat. The settlers got from the sailors on the ships a daily ration of biscuits: in exchange for 'money, sassafras, furs, or love'. Smith was to describe the bad feeling between the settlers and the sailors:[41] the sailors eating every day with good cheer, the settlers having only a little meal and water – plus the victuals given them by the Indians. Although, wrote Smith,

there be deer in the woods, fish in the rivers, and fowls in abundance in their seasons, yet the woods are so wide, the rivers so broad, the beasts so wild, and we so unskilful to catch them, we little troubled them nor they us.

Percy confirms that the 104 colonists left at Jamestown on 22 June 1607 were 'very bare and scanty of victuals'.[42]

The two returning vessels arrived in Plymouth at the end of July 1607, carrying the first letters to reach England from the colony. There was a brief note to the London Council from the Jamestown Council[43] (which from 10 June had included Smith as an active member): the colonists had fortified, sown wheat, built houses, explored, and so on. Virginia, certainly, could 'flow with milk and honey'. Sir Walter Cope, a member of the London Council, wrote on 12 August to Salisbury (Robert Cecil):[44]

If we may believe either in words or letters, we are fallen upon a land that promises more than the Land of Promise. Instead of milk, we find pearl; and gold instead of honey.

Cope had read the account of the Indian chief made ill by 'hot drinks' in the exploration of the James, and fills out the story:

One of their kings sick with drinking our aquavite thought himself poisoned. Newport told by signs that the next day he should be well, and he was so. And telling his countrymen thereof, they came apace, old men and old women, upon every bellyache, to him, to know when they should be well.

Cope's theory about relations with the Indian was that they 'used our

[40] Printed with Smith's *Map of Virginia*. 'Proceedings': 'taken faithfully as they were written out of the writings of' eight named colonists and 'divers other diligent observers there present then'; ed. W.S. (William Symonds). *JV*, 375-464. My three quotations: 380, 381, 384.
[41] Smith-Arber, 444, 930.
[42] *JV*, 143. [43] *JV*, 78-9. [44] *JV*, 108-10.

men well until they found that they began to plant and fortify. Then they fell to skirmishing' – the attack on Jamestown about ten days after the landing. That letter is preserved at Hatfield House. There is also at Hatfield House a letter written by Cope on the very next day[45] pointing out to Cecil that the minerals sent back to England have shown no trace of gold or copper. 'Our new discovery is more like to prove the land of Canaan that the land of Ophir.' In other words, to emphasise gold is to underestimate the prospects of the plantation. (For Ophir, see above, page 22.) Other observers in London were more depressingly metallic, reminding one of Captain Seagull in *Eastward Ho*. Dudley Carleton, writing on 18 August 1607,[46] was supercilious about the planters who had returned with 'much commendation of the air and the soil and the commodities', but with no gold or silver – and no certainty of 'peace with the inhabitants'. Carleton disapproved of the word 'Jamestown' – 'no graceful name'. Jamesfort he would have preferred; 'because it comes near to Chelmsford'.

Spain was of course much concerned with 'the Virginia matter'. James I, speaking to the Spanish Ambassador in September 1607, tried to calm fears by saying that 'he had heard that the land was unproductive, and that those who thought to find great riches there were deceived'.[47] Difficult to guess how much of that was diplomacy, and how much was pessimism about 'Earth's only Paradise'.

The summer and early autumn of 1607 were grim at Jamestown. Evidence comes from Percy, Smith and Wingfield; and from the 1612 compilation of planters' accounts edited by William Symonds.[48] There was the question, again, of rations. It seems that a cup of boiled wheat and a cup of boiled barley (both from the ship's hold) was the actual basic allowance per man per day. The charge went that Wingfield and his special cronies kept the liquor for themselves (Smith). Wingfield said the brandy was reserved for extremities, and the sack for communion. The Symonds contributors accused Wingfield of hogging food also; oatmeal, beef, eggs – and oil. They pointed out that the barley to be boiled had been in the hold for twenty-six weeks, and was mainly worms. Percy says the men drank river water. Some managed to catch sturgeon; but Smith gave the over-eating of sturgeon as a cause of death. In August there were nineteen deaths; including, on the 22nd, Bartholomew Gosnold. Some were due, wrote Percy, to 'swellings, fixes, burning fevers'. Others, to starvation. By 10 September, according to Smith, 46 were dead: 45% of the settlement. Percy gave the most vivid pictures:

[45] *JV*, 111. [46] *JV*, 113-14.

[47] *JV*, 119. For James' diplomacy with Spain concerning America, see Quinn, 'James I and the Beginnings of Empire in America', *Journal of Imperial and Commonwealth History*, Jan. 1974, II, 2.

[48] All in *JV*. Percy's 'Discourse' (Purchas 1625), 144-5. Smith's *True Relation* (1608), 173-4. Wingfield's 'Discourse' (1845), 217-25. Symonds material, 384-5 (see note 40).

our men night and day groaning in every corner of the fort, most pitiful to hear. If there were any conscience in men, it would make their hearts to bleed to hear the pitiful murmurings and outcries of our sick men, without relief every night and day for the space of six weeks; some departing out of the world, many times three and four in a night; in the morning their bodies trailed out of their cabins like dogs to be buried.

Smith portrayed the leaders at Jamestown as 'sick or discontented'; the colonists 'in such despair as they would rather starve, and rot with idleness, than be persuaded to do anything'.

The only ray of hope was that the Indians supplied the colonists with food. Smith tells us that the werowance of Quiyoughcohannock 'did always at our greatest need supply us with victuals of all sorts'; and 'charged his people that they should for ever keep good quiet with the English'. Smith was sent out to trade with the Indians. He went to Kecoughtan; where the Indians, 'thinking us near famished, with careless kindness offered us little pieces of bread, and small handfuls of beans or wheat, for a hatchet or a piece of copper'.

Philip Barbour remarks that 'Smith was one of the few colonists who realised that trade or barter with the Indians was a *sine qua non* of survival'.[49] But Professor Quinn is critical of Smith's handling of that trade:[50]

Smith's tirades against those who gave the Indians too good barter rates and his compliments to himself for his businesslike astuteness seem to show no understanding at all of the relative seasonal plentifulness or scarcity of food in Indian hands.

Quinn's general point is that the Jamestown settlers

seem to have had no idea that in acquiring surplus corn from the Indians, they were causing an upset to the local economy, and that the value of stored corn to the Indians varied very greatly according to whether it was asked of them in September, in December or in May.

The Indians at Roanoke had been antagonised by English demands for food in the winter of 1585/86. And throughout – and in all settlements in North America –

a major element in the deterioration of European-Indian relations was the demand of the settlers for quantities of grain, especially during late winter and spring, which the native economy was not geared to supply.

So, as alderman Robert Johnson wrote in 1612,[51] the Virginia colonists grew 'factious and disordered', 'like the college of English fugitives in Rome'. Harsh words. Smith himself thought that the half

---

[49] *JV*, 437.
[50] Quinn (ed.), *North American Discovery circa 1000-1612*, xxv-xxvi.
[51] *New Life of Virginia*, 10.

dozen of the Council were 'for the most part discontented with each other' – and their malice was (of course) especially directed against him. At all events, the feelings against President Wingfield seemed to unite the fifty or so settlers; it must have been like life in a fourth-rate Cambridge college. The 'Master' had starved the settlers; neglected (as we have seen) his religious obligations; imposed martial penalties – whipping, beating, hanging. And on 10 September 1607 Wingfield was deposed as President, and kept in the 'Discovery'; from which he emerged, if the weather was good, to hear Hunt's Sunday sermon.

Percy thought that 'there were never Englishmen left in a foreign country in such misery as we were, in this new discovered Virginia'. Percy was the same age as Smith, twenty-seven. When Newport arrived back at Jamestown on 2 January 1608, of the 104 settlers he had left twenty-eight weeks before, he found only thirty-eight alive.

Such miseries did nothing to check Smith's exploring itch; indeed, they probably made exploration seem the more attractive. Smith was away from Jamestown with a party in November and December 1607, sixteen persons in all, in two boats, partly exploring, partly looking for food. Their own provisions were cheese, oatmeal and biscuits: now almost a year old. In December Smith was taken prisoner by Opechancanough. In *A True Relation*, London, 1608, Smith told how he gave the chief a compass, and proceeded in 'a discourse of the roundness of the earth, the course of the sun, moon, stars and planets'.[52] The Symonds compilation went further. Smith also showed 'the cause of the day and night, the largeness of the seas, the qualities of our ships, shot and powder, the division of the world, with the diversity of people, their complections, customs and conditions'.[53] At the very end of December 1607 Smith met the emperor Powhatan at Werowocomoco: the first Englishman to see him.

In 1608 Smith described Powhatan as 'proudly lying upon his bedstead a foot high, upon ten or twelve mats, richly hung with many chains of great pearls about his neck'. It 'drew me into admiration, to see such state in a naked savage'.[54] Smith was well entertained – fattened up, in fact – so that he conceived the notion that he was due for sacrifice. It is possible that he was right. Eventually, however, as a hostage for the Indians held at Jamestown, Powhatan entrusted to Smith his young daughter, aged eleven or twelve. This was Matoaka: who 'not only for feature, countenance and proportion much exceedeth any of his people, but for wit and spirit, the only *nonpareil* of his country'.[55] Powhatan had given her the pet name of Pocahontas; which William Strachey tells us means 'Little Wanton'[56] – in the sense of roguish, sportive.

This is the most familiar episode in the whole saga of Smith. The story he published in 1608 was later elaborated. In 1624, we read that Smith was placed with his head on a stone, about – so he thought – to

[52] *JV*, 181. [53] *JV*, 390. [54] *JV*, 185. [55] *JV*, 206.
[56] Strachey, *Virginia Britania*, 113.

have his brains beaten out, when Pocahontas covered his head with hers; and the Emperor relented.[57] It may have been that the intention was to initiate Smith into Powhatan's tribe, and make him a werowans (implying that the English were the subjects of Powhatan) – a ceremony of mock execution and salvation.[58]

It is well known that Henry Adams, anxious to make a reputation as a professional historian, used these differences of text (understandable: the later version was an expansion) to discredit Smith.[59] An unfortunately influential combination of Germanic and American scholarly idiosyncracy. John Smith, like John Foxe, outlives his detractors.

In his book *A Map of Virginia*, published at Oxford in 1612, Smith paid tribute to Indian government, and to Powhatan in particular.[60] The Indians are 'very barbarous'; but they have 'such government as that their magistrates for good commanding, and their people for due obedience and obeying, excel many places that would be accounted very civil'.

They all know their several lands and habitations and limits to fish, fowl or hunt in; but they hold all of their great werowance Powhatan, unto whom they pay tribute of skins, beads, copper, pearl, deer, turkeys, wild beasts and corn.

The Indians have no writing or reading, so 'the laws whereby he ruleth is custom'. 'Yet when he listeth, his will is a law, and must be obeyed. Not only as a king, but as half a god they esteem him.' He is 'very terrible and tyrannous in punishing such as offend him'. Some of the punishments, including scalping, are described. The English were always impressed by Powhatan's abundance of female consorts. 'He hath as many women as he will', says Smith,

Whereof when he lieth on his bed, one sitteth at his head and another at his feet. When when he sitteth, one sitteth at his right hand, and another at his left. As he is weary of his women, he bestoweth them on those that best deserve them.

The reporters of a visit to be made to Powhatan by Newport in February 1608 had a similar passage.[61] Powhatan was sitting on his bed of leather pillows 'embroidered, after their rude manner, with pearl and white beads', wearing a mantle of skins of Irish style, 'at his head and feet a handsome young woman'. 'On each side his house sat twenty of his concubines, their heads and shoulders painted red, with a great chain of white beads about their necks.' The Newport visit

[57] Smith-Arber, 400.
[58] Barbour: *Three Worlds of Smith*, 443-4; *Pocahontas*, 24.
[59] See John Lankford's 1967 preface to his Harper Torchbook anthology, *Captain John Smith's America*.
[60] *JV*, 369-71.   [61] *JV*, 391-2.

appeared to be a success. There was much mirth, feasting, dancing and singing. The English, in return for blue beads, got three hundred bushels of Indian corn. Powhatan received an English boy as a present; and Newport received an Indian servant, Namontacke, who was taken back to England in April, presented as a son of the emperor, and made much fuss of. And the emperor 'carried himself so proudly, yet discreetly, in his savage manner, as made us all admire his natural gifts, considering his education' (wrote one of the Newport observers). It remained for Smith to give a personal description.[62]

He is of personage a tall, well proportioned man, with a sour look. His head somewhat grey, his beard so thin that it seemeth none at all. His age near sixty. Of a very able and hardy body, to endure any labour.

The December of 1607 was piercing at Jamestown itself. However, some rebuilding went on. In the summer, wrote Smith, we had had 'no houses to cover us, our tents were rotten, and our cabins worse than naught'.[63] Things were a trifle better when Newport arrived.

Newport sailed from Gravesend on 8 October 1607, with 120 colonists, and reached Jamestown on 2 January 1608: twelve weeks. Early in 1608 the James (as wide as the Thames) almost froze the whole way across.[64] Worse, on 7 January fire broke out, and only three houses survived the blaze. Hunt lost all his books and possessions, except for the clothes on his back.[65] With the spring, hope returned. On 20 April 1608 Francis Nelson's vessel arrived with 130 colonists and sailors, including eight Europeans: Germans, Swiss, Poles. By that time the fort had been rebuilt, and a reasonable church constructed in wood, sixty feet by twenty four feet with large windows, pews and pulpit of cedar, a communion table in black walnut, a font, and two steeple bells. Hunt, though, was dead by June 1608. He probably died in May. The colonists continued (said Smith) to hold daily prayers, with the reading of a Homily on Sundays.[66]

On 28 March 1608 one of the new colonists, Francis Perkins, gent, who had emigrated with his son, wrote a letter for home[67]. The tone was quite optimistic. The settlers 'are at peace with all the inhabitants of the surrounding country, trading for corn and supplies'. The Indians were teaching the English how to plant maize, and how to make fishing gear. The English are clearing the woods. Perkins sent home an ear of corn, two Indian pots, and some sassafras, 'to use in medicine, or between linens'. He asked in return for some clothes, as he had lost most of his in the fire. This letter was taken by Newport when he sailed back to England on 10 April 1608.

On 2 June 1608 Smith and fourteen others set out in a small open barge to explore the Chesapeake Bay. These explorations continued, on and off, until September, the explorers covering about 3,000 miles

in the barge and reaching Baltimore and Georgetown. Some of the
Indians were 'peevish': but mainly they were 'tractable' and 'civil'.
One of Symonds' contributors gave a glimpse of the expedition:[68]

Our order was, daily to have prayer with a psalm; at which solemnity the
savages much wondered. Our prayers being done, they were long busied
with consultation until they had contrived their business. Then they began in
most passionate manner to hold up their hands to the sun, with a most
fearful song. Then, embracing the Captain, they began to adore him in like
manner, though he rebuked them, yet they proceeded till their song was
finished. Which done, with a most strange furious action and a hellish voice
began an oration of their loves. That ended, with a great painted bear's skin
they covered our Captain. Then one ready with a chain of white beads,
weighing at least six or seven pounds, hung it about his neck. The others had
eighteen mantles made of divers sorts of skins sowed together. All these, with
many other toys, they laid at his feet, stroking their ceremonious hands about
his neck for his creation to be their governor.

Not so gratifying as it sounds, perhaps. The Indians wanted Smith
to stay with them to lead their warfare against a neighbouring tribe.
But even so it seemed no less than appropriate that when Smith
finished his expeditions in September 1608, he became the third
President of the colony (succeeding Ratcliffe).

In September Newport was back in Jamestown: in the third
reinforcement vessel to arrive in 1608. This group of colonists included
two women: the wife of one of the colonists, Mistress Forest,
gentlewoman, and her maid Anne, who was to marry at Jamestown a
carpenter who had been on board (John Laydon) – their child was to
be called Virginia.

In the years before 1660, less than 20% of the settlers in Virginia
were female[69] – one reason, of course, why the population increased so
slowly.

Newport brought news from the London Company that Powhatan
would best be brought under English authority by some form of
'coronation'. No one at Jamestown seemed very keen on the idea, but
it went forward. Smith visited the emperor to ask him to come to
Jamestown to be crowned. According to one of the settlers whose
accounts were edited by Symonds in 1612,[70] Smith was first
entertained by thirty young Indian females, who were almost naked:
the somewhat unconvincing scene brings to the modern reader's mind
the encounter of Parsifal and the Flower Maidens. When Powhatan
arrived he stood on his imperial dignity, and said that the crowners
must come to him. His ire was perhaps soothed by the return of
Namontacke, who had come back with Newport from Gravesend in
the October ship, after three months at the English court (where the

[68] *JV*, 408.
[69] Pomfret, *Founding the American Colonies*, 55. See Thompson, *Women in Stuart
England and America*, 25-30.
[70] *JV*, 413.

Spanish ambassador, doubting the boy's imperial status, had been amused by the honour paid him: 'I hold it for surer that he must be a very ordinary person'.)[71] So Newport had to go up river in November 1608 – 100 miles – to crown Powhatan. Various items of furniture, a bed, basins and jugs, were set up, and Powhatan robed in a scarlet cloak (assured by Namontacke that it was harmless). The crowning was more tricky, the emperor 'neither knowing the majesty nor meaning of a crown, nor bending of the knee'.[72] At last, 'by leaning hard on his shoulders, he a little stooped, and Newport put the crown on his head'. The London Council may have found the news impressive, but to frontiersmen it seemed removed from the realities of power, apart from being slightly ridiculous. Newport left behind a boy, Thomas Savage, to learn the language.

The London Council of the Virginia Company made effective play in England with the coronation. An official pamphlet published in 1610 gave various arguments why the English possess Virginia lawfully.[73] They had a 'real concession' from the 'rural Emperor', 'that hath licensed us to negociate among them, and to possess their country with them'. And Powhatan 'received voluntarily a crown and a sceptre, with full acknowledgement of duty and submission'. The only real effect of the 'coronation' was to increase Powhatan's conceit; because of the gifts, and because he felt his alliance with the English was firmer.

On 29 December 1608 another party set off from Jamestown, in two boats: one contained Smith and a dozen others, the second Percy plus twenty-five. (At that time the population of Jamestown was about 200.) Also, a soldier was sent off with two Indian guides with 'directions how to search for the lost company of Sir Walter Raleigh'.[74] The climax of the expedition was another meeting with Powhatan. And the pages devoted to this winter expedition in the narrative edited by William Symonds in 1612 are an invigorating adventure story. The party stayed for a week at Kecoughtan.

The extreme wind, rain, frost and snow caused us to keep Christmas amongst the savages; where we were never more merry, nor fed on more plenty of good oysters, fish, flesh, wild fowl and good bread; nor never had better fires in England than in the dry, warm, smokey houses of Kecoughtan.

The James River was frozen over in parts. And in the journey along the river

the frost forced us three or four days also to suppress the insolency of those proud savages, to quarter in their houses, and guard our barge, and cause them to give us what we wanted.[75]

[71] *JV*, 163. [72] *JV*, 414.
[73] *True Declaration*, Force, *Tracts*, III, no.1, pp.6-7.
[74] *JV*, 423. [75] *JV*, 423.

At another Indian settlement, the English again needing food,

> the people imparted what little they had, with such complaints and tears from women and children, as he had been too cruel to be a Christian that would not have been satisfied, and moved with compassion.[76]

Early in 1609 the settlement of the emperor was reached. The narrative gives a dialogue between Powhatan and Smith, three speeches to each, very stylised, polished for publication on the classical model. The mood is of wary and respectful co-existence. The 'subtle savage' Powhatan made one especially 'subtle discourse':[77]

> Think you I am so simple not to know it is better to eat good meat, lie well, and sleep quietly with my women and children, laugh and be merry with you, have copper, hatchets or what I want, being your friend, than to be forced to flee from all, to lie cold in the woods, feed upon acorns, roots and such trash, and be so hunted by you that I can neither rest, eat nor sleep.

(We know that some English boys had been sent to live among the Indians, learning the language, 'which many of them already know perfectly':[78] so the general drift of the Powhatan orations can be taken as accurate.) The 1612 narrative includes material on the morality of the dealings with the Indian:[79] a defence against those critics in England who accused the colonists of being too kind. To some, the settlers

> may seem too charitable to such a daily daring treacherous people; to others, unpleasant that we washed not the ground with their bloods, nor shewed such strange inventions in mangling, murdering, ransaking and destroying, as did the Spaniards, the simple bodies of those ignorant souls.

Against such 'hawks' at home, it was pointed out that conditions in Virginia were different from those in Spanish America. It was comparatively 'ill peopled'; and the few Indians were 'idle, improvident, scattered', 'careless of anything but from hand to mouth'.

We also read of the rumour that Smith intended to marry Pocahontas, and make himself a King. Certainly Pocahontas seems to have been a welcome visitor to Jamestown; on one occasion 'she by stealth in the dark night came through the wild woods', to warn Smith of one of her father's intrigues.[80]

Before venturing on this winter journey Smith wrote a letter to the London Virginia Company: a doleful report on the state of the colony, which reached London in January 1609. It was to be printed in 1624 in his *The Generall Historie of Virginia, New England and the Summer Isles*.[81] This is the letter containing the passage, already noted, criticising the sailors, and the ignorance of the settlers in being unable to fish or hunt. The two hundred colonists are 'a many of ignorant, miserable souls, that are scarce able to get wherewith to live, and defend themselves against the inconstant savages'. Thirty carpenters, farmers, gardeners, fishermen, blacksmiths, masons and tree-fellers would be worth 'a thousand such as we have'; plus more 'glass men' from Germany or Poland. Moreover, the minds of the colonists were 'set upon faction' and 'idle conceits'. Smith was President, or, as he later called himself, Governor, from September 1608 until September 1609; and his special strictures were concentrated upon Newport, Ratcliffe and Archer. His criticisms of Jamestown were at bottom a defence of the colony. He was writing to English merchants (Cope and the like) looking for 'profitable returns'; and was aware that 'we feed you but with ifs, and ands, hopes, and some poor proofs'.

The 1612 'proceedings' edited by William Symonds give two speeches by the President to the colonists in 1609. For the first,[82] Smith took as his text Paul's words in II Thessalonians 3:10: 'We commanded you, that if any would not work, neither should he eat.' So, 'you must obey this for a law, that he that will not work shall not eat'. Jamestown was sunk in 'idleness and sloth'; 'the greater part must be more industrious or starve.' Forty industrious settlers cannot maintain 150 'idle varlets'. Such, comments Symonds' contributor, 'was the most strange condition of some 150' that unless they had been compelled to search for food 'they would have all starved, and have eaten one another'. The second speech against idleness[83] had a marginal note in the 1612 text: 'The President's speech to the drones.' Apparently the drones had been stirring up feeling against the Indians, calling them 'savage trash'. As a preacher, Smith was a worthy successor to the late Robert Hunt. His 1624 preface to *The Generall Historie* especially attacked 'cowardice, covetousness, jealousies and idleness'.[84] And in his dislike of 'the rust of covetousness',[85] 'greedy covetousness',[86] Smith was in a tradition of Christian indignation which during the past century had been especially graced by John Colet, Thomas More, Robert Barnes, Hugh Latimer and Thomas Lever. (It is important to remember that in the early seventeenth century 'idle' had the sense of 'wrong headed', as well as of 'lazy'.)

Smith's speeches had their effect. A well was built, of 'excellent sweet water' (there had been none before); clapboard and wainscot were cut, and the church re-roofed, and twenty new houses built; from three sows, sixty pigs were reared; pitch, tar, soap-ashes were made (that is, ashes from which soap was boiled), and there was 'a trial of glass'; the colonists contrived to catch squirrels, turkeys, and deer, and to fish for sturgeon (caviare again). A new settlement was built across the river. On the debit side, there were 'many thousand rats', which had first arrived in the ships.[87]

By the summer of 1609 it seemed that the settlement on the James,

[82] *JV*, 441. [83] *JV*, 447-8. [84] Smith-Arber, 279. [85] *ibid.*, 932. [86] *Ib.*, 937. [87] *JV*, 445-6.

unlike that in Maine, would survive. But prosperity had its dangers. When there was no fear of starvation, the colonists worked only four hours a day: 'the rest in pastimes and merry exercise.'[88]

In October 1609 Smith sailed back to England, never to return to Jamestown. He left behind him nearly 500 colonists; twenty four pieces of ordnance; three hundred muskets; six mares, one horse, six hundred swine, six hundred hens and chickens, and some goats.[89] In 1624 Smith commented that although there were nearly sixty houses at Jamestown, there was only one carpenter. The Germans and the Poles were good workers, and a dozen of the English: the rest 'never did know what a day's work was', being 'poor gentlemen, tradesmen, serving-men, libertines, and such like'.

I confess divers among them had better minds and grew more industrious than was expected. Yet ten good workmen would have done more substantial work in a day, than ten of them in a week.[90]

It should be noted, however, that Smith was not at all against 'gentlemen' as such. Quite the opposite. In the 1620s he wanted gentlemen to go to New England, to hunt and hawk: 'For gentlemen, what exercise should more delight them than ranging daily these unknown parts.'[91] What he disliked were 'gallants', remittance men, men of mode. He advised the New England colonists in 1630 that one hundred good labourers would be 'better than a thousand such gallants as were sent me, that would do nothing but complain, curse and despair'.[92] (The sort of ignorant emigrant who expected 'to find amongst those savages such churches, palaces, monuments and buildings as are in England'.)[93] The London Company had made no 'screening' of settlers: to them it 'was all one to send a workman as a roarer'. So Jamestown was too full of 'loiterers without victuals'; 'the most of them would rather starve than work.' In fact, 'had it not been for some few that were gentlemen both by birth, industry and discretion, we could not possibly have subsisted'.[94]

Two such 'proper gentlemen' had arrived in September 1608: Gabriel Bedell and John Russell. They were very soon among a party of thirty taken by Smith five miles from Jamestown to 'make clapboard, cut down trees, and lie in woods'. The story is told in the 1612 Symonds compilation.[95] Bedell and Russell were unused to this sort of thing, but they soon got the hang of it:

Within a week they became masters, making it their delight to hear the trees

[88] *JV*, 440.
[89] *JV*, 458. For horses in Virginia, 364.
[90] Smith-Arber, 486-87.
[91] *ibid.*, 727 (*Generall Historie*, 1624).
[92] *Ib.*, 929. *Advertisements for the unexperienced planters of New England*, Smith's eighth and last book, written 1630, published 1631. He died in June 1631, aged 51.
[93] *ibid.*, 957. [94] *ibid.*, 930. [95] *JV*, 416.

thunder as they fell; but the axes so oft blistered their tender fingers, that commonly every third blow had a loud oath to drown the echo.

They even took pride in Smith's penalties for swearing. Every oath was noted. And each night, for every oath a can of water was poured down the sleeve. There is the general feel of a rather grim dormitory at a boys' school. A 1612 marginal note here comments: 'one gentleman better than twenty lubbers.' Slightly later, Russell could not be dissuaded from joining Smith's winter journey up the partially frozen James; though he fell ill, and his great weight did not make his body very manageable for his colleagues.[96]

Smith's strictures on the early colonists passed into the folk-lore of Virginia. William Byrd II (1674-1744), writing in 1729[97] argued that the first settlers, 'like true Englishmen', 'built a church that cost no more than fifty pounds, and a tavern that cost five hundred'. The men of Jamestown were 'most of them reprobates of good families'; even the planters of the 1580s were 'idle and extravagant, and expected they might live without work in so plentiful a country'. The Council in Jamestown

were always engaged in factions and quarrels, while the rest detested work more than famine. At this rate the colony might have come to nothing, had it not been for the vigilance and bravery of Capt. Smith, who struck a terror into all the Indians round about. This gentleman took some pains to persuade the men to plant Indian corn, but they looked upon all labour as a curse. They chose rather to depend upon the musty provisions that were sent from England: and when they failed, they were forced to take more pains to seek for wild fruits in the woods than they would have taken in tilling the ground. Besides, this exposed them to be knocked on the head by the Indians, and gave them fluxes into the bargain, which thinned the plantation very much. To supply this mortality, they were re-inforced the year following with a greater number of people, amongst which were fewer gentlemen and more labourers, who, however, took care not to kill themselves with work.

So the 'myth' solidified. In our own day it has been buttressed with the alarming apparatus of 'historical sociology'. A valuable and suggestive article in 1958 by Sigmund Diamond (Columbia University)[98] stressed the problem of recruiting a labour force in Virginia. The Virginia Company was the eighteenth trading company to be founded in England: the previous seventeen dealt with territory where there were extensive settled communities or advanced societies – there was no problem of *importing* a labour force. Edmund S. Morgan took as his theme for a 1968 lecture the labour problem in the

---

[96] *JV*, 424.

[97] Byrd, *History of the Dividing Line* (i.e., between Virginia and North Carolina). Extracts in Pearce, *Colonial American Writing*: this paragraph, 416-17.

[98] 'From Organisation to Society: Virginia in the Seventeenth-Century,' *American Journal of Sociology*, March 1958 (Vol. XLIII, no.5).

first decade at Jamestown.[99] He discussed the attitudes to work in Virginia and Old England. In England, an expanding population meant an employment (and nourishment) problem – underemployment: short working hours. The English government 'discouraged energetic labor and nurtured the workingman's low expectation of himself'.[100] At Jamestown, in addition to the facts of disease and hunger, there were indigenous factors: lack of incentive, in a military style community, for private enterprise; the hope of Indian labour; and the dream of a land of available milk and honey. From the attitudes to work revealed in the criticisms of Smith, the argument runs, arose the southern plantation and the reliance on slavery.

Of course the dominance of the gentry in early Jamestown may have contributed to the lack of aptitude for farming and the homely arts. But perhaps equally important – and Morgan makes the point – was the fact that so many of the early planters were military men.

Or perhaps they were thinking of the six-hour working day on the island of Utopia.

Philip L. Barbour gives a list of the 239 known names among the nearly 300 planters who arrived in Jamestown between 1607 and September 1608.[101]

We have seen that the arrivals in 1608 included two women. The paucity of females in early colonial Virginia, compared with New England, and thus the predominance of bachelors, held by sociologists to be rootless, has been made much of by historians of the family and social structure. (The 102 passengers on the 'Mayflower' in 1620 included 18 wives and over thirty children.)[102] In November 1619 the London Company was to think in terms of one hundred 'maids young and uncorrupt' to be sent to Virginia as matrimonial fodder.[103] Ninety had gone by 1620; and over fifty more in 1621. There were also the Germans, the Swiss and the Poles. Germans, 'skilful in mines', continued to go to Jamestown: two, for example, in 1620.[104] There were Frenchmen also. And in 1622, sixteen Italian glass makers.[105] In 1623 George Sandys had severe things to say about the Virginia Italians – 'a more damned crew, hell never vomited.'[106] One of the Italians had attacked his wife so often that she had to be sent home. Hakluyt had had the conception, if not the actual phrase, of the 'melting pot'; and such Jamestown Europeans had their place in the shaping of 'the new

---

[99] 'The Labor Problem at Jamestown, 1607-18', *American Historical Review*, Vol.76, no.3. Theodore K. Rabb of Princeton made similar points in a lecture at Cambridge University in May 1973: I am grateful to him for drawing my attention to Morgan's essay. The Rabb lecture was printed in December 1974: 'The Expansion of Europe and the Spirit of Capitalism', *Historical Journal*, XVII, 4, pp.675-89.

[100] Page 604.

[101] *JV*, xxv-xxviii.

[102] See below, Chapter 24, p.423.

[103] Kingsbury, *Records*, I, 256.

[104] *ibid.*, III, 305. [105] *ibid.*, 640. [106] *ibid.*, IV, 23.

man, the American'. 'Whence came all these people?' asked Crèvecoeur at the very end of the colonial period:[107]

They are a mixture of English, Scotch, Irish, French, Dutch, Germans, and Swedes. From this promiscuous breed, that race now called Americans have arisen.

Of the white population of British America in the 1770s, not more than 65 per cent were of English stock. Tom Paine in 1776 made much of the point that 'Europe, and not England, is the parent country of America'.[108]

At the end of 1609 the London Council of the Virginia Company listed a 'table of such as are required to this plantation'.[109] Ten 'iron men for the furnace and hammer', ten sawyers, ten fishermen. Six blacksmiths, six carpenters, six shipwrights, six gardeners, six fowlers, six coopers, six vine dressers. Four turners, four brickmakers, four 'sturgeon dressers and preservers of the caviare', four rope makers, four pitch boilers. And two each of the following: surgeons, druggists, armourers, founders, salt makers, ploughwrights, 'press makers', joiners, 'soap ash men', 'mineral men', sugar cane planters, silk dressers, pearl drillers, bakers, brewers, colliers, and 'collar makers for draught'.

Of the nearly 240 known first settlers in Jamestown, about 107 were of the gentry: not less than 45 per cent. Some were Inns of Court men: Archer, Gosnold, Percy, Wingfield. Twenty-five per cent were labourers and artisans: forty-three labourers, fourteen artisans. There at least eight boys; Thomas Savage was thirteen in 1607. There were seven tailors, five surgeons, and four carpenters. Two each of goldsmiths, refiners, bricklayers and blacksmiths. And of the following, one each: mason, tobacco pipe maker, barber, gunner, jeweller, drummer, cooper, gunsmith and fishmonger.

A defence of the first settlers, prepared by four of them, was printed by William Symonds in 1612.[110] We had few men, small boats and small means. Could any similar group 'discover so many fair and navigable rivers, subject so many several kings, peoples and nations to obedience and contribution with so little bloodshed'? The Spanish had found land fruitful and properly manured, and 'infinite numbers of people'. The Indies also had 'precious metals and rich commodities'. But we

chanced in a land even as God made it. Where we found only an idle, improvident, scattered people, ignorant of the knowledge of gold, or silver, or any commodities, and careless of anything but from hand to mouth, but for

[107] *Letters from an American Farmer*, no.3: 'What is an American?', Everyman ed., p.41.
[108] *Common Sense*. A.T. Mason, *Free Government in the Making*, 1956, 138.
[109] *True and Sincere Declaration*, 1610. Brown, *Genesis*, I, 353.
[110] *JV*, 438-40.

baubles of no worth; nothing to encourage us, but what accidentally we found nature afforded.

In spite of all this, the colony might be 'as commodious for England as the West Indies for Spain, if it be rightly managed'.

It was obvious that a stronger hand was needed at Jamestown, and firmer organisation in London. Although it was not signed by James until the end of May 1609, a new Charter for the Virginia Company had been drafted by February – the month in which John Donne was hoping to fill the new post of secretary to the London Council of the Company.[111] The important change in 1609 was that the Company assumed greater control, as against the Crown. In 1606 the small 'Council of Virginia' in London had been appointed by the king. In 1609 it was to have about fifty members, appointed or approved by the shareholders, and responsible to them. The head of the Company in London was the Treasurer: from May 1609 to May 1619 this was Sir Thomas Smythe. In 1609, in addition to fifty-six London Companies, 650 individuals had a financial stake in the Virginia Company (including members of the Plymouth Company; twenty-one peers; and Francis Bacon).[112]

From 1609 the London Council appointed a Governor in Virginia, with more power than the existing President of the Council in Jamestown (who in May 1609 was John Smith). As Robert Beverley was to put it, there was now a 'commissionated Governor', rather than an 'elective President'.[113] His powers were comparatively full and absolute. The Governor appointed was Lord De La Warr, who was Governor until his death in 1618. Rather confusingly, he spent most of the time in England, and the important figures in Jamestown were the Deputy Governors: Sir Thomas Gates, Sir Thomas Dale, Captain George Yeardley, Captain Samuel Argall. Gates was sent in 1609 as 'sole and absolute governor';[114] technically, Deputy Governor. He had been serving in the Netherlands as Captain of a company of English soldiers, and had been given leave of absence by the States General.

The 1609 scheme for emigration was, not to send people 'little by little' but 'to establish ourselves on a large scale all at once'; the words are those of Lord Ellesmere, as reported by the Spanish Ambassador in April (the Ambassador also noted that skilled artisans were to be sent).[115] The initial plan – again according to the Spanish Ambassador – had been to send De La Warr with 800 men. By March 1609, De La Warr not being yet available, the plan was that Gates should sail with 500 men and 100 women, to be followed by De La Warr in January 1610 with 700 men, and some women. 'I confess to your Majesty that I am writing this in anger, because I see the people excited and insolent

[111] *JV*, 247.
[112] 1609 Charter in Bemiss, *Three Charters*.
[113] *History and Present State of Virginia*, ed. Wright, 33.
[114] *True and Sincere Declaration*, 1610, Brown, *Genesis*, I, 345.
[115] *JV*, 260.

over this business': Pedro de Zúñiga to Philip III, 15 March 1609.[116]

A preliminary, 'trial', vessel left England at the beginning of May 1609 and arrived at Jamestown on 13 July. The Captain, twenty-eight years old, was Samuel Argall of Kent, a trained navigator and an experienced soldier (in the Netherlands).[117] A contemporary Dutch historian wrote in 1610[118] that Argall found

> great confusion and dissension among the English there, also among the commanders, resulting from ambition or covetous pride, each striving to rule over the other; but mostly from want of subsistence, and from laziness, for they will not work, and as a result they are dispirited, and live in the hope that the Indians would continue, as had been their wont, to supply and trade with them. They had neglected their sowing time, so their provisions had given out.

Argall told President Smith of the planned supply fleet – the first vessel of which arrived within a month. Argall left Jamestown at the end of August, and reported to the London Council in November.

The supply fleet, the 'Gates fleet', saw the last of England in the second week of June 1609. Six ships left their Thames dock on 15 May, two vessels joined at Plymouth, and the fleet put in at Falmouth: the flagship was the 'Sea Venture', the admiral Sir George Somers, the Vice Admiral Newport; Gates of course was on board, and those present included Gabriel Archer (whose account of the voyage was printed by Purchas in 1625). There were apparently about 500 colonists: men, women and children. Gates carried with him the 'Instructions, Orders and Constitutions' of the London Council.[119] At Jamestown he was to make clear to Smith and the Council that the 'form of government by the first Letters Patents constituted' was now revoked; that he was the governor of the 'country and plantation'; and that there was to be a new council of nine – including Smith and Ratcliffe – for 'consultation' in important matters. He was also to 'take principal order and care for the true and reverend worship of God, that his word be duly preached and his holy sacraments administered according to the constitutions of the Church of England in all fundamental points'.[120] The Reverend Richard Buck was on board, and another cleric: probably Mr Poole (Robert or John). It was important to control the werowances

> whom if you intreat well, and educate those which are young and to succeed in the˙government, in your manners and religion, their people will easily obey you, and become in time civil and christian.

---

[116] *JV*, 254-5.
[117] For the Argall family, Barbour, *Pocahontas*, Ch.6.
[118] Emanuel van Meteren. *JV*, 276.
[119] *JV*, 262-8.
[120] Kingsbury, *Records*, III, 14.

Gates was also advised to make friends with the Indians furthest from Jamestown – the enemies of Powhatan. You won't quarrel with them: the best hope of amity.

Four of the ships arrived at Jamestown on 11 August 1609; another two slightly later. Archer related how the new arrivals met Argall, and heard of the 'distress' of the colony:

Many were dispersed in the savages' towns, living upon their alms for an ounce of copper a day; and fourscore lived twenty miles from the fort, and fed on nothing but oysters eight weeks' space, having no other allowance at all; neither were the people of the country able to relieve them if they would.

Purchas had a marginal note at this point in Archer's narrative: 'Idleness and other vices to blame also.'[121] The Reverend Mr Poole began his ministry – and by the end of September he had become another source of friction:[122]

There is an unhappy dissension fallen out amongst them by reason of their minister; who being, as they say, somewhat a puritan, the most part refused to go to his service or hear his sermons, though by the other part he was supported and favoured. But himself is grown so discontented of his usage there, that by no means he will not stay amongst them.

But the main point of trouble was John Smith: who had been reigning (according to Ratcliffe) 'sole governor, without assistants, and would at first admit of no council but himself'.[123] But in September Smith was severely injured, and hardly expected to live. He sailed for England on 4 October, and George Percy succeeded him as President.

The problem was that Gates did not arrive in Jamestown in August 1609. Nor did Newport, Somers, Buck, John Rolfe, or William Strachey; or the others among the 150 sailors and passengers (including women) aboard the 'Sea Venture'. In a storm at the end of July the ship had run aground in Bermuda; and the survivors did not arrive in Jamestown until the end of May 1610, in two small vessels they had built. Within two weeks Strachey had completed his account of the adventure, circulating in London from the late summer of 1610, and printed by Purchas in 1625: *A true reportory of the wracke, and redemption of Sir Thomas Gates*.[124]

The Tempest began on Monday 24 July 1609; and land was not sighted until Friday 28th. On the Monday, wrote Strachey,

---

[121] *JV*, 282.

[122] John Beaulieu to William Trumbell, 30 November 1609. Historical Manuscripts Commission, Marquis of Downshire, II, 1936, 195. *JV*, 287. No name is mentioned. Barbour, *Three Worlds of Smith*, 462, thinks the minister was William Mease (Mays). One wonders whether Mease had arrived in Virginia so early.

[123] *JV*, 284.

[124] Extracts in Kermode's edition of *The Tempest*, New Arden Shakespeare, 135-40.

a dreadful storm and hideous began to blow from out the north-east, which, swelling and roaring as it were by fits, some hours with more violence than others, at length did beat all light from heaven; which like an hell of darkness turned black upon us, so much the more fuller of horror, as in such cases horror and fear use to overrun the troubled and overmastered senses of all, which, taken up with amazement, the ears lay so sensible to the terrible cries and murmurs of the winds, and distraction of our company, as who was most armed and best prepared was not a little shaken.

The tempest continued: 'not only more terrible, but more constant, fury added to fury, and one storm urging a second, more outrageous than the former.' On the first day the ship had received 'a mighty leak'. The oakum – old tarred ropes, untwisted to make the ship watertight – was washed away, and the ship was five feet deep in water. Gates was 'both by his speech and authority heartening every man unto his labour'. In the five days of danger, much had to be thrown overboard: butts of beer, hogsheads of oil, cider, wine and vinegar; and many trunks and chests of luggage. On the Friday Somers 'cried land'. And the ship was run ashore, 'as near the land as we could, which brought us within three quarters of a mile of shore'. Some things were 'recovered from the wreck': grain, cloth, cables, arms, sails, oars. And how much all this owed to the authority of the Governor!

They had landed on 'the dangerous and dreaded island, or rather islands, of the Bermuda', named, so John Smith tells us, after a wrecked Spanish ship, the 'Bermuda'.[125] Strachey said they were 'called commonly the Devil's Islands; and are feared and avoided of all sea travellers alive'. By 1611 they were called 'Virginiola'. But by 1612 they were called 'Summer Islands: as well in respect of the continual temperate air, as in remembrance of Sir George Summers, that died there.'[126] (Somers died in November 1610 of 'a surfeit in eating of a pig'.)[127]

Strachey built up the paradox of 'those infortunate, yet fortunate, islands'. It was a 'hideous and hated place'; 'no habitation for men, but rather given over to devils and wicked spirits.' But it pleased 'merciful God' to make it 'both the place of our safety and means of our deliverance'. 'The ground of all those miseries was the permissive Providence of God': orthodox thinking from an Emmanuel man. The castaways in fact found the islands 'as habitable and commodious as most countries of the same climate and situation'. 'God sends us all things for our labour; when Adam himself might not live in Paradise without dressing the garden.'

Another member of the company, Sylvester Joudain, had his *A Discovery of the Barmudas* printed in London in 1610.[128] Again there is

[125] *General History*, 1624. Smith-Arber, 633.
[126] Dudley Carleton, 12 February 1611/12. *Court and Times of James I*, 1, 160.
[127] Quoted Barbour, *Pocahontas*, 83, from the 1631 ed. of Stow's *Annals*.
[128] Facsimile reprint 1940. Extract in Kermode (see note 124), 141: from which my quotations are taken. Longer extracts in Wright, *Elizabethans' America*, 195-201.

the theme of 'the fortunate fall'. The 'islands of the Barmudas'

as every man knoweth that hath heard or read of them, were never inhabited by any Christian or heathen people: but ever esteemed and reputed a most prodigious and enchanted place, affording nothing but gusts, storms and foul weather; which made every navigator and mariner to avoid them, as Scylla and Charybdis, or as they would shun the Devil himself.

Yet the shipwrecked English found the air temperate, and the country 'abundantly fruitful of all fit necessaries'. So they lived there comfortably for nine months. The 'most dangerous, infortunate, and most forlorn place of the world' was 'in truth the richest, healthfullest, and pleasing land'.

Gates was back in England in September 1610. In that autumn the story of the Bermuda adventure appeared in London in verse. Twenty-two stanzas about 'the lost flock triumphant', by Richard Rich: *News from Virginia.*[129]

> It is no idle fabulous tale
>   nor is it fained news:
> For truth herself is here arrived
>   because you should not muse.
> With her, both Gates and Newport come,
>   to tell report doth lie:
> Which did divulge unto the world
>   that they at sea did die.

In November 1610, 'by advice and direction of the Council of Virginia', there was published in London *A True Declaration of the estate of the Colonie in Virginia.*[130] The authorship has been attributed both to Sir Dudley Digges[131] and to Francis Bacon.[132] The author had certainly read Strachey: 'The ground of all those miseries was the permissive providence of God.'[133] All is in 'the direct line of God's providence.' *Nimium timet qui Deo non credit*: 'he is too impiously fearful, that will not trust in God so powerful.'[134] The Bermudas are 'those infortunate (yet fortunate) Islands':[135]

These islands of the Bermudos have ever been accounted as an enchanted pile of rocks and a desert habitation for Devils; but all the fairies of the rocks were but flocks of birds, and all the Devils that haunted the woods were but herds of swine.[136]

The 'wondrous preservation' of the English is a demonstration by God

[129] Ed. W.F. Craven, 1937, 'Scholars' Facsimiles and Reprints', New York.
[130] Force, *Tracts*, III, no.1.
[131] Kermode (see note 124), xxviii; following Leslie Hotson.
[132] James, *Dream of Prospero*, 98-101.
[133] Force, 14.
[134] 11. [135] 14. [136] 10.

that 'He will raise our state and build His Church in that excellent climate: if the action be seconded with resolution and religion.'[137] There is nothing in 'this tragical Comedy' to 'discourage us with impossibility of the enterprise'.[138]

As the reverend Lewis Hughes, a Welsh Oxford graduate, was to emphasise in a letter from the Bermuda islands after he had arrived in 1614:[139] 'It hath pleased God to discover them unto and to bestow them upon His people of England.' Hughes advised prospective imigrants to 'have a care to leave their sins behind them, and come hither as it were into a new world, to lead a new life; and for the comfort of their souls let them bring Bibles and other good books.'

The colonists' reports edited by William Symonds in 1612 also have, in the material on the Bermuda sojourn, the theme of the happy preservation, the miracle of survival, the paradise of the Bermudas.[140] William Crashaw dealt with the episode twice in 1613. In his preface to Alexander Whitaker's *Good Newes from Virginia*, Crashaw discussed the 'marvellous and indeed miraculous deliverance' as a sign of the work of Salvation. Bermuda had been thought of as

inaccessible, so not habitable, but so fearful, hideous and hateful, as it seemed a place abandoned of God and man, and given up to the Devil's power and possession, and to be of all known places in the world, a very hell on earth.

But in the event it was found to be 'goodly', 'rich', 'plentiful', 'temperate', and 'healthy': a place of 'safety and security'.[141] In his preface to *A Plain Description of the Bermudas*,[142] the interpretation was repeated. The Bermudas had been thought of as 'a habitation of devils'. They are now known to be 'one of the sweetest paradises':

not only accessible and habitable, but also fertile, fruitful, plentiful, and a safe, secure, temperate and healthful inhabitation for men, and especially for English bodies.

The shipwreck was due to 'the favour of God'. Crashaw went on to recommend the story to those 'that mislike all new inventions, and suspect all new discoveries, and hold it for a rule that whatsoever is new is naught'. God revealed the loadstone; and an 'ordinary seaman' can now go to Virginia more easily than St Paul went to Italy. God revealed printing:

tending to the honour of God, the manifestation of the truth, propagation of the gospel, restoration of learning, diffusion of knowledge; and consequently the discovery and destruction of popery.

---

[137] 27. [138] 11.

[139] Wright, *Elizabethans' America*, 202, 204. For the Bermuda Company, Andrews, *Colonial Period*, I, 119-22.

[140] *JV*, 461-62. [141] A.3.b-B.1.r. [142] Force, *Tracts*, III, no.3.

And God 'discovered to vulgar knowledge' the 'new world of America'.

The first known performance of Shakespeare's *The Tempest* was in November 1611.

John Smith wrote in 1624[143] that the adherents of Virginia could swing between 'the lowest degree of extremity' and 'the highest pinnacles of content'. For Virginia, Smith said, was 'a tabernacle of miracles, and the world's wonder'.

[143] *General History*, 1624. Smith-Arber, 688.

15

The Inconstant Savage, 1607-1610

Edward Maria Wingfield, Esquire, first President of the Jamestown Council, was deposed after four months, in September 1607, and sailed from Virginia with Newport on 10 April 1608, arriving in England six weeks later, 21 May 1608: rejoicing 'that my travels and dangers have done somewhat for the behoof of Jerusalem in Virginia'. He was summoned to meet the London Council of the Company; but apparently no action was taken against him. In the summer of 1608 he wrote his 'Discourse of Virginia', covering the period June 1607 to May 1608. The manuscript survives in the library of Lambeth Palace. It was printed in 1845; and again by Barbour in 1969.[1]

Indian material is rather peripheral in Wingfield's narrative. There are merely occasional glimpses: as when we read that an English boy who had been with the Indians reported that the men and women

spend the most part of the night in singing or howling; and that every morning the women carried all the little children to the river's edge, but what they did there he did not know.[2]

He reports Smith's meeting with the emperor in December 1607, and makes clear that the 'Powhatan' described by Gabriel Archer in the summer of 1607 was the son, and not the 'great Powhatan'.[3]

Captain Gabriel Archer was more descriptive. His 'Description of the now discovered River and Country of Virginia', among the Colonial State Papers in the Public Record Office, was printed in 1860, and again by Barbour.[4] Virginia was naturally flourishing. But

the commodities of this country, what they are *in esse*, is not much to be regarded, the inhabitants having no commerce with any nation, no respect of profit; neither is there scarce that we call *Meum et Tuum* among them, save only the kings know their own territories, and the people their several gardens.[5]

---

[1] Philip L. Barbour (ed.), *The Jamestown Voyages under the First Charter, 1606-1609*, Hakluyt Society, 1969, 2 vols., continuous paging, 213-34. Hereafter cited as *JV*. Quotation in this paragraph, 233-4.

[2] *JV* 216. [3] *JV* 215. [4] *JV* 98-104. [5] *JV* 101.

Archer reported that the emperor had 'at least twenty several kingdoms' under his sway; yet each king was 'potent as a prince in his own territory; these have their subjects at so quick command, as a beck brings obedience'.[6] The Indians 'live commonly by the waterside in little cottages made of canes and reeds, covered with the bark of trees'.[7] Some forty or fifty live in each village; and the villages are not more than a mile or two apart. In appearance, the Indians 'go all naked, save their privities, yet in cool weather they wear deer skins'. They also wear sandals; and some have leather stockings up to the thighs. Their colour is 'tawney'. And they delight in 'dying and painting themselves'. Their hair is black, 'which they wear long on the left side, tied up in a knot'. The chiefs have 'a kind of coronet of deer's hair, coloured red'. The 'common sort' stick long feathers in their knot of hair. Necklaces are worn; either of copper chain, or pearl. Many people are disfigured with disease, with lumps, sores and pustules on the forehead. But the preparation of their food – by the women – is very hygienic. 'They eat often, and that liberally': for the most part, 'sodden wheat, beans and peas' – plus, fish, deer and fowl. The women 'do all the labour, and the men hunt and go at their pleasure'. They are intelligent: 'a very witty and ingenious people, apt both to understand and speak our language.' The men are 'proper, lusty, straight', 'very strong', and 'run exceeding swiftly'. 'The celerity they use in battle is admirable; the king directs the battle, and is always in front.' They have 'many wives' – the emperor the most. But 'as near as I could perceive they keep constant'.

When the Indians saw the English at prayer, 'they observed us with great silence and respect, especially those to whom I had imparted the meaning of our reverence'. Archer 'found they account after death to go into another world: pointing eastward to the element'. Let us hope, said the pious Captain, that God will make the colonists 'authors of His holy will, in converting them to our true Christian faith'.

It is true that the Indians are great thieves. And they are 'naturally given to treachery'. But, in the explorations of 1607, the English in fact found no treachery 'in our travel up the river'. Rather, 'a most kind and loving people'.

Archer's succinct, practical notes may be lacking in the sweep and style of a Hayes or a Hariot. But the alertness is attractive: not everyone would have noted that no Indian had grey eyes.

By 1612, George Percy, Esquire (younger brother of Henry Percy, Earl of Northumberland) had written his 'Observations gathered out of a Discourse of the Plantation of the Southern Colony in Virginia'. This was printed by Samuel Purchas in 1625, in *Purchas his Pilgrimes*; or, *Hakluytus Posthumous*.[8] Percy was a young military man, a trained observer, with basic sense. On the whole, the Indians gave him a

---

[6] *JV* 102.
[7] All further quotations from Archer, *JV* 102-4.
[8] *JV* 129-46. All my Percy quotations, 140-6.

pleasant surprise. He initially assumed they were 'wild and cruel pagans': 'our mortal enemies'. Yet they brought the settlers corn, fish and meat. And although Percy frequently 'began to mistrust some villainy', things seemed to turn out all right in the end. He succumbed to the fascination: meeting an Indian boy of ten 'which had a head of hair of a perfect yellow, and a reasonable white skin, which is a miracle amongst all savages'; and an Indian said to be 160 years old, with sunken eyes, no teeth, grey hair, and a long beard – 'it is a miracle to see a savage have any hair on their faces: I never saw, read, nor heard, any have the like before' (the old man was 'as lusty, and went as fast, as any of us, which was strange to behold').

Many Indians 'murmured at our planting in the country'. But one werowance told his people, 'very wisely of a savage': 'Why should you be offended with them as long as they hurt you not, nor take anything away by force; they take but a little waste ground, which doth you nor any of us any good.'

The Indians worship the sun 'as their God'.

These people have a great reverence to the sun above all other things. At the rising and setting of the same they sit down, lifting their hands and eyes to the sun, making a round circle on the ground with dried tobacco. Then they begin to pray, making many devilish gestures, with a hellish noise, foaming at the mouth, staring with their eyes, wagging their heads and hands in such a fashion and deformity as was monstrous to behold.

William White, a labourer, had lived among the Indians. And

reported to us of their customs in the morning, by break of day. Before they eat and drink, both men, women and children that be above ten years of age, runs into the water, there washes themselves a good while till the sun rises, then offer sacrifice to it, strewing tobacco on the water or land, honouring the sun as their god. Likewise they do at the setting of the sun.

William White made quite a contribution to English opinion about the Indian. Some of his material was published in 1614, in the second edition of Purchas' *Pilgrimage*: the material was heavily edited, with the help of information from the published work of John Smith.[9] White maintained that he had seen a 'sacrifice of children' at Quiyoughcohannock, ten miles from Jamestown, presumably about 1608. There was a festival in the woods:

The people were so painted that a painter with his pencil could not have done better. Some of them were black like devils, with horns and loose hair; some of divers colours. They continued two days, dancing in a circle of a quarter of a mile, in two companies, with antic tricks, four in a rank, the werowance leading the dance. They had rattles in their hands. All in the midst had black horns on their heads, and green bows in their hands. Next them were four or five principal men diversely painted, which with

⁹ *JV* 147-50.

bastinadoes beat forward such as tired in the dance. Thus they made themselves scarce able to go or stand. When they met together they made a hellish noise, and everyone, flinging away his bow, ran, clapping their hands, up into a tree; and tore it to the ground, and fell into their order again. Thus they did twice.

They then took ten 'well favoured children', from 'the properest young boys between ten and fifteen', and danced and sang around them. This was in the morning. In the afternoon, the boys were 'put' to 'the root of a tree', and guarded by the men. Five young men then gathered the boys, who were given crowns of leaves and branches. 'All this while the women weep and cry out very passionately.' The observers did not see 'what else was done with the children'. But there was an altar, 'made of poles set like a steeple'. And there was a fire. White assumed that 'they made a great fire to sacrifice their children to the devil (whom they call Kewase); who, as they say, sucks their blood.' ('Kewasa' means 'he who goes about glowing': association with the sun and moon.)

This was obviously some sort of initiation ceremony. In the final edition of the *Pilgrimage*, in 1617, Purchas noted that this was not a description of Sacrifice. He thought that the Indians had deliberately deceived the English.

Some of the White material was less liable to misinterpretation. He reported that the Indians believe that when the werowance and priests die, they 'do go beyond the mountains towards the setting of the sun, and ever remain there in form of their Oke'; and that the Indians believe that they themselves 'dance and sing with their predecessors'. 'The common people, they suppose, shall not live after death.'

Henry Spelman, the nephew (probably) of the historian Sir Henry Spelman, arrived in Virginia in October 1609, aged barely 16. He spent a year among the Indians: we do not know the details. William Strachey tells us that he was rescued in 1610 by Argall: 'having lived amongst them one whole year, and despaired of ever seeing his native country, his father's house (for he was descended of a gentle family) or Christians any more.'[10] Spelman sailed back to England in March 1611. His 'Relation of Virginia', concerning his experiences in 1609 and 1610, was written in 1613; although it was not printed until 1872.[11] Spelman returned to Virginia. In 1623 he was killed near Washington D.C.

Ten pages of the Spelman 'Relation', on 'the fashions of that country', are description (or purported description) and anecdote, without comment.[12] There is a description of 'their towns and buildings':

The greatest towns have not above twenty or thirty houses in it. Their

---

[10] Strachey, *Virginia Britania*, 46-7, and footnote.
[11] Smith-Arber, ci-cxiv.
[12] *ibid.*, cv-cxiv: from which all my quotations are taken.

buildings are made like an oven, with a little hole to come in at; but more spacious within, having a hole in the midst of the house for smoke to go out at. The kings' houses are both broader and longer than the rest, having many dark windings and turnings before any come where the king is. But in that time when they go a hunting, the women goes to a place appointed before, to build houses for their husbands to lie in at night, carrying mats with them to cover the houses withal.

The young Spelman was impressed by 'the justice and government'.

Concerning their laws, my years and understanding made me the less to look after, because I thought that infidels were lawless. Yet when I saw some put to death I asked the cause of their offense; for in the time I was with the Potomac I saw five executed: four for murder of a child, *id est* the mother and two other that did the fact with her, and a fourth for counseling it as he passed by, being bribed to hold his peace; and one for robbing a traveller of copper and beads. For to steal their neighbour's corn or copper is death; or to lie with another's wife is death, if he be taken in the manner.

Those five convicted of capital offences were bound hand and foot, and a fire made; an officer cut off with a shell 'their long lock which they wear on the left side of their head'. The four murderers were 'beaten with staves till their bones were broken, and, being alive, were flung into the fire'. The thief was 'knocked on the head, and, being dead, his body was burnt'.

The Indian matrimonial *mores* are indicated.

The custom of the country is to have many wives, and to buy them; so that he which have most copper and beads may have most wives; for if he taketh liking of any woman he makes love to her, and seeketh to her father or kinsfolk to set what price he most pay for her.

The marriage ceremony is performed by the father or friends of the woman joining the hands of the two together, and breaking a string of beads over the hands: then there is 'much mirth and feasting'. If a king feels the need of a wife, 'he acquaints his chief men with his purpose, who sends into all parts of the country for the fairest and comeliest maids, out of which the King taketh his choice'. When a wife of the king bears a child,

he keeps her no longer, but puts her from him, giving her sufficient copper and beads to maintain her, and the child while it is young, and then it is taken from her, and maintained by the king's charge; it now being lawful for her, being thus put away, to marry with any other.

When Powhatan (with whom Spelman spent three weeks in November 1609) went hunting, he left his wives in the care of two old men.

Spelman was staying in one Indian village of the Potomac tribe when the chief was away. One of his wives wished to visit her father, and asked Spelman to go with her and carry her child. He refused. She attacked him; he retaliated; another wife joined in; and both beat him 'so as I thought they had lamed me'. On his return, hearing the story, the king struck one of the wives with 'a kind of paring iron'. Spelman fled; but the king was not angry with him, and sent him his child to play with, 'for none could quiet him so well as myself'. The next morning Spelman and the king met: 'I found him kind to me, asking how I did, and whether I was afraid of him last night, because I ran away from him and hid myself.' The two went to the king's house, the Indian 'telling me he loved me, and none should hurt me'; the queen, however, 'looked but discontentedly on me'. Spelman thought that in fact the king was hoping for a gift of copper; which he eventually received, on Spelman's instructions, from Samuel Argall.

Spelman has a section on 'their manner of visiting the sick, with the fashion of their burial if they die'. A priest visits the sick man, setting a bowl of water and a rattle on the ground between them.

The priest, kneeling by the sick man's side, dips his hand into the bowl, which, taking up full of water, he sups into his mouth, spouting it out again upon his own arms and breast. Then takes he the rattle, and with one hand takes that and with the other he beats his breast, making a great noise. Which having done he easily riseth (as loath to wake the sick body) first with one leg then with the other. And being now got up, he leisurely goeth about the sick man, shaking his rattle very softly over all his body; and with his hand he stroketh the grieved parts of the sick. Then doth he besprinkle him with water, mumbling certain words over him.

If the invalid has been wounded, the priest at that point gashes the wound with a flint: 'making it to run and bleed, which he, setting his mouth unto it, sucks out, and then applies a certain root beaten to powder unto the sore.'

For burial, a scaffold is built, three or four yards high, on which the corpse is laid, wrapped in a mat. The kinsmen 'falls a weeping'; and fling beads among 'the poorer people', 'making them to scramble for them, so that many times divers do break their arms and legs'. They then return home and feast and the rest of the day 'they spend in singing and dancing, using them as much mirth as before sorrow'. Of the corpse, nothing is left but bones (presumably the body is gutted, although Spelman does not say so). The kinsfolk remove the bones from the scaffold, and keep them in their houses. The house of the deceased is given for life 'to the wife he liketh best'.

The eating habits of the élite are touched on (after a long section on the planting of corn).

They sit on mats round about the house, the men by themselves and the women by theirselves. The women bring to everyone a dish of meat; for the better sort never eats together in one dish. When he hath eaten what he will, or that which was given him − for he looks for no second course − he sets down his dish by him, and mumbleth certain words in manner of giving thanks. If any left, the women gather it up, and either keeps it till the next meal, or gives it to the poorer sort, if any there be.

There is not very much on personal appearance.

The priests are shaven on the right side of the head, close to the skull, only a little lock left at the ear; and some of them have beards. But the common people have no beards at all, for they pull away their hairs as fast as it grows.

At last a solution to the problem of the beardless Indian!

They also cut the hairs on the right side of their head, that it might not hinder them by flapping about their bow string when they draw it to shoot. But on the other side they let it grow, and have a long lock hanging down over their shoulder.

There is a page on armour, weapons and warfare. And a passage on 'Pastimes':

When they met at feasts or otherwise they use sports much like to ours here in England. As their dancing, which is like our Derbyshire hornpipe; a man first and then a woman, and so through them all, hanging all in a round. There is one which stands in the midst with a pipe and a rattle, with which when he begins to make a noise all the rest giggits about wrying [turning] their necks, and stamping on the ground. They use beside football play, which women and young boys do much play at, the men never. They make their goals as ours; only they never fight, nor pull one another down. The men play with a little ball, letting it fall out of their hand, and striketh it with the top of his foot; and he that can strike the ball furthest wins that they play for.

Finally, Spelman's observations on 'their service to their gods'. 'For the most part they worship the devil'; whom 'the conjurors who are their priests' can make appear. Also, every locality has an 'image which they call their god'. Powhatan has an image called 'Cakeres', standing in his residence of Orapakes. (Powhatan moved from Werowocomoco to Orapakes in 1609 – further away from Jamestown.) Presents of goods or corn are deposited before the image including the crown and the bed sent from England. The Potomac tribe have 'another god whom they call Quioquascacke'. They offer beads and copper to their images 'if at any time they want rain, or have too much'. There is no particular day for worship. Upon necessity – but always at least once in the year –

their priests which are their conjurors, with the men, women and children, do go into the woods, where their priests makes a great circle of fire, in the which after many observances in their conjurations, they make offer of two or three children to be given to their god, if he will appear unto them and show his mind whom he will desire. Upon which offering, they hear a noise out of the circle, nominating such as he will have; whom presently they take, binding them hand and foot, and cast them into the circle of the fire; for be it the king's son, he must be given if once named by their god. After the bodies which are offered are consumed in the fire, and their ceremonies performed, the men depart merrily, the women weeping.

So, in the end, one rather wonders about Spelman. Shades of William White – and even of David Ingram? The manuscript, as we have noted, was not published until 1872; and then in a limited edition.

In 1619 Captain Spelman, under criticism for his friendship with Opechancanough, Powhatan's successor as Emperor, was accused in Jamestown of being 'one that had in him more of the savage than the Indian'![13]

But of course the most famous English observer of the Indians of the James River and York River regions from 1607 to 1609 was John Smith. Smith's first book was entered for publication in London in August 1608, when he was still in Jamestown; Newport probably brought the manuscript back in his voyage from Jamestown on 10 April, arriving in England on 21 May (six weeks). This was: *A True Relation of such occurences and accidents of noate as hath hapned in Virginia since the first planting of that Collony, which is now resident in the South part thereof.*[14] Smith resided in the village of Powhatan – Werowocomoco – in December 1607, and noted the religion of the region.[15] The Indians worship a 'superior power', whom he thought to be called Quiyoughquosicke. Smith lived in a house with seven Indians:

Each with a rattle began at ten o'clock in the morning to sing about the fire, which they environed with a circle of meal; and after, a foot or two from that, at the end of each song, laid down two or three grains of wheat, continuing this order till they have included six or seven hundred in a half circle, and after that two or three more circles in like manner, a hand breadth from each other. That done, at each song they put betwixt every three, two or five grains a little stick; so counting, as an old woman her Pater Noster. One disguised with a great skin, his head hung round with little skins of weasels and other vermin, with a crownet of feathers on his head, painted as ugly as the devil, at the end of each song will make many signs and demonstrations, with strange and vehement actions; great cakes of deer suet, deer, and tobacco he casteth in the fire. Till six o'clock in the evening their howling would continue ere they would depart.

Like Spelman, Smith describes the cure of the sick by the man with the rattle, sucking out 'blood and phlegm from the patient, out of their unable stomach or any diseased place'. He also has material on burial customs.[16]

The death of any they lament with great sorrow and weeping. Their kings

[13] Kingsbury, *Records*, III, 175.
[14] *JV* 165-208. Smith-Arber 1-40.
[15] *JV* 188. [16] *JV* 189.

they bury betwixt two mats within their houses, with all his beads, jewels, hatchets and copper. The other in graves like ours.

Barbour printed the manuscript note, in an early-seventeenth-century hand, in the British Museum copy of *A True Relation*.[17]

This author I find in many errors, which they do impute to his not well understanding the language. For they do acknowledge both God and the Devil, and that after they are out of this world they shall rise again in another world, where they shall live at ease, and have great store of bread and venison and other.

Smith's second book was published in Oxford in 1612 (when Smith was in England), *A Map of Virginia, with a Description of the Countrey, the Commodities, People, Government and Religion. Written by Captaine Smith, sometimes Governour of the Countrey*.[18]

Smith gives a very good description of Indian cooking.[19] They roast their corn 'in the ear green'; and 'bruising it in a mortar of wood with a polt (club), lap it in rolls in the leaves of their corn, and so boil it for a dainty' (i.e. a dish pleasant to the palate). Then it can be boiled with beans. 'Their old wheat they first steep a'night in hot water'; then, by use of sieves, they produce a flour, and mix with water to make cakes, 'covering them with ashes till they be baked, and then washing them in fair water, they dry presently with their own heat'. Or, the 'cakes' can be boiled in water to make a broth.

Their fish and flesh they boil either very tenderly or broil it so long on hurdles over the fire, or else, after the Spanish fashion, putting it on a spit, they turn first the one side then the other.

When the fish is dry, it can be kept for a month or more. Fish or meat broth was eaten 'as commonly' as fish or meat itself. The Indian diet is listed by Smith as follows.[20] March and April are the season for fish, turkey and squirrel; May and June for fish again (crabs, oysters), land tortoises, deer, strawberries, mulberries, acorns and walnuts; July and August for fish again, and for the wheat which was planted in May and June. The provident (such as Powhatan) roast and preserve their meat. They preserve – by grinding – pecans, chestnuts and acorns, and also persimmons (date-plums). Boiled chestnuts (four hours) make bread and broth. Berries are boiled and dried.[21] The chief root for eating is Tuckahoe, rather like a potato, which can be roasted, mixed with sorrell and meal, to make a bread.[22]

Smith criticises the Indians for making 'so small a benefit of their land'.[23]

In appearance, the Indians are

[17] *ibid.*
[18] *JV* 327-74. Smith-Arber, 41-84.
[19] *JV* 351-2. [20] *JV* 357. [21] *JV* 347. [22] *JV* 348. [23] *JV* 354.

generally tall and straight, of a comely proportion, and of a colour brown
when they are of any age, but they are born white. Their hair is generally
black, but few have any beards. The men wear half their heads shaven, the
other half long. For barbers they use their women; who with two shells will
grate away the hair, of any fashion they please. The women are cut in many
fashions agreeable to their years, but ever some part remaineth long.[24]

The heads and shoulders are often 'painted red' – a protection, said
Smith, against heat or cold. The ears of the men are often pierced:
through the hole some wear

a small green and yellow coloured snake, near half a yard in length, which,
crawling and lapping herself about his neck, oftentimes familiarly would kiss
his lips. Others wear a dead rat tied by the tail.

As headgear, they sported a bird wing, and stuffed fowl or bird, or 'the
hand of their enemy, dried'.[25]
    Indian houses are

built like our arbors, of small young springs (branches) bowed and tied; and
so close covered with mats or the barks of trees, very handsomely, that
notwithstanding either wind, rain or weather, they are as warm as stoves, but
very smokey; yet at the top of the house there is a hole made for the smoke to
go into, right over the fire.

At home, the Indians recline on hurdles, raised a foot from the
ground, and covered with mats.[26]
    The economy is based on each household knowing 'their own lands
and gardens; and most live of their own labours'.[27] (Plenty of *meum*
and *tuum*, in fact.)
    The men seem often idle. But the women are very painstaking. The
women and children

make mats, baskets, pots, mortars; pound their corn, make their bread,
prepare their victuals, plant their corn, gather their corn, bear all kinds of
burdens, and such like.

The women 'love children very dearly'. To make the children

hardy, in the coldest mornings they wash them in the rivers, and by painting
and ointments so tan their skins that after a year or two no weather will hurt
them.[28]

    As regards their health, the Indians purge themselves every spring
by drinking bitter root. For the treatment of dropsy, swellings and
aches, they construct a sort of sauna. We again have the description of
the treatment of the sick by the medicine man with his rattle. Smith
notes that 'old ulcers or putrified hurts are seldom seen cured amongst

[24] *Ibid.* [25] *JV* 355. [26] *JV* 356. [27] *JV* 355. [28] *JV* 356-7.

them'. And was hardly surprised that when the Indians met an English surgeon, they came to believe that any English 'plaster' would heal any hurt.[29]

Indian music-making intrigued Smith.[30]

For their music they use a thick cane, on which they pipe, as on a recorder. For their wars, they have a deep platter of wood. They cover the mouth thereof with a skin; at each corner they tie a walnut which, meeting on the backside near the bottom, with a small rope they twitch them together: till it be so taut and stiff that they may beat upon it as upon a drum. But their chief instruments are rattles made of small gourds or pumpions' shells; of these they have bass, tenor, countertenor, mean and treble. These, mingled with their voices, sometimes twenty or thirty together, make such a terrible noise as would affright rather than delight any man.

Their hospitality, at least by English standards, was charmingly generous. Speeches of welcome were made

with such vehemency and so great passions, that they sweat till they drop, and are so out of breath they can scarce speak; so that a man would take them to be exceeding angry or stark mad.

But at night, when the lodging for the visitor has been prepared, 'they set a woman, painted red with oil and pocones, to be his bedfellow'.[31] Pocone, Pochone, Pocan: a Virginia root (pokeberry) bearing berries which stain red. William Strachey gives details:[32]

a small root that groweth in the mountains, which being dried and beat into powder turneth red. And this they use for swellings, aches, anointing their joints, painting their heads and garments with it. For which they account it very precious.

Next, burial customs.[33] There is a distinction between kings, and ordinary folk. For the common sort

they dig a deep hole in the earth with sharp stakes; and the corpse being lapped in skins and mats, with their jewels, they lay them upon sticks in the ground, and so cover them with earth. The burial ended, the women – being painted all their faces with black coal and oil – do sit twenty four hours in the houses mourning and lamenting by turns, with such yelling and howling as may express their great passions.

When the kings die:

their bodies are first bowelled, then dried upon hurdles till they be very dry. And so about most of their joints and neck they hang bracelets or chains, of

[29] *JV* 363-4. [30] *JV* 362-3. [31] *JV* 363.

[32] *Virginia Britania*, 122; note by L.B. Wright, 71.

[33] Unless otherwise indicated the quotations in the next paragraphs are from Smith's section 'Of their Religion': *JV* 364-9.

copper, pearl, and such like, as they use to wear. Their inwards they stuff with copper beads, and covered with a skin, hatchets, and such trash. Then lap they them very carefully in white skins, and so roll them in mats for their winding sheets. And in the tomb, which is an arch made of mats, they lay them orderly. What remaineth of this kind of wealth their kings have, they set at their feet in baskets. These temples and bodies are kept by their priests.

At the residence of Powhatan there was a holy place, three long temples containing tombs, images of kings, and religious images. This, the 'principal place of superstition', was held

so holy as that but the priests and kings dare come into them. Nor the savages dare not go up the river in boats by it, but that they solemnly cast some piece of copper, white beads, or pocones into the river, for fear their Oke should be offended and revenged of them.

Seven priests were resident in that holy place. The faces of the Indian priests were 'painted as ugly as they can devise'. The chief priest of the Powhatan temple wore distinctive headgear: a dozen snake skins stuffed with moss, and skins of weasels and other vermin, all tied together by their tails, the tails meeting in a tassle, around which was a crown of feathers; the actual skins partly covered the face, hanging round the head, neck and shoulders. The 'inferior priests', however, 'could hardly be known from the common people, but that they had not so many holes in their ears to hang their jewels at'.

The Indians have altar stones near their houses, or in the woods and fields. When they return from hunting or fighting they make offering on the altars: 'blood, deer suet, and tobacco.' In times of dangerous storms, tobacco, copper and pocones are cast into the river, with 'many hellish outcries and invocations'. At meal times, there is a sort of blessing:

Before their dinners and suppers the better sort will take the first bit, and cast it into the fire; which is all the grace they are known to use.

In times of harvest, of special danger, or special victory, there are communal 'solemnities':

The manner of their devotion is, sometimes to make a great fire in the house or fields, and all to sing and dance about it with rattles and shouts together, four or five hours. Sometimes they set a man in the midst, and about him they dance and sing, he all the while clapping his hands as if he would keep time. And after their songs and dances ended, they go to their feasts.

The priests of Powhatan's holy place had their special devotions:

most in songs, which the chief priest beginneth, and the rest followed him. Sometimes he maketh invocations with broken sentences, by starts and strange passions. And at every pause the rest give a short groan.

When Smith was a prisoner of the Indians in December 1607, he was subjected to special conjurations. There was a fire in one of the houses, around which Smith was made to sit with the seven Temple priests, while a circle of meal was strewn. There was singing. Then the chief priest laid down grains of wheat, while processing three times round the fire, grains which then were divided into groups with twigs. The party sat for twelve hours, the priests using strange gestures, the prisoner every hour expecting his end. Late in the evening they all ate a large meal. This procedure continued for three or four days.

Smith's assumption was that the Indians 'adore with their kind of divine worship' those things 'able to do them hurt beyond their prevention': fire, water, lightning, thunder. They came to adore English fire arms and English horses. After all, certain needs are essential to men: and in Virginia there is 'no place discovered to be so savage in which the savages have not a religion; deer; and bow and arrows'. But 'their chief God they worship is the devil', Oke.

They say they have conference with him, and fashion themselves as near to his shape as they can imagine. In their temples they have his image evil favouredly carved, and then painted and adorned with chains, copper and beads, and covered with a skin; in such manner as the deformity may well suit with such a god.

To the Indian, said Smith, the person most 'monstrous to behold' is the most 'gallant'.[34]

Certain Indians felt that the religion of the English might have something to offer. Smith reports that the werowance of Quiyoughcohannock 'professed to believe that our God exceeded theirs, as much as our guns did their bows and arrows'. He gave President Smith gifts, intreating him 'to pray to his god for rain; for his god would not send him any'.

Smith printed, in 1612, an account of the yearly 'sacrifice' of children. His informant here was probably William White: we have noted White's version of the event, as printed in 1614. The textual 'sources' here are confusing indeed. However, the Smith of 1612 tells us that at Quiyoughcohannock, ten miles from Jamestown, fifteen boys were painted white. In 1624, when this passage was reprinted in Smith's *Generall Historie*, there was a marginal note here: 'Their solemn sacrifices of children, which they call Black-boys.'[35]

The phrase 'black boys' has tantalised many readers. Philip Barbour ingeniously suggests that the 1624 note is a misprint for 'blake-boys', 'blake' being a northern dialect word for white or pale.[36] That is clever, but unnecessary. The Jamestown Council wrote to the Virginia Company in January 1622 referring to the Indian 'custom of making their children black boys'.[37] The phrase was quoted, and its

[34] *JV* 356. [35] Smith-Arber, 273. [36] *JV* 367.
[37] Kingsbury, *Records*, III, 584.

meaning made clear, in a sermon preached to the Virginia Company in London in April 1622, and printed later in the year: 'the custom of making their children black boys, or consecrating them to Satan.'[38] The writer of the 1624 annotation had read the 1622 literature. The word 'black', after all, has a sense of malignance (blackguard, blackmail, Black Mass) and of rejection (blackball). We have quoted (p.312) William White's use in 1614 of the phrase 'black like devils'.

The boys are then surrounded by dancers, tied to the trees and guarded, and collected by the five young men. 'What else was done with the children was not seen.' They were removed; and the remaining company feasted. The werowance was asked the meaning of the 'sacrifice'. White-Smith interpreted him as saying that some of the boys were dead, the Oke or Devil having them 'by lot', and sucking the blood from their left breast. The others were alive, but 'kept in the wilderness by the young men till nine months were expired, during which time they must not converse with any'. These boys became the 'priests and conjurers'.

This sacrifice they held to be so necessary, that if they should omit it, their Oke or Devil, and all their other Quiyoughcosucks which are their other gods, would let him have no deer, turkeys, corn nor fish; and yet besides he would make a great slaughter amongst them.

The Virginian Robert Beverley, in his *History and Present State of Virginia*, published in London in 1705 (with 14 engravings adapted from White/De Bry), discussed this description by Smith.[39] Beverley says that Smith had seen a ceremonial called 'Huskanawing': 'which, being a ceremony then altogether unknown to him, he might easily mistake some of the circumstances of it.' It was a ceremony of admission for young men destined to be in authority: as members of the 'council', in the 'affairs of government', with 'a great share in the administration'. Such 'great men' are called *Cockarouses*. (A *Werowance*, says Beverley, is a military captain.)[40] The young men chosen are between fifteen and twenty years old; 'the choisest and briskest', 'lively, handsome, well-timbered'. They are kept under confinement in the woods, and are given drugs to destroy their memories. Thus, education and custom blotted out, they achieve 'freedom'. This can induce madness; and, in some cases, death – the basis of the 'sacrifice' interpretation. It seems that in what is now the State of Virginia the 'huskenow' was restricted to males of rich families; in North Carolina all young persons were eligible for the ceremony – including girls.[41]

The werowances and priests, concludes Smith, were esteemed as Quiyoughcosucks. When they die, they

[38] Copland, *Virginias God be Thanked*, 1622, 29.
[39] Beverley, ed. Wright, 206-9.
[40] *ibid.*, 226.
[41] C.R. Feest, 'Powhatan: A Study in Political Organisation', *Wiener Volkerbundliche Mitteilungen*, XIII, viii, 1966, p.73.

go beyond the mountains towards the setting of the sun, and ever remain there in form of their Oke, with their heads painted with oil and pocones, finely trimmed with feathers, and shall beads, hatchets, copper and tobacco, doing nothing but dance and sing with all their predecessors.

The 'common people', however, are not supposed to live after death.

Such was the 'blind idolatry' of the Virginia Indians.

With his *Map of Virginia* in 1612 Smith printed his actual map of Virginia, 12½ inches by 16¼ inches, the plate for the map being cut before August. The map also circulated separately. It was based on the draft map sent with Newport on a vessel which left Jamestown in December 1608.[42] The text also contains a number of Indian words and phrases:[43] 'In how many days will there come hither any more English ships?'; 'I am very hungry, what shall I eat?'; 'Where dwells Powhatan?'; 'Get you gone and come again quickly'; 'Bid Pocahontas bring hither two little baskets, and I will give her white beads to make her a chain.'

Smith had used well his twenty-eight months on the James. His dominant feeling about the Indian he expressed in a letter of 1608: 'inconstant'.[44] The 1612 book has the passage:[45] 'They are inconstant in every thing, but what fear constraineth them to keep.' They are, further,

crafty, timorous, quick of apprehension, and very ingenious. Some are of disposition fearful, some bold, most cautelous,[46] all savage. Generally covetous of copper, beads and such like trash. They are soon moved to anger; and so malicious that they seldom forget an injury.

In 1630, at the end of his life, Smith, stung by charges that he had been cruel to the Indian, could write of the 'simple savages' of Virginia, naturally 'bosom friends' of the English, 'harmless, innocent savages'.[47] But this was hurt, ironical comment, for those who intended to plant in New England.

[42] McCary, *John Smith's Map of Virginia*, 1957.
[43] *JV* 331-4.
[44] Printed 1624. Smith-Arber, 443.
[45] *JV* 354.
[46] *Cautelous*: deceitful, crafty.
[47] Smith-Arber, 928, 931.

16

William Strachey and Virginia, 1609-1612

William Strachey, author of *True Reportory of the Wrack and Redemption ... upon and from the Islands of the Bermudas* (and ancestor of Lytton Strachey) was thirty-seven at the time of the tempest and shipwreck in 1609.[1] He was born in 1572 at Saffron Walden, Essex, sixteen miles from Cambridge; his father had received a grant of arms, and was thus officially of gentry status. The family was also of evangelical piety, for early in 1588, when he was not yet sixteen, William was sent to Cambridge, and the college chosen for him was Emmanuel.

Emmanuel had been functioning for only three and a half years when Strachey went up; the first undergraduates – twenty-six of them – had been admitted in November 1584; the new college buildings were not ready until 1589.[2] In 1583 the site and buildings of the old Dominican Friary had been bought by Laurence Chaderton, Fellow of Christ's, and his brother-in-law, and the estate conveyed to Sir Walter Mildmay, MP: the founder of the College. The Charter was granted in 1584, and Chaderton became the first Master; he remained Master until 1622, and lived until 1640. The College Statutes date from 1585. The preface to the Statutes affirms it to be

an ancient institution in the Church, and a tradition from the earliest times, that schools and colleges be founded for the education of young men in all piety and good learning and especially in Holy Writ and theology, that being thus instructed they may thereafter teach true and pure religion.

St Paul, 'teacher of the Gentiles', and other 'men that were inspired by the divine prompting of the spirit' knew that 'the light of the gospel could not be spread abroad to all posterity to the glory of God and to the salvation of men' without 'noble plants of theology and right good learning':

---

[1] There is a book on Strachey, originally a London PhD thesis: S.G. Culliford, *William Strachey, 1572-1621*, 1965.

[2] I have incorporated here material from my anthology *Puritanism in Tudor England*, 1970, part IX, 'The Puritans and Education'; which includes parts of a new translation of the Statutes of Emmanuel by Dr F. Stubbings, Librarian of the college.

And as those other streams flowed out of the fountains of the garden of Eden to water the earth: so ought schools to be opened like fountains that, arising out of the paradise of God, they may, as with a river of gold, water all regions of our land, yea of the whole earth, with a faith of purest doctrine and with a life of most holy discipline.

Mildmay's purpose was 'to propagate purity of life and religion unto our posterity'. The statutes contained no provision for the study of law and medicine. And they were conservative; in view of the increasing secularisation of the aims of higher education in Tudor England. (The Duke of Somerset, Chancellor of the University, had argued in 1549 for less Divinity and more Roman Law.) Emmanuel was doing for Elizabethan Cambridge what a pious foundation like St Catharine's had intended to do in the late fifteenth century (although the orientation was now very protestant: puritan).

Of the hundred or so Cambridge men who emigrated to New England before 1646, thirty-five were Emmanuel bred.[3] They included Nathaniel Ward, a freshman in 1596; John Cotton, by origin a Trinity man (B.A. 1603), but thereafter Fellow of Emmanuel; Thomas Hooker, who went to Emmanuel in 1604, and became a Fellow; and Thomas Shepard, a freshman in 1620. And, of course, John Harvard (M.A., 1635).

The historian Thomas Fuller, writing in the 1630s, reported an alleged conversation between Mildmay and Elizabeth I.[4] 'Sir Walter, I hear you have established a puritan foundation.' 'No madam, far be it from me to countenance any thing contrary to your established laws, but I have set an acorn, which when it becomes an oak, God alone knows what will be the fruit thereof.'

There appears to be no record of Strachey taking a degree. Presumably he did what sons of the gentry usually did – studied at Cambridge for two years or so, and then went to London, to the Inns of Court: the 'third university'. He was certainly a member of Gray's Inn by 1605. By 1608 he was very short of money: a member of the gentry whose career hasn't gone too well – rather like John Winthrop in the late 1620s. And so he sailed on the 'Sea Venture' in 1609.

Strachey arrived in Jamestown at the end of May 1610, having been named 'secretary' of the colony in Virginia, and left it in September 1611, sixteen months later. By the end of 1612, when he was 40, he had completed the manuscript of *The Historie of Travell into Virginia Britania*:

expressing the cosmography and commodities of the country, together with the qualities, customs and manners of the natural inhabitants; in part gathered and obtained from the industrious and faithful observations and

---

[3] Morison, *Founding of Harvard*, Appendix B, 'English University Men who migrated to New England'.
[4] Fuller, *History of the University of Cambridge*, published 1655. Ed. Prickett and Wright, 278-9.

commentaries of the first planters and elder discoverers: and in part observed by William Strachey, gent.

The dedication of one manuscript copy was to Henry Percy, ninth Earl of Northumberland, elder brother of George Percy. And Strachey permitted himself six lines of preliminary verse – he had been a shareholder in The Children of the Queen's Revels, the company of boy actors which since 1600 had used the Blackfriars Theatre, and which in 1605 had presented *Eastward Ho*: Strachey said he attended the theatre sometimes thrice weekly – odd behaviour in an Emmanuel man. He contributed a commendatory sonnet to the published text of Ben Jonson's *Sejanus* (1605).[5] The 1612 lines concern the Indian:[6]

> Wild as they are, accept them, so were we.
> To make them civil will our honour be.
> And if good works be the effects of minds
> That like good angels be, let our designs,
> As we are *Angli*, make us Angels too.
> No better work can Church or statesman do.

The work remained unpublished until 1849, when it was edited for the Hakluyt Society by R.H. Major. There are three manuscript copies, all apparently made by a secretary about 1612. Major used the British Museum copy, which Strachey dedicated in 1618 to Francis Bacon. The second manuscript is in the Bodleian. The Northumberland copy was sold in 1928 to Princeton (this manuscript has twenty-seven of the John White/De Bry engravings, which Strachey coloured by hand). When the Hakluyt Society financed a new edition, the editors, Louis B. Wright and Virginia Freund, used the Northumberland/Princeton text. Their edition was published in 1953; and my page references are to it. The text runs to 173 pages;[7] and there is an introductory essay of about twenty pages by the editors.

Strachey thought that the James River region is best called 'Virginia'; and that 'the main continent' ought to be named *Britania*. The English claim he took to stretch from St Augustine, Florida to Portland, Maine, and of course to the West: 'for the West thereof the limits are unknown, only it is supposed there may be found the descent into the South-Sea' – America from East to West could be in some places 300 miles, and in others 1000 miles: 'ground enough to satisfy the most covetous.'[8]

Strachey had read the available literature on Virginia – all the accounts, or most of them, thus far discussed here – and he rarely gives specific acknowledgement.[9] So the student who reads Strachey

[5] Sanders, *The Strachey Family*, 15.
[6] *Virginia Britania*, 6.
[7] Convenient extracts in Wright, *Elizabethans' America*, 206-19.
[8] 31-2.
[9] Culliford discusses Strachey's sources, 165-84.

in the chronological sequence of Virginia literature has the sensation throughout of semi-recognition. No doubt he also consulted the experts in London: Hakluyt, surely, and also Thomas Hariot – who may have helped him with the dictionary of words and phrases of 'the Indian language' (the Powhatan dialect of the Algonquian language), running to nearly 900 items, which is found in the Bodleian manuscript.[10]

There are, of course, personal touches which amplify or supercede the earlier literature. The Indian dwellings are 'like garden arbours, at best like our shepherds' cottages'.[11] The broth made by boiling the dregs of maize 'is their kind of Frumenty' (wheat boiled in milk); 'and is indeed like our Ptisane, husked barley, sodden in water.' Strachey was always anxious (sometimes appealingly, sometimes annoyingly) to parade his classical and academic learning. Thus the broth

may be not much unlike that homely *Ius Nigrum* which the Lacedemonians used to eat, and which Dionysius could not abide to taste of, albeit he bought a cook from thence only to make him that broth: for which the cook told him he must have a Lacedemonian's stomack indeed, to eat of the Lacedemonian diet.

(This was apparently a black broth made from the entrails of hares.)[12] The Indians make candles 'of the fattest splinters of the pine or fir tree'; as they do 'in Shropshire between the lordships of Oswestry and Ellesmere'.[13] Strachey ate in Virginia 'as full and luscious a grape as in the villages between Paris and Amiens'; and Dr Lawrence Bohun and others, crushing the grapes by hand, and allowing them to ferment for a week, produced a liquor 'full as good as your French-British wine'.[14] His material on Indian football is a helpful expansion of Henry Spelman's version:[15]

They have the exercise of football, in which yet they only forceably encounter with the foot to carry the ball the one from the other, and spurn it to the goal with a kind of dexterity and swift footmanship, which is the honour of it; but they never strike up one another's heels as we do, not accounting that praiseworthy to purchase a goal by such advantage.

That apart, the game is 'much like that which boys call 'Bandy' in English'. And also (of course) like the description given by Virgil of the game taught to the Italians by the Trojans. They also have a gambling game rather like 'Primero' (except that Primero is played with cards). This is 'a game upon rushes', in which they 'card and discard, and lay a stake too, and so win and lose; they will play at this for their bows and arrows, their copper beads, hatchets, and their leather coats.' There is also detail about Indian songs. Strachey tells us of three types of chant.[16] First, their 'amorous ditties'. Secondly,

[10] 174-207. The edition includes an essay on the dictionary by Fr. J.A. Geary, 208-14.
[11] 78. [12] 81. [13] 115. [14] 121. [15] 84. [16] 85-6.

a kind of angry song against us, in their homely rhymes, which concludeth with a kind of petition unto their *Okeus* and to all the host of the idols, to plague the 'Tassantasses' (for so they call us) and their posterities.

Thirdly, 'a scornful song they made of us the last year at the Falls, in manner of triumph' – when they killed four Englishmen, including De La Warr's nephew, Captain William West, and took prisoners, including Simon Score, a sailor, and a boy called Cob. Strachey prints the words of this song of scorn: four verses of two lines each, each verse also having the refrain: 'Whe, whe, yah, ha, ha, he, wittowa, wittowa.' Strachey also tells us (and this would surely surprise Hariot[17]) that the Indians are 'all of them huge eaters'; an Indian working for the colonists gets 'double the allowance of one of our own men'.[18] The colour of Indian skin he describes as 'brown, or rather, tawny'.[19] Mulberry coloured; or like 'a sodden quince'. Like Smith, Strachey believed that the Indians spring 'from the womb indifferent white'. And are instantly subjected to painting, dying and anointing with yellow and red pigments and juices (because this is the custom; and because it is a protection against insects). The colour is thus artificial. Their facial appearance is more negroid to Strachey than it was to other commentators: 'Their noses are broad, flat, and full at the end; great big lips, and wide mouths, yet nothing so unsightly as the Moors': blackamoors.

The Indians (and this is a novel English emphasis) are also 'most voluptuous'.[20] The women, with the connivance of their husbands:

embrace the acquaintance of any stranger for nothing, and it is accounted no offence. And incredible it is with what heat both sexes of them are given over to those intemperances; and the men to preposterous Venus, for which they are full of their own country disease, the pox, very young.

The venereal disease is treated with sassafras and other herbs: 'which in short time quencheth and mortifieth the indignant poison.' Such excesses Strachey sees as the explanation of Indian infertility.[21] Why is Virginia not as populous as the West Indies? Because of 'their immoderate use and multiplicity of women, and those often full of foul diseases.' Here we are treated to more Emmanuel-style musing. It 'may be a problem in Philosophy': whether 'variety of women' be a 'furtherance or hindrance of many births'. But it seems that in Virginia

the tired body cannot have those sensual helps (as the Turks) to hold up the immoderate desires; many women, dividing the body and the strength thereof, make it generally unfit to the office of increase.

Moreover, the Indians in Virginia seem not to live as long as the

---

[17] For Hariot on Indian moderation in eating, below, Chapter 12, p.239.
[18] 84. [19] 70-1. [20] 112-13. [21] 116.

native population in other parts of America. What is needed is 'greater
moderation' and 'stricter ceremony in their kind of marriage.'
However, the women are 'very painful';[22] a favourite puritan word,
usually applied to preachers: painstaking.

The men bestow their times in fishing, hunting, wars, and such man-like
exercises without the doors, scorning to be seen in any effeminate labour;
which is the cause that the women be very painful, and the men often idle.

The Emperor Powhatan has, in all, over 100 wives, 'according to
the order and custom of sensual heathenism'. Only about a dozen,
however, are operative at any one time: Strachey gives twelve names,
given him by an Indian called Kempes, who died of scurvy after being
resident for nearly a year at Jamestown, where he learnt 'a pretty deal
of English', and also 'came orderly to prayers, and observed with us
the keeping of the Sabbath, both by ceasing from labour, and
repairing to Church'[23] (no doubt to the delight of the Reverend
Richard Buck, who had arrived in Jamestown in May 1610 from
Bermuda, having been, like Strachey, a passenger on the *Sea Venture*:
the third known cleric to be sent to Virginia – Hunt was dead, and the
mysterious puritan had presumably departed). Strachey respected
Powhatan, although he disapproved of him. He was 'proud and
insolent': a 'great tyrant'[24] – and to an Inns of Court man tyranny was
traditionally loathed. Strachey was sure that Powhatan had
massacred the 'lost colony', and was preparing for the Jamestown
settlers 'the same cup which he made our poor countrymen drink of at
Roanoke'. All the same, Powhatan did not seem 'willing to hold any
open quarrel or hostility with us'. And he was frightened:

with the danger and mischief which he saith we intend unto him, by taking
away his land from him, and conspiring to surprise him; which we never yet
imagined nor attempted.

Powhatan was said to be nearly 80. He was 'a goodly old man, not
shrinking':

of a tall stature, and clean limbs; of a sad aspect; round fat visaged; with gray
hairs, but plain and thin, hanging upon his broad shoulders, some few hairs
upon his chin, and so on his upper lip.

He was a ruler of 'subtle understanding and politique carriage'.[25] And
although a 'barbarous and uncivil prince' he has 'majesty':[26]

Such is, I believe, the impression of the divine nature; and howsoever these
(as other) heathens, forsaken by the true light, have not that portion of the
knowing blessed Christian spirit, yet I am persuaded there is an infused kind
of divineness, and extraordinary (appointed that it shall be so by the King of

22 81.   23 61.   24 105-6.   25 57.   26 60-1.

Kings) to such who are his immediate instruments on earth, how wretched soever otherwise under the course of misbelief and infidelity.

Powhatan was guided by Prophecies given him by his priests. He had exterminated, 'not many years since', the Chesapeake Indians because it was foretold 'how that from the Chesapeake Bay a nation should arise which should dissolve and give end to his Empire'. There was also a Prophecy about 'such strangers as should invade their territories, or labour to settle a plantation'. Powhatan and his people would overthrow them twice; 'but the third time they themselves should fall into their subjection, and under their conquest.'[27]

The structure of Powhatan's empire was of subsidiary regions, 'shires as it were', each under a werowance or 'absolute commander': there were over 30 such.[28] Strachey estimated the total population of the confederacy as 3,220.[29] (In fact, it was probably nearer 11,000.) This organisation was basically admirable:[30]

Although the country people be very barbarous, yet have they amongst themselves such government as that their magistrates for good commanding, and their people for due subjection and obeying, excel many places that would be accounted Civil. The form of their commonwealth, by what hath been already delivered, you may well gather to be a *Monarchal government*: where one, as Emperor, ruleth over many kings.

There are no 'positive laws'; 'the law whereby he ruleth is custom.' The weakness is that when Powhatan 'pleaseth, his will is law, and must be obeyed; not only as a king, but as half a god, his people esteem him.' Strachey was most offended by the provision that Powhatan took 80 per cent of the produce of his empire: wheat, vegetables, fish and fowl, roots, skins.[31] This, plus his cruel punishments: he 'doth at his pleasure despoil them both of their lives and goods, without yielding them any reason'.[32] Strachey saw the English as Liberators of the Indian.[33] Under English rule, the Indians will 'enjoy the fruits of their own territories'. They will engage in 'peaceable and frank trade with the English'. True, there will be some Tribute payable; but this will be much less than that to Powhatan, and, in order to pay it, the Indians will be constrained to make better use of their land: they will 'cleanse double as much ground as they do'. The English 'will take of their poorest into their families'. And

their better sort shall by patents and proclamations hold their land as free burghers and citizens with the English, and subject to King James, who will give them Justice, and defend them against all their enemies; whereas now they live in miserable slavery, and have no assurance of their lives or of their goods.

There is a tribute here to Spanish policy in Peru. Strachey had been

[27] 104-5. [28] 63. [29] 69. [30] 77. [31] 87. [32] 91. [33] 91-3.

reading the 1604 translation of José de Acosta: *The Naturall and Morall Historie of the East and West Indies*. The Indians will become 'the more civil; as likewise to enjoy the rest of their own more freely than under Powhatan; they will find themselves in far better estate than now they are' – 'they shall for hereafter be delivered from his tyranny.'

Powhatan was said to have twenty sons and ten daughters. Strachey had seen Pocahontas, 'playful one', 'a well favoured but wanton young girl'.[34] Until they were twelve, Indian girls went naked. And Pocahontas at Jamestown would

get the boys forth with her into the market place and make them wheel, falling on their hands, turning their heels upwards; whom she would follow, and wheel so herself, naked as she was, all the Fort over.

Strachey followed Smith in stressing the inconstancy of the Indian. 'They are inconstant in everything but what fear constraineth them to keep; crafty, timorous' – also short tempered, and slow to forget a grudge.[35] But English deaths are due more to English stupidity than to Indian venom. Strachey said he could not name three Englishmen killed in open conflict:

Let me truly say, how they never killed man of ours, but by our men's folly and indiscretion; suffering themselves to be beguiled and enticed up into their houses without their arms; when then, indeed, they have fallen upon them, and knocked out their brains, or stuck them full of arrows (no force) for their credulity.

Such deaths are to be attributed to English 'weakness' and Indian 'subtlety'.[36]

In generalising about the nature of the Indian, Strachey lapses into his rather sophomoric scholastic manner.[37] The Indians

have many moral goods, such as are *per accidens* plentiful enough amongst them; and as much, poor souls, as they come short of those *bona moralia* which are *per se*.

They are 'healthy enough, which is *Bonum corporis*'.

Nor is Nature a stepdame unto them concerning their *aptas membrorum compositiones*. Only, God wot, I must grant that *Bonum morale* (as aforesaid) which is *per se*, they have not *in medio*, which is *in Virtute*; and then how can they ever obtain it *in Ultimo*, which is *in felicitate*?

Holofernes on the James.

Another plank in the platform of Indian Liberation was deliverance from the power of the Priests. An Indian high priest (*Quiyoughquisock*) 'is no less honoured than Diana's priests at Ephesus'.[38] They are

[34] 72. [35] 74-5. [36] 45. [37] 132. [38] 88.

'ministers of Satan' who persuade the people 'every year to sacrifice still their own children'.[39] We have the familiar material about the ceremony with the adolescent boys, here attributed to the observations of George Percy.[40] The material has the points that the observers did not see what in the end happened to the boys; and that the werowances explained that only one of them died, the rest being held in seclusion to become 'priests and conjurers, to be instructed by tradition from the elder priests'. The habit of child sacrifice Strachey explains is universal 'over all the Indies': Florida and Mexico, for instance (reference again to Acosta); and it was common in Antiquity. The Strachey thesis is that the Indian lay magistrates are wholly swayed by the priests and prophets. It is the priests who

persuade their werowances to resist our settlement, and tell them how much their *Okeus* will be offended with them, and that he will not be appeased with a sacrifice of a thousand, nay a hecatomb of their children, if they permit a nation despising the ancient religion of their forefathers to inhabit among them.[41]

Thus the priests should be captured, and delivered to the Governor of Virginia: who will 'perform the same acceptable service to God that Jehu King of Israel did when he assembled all the priests of Baal and slew them to the last man in their own temple'.[42] All this is conformity with the 'Instructions' given by the London Council of the Virginia Company to Sir Thomas Gates in 1609.[43] The seducers taken care of, the Indian will be amenable to English influence:

We shall by degrees change their barbarous natures, make them ashamed the sooner of their savage nakedness, inform them of the true God and of the way to their salvation, and finally teach them obedience to the King's Majesty and to his Governors in those parts.[44]

The 'ancient religion of their forefathers' teaches that there are two gods.[45] (A touch here of Strachey the Cambridge High Calvinist?) There is *Ahone*, the 'good and peaceable god', who 'intendeth all good unto them, and will do no harm'. He is the great god who

governs all the world, and makes the sun to shine, creating the moon and stars his companions, great powers, and which dwell with him, and by whose virtues and influences the under earth is tempered, and brings forth her fruits according to her seasons.

---

[39] 89.   [40] 98-9.   [41] 90.

[42] 94. Jehu, king of Israel, massacred the worshippers in the temple of the foreign cult of Baal: 'Go in and slay them; let none come forth. And they smote them with the edge of the sword' (II Kings 10:25).

[43] Kingsbury, *Records*, III, 14-15.

[44] 91.   [45] 89.

Ahone does not need to be sacrificed unto. Then there is *Okeus*, whose images are in the temple; as

the presentment and figure of that god (say the priests unto the laity, and who religiously believe what the priests say) which doth them all the harm they suffer, be it in their bodies or goods, within doors or abroad.

The 'displeased Okeus'

looking into all men's actions, and examining the same according to the severe scale of justice, punisheth them with sicknesses, beats them, and strikes their ripe corn with blastings, storms and thunderclaps, stirs up war, and makes their women false unto them: such is the misery and thraldom under which Satan hath bound these wretched miscreants.

To pacify *Okeus*, 'not only their own children, but strangers, are sometimes sacrificed unto him'.

Strachey amplifies earlier material on Indian belief in the immortality of the soul.[46] The 'common people' are not thought to survive after death. The werowances and priests are. It is believed that when

their bodies are laid in the earth, that that which is within shall go beyond the mountains, and travel as far as where the sun sets, into most pleasant fields, grounds and pastures, where it shall do no labour, but, stuck finely with feathers and painted with oil and pocones, rest in all quiet and peace, and eat delicious fruits, and have store of copper, beads and hatchets; sing, dance and have all variety of delights and merriments till that wax old there, as the body did on earth. And then it shall dissolve and die, and come into a woman's womb again, and so be anew born into the world. Not unlike the heathen Pythagoras his opinion, and fable of Metempsychosis. Nor is this opinion more ridiculous or savage than was the Epicures' long since, in time too of morality, who taught that the soul of man, as of brute beasts, was nothing else but lief or the vital power, arising of the temperature and perfection of the body; and therefore died and extinguished together with the body, the soul so being a mere quality in the body, and when the body was to dissolve the soul must likewise become nothing. Nor is it more heathenous than our Atheists, who would (even out of scripture) profanely conclude no immortality of the soul to be; wresting that of Solomon who saith: 'The condition of men and beasts are even as one'; not acknowledging their impious reasoning by fallacies, concluding that which is in some respects so, to be simply so: as because their bodies die alike, therefore the soul of man must perish too. But, alas, well may these poor heathen be pitied and pardoned, until they shall be taught better; neither born under Grace, nor of the Seed of Promise.

Captain Samuel Argall was exploring the Potomac River with Strachey, when Iapassus, the brother of the Potomac chief (the

---

[46] 100. The reference to 'Solomon' in the passage is to Ecclesiastes 3:19: 'A man hath no preeminence above a beast.'

Potomacs were within the confederacy), came on board. One of the crew

was reading of a Bible, to which the Indian gave a very attent ear, and looked with a very wish't eye upon him, as if he desired to understand what he read.

Argall showed Iapassus an illustration in the Bible, depicting the Creation. And Iapassus related an Indian story of creation: 'a pretty, fabulous tale', says Strachey. The interpreter was the 'boy' Henry Spelman.[47] (Was this the occasion of Spelman's 'rescue'?)

We have, said he, five gods in all. Our chief god appears often unto us in the likewise of a mighty great hare. The other four have no visible shape, but are indeed the four winds, which keep the four corners of the earth (and then with his hand he seemed to quarter out the situation of the world). Our god who takes upon this shape of a hare conceived with himself how to people this great world, and with what kind of creatures. And it is true (said he) that at length he devised and made divers men and women, and made provision for them to be kept up yet for a while in a great bag. Now there were certain spirits, which he described to be like great giants, which came to the hare's dwelling place, being towards the rising of the sun, and had perseverance of the men and women which he had put into that great bag; and they would have had them to eat, but the godlike hare reproved those cannibal spirits, and drove them away.

Now if the boy had asked him of what he made those men and women, and what those spirits more particularly had been, and so had proceeded in some order, they should have made it hang together the better. But the boy was unwilling to question him so many things, lest he should offend him.

Only the old man went on, and said how that godlike hare made the water, and the fish therein, and the land, and a great deer which should feed upon the land. At which assembled the other four gods, envious hereat, from the east, the west, from the north and south; and with hunting poles killed this deer, dressed him, and after they had feasted with him departed again east, west, north and south. At which the other god in despite of this their malice to him took all the hairs of the slain deer and spread them upon the earth, with many powerful words and charms, whereby every hair became a deer. And then he opened the great bag, wherein the men and the women were, and placed them upon the earth; a man and a woman in one country, and a man and a woman in another country. And so the world took his first beginning of mankind.

The Captain bid the boy ask him, what he thought became of them after their death.

To which he answered somewhat like as is expressed before of the inhabitants about us. How that after they are dead here, they go up to the top of a high tree; and there they espy a fair, plain, broad pathway, on both sides whereof doth grow all manner of pleasant fruits: as mulberries, starberries, plums, etc. In this pleasant path they run toward the rising of the sun, where the godlike hare's house is. And in the mid-way they come to a house where a woman goddess doth dwell, who hath always her doors open

[47] 101-3.

for hospitality, and hath at all times, ready dressed, green *Uskatahomen* and *Pokahichary* (which is green corn bruised and boiled; and walnuts beaten small, then washed from the shells with a quantity of water which makes a kind of milk, and which they esteem an extraordinary dainty dish) together with all manner of pleasant fruits in a readiness to entertain all such as do travel to the great hare's house. And when they are well refreshed, they run in this pleasant path to the rising of the sun; where they find their forefathers living in great pleasure in a goodly field, where they do nothing but dance and sing, and feed on delicious fruits with that great hare who is their great god.

And when they have lived there until they be stark old men, they say they die there likewise by turns; and come into the world again.

The first Book of *The Historie of Travell into Virginia Britania* begins with a twenty-two page 'Premonition to the Reader':

Wherein (as the foundation to all the succeeding business) is derived down to our times the ancient right and claim which we make to this part of America. And therein both the objections answered, and doubts clearly satisfied, of such who, through malice or ignorance, either have or may hereafter call the lawfulness of the proceeding hereof in question.

Strachey's use of the Madoc, Cabot and Columbus material we have discussed in an earlier chapter. Columbus was a 'great and famous instrument of publishing the Gospel and knowledge of Jesus Christ'. So was Amerigo Vespucci: 'Let the examples of these move us to advance, now opportunity is offered, our profession and faith; as catholic, and more purged from self inventions.'[48]
The Indians are 'barbarous', 'simple', 'innocent'. They 'participate with us of reason, carrying in their nostrils more than the spirit of life, the breath of beasts'. Compare the Indian with the Turk. The religion of the Turk is stronger, and he can defend it with arms; a Christian is in danger in their territory. With the Indian, 'a more easy passage lies open to wound the illusions of Satan, and to gain a poor innocent to partake in our knowledge'. They have 'the practice of all moral policies and offices of virtue, as perfect, peremptory and exact, as the unbelieving Grecians and infidious Romans had'. Yet as Christians we cannot be satisfied even with 'the well ordered powers of philosophy, and all natural knowledges'. We, 'as true Christians, know that the world never was, nor must be only and alone, governed by morality'. But the Indians are of God, 'whose image they bear'. And

albeit in the Old Law, the elected Jew accounted every Jew his neighbour; yet since the time of Grace we are taught to acknowledge every man that bears the impression of God's stamp to be not only our neighbour, but to be our brother, how far distinguished and removed by seas or lands soever from us.[49]

[48] 20. [49] 17-19.

Christian men 'cannot forget that every soul which God hath sealed for Himself, He hath done it with the print of charity and compassion'.[50]

The Indians need 'the supernal light'; the worship of the true God, and of Christ, 'their and our blessed redeemer'.[51] Christ tells us to go and baptise all nations: 'infallibly and mathematically including even these poor savages'.[52] Such actions, by 'men of fervent charity', would be 'meritorious work', 'good works':[53]

And good works, albeit they be not *concausae*, yet they are *consectaria*, as the Schoolman says, of our faith; though not *causa regnandi*, yet are they *via ad regnum*; though they justify not before God, yet they do glorify God in His servants.

A touch of the Emmanuel years again! By the 1580s medieval theology was a favourite extra-curricular study in puritan Cambridge.[54] And Strachey's placing of 'good works' would have won the approval of Cranmer.

By joining with the Indian 'in friendship', by 'keeping company' with him, we communicate the benefits of 'Society'.[55] 'Like doth in time fashion and work into like, as fire worketh wood altogether into fire.' There are those here in England who are 'profane', 'disordered', 'might I not say almost barbarous': shame and compunction strike home to them 'by keeping company':

by conversing, the time or reverence and awe of the better company, or same particular advantage, circumstance, or other, may object that to the most sensual which may strike his proud heart; so as he may find somewhat to be amazed at; about which, whilst his imaginations busy themselves, they may beget further discourse, and arguments of more and more goodness.

We can bring the Indian[56]

from bodily wants, confusion, misery, and those outward anguishes, to the knowledge of a better practice, and improving of those benefits to a more and ever-during advantage, and to a civiler use; which God hath given unto them, but involved and hid in the bowels and womb of their land: to them barren and unprofitable, because unknown.

So the Romans taught us; by 'teaching us even to know the powerful discourse of divine reason, which makes us only men, and distinguisheth us from beasts'.[57] To do so, the Romans offered us 'violence and injury' – a reference here to the *Agricola* of Tacitus, and to Bede. But a venial violence, which the father uses, who beats his

---

[50] 26. [51] 17. [52] 23. [53] 18.

[54] Costello, *Scholastic Curriculum at Early Seventeenth-Century Cambridge.* Puritan casuists such as William Perkins and William Ames (both of Christ's) made use of medieval scholastic theologians.

[55] 19. [56] 25. [57] 24.

child to 'bring him to goodness' (a quotation here from William Symonds' Whitechapel sermon of 15 April 1609, published later in that year).

And a reference to George Peckham's *True Reporte* of 1583, published by Hakluyt in 1589.[58] Peckham, Strachey reminds us, distinguished between two sorts of 'planting'. The first: 'When Christians by the good liking and willing assent of the savages are admitted by them to quiet possession.' The second: 'When Christians, being inhumanely repulsed, do seek to atrain and maintain the right for which they came.' Both sorts 'may be lawfully exercised' in 'regard of the establishment of the Christian religion'. We know that 'the earth is the Lord's, and all that is therein'. God intended His creation to be 'common among men': 'may it not, then, be lawful now to attempt the possession of such lands as are void of Christian inhabitants, for Christ's sake?' We pray, 'thy kingdom come':

which implieth that it would please the great and merciful God that His sacred word might have a powerful passage throughout the world, yea in such sort that all nations might be reduced to the Kingdom of Grace.

One hopes to do this by 'a gentle and fair entreaty'.[59] But suppose the Indians 'practise violence or treason against us'; as they did at Roanoke?

I would gladly know, of such who presume to know all things, whether we may stand upon our own innocency or no, or hold it a scruple of humanity, or make it any breach of charity, to prevent our own throats from the cutting, to draw our swords: *et vim vi repellere*.

The Old Testament clearly shows that when nations would not submit by 'fair entreaty', 'they were *ferro et flammis* compelled thereunto'. We are back with Joshua and the destruction of Jericho: force, fire and sword.

The English thus proceed to 'the raising and building up of a *Sanctum Sanctorum*; a holy house, and a sanctuary to His blessed name, among infidels'.[60]

---

[58] 26-8. See above, pp.217-20.
[59] This particular quotation, 25.
[60] 22.

17

1609: One Merchant and Five Parsons

The Thomas Gates fleet sailed down the Thames on 15 May 1609. Six relevant London orations date from the first months of 1609: a speech early in the year by Robert Johnson; a sermon at Paul's Cross on 24 March by Richard Crakanthorpe; a sermon in early April by Robert Gray; a sermon in Whitechapel on 15 April by William Symonds; a sermon at Paul's Cross on 7 May by George Benson; and (later than the sailing of the fleet) a sermon at Paul's Cross on 25 May by Daniel Price. This chapter is devoted to a discussion of these six set-pieces.

Robert Johnson was a City Alderman, a director of the East India Company, and son-in-law of Sir Thomas Smythe. He was a future Deputy Treasurer of the Virginia Company, under Smythe; and in 1618 was to be listed as one of the six shareholders to have invested more than £200[1] (the others included Sir Edwin Sandys, Lord De La Warr, Henry Wriothesley Earl of Southampton, and William Cecil, son of Robert). Johnson was also a friend of William Crashaw. In his will, 1626, Crashaw named Johnson as an 'honest merchant' suitable to supervise money left by Crashaw for the increase of the stipends of puritan Lecturers in London.[2] Johnson's speech in 1609 was to 'some few adventurers' concerned with Virginia. It was fresh, stylish, practical and optimistic; it was printed in the early spring of 1609, with a dedication to Smythe. *Nova Britannia. Offering most excellent fruits by planting in Virginia. Exciting such as be well affected to the same.*[3]

Johnson's first point was that the Jamestown enterprise was a continuation of the settlements of the 1580s: Virginia is an old colony, now being further succoured, and there has been no 'interruption or invasion'.[4] The first concern of activity in 1609 should be to 'advance and spread the kingdom of God, and the knowledge of his truth, among so many millions of men and women, savage and blind, that never yet saw the true light'.[5] The second concern was the honour of the king and the enlargement of his territory. The third was the defence of the existing Jamestown colonists. (We are treated again to the Cabots, and the Columbus offer to Henry VII.)[6]

[1] Kingsbury, *Records*, III, 85.
[2] P.J. Wallis, *William Crashawe: the Sheffield Puritan*, 1963, 12.
[3] Also in Force, *Tracts*, I, no.6.
[4] A.4.v.   [5] B.1.r.   [6] B.2.r-B.3.v.

Virginia is 'this earthly paradise'.[7] It is 'large and great, assuredly'; the climate 'most sweet and wholesome'.[8] The perfect solution for England's problem of overpopulation. Of course, one does not wish only the dregs to emigrate:

We intend to have of every trade and profession both honest, wise and painful men, whereof our land and city is able to spare and furnish many ... which will be glad to go, and plant themselves so happily, and their children after them, to hold and keep conformity with the laws, language and religion of England for ever.[9]

The inhabitants of the paradise are

wild and savage people that live and lie up and down in troops, like herds of deer in a forest. They have no law but nature; their apparel, skins of beasts – but most go naked. The better sort have houses, but poor ones. They can no art nor science, yet they live under superior command, such as it is. They are generally very loving and gentle, and do entertain and relieve our people with great kindness. They are easy to be wrought to good, and would fain embrace a better condition.[10]

We were once 'poor and naked Britons'. Caesar made us 'tame and civil'. And moreover

we may verily believe, that God hath reserved in this last age of the world an infinite number of those lost and scattered sheep to be won and recovered by our means.[11]

Caesar used force. Can we? For Johnson, 'just conquest by the sword' can be 'honourable'.[12] It is honourable for us 'to subdue the tyranny of the roaring lion, that devours those poor souls in their ignorance and leads them to hell for want of light'. Also, some Indians might put themselves into the position of enemies:

So many as obstinately refuse to unite themselves unto us, or shall malign or disturb our plantation, or whatsoever, belonging to us, they shall be held and reputed recusant, notwithstanding their own good, and shall be dealt with as enemies of the commonwealth of their country.

But the Virginia planters must not fall into the Spanish error, the 'murdering of so many millions of naked Indians'. They must apply 'fair and loving means, suitable to our English nature'. Do those 'fair' means include 'invasion into their right and possessions'? Certainly. For 'our intrusion into their possessions shall tend to their great good'; bringing them 'from their base condition to a far better'. We are not forcing the Indian 'according to our proverb, Out of the frying pan into the fire; but to make their condition truly more happy'. The adventurers intend

[7] B.2.r.   [8] B.4.r.   [9] D.1.v.   [10] B.4.r.-B.4.v.   [11] C.2.r.   [12] C.1.v-C.2.v.

to impart our divine riches, to their inestimable gain, and to cover their naked misery with civil use of food and clothing, and to train them by gentle means to those manual arts and skill which they so much affect, and do admire to see in us.

We require of the Indian 'a quiet residence to us and ours'. That being assured, 'they shall be most friendly welcome to conjoin their labours with ours, and shall enjoy equal privileges with us'.

These extracts may give a unrepresentative impression of the speech as a whole. Johnson seems really more interested in the navy than in the Indian.

In March 1609, the Spanish Ambassador in London forwarded a copy of *Nova Britannia* to Philip III.[13] By April it had been translated into Spanish by an English Jesuit, Father Joseph Cresswell. The Ambassador conveyed his anger about the London interest in Virginia: 'I see the people excited and insolent over this business' – and Prince Henry, the eldest son of James I, whose fifteenth birthday had fallen in February, was being approached to take the title 'Protector of Virginia'. The Virginia promoters 'have seen to it that the ministers in their sermons stress the importance of filling the world with their religion'.

John Smith, at the end of his life, thought that in these early years the Company officials in London (who 'consumed all in arguments, projects and their own conceits') were 'making religion their colour, when all their aim was but present profit'.[14]

In 1612 Johnson published a pamphlet intended as the second part of *Nova Britannia*, with the title *The New Life of Virginia*.[15] The sequel has a more theological flavour. The 'first historian that ever wrote' was Moses. He recorded that 'when the pride of earthly men, in the race and progeny of Noah, began to aspire, and sought to climb the celestial throne' God intervened, and left 'each one to his several ways, to follow the proneness and folly of his own heart'. Thus there sprang up the Gentiles, 'strangers from the commonwealth of Israel', 'guilty of that great conspiracy'; 'a barbarous and unfruitful race of mankind', a 'dispersed crew' with 'inhumane behaviour and brutish conditions' and 'innumerable languages'. But God can rescue a brand from the burning. At length, in Christ, the faithful were 'reduced home to that family of saints and sons of God'. The Indians of America are 'remnants of those scattered Gentiles'. And God 'out of his secret counsel' is beginning to extend to them his grace: who

consist of infinite confused tongues and people, that sacrifice their children to serve the devil, as those heathens did their sons and daughters to Moloch. Yet who can doubt or say, but even among those God may have his special numbers from whose necks he will now remove that heavy yoke of bondage.[16]

[13] Barbour, *Jamestown Voyages*, 256-9.
[14] Written 1630: Smith-Arber, 927-8.
[15] Force, *Tracts*, I, no.7: from which my paging is taken.   [16] 7-8.

The Indians are Gentiles of the worst sort: but they deserve our charity.

And for the poor Indians, what can I say, but God that hath many ways showed mercy to you, make you show mercy to them and theirs. And howsoever they may seem unto you so intolerable wicked and rooted in mischief, that they cannot be moved, yet consider rightly and be not discouraged; they are no worse than the nature of Gentiles; and even of those Gentiles so heinously deciphered by St Paul to be full of wickedness, haters of God, doers of wrong, such as could never be appeased.

And Paul himself lived to see many such become 'true believing Christians'.[17]

The colonists need 'patience and humanity'; to persuade the Indians' 'crooked nature to your form of civility'. Johnson quotes another proverb – 'Look how you win them, so you must wear them.' If you win them 'by way of peace and gentleness, then you shall always range them in love to yourselves, and in peace with your English people'.

Take their children, and train them up with gentleness; teach them our English tongue and the principles of religion; win the elder sort by wisdom and discretion, make them equal with your English in case of protection, wealth and habitation, doing justice on such as shall do them wrong. Weapons of war are needful, I grant, but for defence only; and not in this case. If you seek to gain this victory upon them by strategems of war, you shall utterly lose it and never come near it; but shall make your name odious to all their posterity.[18]

Of our five preachers in 1609, Richard Crakanthorpe and George Benson were former Fellows of Queen's College Oxford. Benson was now a parson in Worcestershire, and Crakanthorpe near Braintree in Essex (he was also chaplain to the Bishop of London, Thomas Ravis). Daniel Price was a graduate of Exeter College Oxford, a popular preacher at the Inns of Court. His sermon has some rather strained legal imagery: God 'hath sent down a Commission from the King's Bench of his Judgment, and another from the Chancery of his mercy'.[19] (Thomas More had used a similar theological/common law parallel in the early 1530s.)[20] Price was also chaplain to Prince Henry. William Symonds was 'preacher' at St Saviour's, Southwark. We have already met Symonds, as the editor in 1612 of the 'proceedings' of the Virginia colony which formed Part II of John Smith's *Map of Virginia*.[21] Robert Gray, 'preacher of the word of God', was surely the

---

[17] 18.   [18] 19.   [19] Price, *Sauls Prohibition staide* ..., London, 1609, B.1.v.

[20] More, *Confutation*, part II, 1533, clxxviii. Concerning predestination: 'God in all His threats reserveth His special prerogative of His mercy, by which His absolute power is never bounden under any rule of His ordinary Justice.' A similar distinction applied to the power of the King is familiar from Bate's Case (1606).

[21] See Chapter 14 above, p.289.

man who matriculated from St John's College Cambridge in 1589: the college which William Crashaw entered in 1588 and Gabriel Archer in 1591 (and where Alexander Whitaker was a child in the Master's Lodge).

Benson mentioned the 'anointed person' of the New Solomon: James I. (Or at least he did in the published text of 1610, which was longer than the actual sermon: 95 pages[22] – he had shortened it for Paul's Cross.) But Crakanthorpe took this as the main theme of his Paul's Cross sermon; he was preaching on 24 March, the sixth anniversary of James' accession. The title of Crakanthorpe's published text (54 pages) announces that 'the sovereignty of Kings is immediately from God'. The King, said the preacher, is 'placed in God's own throne, placed in the stead of God Himself among us'.[23] Both the Old and the New Testaments teach 'the imperial authority of Kings immediately and only derived from God, immediately depending of God, and of God alone'.[24] God made Solomon King over Israel: not the priests, not the people. Solomon was God's 'immediate Vice-gerent, or lieutenant over all Israel', 'immediately representing God's own person'.[25] Lewis IV, Duke of Bavaria, and Holy Roman Emperor (he was crowned by an anti-pope), had decreed in 1338 that his authority came solely and immediately from God. This 'imperial law', commented Crakanthorpe, is worthy of 'engraving in golden letters upon the walls of our houses and posts of our doors'.[26] He also quoted the statute 16 Richard II, c.5, enacted 'of purpose to keep sacred and inviolable the sovereignty and regality of this kingdom'.[27] For Crakanthorpe, orthodox academic High Calvinist, the Deity was a God of sovereign (some might say capricious) will: the Will of His Good Pleasure. The emphasis is on God's 'favour and free love'[28] (to be bestowed where He pleases). Imperial power is similar. And a King, like God, can have a 'secret will'. In an Oxford sermon on predestination, not published until 1620, Crakanthorpe told the story of a King who promises pardon to all who possess his seal – having previously sent his seal to all those he wished to pardon.[29] That is an image of both divine and royal power. Of course, James I was also Constantine.[30] (We remember Hakluyt's use of the Constantine material). And one sign of his inspired Wisdom is 'the honourable expedition now happily intended for Virginia'.[31] After all, Virginia is a 'territory as large and spacious almost as is England'.[32]

William Symonds was preaching in Whitechapel to 'the

[22] Benson. *A Sermon preached at Paules Crosse the Seaventh of May MDCIX.* London, 1609, 11.

[23] Crakanthorpe. *A Sermon at the Solemnizing of the Happie Inauguration of our most gracious and religious Soveraigne ... Preached at Paules Crosse the 24 of March last.* London, 1609, G.3.r.

[24] E.1.v. [25] D.4.v. [26] E.2.v. [27] E.3.r. [28] B.1.v.

[29] *A Sermon of Predestination, preached at Saint Maries in Oxford.* London, 1620, page 16.

[30] 1609 Sermon. B.4.v.

[31] D.2.r. [32] D.2.v.

adventurers and planters for Virginia' (the running title of the published text was *Virginea Britannia*: 54 pages).[33] In the preface, Symonds described himself as a man 'most heartily affected in the cause of Virginia'; a land 'of old times offered to our kings', until Elizabeth 'being a pure virgin, found it, set foot on it, and called it Virginia'. Now James,

> our most sacred sovereign, in whom is the spirit of his great ancestor Constantine, the pacifier of the world and planter of the gospel in places most remote, desireth to present this land a pure virgin to Christ.

The preface ends with a prayer.

> Lord, finish this good work thou hast begun; and marry this land, a pure virgin, to thy kingly son Christ Jesus; so shall thy name be magnified, and we shall have a virgin or maiden Britain, a comfortable addition to our Great Britain.

In the sermon itself, Symonds pictured Virginia as 'more like the garden of Eden, which the Lord planted, than any part else of the earth'.[34] It is certainly no wilderness.

> The land, by the constant report of all that have seen it, is a good land; with the fruitfulness whereof, and pleasure of the climate, the plenty of fish and food, England our mistress cannot compare.

He had seen in London ears of Indian corn ten inches round and fifty inches long.[35] Symonds was to make similar Biblical allusions in his 1612 postscript:[36] 'the land is good',

> there is no cities, so no sons of Anak: all is open for labour of a good and wise inhabitant. And my prayer shall ever be, that so fair a land may be inhabited by those that profess and love the Gospel.

Daniel Price (the published title of whose sermon[37] characterised it as 'the indictment of all that persecute Christ, with a reproof of those that traduce the honorable plantation of Virginia') played with the obvious Old Testament precedent: 'go and possess the land; it is a good land, flowing with milk and honey.' Virginia, he said, equals

> Tyrus for colours, Basan for woods, Persia for oils, Arabia for spices, Spain for silks, Tharsis for shipping, Netherlands for fish, Bononia for fruit, and, by tillage, Babylon for corn; besides the abundance of mulberries, minerals, metals, pearls, gums, grapes, deer, fowl, drugs for physic, herbs for food,

[33] Symonds. *Virginia: a sermon preached at Whitechapel in the presence of … the Adventurers and Planters for Virginia*, April 25, 1609. London 1609. Facsimile reprint 1968, series 'The English Experience', Amsterdam and New York.
[34] 26.   [35] 24.   [36] Barbour, *Jamestown Voyages*, 464.
[37] Price, *Sauls Prohibition staide* …

roots for colours, ashes for soap, timber for building, pasture for feeding, rivers for fishing, and whatsoever commodity England wanteth. The philosopher commendeth the temperature, the merchant the commodity, the politician the opportunity, the divine the piety in converting so many thousand souls.

One should honour the Virginia enterprise if only in remembrance of Elizabeth, 'first godmother to that land and nation'. Also because

that virgin country may in time prove to us as the barn of Britain, as Sicily was to Rome; or the garden of the world, as was Thessaly; or the argosy of the world, as is Germany.[38]

Price has some trenchant reflections on the state of England. His rhetoric is too studiously mannered to be wholly effective, in fact. England is a 'wilderness' now – by implication, the prelude to the Promised Land. The wilderness is a place of Confusion: an image of the world itself, 'a dungeon of condemned persons, scrawling about the globe of the earth, in the theatre of their misery and mortality'.

This world a wilderness, a dry, heathy, thorny, bare, barren wilderness, wherein Satan the serpent, sin the satyr, wrath the lion, lust the leopard ... ; wherein virtue is an exile, conscience a hermit, honesty a stranger, truth a prisoner; a wild wilderness wherein all things are most miserable.[39]

England is bedevilled by 'pride of the court', 'usury of the city', 'dissension in the clergy', 'oppression in the gentry', 'disobedience in the communalty'.[40] The Devils of modern London – a catalogue of unbelief:[41]

to whom nothing is accounted evil, because nothing accounted good; nothing can be a sin, because nothing is a law; the first article of whose creed is in profession that there is no God; the second, that the story of the creation is a fable, the mystery of the incarnation fallible, the doctrine of redemption improbable, of election unprofitable, of predestination unavailable, of the resurrection impossible; the next, that there is no heaven, no hell, adding the corollary that if there be a hell, and they must to it, they hope that they shall not lack company.

London should be Jerusalem, the City of God. But 'it is become murder's slaughter house, theft's refuge, oppression's safety, whoredom's stews, usury's bank, vanity's stage'.[42]

Price was also appalled by what Christopher Hill has authoritatively discussed: 'the lay grip on the church.'[43] He attacked those laymen who had 'engrossed the livings of the church'.[44] This has led to 'the dejected state of the royal priesthood, the clergy'; who now

---

[38] F.3.r-v. [39] B.1.v. [40] E.2.v. [41] E.3.r. [42] F.3.v.
[43] Hill, *Economic Problems of the Church*, 1956.
[44] Price, F.1.v.

could at the most seek 'but ordinary favours' – 'their ancient honours, their honour, lieth in the dust.' The clergy must have 'privileges': 'is not God's cause theirs?' One thinks of John Colet, preaching to the same effect in London a century before.[45] The high conception of the clergy was common to mystical Catholic and clerical Puritan. Price referred to a judgement of Sir Edward Coke, "a religious and good heart', that 'the contempt of the clergy will be the downfall of religion'.

Dr Benson also professed to be pessimistic about England. The preachers were concerned to imply, of course, that the New Jerusalem lay across the Atlantic. England, said Benson, in former times was 'plain and downright'. Nowadays the foreigners have too much influence: 'men that should be mere English are not themselves, but compounded men: Spanish, Dutch, Italian and what not.'[46] Crakanthorpe, Symonds and Gray, in the tradition of Hakluyt and Hayes, put their finger on over-population as the key factor. Gray, whose printed text was titled *A Good Speed to Virginia*[47] (a most unattractive performance), asserted that in the old days 'there was room enough in the land for every man, so that no man needed to encroach or enclose from another' – for one thing, we had civil war and war abroad, which helped.[48] Kingdoms, like bodies, need to be bled. We have a duty to eject 'unnecessary multitudes'; there are in England too many 'degenerate and dunghill minds'.[49] Symonds' material on overpopulation is particularly effective, in its bullying way. The people 'swarm in the land'. There are villains: rich landlords, corn-mongers and shopkeepers. There are heroes: the farmer, the christian merchant, the honest labourer, the deserving poor. Working from the metaphor of a beehive, Symonds presents the ills of his time in a passage which deserves full quotation:[50]

The people, blessed be God, do swarm in the land, as young bees in a hive in June, insomuch that there is very hardly room for one man to live by another ... The mightier, like old strong bees, thrust the weaker, as younger, out of their hives. Lords of manors convert townships in which were a hundred or two hundred communicants, to a shepherd and his dog.

Francis Bacon, speaking in the House of Commons in 1597 about the dangers of enclosure, had imagined an England 'naught but green fields, but a shepherd and his dog'.[51] Symonds continues:

---

[45] Colet, 1512 Sermon in St Paul's to the Canterbury Convocation: in Williams (ed.), *English Historical Documents 1485-1558*, 652-60.

[46] Benson, 26-7.

[47] Gray, *A Good Speed to Virginia*, London, 1609, edited 1937 by W.F. Craven for 'Scholars Facsimiles and Reprints', New York.

[48] B.2.r-v.   [49] B.4.v-C.1.r.

[50] Symonds, 19-22.

[51] D'Ewes, *Journals*, 1693, 557.

The true labouring husbandsman, that sustaineth the prince by the plough, who was wont to feed many poor, to set many people on work, and pay twice as much subsidy and fifteens to the king for his proportion of earth as the landlord did for ten times as much, that was wont to furnish the church with saints, the musters with able persons to fight for their sovereign, is now in many places turned labourer, and can hardly scape the statute of rogues and vagrants. The gentleman hath gotten most of the tillage in his hand; he hath rotten sheep to sell at Michaelmas, his summer-fed oxen at Easter, asking no better price for hay than his beasts, to keep that till spring that they got at grass. By these means he can keep his corn till the people starve; always provided that the poor husbandmen which are left, and the clothier, must buy their feed and wool at such a rate that shall wear them out in a very few years. And were it not that the honest and christian merchant doth often help (who putteth all his estate on the providence of God – which they call venturing) to bring corn into the land (for which he hath many a bitter curse of the cursed cornmongers) we should find an extreme famine in the midst of our greatest plenty. The rich shopkeeper hath the good, honest, poor labourer at such advantage, that he can grind his face when he pleaseth. The poor metal man worketh his bones out, and swelteth himself in the fire; yet for all his labour, having charge of wife and children, he can hardly keep himself from the alms box. Always provided that his masters to whom he worketh will give never a penny towards his living: but they can tell of their own knowledge that if the poor man were a good husband he might live well, for he receiveth much money in the year at their hands – very near fourpence for every sixpennyworth of work. The thoughtful poor women that hath her small children standing at her knee and hanging on her breast, she worketh with her needle and laboureth with her fingers, her candle goeth not out by night, she is often deluding the bitterness of her life with sweet songs, that she singeth to a heavy heart. Sometimes she singeth 'Have mercy on me Lord', sometimes 'Help Lord, for good and godly men do perish and decay', sometimes 'Judge and revenge my cause O Lord': and many such like, which when a man of understanding doth hear, he doth with pity praise God that hath given such means to mock hunger with and to give patience. I warrant you her songs want no passion. She never said 'O Lord' but a salt tear droppeth from her sorrowful head, a deep sigh breatheth as a furnace from her aching heart that weepeth with the head for company with tears of sweetest blood. And when all the week is ended, she can hardly earn salt for her water-gruel, to feed on upon the Sunday. Many such sweets are in England; which I know not how better to interpret than to say the strong old bees do beat out the younger, to swarm and hive themselves elsewhere.

'The honest and christian merchant' who ventures, puts 'all his estate on the providence of God'. The sentiment goes back to Tyndale. *The Obedience of a Christian Man* (1528) had a passage which marks the end of a medieval ideal:[52] 'He that bideth in the world, as the monks call it, hath more faith than the cloisterer: for he hangeth on God in all things.' He must trust God to send him a good employer, good neighbours, a good wife, and a good merchant, 'to send his merchandise safe to land'. His charity is greater than that of the monk: for 'he doth service always unto his neighbour'.

[52] Tyndale, *Works*, Parker Society, I, 280.

The theme was of course especially relevant in the City of London. Benson acknowledged 'the necessity of the merchant's trade; which triumpheth as a Queen in this honorable city'. He continued, in familiar puritan fashion, to condemn fugitive and cloistered virtue, as mistakenly practised by St Francis and those who 'do sequester themselves from the world, affecting a monastical life'. Francis 'joyed in solitariness, and a private life'; but such lives are 'a continual rowing against the stream', and its devotees 'ever quarrelled with human society, like candles turned downwards, choking the flame of themselves with the oil of themselves'.[53] An essay written in 1603 by one of the editors of William Perkins' *Treatise of the Vocations, or Callings of Men* had placed such prejudices elegantly in the framework of a 'world picture'.[54]

The preachers of 1609 did indeed await a Profit. 'My beloved,' exhorted Price at Paul's Cross, 'to the present assurance of great profit, add this future profit: that whosoever hath a hand in this business shall receive an unspeakable blessing'.[55] The balance of riches and covetousness was to be nicely indicated by Ralph Hamor at Jamestown in 1615:[56] 'What more profitable than to purchase great wealth; which most people nowadays gape after overgreedily?''

Such great wealth in Virginia would be set in the context of the godly commonwealth, under a godly colonial governor. It was his responsibility to establish true religion, and to repress heresy and schism. The security of a commonwealth demands a uniformity of doctrine. Benson quoted Calvin on the evils of one state having more than one religion.[57] And Benson took advantage of the occasion to malign the Separatists, 'Brownists and Barrowists, peace-breakers of the Church'; though England was now 'not much molested with them'[58] (for over fifteen years they had sought refuge in Holland, we note). Benson's ironic portrayal of that particular type of 'godliness' was in the tradition of satire to be graced by Ben Jonson, and Thomas Morton of *New English Canaan*; and memorably expressed in 1593 by Richard Hooker in the sharper sections of the Preface to *Of the Laws of Ecclesiastical Polity*.[59] The Barrowists and Brownists (followers of the Cambridge schismatics Henry Barrow and Robert Browne) 'pretend such an abhorring of evil company', scoffed Benson, 'that they look asquint and disdainfully upon all men, as not being holy enough to converse with themselves'. They 'weave unto themselves a garment of righteousness'; and indulge in a sort of spiritual masturbation – 'the varnish of their own hypocrisy deludes them so, that they make love unto themselves, and grow amorous of their own virtues.'

[53] Benson, 25-6.
[54] No.25 in Porter, *Puritanism in Tudor England*.
[55] Price, F.3.r.
[56] Hamor, *True Discourse of the Present Estate of Virginia*, 1615, 48.
[57] Benson, 31.
[58] 27.
[59] Especially Ch.8 of the 'Preface'.

So little love to their equals have these men, that when the rod of God is shaken over our heads they make themselves the only men that are fit to stand in the gap. They blaze the honour of their own preaching as though it were so full of life that they only knew the blood and marrow of the scripture; of their prayers as though they were so effectual that Elias his spirit were only redoubled upon them, and that everyone of them is a second Elizeus.

Their illusion of infallibility means that the 'reverend fathers' of the Church of England are by them 'scorned, disobeyed, resisted'. For 'we of the Church of England are not true members of the Church, nor our Church the true Church of God, because stained (say they) with irreligion and impiety'.[60]

One doubts whether Benson's respect for the 'reverend fathers' of the *Ecclesia Anglicana* would have extended to embrace Crakanthorpe's view of episcopacy and the apostolic succession:[61] bishops having, said Crakanthorpe, 'an assured and undeniable warrant, not only from all antiquity and the renowned practice of the whole primitive church, but even from the apostles themselves and from the divine institution and ordinance of the Lord' (Hooker would have blinked, although the point of view was becoming fashionable in England from the early 1590s). But Benson concurred with Crakanthorpe's dislike of Schism – condemned as 'diabolical', said Crakanthorpe, by Calvin himself, 'a late learned man'. Crakanthorpe (in a passage which reminds one of John Whitgift) condemned the 'new Donatists'[62] who

can abide no spot or wrinkle in the Church; who cry to others, Depart, depart ye, go out from thence and touch no unclean thing; or, Stand apart and come not near us, we are holier than thou.

He echoed Whitgift's dislike of Singularity (individualism) and Popularity (government by majority vote). The presbyterian and separatist (congregational) puritans from the 1570s had been swayed by 'the zeal of opposition and predominancy of popularity and contentious humours'. They would have set the Ark of the Lord 'upon a cart'. But James resolved the discords, and

firmly settled and established the Ark of the Lord upon those holy mountains of Zion on which, even from the most pure and primitive days of the church, and from the apostles themselves, it had ever rested.[63]

Similarly must it rest in Virginia. Gray, outlining the duties of the authorities there (with quotation from Plato's *Laws*, and reference to Alexander the Great) warned that a priority of the Virginia Company must be the provision of clergy.[64] So long, of course, as the clergy are obedient to the civil magistrate:

[60] Benson, 27-8.
[61] Crakanthorpe, C.4.r.
[62] C.3.v.   [63] C.4.v-D.1.r.
[64] Gray, D.3.r.

As the minister, being a subject, must yield his obedience to the magistrate, so the magistrate must be careful to yield him countenance to keep him from neglect, and maintenance to encourage him in his ministry.

The sermons of 1609 make quite clear that there had been debate in England not only about the use of planting colonies, but about the morality. The preachers were nervously sensitive to opposition, actual or potential – from what Price called 'our own lazy, drowsy yet barking countrymen'.[65] On this theme, Symonds rose to his most offensive rhetoric. Some think that the planting of colonies is odious, that the possession of Indian territory is against 'conscience and equity' (such critics 'think themselves to be very wise).[66] Such a critic comes 'dropping out of some anabaptists' spicery' with 'a cankered mouth and a stinking breath', opening 'his school in the fantastical shop of his addle imagination'; in the end he will be 'hissed out of the universities'[67] (did opposition especially come from Cambridge and Oxford, and perhaps the Inns of Court: the three universities of England?). Symonds invoked the noble Roman and the noble Saxon:[68]

Is only now the ancient planting of colonies, so highly praised among the Romans and all other nations, so vile and odious among us, that what is and hath been a virtue in others must be sin in us? And if our objector be descended of the noble Saxon's blood, let him take heed lest while he cast a stone at us he wounds his father, that first brought him in his loins from foreign parts into this happy isle.

That was more about 'use' than morality – a point to be developed later.

Neither Price nor Crakanthorpe had very much to say about the Indian himself. Price stressed that 'a savage country' is 'to become a sanctified country'. The assumption being that the 'Virginian' yearns for the English presence: 'the angel of Virginia crieth out to this land, as the angel of Macedonia did to Paul: O come and help us.'[69] Crakanthorpe said a little more, but did not go beyond the obvious. The Indian lives in 'brutish incivility'. The 'poor and savage and to be pitied Virginians' in 'the blindness of their infidelity and superstition do offer sacrifices, yea even themselves, unto the Devil'. (William White and John Smith have a lot to answer for.) Incivility is to be replaced by 'humanity'; and superstition by 'religion' – 'reducing' the Indian to 'faith and salvation by Christ'.[70] There is the feel that the Virginia enterprise fell into place as an appendix to the Old Testament: the English being

[65] Price, F.2.v.
[66] Symonds, 10.
[67] 13-14.   [68] 15.
[69] Price, F.2.v-F.3.r.
[70] Crakanthorpe, D.2.v.

the means or furtherers of so so happy a work, not only to see a new Britain in another world, but to hear also those as yet heathen, barbarous and brutish people, together with the English, to learn the speech and language of Canaan.[71]

The Old Testament imperative was stressed by Symonds and Gray. Indeed Symonds began his sermon with the Book of Genesis. His text was Chapter 12, verses 1 to 3:

Now the Lord had said unto Abraham, Get thee out of thy country, and from thy kindred, and from thy father's house, unto a land that I will show thee. And I will make of thee a great nation, and I will bless thee, and make thy name great; and thou shalt be a blessing. And I will bless them that bless thee, and curse him that curseth thee; and in thee shall all families of the earth be blessed.

By page 9 (out of 54) we have been taken through the Bible to the words of Christ to his Disciples, as given by Mathew: 'Go ye therefore, and teach all nations, baptising them in the name of the Father, and of the Son, and of the Holy Ghost.' Symonds was preaching to the new children of Israel; reminding them of the directive to Abraham. He was of course aware of the 'black legend' of Spanish policy in the Americas. There are those who 'tear in pieces, murder and torment the natural inhabitants, with cruelties never read nor heard of before', who 'burn millions of them, and cast millions into the sea', or 'bait them with dogs, that shall eat up the mothers with their children': such atrocities are the work of 'purple Rome', that is, 'Antichrist and his fry'.[72] Every Spanish or Portuguese vessel crossing the Atlantic has its cargo of Jesuits and Friars. This of course is a bad thing. But Symonds is forced to compare such active faith with the 'snorting idleness of the ministry' in England.[73]

Symonds' conception of the Indian was sombre. Virginia is 'a waste country, where the people do live but like deer in herds'. Like the deer, they are naked: they 'have not as yet attained unto the first modesty that was in Adam, that knew he was naked'. They 'know no god but the devil, nor sacrifice, but to offer their men and children unto Moloch'.[74] Thus 'their god is the enemy of mankind, "that seeketh whom he may devour"'. Fortunately they are no match for an armed European Christian: 'a mat is their strongest portcullis, a naked breast their target of best proof, an arrow of reed on which there is no iron their most fearful weapon of offense.'[75]

One thing is quite clear. The English must not marry the Indians.[76]

Then must Adam's posterity keep to themselves. They may not marry nor give in marriage to the heathen, that are uncircumcised. And this is so plain

---

[71] D.3.r.
[72] Symonds, 14.
[73] 54. [74] 15. [75] 25. [76] 35.

that out of the foundation arose the law of marriage among themselves. The breaking of this rule may break the neck of all good success of this voyage; whereas by keeping the fear of God, the planters in short time, by the blessing of God, may grow into a nation formidable to all the enemies of Christ.

Symonds is arguing, in Old Testament terms, for the cohesion and integrity of an elect nation in covenant with God, and faced with 'heathen'. The 'rule' has no relevance to colour; except in so far as the mark of the Faith was whiteness. Whiteness is of course an image of purity: blackness an image of darkness and evil. It was to be a common belief in later seventeenth century England that at the resurrection, negroes will appear white. Sir Thomas Browne, M.D., wrote in the reign of Charles II that: 'Some Negroes who believe the Resurrection, think that they shall rise white.'[77] It seems that in the early seventeenth century, colour was invoked more often than not for literary rather than ethnological purposes. Here is William Strachey saluting in sonnet form the London Council of the Virginia Company in 1612:[78]

> And where white Christians turn in manners Moors
> You wash Moors white with sacred Christian blood.

To comment on the assumptions, allusions and traditions behind that couplet would require a separate essay!

The Colonist John Rolfe, anxious to marry Pocahontas in 1614, was to be tortured by the Old Testament 'rules' mentioned by Symonds in 1609.[79]

Robert Beverley of Virginia, born in 1673, wrote in 1705:[80]

Intermarriage had been indeed the method proposed very often by the Indians in the beginning, urging it frequently as a certain rule that the English were not their friends if they refused it. And I can't but think it would have been happy for that country, had they embraced this proposal.

Two 'certain rules' in collision! Beverley thought marriage a 'kind method' of conversion. And it would have lessened that Indian 'jealousy' of the English which Beverley took to be the First Cause of animosity. William Byrd II, writing in the 1720s, elaborated the point, in his discussion of early years in Jamestown:[81]

They had now made peace with the Indians, but there was one thing wanting to make that peace lasting. The natives could by no means persuade themselves that the English were heartily their friends, so long as they disdained to intermarry with them. And, in earnest, had the English

---

[77] Browne, *Christian Morals*, part II, section VI.
[78] Quoted by Wright, introduction to *Virginia Britania*, xxvi.
[79] See above, pp.111-12.
[80] *History and Present Estate of Virginia*, 38.
[81] 'History of the Dividing Line': Pearce, *Colonial American Writing*, 417-18.

consulted their own security and the good of the colony – had they intended either to civilise or convert these Gentiles – they would have brought their stomachs to embrace this prudent alliance.

Morals and all considered, I can't think the Indians were much greater heathens than the first adventurers, who, had they been good Christians, would have had the charity to take this only method of converting the natives to Christianity. For, after all that can be said, a sprightly lover is the most prevailing missionary that can be sent amongst these or any other infidels. Besides, the poor Indians would have had less reason to complain that the English took away their land, if they had received it by way of portion with their daughters. Had such affinities been contracted in the beginning, how much bloodshed had been prevented, and how populous would the country have been, and consequently how considerable? Nor would the shade of the skin have been any reproach at this day; for if a Moor may be washed white in three generations, surely an Indian might have been blanched in two.

Of course, an eighteenth-century Virginia planter was hardly likely to be obsessed by the Book of Ezra.

Symonds dealt brusquely with scruples about two points: the dispossession of the Indian, and the use of force in colonisation,[82] There are those who maintain that rulers 'must not make offensive wars', even 'if it were to gain the whole world to Christ' (such people as Erasmus, he might have conceded). Nonsense. We whip children to educate them – an observation to be approvingly quoted by William Strachey in 1612.[83] And 'what wrong I pray you did the apostles in going about to alter the law of nations, even against the express commandment of the prince, and set up the throne of Christ?' Some argue that Virginia 'is possessed by owners that rule and govern it in their own right; then with what conscience and equity can we offer to thrust them, by violence, out of their inheritance?'[84] In his own exposition of true conscience and equity, Symonds developed his commendation of 'the strong title of the sword', a title 'magnified by historians, politicians and civilians'; albeit to the loathed objectors no more than 'a spider's web, or the hatching of a cockatrice his egg'. History shows us many admirable 'conquering and subduing nations'.[85] We look at Assyria, Persia, Greece and Rome. More important, we consult the stories of the Old Testament – true histories. Did not God approve of Cyrus, Jacob, Joseph, David, Solomon and Joshua?[86] (Joshua, as we have seen in Chapter 5, was regarded as an honorary member of the Virginia Company.)

Gray was especially at home in the Old Testament. His basic dogma was that every 'example' approved in the Bible was a 'precept':[87] that is, a rule of action for 1609 (a much discussed – and disallowed – conception of the interpretation of scripture). Joshua told

[82] Symonds, 13-14.
[83] *Virginia Britania*, 24.
[84] Symonds, 10.
[85] 11. [86] 13.
[87] Gray, B.3.r. See above, pp.98, 113-15. Below, 365-72.

his people to 'enlarge their territories and dilate their borders by destroying God's enemies'.[88] Thus 'the children of Joshua' have an 'express commandment' to 'destroy those idolators and possess their land':[89]

As every example in the scripture, as I said, is a precept, we are warranted by this direction of Joshua to destroy wilful and convicted idolators rather than let them live, if by no other means they can be reclaimed.[90]

Also, David 'doth promise a blessing to those that shall take the children of the idolatrous Babylonians and dash them against the stones'. Thus there is a firm direction for all Christians: 'they that have taken arms against such a people are said to fight the Lord's battles.'[91]

The tradition of Christian thought, Gray claimed, is firm on this point. All true writers on affairs of state

do with one consent hold and maintain that a Christian king may lawfully make war upon a barbarous and savage people, and such as live under no lawful or warrantable government, and may make a conquest of them, so that the war be undertaken to this end, to reclaim and reduce those savages from their barbarous kinds of life and from their brutish manners to humanity, piety and honesty.

St Augustine wrote that war was warranted if undertaken in the interests of peace, and for the suppression of 'lewd and wicked men'. Augustine, had he been resident in London in 1609, would confirm that 'we might lawfully make war upon the savages of Virginia'.[92]

Milton, in his *History of Britain* (published 1671) was to reflect on 'the necessity of war and dominion'.[93] There are 'wasting and ruining wars', pursued by 'greedy and violent men', 'wild beasts and destroyers' compelled by 'ambition and the love of rapine'. But war can be used 'not to destroy but to prevent destruction, to bring in liberty against tyrants, law and civility among barbarous nations' – by the Miltonic hero of 'just and true valour': with 'recourse to the aid of Eloquence'.

Gray reminded his congregation of the reports that the Indian was 'by nature loving and gentle'. Also, that he was 'desirous to embrace a better condition'. Desirous, that is, of conversion: 'Oh how happy were that man that could reduce this people from brutishness to civility, to religion, to Christianity, to the saving of their souls.'[94] The English should emulate Columbus, adept at winning over the Indian. They must 'first try all means before weapons': 'weapons should always be the last means.' If the sword is resorted to, it must not be because of 'ambition, or greediness, or gain, or cruelty, or any private respect whatsoever'; but because of 'necessity of preserving our own

[88] C.1.r. [89] C.3.r. [90] C.2.r. [91] C.1.r-v. [92] C.4.r-v.
[93] Beginning of Book II: ed. French Fogle, Yale, 1971, 40.
[94] Gray, C.2.v.

lives' against 'the enemies of God'. Bloody cruelty is always to be eschewed.[95] The object of any use of force must be to bring the Indian

to a civil and Christian kind of government, under which they may learn how to live holily, justly and soberly in this world, and to apprehend the means to save their soul in the world to come, rather than to destroy them or utterly to root them out. For a wise man, but much more a Christian, ought to try all means before they undertake war. Devastation and depopulation ought to be the last thing which Christians should put in practice.[96]

By nature the Indian may be loving and gentle. By fact he is 'barbarous and savage'. Gray comments on colonists' literature available in 1609:[97]

The report goeth that in Virginia the people are savage and incredibly rude; they worship the devil, offer their young children in sacrifice unto him, wander up and down like beasts, and in manners and conditions differ very little from beasts, having no art, nor science, nor trade to employ themselves or give themselves unto.

Such a negative view of the American Indian was to appeal to Thomas Hobbes, who used the example of the Indian on three occasions. In noting the disadvantages of a state of perpetual war he pointed out that 'they in America are examples hereof, even in the present age', with an existence 'fierce, short-lived, poor, nasty, and deprived of all that pleasure and beauty of life which peace and society are wont to bring with them'.[98] No *douceur de vivre*. In *Leviathan* (published 1651) Hobbes argued that for the study of philosophy it is necessary to have both leisure and a sophisticated method. 'The savages of America are not without some good moral sentences; also they have a little arithmetic, to add and divide in numbers not too great: but they are not, therefore, philosophers'.[99] The most familiar section of *Leviathan* is that in which Hobbes portrayed the 'natural condition of mankind' as 'solitary, poor, nasty, brutish and short': a 'condition of war'.[100]

It may peradventure be thought, there never was such a time, nor condition of war as this; and I believe it was never generally so, over the world: but there are many places, where they live so generally now. For the savage people in many places of America, except the government of small families, the concord whereof dependeth on natural lust, have no government at all; and live at this day in that brutish manner.

The 'brutish manner' is a series of negatives: no 'industry', 'culture of the earth', 'navigation', 'commodious building', 'instruments of

[95] C.3.r. [96] C.2.r. [97] C.2.v.
[98] Hobbes, 'Philosophical Rudiments', *English Works*, ed. W. Molesworth, II, 12.
[99] *Leviathan*, IV, 46.
[100] *ibid.*, I, 13.

moving and removing', 'knowledge of the face of the earth', 'account
of time', 'arts', 'letters', 'society'. These passages need not be taken as
more than casual. Hobbes had no sustained knowledge of the literature
of the New World (unlike Locke). He was demonstrating that the 'state
of nature' was not what the conventional Natural Law school thought it
was – Grotius had written that 'certain tribes in America' were in a
condition of 'community of property arising from extreme
simplicity'.[101] However, there is no reason to think that Hobbes hadn't
read such interpreters of the American experience as Robert Gray.

So much for Gray's certainties and qualifications about the use of
force in missionary activity. An equally important consideration was
that of the right of the English to take over Indian territory: 'the moral
and legal justifications for dispossessing the Indians.'[102] There is a
distinction between fact and theory. In fact the Indians, said Gray,
may have a 'rightful inheritance'. And in fact the English have no
'intendment' to take this away by force; because the Indians 'have
offered to yield into our hands on reasonable conditions more land
than we shall be able this long time to plant and manure', and thus we
possess by 'lawful grant'.[103] These 'facts' did not deter Gray from
theological and legal exposition. 'The Lord hath given the earth to the
children of men': 'So may man say to himself, The earth was mine,
God gave it to me and my posterity, by the name of the children of
men.' *Was* mine; because

is the greater part of it possessed and wrongfully usurped by wild beasts and
unreasonable creatures, or by brutish savages, which by reason of their
godless ignorance and blasphemous idolatry are worse than those beasts
which are of most wild and savage nature.

It is a sin in man to

stay and take it not out of the hands of beasts and brutish savages, which
have no interest in it, because they participate rather of the nature of beasts
than men.

A supporting text here: I Kings 22, verse 3. 'And the King of Israel
said unto his servants, Know ye that Ramoth in Gilead is ours, and we
be still, and take it not out of the hand of the King of Syria?'[104]

Similarly the English are still, and take not Virginia out of the hand

[101] Grotius, *Bellum et Pacis*, Book II, Ch.11, para.2. I am indebted to Quentin
Skinner for this reference; and, more generally, for his painstaking consideration of a
query I raised in 1967 about Hobbes' knowledge of the literature concerning the
Indian. See Richard Ashcraft, 'Leviathan Triumphant: Thomas Hobbes and the
Politics of Wild Men', in Dudley and Novak (eds.), *Wild Man Within*, 1972.
[102] The title of an essay by Wilcomb E. Washburn, of the Smithsonian Institution,
in Smith (ed.), *Seventeenth-Century America*.
[103] Gray, C.4.r.
[104] B.1.v.

of the Indian. Experience and legal precedent, no less than the word of God, indicate the error of such hesitancy.

Some affirm, and it is likely to be true, that these savages have no particular propriety in any part or parcel of that country, but only a general residency there, as wild beasts in the forest; for they range and wander up and down the country without any law or government, being led only by their own lusts and sensuality. There is not *meum* and *tuum* amongst them. So that if the whole land should be taken from them, there is not a man that can complain of any particular wrong done unto him.[105]

The appeal there was to the 'Law of Nations'.

The 'lawfulness' of English occupation was also discussed in a pamphlet published in November 1610 'by advice and direction of the Council of Virginia': *A True Declaration of the estate of the Colonie in Virginia, With a confutation of such scandalous reports as have tended to the disgrace of so worthy an enterprise.*[106] (The author was probably Sir Dudley Digges: though some attribute it to Bacon.) The author argues that the Indians break 'the law of nations' if they repel or attack a 'peaceable stranger'. The 'Ethiopians, Egyptians, and men of China' have been guilty of such inhospitality. The Indians have treated the English 'as Ammon did the servants of David': 'If in him it were a just cause to war against the Ammonites, it is lawful in us, to secure ourselves against the infidels.' Possession was by permission of Powhatan: a 'lawful possession, as Pharoah gave Goshen to Israel, or Ephron sold his cave to Abraham.'

If any man allege that yet we can possess no farther limits than was allotted by composition; and that *fortitudo sine iustitia est iniquitatis materia*, fortitude without justice is but the firebrand of iniquity, let him know that Plato defined it to be no injustice to take a sword out of the hand of a mad man, that Augustine hath allowed it for a lawful offensive war *quod ulcisitur iniurias*, that revengeth bloody injuries. So that, if just offences shall arise, it can be no more injustice to war against infidels than it is when, upon just occasions, we war against Christians.

So the 'scrupulous conscience' is answered. As a clinching point:

The Church of Geneva in the year 1555 decided in a Synod, whereof Calvin was President, to send Peter Richier and William Quadrigarius under a French captain to Brazil.

This was a reference to the episode in 1556 discussed in Chapter 7, the sending of the Geneva pastors Pierre Richier and Guillaume Chartier to the French settlement on an island in the Bay of Rio de Janeiro. The Church of Geneva would not

[105] C.3.v-C.4.r.
[106] Force, *Tracts*, Vol.III, no.1.

after a synodical consultation, have sent their ministers to such an adventure, had not all scruples, in their judgement, been cleared by the light of scripture.

There is 'room sufficient' in Virginia for both English and Indian, 'the extent of an hundred miles being scarce peopled with 2,000 inhabitants'. We can 'possess part of their land, and dwell with them':

partly because there is no other moderate and mixed course to bring them to conversion but by daily conversation, where they may see the life and learn the language each of other.

And partly because 'there is no trust to the fidelity of human beasts'.
Early in 1609 – the time of our sermons – John Donne, aged 36, was living in London, looking for a job (he was not ordained until 1615). He was interested in the post of secretary to the London Council of the Virginia Company (his father-in-law was a shareholder). That particular hope came to nothing. By 1622 he was Dean of St Paul's, and an honorary member of the Virginia Company and of the London Council. And in November 1622 he was invited to preach the annual Company sermon at St Michael's, Cornhill (followed by a feast in the Merchant Taylors' Hall).[107] His text was Acts 1:8: 'Ye shall receive power, after that the Holy Ghost is come upon you: and ye shall be witnesses unto me both in Jerusalem, and in all Judaea, and in Samaria, and unto the uttermost part of the earth.' Donne took as his theme the lawfulness of the English presence in Virginia. The Law of Nations, he said (he had been a student at the Inns of Court) makes clear that territory uninhabited, or abandoned, or derelict can be rightfully possessed; and so can territory which is underpopulated, for the earth is meant for all men – a man in a fishing boat doesn't own the ocean: no more do the Indians possess America. Those who occupy the earth must see that it is 'improved', 'to the best advantage of mankind in general'. If this is not done, 'the Law of Nations may justify some force'. This is especially true for England, where God is on our side, and the English conscience is directed by the Holy Ghost: 'When the Holy Ghost is come upon you you shall have power, a new power.' The Virginia Company, acknowledged Donne – in the only passage in this sermon which is at all well known – has

made this island, which is but as the suburbs of the Old World, a bridge, a gallery, to the New: to join all to that world which shall never grow old, the kingdom of heaven.

Robert Gray's text was entered at Stationer's Hall on 3 May 1609, twelve days before the departure of the Gates' fleet; with a dedication, signed on 28 April, to 'the right noble and honorable earls, barons and

---

[107] Sermon 13 November 1622. *Sermons*, ed. Potter and Simpson, IV, no.10. R.C. Bald, *John Donne*, 1970, 436-7.

lords, and to the right worshipful knights, merchants and gentlemen, adventurers for the plantation of Virginia'. Gray much regretted that he was not able to join the adventure in person, nor did his finances allow him to invest in it. But a colonist need have no scruples about his 'good speed to Virginia': let him

examine his own heart, and if he find that he is drawn to partake in this business to draw the savages from their barbarous kind of life to a more civil, honest and christian kind of life, let him not doubt of the lawfulness of it, but let him cheerfully and liberally put helping hand to this business.[108]

For people which have no knowledge of God 'and His worship', who 'give that honour to the insensible and unreasonable creature which is only due to the omnipotent and almighty creator' cannot but be 'odious' in the sight of God.[109]

Of the five preachers in 1609, Benson is the only one who approaches Erasmian ideals of fairness and consideration. Of course, he has no time for those who condemn colonisation as usurpation. One authority, indeed, said that the Israelites were usurpers in the Promised Land, as the Goths and Vandals were in Christendom. That authority was Machiavelli![110] But Benson felt the appeal of Las Casas more openly than did his four colleagues: indeed, he mentions him by name, and repeats his message.

There were a people of the like quality with the natural inhabitants of Virginia, poor and naked things (I call them so, the more to endear your affections); when they were conquered there was that cruelty used unto them, that scandal was given unto the name of Christ; the name of Christianity grew odious unto them; by reason of that cruelty, they would let it have no room in their thoughts.

The English now have in their hands 'the key of the kingdom of God'. Benson hopes 'our English are of that metal' that 'they will not keep those weak ones out, but rather make way for the gospel, as I hope they may, by their gentle and humane dealing'.[111]

In spite of Benson, it might have seemed in 1609 that in the London pulpit the spirit of Sepúlveda had triumphed. That it did not was the contribution of William Crashaw in 1610.

[108] Gray, C.4.v.
[109] C.1.r.
[110] Benson, 60.
[111] 92.

18

1610: William Crashaw

In 1609 Thomas West, Baron De La Warr, aged thirty-two, was chosen as 'Lord Governor and Captain General of Virginia' by the Council of the Virginia Company in London. The actual commission was not issued until February 1610; but when Gates left London for Virginia in May 1609, he did so as Deputy Governor – or, more correctly, as interim Governor. De La Warr did not sail until April 1610. On 21 February 1610 a sermon was preached at the Temple Church to De La Warr, members of the Virginia Company, and intending colonists. The preacher was a shareholder; William Crashaw, Bachelor of Divinity and Preacher at the Temple. Later in 1610, on the instructions of 'L.D.' (possibly Leonard Digges), but without leave from Crashaw, the sermon was published, and dedicated to the Lords, Knights and Burgesses 'now happily assembled in Parliament', because of the 'care of many of them to advance the propagation of the gospel'. The text of *A Sermon preached in London before the right honourable the Lord Lawarre, Lord Governour and Captaine Generall of Virginia, and others of his Majesties Counsell for that Kingdome, and the rest of the adventurers in that plantation*, ran to 83 pages. The printer gave it the running title *A New-yeeres Gift to Virginea* (the New Year then beginning on 25 March).

Crashaw, former Fellow of St John's College, Cambridge, was 37, and had been for five years Preacher at the Temple Church (the college chapel, as it were, of the Inner and Middle Temple), speaking every Sunday and Thursday in term from the pulpit which in the mid-1580s had housed the debate between Walter Travers and Richard Hooker. He was born in Yorkshire in 1572, and educated in Sheffield before entering St John's as a sizar (poor student) in 1588. He graduated in 1592, when he was 19, and taught for a spell in Sheffield – until 1594, when he returned to St John's as a Fellow, age 21. After ordination in 1597 he became 'preacher of God's word' in Yorkshire; first at Bridlington, then at Beverley – where he had a large house and a stipend of over £32 a year (the average English country parson had about £8). In 1600 he became rector of Burton Agnes, near Bridlington, one of the few very wealthy livings in England, worth £200 pa. Crashaw spent most of his money on books, being an avid collector of both printed volumes and manuscripts, some surviving from the dissolved religious houses; he was here in the tradition of such committed antiquarians as John Bale, John Leland and John Dee. He also became chaplain to Lord Sheffield, Lord Lieutenant of Yorkshire and President of the Council of the North; and a friend of Tobias Matthew, Bishop of Durham from 1595 until his election as Archbishop of York in 1606. Crashaw was appointed to the Temple in 1605. The Inns of Court were the 'third university of England' – larger, and more *chic*, than Oxford and Cambridge. Crashaw found the company comfortable and delightful for a scholar. In 1612 he helped William Symonds with the editing of the material in the second part of John Smith's *A Map of Virginia*. We may assume that Raleigh Crashaw, gent, who had arrived in Jamestown in September 1608, was some sort of kinsman. In 1612 also, when he was forty, Crashaw married; and in 1613 he left the Temple, returning to Burton Agnes. 1613 was the year of the birth of his son Richard, the poet, who went up to Pembroke College Cambridge in 1631. William returned to London in 1618, to a parish in Whitechapel, and died in 1626 at the age of 53.[1]

Crashaw lived for nine years at St John's. When he matriculated in June 1588, aged 15.9 (about average), the Master of the College was a Lancashire man, William Whitaker, biblical scholar and interpreter, and a prime hammer of the papists. Whitaker's protégé among the Fellows was Henry Alvey, whose pupil Crashaw became in 1591, when he was 19. He considered Alvey 'my father in Christ', and left him a silver pot in his will. Alvey was a vehement campaigner within the university on behalf of puritans in trouble with Authority. And he was one of the clerics who had been connected in the 1580s with the move to establish within the English Church a presbyterian network of organisation. In fact, in 1589, when William Crashaw was in his second year, a secret clerical meeting had been held in the Master's Lodge, the members including Thomas Cartwright, a St John's man by origin. The anglican authorities defined this meeting as a 'Presbytery'. It was also said that Alvey had established a secret 'presbytery', or puritan inner-ring, within the college itself. Such was the allegiance of Crashaw when he graduated in 1591. Whitaker died in 1595, the year following Crashaw's return to St John's as a Fellow. Rather more than half the dons, including Crashaw and the

[1] Crashaw Bibliography. P.J. Wallis, 'The Library of William Crashaw', *Transactions Cambridge Bibliographical Society*, vol.2, part 3, 1956, 213-28. P.J. Wallis, *William Crashawe: the Sheffield Puritan*, 1963 (reprinted from *Transactions Hunter Archaeological Society*, vol.8, parts 2-5, 1960-3.) C.W. Previté-Orton, 'The Southampton Mss: a catalogue', *The Eagle*, St John's College Cambridge, June 1918. K.J. Larsen, 'The Religious Sources of Richard Crashaw's Sacred Poetry', Cambridge PhD Thesis, Faculty of English, 1969.

In 1973 Mr R.M. Fisher, then a research student at Clare College Cambridge, lent me his essays on 'Crashaw's Library', 'Crashaw as Preacher at the Temple', and 'Crashaw and the Middle Temple Globes'.

Mr Graham Harding, then a research student at St John's College Cambridge, was also helpful.

mathematician Henry Briggs, thought Alvey the obvious successor. Their campaign was unsuccessful; and Alvey was to become Provost of Trinity College Dublin.

Also in 1595 there were theological disputes in the university at large. The High Calvinism personified in Whitaker, and in William Perkins of Christ's, came under attack; by those who, in the eyes of the Whitaker-Perkins party (which included Crashaw), undermined among other things 'the comfortable certainty of true faith' (as expounded by Calvin in his discussions of Christian *securitas*). These debates were echoed in Crashaw's Virginia Company sermon. The quibbles today may seem minute; but they involved epic conceptions of the qualities of the Creator and the Creation, and the relationship between them. Those were the intellectual issues alive in Cambridge when Crashaw was ordained (1597). Perkins died in 1602; and Crashaw became one of the six editors of his work for the three volume Cambridge edition. Before 1609 he prepared five Perkins items for the Press (one of them he dedicated to Coke); some were sermons and lectures which Crashaw himself had taken down in shorthand.[2]

In 1620 an anonymous benefactor (Crashaw?) gave two gifts of books to Virginia for the proposed College: Augustine's *City of God*, and the three volume Cambridge Perkins.[3]

Perkins was an influential exponent of the art of plain preaching. Crashaw's 1610 Sermon, as one would expect, is in the Perkins manner. It has some of his tricks; the insistance on the practical application and use of the scriptural points of doctrine, the knack of the imaginative but homely parable. (George Benson's Paul's Cross Sermon of May 1609 had also sustained a Perkins-like plan; and was, again in the manner of the Master, the most stylish of the five sermons discussed in Chapter 17.)

By the time he left the Temple Church in 1613, Crashaw had collected a library of 4,000 printed books and 200 volumes of manuscripts (including works of Wyclif). It had cost him £2000. What to do with it, now he was a married man? Some items he kept. Other volumes he tried to sell; and after a few disappointments he found a buyer in another old member of St John's, Henry Wriothesley, Earl of Southampton, member of the Virginia Company (and patron of Shakespeare). The intention was to present the collection to St John's, where a new library was being built. In the event Henry died in 1624, before the library was quite ready, and the bequest was made by his son Thomas: 2000 printed books, and 162 volumes of manuscripts. These are still in the college; with the original Crashaw binding, stamp, motto and signature.

Another memorial of Crashaw is in the library of the Middle

---

[2] Volume 2 of the Cambridge Perkins edition included two Crashaw letters: prefaces to *Treatise on Christian Equity*, dated September 1603. In vol. 3 came a further four letters; and also a 1607 letter written jointly by Crashaw and another of the editors, Thomas Pierson.

[3] Kingsbury, *Records*, I, 421.

Temple; a pair of globes, one celestial, one terrestial, made in 1603 by Emery Molyneux: the latter of course had North America, and Molyneux had read Hakluyt and De Bry, and consulted Hariot and Raleigh.[4] Crashaw had bought this pair in 1603, on one of his trips to London from Burton Agnes.

As an appendix to the published text of Crashaw's sermon were grouped nine biblical quotations. Three were suggested as messages from God; three as messages from England; and three as messages from Virginia.

England says to God: 'Lord here I am: Send me' (Isaiah 6:8). England says to Virginia: 'Behold, I bring you glad tidings: Unto you is born a Saviour, even Christ the Lord' (Luke 2:10-11); and 'Come children, hearken unto me: I will teach you the fear of the Lord' (Psalm 34:11).

Virginia says to God: 'God be merciful to us, and bless us, and cause the light of thy countenance to shine upon us: let thy ways be known upon earth, and thy saving health among all nations' (Psalm 67:1-2). Virginia says to England: 'How beautiful are the feet of them that bring glad tidings, and publish salvation' (Isaiah 52:7); and 'Blessed be he that cometh to us in the name of the Lord' (Psalm 118:26).

God says to Virginia: 'He that walketh in darkness, and hath no light, let him trust in the name of the Lord, and stay upon his God' (Isaiah 50:10). God says to Europe: 'The Kingdom of God shall be taken from you' – 'too true', comments a marginal note: 'for the greater part is overrun either with Turkism or Popery' – 'and given to a nation that shall bring forth the fruits thereof' (Matthew 21:43). And God says to England: 'But I have prayed for thee that thy faith fail not: therefore when thou art converted strengthen thy brethren' (Luke 22:32).

Crashaw took this last, Lucan, text as the text for his sermon; the first third of which was a statement of the High Calvinist version of the certainty of God's covenant, the truth of His purpose, and the nature of conversion – a leisurely and limpid exegesis of the mysteries of Christian assurance, as expounded by Whitaker and Perkins in Cambridge in the 1590s. This biblical and theological approach to the Virginia enterprise was expected by the congregation. Symonds' sermon of 1609 had run to 54 pages; not until page 10 did he pause from biblical exegesis. Daniel Price and George Benson, following Perkins, broke their material down into 'doctrine' and 'the use of the doctrine'; not until page 25 (out of 95) did Benson progress from the doctrine to the use.

Thus members of the Virginia Company in February 1610 began by hearing about 'the true cause of a Christian man's standing in the state of grace'. The cause is 'out of us, even in God': 'it is the

[4] Quinn, 'The Molyneux Globes', *Roanoke Voyages*, 850-51.

stableness of His purpose, the immutability of His word, and the certainty of His love.'[5] The papists – 'the adversaries of the grace of God' – maintain that a man may fall from grace 'both finally and totally'; others, also in error, that he may fall 'totally, but not finally'. The Reformed protestant Church of England, said Crashaw, teaches what Christ himself taught: that 'a Christian truly converted and called to the state of grace, cannot fall away totally nor finally'. This is a 'doctrine of unspeakable comfort to the Christian soul'.[6]

The Virginia enterprise is for 'sanctified men'. True, there are those involved who have hope merely of

great profit, of winning a goodly country for Englishmen to live in (which now by multitudes are thrust out at home) and of living a more free and pleasant and contented life.[7]

But most of those are 'unconverted and unsanctified men'. Tell them of making a profit of 20 per cent –

Tell them of getting twenty in the hundred, and how they bite at it, oh how it stirs them! But tell them of planting a Church, of converting ten thousand souls to God, they are senseless as stones; they stir no more than if men spoke of toys and trifles; nay, they smile at the simplicities, and laugh in their sleeves at the silliness of such as engage themselves in such matters.[8]

The 'principal ends' of the enterprise are 'the plantation of a Church of English Christians there, and consequently the conversion of the heathen from the Devil to God'.[9] Such conversion is a plain and necessary duty for every converted Christian: every Christian endowed with grace. 'Remember the end of this voyage is the destruction of the Devil's kingdom, and propagation of the Gospel.'[10] Godliness is of 'a large, a liberal, a communicating and diffusive nature': 'grace is of a high and royal nature, and enlargeth his heart that possesseth it.' Thus

as many as are indued with true saving and sanctified grace, will say with their tongues, pray in their hearts, and endeavour with their best assistance that the poor savages in Virginia were as good Christians as we ourselves.[11]

Thus not to assist the Virginia enterprise can be a sign of Reprobation: 'whosoever is of ability, and knows the true grounds and ends of this voyage, if he assist it not, discovers himself to be an unsanctified, unmortified and unconverted man.'[12] The superficial

---

[5] B.1.v.

[6] A.4.v. I treated such subtleties in *Reformation and Reaction in Tudor Cambridge*, 1958, 1972: part III; and in *Puritanism in Tudor England*, 1970, part XIV: 'William Perkins'. I am not convinced by Father Kenneth Larsen's argument (see note 1) that William Crashaw's anglicanism was traditional and moderate – a stress on Richard's supposed similarities to his father.

[7] K.1.v.   [8] C.2.r.   [9] C.3.r.   [10] B.4.r.   [11] C.2.r-v.   [12] D.2.r.

implication might seem to be that no man not a member of the Virginia Company can be saved! Crashaw had guarded himself by the phrase 'knows the true grounds and ends of this voyage':

lest any man, mistaking or abusing my words, should here cavil and say, Belike then this man holds all damned that are not adventurers to Virginia, and it is a sure sign of a profane man if he be not an undertaker in that action, or the like: take notice that my assertion is qualified with these two limitations.

First, 'that a man must know the true state of this business, and true grounds and ends both of His Majesty's gracious grants and of the undertakers' adventure'. Secondly, 'he must be of ability to contribute':

for a man is bound first to maintain himself and his family, and to bear his part of the needful burdens of the Church and State where he lives; then, out of that which remains such actions as this do challenge a part.[13]

There are various discouragements to the Virginia enterprise. For one thing, 'the country is ill reported of by them that have been there'. Or by some of them. Bad news does not come from the 'better part'; it comes from 'the greater part (which generally is the worst part)' – 'the vulgar and viler sort, who went thither only for ease and idleness, for profit and pleasure, and some such carnal causes'. Similarly there were those who denied that Canaan was 'a good land, and they should overcome the heathen and enjoy it'.[14] Of course, there are important differences between God's command to the Israelites and his intentions for the English:[15]

The Israelites had a commandment from God to dwell in Canaan; we have leave to dwell in Virginia. They were commanded to kill the heathen; we are forbidden to kill them, but are commanded to convert them. They were mighty people, ours are ordinary; they armed, ours naked; they had walled towns, ours have scarce hovels to cover them; that land flowed with milk and honey, ours abounds with as good or better; they sent men to search that, so we to search this; they brought of the commodities, so have we; many slandered that country, so they do ours; more believed the slander than the truth, and so they do of ours; yet some stood boldly for the truth, and so there do in ours, and better than those that deprave it.

The Old Testament 'commandment' to occupy Canaan and exterminate the heathen is not a rule for Englishmen in 1610. Thus did Crashaw deny the use of Old Testament 'precept' by the likes of Robert Gray: an important difference in both Biblical interpretation and colonial policy.

There are, of course, difficulties in the Virginia voyage. There is the distance: but that is 'nothing to speak of' – 'a two months' voyage, and

[13] D.1.r-v. [14] F.2.r-v. [15] F.3.r-v.

we hope shall shortly be able to say a month's'.[16] There is the crossing itself: but in truth this is

the easiest, fairest and safest that hath been discovered to any place. We come not near the sun, nor under the equinoctial line, to distemper our bodies. We have no straits to pass through. We come near no enemies' country. No rocks, shelves, sands, nor unknown islands lie in our way. We are not in danger of the Turk's galleys, nor other enemies of Christian religion, who never yet did peep out of the Straits of Gibraltar. We fear no congealed seas nor mountains of ice to immure us, but after we are out of our own doors (the narrow seas) we keep a fair course, betwixt the sun in the south on the left hand and the ice in the north on the right, upon the main ocean, where we have room enough. And it is hard to name any other great voyage from this land but the passage is subject either to the untemperate heat of the sun on the one side, or the danger of the ice on the other side; witness the voyages to the East Indies, and others into the south, and to Muscovy, Danske, and others into the north and east. Only this passage into Virginia, being unto the West South West, or thereabouts, is in that true temper so fair, so safe, so secure, so easy, as though God Himself had built a bridge for man to pass from England to Virginia.[17]

(Crashaw would appear to have been reading George Peckham's 1583 *True Reporte*).[18] Another potential discouragement was the climate. But in fact not:

Examine the truth, look into the maps and cards, or, if thou hast not skill in them, look into our Patents, or if thou canst not read, or hast them not; ask and enquire of travellers by sea or land, if the land that lieth between the 34th and 45th degree of northerly latitude from the equinoctial line[19] be not far enough from the Torrida Zona and from the distempering heat of the sun. And though the middle of Virginia seem to be in the same position with the heart and middle of Spain, as Toledo or thereabouts,[20] yet it falls out, for reasons not yet fully discerned, it is not so hot as Spain, but rather of the same temper with the south of France, which is so temperate and indifferent as if our own were something nearer unto it we would be well content with it. And a further evidence that all this is true we have from the experience of a Virginian that was here with us in England, whose skin, though he had gone naked all his life till our men persuaded him to be clothed, was so far from a Moor's, or East or West Indian's, that it was little more black or tawney than one of ours would be if he should go naked in the south of England.[21]

There is a marginal note at this point: 'Their skins not black.' For an Elizabethan or Jacobean Englishmen 'Moor' probably meant 'Blackamoor', negro.[22] Or, at any rate, this was popular language. Dons knew better. George Abbot wrote in 1599 that the inhabitants of

[16] E.1.r.   [17] E.1.r-v.
[18] Passage on the advantages of the voyage, Everyman Hakluyt, VI, 70-1.
[19] That is, between Maine and South Carolina.
[20] Toledo is about the same latitude as Philadelphia.
[21] E.2.r.
[22] See Jones, *Elizabethan Image of Africa*, 1971.

the Torrid Zone are called 'Negroes, as them whom no men are blacker': they 'are not only blackish, like the Moors, but are exceedingly black'.[23]

To continue with Crashaw's inventory of possible discouragements. There were in circulation stories of miseries on the James. The fare of the colonists, 'their diet, their drink, their apparel, their houses, their bedding, their lodging, are all so poor, so pitiful, that no Englishmen are able to endure it.' Here Crashaw appeals to the virtues of our 'forefathers'. They

exposed themselves to frost and cold, snow and heat, rain and tempests, hunger and thirst, and cared not what hardness, what extremity, what pinching miseries they endured, so they might achieve the ends they aimed at.

Compare that with the 'fashion of life' we have in England in 1610.

Let us not deceive ourselves. Stately houses, costly apparel, rich furniture, soft beds, dainty fare, dalliance and pleasures, huntings and horse races, sports and pastimes, feasts and banquets, are not the means whereby our forefathers conquered kingdoms, subdued their enemies, converted heathen, civilised the barbarians, and settled their commonwealths.

Those who go to Virginia 'with purpose to live for the present, as they lived in England' are not worthy to be counted 'Fathers and Founders of a new Church and Commonwealth'. Our forefathers were a 'strong, valiant, hardy, patient and enduring people'.[24] Had they been

such mecocks and milksops as we are now, they had never expulsed the Danes, nor overcome the French. We had never quartered the arms of France, nor crowned our kings in Paris. We had never taken so many foreign kings in the field, and sometimes on their own ground. We had never made the mightiest Emperors seek alliance and marriages with us, and some of them to come in person into our land, and fight under the banners and pay of our kings.[25]

Nowadays the English have Peace and Plenty. But we abuse them[26]

by want of exercise of arms and activity, want of trades and labour; by our idleness, laziness and lasciviousness, wherein cities have laboured to match the court, and the country envies the cities. And so now at last all turn after state and pomp and pleasures; and if any occasion fall out that men should be put to any hardness, in cold and heat, by land or sea, for diet and lodging, not one of a hundred is found that can endure it.

Faced with hardship, we prefer 'the fireside in England'.

---

[23] Abbot, *Briefe Description of the whole Worlde*: section 'De Reliquis Africae regionibus maritimis'.
[24] F.4.r-v. [25] G.1.r. [26] F.4.v.

Later in the sermon, discussing the value of English prayers for Virginia, Crashaw invoked the spirit of Agincourt: Marginal Note, 'See the English Chronicle'.[27]

It is very memorable how when our noble Henry V was to give the French battle at Agincourt, where were scarce ten thousand.Englishmen, weak and sickly, against sixty thousand French, in which army was the principal chivalry of France, that valorous King, rising up from his private prayers, and having purposely put off the battle till nine of the clock, at that hour he went in person about all the host, and cheering up his people with princely words, he bade them stand to him and fight valiantly, and fear not (saith he) but be valiant and assured of victory: for at this hour they are praying for us in every church in England.

Such memories are a rebuke to 'the pusillanimity, the baseness, the tenderness and effeminateness of our English people'. Compare the Hollanders: who 'an hundred years ago' were dull, base, poor and servile; but who now, with Industry and Unity, have 'shaked off that dull and lazy humour' and have become 'the wonder of nations'. Where, oh where, is 'the ancient valour of English blood'.[28]

Crashaw's disarming rhetoric was next turned against those interested in Virginia only for Profit. Profit 'is not the principal end of this action'. Obviously not: 'If it were, what should so many of the nobility, of the gentry, and especially of the clergy, have their hands in it? It is not fit for them to be merchants.'[29] Not that Crashaw had a lack of respect for the mercantile community. In his will he left money for the maintenance of preachers in the City of London; the money to be put into the hands of honest merchants of London, preferably approved by Sir Edwin Sandys, who would then pay the clerical stipends.[30] (We remember that John Colet, a century before, had found the truest piety in the high mercantile bourgeoisie of the City of London.)[31]

But, if the intention be right, temporal benefit will duly follow:

though we do not intend our profit in this action, yet if we intend God's honour, and the conversion of souls, God will assuredly send us great profit, which we may take lawfully and thankfully as his blessing.

Daniel Price had almost said that, but not quite. Crashaw quoted words of Christ, as relayed by Matthew (6:33): 'Seek ye first the kingdom of God and His righteousness; and all other things shall be added unto us.' So, in the Virginia venture,

if we first and principally seek the propagation of the gospel and conversion of souls, God will undoubtedly make the voyage very profitable to all the

---

[27] I.4.v-K.1.r.   [28] F.4.v-G.1.v.   [29] G.3.v.

[30] Wallis, *William Crashawe: Sheffield Puritan*, 12.

[31] Or so Erasmus said: Letter about Vitrier and Colet. Olin (ed.), *Christian Humanism and the Reformation: Erasmus*, 180.

adventurers and their posterities, even for matter of this life. For the soil is good, the commodities many and necessary for England, the distance not far off, the passage fair and easy; so that there wants only God's blessing to make it gainful. Now the highway to obtain that is to forget our own affections, and to neglect our own private profit in respect of God's glory; and he that is zealous of God's glory, God will be mindful of his profit; and he that seeks only or principally spiritual things, God will reward him with both those spiritual and temporal things.[32]

One imagines that this, no less than the Calvinist dogma of Christian security, was a doctrine 'of unspeakable comfort' to Crashaw's congregation.

One final possible discouragement was the 'poor and small' beginning in 1607; the mere 'handfuls of men'. But many great states have had small beginnings. Only seventy Israelites went into the wilderness. Also 'look at the beginning of Rome, how poor, how mean, how despised it was; and yet, on that base beginning, grew to be the mistress of the world'.[33] Small; but what about the quality – are not the colonists 'disordered men', 'raked up out of the refuse'?[34] Well: 'this is true for some, not all; and so it is in every town in England.'[35] And look at the followers of David (I Samuel 22:2): 'There gathered unto David all men that were in trouble, and all that were in debt, and all that were vexed in mind: and David was their Prince, and they were about four hundred men.' A 'strange kind of people, and a poor number', one might think,[36]

to be the founders and reformers of such a kingdom. But thus hath God used to set on foot and lay the beginnings of greatest matters, that His power might be seen in weakness, and that it might appear to be the work of God and not men's, and that therefore the glory might be His. Thus deals He in things natural, human, politic and spiritual. For the first, we see He made this goodly world out of a rude and confused chaos, and the beautiful sun and stars out of a deformed heap. For the second, we see the mightiest emperors of the earth, that have made the nations tremble, were at the first crying infants, kept and carried in the arms of silly women. And thirdly, the glorious church of the New Testament, which now hath kings to be her nursing fathers and queens her nursing mothers and princes to lick the dust off her feet, was it not begun by twelve poor men, not worthy to be looked at, and taken most of them from base, and some from bad, occupations.

The nursing father and mother image was from Isaiah, 39:23: 'And kings shall be thy nursing fathers, and their queens thy nursing mothers: they shall bow down to thee with their face toward the earth, and lick up the dust of thy feet.' It had been a favourite text of Thomas Cartwright in his campaign for the primacy of the church over the magistrate.[37]

And so, even though the colonists may be 'the most disordered men

___

[32] G.3.r-v.   [33] E.2.r-v.   [34] E.2.v.   [35] E.3.v.   [36] E.4.r.
[37] Cartwright: in Whitgift, *Works*, Parker Society, III, 189.

that can be raked up out of the superfluity, or, if you will, the very
excrements of a full and swelling state',[38] they can become 'new men',
in a 'new mould'. (What, mused Crèvecoeur in the 1760s, is 'the
American, this new man?': 'Here individuals of all races are melted
into a new race.')[39] The most disordered men,

if they be removed out of the fat and feeding ground of their native country,
and from the licentiousness and too much liberty of the states where they
have lived, into a more bare and barren soil, as every country is at the first,
and to a harder course of life, wanting pleasures, and subject to some
pinching miseries and to a strict form of government and severe discipline, do
often become new men, even as it were cast in a new mould.[40]

Commonwealths 'of long continuance' may be 'ripe and rotten for
want of reformation'.[41] There could be hope of order in a 'new
government'. Crashaw had definite instructions for the New Order in
Virginia:[42]

Suffer no papists: let them not nestle there; nay, let the name of the Pope or
Popery be never heard of in Virginia. Take heed of atheists, the devil's
companions, and if thou discover any, make them exemplary, and (if I may
be so bold as to advise) make atheism and other blasphemy capital: and let
that be the first law made in Virginia. Suffer no Brownists nor factious
separatists. Let them keep their conventicles elsewhere; let them go and
convert some other heathen; and let us see if they can constitute such
churches really, the Ideas whereof they have fancied in their brains; and
when they have given us any such example, we may then have some cause to
follow them – till then we will take our pattern from their betters. Especially
suffer no sinful, no lewd, no licentious men, none that live not under the
obedience of good laws. And let your laws be strict, especially against
swearing and other profaneness. Let the Sabbath be wholly and holily
observed, public prayers daily frequented, idleness eschewed, and mutinies
carefully prevented. Be well advised in making laws; but being made, let
them be obeyed, and let none stand for scarecrows, for that is the way to
make all at last to be condemned. This course take, and you shall see those
who were to blame at home will prove praiseworthy in Virginia. And you will
teach us in England to know (who almost have forgot it) what an excellent
thing execution of laws is in a commonwealth.

The Papists were followers of Antichrist, the atheists were children
of hell. The Devil of course was an enemy of the Virginia venture, 'and
who can blame him?':

For we go to disinherit him of his ancient freehold, and to deliver from out of
his bondage the souls which he hath kept so many years in thraldom ... And
for his pleading of possession, we care not. The possession is his, but the right
is Christ's; and we are for Him, and therefore doubt not but to bring from

---

[38] E.4.v.
[39] Crèvecoeur, *Letters from an American Farmer*, published 1782. Everyman ed., 43.
[40] E.4.v-F.1.r.   [41] F.1.v.   [42] L.1.r-v.

heaven such an injunction out of the highest Court of Equity as shall remove him out of possession, maugre his malice.[43]

(We have seen from Daniel Price that no preacher in favour at the Inns of Court could resist a comparison between the Deity and the English Bench.)

The enemies of the Virginia expedition have been thus far predictable. Crashaw's last enemy is rather unexpected: Actors. Presumably rumours had reached him of *Eastward Ho*:

As for players (pardon me, right honourable and beloved, for wronging this place and your patience with so base a subject) they play with princes and potentates, magistrates and ministers, nay with God and religion and all holy things. Nothing that is good, excellent or holy can escape them; how then can this action? But this may suffice, that they are Players. They abuse Virginia, but they are but Players. They disgrace it, true, but they are but Players, and they have played with better things, and such as for which, if they speedily repent not, I dare say vengeance waits for them. But let them play on. They may make men laugh on earth, but He that sits in heaven laughs them to scorn, because like the fly they so long play with the candle till first it singe their wings, and at last burns them altogether. But why are the Players enemies to this plantation and do abuse it? I will tell you the causes. First, for that they are so multiplied here, that one cannot live by another, and they see that we send men of all trades to Virginia, but will send no Players; which if we would do, they that remain would gain the more at home. Secondly, as the Devil hates us because we purpose not to suffer heathens, and the Pope because we have vowed to tolerate no papists, so do the Players: Because we resolve to suffer no idle persons in Virginia, which course, if it were taken in England, they know they might turn to new occupations.[44]

(With regard to the first cause: after Crashaw's marriage in 1612 one of his enemies suggested that he would have been glad for certain clerics to be sent to Virginia, 'that you might have stepped into one of their rooms with your wife'.)[45]

At all events, it is clear that for Crashaw the Virginia adventurers were part of the establishment of the Kingdom of Christ in England itself. They could 'rectify and reform many disorders which in this mighty and populous state are scarce possibly to be reformed without evacuation'; as well as being 'the first beginners of one of the bravest and most excellent exploits that was attempted since the primitive times of the Church' – and also helping to 'wipe off the stain that sticks upon our nation' because of our refusal of the offer of Columbus, 'either for idleness, or some other base fears, or foolish conceits'.[46] King James and Prince Henry, in making themselves 'fathers and founders of this plantation and protectors of this royal enterprise' have shown themselves 'new Constantines or Charles the Great'.[47]

[43] H.1.v-H.2.r. [44] H.4.r.
[45] Quoted Wallis, *William Crashawe: Sheffield Puritan*, 37.
[46] K.3.r. [47] I.2.r.

And thou Virginia, whom though my eyes see not my heart shall love, how hath God honoured thee. Thou hast thy name from the worthiest Queen that ever the world had. Thou hast thy matter from the greatest King on earth. And thou shalt now have thy form from one of the most glorious nations under the sun, and under the conduct of a general of as great and ancient nobility as ever was engaged in action of the nature. But this is but a little portion of thy honour. For God is coming towards thee, and in the mean time sends to thee and salutes thee with the best blessing heaven hath, even His blessed gospel. Look up therefore, and lift up thy head, for thy redemption draweth nigh. And He that was the God of Israel, and is still the God of England, will shortly I doubt not bring it to pass that men shall say, Blessed be the Lord God of Virginia.[48]

There is a basic doubt about the enterprise, which Crashaw discusses with precision. Is it lawful? Many have been moved to ask this; some for 'conscionable and Christian reasons'. It is a 'principle of Justice' that 'a Christian may take nothing from a heathen against his will; but in fair and lawful bargain'. (Marginal Note: 'A Christian may not do wrong to a heathen.')[49] This truth stands unless 'God hath given a plain and personal charge to the contrary' – as he did to the Israelites about the 'cursed Canaanites', 'whom they were commanded to kill, and have nothing to do withal'. But 'we have no such commandment touching the Virginians'. And thus, as the instructions of the Virginia Company make clear,

we will take nothing from the savages by power nor pillage, by craft nor violence; neither goods, lands nor liberty, much less life – as some of other Christian nations have done, to the dishonour of religion. We will offer them no wrong, but rather defend them from it.

We will 'exchange with them for that which they may spare, and we do need'. Most crucially, they can spare

land and room for us to plant in, their country being not replenished by many degrees, insomuch as a great part of it lieth wild and uninhabited of none but the beasts of the field, and the trees that have grown there it may be a thousand years.[50]

This is fortunate; for 'as the present state of England stands, we want room, and are likely enough to want more'. The Indians can also spare timber, crystal, wine, copper, iron, pitch, tar, ashes for soap, and sassafras. What can the English give in return? Out of our 'humanity and conscience' we can give 'such things as they want and need, and are infinitely more excellent than all we take from them'; that is, 'Civility for their bodies' and 'Christianity for their souls'.[51]

Marginal Note: 'Civility and skill in trades and tools for trades; and government.'[52]

---

[48] L.1.v-L.2.r.   [49] D.3.r.   [50] D.3.v.   [51] D.4.r.   [52] *ibid.*

For he that hath a thousand acres and, being a civil and sociable man, knows how to use it, is richer than he that hath twenty thousand and being a savage cannot plough, till, plant nor set, and so receives no more profit than what the earth of itself will yield by nature. So that we are so far from disinheriting them of their possessions, or taking anything from them, that contrariwise we will make them much richer, even for matters of this life, than now they are; as they themselves will hereafter confess.[53]

So the secular aims of the enterprise are 'of a high and excellent nature'; not mere 'profit and pleasure'. That is why it has such honourable support:[54]

What voyage ever was there which had so many honourable undertakers, and of so many sorts and callings, both of the clergy and laity; nobility, gentry and commonalty; city and country; merchants and tradesmen; private persons and corporations? As though every kind and calling of men desired to have their hands in so happy a work.

The enterprise is also 'comfortable to the conscience of the doer'. Matthew reports Christ as saying (10:42): 'whosoever shall give to drink unto one of those little ones a cup of cold water only in the name of a disciple, verily I say unto you, he shall in no wise lose his reward.' How liberally shall the Virginia adventurers be rewarded for 'the relief of distressed and miserable souls'![55] What joy there will be among 'the glorious and innumerable multitude of holy angels' when the news reaches heaven 'that England hath enterprised the conversion of Virginia, whereby so many thousand souls shall be brought to heaven'![56] The angels might of course comment that it is about time. Many critics think it 'no small stain to our religion, that we have sent none into heathen countries to convert the savages'. This venture will 'discharge us and our religion for ever of that imputation'. The politic papists for the last hundred years have sent men 'into the West and East Indies to preach Christ; which, if they had done without other abominable idolatry and superstition, their fact had been most honorable.' In their way they have been successful: 'such is their government, and such their obedience to their superiors, wherein we may worthily learn of them.'[57]

We go to Virginia to erect temples for the Holy Ghost, 'that is, to prepare the souls of men for him to dwell in'; to erect the throne of Christ, 'even there where Satan's throne is'.[58] Satan rules over the Indians: Crashaw makes the point twice.[59] Also in 1613 he was to write of Virginia: 'Satan visibly and palpably reigns there, more than in any other known place of the world.'[60] The more dramatic the challenge, the more reputable the conversion. We go to enlarge the Kingdom of God, and 'to accomplish the number of his elect'.[61]

[53] D.4.r-v. [54] I.1.r. [55] I.1.v. [56] I.4.r. [57] K.2.r-v. [58] I.2.r. [59] I.2.r.K.3.v.
[60] Preface to Whitaker, *Good News from Virginia*, C.2.r.
[61] I.2.r.

Opinions have always varied in Christian thought about whether the number of the elect is small, or not so small. This debate was now focused on the unsuspecting American Indian. In 1609, as we have seen, the layman Robert Johnson believed that God had reserved 'an infinite number of those lost and scattered sheep'.[62] Writing from Jamestown in 1615, Ralph Hamor was more cautious about the Indians; 'of whom undoubtedly, as in other parts of the world, He hath predestined *some* to eternal salvation.'[63] Crashaw does not commit himself in these matters of dogmatic mystical mathematics.

God will incline the hearts of the Indians 'lovingly to call and invite us, and to use our men well: when they themselves are well used'.[64] In fact we have already been given 'favour in the eyes of the savages, who rather invite us than resist us'. And the Indians are 'a people inclinable (as we see by some experience already) first to civility, and so to religion'.[65] (The conversion of souls comes 'after they first be made civil men'.)[66] The Indians 'invite us, and use us well'; and 'when they are converted, and love their own souls, then they will love us also, and eternise their names who brought the gospel to them'.[67]

We English were once like the Virginia Indians. Time was

when we were savage and uncivil, and worshipped the Devil, as they do now. Then God sent some to make us civil, others to make us Christians. If such had not been sent us, we had yet continued wild and uncivil, and worshippers of the Devil. For our civility, we were beholden to the Romans; for our religion, to the apostles and their disciples ... In what a case had we been if God had not sent some to civilise and convert us. And shall not we now labour to procure the same to others?

Marginal Note: 'We must do as we have been done unto.' If we do not – Crashaw brings us back to Luke 22:32 – we cannot ourselves have been 'truly and effectually converted'.[68]

In a moving passage, surely designed to counteract the bleak conception of the Indian purveyed by such as Robert Gray, Crashaw points out that the Virginia Indians are 'our brethren':[69]

The same God made them as well as us, of as good matter as He made us; gave them as perfect and good souls and bodies as to us; and the same Messiah and Saviour is sent to them as to us. For if a Virginian having our language had learned our religion, professed our faith, craved baptism, and challenged salvation by Christ, could either man deny him baptism, or would God deny him salvation? Surely God would not the one, and man may not the other. So then they are our brethren; wanting not title to Christ, but the knowledge of Christ. O thrice happy then are they that carry the knowledge to them.

[62] *Nova Britannia*, C.2.r.
[63] Hamor, *True Discourse of the Present Estate of Virginia*, 46-7. My italics.
[64] I.3.r.   [65] C.3.v.   [66] K.1.v.   [67] H.1.r.   [68] C.4.v.   [69] C.3.r-v.

Crashaw held 'every man bound to assist' the Virginia plantation; with prayers; with money; or in person. 'I will press none to go in person':[70] but

those whose consciences and resolutions do press themselves, I doubt not to affirm that they adventure their lives in the most worthy action that was attempted in the Christian world these many years.

One person there was whose conscience at that time was pressed. This was a close friend of Crashaw, twenty-five years old, newly ordained, serving his first pastoral charge in Yorkshire: Alexander Whitaker of Trinity College Cambridge, son of the late Dr William Whitaker, Master of St John's.

[70] D.1.r.

PART THREE

19

Alexander Whitaker, Cambridge Apostle to Virginia 1611-17

The Reverend Alexander Whitaker arrived in Jamestown in May 1611, one of the three hundred people in three ships under Sir Thomas Dale (who, like Sir Thomas Gates, was a soldier released from the service of the States General of Holland). Whitaker seems to be the fourth cleric to arrive in Jamestown, four years after the founding of the settlement. There had been Robert Hunt, who died in 1608; the 'puritan' who occasioned discord in 1609 (probably Mr Poole); and Richard Buck, who had arrived in May 1610. Buck was a protégé of William Crashaw, who thought him an 'able and painful preacher', though an Oxford man.[1] Buck married at Jamestown, and had four children: a daughter Mara (Ruth 1:20) born in 1611; and three sons – Gershom (eldest son of Moses, Exodus 2:22), born in 1614, Peleg (grandson of Shem, Genesis 10:25), born in 1620, and a mentally retarded boy born in 1617, baptised Benoni, 'son of my sorrow'.[2] Another Crashaw discovery arrived in the late summer of 1611. This was Nicholas Glover, a graduate of Jesus College Cambridge (BA 1588) who had been a 'godly preacher' in the Bedfordshire/Huntingdonshire area. Glover was a bachelor in his mid-forties, and not in good health. Like Hunt, he died within a year of arriving on the James.

At the end of 1609 the London Council of the Virginia Company had been thinking in terms of 'four honest and learned ministers' in Virginia.[3] (At that point, only Poole was there.) When Whitaker died in 1617, there remained only three clerics known to us by name: Richard Buck, William Mease, and William Wickham (who was probably in Presbyterian orders.) Of the clergy in Virginia during the seventeen years before the dissolution of the Virginia Company (1624) we know the names of only twenty-two.[4] Complaints about the

---

[1] Crashaw, Epistle Dedicatory (to Ralph, Baron Eure) in Whitaker, *Good Newes from Virginia*, 1613.

[2] Brydon, *Virginia's Mother Church*, 22-3.

[3] *True and Sincere Declaration*. Brown, *Genesis*, I, 353.

[4] Robert Hunt (May 1607); Poole (August 1609); Richard Buck (May 1610); Alexander Whitaker (May 1611); Nicholas Glover (late 1611); William Mease (1612?); William Wickham (1615?); George Keith (1617); Samuel Maycock (1618); Robert Pawlett (1619); Thomas Bargrave (1620?); Thomas White (1621); Hawte Wyatt (1621); Jonas Stockham (1621); Francis Bolton (1621); Robert Staples

shortage of clergy were persistent in seventeenth-century Virginia. Seventy English clerics petitioned the House of Commons in 1641 complaining about the 'want of able and conscionable ministers' in Virginia;[5] in 1645 the Virginia Assembly at Jamestown noted the 'scarcity of pastors' – some of them having charge of two or three cures;[6] the Virginia Laws of 1658 confirmed that 'there are many places destitute of ministers, and like so to continue'.[7] And the deaths of Hunt and Glover indicate that some of the clerics provided were hardly frontier material. So the colony made use of laymen. Indeed, the word 'minister' is often used of a lay lecturer, who preaches and baptises.[8] (Of the twenty-two known names before 1624, some were probably not ordained priests.) The Jamestown Assembly in 1661 ordered that parishes with no incumbent were to have 'readers', of 'sufficient abilities to read the prayers and homilies of the church (where they can be procured) and to catechise children and servants' – as in the reign of Elizabeth, when there was in England a lack of 'orthodox reformed ministers'.[9]

It has been calculated that in 1650 there was in Virginia one cleric to every 3239 inhabitants; and in Massachusetts, one to every 415.[10]

Alexander Whitaker was born in Cambridge in 1585 to William Whitaker, sometime Fellow of Trinity, and Susan (Culverwell) Whitaker, offspring of a wealthy London merchant family. The boy was presumably named Alexander after his great-uncle, Alexander Nowell, Dean of St Paul's (whose Latin Catechism, a required text in the Elizabethan Church, his nephew William Whitaker had translated into Greek.) Alexander Whitaker's uncles were Samuel, Nicholas and Ezekiel Culverwell; Thomas Gouge; Arthur Dent; and Laurence Chaderton, who had become the first Master of Emmanuel in 1584. (The annals of the Culverwell family reveal an unusually striking link between London trade, colonial expansion, Cambridge education, and puritan piety. 'Here's to us and all like us:') William Whitaker had given up his Fellowship in 1577 to marry Susan, and so lived privately in Cambridge. He was elected Regius Professor of Divinity in 1580. His lectures on biblical interpretation remain the most extensive Tudor treatment of the subject, and he is one of the

(1621); William Leate (1622); Patrick Copland (1622); David Sandys (1622: matriculated St John's, Cambridge 1611, MA Trinity 1615, ordained priest 1620, age 25); Greville Pooley (1622); John Pemberton (1622); Hopkins (1622). This list derives from my delvings in Kingsbury's *Records*; supplemented by the lists in Brydon, *Virginia's Mother Church* (1947), 47-9, 419-21. Some of my names are not in Brydon. See also Babette M. Levy, *Early Puritanism in the Southern and Island Colonies*, Ch.2 (this book was published in 1960 in Vol.70, pt.1 of *Proceedings of the American Antiquarian Society*, 69-348; the bibliography of source material is very good).

[5] Force, *Tracts*, I, no.13.
[6] Hening, *Statutes*, I, 289-90.
[7] *ibid.*, 478.
[8] *ibid.*, 290 (1645).
[9] *ibid.*, II, 29.
[10] Rutman, *American Puritanism*, 51, 87.

four talents of the sixteenth-century English tradition still worth reading on this regard; the other three being William Tyndale, John Jewel, and William Perkins. After ten years without a residential college attachment, William was elected Master of St John's in 1587 (Heads of Houses were allowed to commit matrimony). The family moved into the Master's Lodge in February 1587; and later in the same year, when Alex was two, another son – Samuel – arrived.

The Master's Lodge of St John's was Alex's home until the death of his father in 1595. In 1589, when he was four, his mother died. But in April 1591 the Master married again. His new wife, Joan, was the widow of Dudley Fenner, a graduate of Peterhouse Cambridge, who had renounced his Anglican orders in the late 1570s and crossed to Antwerp to be reordained in the Reformed Church; he died, aged thirty, in 1587, as chaplain to the congregation of English residents (and soldiers) at Middelburg. Joan brought her two children to St John's: a son, More Fruit Fenner, born in 1583, and a daughter, Faint Not, born in 1585. So Alex and Samuel had playmates. The members of the College presumably helped to entertain the Master's children; especially the junior members – the 'scholars', 'students', 'young gentlemen', 'boys' or 'lads' (the word 'undergraduate' was not common until the 1630s). William Crashaw was at the College from 1588 to 1592; and again in the final year of William Whitaker's Mastership, being admitted Fellow in 1594 – the year in which Samuel Purchas was a freshman. Gabriel Archer also was a member of the college for about two years, from 1591.

William Whitaker died on 4 December 1595 at the age of forty-eight, when Alex was ten. His funeral was one of the most splendid of the decade in the University; the court of the College hung with mourning drapes, a procession to Great St Mary's Church of representatives of the whole University, and a final laying of the body to rest after a Latin oration. The position of the children was precarious. Just after William's death, Joan bore a son, baptised on 11 December 1595 in St Clement's Church, with the name Jabez – 'because I bore him with sorrow',[11] – the Hebrew means, 'he makes sorrowful'. In time, Alex was to find helpful 'some means of his own left him by his parents'.[12] But is doubtful whether these were very ample means. It is certain that soon after William's death, Dean Nowell was much concerned about the poverty of the Whitakers. They probably made do only with the Dean's help. William Whitaker was said to have had eight children by his two wives. Only Alexander, Samuel and Jabez are known by name. There was also a daughter who went to Virginia in 1625.[13] The other four children are not traceable. It is possible that Thomas Whitaker, born about 1578, who went up to Trinity in 1594 and became a schoolmaster in Burnley until his death in 1626 was the son of William and Susan, presumably

[11] Cooper, *Athenae Cantabrigienses*, II, 197.
[12] Crashaw, Ep.Ded. to *Good Newes from Virginia* (see note 1).
[13] Kingsbury, *Records*, IV, 511.

their first born. The Whitakers were a Lancashire family, and the family estate of Holme was four miles south east of Burnley (near the Yorkshire border: only ten miles from the moors now known as the setting for *Wuthering Heights*).[14] The William Whitaker born about 1592, going up to St John's in 1609, and becoming a parson in Lincolnshire from 1620 to 1642, may have been a son of William and Joan.

Alexander and Samuel disappear from history for over two years after their father's death. Then, in 1598, the two boys were sent to Eton; of which College William Whitaker, during his years as Master of St John's, had been a Fellow.

Samuel, who was only eleven, went to Eton as a chorister. Alexander was thirteen, and became a foundation scholar – the foundation instituted by Henry VI for the 'poor and needy' in the 1440s.[15] Alexander remained at Eton for four years; studying Latin grammar and Latin set authors, composing Latin prose and (in his final year) Latin verse. There were, of course, diversions. The boys played tennis, and drank beer, and performed plays at Christmas. The College was visited by the Queen in 1601, in which year there was also a visit by the Duc de Biron, before whom a Latin oration was delivered by a puny prefect called John Wilson, later a Fellow of King's College Cambridge, later still pastor of the church at Boston Massachusetts, and a member of the first Board of Overseers at Harvard. Alexander Nowell died in 1602; and the autumn of that year the seventeen-year-old Alexander Whitaker left Eton for Cambridge – for his father's old College, Trinity.

When Alexander arrived at Trinity as a scholar, the College (founded by Henry VIII in 1546: a grandiose Renaissance gesture) was the largest in Cambridge, with nearly sixty graduates and over three hundred students. (John Dee of St John's had been one of the first Fellows in 1546.) For almost ten years the princely Thomas Nevile, Dean of Canterbury, had been Master; and the Great Court of Trinity, as it imposingly stands today, was Nevile's 'grand design'. (Compare it with the Old Court of Corpus, built in the 1350s, to sense the difference between the Middle Ages and the aspirations of the Tudors). Nevile built with the determination (and some of the technique) of a millionaire American dilettante, pulling down whole wings, building anew on a grand scale, and financing out of his own private fortune perhaps the most beautiful secular edifice in Cambridge: the second Court of Trinity, which bears his name. When Alexander joined the College, the turrets of the Great Gate were complete, the Edward III gateway had been moved stone by stone to its present site, and a new library and the greater part of the Master's

[14] The historian and topographer Thomas Dunham Whitaker was born in the Whitaker manor house in 1759; his valuable account of William Whitaker is in Book VI, Ch.1 of his *History of the original parish of Whalley*, 1801: second ed., 1806, 467-71 (Chart of the Whitaker family, 337-8).

[15] Sterry, *Annals of Eton College*, 1898; *Eton College Register 1441-1698*, 1943, 362.

Lodge were ready for use; the elegant *quattrocento*-style fountain which still stands in the Great Court was erected in Alexander's freshman year; by 1604 the dining Hall (modelled on that of the Middle Temple) was finished; by 1605, when Alexander commenced B.A., the kitchen and the Fellows' Parlour. Under such a Master, the College was excitingly noisy with the sound of axe and hammer, the travails of masons, carpenters, joiners, plumbers, tilers and bricklayers; but relatively undisturbed by religious convulsions such as had racked the St John's of Alexander's boyhood and William Crashaw's adolescence.

A few weeks after Alexander came into residence – in October 1602 – William Perkins died in Cambridge at the age of forty-three. For John Cotton, a seventeen-year-old Trinity undergraduate, his passing was a blessed relief, for the youth had been tortured by the spiritual self-questioning which the sermons of Perkins had prompted:

as he was walking in the fields, he heard the bell tolling for Master Perkins, who lay a dying, whereupon he was secretly glad in his heart that he should now be rid of him who had (as he said) laid siege to and beleagured his heart.[16]

Three years later a sermon by Richard Sibbes of St John's, Perkins' successor as Lecturer at St Andrew's Church, opposite Christ's,[17] was to convert Cotton to a true and lively faith.

Cotton had gone up to Trinity a year or two before Alexander, though they were the same age. An exact contemporary of Alexander's was William Wickham, later to assist Alexander in Virginia, although he does not appear to have been ordained according to the Anglican Ordinal (either he was never priested, or perhaps, by 1615, when he went to the James, he had been ordained in the Presbyterian fashion). In 1603, when Whitaker and Cotton were eighteen, there arrived in Trinity a boy of fifteen, John Winthrop.

Winthrop remained in Cambridge for only about eighteen months. He had come up from the family seat, Groton, in Suffolk. He was already quite adept in the subtleties of the puritan spiritual life.[18] 'About ten years of age', he later wrote (that is, about 1598),

I had some notions of God; for in some fighting or danger I have prayed unto God and found manifest answer; the remembrance whereof, many years after, made me think that God did love me; but it made me no whit the better.

(Before the age of ten he had been 'very lewdly disposed; inclining into and attempting ... all kinds of wickedness, except swearing and

---

[16] Clarke, *Lives of Thirty-two English Divines*, 218.
[17] A recent American writer presents a peripatetic Perkins: lecturer at Cambridge and preacher at St Andrews University (Little, *Religion, Order and Law*, 1969, 106).
[18] R.C. Winthrop, *Life and Letters of John Winthrop*, I, 56-7.

scorning religion, which I had no temptation unto, in regard of my education.') After he was twelve (1600)

I began to have some more savour of religion; and I thought I had more understanding in divinity than many of my years, for in reading of some good books I conceived that I did know divers of those points before, though I knew not how I should come by such knowledge. (But since, I perceived that it was out of some logical principles, whereby out of some things I could conclude others.) Yet I was still very wild and dissolute. And as years came on, my lusts grew stronger; but yet under some restraint of my natural reason.

At Cambridge he was ill, feeling himself 'neglected and despised':

Being in Cambridge, I fell into a lingering fever, which took away the comforts of my life. For, being there neglected and despised, I went up and down mourning with myself; and, being deprived of my youthful joys, I betook myself to God, whom I did believe to be very just and merciful, and would welcome any that would come to Him, especially such a young soul, and so well as I took myself to be. So as, I took pleasure in drawing near to Him.

(In 1629, in an essay justifying the intended emigration to New England, Winthrop was to draw attention to the 'scorn and contempt' which such as he felt themselves to attract:[19] disgruntled gentry, in a poor financial way, seeing their type of piety waning in both England and Europe – and resenting increasing government paternalism.) By April 1605 Winthrop had left Trinity, and had got married, aged seventeen, at Great Stambridge, Essex. The officiating cleric was Alexander's uncle, Ezekiel Culverwell, and in Culverwell's parish Winthrop 'first found the ministry of the word to come home to my heart with power'.[20] Ezekiel's pastoral concern was reinforced in the young bridegroom by the reading of Perkins. That of course was the storm before the calm. For there is always, in the stylised tradition of the puritan pilgrim's progress, a tide in the affairs of spiritual men which taken at the flood leads on to fortune – to that perfect assurance about which Crashaw preached to the Virginia Company in 1610. Winthrop decided he could 'no longer dally with religion'.[21]

Now I grew full of zeal, which outran my knowledge, and carried me sometime beyond my calling ... I had an unsatiable thirst after the word of God; and could not miss a good sermon, though many miles off, especially of such as did search deep into the conscience.

On 20 April 1605, when he was 18.3, he 'made a new convenant with the Lord': 'Of my part, that I would reform these sins by his grace'; 'of the Lord's part, that he would give me a new heart.'[22] That was the personal covenant. Robert Browne in 1580 had illustrated in his congregation in Norwich the corporate spiritual covenant: 'a covenant

---

[19] *ibid.*, 310. [20] *ibid.*, 60. [21] *ibid.*, 60-1. [22] *ibid.*, 65-6.

was made and mutual consent was given to hold together', to 'join themselves to the Lord in one covenant and fellowship together'.[23] From the personal, to the congregational. And from there to the political: to the document signed aboard 'the Mayflower' at Cape Cod on 11 November 1620 by the forty-one 'pilgrims', in which they did 'solemnly and mutally, in the presence of God and one another, covenant and combine ourselves together into a civil body politic'.[24]

The undergraduate Alexander Whitaker may have been touched by the same concerns as exercised Cotton and Winthrop. It would have been odd for a son of the great Dr Whitaker not to have thought on these things.

In January 1604, ten months after the accession of James, Alexander's uncle Laurence Chaderton went down from Emmanuel to Hampton Court as a member of the puritan delegation to the conference before the new monarch; there to suggest, among other things, that the use of the surplice be made optional. By that time it had been brought to official notice that in Emmanuel, founded all but twenty years before, the Book of Common Prayer was disregarded in favour of 'a private course of public prayer'; that the surplice was not worn in the chapel; and that the bread and wine were received by members of the college 'sitting upon forms about the communion table'.[25] The puritan pleas were unsuccessful; and official rigidity was not only continued but intensified (much to the distress of Francis Bacon). The new ecclesiastical canons of 1604 attempted to enforce and tighten the existing regulations about liturgy and discipline. Colleges were to observe 'the order, form and ceremonies ... as they are set down and prescribed in the Book of Common Prayer, without any omission or alteration'; the surplice was to be worn in chapel; and the communion to be received by the congregation 'kneeling reverently and devoutly upon their knees, according to the order of the communion book'.[26] This restatement of the basic liturgical discipline which had been in theory obligatory for forty five years occasioned much searching of conscience in Cambridge. Samuel Ward, Fellow of the College, noted in his diary that Wednesday 18 January 1605 was the fell day when 'the surplice was first urged by the Archbishop to be brought into Emmanuel'.[27] (In 1610 Ward became third Master of Sidney Sussex College, founded in 1596; the House which was to nurture not only Oliver Cromwell, but also John Wheelwright, the founder of New Hampshire.)

In Trinity, where Alexander Whitaker was in his third year, no new

---

[23] Porter, *Puritanism in Tudor England*, 110-11.

[24] Text and names given by Nathaniel Morton, *New England's Memorial*, Cambridge, Mass., 1669. In Everyman Library *Chronicles of the Pilgrim Fathers*, 1910, 23-5. See below, pp.423-24.

[25] British Museum, Harleian Mss, 7033, p.850.

[26] 'Constitutions and Canons Ecclesiastical' 1604: xvi, xvii, xxiii.

[27] *Two Elizabethan Puritan Diaries* (Richard Rogers and Samuel Ward), ed. M.M. Knappen, Chicago 1933, 130.

enforcement was necessary. And, in any case, Authority had not yet wholly succumbed to the Laudian conviction that external Formality is the surest sign of inward Grace. James I visited Cambridge in 1615, with Prince Charles. (The University, whether by accident or design, neglected to invite the Queen; James' roving eye for glamorous young men was given a scope in Cambridge which might have worried her.) Every College was 'new be-painted'; except, a contemporary versifier tells us, the 'pure house of Emmanuel', which as its contribution to the festivities 'conceived a tedious mile of prayer'. It was pointed out to the King that the kitchen of Emmanuel faced east, and the chapel north. James, with his usual good sense, commented to Chaderton that 'God will not turn His face away from the prayers of any holy and pious man, to whatsoever region of heaven he directs his eyes. So, Doctor, I beg you to pray for me'.[28] Chaderton, a good conforming puritan, knew just as well as the Supreme Governor that men 'who dislike the government of the Church by Bishops will substitute something far less beneficial to Church and State'.[29] Crashaw in 1610, like Wingfield in 1606, had wished no 'factious separatists' in Virginia: the likes of John Robinson, who resigned his Cambridge Fellowship at Corpus Christi in 1605 and was soon to convince himself that he must 'proclaim to all the world separation from whatsoever riseth up rebelliously against the sceptre of His Kingdom; as we are undoubtedly persuaded the communion, government, ministry and worship of the Church of England do'.[30] That decision made, Robinson advanced to meet his destiny as pastor to the Pilgrim Fathers. Such a decision no Culverwell or Whitaker had ever made.

In 1609, when he was twenty four, Alexander Whitaker was ordained priest; having taken his M.A. degree in 1608 (the year in which Samuel, although academically three years Alexander's junior, was elected a Fellow of King's). At the time of his ordination, in accordance with the canons of 1604 (based on Articles of Archbishop Whitgift twenty years before) Alexander was required to 'willingly and *ex animo* subscribe' to three articles:[31] recognising the King as Supreme Governor of the Church of England; approving the thirty-nine articles as 'agreeable to the word of God'; and – most disliked by the factious – affirming that the Prayer Book

containeth in it nothing contrary to the word of God, and that it may lawfully be used; and that he himself will use the form in the said book prescribed, in public-prayer and administration of the sacraments, and none other.

Thus Alexander began his career as a pastor in the Church of England. His parish we do not know. We know that it was in the North; and that pastor and parish were well known to Ralph, Baron

[28] William Dillingham, *Life of Chaderton*, tr. E.S. Schuckburgh, 1884, 11.
[29] *ibid.*, 10.
[30] Robinson, *Works*, ed. R. Ashton, 1851, III, 406.
[31] 1604 Canons: xxxvi.

Eure, a man of influence in the northern province, who had a house at Malton, Yorkshire, twenty miles from York. This, together with Crashaw's Yorkshire standing, make it reasonable to assume that the living was in Yorkshire. (Lord Eure was a shareholder in the Virginia Company.) It was worth £40 a year – wealthy: and in a cheap county. Crashaw tells us[32] that Whitaker was

well approved by the greatest, and beloved of his people, and had competent allowance to his good liking, and was in as good possibility of better living as any of his time.

A successful and edifying career as a learned 'godly pastor' lay before him, surely.

But Alexander remained in his parish for less than two years. During that period he increasingly strongly 'entertained a purpose of going to Virginia'; and this, said Crashaw, 'merely of himself', without any pressure or inducement. The published motive was missionary. The stresses which had driven Alexander Nowell to Germany and Switzerland in the reign of Mary, the considerations which were to inspire Winthrop and Cotton to brave the ocean and the wilderness in search of the spiritual Utopia (the wilderness being a place at once of iniquity, of trial and redemption), are not fully applicable to the musings of Whitaker in 1610. Alexander himself was to refer in 1613, from Jamestown, to his mission as apostle to the gentiles in 'the barbarous country of Virginia, where the name of God hath been yet scarce heard of'.[33] Crashaw paints a picture of Whitaker's 'serious deliberation', his 'many distractions and combats with himself', his 'many inward temptations, and outward discouragements and dissuasions' counterblancing his missionary urge. On the James he would be almost an individual clergyman, ploughing a lonely furrow. This could be no communal, almost family, affair like the Marian exile or the Atlantic migrations of the 1630s (let alone the activities of the Spanish and Portuguese Religious Orders). But he won his inward battle, and 'settled his resolution that God called him thither, and therefore he would go'. The decision made, those who wished him well urged him to reconsider. He was subject to 'the earnest disssuasions of many his nearest friends; and the great discouragements which he daily heard of, touching the business and the country itself'. These were to no effect. Alexander asked Crashaw to arrange that he might be sent to the colony for a provisional period of three years. (In theory the salary would be as large or larger than his Northern stipend: although in fact the Virginia Company was always rather slow in paying the handful of clerics under its jurisdiction.)

And in March 1611 the Reverend Alexander Whitaker, not yet twenty-six, sailed from London with Sir Thomas Dale.

[32] Crashaw quotations from Ep.Ded. to *Good Newes from Virginia*.
[33] Whitaker, *Good.Newes from Virginia*, 15.

The arrival of Dale at Jamestown in May 1611 did a little to ease the confusion in the Colony. The Bermuda group – Thomas Gates, John Rolfe, William Strachey and Richard Buck among them – had finally arrived in Jamestown on 23 May 1610; followed on 16 June by Lord De La Warr, Governor (who had sailed from England in April). The ghastly winter of 1609/10 – the notorious 'starving time' – had reduced the population to five dozen.

Robert Beverley, born in Virginia in 1673, has this passage on that time in his *The History and Present State of Virginia*, published in 1705:[34]

They who remained alive were all near famished, having brought themselves to that pass, that they durst not stir from their own doors to gather the fruits of the earth, or the crabs and mussels from the waterside; much less to hunt or catch wild beasts, fish or fowl, which were found in great abundance there. They continued in these scanty circumstances till they were at last reduced to such extremity as to eat the very hides of their horses, and the bodies of the Indians they had killed; and sometimes also, upon a pinch, they would not disdain to dig them up again to make a homely meal of after they had been buried. And that time is to this day remembered by the name of the Starving Time. Thus a few months indiscreet management brought such an infamy upon the country, that to this day it cannot be wiped away.

'Indiscreet' by necessity – the 'government' was shipwrecked in Bermuda: John Smith had left in October 1609, leaving George Percy as the fourth and final 'President of the Council'.

De La Warr brought 150 colonists and provisions for one year. He made a speech to the planters, criticising their 'sluggish idleness': and

heartening them with relation of that store he had brought with him; constituting officers of all conditions to rule over them, allotting every man his particular place to watch vigilantly and work painfully.

This oration – as reported in a pamphlet published in London in November 1610 'by advice and direction of the Council of Virginia'[35] – helped to cure 'the idle and restive diseases of a divided multitude'.

Those that knew not the way to goodness before, but cherished singularity and faction, can now chalk out the path of all respective duty and service, every man endeavouring to out-strip each other in diligence, the French preparing to plant the vines, the English labouring in the woods and grounds. Every man knoweth his change, and dischargeth the same with alacrity.

The praiseworthy routine of labour (like that of the Utopians) was based on a six hour day: a thirty-six hour official work week. This, so the London Council thought, was all that the colonists or the shareholders 'need desire'. The hours were 6 a.m. to 10 a.m.: and 2

---

[34] Ed. L.B. Wright, 34-5.
[35] 'True Declaration of the Estate of the Colonie in Virginia'. Force, *Tracts*, III, no.1, 19-20.

p.m. to 4 p.m. At 10 a.m. and 4 p.m. 'they enter into the church, and make their prayers unto God. Next, they return to their houses and receive their proportion of food.' (The houses, we learn, are 'covered above with strong boards, and matted round within, according to the fashion of the Indians'.) The London Council emphasised that colonisation does not exclude 'Gentlemen, whose breeding never knew what a day's labour meant':

though they cannot dig, use the square, nor practice the axe and chisel, yet may the staid spirits of any condition find how to employ the force of knowledge, and exercise of counsel, the operation and power of their best breeding and qualities.

De La Warr's health suffered in Jamestown (diarrhoea, cramp, gout and scurvy); and he left in March 1611, not yet 34, leaving George Percy as interim 'governor' until the arrival of Dale (with Whitaker) in May. Gates, who had made a short visit to London, returned in April. And the Gates/Dale regime from the summer of 1611 dragged the colony to survival: 'the first ragged government,' wrote William Strachey, 'was prudently changed into an absolute command.'[36] Gates was governor from June 1611 to March 1614; Dale from March 1614 to April 1616.

In June 1611 Gates and Dale confirmed edicts issued by Gates in May 1610; and in 1612 this body of laws, running to sixty pages, edited by Strachey, was published in London: *For the Colony in Virginea Britannia. Lawes Divine, Moral and Martiall.*[37]

The Gates legislation had included the following provisions.[38] The authorities should ensure that God 'be duly and daily served'; that the settlers should 'diligently frequent morning and evening prayer' which were held daily; and that they should hear sermons – presumably by Mr Buck. The clergy were to be held in 'reverend regard' (Mr Buck again). The settlers were to 'sanctify and observe the Sabbath', in which there was to be a sermon at both matins and evensong, 'catechising' (a spiritual seminar), and private prayers in each household. There was also to be a sermon preached every Wednesday. In each settlement there were to be people rather like Churchwardens: the pastor was to 'choose unto him four of the most religious and better disposed, as well to inform of the abuses and neglect of the people in their duties and service to God'. (George Herbert was to recommend that if the parson is asked to judge any controversy in the parish, 'he never decides it alone, but sends for three of four of the ablest of the parish to hear the cause with him'.)[39] The penalties for colonists who fell short of these requirements

[36] Strachey, *Virginia Britania*, 90.
[37] Page references to Force, *Tracts*, III, no.2.
[38] 10-12.
[39] *A Priest to the Temple; or, the Country Parson*, Ch.23, 'The Parson's Completeness': 'The Country Parson desires to be all to his parish, and not only a Pastor, but a lawyer also, and a physician.' *Works*, ed. F.E. Hutchinson, 259-60.

included whipping, public penance in the church, and a period of service in the boats. There were heavy penalties for blasphemy (beginning with a bodkin through the tongue; and, finally death). The death penalty was to be imposed for murder; sodomy ('horrible and detestable'); adultery; rape of 'woman, maid or Indian'; perjury; embezzlement; robbery; treason – and for soldiers offending or ill-treating the Indian (by setting fire to an Indian house, for example).[40]

Alderman Robert Johnson, writing in 1612, praised the laws of 1610 forbidding 'injurious violence against the Indian'.[41]

Military rules, really, for a beleagured and slack settlement. Every settler was to

give up an account of his and their faith and religion, and repair unto the minister, that by his conference with them, he may understand and gather whether heretofore they have been sufficiently instructed and catchised in the principles and grounds of religion.[42]

Henry VIII had made it clear in 1530[43] that there should be in England

unity and agreement in one persuasion of faith and religion, the dissension wherein, as being ground and fundament, moveth, confoundeth and totally subverteth all the rest.

The community 'faith' was the 'fundament'; the basic foundation of any commonwealth, Catholic, Protestant or Puritan, especially, the Virginia Company had come to realise; of a commonwealth on the frontier. John Smith was to write in 1630 of the dangers of 'factions in religion', 'divisions and opinions', to a 'well settled commonwealth' – which should have 'one religion'; that is, acknowledge 'the prime authority of the Church of England'.[44]

In 1611 all this was confirmed as suitable for 'select, painful and religious adventures;[45] and other requirements were added. The captains of the watch were to recite every morning and evening the text of a prayer which would have taken twenty minutes to read.[46] It acknowledged that God has 'honoured us to choose us out to bear Thy name unto the gentiles', the 'highest end of our plantation' being 'to set up the standard and display the banner of Jesus Christ, even here where Satan's throne is Lord'. The Indian must never have occasion to comment, 'Where is now your God?' Let

Dagon fall before Your ark, let Satan be confounded in Thy presence, and let the heathen see it and be ashamed, that they might seek Thy face; for their God is not as our God ... As the smoke vanisheth, so let Satan and his

[40] 12.
[41] *The New Life of Virginia*. Force, *Tracts*, I, no.7, p.13.
[42] 17.
[43] May 1530. Quoted in Cooper, *Annals of Cambridge*, I, 342.
[44] Smith-Arber, 959-60.
[45] 29. [46] 63-8.

delusions come to naught, and as wax melteth before the fire, so let wickedness, superstition, ignorance and idolatry perish at the presence of Thee our God ... Lord, bless England, our sweet native country; save it from popery, this land from heathenism, and both from atheism.

Such were the 'religious' fundamentals for 'the first seed-plot and settlement of such a temporary kingdom and state as may reduce and bring poor misbelieving miscreants to the knowledge of the eternal kingdom of God'.[47]

Ten years later one of the charges against the reign of Sir Thomas Smythe as Treasurer of the Virginia Company was that he 'suffered a Book of Laws for government of the Colony chiefly extracted out of the Laws for governing the army in the Low Countries'. (This derivation is doubtful.)[48]

When Gates left London for Virginia in May 1609 he had carried instructions from the London Council of the Virginia Company,[49] to be observed when he arrived at Jamestown (in the event, May 1610). He was to endeavour the conversion of the Indians, 'which the better to effect you must procure from them some convenient number of their children to be brought up in your language and manners'. This could be done by force, by taking them prisoner, in order to remove them from the baleful influence of the Priests. For the Indians are 'so wrapped up in the fog and misery' of priestly 'iniquity', and

so terrified with their continual tyranny, chained under the bond of death unto the Devil, that while they live among them to poison and infect them their minds, you shall never make any great progress in this glorious work, nor have any civil peace or concur with them.

The opinion, we have seen, of Gates' fellow voyager William Strachey. The English could deal 'sharply' with the Priests, and 'proceed even to death' – in case of 'necessity or conveniency'. The Virginia Company Council 'pronounce it not cruelty or breach of charity'; while 'referring the consideration of this, as a weighty matter, of important consequence, to the circumstances of the business and place, in your discretion'.[50] The werowances, on the other hand, should be well treated, and their sons educated in English 'manners and religion' – thus in time becoming 'civil and Christian'. But Powhatan was 'no way' to be trusted: 'it is clear even to reason, besides our experience, that he loved not our neighbourhood.' It may not be wise to take him prisoner; but he must become a 'tributary', acknowledging 'no other lord but King James'.[51]

In civil cases, Gates was instructed not to emphasise too much 'the niceness and letter of the law'; to act 'rather as a chancellor than as a

---

[47] 42.
[48] Kingsbury (ed.), *Records*, IV, 83 (1623). See Andrews, *Colonial Period*, I, 115.
[49] Kingsbury (ed.), *Records*, III, 12-24.
[50] 14-15.   [51] 18-19.

judge', upon the 'natural right and equity', in a 'summary and arbitrary way of justice discreetly mingled with those gravities and forms of magistracy. as shall in your discretion seem aptest for you and that place'. In cases of rebellion and mutiny 'and in all such cases of present necessity' – criminal and capital cases – he was to 'proceed by martial law according to your commission, as of most dispatch and terror, and fittest for this government'.[52]

The London Virginia Council instructed Gates in 1609 to

take principal order and care for the true and reverend worship of God, that His word be duly preached and His holy sacraments administered according to the constitutions of the Church of England in all fundamental points.[53]

This was confirmed by the first meeting of the General Assembly at Jamestown in 1619:[54]

All ministers shall duly read divine service and exercise their ministerial function according to the ecclesiastical laws and orders of the Church of England.

Virginia thus came within 'the Laws of Ecclesiastical Polity'. In 1619 also, the London Council gave directions for the new settlement at Berkeley.[55] Morning and evening prayer were to be 'according to the English Book of Common Prayer'; holy days and festivals were to be 'kept which are authorised and appointed by the laws and statutes of the realm of England'; the 'rules and ceremonies authorised and appointed by the ecclesiastical laws or canons of this realm of England and Book of Common Prayer' were to be 'in all things observed and kept according as it is used in the Church of England'. The dangers – the London Council noted in 1621[56] – were a lack of respect for 'honour and rights belonging to the Church and ministry'; and 'factions and needless novelties'. In 1643 the Assembly was to order that 'nonconformists' be 'compelled to depart the Colony with all conveniency' (as infringing 'purity of doctrine, and unity of the Church').[57]

The disciplinary regime of the Church of England, in England and Virginia, was strict. Much of what some historians of colonial America label as 'puritan' is in fact a feature of the Anglican parish.[58] In 1632 the Jamestown General Assembly, for example, thought that 'the laws of England against drunkards are thought fit to be published and daily put in execution'; that is, for every offence, five shillings

[52] 15. [53] 14.
[54] Kingsbury, *Records*, III, 172.
[55] *ibid.*, 208.
[56] *ibid.*, 469.
[57] Hening, *Statutes*, I, 277.
[58] See Emmison, *Elizabethan Life: Morals and the Church Courts*; Brinkworth, *Shakespeare and the Bawdy Court of Stratford*.

must be paid to the churchwardens.[59] The fine for missing church on a Sunday or Holy Day was eleven shillings. (The minister must preach one sermon every Sunday; and before the Sunday Evensong put aside a half hour to 'examine, catechise and instruct the youth and ignorant persons of his parish'.) The churchwardens were to present drunkards, swearers, blasphemers, adulterers, fornicators, slanderers, and those not observing the Sabbath.[60] In 1643 it was laid down that there should be no travelling on the Sabbath – except to Church; and no shooting – except for defence against the Indians.[61]

In 1609, Gates was instructed to ensure that the settlers who 'attend any work in or near about every town' were to

eat together at seasonable hours in some public place, being messed by six or five to a mess, in which you must see there be equality, and sufficient, so that they may come and return to their work without any delay, and have no cause to complain of measure, or to excuse their idleness upon the dressing or want of diet.[62]

A bell was rung to summon them to the meal, and again at the end of the break – which was to be three hours in summer, and two hours in winter.

Gates was also instructed to think in terms not merely of Jamestown, though that should be the port and the chief plantation, but to establish at least three further forts further along the James (or to the south: North Carolina). In July 1611 Thomas Dale, taking Whitaker with him, went seventy miles up the James, partly to inspect possible settlement sites. Whitaker wrote a letter to Crashaw on 9 August 1611 meditating, among other things, upon this trip.[63] (We know that Whitaker had written an earlier letter to Crashaw, within a week of his arrival: but this has not survived.) Whitaker supposed 'it would be unsavoury to the conceit of a scholar, and your heavenly meditations, to hear what corn we have set, what boats we have built, etc.' But he ought to know 'how God hath continued His goodness towards me, and preserved me safe hitherto with great hope of good success to our purposes'. And he would be interested to hear of the adventure along the James, and of their seeing on the shore

a mad crew dancing like Antics, or our morris dancers, before whom there went Quiockosite, or their priest, who tossed smoke and flame out of a thing like a censer.

'All which things made me think that there be great witches amongst them, and they very familiar with the Devil' – both Whitaker and Crashaw were familiar with William Perkins' treatise on witchcraft.

[59] Hening, *Statutes*, I, 167.
[60] *ibid.*, 155-7.
[61] *ibid.*, 261.
[62] Kingsbury, *Records*, III, 21.
[63] Brown, *Genesis*, I, 497-500.

Whitaker's thoughts at this stage about the beauties of Virginia were made sombre by his conviction that the flourishing bay tree was an image of Evil.

I should more admire Virginia, with the inhabitants, if I did not remember that Egypt was exceeding faithful; that Canaan flowed with milk and honey before Israel did overrun it; and that Sodom was like the garden of God in the days of Lot.

However, he believed that God had 'spared' the Indian; and that He had 'enriched the bowels of the country with the riches and beauty of nature, that we, wanting them, might in the search of them communicate the most excellent merchandise and treasure of the Gospel'. And God had been very lenient to the English colonists since 1607: 'I marvel more that God did not sweep them all away at once.' The 'sins of our men were intolerable'. We need 'discretion and learning, zeal with knowledge'. We do not need either 'bad livers' (he means people who live badly), or 'ceremonies' (a liturgical touch). Obviously Whitaker's leaving England was due in some degree to his dislike of 'the laws of ecclesiastical polity': especially those associated with the conventions of external piety expressed in the Book of Common Prayer (as interpreted by the Canons of 1604). Whitaker, in a passage again critical of the Established Church, pressed upon Crashaw the duty to send to Virginia 'any young, godly, and learned ministers whom the Church of England hath not, or refuseth to, set a work'. A sense of Miltonic indignation there, however slight. In Virginia Whitaker had bloomed 'beyond my friends' opinion, and my own hopes'. 'I think I have fared better for your prayers, and the rest.'

The appeal for 'young' pastors was hardly satisfied by the arrival later in that month of the aging and ill Nicholas Glover.

Glover came with Gates. Now both Dale and Gates were together in Jamestown, Gates having the superior authority. This left Dale free to consolidate his plans for a new settlement along the James. Ralph Hamor, 'recorder' of the colony (whose son had gone up to Emmanuel in 1607) wrote the account of this venture.[64] Dale set off with a party at the beginning of September 1611;

and in a day and a half landed at a place where he purposed to seat and build; where he had not been ten days before he had very strongly impaled seven English acres of ground for a town: which in honour of the noble Prince Henry ... he called by the name of *Henrico*.

Henry had been invested Prince of Wales in June 1610. He died in November 1612.

The new fort was on the Dutch gap peninsula – formed by a loop bend of the James fifty miles up from Jamestown, twenty miles below the site of Richmond. And by building a palisade across the neck of

[64] Hamor, *True Discourse of the Present Estate of Virginia*, 1615, 29-31.

the peninsula, Dale made of Henrico almost a little island (not unlike Jamestown). No sooner was the site 'thus fenced, and in a manner secured from the Indians', than Dale built at each corner of the fort 'very strong and high commanders, or watch towers'. And within the fort

a fair and handsome church, and storehouses, which finished he began to think upon convenient houses and lodgings for himself and men, which with as much speed as was possible, were more strongly and more handsome than any formerly in Virginia contrived and finished. And even in four months' space, he had made Henrico much better and of more worth than all the work ever done since the colony began.

That is, by Christmas 1611. Hamor, who was writing in the spring of 1614, praised the 'three streets of well-framed houses, a handsome church, and the foundation of a more stately one laid – of brick, in length an hundred foot, and fifty feet wide': twice the size of the then church at Jamestown. Moreover, from the first the new settlement had been planned to include ground on the south bank of the James; until by 1614 some twelve miles of territory had been enclosed there, 'especially for our hogs to feed in'. Alexander Whitaker, first minister of Henrico, chose to live on this south bank: 'here hath Mr Whitaker chosen his parsonage, or Church land, some hundred acres impaled, and a fair framed parsonage house built thereupon, called Rock Hall.' This location enabled him the more easily to minister, from 1612, to the settlement of Bermuda Hundred, about five miles from his house, where the Appomattox joins the James. About 1615 his Trinity contemporary William Wickham joined him to care for that region of the James. Wickham seems to have been assigned responsibility in Henrico itself, while Whitaker concentrated on Bermuda Hundred.

To the year 1612 belongs Alexander Whitaker's essay *Good Newes from Virginia*, the preface to which was dated at Henrico, 28 July (after Whitaker had been in Virginia for just over thirteen months). This piece, of some forty-five pages, was sent over to London by Whitaker to his distant relation Sir Thomas Smythe, Treasurer (Head) of the Virginia Company. (Sir Thomas' deceased wife had been a Culverwell, a cousin of Alexander's mother.) Whitaker's letter to Smythe was published as a preface to the text:

Since the affairs of this colony have now taken better footing, and are advanced by the helps of so many honorable adventurers, I was greatly emboldened to write these few lines of exhortation, to encourage the noble spirits of so many worthy men to go forward in well-doing. Wherefore (honoured Sir) since all the dispatches of our affairs pass through your hands, I request you to accept of my poor endeavours, and to publish it to the view of our adventurers, that the prejudicate opinion of some, and the disheartened mind of others, may be reformed.

Smythe and the London Council asked Crashaw to authenticate the genuineness of the manuscript; because, explained Crashaw in 'The Epistle Dedicatorie',

the man was once so well known to me (as he is still; and ever shall be beloved of me) I was desired of them that may command me, to peruse the original itself, and for that I had (as they probably thought) some knowledge of his hand, to consider whether truly or suspiciously it bore his name.

Crashaw reported 'a great part of it written, and all of it subscribed, with his own hand'. Whitaker, Crashaw further commented, had intended the manuscript not to be printed; but 'rather for the private use and encouragement of such whose purses here, or persons there, were engaged in the action'. Crashaw builds Whitaker up as a Hero, worthy of his father:

I dare say, if he had thought we would have published it, he would otherwise have adorned it. For I know (and so do others that know him) he is able to have written it in Latin or in Greek, and so to have decked it both for phrase and style, and other ornaments of learning and language, as might show him no unworthy son of so worthy a father. And I dare say, if he live (be it in England or Virginia) he will in due time manifest to the world by true and good evidence that God hath made him heir, as of divers of the holy virtues, so of a good part of the learning of his renowned father.

As it is, the work is not ornamentally decked; it is, approvingly noted the editor of Perkins, 'plain, but pithy and godly'. After 'mature consideration' the London Council decided to print it: 'That so the naked and plain truth may give a just affront to the cunning and coloured falsehoods devised by the enemies of this plantation.' (The friends of the plantation, shareholders named in the 'Third Charter' of March 1612, included George Abbot, Archbishop of Canterbury; William James, Bishop of Durham; Henry Parry, Bishop of Worcester; John Bridges, Bishop of Oxford; and George Montaigne, Dean of Westminster (to be Bishop of Lincoln in 1617).) *Good Newes from Virginia* was published in London in 1613 – the same year in which a son was born to William Crashaw, baptised Richard.

Whitaker's book has an opening text; and was probably based on a sermon preached in Virginia. An Old Testament text, Ecclesiastes 11:1: 'Cast thy bread on the waters; for thou shalt find it after many days.' In the manner of the sermons discussed in earlier chapters, the biblical material is given primacy; Virginia is not mentioned until quarter of the way through. Alexander – and here he certainly was the son of his father, the Cambridge lecturer on biblical interpretation – discusses the rhetorical and figurative language of scripture, the 'soul and substance' of the literal text, the 'agreement of the text with the words following', the nature of words – and the 'plain meaning' of them; the 'parts', 'points' and 'rules' of Biblical criticism. The Henrico colonists may well have thought themselves in the Cambridge

'Common Schools'. After the 'doctrine', the 'use' of it (a method taught by Perkins).

This is the doctrine; and I beseech God to stir up your minds to the practice of liberality in all things towards all men. And remember the poor estate of the ignorant inhabitants of Virginia. Cast forth your alms, my brethren of England, and extend your liberality on these charitable works, which God hath called you to perform.

Those 'that cannot help on monies, by reason of their poverty, may venture their persons hither'.[65] Those who could do neither could usefully pray for the prosperity of the plantation.

Whitaker put this call for Liberality in the theological context of 'works of charity'; the rules of right giving, of 'meritorious' and 'principal' 'good works'[66] – and he quotes the division of Works of Charity given by the 'great schoolman' St Thomas Aquinas (although unlike Strachey he refrained from remembering the Latin phrases). The 'principal point of perfect charity is, that we give in faith'.[67]

Our liberality, grounded on faith and practised in love, will be a means to help our souls forward in their passage to heaven, for they are the highway and trodden path wherein we must walk to everlasting life. Therefore, the more any man abounds in good works, the more comfortable shall be his passage: ... they are such necessary fruits of faith, that faith cannot go without them. For where no good works are, there is no faith; and where true saving faith is, there will be showed good works; yea, we cannot hold true faith from doing good. Read for the proof of this, the Epistle of St James, and the first Epistle of St John.[68]

England was too full of 'covetous hearts'.[69] Whitaker gives an orthodox warning about the vocation of wealth, the 'calling of the rich man':[70] God,

lending his treasures to the rich men of the world, hath showed to them an example of His liberality; to this end, that they might be open-handed to others, distributing as faithful stewards of His gifts, according to the necessity of the saints.

'Liberal minded and open-minded';[71] especially because of the duty of Christian compassion to the Indian. In one of the most eloquent passages of his sermon, Whitaker rendered due praise to the Indian:[72]

If any of us should misdoubt that this barbarous people is uncapable of such heavenly mysteries, let such men know that they are far mistaken in the nature of these men. For besides the promise of God, which is without respect of persons ... let us not think that these men are so simple as some

[65] *Good Newes from Virginia*, 18-19. Wright has extracts from *Good Newes* in *Elizabethans' America*, 218-24.
[66] 16-17. [67] 29. [68] 36. [69] 22. [70] 5-6. [71] 21. [72] 25.

have supposed them. For they are of body lusty, strong and very nimble; they are a very understanding generation, quick of apprehension, sudden in their despatches, subtle in their dealings, exquisite in their inventions, and industrious in their labour. I suppose the world hath no better mark-men with their bows and arrows than they be. They will kill birds flying, fishes swimming, and beasts running. They shoot also with marvellous strength; they shot one of our men, being unarmed, quite through the body, and nailed both his arms to his body with one arrow.

Their religion is worthy of note.[73]

They acknowledge that there is a great, good God; but know him not, having the eyes of their understanding as yet blinded. Wherefore they serve the Devil, for fear, after a most base manner, sacrificing sometimes (as I have here heard) their own children to him.

Not much evidence of research there; the passage could have been composed in England. However, Whitaker had something to show: 'I have sent one image of their God to the Council in England; which is painted on one side of a toadstool, much like unto a deformed monster.' True to the spirit of the Virginia Company in its Gates/Strachey phase, the Indian priests become the generalised villains: 'no other but such as our English witches are'; 'a generation of vipers even of Satan's own brood.'

The manner of their life is much like to the popish hermits of our age. For they live alone in the woods, in houses sequestered from the common course of men; neither may any man be suffered to come into their house, or to speak with them, but when this priest doth call him. He taketh no care for his victuals, for all such kind of things, both bread and water, etc, are brought unto a place near unto his cottage, and there are left, which he fetcheth for his proper need. If they would have rain, or have lost anything, they have their recourse to him, who conjureth for them, and many times prevaileth. If they be sick, he is their physician; if they be wounded, he sucketh them. At this command they make war and peace; neither do they anything of moment without him:[74]

However, the Indians can 'do by nature the things contained in the law':

There is a civil government amongst them which they strictly observe, and show thereby that the Law of Nature dwelleth in them. For they have a rude kind of commonwealth, and rough government; wherein they both honour and obey their kings, parents and governors, both greater and less; they observe the limits of their own possessions, and encroach not upon their neighbours' dwellings. Murder is a capital crime scarce heard of amongst them. Adultery is most severely punished, and so are their other offences. These unnurtured grounds of reason in them may serve to encourage us to

[73] 25.   [74] 26.

instruct them in the knowledge of the true God, the rewarder of all righteousness, not doubting but that He that was powerful to save us by His word when we were nothing, will be merciful also to these sons of Adam in His appointed time: in whom there be remaining so many footsteps of God's image.[75]

The footsteps of course are fairly faint. The Indians 'live naked in body, as if the shame of their sin deserved no covering'. They 'esteem it a virtue to lie, deceive and steal, as their master the Devil teacheth them'.[76] They are 'to be feared of those that come upon them without defensive armour'. But in fact they are 'faint hearted'. Some of their 'petty kings', through fear, have 'desired our friendship, and those keep good quarter with, being very pleasant amongst us, and, if occasion be, serviceable unto us'. The colonists should utilise that timidity:

If we were once the masters of their country, and they stood in fear of us (which might with few hands, employed about nothing else, be in short time brought to pass) it were an easy matter to make them willingly to forsake the Devil, to embrace the faith of Jesus Christ, and to be baptised.[77]

The inadequacies of the Life of Nature should spur the missionary work:

If this be their life, what think you shall become of them after death, but to be partakers with the Devil and his angels in hell for evermore. Wherefore my brethren, put on the bowels of compassion, and let the lamentable estate of these miserable people enter into your consideration. One God created us; they have reasonable souls and intellectual faculties as well as we; we all have Adam for our common parent. Yea, by nature the condition of us both is all one: the servants of sin, and slaves of the Devil. Oh remember, I beseech you, what was the state of England before the Gospel was preached in our country?[78]

The voice of William Crashaw was heard, via Whitaker, along the James.

Whitaker ended his 'good news' with a kind of postscript to the sermon: eight pages devoted to a fresh and charming description of the beauty and riches of Virginia – its rivers, its climate (not so cold as England nor so hot as Spain), its soil and minerals, its trees, plants and herbs, its beasts, birds and fish. Like his father, and his great-uncle the Dean, Alexander rejoiced in his skill as an angler: 'I have caught with mine angle pike, carp, eel, perches of six several kinds, cray fish and the torope or little turtle, besides many other smaller kinds.'[79] He wrote of the 'great ridge of high hills' a week's journey from Henrico:[80] the Appalachians. And he was pleased with his success at planting corn; though he needed help, 'having not a body inured to such labour'.[81]

[75] 26-7.   [76] 25.   [77] 40.   [78] 24.   [79] 42.   [80] 38.   [81] 43.

The work was predictably rounded off by a request to the members of the Virginia Company that they pray for the Church in Virginia; 'and pray also for me, that the ministration of His gospel may be powerful and effectual, by me, to the salvation of many, and advancement of the kingdom of Jesus Christ'.[82]

It may be noted here that *Good Newes from Virginia* was one of the books in the library of William Brewster (a Peterhouse man) at Leiden.[83]

Within a year the prayers of the Virginia Company were strikingly (even melodramatically) answered. In the spring of 1614 Pocahontas, now aged nineteen, became a convert to Christianity. Dale and Argall had had a showdown with the Indians in 1613, demanding that they surrender their weapons: 'if they would do this, we would be friends; if not, burn all.' The Indians fired their arrows at the English, so Dale 'killed some, hurt others, marched into the land, burnt their houses, took their corn' – and proposed 'to burn all, if they would not do as we demanded'. There followed a truce, a 'bargain' (with the help of 'the God of battles'). And Pocahontas was taken under Dale's custody: 'Powhatan's daughter I caused to be carefully instructed in Christian religion; who, after she had made some good progress therein, renounced publicly her country idolatry, openly confessed her Christian faith; was, as she desired, baptised.'[84]

Pocahontas had been sent to live at Henrico. The baptism, one assumes, was performed by Alexander Whitaker. She was given the name 'Rebecca'. Further, in April 1614 Richard Buck conducted at Jamestown the marriage of Rebecca to John Rolfe. (The fact that Pocahontas had married an Indian, Kocoum, in 1610, was apparently not a 'just impediment'.) The bride was given away by a 'brother' of Powhatan, Opachisco; and two of her brothers attended the ceremony.

Rolfe had been among those shipwrecked in Bermuda in 1609. His wife had died shortly after the arrival at Jamestown in 1610, and so had his baby daughter (but not before she had been baptised as 'Bermuda' by Buck). Rolfe's main interest in Virginia was tobacco: to improve the native root, *Nicotiana Rùstica* (which William Strachey thought weak and bitter) by importing *Nicotiana Tabacum* from the West Indies.[85] He succeeded in 1612; and his first shipment reached London in 1614.

Rolfe's letter to Sir Thomas Dale, 'patron and father of us in this country', about the 'mighty war in my meditations' occasioned by his passion for Pocahontas (the mental debate about the Book of Ezra) has already been discussed: in Chapter 5, pp.110-11.[86]

[82] 44.

[83] Barbour, *Three Worlds of Smith*, 342.

[84] June 1614 letter of Dale; in Hamor, *True Discourse*, 53-5.

[85] Strachey, *Virginia Britania*, 123.

[86] Perry Miller made effective use of the letter in 'The Religious Impulse in the Founding of Virginia', *William and Mary Quarterly*, October 1948 (3rd series, V, 4),

The baptism and the marriage were a symbolic turning point in the history of the seven-year-old colony. From the Indian point of view, writes Nancy O. Lurie,[87] the 'strengthening of the social bond between Indians and Europeans helped solidify Powhatan's power and prestige among the confederated tribes, as he was thus enduringly allied with the whites'. Whitaker, writing to his cousin William Gouge in June 1614 was also optimistic:[88]

> Sir, the colony here is much better. Sir Thomas Dale, our religious and valiant Governor, hath now brought that to pass which never before could be effected. For by war upon our enemies, and kind usage of our friends, he hath brought them to seek for peace of us; which is made, and they dare not break. But that which is best, one Pocahontas, or Matoa, the daughter of Powhatan, is married to an honest and discreet English gentleman, Master Rolfe, and that after she had openly renounced her country idolatry, confessed the faith of Jesus Christ, and was baptised: which thing Sir Thomas Dale had laboured a long time to ground in her.

Ralph Hamor, who sent all these letters to England, with his own commentary, emphasised that 'after five year's intestine war with the revengeful, implacable Indians, a firm peace (not again easily to be broken) hath been lately concluded' – 'even with that subtle old revengeful Powhatan'.[89] Hamor gave most of the credit to Captain Samuel Argall then aged 33:[90] who

> by his best experience of the disposition of those people, partly by gentle usage and partly by the composition and mixture of threats, hath ever kept fair and friendly quarter with our neighbours bordering on other rivers – of affinity, yea consanguinity no less near than brothers to Powhatan – such is his well-known temper and discretion. Yea to this pass hath he brought them, that they assuredly trust upon what he promiseth, and are as careful in performing their mutual promises, as though they contended to make that maxim That there is no faith to be held with infidels, a mere and absurd paradox. Nay, as I have heard himself relate, who is *fide dignus*, they have even been pensive and discontented with themselves because they know not how to do him some acceptable good turn.

And so an English M.P., speaking in May 1614 in the House of Commons, could stress that the conquest of Virginia was 'just' (unlike the Spanish conquest) because of our 'merciful and respective' usage of the Indian.[91]

Alexander Whitaker had contracted in 1611 to remain in Virginia

---

reprinted (1956) in his *Errand into the Wilderness*, ch.4, 'Religion and Society in the Early Literature of Virginia'.

[87] In Smith (ed.), *Seventeenth-Century America*, 48. For the policy and motives of Powhatan from 1606 see also Craven, *White, Red, and Black*, 44-8.

[88] Hamor, *True Discourse*, 59-61.

[89] *ibid.*, 2.

[90] *ibid.*, 3.

[91] Brown, *Genesis*, II, 693.

for three years. He now elected to 'abide in my vocation here until I be lawfully called from hence'.[92] As things turned out, he was now at the halfway mark of his ministry. In his letter to William Gouge in 1614, Whitaker gave a glimpse of the routine of his 'preaching ministry' at Henrico. (William was the son of Thomas Gouge, shareholder in the Virginia Company, and Elizabeth Culverwell Gouge, the sister of Alexander's mother.)

Every Sabbath day we preach in the forenoon, and catechise in the afternoon. Every Saturday at night I exercise in Sir Thomas Dale's house. Our church affairs be consulted upon by the minister and four of the religious men. Once every month we have a communion; and once a year a solemn Fast.

This passage was printed in 1615 (page 60) in the second issue of Ralph Hamor's *A True Discourse of the Present Estate of Virginia*: it had not been in the first. (The 1860 reprint published at Albany, N.Y., is of the second issue; the 1957 facsimile edition – Virginia State Library Publications No.3, Richmond, Va. – is of the first.) This spiritual routine was really 'according to the constitutions of the Church of England in all fundamental points'; with a marked bias in the 'puritan' direction. (So marked, perhaps, as to have made desirable Whitaker's departure from Yorkshire.) By the Canons of 1604 (LIX) the minister had to 'catechise' every Sunday for thirty minutes before evening prayer; that is, to instruct the 'youth and ignorant persons' in the Commandments, the Creed, and the Catechism contained in the Book of Common Prayer, so Whitaker was orthodox there, although one imagines his instruction was not so confined by the Liturgy. There were various 'catechisms' in more or less official circulation in England, including one already mentioned, by Alexander's great-uncle Alexander Nowell. In 1622 someone presented the Quarter Court of the Virginia Company in London with the Catechism of Zacharias Ursinus, to be sent to the colony.[93] The Prayer Book catechism had the advantage of brevity. To preach every Sunday was hardly customary among the majority of incumbents in England, and Authority was slightly suspicious of over-sermonising; but the 'godly pastors' had always tried to do so. Monthly communion was the practice of Calvin at Geneva. By the 1604 Canons, the' laity were bound to receive communion three times a year at least (XXI,XXII) – except at the Colleges of Oxford and Cambridge, the requirement for all members thereof being at least four times (XXIII). But the Canons had the ideal of 'oftentimes receiving the communion' (XIII); and the communion service was to be celebrated every month at Oxford and Cambridge Colleges (XXIII). (The 'pilgrim' church at Leiden from 1609 celebrated the Lord's Supper every Sunday; a practice they were unable to follow at first in New Plymouth, as there

[92] Hamor, *True Discourse*, 60-1.
[93] Kingsbury, *Records*, I, 589.

was no cleric on the 'Mayflower.') Canon LXXII recognised 'solemn fasts' (and 'fasting days' were in the calendar: LXIV); but such were to be held only at 'the license and direction' of the Bishop. Also, only the Bishop could authorise 'prophecies or exercises' (put on a level with exorcisms): LXXII. Such 'prophesyings' – meetings to discuss scripture – were banned in the Province of Canterbury from the 1570s, because of the danger of lay participation; but they continued in the North. So Whitaker's routine in Henrico was very like that of his Yorkshire parish: the 'exercise' in Henrico was a prayer and study meeting with his parishioners – a feature again of English 'puritan' pastors, on the fringes of illegality, perhaps.

The four 'religious men' spring from Gates' 1610 requirements. To some readers in England they would seem suspiciously like 'elders', as in the Church of Scotland. One thinks also of the four Elders whom the Reverend Lewis Hughes of Bermuda was to institute as part of his church government in 1617,. in the convenient absence of the Governor:

I have, by the help of God, begun a church government by Minister and Elders. I have made bold to choose four Elders for the town publicly, by lifting up of hands, and calling upon God, when the Governor was out of the town.[94]

Hughes was a Welshman, twenty-four years older than Whitaker, who had gone up to Jesus College Oxford in 1582. The 'precedent' for his action was the presbyterian form of government allowed by Elizabeth I in the Channel Islands.

Virginia was, by necessity (and perhaps even from conviction) a community in which the laity played a greater part than in England. Whitaker's four 'religious' laymen are a hint of the development of the lay Vestry (the governing body of the parish) in Virginia from the 1630s.[95]

Compulsion was greater than in England; again, the feel of the military garrison on the frontier. In 1618 it was to be decreed in Virginia that a settler who missed attendance at church on Sunday was to be imprisoned for one night and made 'a slave the week following' (there were as yet no negroes in Virginia: the equation of black skin and slave status is a later development). For a second offence, the transgressor was to be a slave for a month; and after the third, for a year and a day.[96] But, as the General Assembly at Jamestown confirmed in 1619, all was to be 'according to the ecclesiastical laws and orders of the Church of England'.[97]

[94] Manchester Papers. Historical Manuscripts Commission, 8th Report, Appendix, part II, 1881, p.32. For Hughes and puritanism in Bermuda see Andrews, I, 229-35; W.F. Craven, *William and Mary Quarterly*, January 1937.

[95] Brydon, *Virginia's Mother Church*, 90-102.

[96] Kingsbury, *Records*, III, 93.

[97] *ibid.*, 172.

But Whitaker had boasted to Crashaw in his letter of August 1611 that 'we have no need of ceremonies'.[98] Archbishop Cranmer had written in 1549, in one of his essays prefacing the Prayer Book ('Concerning Ceremonies, why some be abolished and some retained')[99] that 'the keeping or omitting of a ceremony, in itself considered, is but a small thing'; and that 'we think it convenient that every country should use such ceremonies as they shall think best, to the setting forth of God's honour and glory': 'in men's ordinances it often changes diversely in diverse countries'. Such words sounded a different note by the James than by the Thames – or the Cam. In a forthright phrase to Gouge in 1614 Whitaker expressed surprise that 'so few of our English ministers that were so hot against the surplice and subscription come hither, where neither is spoken of'. This phrase was printed in the first issue of Hamor's book in 1615 (page 60). In the second issue the passage was omitted and carefully replaced – without disturbing the layout of the page – by the description of the spiritual routine at Henrico, already discussed. A little too dangerous for England in 1615. John Smith quoted the deleted phrase in 1624, in his *Generall Historie*; and the whole passage, as written by Whitaker, appeared in print in 1625 in the pages of the Johnian Samuel Purchas (*Hakluytus Posthumus* or *Purchas His Pilgrimes*). Whitaker thought a surplice would look rather inappropriate by the banks of the James. (John Gadsby Chapman, in portraying the Baptism of Pocahontas in his series of oil paintings of 1840 in the Rotunda of the Capital Building in Washington D.C., gave the cleric a surplice; this looks well, but is inaccurate). Whitaker would never have gone so far as Mr Hughes in Bermuda, who boasted that 'the Book of Common Prayer, I use it not at all', and drew up his own private liturgy on the Geneva model, a manuscript of seventeen pages, so that 'the service of God in these islands may be so established now, as hereafter there be no such bitter contention about it, as is in England'.[100] It was not to be expected that the nephew of Arthur Dent, Ezekiel Culverwell and Laurence Chaderton would be a strict conformist to the letter of Anglican orthodoxy. The puritan 'godly pastors', like Anglo-catholic parish priests in the nineteenth century, passed easily into nonconformity; that is, they did not scrupulously observe the regulations about vestments, ornaments and ceremonies. But Whitaker was a Cambridge conformist, in the moderate – and pastoral – puritan tradition within the 'laws of ecclesiastical polity'.

In the spring of 1617 Alexander Whitaker was drowned in a crossing of the James River, aged thirty-two. Later in the same year Samuel Whitaker, who had spent a quiet life at Cambridge as a Fellow of King's died equally quietly, and was buried in the College Chapel. A curious but happy irony, that two lives so very differently

[98] Brown, *Genesis*, I, 499-500.
[99] Porter, ed., *Puritanism in Tudor England*, 19-21.
[100] See note 94.

spent should have been terminated in such fraternal sequence.

Also in the spring of 1617 Rebecca Rolfe, 'a Virginia lady born' was buried in the chancel of St George's Church, Gravesend, Kent: on 21 March.

Pocahontas had arrived in England in June 1616, aged about 21. She had travelled from Jamestown, with Rolfe, their baby son Thomas, and about a dozen Indians, including her brother-in-law Uttamatomakkin (who had married another daughter of Powhatan). John Chamberlain wrote to Sir Dudley Carleton on 22 June:[101]

> Sir Thomas Dale is arrived from Virginia, and brought with him some ten or twelve, old and young, of that country; among whom is Pocahontas, daughter of Powhatan, a king or cacique of that country, married to one Rolfe, an Englishman. I hear not of any other riches or matter of worth, but only some quantity of sassafras, tobacco, pitch, tar and clapboard; things of no great value, unless there were plenty, and nearer hand. All I can hear of it is, that the country is good to live in, if it were stored with people, and might in time become commodious: but there is no present profit to be expected.

Pocahontas (who was given an allowance of £4 a week by the Virginia Company), lived first off Fleet Street, in a tavern already called the 'Bell Savage' (Belle Sauvage); and then six miles away, at Brentford, where she had a rather embarrassing reunion with John Smith. One hopes she met Hakluyt; who died in London on 23 November. She certainly met the reverend Samuel Purchas, and was grandly entertained by the Bishop of London, John King. Her portrait was drawn by the Dutch engraver Simon van de Passe.[102] In January 1617 Chamberlain wrote again about the 'Virginian woman Pocahontas'.[103] She had been presented to James I; and 'well placed at the Masque' – the masque, on 6 January 1617, was 'The Vision of Delight' by Ben Jonson. Her return to Virginia had also been planned, though 'sore against her will': 'if the wind would come about to send them away.'

Samuel Purchas met Uttamatomakkin (called Tomocomo by the English) frequently at the house of his friend Theodore Goulston, M.D.[104] 'where I have both seen him sing and dance his diabolical measures; and heard him discourse of his country, Sir Thomas Dale's man being the interpreter'. Tomocomo was very eager to argue for the Indian religion, preferring 'his God to ours', the God of the St John's of William Whitaker. He was, commented Purchas, 'a blasphemer of what he knew not'; and argued that the 'Okee, or devil' had 'taught them their husbandry', and 'to wear their devil-lock at the left ear'. He

[101] *Court and Times of James I*, I, 415; Wright, *Elizabethans' America*, 225.

[102] This, or copies of it, frequently reproduced: Plate 3 in Washburn, ed., *The Indian and the White Man*. Plate 4 is an 18th century version of Pocahontas: a well mannered young lady. Plate 5 is 19th century: a daughter of the wilderness.

[103] *Court and Times of James I*, I, 388. For Pocahontas in England, see Barbour, *Pocahontas*.

[104] *Purchas His Pilgrimes*, Glasgow ed., XIX, 118-19.

had also been surprised 'at the sight of so much corn and trees in his journey from Plymouth to London; the Virginians imagining that defect thereof had brought us thither.'

Purchas tells something of the last days of Pocahontas. Argall's ship, returning to Virginia, had left London and put in at Gravesend, where she came 'to her end and grave;· having given great demonstration of her Christian sincerity, as the first fruits of Virginian conversion'.

Rolfe sailed from Gravesend with the baby Thomas at the end of March 1617. But in the passage to Plymouth he found 'much fear and hazard' of the child's health 'being not fully recovered of his sickness; and lack of attendance, for those who looked to him had need of nurses themselves'. So the boy was left behind at Plymouth, from where Rolfe sailed on 10 April. This was related by Rolfe in a letter from Jamestown on 8 June to Sir Edwin Sandys, 'a father to me, my wife and child'.[105] The colony was 'in good estate'; 'the Indians very loving and willing to part with their children'; 'my wife's death is much lamented, my child much desired' – but the soul of Pocahontas 'I doubt not, resteth in eternal happiness'. The warnings of the Book of Ezra had been scotched.

In March 1618 Governor Argall wrote to London:[106]

Powhatan goes from place to place visiting his country, taking his pleasure in good friendship with us; laments his daughter's death, but glad her child is living. So doth Opechancanough. Both want to see him; but desires that he may be stronger before he returns.

Powhatan died later in 1618, and was succeeded by Opitchapan, although Opechancanough was the real power in the Empire. Argall wrote to the London Company to give them 'warning that Opechancanough and the natives have given their country to Mr Rolfe's child, and that they will reserve it from all others till he comes for years'. London was not impressed. Rumour had it that this was a device of the colony 'to some especial purpose for yourself'. Whatever the case, 'we shall little esteem of any such conveyance'.[107]

Thomas Rolfe did not go to Virginia until 1635, when he was twenty. John Rolfe had died in March 1622; possibly in the massacre organised by Opechancanough – although more probably of natural causes. He had married an English girl in Virginia in 1620, Joan Pierce. They had one daughter.

* * *

A final tribute to Alexander Whitaker is best left to William

[105] Kingsbury, *Records*, III, 70-3.
[106] *ibid.*, 92.
[107] *ibid.*, II, 52-3.

Crashaw, who noted, in the Epistle Dedicatory to *Good Newes from Virginia*, that Whitaker

without any persuasion, but God's, and his own heart, did voluntarily leave his warm nest; and to the wonder of his kindred, and amazement of them that knew him, undertook his hard, but in my judgement heroical, resolution to go to Virginia and help to bear the name of God unto the Gentiles. Men may muse at it, some may laugh, and others wonder at it. But will you know the reason? God will be glorified in His own works; and what He hath determined to do, He will find means to bring to pass, for the perfecting therefore of this blessed work.

As John Rolfe wrote in 1616, before he sailed from Jamestown with Pocahontas, 'what need we then to fear' in our 'zealous work' in the land of Virginia,[108] 'but to go up at once as peculiar people, marked and chosen by the finger of God to possess it'.

Postscript

After this Chapter was in page proof, it was drawn to my attention that Alexander Whitaker's will, signed on 16 February 1611 in the presence of Richard Culverwell and Caleb Gouge, and proved on 4 August 1617, is preserved in the London Guildhall Library: Ms 9172/29 (Commissary of London: Wills 1616-17), item 75. £5 are bequeathed to each of his two brothers, Jabez and William, and £5 to each of his three sisters – Susanna, Mary and Frances. William Gouge receives £2. Samuel, the executor, is to have Alexander's 'bill of adventure to Virginia, with all the profits thereunto belonging'. Alexander owes £4 to a York linen draper. And is owed over £100: £24 from Samuel and £16 from his cousin Anthony Culverwell; £60 in miscellaneous amounts, to be gathered by William Crashaw; and £7 for a chest of viols sold to Sir Henry Griffith of Burton Agnes, in the East Riding of Yorkshire (whose son was to enter St John's Cambridge in 1619). Crashaw was rector of Burton Agnes 1600-1605, and 1613-18. Two of the sisters were married: Mary to Randolph Clark; and Susanna to John Lothrop (1584-1653), a Yorkshireman who graduated from Queens', Cambridge (B.A. 1607, M.A. 1609), and was to sail to Plymouth Colony in 1634, becoming the first minister of Scituate, and then minister at Barnstable. Susanna apparently died in the early 1630s, when John was in prison.

[108] Rolfe, 'True Relation of the State of Virginia', ed. H.C. Taylor. For the Rolfe family, Barbour, *Pocahontas*, 214-15, Appendix II.

20
Temperate Government and Doubtful Times, 1616-1619

When John and Rebecca Rolfe sailed to England in April 1616, the plantation on the James River had survived for nine years. They sailed under Samuel Argall, with, among the passengers, Sir Thomas Dale, who, with Gates, had controlled the colony for five years (since his arrival with Whitaker in May 1611) and who was leaving Virginia for ever. The then acting governor was George Yeardley; who had acquired a wife with the W.C. Fieldsian name of Temperance Flowerdieu.

Rolfe wrote a report on the condition of the colony in 1616: 'A True Relation of the State of Virginia', which was paraphrased in 1617 by Samuel Purchas (in the third edition of *Purchas his Pilgrimage*) but not printed in full, from the manuscript, until 1951 (edited by the owner, Henry C. Taylor; New Haven; with essays on the manuscript by F.L. Berkeley and on Rolfe by J.M. Jennings).[1]

The manuscript was dedicated to William Herbert, Earl of Pembroke (of Wilton, Wiltshire). Herbert had been on the London Council of the Virginia Company since 1609. He was a nephew of Sir Philip Sidney; friend of Inigo Jones, John Donne, George Chapman, and Ben Jonson; and in 1623 the 'first folio' of Shakespeare was to be dedicated to William and his younger brother Philip, 'the most noble and incomparable pair of brethren' (William naturally has also been taken to be the 'Mr W.H.' of the Sonnets).[2]

Rolfe condemned the balance of power at Jamestown in the first three years: 'aristocratical' rule, by the Council with a President chosen therefrom, which meant 'envy, dissension and jars'. 'All would be Caesars, none inferior to other.' Then, in the reorganisation of 1609, the King granted 'a more absolute government'. But the basic problem remained 'emnity with the Indians'. Peace came by 1614:

which still continueth so firm, that the people yearly plant and reap quietly, and travail in the woods a fowling and hunting as freely and securely free from danger or treachery as in England. The great blessings of God have followed this peace; and in it, next under Him, hath bred our plenty. Every man sitteth under his fig tree in safety.

[1] Quotations from the New Haven edition, 34-41.
[2] The article on Herbert in *Dictionary of National Biography* was by Sidney Lee (1891).

The plantations on the James were 'all our own ground, not so much by conquest, which the Indians hold by a just and lawful title, but purchased of them freely, and they very willingly selling it'.

There were five settlements in addition to Jamestown. They included Kecoughtan (Elizabeth City: today, Hampton) where the population was only twenty, the minister William Mease; Henrico, with twenty-two farmers and sixteen soldiers, where William Wickham 'in his life and doctrine gives good examples and godly instructions to the people'; and Bermuda Hundred, on the south side of the River from Henrico, the residence of Yeardley, where Alexander Whitaker 'a good divine', 'son to that reverend and famous divine Dr Whitaker', has 'the ministerial charge'. The population of Bermuda Hundred was 120; being over one third of the total population of English Virginia. Buck was still in Jamestown: 'a very good preacher' to the fifty colonists there. So there were four ministers in 1616: Whitaker, Buck, Wickham and Mease.

Rolfe gives the population of the colony as 351. In 1611 it had been 450: by 1618 it was to be 600, and by Easter 1619, 1000.[3] Of the 351, 205 were soldiers and labourers (58%); 81 were farmers (23%); and there were 65 women and children (19%). Rolfe also tells us that there were 6 horses, 216 goats, and 144 head of cattle.

There were those patrons of Virginia in England who were fickle, and 'withdrew themselves', so that 'this action was almost sunk down in forgetfulness'. Others (such as William Herbert, Earl of Pembroke) 'mightily upheld this Christian cause'. Similarly,

Caleb and Joshua, in the very heat of the grudgings, murmurs and assemblies of the children of Israel, stood stoutly for the Lord's cause; commending the goodness of the land they discovered to the faces of their opposers, and the easiness to obtain it, even to the peril of their lives.

'The Lord's cause' was the propagation of the Gospel to the Indians. It is to be lamented 'how lightly the works of God are nowadays generally regarded', and 'the works of the world, as though they were eternal, hungered for and thirsted after with unsatiable greediness'. But surely

there can be no heart (if not hardened as the nether mill-stone) but would even break itself to pieces and distribute to many poor souls some part thereof to purge them from their lees of sin, and to settle them in the right paths of holiness.

Some of the Indians have been 'won to us already': 'by piety, clemency, courtesy and civil demeanour.' There is no mention of Pocahontas: but Rolfe's heartfelt sympathy shines through the promotional vocabulary – the tortured urge to

[3] Andrews, I, 134, 136.

convert and bring to the knowledge and true worship of Jesus Christ
thousands of poor, wretched and misbelieving people, on whose faces a
Christian cannot look without sorrow, pity and commiseration, seeing they
bear the image of our heavenly creator, and we and they come from one and
the same mould. Especially we knowing that they, merely through ignorance
of God and Christ, do run headlong, yea with joy, into destruction and
perpetual damnation. For which knowledge we are the more bound and
indebted to Almighty God; for what were we before the Gospel of Christ
shined amongst us?

Rolfe arrived back in Jamestown in May 1617, after an absence of
just over a year. After three weeks (during which Argall had
succeeded Yeardley as Governor) Rolfe wrote to Sir Edwin Sandys[4]
reporting that the buildings, fortifications and boats were 'much
ruined' and in 'great want'. However, Yeardley and Argall were
'repairing and making straight' what was 'decayed and crooked'. 'All
men cheerfully labour about their grounds, their hearts and hands not
ceasing from work, though many have scarce rags to cover their naked
bodies.' There was 'great plenty' of English wheat and barley, Indian
corn, tobacco, hemp and flax; 'the cattle thrive, and increase
exceedingly well; the ploughs yearly work; and oxen are plentiful.' So
on the whole the 'colony' was 'in good estate; and enjoying a firmer
peace and plenty.'

By this time Whitaker had been drowned. His death was reported
by Argall, 'principal Governor of Virginia', in a letter to the London
Council on 9 June 1617:[5] 'Mr Whitaker being drowned.' So the
colonists 'want ministers'; in the mean time Argall 'will use his best
endeavours', and hopes that Archbishop Abbot will 'give Mr
Wickham power to administer sacraments'. A replacement of course
was hoped for. By 1619 the names of George Keith, Samuel Maycock
and Robert Pawlett had appeared on the records; Pawlett was also a
medical doctor. William Mease apparently left in 1620. A 1625
'Discourse' on the policy of the Virginia Company stated that since
1619 'there were sent out more than eight able ministers'.[6] It is
difficult to keep track of the possible comings and goings: but the
names seem to include Thomas Bargrave, Thomas White, Jonas
Stockham, Hawte Wyatt, Francis Bolton, Robert Staples, Patrick
Copland, David Sandys, Greville Pooley, John Pemberton, and a Mr
Hopkins.

The *dramatis personae* were changing. Powhatan died in April 1618.
Opitchapan (Itopatin) was his technical successor; but by 1620
Opechancanough had supplanted him. Also in April 1618 Lord De La
Warr sailed for Virginia to resume his Governorship; but he died
during the passage, and the London Council appointed as his
successor George Yeardley (characterised by Alistair Cooke as 'lazy,

---

[4] Rolfe to Sandys, 8 June 1617. Ferrar Papers, Magdalene, Cambridge. Kingsbury, *Records*, III, 70-3.

[5] *ibid.*, III, 74.

[6] *ibid.*, IV, 522.

inefficient, bewildered, kindly, and honest')[7] who was knighted by James I at Newmarket in November 1618. In April 1619 Thomas Smythe was replaced as Treasurer of the Virginia Company by Edwin Sandys (who was amicably succeeded in June 1620 by Henry Wriothesley, Earl of Southampton). In November 1618 Yeardley's appointment as Governor of Virginia was confirmed by the Quarter Count of the Virginia Company in London.

From 1612 – the year of the third Charter of the Virginia Company – there was, besides the Council, a weekly 'Court' of representatives of the Council together with fifteen members of the Company, and in London, every January, May, June and November, 'Great and General Courts of the Council and Company of Adventurers for Virginia', which all shareholders could attend, regardless of the extent of their investment (a single share was £12.10s): sometimes the Quarter Courts attracted 200 members.[8] Charles I in 1625 was retrospectively to condemn this 'popular government': where 'affairs of the greatest moment were, and must be, ruled by the greater number of votes' (quite unsuitable for the government of a colony).[9] In the early 1930s Charles Andrews stressed the significance of the 1612 arrangements as having

a direct relation to the adoption of a popular form of government for Virginia and so eventually for all the royal colonies in America. Such adoption marks the beginning of the idea of generality control in America and so has a bearing on the growth of an American ideal.[10]

Yeardley was given Instructions by the Company; the 'Great Charter' of Virginia 'myth'. One of the provisions was for the abolition of martial law in the colony. Another (in fact a separate order from the so-called 'charter') was for the summoning at Jamestown of a General Assembly.[11]

Sir George Yeardley sailed in January 1619 and arrived at Jamestown in April. On 30 July – shortly after the twelfth anniversary of the founding of Jamestown – the General Assembly met in the parish church: the Governor; the Jamestown Council; and twenty two burgesses. Two burgesses were elected from each of four 'boroughs' and seven 'plantations'. The boroughs were Jamestown; Kecoughtan; Henrico; and Charles City, reckoned 'the most commodious place for health, security, profit and conveniency'[12] (Charles City was near Henrico, and contained Bermuda Hundred). The Speaker was John Pory. Pory had come to Virginia in 1619 as Yeardley's secretary. He had been at Gonville and Caius College, Cambridge, from 1588 to

[7] *America*, 1973, 67.
[8] Craven, *Dissolution of the Virginia Company*, 30-1.
[9] Royal Proclamation, 13 May 1625. Jensen, *American Colonial Documents*, 235.
[10] Andrews, I, 103.
[11] Craven, *Dissolution*, 52-4, 67-80.
[12] Kingsbury, *Records*, III, 540.

1595, and had been an MP in the first Parliament of James I. He was now in his late forties. Buck recited the opening prayer. The session ended five days later. Meetings ended at 4 p.m. because of the heat; many burgesses were ill, and one died. The 'House of Burgesses' did not meet separately until 1663. Pory's report of the proceedings survives in the Public Record Office.[13]

At the final session, on 4 August,[14] Pory was asked to forward certain apologies to the Treasurer, Council and Company in England. Heat and sickness had made the sessions abrupt. In such a short time the Assembly could send back to London only imperfect things: 'titles rather than laws, propositions rather than resolutions, attempts than achievements.' But perhaps the Treasurer and Council in London 'will accept our poor endeavour, and their wisdom will be ready to support the weakness of this little flock' (a Pauline phrase, which had been much liked by William Tyndale, with its associations of the 'godly remnant': the purged élite). The Assembly acknowledged that it was the right of the London Company to allow or abrogate any legislation passed in Jamestown:

Yet that it would please them not to take it in ill part if these laws which we have now brought to light do pass current and be of force till such time as we may know their farther pleasure out of England; for otherwise this people (who now at length have gotten the reins of former servitude into their own swinge) would in short time grow so insolent as they would shake off all government, and there would be no living among them.

Indeed, Rolfe thought that 'the present government', the 'most temperate and just that ever was in this country', was 'too mild indeed for many of this colony, whom unwonted liberty hath made insolent'.[15]

The General Assembly was then prorogued until 1 March 1620. The laws enacted were based on the instructions and edicts of the past eight years. There was material 'against idleness, gaming and excess in apparel'; against gambling, cards, dice, and swearing. And against drunkenness: for a first offense, private reproof by the Minister; for a second, public reproof; for a third, twelve hours in chains.[16] Again, the requirements of a disciplined frontier society. (James Oglethorpe was to ban Spirits in Georgia in 1738: Savannah, it seems, was 'poisoned' with rum, and many of the inhabitants drunk by breakfast.[17] The liquor laws of Massachusetts, 1648, were comparatively liberal.) All this was in the spirit of orthodox English legislation; one is reminded of Tudor and Stuart regulations for Cambridge and Oxford.

The clergy were to 'read divine service and exercise their ministerial function according to the ecclesiastical laws and orders of the Church

---

[13] *ibid.*, 153-77.
[14] 176-7.   [15] 170.   [16] 164-5.
[17] *Calendar of State Papers, Colonial Series, America and West Indies*, vol. xliv, 1738, ed. K.G. Davies, 1969, 121.

of England'. Every Sunday afternoon those children not ripe for Communion were to be 'catechized'. Every Sunday morning and evening there was a service with a sermon, at which attendance was compulsory ('and all such as bear arms shall bring their pieces, swords, powder and shot'). Each absence incurred a fine of three shillings (in the case of servants, a beating). 'All ministers in the Colony' were to present to the Council every March a record of baptisms, marriages, and burials (as in England, *mutatis mutandis*, in the 1604 Canons). The committers of 'ungodly disorders' (sexual offences seem to be meant) were to be presented to the Minister by the Churchwardens (again, as in England). If two warnings occasioned no amendment, the offender was to be 'suspended from the church for a time by the minister'. If still unrepentant, the name of the offender was to be brought before the Governor at one of the four yearly meetings of the clergy: Christmas, the Annunciation of the Blessed Virgin (25 March), mid-summer, and St Michael and all Angels (29 September). If the Governor approved, the offender was to be excommunicated, his person apprehended, his good seized.[18]

And now the laws concerning the Indian. Anyone trading in the Bay must promise that 'neither himself nor his company shall force or wrong the Indians'. Any settler ('servants only excepted') was at liberty to trade with the Indians; although no one could 'purposely go to any Indian towns, habitations, or places, or resorts' without leave of the Governor or the local Commander. Anyone stealing 'any canoes or other things from the Indians' was to return them, and either pay a fine (£2 for a servant, £5 for a freeholder) or be whipped. No one was to sell or give to the Indians 'any of the greater hounds', or 'any English dog of quality, as a mastiff, greyhound, land or water spaniel, or any other dog or bitch whatsoever of the English race'. Nor to sell or give any 'piece, shot or powder, or any other arms, offensive or defensive': the penalty for this was hanging, 'without all redemption'.[19]

It was enacted that 'for laying a surer foundation of the conversion of the Indians to Christian Religion', each settlement ('town, city, borough and particular plantation') should

obtain unto themselves by just means a certain number of the natives' children to be educated by them in true religion and civil course of life; of which children the most towardly boys in wit and graces of nature to be brought up by them in the first elements of literature, so to be fitted for the college intended for them, that from thence they may be sent to that work of conversion.

There had been earlier orders to draw 'some of the better disposed of the Indians to converse with our people, and to live and labour

---

[18] Kingsbury, *Records*, III, 171-3.
[19] 170-3.

amongst them'. The General Assembly ('who know well their dispositions') was rather cautious. They thought it fit

to enjoin, least to counsel, those of the Colony, neither utterly to reject them, nor yet to draw them to come in. But in case they will of themselves come voluntarily to places well peopled, there to do service in killing of deer, fishing, beating of corn, and other works, then that five or six may be admitted into every such place, and no more; and that with the consent of the Governor. Provided that good guard in the night be kept upon them; for generally (though some amongst many may prove good) they are a most treacherous people, and quickly gone when they have done a villainy. And it were fit a house were built for them to lodge in apart by themselves; and lone inhabitants by no means to entertain them.[20]

The men of the Assembly knew that in fact they lived in 'doubtful times between us and the Indians'.[21] But they did not wish to take a dogmatically 'hard' line. In May 1618 Governor Argall had issued an edict: 'No trade with the perfidious savages, nor familiarity, lest they discover our weakness.'[22] The Assembly, fourteen months later, was more confident. (In 1618 there had been trouble with the Chickahominy tribe, and the London Council advised a 'sharp revenge'; though in general they wished the colonists to 'maintain amity').[23] There was also the question of Opechancanough – and of Henry Spelman.

At the final session of the General Assembly, 4 August 1619, Captain Henry Spelman, now aged· twenty-four, appeared for questioning.[24] A certain Robert Poole, employed as an Interpreter, had been present at a meeting between Spelman and Opechancanough; and Poole had sworn under oath that Spelman had spoken 'unreverently and maliciously' about Yeardley: thus bringing into contempt the dignity of the Governor, and the honour of the colony. Spelman admitted only a remark to Opechancanough that 'within a year there would come a Governor greater than this that now is in place'. The Assembly – who had received other complaints, not only that of Poole – concluded that Spelman

hath alienated the mind of Opechancanough from this present Governor and brought him in much disesteem both with Opechancanough and the Indians; and the whole Colony in danger of their slippery designs.

If the 'rigour and extremity of the law' were applied, then Spelman would die. But in examination he had raised doubts about Poole's indictment. Some individual members of the Assembly were in favour of severity. But 'the whole court' came to the verdict that

[20] 165-6.   [21] 161.
[22] Kingsbury, *Records*, III, 93.
[23] *ibid.*, 147.
[24] *ibid.*, 174-5.

for this misdemeanour he should first be degraded of his title of Captain, at the head of the troop, and should be condemned to perform seven years' service to the Colony; in the nature of Interpreter to the Governor.

When the sentence was read to Spelman he

muttered certain words to himself; neither showing any remorse for his offenses, nor yet any thankfulness to the Assembly for their so favourable censure, which he at one time or another (God's grace not wholly abandoning him) might with some one service have been able to have redeemed.

But then Spelman 'had in him more of the savage than of the Christian'. Of all the Jamestown settlers he was the one who had, since 1609, most completely 'gone native'. The first of the Lone Rangers later to be potent figures of American 'Myth'. (John Smith is better known; but Smith was in Virginia for only two years.)

Yeardley in fact was more tolerant of Spelman, thinking his 'fault' to proceed 'much of childish ignorance'. And he 'pardoned the punishment, upon hope of amendment'. As a probationary measure, Spelman was sent as an interpreter to the Potomac tribe, 'to trade for corn'.[25] And within six months it was revealed that Poole was dishonest. Yeardley sent him in September with an invitation to Opechancanough to visit Jamestown. Slightly later, John Rolfe was asked to take a shallop up the Pamunkey (York) River, with Spelman, to visit Opechancanough also. (Rolfe claimed that Opechancanough 'professeth much love to me, and giveth much credit to my word'.) They found that the Indians had become 'very weary' of Poole; and had in fact 'accused and condemned' him as 'an instrument that sought all the means he could to break our league'. Rolfe concluded that the fears of the Colony had been occasioned by the fact of 'all messages being untruly delivered by Poole on both sides'. And in a letter to Sandys in January 1620,[26] in which the above is related, Rolfe concluded that the relations of the English with the Potomac tribe, at least, could be from henceforth 'in great love and amity: to the great content of the colony'.

Not everyone was as confident as Rolfe. Yeardley and the Council, writing from Jamestown in November 1619,[27] pointed out that Opechancanough had of late 'stood aloof, upon terms of doubt and jealousy', and could not be drawn to a 'treaty' in spite of the blandishments of Yeardley. Openchancanough had made various complaints to Yeardley, some of which were discussed by the General

[25] *ibid.*, 242.

[26] Rolfe to Sandys, January 1620. Ferrar Papers, Magdalene. Marginal notes by John Ferrar. Kingsbury, *Records*, III, 241-8: Poole material, 244-5.

[27] Ferrar papers, Magdalene. Marginal notes by Nicholas Ferrar. Kingsbury, *Records*, III, 226-9. This passage, 228.

Assembly on 30 July 1619;[28] the seizure by English parties of canoes and corn. The offending Captain was rebuked.

In 1619 the whole question of relations with the Indians seemed to be in an uncertain and tricky state.

The November 1619 letter of Yeardley and the Jamestown Council also reported a request from Opechancanough,[29] relayed by Nenemettanan (whom the English called 'English Jack', 'Jack of the Feathers'). Opechancanough wished to revenge himself on an Indian tribe for 'murdering certain women of his country, contrary to the Law of Nations'; and wanted ten English soldiers to help him. He would provide Indian shoes; his warriors would carry the Englishmen's armour; and the Indians and the English between them would agree to 'share all the booty of male and female children, of corn and other things; and to divide the conquered land into two equal parts between us and them'. This was an offer which Jamestown could not refuse. The campaign was 'lawful and well grounded'; the help required was small, 'and not of consequence enough for Opechancanough to put any treacherous disaster upon'. It would oblige him, at a difficult time. And English aid might, 'at least for the present',

win amity and confidence from Opitchapan the great king; from Opechancanough his brother; and likewise from their subjects of these three rivers of Roanoke, Powhatan (James) and Pamunkey (York).

It was also thought that

the children taken in their war might in time serve as well for private uses of particular persons as to furnish the intended college; this being a fair opportunity for the advancement of this blessed work, seeing those Indians are in no sort willing to sell or, by fair means, to part with their children.

By 1619 the question of educating the Indian – and of education in general in Virginia – was exercising the mind of the Virginia Company in London.

By one of the ironies – perhaps the most trenchant irony – in American history, the same month which saw the prorogation of the General Assembly at Jamestown (the traditions of Westminster transplanted to Virginia) saw also the arrival of the first negroes. (Nothing is known of the fate of the negroes – possibly three hundred or more – who were in Drake's fleet when he arrived off Roanoke in June 1586: some may have been put ashore, in what is now North Carolina, but there is no evidence for this.)[30] The Assembly ended on 4 August 1619. At 'the latter end of August' a Dutch vessel arrived in Chesapeake Bay from the West Indies. The captain, wrote Rolfe in his

[28] Kingsbury, *Records*, III, 157.
[29] *ibid.*, 228.
[30] Quinn, *England and Discovery of America*, 433-4.

1620 letter to Sandys, 'brought not anything but twenty and odd negroes'. He needed provisions. And Yeardley, at 'the best and easiest rate' possible, 'bought' the negroes for 'victuals'.[31] By 1625 there were 23 negro 'servants' in Virginia. (There were also 487 white 'servants' and 2 Indian 'servants': most of them in the service of 48 families.)[32]

It was not without significance for the development of North America that John Smith, in a book published at London in June 1616,[33] had drawn a distinction between the 'poor savages' of Virginia and New England, and the 'black brutish Negers' of Africa.

---

[31] Kingsbury, III, 243. For a critical assessment of Rolfe's information, Craven, *White, Red, and Black*, 1971, 77-81.

[32] Sigmund Diamond, *American Journal of Sociology*, March 1958 (XLIII, 5), 472.

[33] *Description of New England*, Smith-Arber, 191. In 1630 Smith wrote about Negroes: 'as idle and devilish people as any in the world', and yet in Spanish America the 'best servants' (Smith-Arber, 955). Milton in 1641 imagined the damned in Hell providing for the Prelates a 'raving and bestial tyranny', treating them as 'their slaves and negroes' (*Of Reformation in England*, final paragraph). In 1599 George Abbot described the natives of the Zona Torrida as 'not only blackish, like the Moors', but 'exceedingly black': *Nigritae*, 'named Negroes, as them whom no men are blacker' (*Briefe Description of the whole Worlde*: 'De Reliquis Africae regionibus maritimis'). See further, Jones, *Elizabethan Image of Africa*, 1971; Jordan, *White Over Black*, 1968.

21

Pilgrims, Strangers and Savages,
1617-1621

In 1617 some members of the community of English religious exiles at
Leiden had begun to think of emigrating to 'those vast and unpeopled
countries of America, which are fruitful and fit for habitation, being
devoid of all civil inhabitants'. The story was told by one of them,
William Bradford: born in 1590, of ordinary Yorkshire farming and
shop-keeping stock. His *History of Plymouth Plantation*, begun in 1630 in
New England, was not published until 1856;[1] but New England
historians had previously made use of it. *New Englands Memoriall*
(Cambridge, Mass., 1669) by Bradford's nephew Nathaniel Morton is
for the period before 1647, where Bradford ended, essentially the work
of the uncle (who died in 1657).

The inhabitants of America, Bradford assumed, far from being
'civil', were 'savage and brutish men which range up and down, little
otherwise than the wild beasts of the same'.[2] He had probably been
reading Robert Johnson's *Nova Britannia*, 1609, with its 'wild and
savage people that live and lie up and down in troops, like herds of
deer'.[3] (The comparison with herds of deer had also been made by
William Symonds in his 1609 sermon.)[4] But Bradford had also been
reading the gloomier Spanish and Italian material. The 'savage
people', he wrote, are

cruel, barbarous and most treacherous, being most furious in their rage and
merciless where they overcome; not being content only to kill and take away
life, but delight to torment men in the most bloody manner that may be;
flaying some alive with the shells of fishes, cutting off the members and joints
of others by piecemeal and broiling on the coals, eat the collops of their flesh
in their sight whilst they live, with other cruelties horrible to be related.

A rather selective characterisation for a man who owned a copy of the
Decades of Pietro Martire! But Bradford was in fact concerned to draw

---

[1] Edited S.E. Morison, 1952, Modern Library. Quotation, p.25. Hereafter cited as
PP (Plymouth Plantation). Good essay on Bradford by Jesper Rosenmeier, reprinted
in Bercovitch (ed.), *The American Puritan Imagination*.
[2] Quotations in this paragraph, *PP* 25-7.
[3] Above, p.340.
[4] Above, p.351.

an analogy with the Spaniards. The truce in the Netherlands signed in 1609 was due to expire in 1621; preparations for war had begun; and 'the Spaniard might prove as cruel as the savages of America'. The English might be safer away from the Low Countries.

The aim of Bradford and his friends in 1617 was to 'live as a distinct body by themselves under the general Government of Virginia'.[5] In other words, to apply for a patent from the Virginia Company for a 'private plantation' – a feature of the Company's policy from 1616.[6] They hoped also to be granted freedom of religion. Two agents were sent from Leiden to London: Robert Cushman, by origin a Canterbury man; and John Carver, who had been a London trader. On 12 November 1617 one of the members of the London Virginia Council, Sir Edwin Sandys, wrote to pastor John Robinson and Elder William Brewster at Leiden to say that the meeting had been satisfactory.[7] Robinson and Brewster replied on 15 December:[8] the Leiden community has experience of 'the difficulties of a strange and hard land'; they are a people 'industrious and frugal'; and

we are knit together as a body in a most strict and sacred bond and covenant of the Lord, of the violation whereof we make great conscience, and by virtue whereof we do hold ourselves straitly tied to all care of each other's good and of the whole, by every one and so mutually.

In his *History*, Bradford was careful to place the story of Leiden and Plymouth in the general context of the Protestant Reformation, and indeed earlier: we are asked to read the Church historian Socrates 'Scholasticus' of Constantinople (380-450). Naturally, England was 'the first of nations whom the Lord adorned' with the 'light of the gospel'. The Day of the Lord has come: Satan, the Man of Sin, has been revealed. But Satan fights his rear-guard action against the 'Saints'. He spreads dissension: as among the English exiles at Frankfurt in the reign of Mary, where the 'poor servants of God' who 'laboured to have the right worship of God and discipline of Christ established in His Church according to the simplicity of the Gospel' were thwarted by the 'episcopally minded' (a reference to 'a book that deserves better to be known and considered': William Whittingham's *Brieff Discours off the Troubles begonne at Franckford*, 1575). And in England since 1558 the 'sincere servants of God', those wishing to see 'the churches of God revert to their ancient purity, and recover their primitive order, liberty and beauty', have been persecuted; and given – 'opprobiously and most injuriously' – the name of 'Puritan'.[9]

Yet there was in England 'travail and diligence of some godly and zealous preachers': and 'many became enlightened by the word of

[5] *PP* 29.
[6] Craven, *Dissolution of Virginia Company*, 57-8.
[7] *PP* 31-2.
[8] *PP* 32-4.
[9] *PP* 3-7. For the word 'puritan', Porter, *Puritanism in Tudor England*, 1-7.

420 *Part Three*

God'. Bradford's personal experience was confined to the 'north parts': where Nottinghamshire, Lincolnshire and Yorkshire meet – the Gainsborough area. The godly here were scorned, but bore this for 'sundry years'. Then – about 1606 – they decided to shake off the 'yoke of antichristian bondage'; and 'as the Lord's free people joined themselves (by a covenant of the Lord) into a church estate'.[10] They thus followed the tradition formalised by the congregation of Robert Browne at Norwich in 1580, and described in a book published by Browne in 1590.[11] Bradford, aged 16, joined one of these congregations in 1606. This was at Scrooby, a post-halt on the Great North Road, where William Brewster was post-master and bailiff of the manor (a manor belonging to the Sandys family). Brewster had gone up to Peterhouse, Cambridge, from Scrooby, in 1580. He remained there for only a short time; but he was to be the sole Cambridge man on the 'Mayflower'. One of the clerics associated with the Scrooby congregation was a local man, John Robinson, who had married in Nottinghamshire in 1604, thus forfeiting his Fellowship at Corpus Christi College Cambridge, which he had entered as a sizar (poor student) in 1592. The congregations 'continued together about a year, and kept their meetings every Sabbath in one place or other, exercising the worship of God amongst themselves'. But Authority was too troublesome; and 'by a joint consent they resolved to go into the Low Countries'[12] – again following the precedent of Robert Browne, a quarter of a century earlier. The decision followed much discussion. How would they fare in Holland, these folk used to 'plain country villages', a 'plain country life' and the 'innocent trade of husbandry'?[13] But in 1608 they emigrated; and eventually about 125 members of the congregation based at Scrooby reached Amsterdam – including Robinson, Brewster and Bradford. Amsterdam was unsatisfactory. The English Church established in the 1590s was now bedevilled by contention. And in the spring of 1609 the new immigrants went on to Leiden.

With 'hard and continual labour', the English survived at Leiden. A house was bought in which the congregation met, and Robinson lived, preaching three times a week. Bradford portrayed Robinson as a 'common father' (like Marcus Aurelius; or John Zizka, the Hussite leader in the 1420s of the Czech town of Tabor). Robinson stressed the 'common good', and the danger of individuals becoming 'close and cleaving to themselves'.[14] Brewster was the Elder, 'called and chosen by the church', and John Carver the (lay) Deacon. But in time the community came to desire 'a better and easier place of living'. Economic pressures had forced some members back to England. It was impossible, in a populous and foreign country, to guarantee the integrity of English youth: 'their posterity would be in danger to degenerate and be corrupted.'[15] And they disliked living in exile.

[10] *PP* 8-9.
[11] *True and Short Declaration*. Porter, *Puritanism in Tudor England*, part V.
[12] *PP* 10. [13] *PP* 11, 16. [14] *PP* 17-19. [15] *PP* 24-5.

Edward Winslow (who came from London to Leiden in 1617, aged 21, helping Brewster with his printing-press) wrote, in 1646,[16] that many had found it 'grievous to live from under the protection of the State of England'. Would we not 'lose our language and our name of English'?

Of course, added Winslow, there was also the desire to 'enlarge' the Church of Christ. Bradford had also noted the missionary motive. As with Winslow, it was at the bottom of the list:[17]

Lastly (and which was not least) a great hope and inward zeal they had of laying some good foundation, or at least to make some way thereunto, for the propagation and advancing the gospel of the Kingdom of Christ in those remote parts of the world.

Not a very confident expression of a 'great hope'! We can enlarge the Church, Winslow wrote, 'if the Lord have a people among the natives'. In other words, if any Indians are Elect. The first planters of Plymouth were loath to make such an assumption. This, together with the absence of clerics in the early years, and the fact that the main motive of the Plantation was to preserve from contamination a unique and separated community, meant that there was no attempt actively to convert the Indian. The Indian was accepted, without undue inquisitiveness: sometimes useful, sometimes a nuisance, sometimes a danger. Indian relations were a matter of diplomacy, not theology.[18]

So, in Plymouth, relations with the Indian were practical; and tended to be sensible and just.

The English in Leiden knew of the 1597 venture, approved by the Privy Council, to settle the Francis Johnson (London) separatist congregation on the Magdalen Islands in the Gulf of St Lawrence. The attempt failed; which is why Johnson went to Amsterdam.[19] They were to be dismayed in 1619 by news of the failure of a Virginia expedition from the English congregation at Emden (whither Johnson had removed in 1613). Francis Blackwell was in charge of this ship. Samuel Argall reported (according to Robert Cushman) that the vessel reached Chesapeake Bay in March 1619, after weeks of 'long seeking and beating about'. Blackwell and the Captain were dead; and of the 180 passengers and crew, 'packed together like herrings', only fifty reached Jamestown alive.[20] But Blackwell, once an Elder of the Amsterdam church, had received the blessing of Archbishop Abbot for his Virginia passage. If such a catastrophe follows such a

[16] Everyman Library, *Chronicles of the Pilgrim Fathers*, 1910 (introduction by John Masefield), 360. Hereafter cited as Everyman *Chronicles*. The Winslow quotations in the next paragraph are also on p.360.

[17] *PP* 25.

[18] Alden Vaughan writes (*New England Frontier*, 338) that the new England Puritans 'treated the Indians not as a race apart, but as fellow sinners in God's great universe'. That is not my impression of early Plymouth.

[19] Quinn, *England and Discovery of America*: ch.13, 'The First Pilgrims'; ch.12, 'England and the St Lawrence, 1577-1602'.

[20] *PP* 356-7.

blessing, wrote Bradford, 'happy are they that miss the same'![21] The men of Leiden spurned prelatical approval; but the Blackwell adventure showed that the Virginia Company might have something to offer the exiled saints.

Edwin Sandys became Treasurer of the Virginia Company in April 1619. The Leideṅ community received their patent in June. The text has not survived; but it can be assumed that land was granted for a plantation within the Company's boundaries (which reached north to Manhattan); that no specific place of settlement was mentioned; and that the leader of the settlers had authority to make regulations for local well-being, under the supervision of the Jamestown Governor and Council.[22] Robinson, 'strengthening them against their fears and perplexities, and encouraging them in their resolutions', preached on a text from I Samuel Chapter 23.[23] The Philistines were beseiging the town of Keilah, and David asked the Lord: 'Shall I go and smite these Philistines?' 'And the Lord answered him, and said, Arise, go down to Keilah; for I will deliver the Philistines into thine hand.' Only a minority of the Leiden congregation was anxious (or suitable) to settle in America. So the Pastor would, for the moment, remain; and Brewster would spiritually lead the ·Leiden emigrants. So the group left Leiden: 'they knew they were pilgrims', comments Bradford at this point.[24] Bradford gives a reference to Hebrews 11:13-16. That text concerns Old Testament exiles who 'died in faith', having seen the promises of God 'afar off'; and 'confessed that they were strangers and pilgrims on the earth'. Those who use such language 'declare plainly that they seek a country'. Their hearts are not in the country they have left: 'they desire a better country, that is, an heavenly: wherefore God is not ashamed to be called their God: for He hath prepared for them a city.'

The 'pilgrims' eventually left Holland (from Delft) on 22 July 1620. They had received a second patent from the Virginia Company, which probably (again it has not survived) gave them more autonomy that the patent of 1619. But perhaps their future would be freer in those 'northern parts of Virginia' which in 1606 had been placed under the authority of the Plymouth members of the Virginia Company – and which had not been colonised after the failure in 1608 of the settlement in Maine. John Smith had explored the northern coast in the spring and summer of 1614. And in 1616 he published *A Description of New England* (the name based on Drake's 'Nova Albion'); with a map giving various new places names, including 'Plimoth'. (Smith thought of himself as 'he that brought New England to light'.)[25]

[21] *PP* 358.

[22] Andrews, *Colonial Period*, 1, 259.

[23] *PP* 36.

[24] *PP* 47. The passage was printed by Nathaniel Morton in 1669. For the development of the 'myth' of the 'Pilgrim Fathers' from the late 1760s. Craven, *Legend of the Founding Fathers*, 1956; Cornell paperback 1965, 35-7, 97-101, 107-11, 133, 150-1.

[25] Smith-Arber, 279 (Preface to 1624 *General History*).

Moreover, four months before the pilgrims left Holland, various members of the Virginia Company concerned with the north (rich in fishing) had petitioned for a new charter for the region. That Charter was granted in 1620, to 'the Corporation established at Plymouth in the County of Devon for the planting, ruling, ordering and governing of New England' (usually called the Council of New England). They had the power to issue patents. The pilgrims probably prefered to settle in the area controlled by the Council for New England. Unfortunately, the Charter was not granted until November 1620, and the 'Mayflower' left Plymouth on 16 September. So technically the pilgrims reached America with the authority of their Virginia Company grant; they anchored (whether intentionally or not is a disputed matter) in Cape Cod Bay, where that patent was invalid; their situation was legalised in June 1621 by a patent from the New England Council.

There were 102 passengers on the 'Mayflower' when the vessel left Plymouth, including some hired hands, and a crew of about three dozen.[26] One servant died during the passage; but there were two births (Oceanus Hopkins and Peregrine White). So 103 reached Cape Cod. (102 landed at Plymouth: Dorothy Bradford was drowned while the 'Mayflower' was anchored at Provincetown Harbour.) There were eighteen wives and about thirty-two children (including Love Brewster, Wrestling Brewster, Remember Allerton, Resolved White and Humility Cooper). Of the males, two dozen were not from Leiden. They were planters and servants, some sympathetic to the pilgrims, some not, who had been hired by the London merchants who financed and organised the expedition. The actual 'pilgrims' were seventeen males; eight wives (including Mary Brewster, Catharine Carver and Elizabeth Winslow); and sixteen children – forty-one in all. (More had departed from Holland, but had been left behind in England.) It had been agreed at Leiden, 'by mutual consent and covenant', that those departing should be in America 'an absolute church of themselves'.[27] And Robinson pointed out to them, in a letter of July 1620, that they must have a 'course of civil community': 'you are become a body politic, using amongst yourselves civil government.'[28]

On 11 November the 'Mayflower' anchored in Cape Cod Bay, in Provincetown Harbour. The pilgrims knew that their existing patent did not apply there; and so (in the words of Bradford), 'none had power to command them'. The 'strangers' on board had been making 'discontented and mutinous speeches'. The pilgrims needed something 'as firm as any patent, and in some respects more sure'.[29]

---

[26] Bradford's list and comments, *PP* 441-8. Andrews, *Colonial Period*, I, 268-71. One of the passengers, a girl of four, survived until 1699. Bradford made much of the longevity of the pilgrims who survived the first winter.

[27] *PP* 36.

[28] *PP* 369-70.

[29] *PP* 75.

So they drew up the 'compact' which was signed on board on 11 November, and first printed in 1622.[30] Those who signed, 'loyal subjects' of James I, had 'undertaken for the glory of God, and advancement of the Christian Faith, and honour of our King and Country, a voyage to plant the first colony in the northern parts of Virginia' – so much for the 1607 settlement on the River Sagadahoc! They now

solemnly and mutually in the presence of God and one of another covenant and combine ourselves together into a civil body politic for our better ordering and preservation and furtherance of the ends aforesaid; and by virtue hereof to enact, constitute and frame such just and equal laws, ordinances, acts, constitutions, offices from time to time as shall be thought must meet and convenient for the general good of the colony.

The 'covenant' – once personal, then ecclesiastical – had become political. The names of the forty-one signers were first printed by Nathaniel Morton in 1669.[31] They were, of course, all male: the 17 pilgrims, 17 other settlers, 3 hired men, and 4 servants. From the point of view of the unity of the plantation, it was a very common-sensical document.

Bradford, 'being thus arrived at Cape Cod' (so called by 'Gosnold and his company, Anno 1602'), and considering the landscape, found relevant the Biblical image of the Wilderness: 'a hideous and desolate wilderness, full of wild beasts and wild men – and what multitudes there might be of them they knew not.' But there was the comfort of Psalm 107: 'O give thanks unto the Lord, for he is good ... Let the redeemed of the Lord say so, whom he hath redeemed from the hand of the enemy ... They wandered in the wilderness in a solitary way ... Then they cried unto the Lord in their trouble, and He delivered them out of their distresses.' And Bradford recalled the description in the Acts of the Apostles (28:2) of the welcome given to the shipwrecked Paul by the natives of Malta: 'and the barbarous people showed us no little kindness: for they kindled a fire, and received us every one, because of the present rain, and because of the cold.'[32]

What might the English expect of the 'savage barbarians' of New England?

A party of sixteen men, under Captain Miles Standish, landed on 15 November, marched for about a mile, and had their first glimpse of the Indians:[33]

They espied five or six persons with a dog coming towards them, who were savages; but they fled from them and ran up into the woods, and the English

[30] *A Relation or Iournall*, ed. Cheever, 30-31. See note 34.
[31] *New Englands Memoriall*. Everyman *Chronicles*, 24. Nathaniel had access to the original document and signatures.
[32] *PP* 61-3.
[33] *PP* 64-6.

followed them, partly to see if they could speak with them, and partly to discover if there might not be more of them lying in ambush. But the Indians seeing themselves thus followed, they again forsook the woods and ran away on the sands as hard as they could.

The English followed the footprints; and continued to do so on 16 November, 'hoping to find their dwellings'. On 17 November they saw 'new stubble where corn had been set the same year'. They also came across the remains of a dwelling, with a European ship's kettle among the contents. Nearby were new mounds of sand, which the English dug into and found Indian baskets, 'handsomely and cunningly made',[34] filled with corn and ears of corn – thirty-six ears, 'fair and good, of divers colours, which seemed to them a very goodly sight (having never seen any such before).' They decided to take the kettle back to the 'Mayflower', and as much corn as they could carry: if Indians were encountered, 'we would give them the kettle again, and satisfy them for their corn'.[35]

There was a second exploring expedition, this time of thirty men, on 28 November. This 'second expedition' is most fully described in the *Relation* published in 1622 (London): *A Relation or Iournall of the beginning and proceedings of the English Plantation setled at Plimoth in New England*. The material had left Plymouth in December 1621; and the London editor ('G. Mourt') was George Morton, who was to emigrate to Plymouth in 1623 with his son Nathaniel.

It was snowing, and the ground was now frozen.[36] Two Indian houses were found –

made with long young sapling trees, bended and both ends stuck into the ground; they were made round, like unto an arbor, and covered down to the ground with thick and well-wrought mats; and the door was not over a yard wide, made of a mat to open; the chimney was a wide open hole in the top, for which they had a mat to cover it close when they pleased.

The houses were matted outside, and also inside (with 'newer and fairer mats'). The explorers found wooden bowls, trays and dishes, earth pots, baskets made of crab shells, and an English bucket. And also a skeleton, 'embalmed' in 'fine and perfect red powder' in a sack. 'The skull had fine yellow hair still on it, and some of the flesh unconsumed.' In another bundle were the remains of a child. Some thought the adult remains were Indian; others argued that 'the Indians have all black hair, and never was any seen with brown or yellow hair'. No live Indians were seen on this expedition.

[34] 1622 *Relation*, ed. Cheever, 34. George B. Cheever's volume, 1848, printed the *Relation*; with his own 'Historical and Local Illustrations of Providences, Principles and Persons'; the spine title was 'The Plymouth Pilgrims'. All references to the *Relation* are to this edition: hereafter cited as *Rel.*

[35] *Rel.* 34.

[36] *Rel.* 36-40.

A third party left the 'Mayflower' on 6 December:[37] ten men, including 'three of London', and Standish, Bradford, Carver and Winslow; plus 'two of our seamen', and two mates, a gunner, and three sailors 'of the ship's company' – eighteen in all. It was 'very cold and hard weather': 'the water froze on our clothes and made them many times like coats of iron.' As the shallop approached the shore 'they saw some ten or twelve Indians very busy about something'. The English, once landed, constructed a barricado, 'and got fire wood, and set out our sentinels': 'we saw the smoke of the fire which the savages made that night, about four or five miles from us.' On 7 December, it was revealed that the Indians had been cutting up 'a great fish – like a grampus' (whale); 'being some two inches thick of fat, like a hog: some pieces whereof they had left by the way.' During the night of 7th/8th a 'hideous and great cry' was heard. The party assumed it was wolves, discharged two muskets, and the noise stopped. They rose at 5 a.m., and had prayers, and breakfast. Then

they heard a great and strange cry, which they knew to be the same voices they heard in the night, though they varied their notes; and one of the company being abroad came running in and cried 'Men, Indians! Indians!' And withal, their arrows came flying amongst them.

Very unlike the home life of St Paul on Malta. The 'barbarous people' of Cape Cod, wrote Bradford in his discussion of Acts 28:2, were 'readier to fill their sides full of arrows than otherwise'.[38] The Indians came near, 'wheeling about upon them', continuing their 'dreadful' cries; at least forty of them. The English aimed muskets, 'let fly amongst them, and quickly stopped their violence'. The Indians fled. The English pursued for a time, shooting and shouting – to show they were not afraid. God was on the side of the muskets. Bradford concluded his account of the 8 December incident:

Thus it pleased God to vanquish their enemies and give them deliverance; and by His special Providence so to dispose that not any of them were either hurt or hit, though their arrows came close by them, and on every side of them, and sundry of their coats, which hung up in the barricado, were shot through and through. Afterwards they gave God solemn thanks and praise for their deliverance, and gathered up a bundle of their arrows, and sent them into England afterward by the master of the ship; and called that place The First Encounter.

On Monday 11 December a small group 'sounded the harbour' of Plymouth, 'marched also into the land,[39] and returned to the 'Mayflower'. On Saturday 16th the 'Mayflower' anchored in Plymouth Harbour. And on Monday 18th 'we went aland, manned

[37] *PP*68-70; *Rel.* 42-6. Bradford's account is based on the *Relation*, which he may have written himself.
[38] *PP* 62.
[39] For 'Plymouth Rock', Craven, *Legend of Founding Fathers*, 37-8.

with the master of the ship, and three or four of the sailors': this was another exploring expedition. On Saturday 23rd, 'as many of us as could went on shore, felled and carried timber, to provide themselves stuff for building'. Sunday 24th: 'our people on shore heard a great cry of some savages (as they thought) which caused an alarm, and to stand on guard, expecting an assault; but all was quiet.' Monday 25th: some of the workmen 'heard a noise of some Indians which caused us all to go to our muskets, but we heard no further, so we came aboard again' – and were given beer by the captain.[40]

The first few months were appalling. Bradford noted that fifty-one of the planters died 'soon after their arrival, in the general sickness that befel'.[41] That was precisely half: fifty-one survived. But until the end of March the Indians remained at a distance. Bradford wrote that they 'came skulking about them, they would sometimes show themselves aloof off, but when they approached them, they would run away'.[42] On 16 February Indians were seen approaching the plantation, and the alarm was given. On the 17th two Indians appeared a quarter of a mile away 'and made signs unto us to come unto them'. The planters made signs for the Indians to come to them, armed themselves, and sent Standish and another man, with muskets, to parley. The two Indians departed. A 'noise of a great many more was heard'; and 'this caused us to plant our great ordnances in places more convenient'.[43]

The story develops in March 1621. On Friday 16th 'there presented himself a savage, which caused an alarm'.[44] He was 'a tall straight man, the hair of his head black, long behind, only short before, none on his face at all'. He was 'stark naked, only a leather about his waist, with a fringe about a span long'. He also spoke English, 'for he had learned some broken English among the Englishmen that came to fish'. This was Samoset, an Algonkian chief from Maine. He was given 'strong water, and biscuit and butter and cheese and pudding, and a piece of a mallard'. He stayed the night at Plymouth and told the settlers about the Indians of the region. Their neighbours were the 'Massasoits': the Wampanoag Indians, whose territory extended from Plymouth to east Narragansett Bay, and whose Great Chief, Massasoit, lived at Sowams near Narragansett Bay (Barrington, Rhode Island). Thus far the planters had seen only the Nauset Indians of Cape Cod, who were 'much incensed and provoked against the English' – there had been ugly incidents shortly before 1620 with English traders on Martha's Vineyard and east Cape Cod.

All the New England tribes were of the Algonkian family. The Nausets of Cape Cod, and the Wampanoag, were neighbours of Plymouth. The Massachusetts were to the north. The Narragansetts were in Rhode Island; and, further west, the Pequots ('destroyers') in Connecticut – they had migrated from the upper Hudson.[45]

[40] *Rel.* 47-50. [41] *PP* 443-7. [42] *PP* 79. [43] *Rel.* 56. [44] *Rel.* 57-8.
[45] Vaughan, *New England Frontier*, ch.2: 'The Indians of New England'.

Samoset also said that the Indian name for Plymouth was Patuxet, and that 'about four years àgo all the inhabitants died of an extraordinary plague, and there is neither man, woman nor child remaining'. This is the first reference to the pestilence of (about) 1617 which destroyed the Indians of the Plymouth area. Bradford wrote of the 'wasting plague', the 'late great mortality'.[46] The Indians 'not being able to bury one another, their skulls and bones were found in many places lying still above the ground where their houses and dwellings had been; a very sad spectacle to behold'. John Smith observed in 1622 that where, in 1614, he had seen one hundred or two hundred Indians, it appeared that now 'there is scarce ten to be found'.[47] Thomas Morton, who was to arrive in the region in 1625, described the Indian skulls and bones he saw in the 'forest near the Massachusetts': 'it seemed to me a new-found Golgotha.'[48] To Smith and to Thomas Morton this was the work of Providence. The paucity of Indians, wrote Morton, makes New England 'so much the more fit for the English nation to inhabit in, and erect in it temples to the glory of God'. Smith reported that 'God had laid open this country for us, and slain the most part of the inhabitants by cruel wars and a mortal disease'. Smith was here retailing the sentiments of the men of Plymouth. Nathaniel Morton, who went to Plymouth, a boy of ten, in 1623, was to make much of the theme in 1669, in *New Englands Memoriall*. His mother's sister married the widowed Bradford at Plymouth. Nathaniel's book, as we have noted, was based on his uncle's manuscript History; but Nathaniel was more addicted to the pointing of Biblical morals (and much harsher to the Indian). Nathaniel referred to Exodus 23, verses 28 and 30:[49]

I will send hornets before thee which shall drive out the Hivite, the Canaanite and the Hittite from before thee. By little and little I will drive them out before thee, until thou be increased and inherit the land.

He was also fond of verse 8 of Psalm 80: 'Thou hast brought a vine out of Egypt: thou hast cast out the heathen and planted it.' Thus at Plymouth 'God made way for His people, by removing the heathen, and planting them in the land.'[50] God's bounty was not confined to Plymouth, but embraced the whole of New England:[51]

God hath very evidently made way for the English, by sweeping away the natives by some great mortalities; as first, by the plague here in Plymouth jurisdiction; secondly by the smallpox in the jurisdiction of the Massachusetts, a very considerable people a little before the English came into the country; as also at Connecticut.

[46] *PP* 87.
[47] *New Englands Trials*, 1622. Everyman *Chronicles* 251.
[48] *New English Canaan*. Force, *Tracts*, II, no.5, p.19.
[49] Everyman *Chronicles*, 43.
[50] *ibid.*, 36.   [51] *ibid.*, 43.

All part of God's marvellous works in the beginning and planting of New England.

It appears that in 1620 there were no more than 18,000 Indians in New England. The Narragansetts of Rhode Island, untouched by the pestilence, numbered about 4,000. The Wampanoag and the Massachusetts had been reduced to about 500. (The Powhatan Confederacy in Virginia may have been about 11,000; the Cherokee of Georgia about 22,000. It was once thought that there were less than 1,000,000 Indians in North America by the sixteenth century. Recent work tends considerably to expand that figure. A recent estimate (1966) is between 9,800,000 and 12,250,000.)[52]

At the practical level, Samoset's account of the plague made clear to the planters of Plymouth in March 1621 that 'there is none to hinder our possession, or to lay claim unto it'.[53] (In any case, the Plymouth area had probably been used only as a game reserve.)

Samoset left Plymouth on the morning of Saturday 17 March. He was given a knife, a bracelet and a ring. On the Sunday he reappeared, with 'five other tall, proper men'.[54] They wore deer skins. And

they had most of them long hosen up to their groins, close made; and above their groins to their waist another leather; they were altogether like the Irish trouses. They are of complexion like our English gypsies; no hair, or very little, on their faces; on their heads long hair to their shoulders, only cut before, some trussed up before with a feather (broad-wise, like a fan), another a fox tail hanging out.

They had left the bows and arrows a quarter of a mile away (an arrangement the planters had made with Samoset). They were entertained, ate English food, 'sang and danced after their manner, like Anticks', and 'made semblance unto us of friendship and amity'. Some had their faces painted black from the forehead to the chin, in strokes three inches broad. They were quickly dismissed, 'because of the day'. On the following Wednesday two or three Indians approached, and 'made semblance of daring us, as we thought'.[55] Standish was dispatched with his musket. The Indians 'whetted and rubbed their arrows and strings, and made show of defiance'. But they fled when Standish approached.

The planters regarded these Indian visits as tiresome interruptions to the work of drawing up laws and orders, and of digging, and sowing seed.[56]

At noon on Thursday 22 March, 'a very fair warm day', the

[52] On Indian demography before Columbus, see Wilbur R. Jacobs in *William and Mary Quarterly*, January 1974 (Series 3, vol.XXXI, no.1, pp.123-32). It is fashionable among recent American scholars to give the highest possible estimates of Indian numbers before the arrival of the Europeans. The subsequent decline in numbers is thus greater, and the European 'conquest' the more pernicious.
[53] *Rel.* 58. [54] *Rel.* 59. [55] *Rel.* 60. [56] *ibid.*

planters had been meeting for an hour 'about our public business' when Samoset arrived again. He brought with him Squanto, a native of Patuxet, who had been kidnapped onto an English vessel in 1614, and had spent two years in London, thereafter being employed by voyagers to Newfoundland and the New England coast. They told the English that Massasoit (properly Ousamequin, 'yellow feather'), the 'great chief', was arrived: (*Sachem*: a word technically applicable only to the chief of a whole tribe, as here, but often indiscriminatingly used by the English.) The chief appeared on the top of a nearby hill with sixty men. They seemed unwilling to approach, and the planters did not advise Governor John Carver to trust himself to them. So Winslow was sent, with Squanto, 'to signify the mind and will of our Governor, which was to have trading and peace with them'. (Samoset had brought some skins to barter.) Winslow took knives, a copper chain with a jewel, 'a pot of strong water', and biscuit and butter; and Winslow declared to Massasoit

that King James saluted him with words of love and peace, and did accept of him as his friend and ally, and that our Governor desired to see him, and to truck with him, and to confirm a peace with him, as his next neighbour.

Massasoit and twenty men entered Plymouth, Winslow remaining behind as hostage. The Chief was greeted by Standish, who

conducted him to a house then in building, where we placed a green rug and three or four cushions; then instantly came our Governor, with drum and trumpet after him, and some few musketeers. After salutations, our Governor kissing his hand, the King kissed him; and so they sat down.

Massasoit drank 'a great draught' of 'strong water', that 'made him sweat all the while after'. Massasoit was 'a very lusty man, in his best years' (he lived until 1661), 'an able body, grave of countenance, and spare of speech'. He wore a chain of white bone beads round his neck, and also a knife attached to a string, and 'a little bag of tobacco, which he drank and gave us to drink'. His face was 'painted with a sad red, like murrey' (mulberry); and 'oiled both head and face, that he looked greasily'. All the Indians had painted faces: black, red, yellow, white. Massasoit 'marvelled much at our trumpet, and some of his men would sound it as well as they could'.[57]

A 'peace' with the Wampanoag was concluded, which was basically to endure for fifty years, until the reign of Massasoit's son Metacom – known to the English as 'King Philip'. These were the terms of the 'peace'. No Indian was to injure the English, or visit Plymouth carrying bow and arrow; an offending Indian was to be punished by the English. Goods stolen from the English were to be returned. The English were to return anything stolen from the Indians, and were not to carry arms when visiting the Indians. Massasoit was to help the

[57] *Rel.* 60-3.

English in case of war; the English would aid him 'if any did unjustly war against him'. Massasoit was to announce the treaty to neighbouring Indian tribes: so that they would not wrong the English, but 'might be likewise comprised in the conditions of peace'. The 'conditions' were printed in the *Relation* of 1622.[58]

In the reports from Plymouth published in London, the planters were at pains to stress their observance of the formalities of fair play in dealing with the Indian. In September 1621 ten men and three Indians (including Squanto) made an expedition to Massachusetts Bay. Squanto was keen to relieve the Indian women of their beaver coats: he 'would have had us rifled the savage women, and take their skins, and all such things as might be serviceable for us; for (said he) they are a bad people, and have often threatened you'. The reply of the English (as given in the 1622 *Relation*) was: 'Were they never so bad, we would not wrong them, or give them any just occasion against us.' Indian murmurings should not be taken too seriously – but Squanto was assured that 'if they once attempted anything against us, then we would deal far worse than he desired'.[59] In Plymouth, there were cases of murderers of Indians themselves being executed. In 1638, for example, four men were indicted for killing an Indian, and robbing him of cloth coats and wampumpeag (wampum: beads made from clam and whelk shells, strung together, and used instead of money). One escaped; the other three were found guilty by a jury of twelve, and hung.[60]

After the drawing up of the 'peace' Samoset and Squanto stayed the night in Plymouth. Massasoit 'and all his men lay all night in the woods, not above half an English mile from us; and all their wives and women with them'. The planters 'kept good watch'; but 'there was no appearance of danger'.

We cannot yet conceive but that he is willing to have peace with us, for they have seen our people sometimes alone two or three in the woods, at work and fowling, when as they offered them no harm, as they might easily have done; and especially because he hath a potent adversary, the Narragansetts, that are at war with him, against whom he thinks we may be some strength to him, for our pieces are terrible unto them.

The Indians left the area in the Friday morning, after Massasoit's kettle had been filled with pease (a mash of dried peas), 'which pleased them well'. Squanto went fishing, and caught by hand some eels, 'fat and sweet', for the English. And the planters were able to proceed with their 'common business': from which 'we had been so often hindered by the savages coming'.[61]

Squanto remained mostly at Plymouth: 'a special instrument sent

[58] *Rel*. 62. *PP* 80-1.
[59] *Rel*. 91.
[60] *Records of Plymouth Colony*, ed. Shurtleff, I, 96-7.
[61] *Rel*. 63-4.

of God for their good, beyond their expectation', wrote Bradford.[62] He taught the settlers where to fish, and how to plant and tend corn. He died in December 1622, desiring Governor Bradford 'to pray for him, that he might go to the Englishman's God in heaven'.[63]

In June 1621 a small party, including Winslow and Squanto, left Plymouth to visit Massasoit at Sowams, near Narragansett Bay, forty miles west; to explore, and 'to continue the league of peace and friendship'.[64] There was one complaint. Indians – men, women and children – had fallen into the habit of visiting Plymouth 'often, and without fear'. The English were new to the site, 'and not knowing how our corn might prosper, we could no longer give them such entertainment as we had done, and as we desired still to do.' But Massasoit would be welcome, and any 'special friend' – Winslow took a copper chain, to be worn by an authorised messenger. He also carried a gift from Bradford to Massasoit, 'a horseman's coat of red cotton, and laced with a slight lace'. They reached Sowams, situated on a river which 'cometh unto the sea at the Narragansett Bay, where the Frenchmen so much use'. Massasoit was delighted with the coat and chain: 'he was not a little proud to behold himself, and his men also, to see their king so bravely attired.' He said that 'we were welcome, and he would gladly continue that peace and friendship which was between him and us; and, for his men, they should no more pester us as they had done.' He promised also to send skins to Plymouth. He then talked of James I: the region of Narragansett Bay 'was King James his country, and he also was King James his man'. He also marvelled that James 'would live without a wife' (Queen Anne had died in 1619). The Plymouth party did not much enjoy the visit, because in two nights and one day they were given only one meal (of fish); and they could not sleep because of the 'barbarous lodging', the lice and mosquitoes, and the 'barbarous singing' of the Indians, who 'use to sing themselves to sleep'. (Bradford, writing in the 1640s, noted that the Indians did not have as much corn then as since – the English having later given them hoes.) However, the peace appeared secure.[65]

The peace was extended on 13 September 1621 when other Indian chiefs came to Plymouth and put their mark on a document (printed by Nathaniel Morton in 1669)[66] acknowledging themselves to be 'loyal subjects of King James': the nine subscribers included Massasoit's brother; Corbitant, thought likely to be Massasoit's successor; and two chiefs of the Massachusetts tribe.

At the end of 1621, Winslow wrote a letter, printed in 1622,[67] describing the harvest at Plymouth. In the spring the planters had sown twenty acres of Indian corn, and six acres of barley and peas. 'Our corn did prove well, and God be praised we had a good increase

[62] *PP* 81.   [63] *PP* 114.   [64] *Rel.* 67-72.   [65] *PP* 87.

[66] Everyman *Chronicles* 44-5.

[67] *Rel.* 95-8.

of Indian corn.' Winslow noted that it had pleased God 'to possess the Indians with a fear of us, and love unto us'.

We have found the Indians very faithful in their covenant of peace with us, very loving and ready to pleasure us. We often go to them, and they come to us; some of us have been fifty miles by land in the country with them.

There is now peace among the Indians themselves, due to the English. And 'we for our parts walk and peaceably and safely in the wood, as in the highways in England; we entertain them familiarly in our houses, and they are friendly bestowing their venison on us'. Governor Bradford thought rejoicing was in order:

Our harvest being gotten in, our Governor sent four men on fowling, that so we might after a more special manner rejoice together, after we had gathered the fruit of our labours. They four in one day killed as much fowl as, with a little help beside, served the company almost a week; at which time, amongst other recreations, we exercised our arms, many of the Indians coming amongst us, and amongst the rest their greatest king Massasoit, with some ninety men, whom for three days we entertained and feasted. And they went out and killed five deer, which they brought to the plantation, and bestowed on our Governor, and upon the Captain, and others.

The first 'Thanksgiving', 1621. No precise date was given. If it was before the end of November, when the first reinforcements arrived at Plymouth, the ninety Indians would have outnumbered the planters, only fifty-one of whom had survived.

22

Education in Virginia

The main part of this Chapter covers the years 1618 to 1622, and considers three educational schemes: for a *university* for the sons of planters, at Henrico; for an Indian *college*, in the Henrico area; and for a *school* for English boys at Charles City (near Henrico). The schemes had one thing in common. They all came to nothing.

The English were perhaps aware of the Schools and Universities of Spanish America – the Franciscan Schools in Mexico, dating from the 1520s; the Franciscan and Dominican Colleges in Mexico City from the 1530s, which were open to Indians; the University in Mexico City, 1553, also open to Indians. On 18 November 1618 the London Council of the Virginia Company wrote to Governor Yeardley, who was preparing to sail to Virginia, about the funds which had been raised in England (by way of royal letters to the Bishops) 'for the building and planting of a college for the training up of the children of those infidels in true religion, moral virtue and civility'.[1] Preparations were to be begun for the construction of the Indian college. Also, a site should be chosen, at Henrico, 'for the planting of a university' 'in time to come'. 10,000 acres 'within the territory' of Henrico were to be 'set out for the endowing' of both the Indian 'college' and the projected 'university'. A year later, in November 1619, the minutes of the Quarter Court (sixty-five members present)[2] added that 9,000 acres were intended to support the English 'university', and 1,000 the 'college for the conversion of infidels'.

The letter of November 1618 also instructed that the 'cities' of Jamestown and Charles City, and the 'boroughs' of Henrico and Kecoughtan, were each to set aside 100 acres as glebe land for the maintenance of 'godly, learned and painful ministers'. This, plus a yearly levy, should give each minister £200 a year. (It was a fortunate parson in England who got more than £10 a year.) At the end of November 1618 the Reverend Thomas Lorkin, a sort of professional private tutor, wrote to a friend that there was a possibility of his going to Virginia, with a stipend of £200 a year.[3] He also mentioned that

[1] Kingsbury (ed.), *Records*, III, 102. Unless otherwise stated, the references in this chapter are to these volumes.
[2] I, 268.
[3] *Court and Times of James I*, II, 109-10.

'the Virginia Company means to erect a college'. In the event he remained at home – perhaps when he discovered that an Indian school was what the Company had most in mind.

The area chosen for the 'college land' was on the north bank of the James, above Henrico, towards Richmond; about ten miles in length. In addition to the 10,000 acres subsiding education, there were 3,000 acres for the Virginia Company, and 1,500 acres of 'common land' for Henrico.[4] Fifty tenants for the land were selected in London in the summer of 1619, and arrived in Virginia in November; farmers, but also carpenters, potters, brickmakers and bricklayers, and so forth. Half the profits of the educational land were to go towards the building of the Indian college and the English university, 'and for maintenance of the tutors and scholars'. One of those in charge of this emigration was Lieutenant Jabez Whitaker, aged 23, half-brother of Alexander. Sir Edwin Sandys, who had become Treasurer of the Virginia Company in April, was determined that before any building began, the Company must have proof that sufficient revenue would be raised in Virginia.[5] He also moved, in June 1619, that a committee be appointed in London to supervise the Indian college: 'of choice gentlemen, and other of his Majesty's Council for Virginia, concerning the college; being a weighty business, and so great that an account of their proceedings therein must be given to the state.' The Company Court (present, 28) approved seven names, including the Deputy Treasurer, John Ferrar.[6] (John Ferrar and his brother Nicholas – later of Little Gidding – were sons of the merchant Sir Nicholas Ferrar, who died in April 1620. The family was prominent in the administration of the Virginia Company. A third son, William, had gone to Virginia in 1618.)

But time dragged on. We have seen that the Jamestown General Assembly in July/August 1619 had asked each 'town, city, borough, and particular plantation' to take in some Indian boys, with the intention that the brightest of them would be 'fitted for the college intended for them'.[7] Two years later (24 July 1621) the London Council sent out an instruction, in almost exactly the same words; with the addition that 'we purpose to speed' the 'fabric' of the college, 'as soon as any profit returned from the tenants shall enable us'.[8] This in spite of the fact that on 28 June 1620, at a meeting of the Quarter Court held at the house of John Ferrar, the Charter for 'the deputies of the college' was read, confirmed, and sealed.[9] (One of the two Deputies, George Thorpe, was by that time in Jamestown, having sailed from England in March.)

From 1619 various benefactions were made for the intended Indian college. In 1619 Nicholas Ferrar Senior drew up his will, leaving £300.

to the college in Virginia; to be paid when there shall be ten of the infidels' children placed in it. And in the mean time, four and twenty pounds by year,

[4] Hatch, *First Seventeen Years*, 53.
[5] I, 220. [6] I, 231. [7] III, 165-6. [8] III, 470. [9] I, 382.

to be distributed unto three discreet and godly men in the colony, which shall honestly bring up three of the infidels' children in Christian religion, and some good course to live by.[10]

In 1619 also a 'person unknown' gave 'for the use of the college' a communion cup, a plate of silver gilt for the communion bread, a 'crimson velvet carpet with gold lace and fringe', and a 'linen damask table cloth' (both the latter intended as church furnishings.)[11] At the Quarter Court in November 1620,

> a stranger stepped in, presenting a map of Sir Walter Raleigh's containing a Description of Guiana, and, with the same, four great books, as the gift of one unto the Company that desired his name might not be made known. Whereof one book was a treatise of St Augustine, Of the City of God, translated into English. The other three great volumes were the works of Mr Perkins, newly corrected and amended. Which books the donor desired they might be sent to the college in Virginia, there to remain in safety to the use of the collegiates thereafter, and not suffered at any time to be sent abroad, or used in the meanwhile.

The Earl of Southampton (Henry Wriothesley) who had succeeded Sandys as Treasurer in April 'desired the party that presented them to return deserved thanks from himself and the rest of the Company to him that so kindly bestowed them'.[12] The three volume Cambridge edition of Perkins, containing thirty-eight works, had been printed three times: 1608/1609, 1612/1613, and 1616/1618.

One is tempted to think that the donor was William Crashaw, one of the editors. Whoever he was, he made a further gift in January 1622: a small Bible 'with a cover richly wrought'; a 'great Church Bible'; the Book of Common Prayer; and the Catechism of the German Calvinist Zacharias Beer (Ursinus: 1534-1583).[13] And in 1622 a former Fellow of Clare College Cambridge left in his will £100 'for the education of infidels' children'. This was George Ruggle. Ruggle had gone up to St John's in 1589, when William Crashaw was in his second year; he transferred to Trinity in 1593 and was a Fellow of Clare from 1598 to 1620. Nicholas Ferrar Junior (later of Little Gidding) had been sent to Clare in 1606 in order to be under Ruggle's care; and at the meeting of the Quarter Court on 20 November 1622 it was Ferrar, then aged 30, who announced the bequest ('which he said he could not without great grief mention'). (Nicholas Ferrar Jr. was Deputy Treasurer of the Company from May 1622.) Ferrar also told the members that Ruggle had been

> a man second to none in knowledge of all manner of humanity, learning, and was so generally reputed in the University, of singular honesty and integrity of life, sincere and zealous in religion, and of very great wisdom and understanding.

---

[10] III, 117. [11] III, 575. [12] I, 421-22. [13] III, 576. I, 589.

He had left Clare in 1620, and for the last three years of his life, said Ferrar, had been 'wholly almost spent and exercised in Virginia business'; he had advised the Ferrars; and written 'sundry treatises for the benefit of the plantation' (in particular a manuscript 'concerning the Government of Virginia' which had been highly thought of by Sandys).[14] Ferrar did not mention that Ruggle also had a reputation as a Cambridge University playwright. He was the author of the Latin play performed before James I in Cambridge in 1615: *Ignoramus*, an attack on lawyers, which much annoyed Edward Coke, but delighted the King (he saw it again two months later, in spite of the fact that it was six hours long).

But the most revealing story of benefactors to Indian education is that concerning the generosity of a donor going under the signature 'Dust and Ashes'. We pick up the story on 3 November 1619, when, at a meeting of the Quarter Court, Sandys announced that an 'unknown gentleman' had offered to send him £500 'for the converting and education of three score infidels' children, whensoever he shall require the same'.[15] Shortly afterwards, Sandys received the actual money, in gold, in a box. On 2 February 1620 a letter concerning the benefaction was read, and written into the minutes.[16] It was signed 'Dust and Ashes':

I am encouraged to tender my poor mite, and although I cannot with the princes of Issachar bring gold and silver covering, yet offer here what I can, some goats' hair, necessary stuff for the Lord's tabernacle, protesting here, in my sincerity, without papistical merit or pharisaical applause; wishing from my part as much unity in your honourable undertaking as there is sincerity in my designs. To the furtherance of which good work – the converting of infidels to the faith of Christ – I promised by my good friends £500; for the maintenance of a convenient number of young Indians, taken at the age of seven years or younger, and instructed in the reading and understanding of the principles of Christian religion unto the age of twelve years; and then, as occasion serveth, to be trained and brought up in some lawful trade, with all humanity and gentleness, until the age of one and twenty years; and then to enjoy like liberties and privileges with our native English in that place.

Also, the Company was to receive a further £50 to be given to 'two religious persons' in Virginia, who every three months were to inform Sandys that the plan was being executed, and to send him the name of the children and of 'their foster fathers and over-seers'. If Sandys had any suggestions, he was to inform a known 'friend'; who is under a pledge of secrecy – and Sandys was in turn asked not to reveal the name of the friend. All very cloak and dagger.

Two years passed for 'Dust and Ashes'. And on 28 January 1622 'D and A' wrote another letter, this time to the Company.[17] It was brought to the Quarter Court on 30 January 'by an unknown messenger': 'D and A' laments the fact that shortly after his first letter

---

[14] II, 136. [15] I, 257. [16] I, 307-8. [17] I, 585-6.

he had sent the £550 to Sandys. He had not strictly detailed the bestowing of the money; but showed his 'intent' for the conversion of Indian children. But the money appears to him to have gone to the 'gentlemen' of one of the 'particular' (private) plantations established in Virginia from 1617: Southampton Hundred as it was called from 1620, because Henry Wriothesley (Earl of Southampton) had bought it in that year from Sir Thomas Smythe (the original name had been Smith's Hundred; on the north shore of the James, by the Chickahominy River). These 'gentlemen' have 'undertaken the disposing of the said £550'. So the money has been 'detained by a private hundred'; and 'D and A's' intent ignored – the intent of

the erecting of some school, or other way, whereby some of the children of the Virginians might have been taught and brought up in Christian religion and good manners.

The letter is an appeal to the whole body of the Company to see that the money ('a great and the most painfully gained part of my estate') is 'faithfully converted to the work intended'. However, there is another possibility. The £550 might be used to

procure that some of the male children of the Virginians (though but a few) be brought over to England, here to be educated and taught; and to wear a habit as the children of Christ's Hospital do.

In fact 'D and A' wants the boys (eight or ten, he is thinking of) to be placed in Christ's Hospital, London, or else in a 'Virginian School or Hospital' in London. This could be augmented by the gifts of other benefactors; but 'D and A' would give another £450, making a total gift of £1000, on condition that he appoint 'the first Tutor or Governor'. If the Company doesn't like this idea, then let the £550

be wholly employed and bestowed upon a free school to be erected in Southampton Hundred (so it be presently employed), or such other place as I or my friends shall well like of; wherein both English and Virginians may be taught together.

One condition. The Master of the School should not be appointed until he had brought to the London Company 'sound testimony of his sufficiency in learning, and sincerity of life'.

So Sandys entered into a 'narration'[18] about the fate of the £550; observing in passing that the donor might have received 'more clear satisfaction' had the Company not been put to 'so great inconvenience by his modesty and eschewing of show of vain glory by concealing his name'.

In the spring of 1620, we are told, Sandys had brought the money-chest to a meeting of the Company Court, and there had been 'large

[18] I, 587-9.

and serious deliberation'. It was eventually decided to send the money to Southampton Hundred and to the 'particular plantation' of Martin's Hundred, on the opposite site of the River James, 'each to undertake for a certain number of the infidels' children to be brought up by them and amongst them in Christian religion and some good trade to live by'. Martin's Hundred asked to be excused, pleading weakness and confusion – the patent of John Martin (brother-in-law of Sir Julius Caesar) was under fire; and his plantation was criticised in the 1619 Jamestown General Assembly, when he had to make a personal appearance to justify himself. Southampton Hundred was not very enthusiastic either; and offered to raise £100 if the 'D and A' money could be sent elsewhere! However, the men of Southampton Hundred eventually decided to accept the money; but to use it to subsidise an iron works (requiring eighty workmen), 'whereof the profits accruing were intended and ordered in a rateable proportion to be faithfully employed for the education of thirty of the infidels' children in Christian religion'. The iron works was conceived to be a scheme 'whereon the eyes of God, angels and men were fixed'. Matters were helped by the fact that Yeardley, apart from being Governor of the colony, was also Captain of Southampton Plantation. In fact Yeardley was not too optimistic about the education idea in general: he thought

how difficult a thing it was at that time to obtain any of their children with the consent and good liking of their parents, by reason of their tenderness of them, and fear of hard usage by the English.

And the English technical expert sent out to be in charge of the ironworks died shortly after reaching Virginia.

This had been in the summer of 1620. Sandys maintained that since that time (a year and a half) 'care had been taken to restore that business' – the ironworks – 'with a fresh supply'. So he felt that 'D and A' had received 'good satisfaction'; the more so as the Company had themselves subsidised the iron works to the tune of over £500.

Sandys ended by considering 'D and A's' latest proposals. The Education in England idea he felt would not work: 'upon experience of those brought by Sir Thomas Dale' (presumably with the Rolfes in 1616). As to the building of a school: none of the buildings there intended had yet been built; and 'through their doting so much upon tobacco', no workmen would undertake building work except 'at intolerable rates'. The £550 would in 1622 finance only a 'small fabric'.

But if 'D and A's' friend would appear, or even 'D and A' himself, then a meeting could be arranged with representatives from Southampton Hundred:

that all things being debated at full, and judiciously weighed, some constant course might be resolved on and pursued for the proceeding in and perfecting of this most pious work, for which he prayed the blessing of God to be upon the author thereof. And all the Company said Amen.

By 1623 the London Company had become aware that 'the greatest part of the stock' belonging to the 'Dust and Ashes' fund had been 'wasted', because the iron works project had failed: 'the fifty men sent over' were 'not able to manage an iron work; and so turned good honest tobacco mongers'.[19] Twenty-six years later, in 1649, Virginia promoters were still hoping to build furnaces and mills, and appealing for skilful 'iron men'.[20]

So much for the bringing up of Indian boys in civility and true religion. The colonists, of course, were more concerned with the education of their own boys, not relishing the expense, or the prospect, of sending them to school in England.

The plan for a 'free school' at Charles City for the sons of Virginia planters dates from 1621 (and ends in 1622). The story began, rather oddly, at the Cape of Good Hope. Some English ships outward bound to the East Indies encountered a vessel returning from India, the 'Royal James'. The Captain of the 'Royal James' was Martin Pring (whom we last met crossing to Maine in 1606). The 'preacher' was Patrick Copland, a missionary from Aberdeen with ten years' experience in the East. The outgoing Englishmen told Copland and Pring of 'the prosperity of Virginia'. And Copland persuaded the crew and passengers of the 'Royal James' into a collection for a pious work in Virginia.[21] Over 140 persons contributed: Pring gave £6.13.4, Copland £5; three merchants on board gave £5 each; the Purser gave £1.5.0, a boatswain and a surgeon £1 each. In all, Copland raised £78.8.6 (the contributions of the mariners ranged from 18 shillings to one shilling).[22] And it was decided that the money should be used for the building in Virginia 'either of an East Indian Church, or School; at the choice of the Company'[23] (the Virginia Company).

The Virginia Company in October 1621 appointed a committee of six to consider, including the brothers John and Nicholas Ferrar. Copland met the Committee on 30 October.[24] He said he hoped to persuade the East India Company to increase the sum, and he had written to various merchants in the East Indies 'to stir them up to the like contribution towards the performance of this pious work' (they had recently subsidised a Church in Wapping to the tune of £400). A member of the committee trumped this by announcing an anonymous gift of £30, bringing the sum available to £108.8.6. It was thought that the sum was not enough for a Church; and in any case in Virginia there was 'a greater want of a school than of churches'. A school would be more acceptable to the planters: 'through want thereof they have been hitherto constrained, to their great cost, to send their children from thence hither to be taught.' Thus opinion went towards

[19] IV, 141.
[20] *Perfect Description of Virginia*, 1649. Force, *Tracts*, II, no.8, pp.4-5, 20.
[21] III, 531. [22] III, 537-8. [23] I, 558-9. [24] I, 538-41.

'the erecting of a public free school': 'for the educating of children, and grounding of them in the principles of religion, civility of life, and humane learning' – the 'rudiments of learning', that is. It should obviously be in one of the four 'cities'; and Charles City was the most 'convenient' – 'it matcheth with the best in wholesomeness of air, as also for the commodious situation thereof, being not far distant from Henrico, and other particular plantations.' It could be close to the projected university:

have dependence upon the college in Virginia, which should be made capable to receive scholars from the school into such scholarships and fellowships as the said college shall be endowed withal, for the advancement of scholars as they arise by degrees and deserts in learning.

The committee thought that 1,000 acres in the area should be devoted to the school, and five apprentices and an overseer sent to farm the land and erect the schoolhouse. The Governor in Virginia should be urged that 'speedy building' would be appreciated – those planters donating most would receive most preference in the selection of entrants. And, 'forthwith', a 'good schoolmaster' must be chosen in England.

These recommendations would be presented to the Quarter Court scheduled for 21 November 1621.

Three days before the Quarter Court, a 'preparative Court' met – thirty members, under John Ferrar, and approved the recommendations.[25] They also elected Copland a 'free brother' of the Company, and allotted him 300 acres in Virginia without rent.

At the Quarter Court on 21 November, the £100.8.6 was presented to Henry Wriothesley, Earl of Southampton.[26] The recommendations were all approved. And it was decided that the school should be called 'The East India School'. It was also minuted that an 'usher' (of lower status than a 'schoolmaster') should be sent over 'presently'.

At the next Quarter Court, 30 January 1622, a messenger arrived bringing an anonymous gift for the school of £25.[27] So there was now £125.8.6. (This was the Court at which Sandys made his 'narration' about 'Dust and Ashes').

The question of the 'usher' now took primacy. On 13 February 1622 Copland told a meeting of members of the Company[28] that 'a very good scholar', whom he 'well knew', had 'offered himself to go'; and said that the scholar – whose name we know was Dike[29] – had 'good testimony for his sufficiency in learning and good carriage'. This was probably Nathaniel Dike, the son of a puritan preacher in Essex, who had gone up to Christ's College Cambridge in 1608, taking his M.A. in 1615, and who by 1622 was about 30. A committee was appointed to interview the gentleman: Copland and five others. During the next fortnight Mr Dike made it clear to Copland that he would not be pleased to go to Virginia as 'usher': he wanted the title –

[25] I, 550-1. [26] III, 539-40. [27] III, 540. [28] I, 600. [29] I, 616.

and the stipend – of 'Master of the said school'.[30] A Court of the Company, meeting on 27 February, did not take this well.[31] Provision for the stipend of the usher was under way; the post had been talked about, and 'many sufficient scholars were interested'. However, as Dike was 'specially recommended by Mr Copland, whom the Company do much respect', he could have until the next Quarter Court to decide whether to accept the position or not: he will have first refusal. It was also recommended that a committee of four, including Copland, should meet Dike again and 'confer with him about the method of teaching, and the books he intends to instruct children by'. By 13 March all seemed to have been organised. Dike should go with the status of 'Master'; but this would have to be confirmed by a certificate from the Governor in Virginia 'of his sufficiency and diligence in framing up of youth committed to his care'. He would serve five years, and thereafter 'during his own pleasure' – with a year's notice of replacement. He himself was to be 'furnished with books fit for the school'; and the Company will provide 'good store of books' for the children. The Company would also like him to have an assistant, to 'teach the grounds of arithmetic, whereby to instruct the children in all matters of account'.[32]

Dike got cold feet. And on 10 April 1622 the Company was informed that he had 'shown a willingness to resign that place, by reason of some other hopes he had to prosper himself here in England'.[33] He had been under consideration for two months; so he was voted £3 as compensation.

By June the Company had decided that they could not afford to send an 'usher' to Virginia.[34] Also, 'upon a second consideration, it was thought good to give the Colony the choice of the Schoolmaster or Usher, if so there be any there fit for the place'. If not, the authorities in Virginia were to tell London how much the colonists could afford to pay: and 'we will do our best to procure from hence an honest and sufficient man'.

The whole scheme was wavering. The Company certainly had five apprentices to hand by June 1622, and a carpenter and his wife to 'oversee' them. They would be sent over soon, and must be 'kept together for cultivating the land and building of a house'. But doubts had arisen in Virginia about the choice of Charles City for the land and the schoolhouse. This site, said London, is not 'absolutely required'. And local choice again was granted – rather a sign of desperation. If 'another place shall be judged more convenient by the Colony, it is left to your choice'.

The only survival of that particular plan for a planters' school in Virginia is the flysheet which Copland published in London in 1622, 'A Declaration how the monies ... were disposed, which was gathered by M. Patrick Copland ... towards the building of a free school in Virginia'.[35] This listed the names and contributions of the 'gentlemen

[30] I, 606. [31] I, 606-7. [32] I, 616-17. [33] I, 629. [34] III, 650. [35] III, 537-40.

and mariners' in the 'Royal James'; summarised the resolutions of the General Court of 21 November 1621; and mentioned the £25 gift of 30 January 1622. The leaflet was printed *pour encourager les autres*:

For public actions of virtue, besides that they are presently comfortable to the doers, are also exemplary to others. And as they are more beneficial to others, so are they crowned in us. Our principal care should be, that while our souls live in glory in heaven, our good actions may live upon earth, and that they may be put into the bank and multiply, while our·bodies lie in the grave and putrify.

The appeal was clinched by two Biblical texts. From the Old Testament: 'They that be wise shall shine as the brightness of the firmament; and they that turn many to righteousness, shall shine as the stars for ever and ever' (Daniel, 12:3). And words of Christ: 'whosoever shall receive such a little child in my name, receiveth me' (Matthew 18:5).

Also, we noted the request of the Virginia Company in February 1622 that Mr Dike, the intended schoolmaster, should be questioned about his 'method of teaching, and the books he intends to instruct children by'. The committee were surely swayed by a new book on educational theory by John Brinsley, who was living in London at the time, having been ousted from his headmastership of the school at Ashby-De-La-Zouch, Leicestershire, by the ecclesiastical authorities. The Reverend John Brinsley was in his late fifties, and had entered Christ's College Cambridge as a scholar in 1581; the year in which William Perkins, having been at the college for four years, took his B.A. Perkins was resident at Christ's throughout Brinsley's academic career. Brinsley left Cambridge in 1588, was ordained, but found his vocation as a teacher. By 1622 he had had 'long experience of the manifold evils which grow from the ignorance of a right order of teaching'. And to the work of planning such a true method 'I have betaken me almost wholly, for many years'. His book of 1622 was published in London, dedicated to the Lord Deputy of Ireland, the Lord President of Wales, the Governors of Guernsey and Jersey, and the Treasurer, Council and Company for Virginia and the Sommer Islands:[36]

A Consolation for our Grammar Schooles: or, A faithfull and most comfortable incouragement, for laying of a sure foundation of all good Learning in our Schooles, and for prosperous building thereupon. More especially for all those of the inferiour sort, and all ruder countries and places; namely, for Ireland, Wales, Virginia, with the Sommer Ilands, and for their more speedie attaining of our English tongue by the same labour, that all may speake one and the same Language. And withall, for the helping of all such as are desirous speedilie to recover that which they had formerlie

---

[36] Reprint (facsimile) 1943; introduction by T.C. Pollock, School of Education, New York University. Page references in notes 36-41 are to Brinsley.

got in the Grammar Scholles; and to proceed aright therein, for the perpetual benefit of these our Nations, and of the Churches of Christ.

Brinsley was the advocate of 'a right order of teaching'; 'the shortest, surest and most easy.' He was writing for 'the common sort of teachers', the 'poor, painful and honest-minded schoolmaster'[37] in 'our meaner and ruder schools', the 'weakest', most 'common country school' (not for 'the renowned schools of Westminster, Eton, Winchester').[38] William Whitaker and William Perkins are among the authors he quotes with approval. So are Erasmus, Roger Ascham, and Peter Ramus. His actual curriculum and advice does not begin until page 52, and runs to only 34 pages; it is basically a book list, with advice, on surprisingly traditional lines. Nearly half the book was the Preface: attractive and eloquent, but wholly devoid of terseness. This was an appeal for the bringing of light to places 'which now sit in such palpable darkness, and in the shadow of death, and wholly under the slavery of Satan' – such 'dark places' as 'the ignorant country of Wales; and more especially that poor Irish nation; with our loving countrymen of Virginia'.[39] The 'inhumanity' among 'many of the Irish, the Virginians, and all other barbarous nations' springs from 'their extreme ignorance of our holy God, and of all true and good learning'.[40] The use of a right method of teaching will produce 'a change from raw and rude behaviour unto all commendable qualities; as if they had been cast in a new mould'.[41]

The Dedicatory Epistle is especially concerned with 'the poor natives in Virginia'. The Indians are again linked with the Irish: the one 'nourished long in fearful superstition and idolatry', the other 'bred in a manifest and most palpable, and even a visible, adoring of Satan'. Brinsley believes that many Englishmen are nervous of crossing to Virginia because of the danger of themselves 'falling away from God to Satan, and that themselves or their posterity should become utterly savage'. For the reducing of a barbarous people to 'civility' God has ordained 'schools of learning'. The two purest tongues are English and Latin. And English and Latin must be 'propagated to the rudest Welsh and Irish, yea to the very heathen and savage'. So 'a loving civility' will be certain, in obedience to the King and the laws; and the way prepared 'to pull them from the power and service of Satan'. Brinsley is concerned to emphasise to the Virginia Company that there must be 'no wrong offered to the poor savage there, nor scandal given to them'.

The essay on the Right Order of Teaching is presented 'more specially' to the English in Virginia: as 'their sea card and compass to keep them in their right course to their intended point', so that 'they may sail securely amongst the most dangerous rocks and perilous tempests'.

Brinsley's emphasis on the Indian, rather than on the sons of the

---

[37] 1-2.   [38] 22; 25-6.   [39] 14-15.   [40] 3.   [41] 7.

English colonists, may have made its mark on Copland. He had had effective experience in bringing to civility and religion the natives encountered by the East India Company. In 1613 he had brought to England 'an Indian youth, born in the Bay of Bengala'. Within a year Copland had taught the boy 'to speak, to read, and write the English tongue and hand, both roman and secretary'. James I and 'many of the nobility wondered at his hand'. And during three years Copland 'taught him the grounds of religion, and to learn most of St Paul's Epistles by heart, and to give a public confession of his faith the day he was baptised'[42] – 22 December 1616, at St Denis, Fen Church Street. The boy, Peter Pope, returned to India. By 1620 he was adept in Latin; in that year he wrote three letters in both Latin and English, one to Captain Thomas Smith, and two to Captain Pring. Copland and Pring brought the letters back to England on the 'Royal James' in 1621; and Copland printed the letters as an Appendix to the published version of the sermon he preached to the Virginia Company on 18 April 1622.

Copland decided to go in person to Virginia. And on 3 July 1622 the Virginia Company announced that he was to have a parsonage there.[43] And also that he was to be 'Rector' of the intended Indian College. London had not yet received news of the Massacre of March 1622. That, and the discords which were to result in the dissolution of the Virginia Company in May 1624, postponed any educational hopes in Virginia.

Copland, however, appears to have arrived in Virginia in the winter of 1622.[44] Shortly afterwards, he went to Bermuda: where by the 1640s he was concerned with the setting up there of a 'covenanted' church – 'the culmination of many years of effort to convert Bermuda into a Puritan sanctuary'.[45] He was banished to the Bahamas in 1649.

By his will of 1635, a Virginia planter named Benjamin Symmes, 'the forefather of the American system of free education', left 200 acres, and the increase and milk of eight cows, to provide for the education of settlers' sons in Elizabeth County on the seaboard of Chesapeake Bay.[46] In 1643 the General Assembly at Jamestown acknowledged Symmes' founding of a 'free school'.[47] And by 1649 a Virginian could pay tribute to the Symmes 'free school': 'with two hundred acres of land, a fine house upon it, forty milch kine, and other accomodations to it.'[48] 'Free' because fees were demanded only from those parents who could afford to pay. (Wealthy parents may have preferred to keep their offspring at home.) The 1649 writer also said

[42] Copland, *Virginias God be Thanked*, 1622, 20-30.

[43] Kingsbury, II, 91.

[44] IV, 15.

[45] Andrews, *Colonial Period*, I, 231-2.

[46] Helen Jones Campbell, 'The Syms and Eaton Schools and their Successor', *William and Mary Quarterly*, ser.2, vol.20, no.1, Jan.1940, pp.1-61. For this paragraph see Wright, *Cultural Life*, 100.

[47] Hening, *Statutes*, I, 252.

[48] *Perfect Description of Virginia*, 1649, Force, *Tracts*, II, no.8, p.15.

that in the colony there were 'other petty schools'. We do not know the details. Another benefaction came in 1659, by the will of Thomas Eaton, who left 500 acres, some cattle and two negroes for another school in Elizabeth County. The Symmes and Eaton schools taught reading, writing and arithmetic, and maybe a little Latin. They were merged in 1805, to form Hampton Academy (Hampton was Elizabeth City, which was Kecoughtan). Winchester school, in northern Virginia, sprang from a bequest of land and books by a Virginia parish parson in 1702.

The straggling and small settlements and plantations of Virginia, the shortage of graduate settlers, the traumatic early history (the constant possibility and fear of defeat and failure: the interaction of incompetence between London and Jamestown) – these things did not foster any systematic educational programme. In 1671 Governor Sir William Berkeley (who had been in Virginia for thirty years) lauded the fact that along the James 'there are no free schools nor printing':[49]

learning has bought disobedience and heresy and sects into the world, and printing has divulged them and libels against the best government. God keep us from both!

However, there were six schools in Virginia by 1690.[50]

Things were better in early Massachusetts – for one thing, there was no dependence on, or supervision by, London.[51] Boston was founded in 1630: the Boston Latin School dates from 1635.[52] Daniel Maude became Master of the Boston School in 1636. Daniel's father had been at St John's College Cambridge from 1564, becoming a Fellow in 1570, and then leaving Cambridge for Yorkshire, to become Master of Halifax School, and then the first Master of Wakefield School. The father sent his four sons to Cambridge: the first to Emmanuel, the second to St John's, the fourth to Clare. Daniel, the third son, went to Emmanuel in 1603, and took his M.A., and was ordained, in 1610. He went to New England in 1635. The Master of the Boston School from 1650 until 1667 was Robert Woodmansey, who had matriculated from St John's in 1609, but transferred to Magdalene: B.A. 1613, M.A. 1616. The most famous colonial Master of the Boston School was Ezekiel Cheever, a schoolmaster in New England for seventy years. Cheever died in 1708, aged 102. He had been Master of the Newhaven School in 1638, aged 22; he then taught at Ipswich and Charlestown, and went to the Boston School in 1670, when he was 54. He had gone up to Emmanuel from Christ's Hospital in 1633, aged 17. Perhaps the air of Emmanuel encouraged longevity:

[49] Quoted Hawke, *Colonial Experience*, 297.

[50] Cremin, *American Education: The Colonial Experience*, 1970, 183.

[51] I am not, of course, thinking of matters of capital and shipping: the role played by London here is emphasised by modern scholarship.

[52] Wright, *Cultural Life*, 101-3; Holmes, *Tercentenary History of the Boston Public Latin School 1635-1935*.

the first Master of the College, Laurence Chaderton, died in 1640 at the age of 103.

There were twenty-three schools in Massachusetts in 1690.[53]

In the 1640s the General Court of Massachusetts ordained that every child should have some 'honest trade or calling'.[54] That was equally an imperative in Jamestown; where in 1646, for 'the better educating of youth in honest and profitable trades and manufactures', the General Assembly ordered that from each of the eleven counties two poor children, boys or girls, not less than seven years old, should be sent to Jamestown, installed in a specially built hostel, and employed in 'carding, knitting and spinning' in 'the public flax houses'.[55] And, in general, the county authorities were to 'bind out children to tradesmen or husbandmen to be brought up in some good and lawful calling', following 'laudable custom in the kingdom of England'; to 'avoid sloth and idleness', and 'for relief of such parents whose poverty extends not to give them breeding'. (It was regrettable that the settlers 'either through fond indulgence or perverse obstinacy are most averse and unwilling to part with their children'.) The Ethic of Work was a necessity, not a Cultural Trait, in Virginia! Thus far Boston and Jamestown were alike in the 1640s. But the General Court of Massachusetts went on to say that every township of fifty householders should have a schoolmaster to teach reading and writing, and every township of one hundred householders should establish a Latin Grammar School, in which boys could be prepared for Harvard. In New England, children and apprentices should be able to 'read and understand the principles of religion, and the capital laws of the country'.

In Virginia, the wealthier planters, perhaps far from any township, looked for tutors, or relied on the parson. (If they could find a parson: there were nearly fifty parishes in Virginia in 1660, but only ten official clerics.)[56] Or the boys were sent to school in England. William Fitzhugh intended in 1690 to send his eldest son to London; but he met a French Huguenot minister, who agreed to board and lodge the young man, and teach him Latin. It was a reasonable arrangement, in spite of the lack of dictionaries and grammars, and the fact that the household spoke only French. A younger son was sent to England in 1698 – he, at the age of eleven, could not read or write English, having also been with 'the ingenious French gentleman'.[57]

The Jamestown General Assembly in 1661 raised once again the question of a central 'College, and free school': for 'the advance of learning, education of youth, supply of the ministry, and promotion of

[53] Cremin, 183.
[54] Wright, *Cultural Life*, 103.
[55] Hening, *Statutes*, I, 336-7.
[56] W.S. Seiler, 'The Anglican Parish in Virginia', in Smith (ed.), *Seventeenth-Century America*, 129.
[57] Davis, *Fitzhugh*, 271, 361.

piety' (in face of the fact of 'the want of able and faithful ministers in this country').[58] Nothing effective happened for another thirty years. In 1693 the College of William and Mary received its Charter from London. The site chosen was Middle Plantation, seven miles inland from Jamestown: 'middle' between the James and the York rivers, first settled in 1630. The foundation stone was laid in 1695. £2,500 had been subscribed in England and Virginia; an arrangement had been agreed about export taxes on tobacco; and King William and Queen Mary had given £2,000 and granted 20,000 Virginia acres.[59] Robert Beverley of Virginia, in a book published in 1705, was gloomy about the College.[60] The plan was for one hundred students, but there were fewer in 1700 than there had been at the beginning – many of the Virginia planters 'choose to send their sons to England, and others to keep theirs at home'. (Beverley had been sent to England.) The Head of the College lived several miles away, and the quadrangle, fine though the design was (traditionally by Wren), was unfinished, and the boys were taught in the 'little school house' nearby. Indeed, in its early years William and Mary was a Grammar School rather than a University.

In 1699 Middle Plantation became the capital of the Colony and was renamed Williamsburg. (William III died in 1702: Mary had died in 1694.) Beverley strongly disapproved of this 'wild project' of the 'arbitrary and imperious' Francis Nicholson, Governor from 1698 to 1705, who 'flattered himself with the fond imagination of being the founder of a new city': a city which by 1705 was largely 'imaginary', although the noise of the construction work meant that 'the students are interrupted in their study, and make less advances than formerly'.[61]

The contrast is unavoidable between the length of time taken to found a University in Virginia (1618-93), and the brisk establishment of Harvard. The General Court of Massachusetts voted funds for a College in October 1636; it was decided in 1637 to build the College at Newtown; in May 1638 Newtown was renamed Cambridge; and students entered the College in the autumn of 1638. In September 1638 there died in Massachusetts an M.A. of Emmanuel, aged thirty, who left to the College £850 and his library of 400 volumes. That was John Harvard, who had gone up to Emmanuel in 1627, at the ripe age of twenty. In March 1639 the College was named Harvard. The first effective President of Harvard (1640) was Henry Dunster, who had matriculated from Magdalene College Cambridge in 1627, and had taught in his Lancashire birthplace, Bury, after taking his M.A. in 1634. In October 1642 nine young men graduated from Harvard. By 1650 there were fifty students there. Dunster thought in terms of a

[58] Hening, *Statutes*, II, 25.
[59] Wright: *Cultural Life*, 118-19; and *First Gentlemen of Virginia*, 106-12.
[60] *History and Present State of Virginia*, ed. Wright, 97-105, 265-7.
[61] *ibid.*, 86, 100, 105.

University for the whole of British America; in the event, colonial Harvard catered exclusively for New England.[62]

From about 1655 (with the help of the New England Society: a missionary enterprise founded in London in 1649) there was provision for Indian students at Harvard. Indeed, a building was erected for the purpose in the 1650s in Harvard Yard; two stories high, with two 'staircases' or 'entries', and accommodation for twenty young men. It was probably never intended that more than six Indians should reside there; the building was always used for ordinary Harvard students, and was demolished in 1693, having decayed beyond repair. There were Indian students at colonial Harvard (four in the 1660s and 1670s); but only one actual Indian graduate (Class of 1665 – another Indian in that Class was drowned before graduation). An Indian in the Class of 1716 also died before graduating – he had earlier been rusticated for excessive drinking.[63]

There was also provision for Indians at William and Mary.[64] This was financed by 'the Charity of the Honorable Robert Boyle, Esquire'. Robert Boyle, scientist, philosopher, and religious thinker, was born in Munster in 1627, son of the Earl of Cork. He died in 1691, leaving the greater part of his estate for missionary activity. His executors invested in land; one of their purchases was the extensive 'manor' of Brafferton, Yorkshire, which brought in £270 a year. The allotment of the Brafferton income was worked out in 1698 by Bishop Henry Compton of London, and the Earl of Burlington and Cork. £90 a year was to go to New England (through the New England Company): half of that to Harvard. The remainder went to William and Mary for Indian education. (Compton was Chancellor of William and Mary: a College, wrote Beverley, 'begun in an episcopal way, and carried on wholly by zealous conformists to the Church of England'.)[65] The College was to provide lodging, clothes, food, laundry and books for the Indians 'from the first beginning of letters till they should be ready to receive Orders, and be thought sufficient to be sent abroad to preach and convert the Indians'. By the 1720s a building had been provided for them, and one of the six professors appointed Indian 'Master'. The building was called 'Brafferton'.

It was difficult to recruit Indians for William and Mary. The sons of chiefs might be placed there as hostages; or the chiefs could be bribed – by promise of remission of tribute, for instance. But by 1712 there were twenty boys there; four of them from 'some years ago'. At that time, they lived in the town of Williamsburg, some of them as

---

[62] Wright, *Cultural Life*, 117.

[63] Wright, *Cultural Life*, 117; Morison; *Harvard in Seventeenth Century*, ch.17; *Three Centuries of Harvard*, 38. Sibley, *Harvard Graduates*, II, 201-4; VI, 142-4. Vaughan, *New England Frontier*, 281-7.

[64] Indians at William and Mary: Kellaway, *New England Company*, 173-4; H.L. Ganter, *William and Mary Quarterly*, January 1935 (series 2, vol.15, no.1), 17-21, and October 1935 (no.4), 366-9.

[65] *History and Present State of Virginia*, ed. Wright, 99-100.

servants; and they tended to die. Their education did not then go beyond the grammar school level. But during the eighteenth century, eight or ten Indian boys went every year to the 'Indian School of the College of William and Mary'.

William Byrd II by 1729 was pessimistic about 'Mr Boyle's Charity'.[66] It had had 'bad success' in 'converting any of these poor heathens to Christianity'.

Many children of our neighbouring Indians have been brought up in the College of William and Mary. They have been taught to read and write, and have been carefully instructed in the principles of the Christian religion till they come to be men. Yet after they returned home, instead of civilising and converting the rest, they have immediately relapsed into infidelity and barbarism themselves. And some of them too have made the worst use of the knowledge they acquired among the English, by employing it against their benefactors. Besides, as they unhappily forget all the good they learn, and remember the ill, they are apt to be more vicious and disorderly than the rest of their countrymen.

Perhaps Sir Edwin Sandys had the same sort of outlook in 1622.

For white Virginians, William and Mary became increasingly attractive in the eighteenth century. By 1760 its library had about 3,000 books – but Harvard had 5,000, and William Byrd II, 5,000. In 1711 there was founded at William and Mary a chair of 'Natural Philosophy and Mathematics' – the first scientific chair in North America.[67] Thomas Jefferson, who entered the College in 1760, aged 16.11 (having learned Latin, Greek and French under two successive clerics since he was nine) was especially impressed by the lectures of the mathematics Professor.

By 1770 there were eight Universities in the thirteen colonies: Harvard and William and Mary; the College in Connecticut, founded in 1701, moving to New Haven in 1716, and named after the London merchant Elihu Yale, who had sent goods (including a portrait of George I) which raised £500 at a sale; the College of New Jersey, an achievement of Scots Presbyterians, 1746 – Princeton; King's College, New York City (Columbia) 1754; the College of Philadelphia (University of Pennsylvania) 1755; Rhode Island College (Brown) 1764; and Queen's College New Jersey (Rutgers) 1766.

But what of the Indian?

There is to hand a Reuter report of White House approval for a grant to establish in the United States 'the first College exclusively for Indians'. The date: July 1968.

---

[66] Byrd, 'History of the Dividing Line': Pearce, *Colonial American Writing*, 433.
[67] Wright, *Cultural Life*, 224.

23

The Judicious Master Thorpe, 1620-1622

In his sermon to the Virginia Company at Bow Church, Cheapside, on 18 April 1622, Patrick Copland paid tribute to his 'religious' and 'judicious' friend George Thorpe, then in Virginia as 'over-seer of your college lands'.[1] Master George Thorpe, Esquire, of Gloucestershire, is not in the *Dictionary of National Biography* (1898) nor in the *Dictionary of American Biography* (1936). It seems just that a separate chapter should here be devoted to him.

Thorpe was listed as a shareholder in the Virginia Company in 1618, the amount of his 'holding' being £25.[2] A modest investment; though there were some prominent 'adventurers' who had risked less – £12.10s in the case of Lionel Cranfield, Raleigh Crashaw, and George Montaigne, £13.6.8 in the case of Bishop John Thornborough of Worcester. £25 is the sum noted also for the towns of Chichester and Dover, and the Companies of Barber Surgeons and Embroiderers. William Crashaw had invested £37.10s; Archbishop Abbot and Bishop Arthur Lake of Bath and Wells £75 each; Ralph Hamor £133.6.8; Alderman Robert Johnson £241; Sir Edwin Sandys £287.10s; the Company of Grocers £487.10; Thomas West, Baron De La Warr, £500; William Herbert, Earl of Pembroke, £400; Henry Wriothesley, Earl of Southampton, £350; William Cecil, Earl of Salisbury, £333.6.8; David Cecil, Earl of Exeter, £220; Thomas Howard, Earl of Suffolk, £133.6.8.

By the beginning of 1619 a Gloucestershire group – Thorpe, Sir William Throckmorton, John Smyth, and Richard Berkeley – had procured a 'patent for plantation in Virginia' – a copy of the patent 'written by the Virginian boy of me, George Thorpe' was sent to Yeardley.[3] This was a 'particular plantation'; and the first settlers for it arrived in Virginia in November 1619 – the site being 'Berkeley Hundred', an area of 12½ square miles up towards Charles City, but on the north bank of the River James. Shortly thereafter a new charter

---

[1] *Virginias God be Thanked*, 1622, 12. My attention was drawn to Thorpe by W.F. Craven's article 'Indian Policy in Early Virginia', *William and Mary Quarterly*, January 1944 (3rd series, vol.1, 65-82).

[2] Kingsbury, ed., *Records*, III, 89. Unless otherwise stated, all the references in this chapter are to the Kingsbury volumes.

[3] III, 136.

placed the management directly in the hands of Thorpe, together with William Tracy: to be 'sole governors and directors of all manner of businesses there'.[4] Thorpe sailed for Virginia in March 1620; and Tracy followed in the autumn with a substantial body of settlers.[5] Before leaving London Thorpe had been appointed a member of an eight-man Committee of the Council for Virginia, chaired by Southampton. And in June 1620 (by which time Thorpe was in Jamestown) the London Quarter Court named him as one of seven new 'Councillors of State' in Virginia.[6] He was also one of 'two new officers' called 'Deputies', in charge of 'public land'. The 'public land' devoted to the Company was to be in the charge of Thomas Newse; and to Thorpe, 'well known to the Company for his sufficiency', was assigned the government of 'the college land'.[7] He had originally gone to Virginia, of course, in the interest of Berkeley Hundred. But he became a 'spur' to the project of the 'college land', the first tenants for which, as we have seen, arrived in Virginia in November 1619. Eventually the 'public lands' beyond Henrico were laid out: including the 10,000 acres of 'university and college' land.[8]

In December 1620, six months after his arrival in Virginia, Thorpe wrote to Sir Thomas Smythe.[9] There had been stories in England of inordinate illness in the colony:

Be not discouraged therein, for I thank God I never had my health better in my life than I have had since my coming into this country, and I could say the like of divers others, and am persuaded that more do die here of the disease of their mind than of their body, by having this country's victuals over-praised unto them in England, and by not knowing they shall drink water here.

However, the settlers 'have found a way to make so good drink of Indian corn as I protest I have divers times refused to drink good strong English beer, and chosen to drink that.' (Is this the first recorded reference to bourbon whisky?) Thorpe reassures Smythe that if he sends his second son to Virginia (Smythe had three sons) he will be 'as good a man of living, every way, as his elder brother' (provided he has 'a competent number of servants' and 'a reasonable stock of cattle'). He asks Smythe to care for 'my poor wife and children, unto whom I have written to come over hither', and to whom he intends to send a note 'of what is fit for her to bring for her journey and for this country'.

Thorpe quickly made a good impression on Governor Sir George Yeardley, who wrote to Treasurer Sandys that Thorpe would be the best person to succeed him as Governor in November 1621.[10]

[4] III, 378.
[5] Hatch, *First Seventeen Years*, 44-5.
[6] I, 383. [7] I, 349.
[8] See Chapter 22, p.434, 435.
[9] III, 417-18. [10] III, 124.

Being, I am assured, you tender most deeply the welfare of this plantation, you would be pleased, my time of three years being expired in the government, to commend unto the good regard of the Company this worthy person Captain Thorpe, whom I do find to be a man most jealously affected unto the well proceeding of the whole plantation; and being it pleaseth God to give him health and strength, having also been well seasoned to the country, assuredly will be the most fit man to be Governor of Virginia.

He was to mention Thorpe's name again as a possible successor in a letter to Sandys in May 1621: he was, again, 'well seasoned to the country'.[11] But in fact the Governor named in June 1621 was Sir Francis Wyatt.

We know of two letters written by Thorpe from Jamestown in May 1621. A passage from one of them was to be quoted by Copland in his 1622 Virginia Company sermon.[12] The passage runs

No man can justly say that this country is not capable of all those good things that you in your wisdoms, with your great charge, have projected, both for her wealth and honour; and also of all other good things that the most opulent parts of Christendom do afford. Neither are we hopeless that this country may also yield things of better value than any of these.

The second was to Sir Edwin Sandys, and is preserved in the Ferrar Papers at Magdalene College Cambridge.[13] Thorpe mourns that 'so slender hath been the harvest of our labours'. And the reason surely is that 'God is displeased with us that we do not as we ought to do: take His service along with us by our serious endeavours of converting the heathen that live round about us, and are daily conversant amongst us'. There is

scarce any man amongst us that doth so much as afford them a good thought in his heart, and most men with their mouths give them nothing but maledictions and bitter execrations, being thereunto falsely carried with a violent mispersuasion (grown upon them I know not how) that these poor people have done unto us all the wrong and injury that the malice of the Devil or man can afford.

In Thorpe's opinion, 'if there be wrong on any side it is on ours: who are not so charitable to them as Christians ought to be'. The main fault of the Indians is that they are 'a little craving, and that in a niggardly fashion, for they will commonly part with nothing they have'. But they are ('especially the better sort of them') of 'peaceful and virtuous disposition'. And – another good thing – 'they begin more and more to affect English fashions'; if the Company would send over 'something in matter of apparel and household stuff' for the chiefs, 'I am persuaded it would make a good entrance into their

[11] III, 452.
[12] *Virginias God be Thanked*, 12. Letter of 17 May 1621.
[13] III, 446-7.

affections, they being, as I think, first to be dealt with by the book of the world, as being nearest to their sense'. Thorpe recommends also that the Virginia Company

make some public declaration of their intent and desire of the conversion of this people, and therewithal a testification of their love and hearty affection towards them, to be sent hither and published, thereby to mollify the minds of our people.

The iron works project is going badly. But Thorpe has imported 'a mason of my own that hath built many iron furnaces in England, and I hope shall perform this here, whereunto my help and often presence shall not be wanting'. The settlers have begun to plant vines; Thorpe has planted 'near ten thousand' for 'the college'. Most of the silk worm seed has perished – but not quite all, and there is still hope there.

Some things Thorpe especially requires. Some new pikes; those in Virginia are worn out in 'fighting with the natives' – and the colony was fearing a Spanish attack. A copy of John Gerard's *The Herball or Generall Historie of Plantes* (1597): 'thereby to make comparison of the simples of the country.' And, most important, Law books. 'In the matter of our government here we are many times perplexed; sometimes for lack of legal officers, and sometimes for want of books.' So Thorpe asks for *Le plees del Coron* (the Pleas of the Crown) by Sir William Stanford (1509-1558), first published in 1557; a volume on 'precedents'; 'the new book of the abridgement of Statutes'; and 'what other Law books you shall think fit'. (John Harvard's library was to include similar tomes.)

Thorpe had his enemies in Virginia, and was afraid that bad reports had reached Sandys.

I pray you judge charitably till you be better informed; for I thank God I have the testimony of a good conscience that I have done no man wrong. Only I do desire to bring drunkenness and some other sins out of fashion, and if I live I doubt not but I shall do it.

These unfavourable reports were presumably the reason for Sandys' rejecting Yeardley's recommendation of Thorpe as his successor.

The new Governor, Wyatt, received his instructions on 24 July 1621.[14] His appointment as Governor was to date from 18 November. London was worried about the excessive emphasis in Virginia on tobacco – a 'useless' commodity,[15] although 'a small quantity' should be planted, using 'all possible care that the proportion limited may be improved in goodness as much as may be'.[16] The settlers would be better employed sowing and planting corn, and building enclosures for cattle, swine and poultry.[17] The London Company was interested in mulberry trees and silk; vines (vine growers had been sent out);

---

[14] III, 468-82. [15] Item 18. [16] Item 25. [17] Item 14.

salt, pitch, tar and ashes for soap; dyes, gums and drugs; and walnut oil. The 'Dutchmen' sent over for 'the erecting of sawing mills' should be cherished,[18] and the Italians, in Virginia 'for the erecting of a glass furnace'.[19] The 'iron works' is a venture 'so necessary as few other are to be valued in comparison thereof': and John Berkeley of Gloucestershire has been dispatched, an 'industrious and intelligent gentleman many ways, but especially for Iron Works'.[20] (He was presumably Thorpe's 'mason of my own'.) The planters should explore 'every day further by the sea coast and within land' – and especially look for furs, and 'find good fishing between James River and Cape Cod'.[21] The settlers must 'apply themselves to an industrious course of life', in 'several degree and profession', and 'no man be suffered to live idly, the example whereof might prove pernicious to the rest'. In particular, three things should be suppressed: 'too much gaming'; the 'odious vice of drunkeness'; and 'all kind of riot both in apparel and otherwise' – no one, except members of the Jamestown Council, and the heads of hundreds and plantations and their wives and children, should 'wear any gold in their clothes, or any apparel of silk, until such time they have it of the silk there made by silkworms, and raised by their own industry'.[22] The 'service of Almighty God and observance of His divine laws' must be specially regarded, especially as 'our general endeavours and designs have not yet effected a due establishment of the honour and rights belonging to the Church and Ministry'. There must be 'due order in administering of all services according to the usual form and discipline of the Church of England', an avoidance of 'all factious and needless novelties, tending only to the disturbance of peace and unity', and maintenance and respect for 'such ministers as have been or shall be sent from time to time'. Thus the example of the people in Virginia 'may be a means to win the infidels to God'.[23]

Especial care was to be taken that 'no injury or oppression be wrought by the English against any of the natives' (although of course 'all manner of insolence' by the Indians was to be 'severely and sharply punished').[24] The best means were to be used

to draw the better disposed of the natives to converse with our people, and labour among them with convenient reward; that thereby they may grow to a liking and love of Civility, and finally be brought to the knowledge and love of God and true religion, which may prove also of great strength to our people against the savages, or other invaders whatsoever. And they may be fit instruments to assist afterwards in the more general conversion of the heathen people which we so much desire.[25]

For 'the laying of the surer foundation for the said conversion', each 'town, city, borough and other particular plantation' should obtain[26]

---

[18] Item 18. [19] Item 28. [20] Item 21. [21] Item 44. [22] Item 3. [23] Item 1. [24] Item 2. [25] Item 5. [26] Item 6.

by just means a certain number of the children of the natives, to be educated by them in true religion and a civil course of life. Of which children the most towardly boys in will and graces of nature to be brought up by them in the first elements of literature, so to be fitted for the college; in the fabric whereof we purpose to proceed as soon as any profit returned from the tenants shall enable us.

The 'business of the college' would ensure for Virginia 'a particular blessing of God', and 'the love of all good men here to the plantation'.

When Wyatt arrived in October 1621, he found the colony 'in very great amity and confidence with the natives'. The Indians were apparently 'in some jealousy whether our new Governor would continue the League or not'.[27] So Wyatt used Thorpe as an intermediary. Thorpe, who had studied the language in England with his Indian 'boy', knew Opechancanough. He had met him by June 1621, and paid another visit in July, because Opechancanough 'hath divers times sent for me, as he saith out of a desire he hath to be further informed of some things by me offered unto him at our last meeting'.[28] Wyatt sent Thorpe again to Opechancanough,[29] who

gave him very good hope of their entertaining of some of our families to live amongst them, and of their sending to cohabit with us; and did confirm a former promise of sending one to be our guide beyond the falls to certain mines.

Thorpe reported that Opechancanough 'had some knowledge of many of the fixed stars, and had observed the north star and the course of the constellation about it, and called the Great Bear 'Manguahaian', which in their language signifies the same'. Thorpe also found 'more motions of religion in him than could be imagined in so great blindness, for he willingly acknowledged that theirs was not the right way, desiring to be instructed in ours, and confessed that God loved us better than them'. Opechancanough, according to Thorpe, thought 'the cause of His anger against them was their custom of making their children black boys'. In his Cheapside sermon to the Virginia Company on 18 April 1622 Patrick Copland quoted and elucidated this material:[30] Opechancanough 'thought the cause of His anger against them was the custom of making their children black boys, or consecrating them to Satan'. The use of the 'black boy' phrase in John Smith's *Generall Historie* of 1624 has already been noted.[31] In the early eighteenth century Robert Beverley of Virginia reported that it was a rumour in England among the 'common people' that Virginia 'turns all people black who go to live there'.[32]

[27] III, 584 (Jamestown to London, January 1622).
[28] III, 462 (Thorpe to Sandys, 27 June 1621).
[29] III, 584.
[30] *Virginias God be Thanked*, p.322.
[31] Chapter 15, p.0.
[32] Wright, introduction to Beverley, *History and Present State of Virginia*, xvii.

Opechancanough broke off his meeting with Thorpe. He was 'in the midst of his hunting'; and referred Thorpe, 'touching all matters, to a further conference at Pomeiock when he had ended his hunting'.[33]

A second tribute to Thorpe, in addition to the sermon by Copland, was printed in London in 1622. This was by the London Secretary of the Virginia Company, Edward Waterhouse.[34]

That worthy religious gentleman Master George Thorpe Esquire, deputy of the college lands, sometimes one of his Majesty's pensioners, and in one of the principal places of command in Virginia, did so truly and earnestly affect their conversion, and was so tender over them, that whosoever under his authority had given them but the least displeasure or discontent, he punished them severely. He thought nothing too dear for them, and, as being desirous to bind them unto him by his many courtesies, he never denied them anything that they asked him; insomuch that when these savages complained unto him of the fierceness of our mastiffs, most implacable and terrible unto them ... he, to gratify them in all things, for the winning of them by degrees, caused some of them to be killed in their presence, to the great displeasure of the owners, and would have had all the rest gelded (had he not been hindered) to make them the gentler and the milder to them.

Thorpe was 'kind and beneficial' not only to the 'common sort' but also to Opechancanough,

to whom he oft resorted, and gave many presents which he knew to be highly pleasing to him. And whereas this king before dwelt only in a cottage, or rather a den, or hog sty, made with a few poles and sticks, and covered with mats after their wild manner, to civilise him he first built him a fair house according to the English fashion; in which he took such joy, especially in his lock and key, which he so admired, as, locking and unlocking his door an hundred times a day, he thought no device in all the world was comparable to it.

Waterhouse then gave his adaptation of the January 1622 report of the Thorpe/Opechancanough conversations. Thorpe

intimated to him matters of our religion. And thus far the pagan confessed, moved by natural principles, that our God was a good God, and much better than theirs, in that He had with so many good things, above them, endowed us. He told him if he would serve our God he should be partaker of all those good things we had, and of far greater than sense or reason ever could imagine. He won upon him, as he thought, in many things, so as he gave him fair hearing and good answer and seemed to be much pleased with his discourse, and in his company. And both he and his people, for the daily courtesies this good gentleman did to one or other of them, did profess such outward love and respect unto him, as nothing could seem more.

Thorpe's example helped to inspire Copland's sermon of 18 April 1622, which was printed in May under the title: *Virginias God be*

[33] III, 584. [34] III, 552.

thanked; or a sermon of thanksgiving for the happy success of the affairs of Virginia this last year. It was a flat and army-chaplain type effort. But the material is appealing. Copland reminded his audience, members of the Virginia Company, of the safe arrival at Jamestown in November and December 1621 of nine ships, with eight hundred settlers on board – men, women and children. (By March 1621 the population of the colony had declined to about 840: two years before it had been 1,000.)[35] Copland, like William Symonds and Robert Gray, was obsessed by the danger of over-population. Emigration was the equivalent of bleeding in medicine. Some Londoners are starving.

I have heard many of the painfullest labourers of your city, even with tears, bemoan the desolate estate of their poor wives and children. Who, though they rise early, taw and tear their flesh all the day long with hard labour, and go late to bed, and feed almost the week long upon brown bread and cheese, yet are scarce able to put bread in their mouths at the week's end, and clothes on their backs at the year's end. And all because work is so hard to come by, and there be so many of the same trade that they cannot thrive one for another.[36]

But the enterprise in Virginia was thriving. Copland mentioned a Persian who had lived in Virginia for seven years, and said that of the eighteen countries to which he had travelled 'all of them in my mind come far short of Virginia, both for temperature of air and fertility of the soil'.[37] More important, God had worked

to mollify the hearts of savages, and to make some of them voluntarily to remove from their own warm and well-seated and peopled habitations, to give place to strangers whom they had never before seen.

Powhatan had done this 'at the first plantation of the English'. Similarly, Opechancanough had given to Yeardley the 'right and title' of his possessions.[38] Thus there was now 'a happy league of peace and amity soundly concluded and faithfully kept between the English and the natives'. And 'the fear of killing each other is now vanished away'.[39]

This address of 18 April 1622 is the most ironical sermon in English history. Twenty-seven days earlier – the news took eighteen weeks to reach London – Opechancanough had organised an Indian uprising in which nearly 350 colonists had been massacred. Those murdered included George Thorpe.

[35] Andrews, I, 136.
[36] *Virginias God be Thanked*, 34.
[37] *ibid.*, 14. [38] *ibid.*, 25-6. [39] *ibid.*, 9-10.

24

The Massacre and After: 1622-1625

The 'official' account of the massacre was written by Edward Waterhouse, and printed in London in the autumn of 1622.

A Declaration of the State of the Colony and Affairs in Virginia. With a Relation of the Barbarous Massacre in the time of Peace and League, treacherously executed by the Native Infidels upon the English, the 22 of March last. Together with the names of those that were then massacred.[1]

The settlers had thought that 'all their affairs were full of success, and such intercourse of familiarity, as if the Indians and themselves had been of one Nation'. There had been peace for five years. But Opechancanough had been plotting since at least the summer of 1621. The 'true cause' of the conspiracy (apart of course from 'the instigation of the Devil') was 'the daily fear that possessed them that in time we, by our growing continually upon them, would dispossess them of their country, as they had been formerly of the West Indies by the Spaniard'.[2]

Robert Beverley in 1705 gave a more sober account of the 'original cause' of the 'misfortunes':[3] from 1607,

the English had a very advantageous trade with the Indians; and might have made much greater gains of it, and managed it both to the greater satisfaction of the Indians and the greater ease and security of themselves, if they had been under any rule, or subject to any method, in trade, and were not left at liberty to outvie or outbid one another. By which they not only cut short their own profit, but created jealousies and disturbances among the Indians, by letting one have a better bargain than another. For they being unaccustomed to barter, such of them as had been hardest dealt by in their commodities thought themselves cheated and abused; and so conceived a grudge against the English in general, making it a national quarrel.

Back to Waterhouse. The Indians in March 1622 planned to

---

[1] Kingsbury, *Records*, III, 541-71. John Smith's account of the massacre in his 1624 *Generall Historie*, book 4 (Smith-Arber, 572-87) is wholly from Waterhouse. In this chapter, unless otherwise stated, all page references are to Kingsbury, vol.III.

[2] 554, 556.

[3] *History and Present State of Virginia*, 29.

'subvert the whole colony' in one day and 'at one instant of time';
'though our several plantations were an hundred and forty miles up
one river, on both sides' (i.e., 70 miles along the river). Waterhouse
explains to his readers that the 'wild, naked natives' live 'not in great
numbers together, but dispersed, and in small companies' – never
above 200, and mainly 40 or 50 – 'and many miles distant from one
another'.[4] Wilcomb E. Washburn has recently emphasised the
contrary point that it was the English who were scattered, and restless
and individualistic. The Indians lived in a 'group centered society';
defined settlements, living off the adjoining land. The Indians were
the 'urban' element.[5]

According to Waterhouse, the Indian 'small and scattered
companies'

> had warning given from one another in all their habitations to meet at the
> day and hour appointed for our destruction, at all our several towns and
> places seated upon the River. Some were directed to go to one place, some to
> another, all to be done at the same day and time. Which they did
> accordingly: some entering their houses under colour of trucking, and so
> taking advantage; others drawing our men abroad upon fair pretences; and
> the rest suddenly falling upon those that were at their labours.

The plot would have completely failed 'had any the least
foreknowledge been in those places where the massacre was
committed'. Some places had warning – the work, Waterhouse says,
of converted Indians, such as the one living in an English settlement
on the south bank of the River, opposite Jamestown, who heard of the
plot from his brother, and warned his master, who rowed across to
Jamestown before dawn. Thus 'thousands of ours were saved by the
means of one of them alone which was made a Christian'[6] – a fact to
balance the deaths of the 347 settlers listed by Waterhouse: out of a
population which he gives as over 4,000.

Or rather, he writes that 'eleven parts of twelve' remain alive.[7] So,
taking the 347 dead as one twelfth of the Virginia population, we
calculate a total population before the massacre of 4,164. Population
figures for a colony in the seventeenth century, even more than for a
homeland, are notoriously nightmarish to assess; but Waterhouse was
wildly out. He was probably influenced by the fact that in the three
years 1619-1621 over 3,500 emigrants had left England for Virginia.[8]
But an alarming proportion of these had died; whether on the voyage
or shortly after arrival. A London document of 1625 gave the
population on the eve of the massacre as 'about 2000';[9] but this was a
propaganda piece lauding the policy of the Virginia Company under
Sandys and Southampton. A note made in London late in 1622 gives

[4] 554.
[5] *Virginia under Charles and Cromwell*, 54.
[6] 554-5.   [7] 554.   [8] 536-7.
[9] Kingsbury, IV, 522.

an estimate of 'rather under' 1240 for 'about the time of the massacre'.[10] C.M. Andrews took this to mean *before* the massacre.[11] Others have read it as referring to the survivors; even if they are right (which is probable) the pre-massacre population was not more than 1,600. (The figure of 347 victims seems exact.) 1621 – the fifteenth year of settlement – had been the first year in which the population reached four figures. By 1625 there were probably less than 1,200 settlers in Virginia.[12]

March 22 was a Friday. For some days previously the Indians 'came unarmed into our houses, without bows or arrows, or other weapons, with deer, turkeys, fish, furs and other provisions, to sell and truck with us, for glass, beads and other trifles'. In some places they 'sat down at breakfast with our people at their tables'. So when the 'cruel execution' came, 'few or none discerned the weapon or blow that brought them to destruction'.

In which manner they also slew many of our people then at their several works and husbandries in the fields, and without their houses, some in planting corn and tobacco, some in gardening, some in making brick, building, sawing, and other kinds of husbandry. They well knowing in what places and quarters each of our men were, in regard of their daily familiarity and resort to us for trading and other negociations; which the more willingly was by us continued and cherished for the desire we had of effecting that great masterpiece of works, their conversion.

So the 347 fell: including 42 women and 26 boys and children. And

not being content with taking away life alone, they fell after again upon the dead, making as well they could a fresh murder, defacing, dragging and mangling the dead carcasses into many pieces, and carrying some parts away in derision, with base and brutish triumph.[13]

So they did with George Thorpe, living at Berkeley Hundred, five miles across the river from Charles City. (In all, eleven settlers were killed at Berkeley Hundred, including a woman and a child: and a Thomas Thorpe.)[14] They

not only wilfully murdered him, but cruelly and foully, out of devilish malice, did so many barbarous despites and foul scorns after to his dead corpse, as are unbefitting to be heard by any civil ear.

One detail of the story Waterhouse cannot resist underlining:[15]

when this good gentleman, upon his fatal hour, was warned by his man (who

[10] Kingsbury, III, 537.
[11] Andrews, *Colonial Period*, I, 139.
[12] *ibid.*, 136-40.
[13] Kingsbury, III, 551.
[14] 567.   [15] 553.

perceived some treachery intended to them by these hellhounds) to look to himself – and withal ran away for fear of the mischief he strongly apprehended and so saved his own life – yet his master, out of the conscience of his own good meaning and fair deserts ever towards them, was so void of all suspicion, and so full of confidence, that they had sooner killed him than he could or would believe they meant any ill against him.

For Waterhouse, Thorpe had been 'too kind and beneficial'. And in his story of the Indian fear of English mastiffs,[16] 'implacable and terrible unto them', he comments approvingly on the canine implacability: 'knowing them by instinct, it seems, to be but treacherous and false-hearted friends to us, better than ourselves.' His portrait of Thorpe, quoted in the preceding chapter, is thus, in intention, a warning.

Waterhouse records no deaths at Jamestown or Elizabeth City. It was the plantations, hundreds and farms down the River which suffered; such as Captain Berkeley's plantation, nearly seventy miles from Jamestown, towards Richmond – the furthest of the frontier outposts. The college lands were almost as far: and seventeen of the 'college people' were killed.[17] In all, there were nearly eighty English settlements along the James.

The 'greatest cause' of the massacre Waterhouse suggested to be the colonists' 'desire to draw those people to religion by the careless neglect of their own safeties'. The 'hearts' of the English were 'ever stupid': 'averted from believing anything that might weaken their hopes of speedy winning the savages to civility and religion by kind usage and fair conversing among them.' Waterhouse, a High Calvinist lawyer, was suspicious of facile conversion. We have quoted his description of Indian conversion as 'that great masterpiece of works' – a contemptuous description: Faith, not Works, is alone sufficient. The Deity, after all is inscrutable, and not bound by the laws of nature: He will effect the conversion of the Indian 'in His good time, and by such means as we think most unlikely'.[18]

Waterhouse was as shocked by the killing of the 347 English along the James in 1622 as modern readers are assumed to be by the murder of 153 Indians at Wounded Knee, South Dakota, in 1890. (Waterhouse's *Relation*, unlike Mr Dee Brown's 1971 *Bury My Heart at Wounded Knee*, was addressed to a reading public innocent of the Book-of-the-Month Club, the Popular Science Book Club, and the Playboy Book Club.) Waterhouse was urgently concerned to reveal 'the bloody and barbarous hands of that perfidious and inhumane people'.[19] The Indians are a 'viperous brood', 'wicked infidels', 'hell hounds', 'treacherous and false hearted'. Venereal disease was 'the Indian disease'.[20] Columbus used 'fair usage' to the Indian. Like Thorpe, he was deceived. Waterhouse recommends us to read Oviedo's judgment

---

[16] 552.
[17] List of the dead, 565-71.
[18] 553-4   [19] 551.   [20] 560.

on the Indians of the West Indies, 'that you may compare and see in what, and how far, it agrees with that of the natives of Virginia'.[21]

They are (saith he) by nature slothful and idle, vicious, melancholy, slovenly, of bad conditions, liars, of small memory, of no constancy or trust. In another place he saith, The Indian is by nature of all people the most lying and most inconstant in the world, sottish and sudden; never looking what dangers may happen afterwards; less capable than children of six or seven years old, and less apt and ingenious. This is the general disposition of most of them, though there be some (says he) that be wise and subtle.

Thus 'savages and pagans are, above all other, for matter of justice ever to be suspected'.[22]

But the loss of blood in Virginia can be beneficial: it can 'make the body more healthful'. For 'betraying of innocency never rests unpunished'. We now have the right to punish: 'our hands which before were tied with gentleness and fair usage are now set at liberty by the treacherous violence of the savages: not untying the knot, but cutting it.'[23] The 'fault is on their sides, not on ours, who have used so fair a carriage, even to our own destruction'.[24] So we can claim for Virginia more men and more munitions. The Indians 'who before we used as friends may now most justly be compelled to servitude and drudgery'. The meanest settlers can

employ themselves more entirely in their arts and occupations, which are more generous, whilst savages perform their inferior works of digging in mines, and the like; of whom also some may be sent for the service of the Sommer Islands.[25]

Waterhouse writes in terms of Conquest and Invasion. We may now

by right of war, and law of Nations, invade the country; and destroy them who sought to destroy us. Whereby we shall enjoy their cultivated places, turning the laborious mattock into the victorious sword (wherein there is more both ease, benefit and glory) and possessing the fruits of others' labours. Now their cleared grounds in all their villages (which are situated in the fruitfullest places of the land) shall be inhabited by us; whereas heretofore the grubbing of woods was the greatest labour.

Virginia will be more abundant; for the Indian used to kill the deer, the turkey and the hen – and we can 'orderly' use their fishing weirs:[26] Moreover –

the way of conquering them is much more easy than of civilising them by fair means, for they are a rude, barbarous and naked people, scattered in small companies, which are helps to Victory, but hindrances to Civility. Besides that, a conquest may be of many, and at once. But Civility is in particular,

---

[21] 562. [22] 559. [23] 556. [24] 559. [25] 558-9. [26] 557.

and slow, the effect of long time and great industry. Moreover, victory of them may be gained many ways: by force; by surprise; by famine in burning their corn; by destroying and burning their boats, canoes and houses; by breaking their fishing weirs; by assailing them in their huntings, whereby they get the greatest part of their sustenance in winter; by pursuing and chasing them with our horses, and bloodhounds to draw after them, and mastiffs to tear them, which take this naked, tanned, deformed savages for no other than wild beasts, and are so fierce and fell upon them, that they fear them worse than their old Devil they worship, supposing them to be a new and worse kind of Devil than their own. By these and sundry other ways, as by driving them (when they fly) upon their enemies who are round about them, and by animating and abetting their enemies against them, may their ruin or subjection be soon effected.

Take advantage of enmities and quarrels amongst the Indians themselves. It is the 'maxim of the politician': Divide and Conquer. Thus the Romans overcame Britain, Pizarro became master of Peru, and Cortez gained Mexico.[27]

The first reaction of the Virginia Company in London to the massacre was a letter dated 1 August 1622 to Wyatt and the Virginia Council from Sandys and the Council for Virginia in London.[28] The letter was critical of the administration in Jamestown: 'surprised by treachery in a time of known danger'; 'deaf to so plain a warning as (we now too late understand) was last year given';[29]

not to perceive anything in so open and general conspiracy, but to be made in part instruments of contriving it, and almost guilty of the destruction by a blindfold and stupid entertaining of it, which the least wisdom or courage sufficed to prevent, even on the point of execution.

(An occasion of Opechancanough's 'great suspicion and jealousy' had been the death on 6 March of Nenemettanan, shot in error by two English boys: Nenemettanan, 'Jack of the Feathers', had been for six years a friendly intermediary between the English and the Indians, and an acquaintance of Thorpe.)[30] So the massacre was a punishment of God upon the colonists: in particular for.

those two enormous excesses of apparel and drinking, the cry whereof cannot but have gone up to heaven, since the infamy hath spread itself to all that have but heard the name of Virginia, to the detestation of all good minds, the scorn of others, and our extreme grief and shame. In the strength of those faults, undoubtedly, and the neglect of the divine worship, have the Indians prevailed.[31]

So what to do now? 'You have conquered Sparta, now adorn it.' The Company is sending out more arms, and four hundred young

[27] 557-8. [28] 666-73. [29] 666.
[30] Barbour, *Pocahontas*, 205.
[31] 666.

men: 'the multitude of people is the strength of a kingdom.' One obvious fault in Virginia had been the 'inordinate straggling' of the settlements:[32]

We think it fit that the houses and buildings be so contrived together as may make, if not handsome towns, yet compact and orderly villages; that this is the most proper and succesful manner of proceeding in new plantations.

Charles City, Henrico, the iron works and the college land must be replanted; and the new settlers can replenish the ranks of 'the college tenants, and those belonging to the iron works' (the iron works to be under the supervision of Maurice Berkeley).[33] The 'college affairs' are especially pressing, 'not only as a public, but a sacred business'. (We remember that in July 1622, before London had heard of the massacre, Copland had been named Rector of 'the intended college for the conversion of the infidels'.)[34] There must be 'building of convenient houses, planting of orchards, gardens, etc, on the college land'.

As for the brick-makers, we desire they may be held to their contract made with Mr Thorpe, to the intent that when opportunity shall be for the erecting of the fabric of the college, the materials be not wanting.[35]

The Virginia Company has 'zealously affected' the saving of Indian souls. But now: 'we cannot but, with much grief, proceed to the condemnation of their bodies.' The 'innocent blood of so many Christians doth in justice cry out for revenge'. Thus –

we must advise you to root out from being any longer a people, so cursed a nation, ungrateful to all benefits and uncapable of all goodness. At least to the removal of them so far from you, as you may not only be out of danger, but out of fear of them, of whose faith and good meaning you can never be secure. Wherefore, as they have merited, let them have a perpetual war without peace or truce. And although they have deserved it without mercy too, yet remembering who we are rather than what they have been, we cannot but advise not only the sparing, but the preservation, of the younger people of both sexes; whose bodies may by labour and service become profitable, and their minds, not overgrown with evil customs, be reduced to Civility, and afterwards to Christianity.

So burn their corn; provoke their enemies; maintain

continually certain bands of men of able bodies, and inured to the country, of stout minds and active hands, that may from time to time, in severed bodies, pursue and follow them, surprising them in their habitations, intercepting them in their hunting, burning their towns, demolishing their temples, destroying their canoes, plucking up their weirs, carrying away their corn,

[32] 669. [33] 670. [34] Kingsbury, II, 91.
[35] Kingsbury, III, 671.

and depriving them of whatsoever may yield them succour or relief. By which means, in a very short while both your just revenge and your perpetual security might be certainly effected.[36]

Anyone taking Opechancanough prisoner will have 'a great and singular reward from us'. As for the Indians 'whom God used as instruments of revealing, and preventing the total ruin of you all' – they can best be thanked by 'a good and careful education', 'whereby they may be made capable of further benefits and favours'.[37]

No ship had been able to leave Jamestown until about a month after the massacre. The letter to London carried by that vessel, from Wyatt and the Jamestown Council,[38] acknowledged receipt of letters of late November and early December 1621, which had not arrived in Jamestown until the middle of April: eighteen weeks. The last letter from Jamestown had left in January 1622. Since when

it hath pleased God for our manifold sins to lay a most lamentable affliction upon this plantation by the treachery of the Indians; who on the 22nd of March last attempted in most places, under the colour of unsuspected amity, in some by surprise, to have cut us off all, and to have swept us away at once throughout the whole land; had it not pleased God of His abundant mercy to prevent them in many places, for which we can never sufficiently magnify His blessed name. But yet they prevailed so far that they have massacred in all parts above three hundred men, women and children; and have since not only spoiled and slain divers of our cattle, and some more of our people, and burnt most of the houses we have forsaken, but also have enforced us to quit many of our plantations, and to unite more nearly together in fewer places, the better for to strengthen and defend ourselves against them.[39]

(This was to breed disease. Epidemics followed the massacre. The population by 1624 was just over 1,000, in spite of the new settlers sent across in 1622 and 1623. In all, nearly 8,000 colonists crossed to Virginia between 1607 and 1624: in the three years 1620 and 1622, 3,000 immigrants died.[40] The shipboard diseases – cholera, dysentery, typhoid fever – exacerbated the fevers, the respiratory disorders and the dietary deficiences which were prevalent in the plantations, perhaps more lethal than malaria.)[41]

After the massacre, most of the cattle had been brought to Jamestown, 'the island being the securest place for them which we hold in all the River'. All settlements had been abandoned except seven: Jamestown; the plantations on the other side of the river from Jamestown; Kecoughtan; Newport Mews; Southampton Hundred; Flowerdie Hundred; and two other plantations. The 'frontier' had contracted. What the colony really needed – and had always needed – was a really 'defensible' settlement site.[42] The more so now:

[36] 672. [37] 673. [38] 611-15. [39] 612.
[40] Kingsbury, IV, 525; III, 537.
[41] Pomfret, *Founding the Colonies*, 42.
[42] Kingsbury, III, 612.

since this late woeful experience hath taught us that our first and principal care should have been for our safety, by the neglect whereof the plantation, though it hath seemed to go in a hopeful and flourishing course, yet hath all this while gone but so much out of the way.

Wyatt intended to find such a site during the summer. Another danger was 'extreme famine'. We need corn: 'to feed so many mouths as are here, two third parts whereof are women, children and unserviceable people.'[43] The season for planting corn was almost lost; the colonists must give priority to defence.

Neither can we now plant corn in so many places as we could wish, especially near our houses, by reason it spreadeth all over the ground like a thick grove, that the Indians may hide themselves therein, who will from time to time peek out many of our people whilst they are about their weeding and dressing thereof; and we have great reason to doubt, since they have heretofore practised the like, that where we do plant any corn they will either cut it down, or destroy it in summer before it be ripe, or by stealth share with us at harvest.

We can get corn from friendly Indians by trade, or from enemies by force: both methods are 'uncertain and hazardous'. There is also a lack of weapons; a third of the able-bodied men have none. Fortification engineers are needed; and spades, shovels, and pickaxes. We can repay with 'very good tobacco'.[44]

A very practical letter; of distress, but not despair. In reply to the criticisms from London, the Jamestown Council was to admit[45] that the settlers had been too optimistic in 'security': the result of 'the Indians coming daily amongst us, and putting themselves into our powers'. Otherwise Jamestown was stung by the 'disgraceful reproofs'. Would it were not that 'the covetousness of some at home did not minister swell to our drunkenness here, filling the country with wine not only in quantity excessive but in quality base and infectious'. For apparel, 'we know no excess, but in the Purists'.

On 7 May 1622, eleven weeks after the massacre, Wyatt authorised Ralph Hamor in Jamestown to voyage in Chesapeake Bay in 'The Tiger' and 'trade with the Indians for corn':[46] and 'in case he can get no trade with them, or not such as he expecteth, then it shall be lawful to take it from them, if he be able, by force.' Later in the year Hamor was similarly authorised to sail down the Potomac River in 'The Tiger'.[47] The Potomac tribe were traditional allies of the English (in the sense that they were enemies of the Pamunkey tribe). Nevertheless, Hamor was instructed to make a decision

either in the setting free of the king of Potomac and his son, or detaining and

[43] 613.   [44] 614.
[45] Kingsbury, IV, 11. January 1623.
[46] Kingsbury, III, 622.
[47] 697.

keeping them or any other Indians prisoners, as occasion shall be offered, and them or more in bringing to James City.

In fact the Potomac king and his son were brought to Jamestown. And there were those colonists who were offended by this. One of the complaints has been preserved:[48]

We ourselves have taught them how to be treacherous by our false dealing with the poor king of Potomac, that had always been faithful to the English; whose people was killed, he and his son taken prisoners, brought to Jamestown, brought home again ransomed, as if had been the greatest enemy they had.

The writer was Peter Arundel. And he thought a 'just revenge' was the death in the Potomac country of Captain Henry Spelman, 'the best linguist of the Indian tongue of this country's'. In April 1623 Spelman was sent trading in 'The Tiger', with a pinnace directed by John Pountis, a member of the Jamestown Council, with over 30 armed men on board. Spelman thought danger was ahead.

He had warning of it by an Indian. He and his men coming with their armour, the king of that place asked why he came so armed. Spelman told him of his distrust, and showed him the man that gave him warning. Whereupon the king in his presence caused the fellow's head to be cut off and cast into the fire before the said Captain his face; a bad reward, to betray him that had given him so faithful a warning. But his own life paid for it; for the next day he and his men, coming ashore disarmed, thinking to trade, were all cut off by the Indians. They took Mr Pountis his shallop and hewed her to pieces; and came with sixty canoes to take the unlucky ship 'The Tiger', who had but four sailors and some few land men, who whiffed up sails, and went faster than their canoes.

Arundel lamented that 'if we had sufficient provision, we should not need to seek after the Indians'.

The English in turn had their revenge.[49] In the autumn of 1623 Wyatt

set forward to the river of Potomac to settle the trade with our friends; and to revenge the treachery of the Pascoticons and their associates, being the greatest people in those parts of Virginia, who had cut off Captain Spelman, and Mr Pountis his pinnace. In which expedition he put many to the sword, burnt their houses, with a marvellous quantity of corn carried by them in to the woods, as it was not possible to bring it to our boats.

In the autumn of 1622 Jamestown received the reproving letter from the London Council. And the policy had begun of 'setting upon the Indians in all places':[50] Campaigns were mounted against the tribes

[48] Kingsbury, IV, 89.
[49] *ibid.*, 450.
[50] *ibid.*, 9-10.

that were confederate with Opechancanough: Yeardley against Opechancanough's seat of Pamunkey, and against the Weanoc, Nansemond and Warraskoyack; Captain John West against the Powhatan; Captain William Powell against the Chickahominy; Mr Trevor against the Topahanock – and Hamor, in his Potomac voyage, decimated the Nacotchtanke. We 'have slain divers, burnt their towns, destroyed their weirs and corn'. But it had become

most apparent that they are an enemy not suddenly to be destroyed with the sword, by reason of their swiftness of foot, and advantages of the woods, to which upon all our assaults they retire. But by the way of starving, and all other means that we can possibly devise, we will constantly pursue their extirpation. By computation, and confession of the Indians themselves, we have slain more of them this year than have been slain before since the beginning of the colony.

This news was given in a letter to Henry, Earl of Southampton, signed at Jamestown on 20 January 1623 by Wyatt and five others (including Yeardley and Hamor). The great failure has been the iron works, which must now be abandoned, so many of the workmen being slain: Maurice Berkeley is returning to England to report.[51] The men sent 'for the building of the East Indie school' (four of whom died) have for the moment been placed amongst the 'college tenants': as soon as convenient they will move to Martin's Hundred, 'according to Mr Copland's request to the Governor'.[52] The college tenants themselves,

with much difficulty, we are now about to resettle, and have engaged ourselves to supply them with corn until harvest, having strengthened them with divers of the Old Planters.[53]

The reverend William Leate had arrived in the late summer of 1622: a 'minister', said the London Council, 'recommended unto us for sufficiency of learning and integrity of life'.[54] By the end of the year he was dead; though 'the little experience we had of Mr Leate made good your commendations of him'.[55] It is uncertain how many clerics were in Virginia at the beginning of 1623. Thomas White, certainly, who had arrived at the end of 1621; Patrick Copland. Richard Buck, William Wickham and Robert Pawlett? – perhaps they were still alive.

The letter from Jamestown of January 1623 ended with an appeal to London not to

judge of us by the events of things which are ever uncertain, especially in a new plantation, nor by reports of branded people, some of whom have deservedly undergone several kinds of punishment, nor of the malicious and unknowing.

[51] *ibid.*, 12, 14. [52] *ibid.*, 15. [53] *ibid.*, 16.
[54] Kingsbury, III, 657.
[55] Kingsbury, IV, 15.

Give credit, rather, to the 'public informations' from the Governor and his Council.[56]

The attitude of official Jamestown towards the Indian continued unrelenting. The spur was necessity, rather than continuous hatred. There was still 'very great want of corn', especially as, in 1623, 'our numbers do daily increase', and one must 'provide for the future'. Wyatt continued to issue instructions for captains to investigate the Bay and the Rivers, in search of corn, peas, beans, or whatever, to be obtained by

trade, or take by force of arms, or any other ways and means, from the Indians there inhabiting, as subjects or confederates with Opechancanough, or as those who had their hands in the cruel and treacherous murdering of our people.[57]

By the early summer of 1623 some Indians were again 'resorting to private plantations, and treating with them', which occasioned a proclamation from Wyatt[58] that no one other than 'the chief commander of any plantation' shall

hold any conference with any Indians (if at any time they shall in peaceable manner resort unto them and desire a parley) without first giving notice thereof to his Commander. And that no Commander of any plantation shall in any wise give them pledges. Whereupon if they shall stand out, to shoot or kill them by any means they can. But if they shall voluntarily come in and yield themselves unto him, then to take and keep them safely guarded, until they can give notice thereof to the Governor, or send them unto him.

No settler was to go out into the fields to work unarmed, and without armed sentries posted. Deer should not be hunted without the Commander's permission, and the hunters must be in 'sufficient parties'; the danger lay in straggling. And

generally in all points to be very careful and watchful, to prevent their treacheries, knowing that (with God's assistance) they cannot hurt us through their strength, but of our own carelessness; being well assured that their perfidious craft is much more dangerous than open violence.

The Indians were 'base savages'.[59] And in March 1624 the General Assembly at Jamestown (the burgesses of which included Jabez Whitaker and Raleigh Crashaw) decreed[60] that from the following June 'all trade for corn with the savages, as well public as private' was prohibited (Edict 17). That (Edict 23) 'every dwelling house shall be palisaded in for defence against the Indians'. And that (Edict 32) at the beginning of July 1624 'the inhabitants of every corporation shall fall upon their adjoining savages, as we did the last year'.

The 1624 General Assembly also confirmed proclamations by Wyatt against swearing and drunkenness (churchwardens to be the

[56] *ibid.*, 17. [57] *ibid.*, 6-7. [58] *ibid.*, 167-8. [59] *ibid.*, 172. [60] *ibid.*, 580-5.

enforcing officers) (Edict 19); enacted requirements that every plantation was to have a 'house or room' set aside for worship, that those absent from Sunday service were to pay an amount in tobacco, that no 'minister' was to be absent from his cure more than eight weeks in the year, and that there should be 'an uniformity in our church, as near as may be, to the·Canons in England, both in substance and circumstance' (1-5: the Canons were those of 1604). The 'Old Planters' (those dating from 1614 or earlier, the first eight years of the colony) were to be exempt from military service and from taxes ('Church duties excepted': Edict 10). And the Governor was not to 'lay any taxes or impositions upon the colony' except 'by the authority of the General Assembly' (Edict 8).

Thus far we have considered official reactions to the massacre: in London and Jamestown. There were other voices. In Virginia, there was that of Captain John Martin.

John Martin's 'The manner howe to bringe in the Indians into subjection without makinge an utter exterpation' of them, a manuscript now in the British Museum, is dated 15 December 1622.[61] This succinct essay is laid out step by step in the manner recommended by William Perkins. There are reasons 'why it is not fitting utterly to make an extirpation of the savages yet'.

My reasons are grounded twofold: first upon Holy Writ and my own experience. Secondly, other necessary uses and profit that may return by the same.

Holy writ says that God advised

the Children of Israel (though they were of far greater numbers than we are yet in many ages like to be, and came into a country where were walled towns) not to utterly destroy the heathen: lest the woods and wild beasts should over-run them.

Martin's own observation

hath been such as assureth me that if the Indians inhabit not amongst us under obedience (and, as they have ever, kept down the woods, and slain the wolves, bears and other beasts, which are in great number) we shall be more oppressed in short time by their absence, than in their living by us: both for our own security, as also for our cattle.

And if

they shall be brought into subjection, and shall be made to deliver hostages for their obedience, there is no doubt by God's grace but of the saving of many of their souls. And they, being natives, are apter for work than yet our English are; knowing how to attain great quantity of silk, hemp and flax, and most exquisite in thereof for our uses; fit for guides upon discovery into other

[61] Kingsbury, III, 704-7.

countries adjacent to ours; fit to row in galleys and frigates; and many other pregnant uses too tedious to set down.

There must of course be strict supervision: to prevent 'the main body of the enemy from having the sinews of all expeditions' (such as food). They must be kept from planting corn and fishing. This to be effected

by having some two hundred soldiers on foot continually harrowing and burning all their towns in winter, and spoiling their weirs. By this means our people securely may follow their work; and yet not to be negligent in keeping watch.

They must be kept from their 'accustomed trading for corn', by ten shallops 'that in May, June, July and August may scour the Bay, and keep the rivers that are belonging to Opechancanough'.

By this ariseth two happy ends. First, the assured taking of great purchases in skins and prisoners. Secondly, in keeping them from trading for corn on the eastern shore, and the southward, from whence they have five times more than they set themselves.

The enemy Indians will be forced to 'yield to obedience'. Their alternative is to seek refuge with their neighbours: but they will not receive them. 'At the Northwest end of his dominions the Monacans are their enemies. On the Northernmost side, the Potomacs and other nations are their enemies.' The prevention of Indian trade 'with the eastern shore' will assure corn for us. This

is best known to myself, for that by sending and discovering those places, first I have not only reaped the benefit, but all the whole colony since; who had perished had it not been discovered, before Sir George Yeardley came in, by my ancient, Thomas Savage, and servants.

(Yeardley had arrived as Governor in 1619.) The Indians of that area are 'more industrious than any other Indians in our Bay'. We can use them for getting skins: 'my ancient and servants have seen in trade at one time forty great canoes laden with these commodities.' There must be 'two especial irrevocable laws':

First, that none, of what rank soever, do ever trink or trade in the late precinct of Opechancanough, nor any bordering neighbours that aided him in this last disaster. Secondly, for our own people to set and sow a sufficient proportion of corn for their own uses; and yearly to lay up into a granary a proportion, for which if they have no use for themselves the next year, then to be sold, and every man to have his due paid him.

Two granaries must be built. Thus

the savages shall be frustrated of all means of buying any manner of victuals and clothing, but what they shall have from us for their labour and industry;

as also being disabled from hiring any auxiliaries if at any time they would rebel.

For

the infinite trade they have had in this four years of security enabled Opechancanough to hire many auxiliaries; which in former times I know for want thereof Powhatan was never able to act the like.

And the colony will have the benefit of the storing of corn.

In a second paper dated 15 December 1622, Martin proposed that Virginia 'may be made a Royal Plantation'.[62] The English part of Virginia ('in which we are seated and fit to be settled on for many hundred years') is defined thus:

Is within the territories of Opechancanough (it lieth on the west side of Chesapeake Bay) who commandeth from the southernmost part of the first river to the southernmost part of the fourth river, called Potomac, which lieth north next hand to our river: some fifty leagues in latitude. In longtitude it extendeth to the Monacan country next hand west and by north of equal length with the latitude. His own principal seat is in the second river, called Pamunkey, in the heart of his own inhabited territories. This revolted Indian king in his square commandeth thirty two kingdoms under him, every kingdom containing the quantity of one of our shires here in England.

(The Pamunkey is the York River.) Martin wanted the King, the Privy Council and the Virginia Company to arrange that thirty-two English shires should each dispatch one hundred men to possess the thirty-two kingdoms; living 'under the command of some noble general fit for so royal a plantation', with some 'worthy gentleman' from each shire as a Deputy Lieutenant. If the Opechancanough areas are thus possessed – with JPs, iron workers, tanners, weavers and husbandmen –

it will not only quite frustrate and disable the Indians (our enemies) ever to subsist of themselves, but force them to have their dependency upon us for food and clothing, which their industry will well acquit to the whole kingdom in short space. And all other borderly kingdoms, seeing their villainies and treacheries so rewarded, will be ever afraid to enterprise the like against our nation when it shall so increase that they must stretch further their possessions and territories.

One of the critics in England of the organisation of the Virginia Company in London was a soldier and small merchant, Captain John Bargrave: related, presumably, to the Reverend Thomas Bargrave who had died in Virginia in 1621. At the end of 1623 he wrote a paper on Planting in Virginia – after seven years' study, he said, of 'the

---

[62] 707-9.

abuses of the Virginia Company'.[63] His essay – 'A Form of Polisie to plante and governe many Families in Virginea'[64] makes only slight and casual mention of the Indian. The theme is 'the uniting of Virginia to the Crown of England', to avoid the unfortunate facts both that there has been too much 'popular liberty' in Virginia, and that legislation there has been 'tyrannical': not 'consonant to the laws of England'. It is a rather stilted exercise, making ostentatious parade of the rules of Aristotle, with approving nods to Cicero and King Alfred. Minor concerns of Bargrave are that the settlers should not 'imitate the Irish in their wild and barbarous manners'; and that, because 'a set and frugal habit is the best means to advance and growing commonwealth', the three plantations (Bargrave wants a southern, and middle and a northern plantation: the latter being 'New England') should banish 'superfluity' and require that 'every degree may be known by their habits':

We do charge and command you to set down amongst yourselves certain frugal and unchangeable fashions for each degree to wear; giving to the Old Planters some note of honour to distinguish them from others.

His few references to the Indian are in the main conventional enough. The 'natural Virginians' must be made 'tame and civil'; cohering, 'according to our form', in 'religion, discipline, government ecclesiastical and civil'. These 'savage people' should be exposed to 'the true word and service of God and Christian faith', according to 'the doctrine, rites, religion, and ecclesiastical form of government now professed and established in England'. There is no doubt that a prime motive of colonisation is 'the honour we shall do to God in converting of the infidels to the knowledge and worship of Him'. But there is a sting in the tail: the Indian must be 'drawn' – and by 'gentle usage'.[65]

The story of the end of the Virginia Company is not, in detail, my concern. Wesley Frank Craven's *Dissolution of the Virginia Company: the failure of a colonial experiment* remains definitive (1932, reprinted 1964). A major point of controversy was: were things better with the Company, and in Virginia, before 1619, under Thomas Smythe, or after 1619, under Sandys and Southampton? Jamestown tended to approve of Sandys – people like Ralph Hamor and Jabez Whitaker. During the 'Second Government' there had been 'the liberty of a General Assembly'; young women had been sent over for wives, and youths for servants; the 'bloody laws' had been ended, and the government ordered in English fashion; the population had risen.[66] And, thus, there was strong criticism of 'those twelve years of Sir Thomas Smythe his government': merciless laws, hard times,

[63] Kingsbury, IV, 435.
[64] Kingsbury, IV, 408-35.
[65] This sentence, *ibid.*, 431.
[66] *ibid.*, 522-3.

conditions of servitude, fearful Indians. The critics of Sandys – led by Alderman Robert Johnson, who had been deputy treasurer to Smythe – expressed nostalgia for the days of the 'old planters'. The country was 'recovered or procured from the savages'. And, as part of the 'growth of perfection' in Virginia:

The natives of the country in so awful an alliance and amity with them, that many of those heathens voluntarily yielded themselves subjects and servants to our gracious sovereign, and, priding themselves in that title, did, together with most of the rest, pay a yearly contribution of corn for sustentation of the colony, and were kept in such good respect and correspondency that they became mutually helpful and profitable each to other.

The colony was governed with 'unanimity, moderation, integrity and judgement'.[67] Since 1619, misery. Robert Johnson wrote in May 1623 a paper relating 'disorders in the company and colony in the four last years'.[68] In London,

inviting of strangers, yea of women, to be present in a latticed gallery which looks into the place where the Courts these last four years have been kept, there to be spectators of their courses, and hearers of their calumnies, etc, to the end the rumour thereof might be more generally spread.

In emigration policy, the mistake of

transporting of great multitudes of people to Virginia without sufficient provision of victuals to feed them or of houses to entertain them at their arrival; and it is mortal for newcomers to lay of the ground.

The food sent over has been bad: 'especially the meal, being so mean and base.' The passengers travelling in summer, in ships overloaded with people and goods, have landed 'half starved, and bring with them their own deaths, and infect others in the colony'. Johnson claimed that in the three years before the massacre, 3,000 emigrant colonists died, because of overcrowding on the ships, and bad food and accommodation in Virginia. There have been too many 'wild and vast projects': including the iron works. The 'Old Planters' have been removed from 'their habitations and cultivated lands and places of security; whereby many of them were extremely impoverished, and many perished in the late massacre'. There are too many laws in the Company, and not enough in the Colony:

For though the planters three years since in a parliamentary fashion were assembled, and made laws to govern themselves, yet have they not been confirmed here; and the Council in Virginia gave it for a reason that they make no new laws because those formerly made are not yet here ratified or disallowed.

[67] *ibid.*, 4-5.
[68] *ibid.*, 174-82.

And – crucially – there has been 'often neglect and little regard showed to his Majesty's most gracious advertisements and directions for choice of officers agreeable to his princely pleasure and liking'.

The 'wild and vast projects', and the scattered and weak pattern of settlement on the James, had forced Yeardley from 1619

to make a dishonorable peace with the natives, leaving unrevenged the death of some of our people barbarously murdered by the Virginians; and the strength of the colony, at a most unseasonable time, divided into so many small bodies that it did even invite the savages to execute the late horrid massacre.

In a private conversation in May 1623 Bargrave reported[69] 'a marvellous ill affection in Sir Edwin Sandys to the happy frame of a monarchy'. Sandys carried a 'malicious heart' to Monarchy; and had observed that 'if our God from Heaven did contitute and direct a form of government, it was that of Geneva'. He had asked Archbishop Abbot 'to give leave to the Brownists and Separatists of England to go' to Virginia. (Abbot disapproved: 'those Brownists by their doctrine claiming a liberty to disagreeing with the government of monarchs.') Moreover, Sandys intended to make Virginia 'a free, popular state'. And in fact at the moment it 'inclines into, if not directly being, a "popular" government'. ('Popular': government by majority vote – 'democratic'.)

As a way of resolving the 'discords and contentions' within the Virginia Company, some members of the Company made the mistake of appealing to the House of Commons. This naturally angered James I. On 28 April 1624 the King wrote to the Speaker.[70] He claimed that the affairs of the Company were 'in a good way to be composed' by himself and the Privy Council:

As for these businesses of Virginia and the Bermudas, ourself have taken them to heart, and will make it our own work to settle the quiet and welfare of those plantations, and will be ready to do anything that may be for the real benefit and advancement of them.

Thus 'we hold it very unfit for the Parliament to trouble themselves with those matters; which can produce nothing but a further increase of schism and faction'. The Virginia Company was dissolved by decree of the Court of King's Bench on 24 May 1624, eighteen years after the first Charter (April 1606). The tradition arose that the dissolution was all a Spanish plot, engineered by Gondomar.[71]

The dissolution was confirmed in July by royal Letter Patent[72] addressed to the anti-Sandys group, including Sir Nathaniel Rich, Sir

[69] To Sir Nathaniel Rich, who took notes. *ibid.*, 194-5.
[70] *ibid.*, 477-8.
[71] Beverley, *History and Present State of Virginia*, 9-10.
[72] Kingsbury, IV, 490-7.

Samuel Argall, Alderman Robert Johnson, and John Pory Esquire. It recited the story of the Letters Patent of 1606, and the intention of

propagating religion to such people as then lived in darkness and miserable ignorance of the true knowledge and worship of God, and might in time bring the infidels and savages in those parts to human civility, and to a settled and quiet government.

However, the 'courses taken for the settling' of the plantation had not had 'that good effect which we intended'. The affairs of the colony have been investigated by commissioners in Virginia; who found

that our subjects and people sent to inhabit there and to plant themselves in that country were most of them, by God's visitation, sickness of body, famine, and by massacres of them by the native savages of the land, dead and deceased; and those that were living of them lived in miserable and lamentable necessity and want.

Virginia is 'fruitful and healthful', and could produce 'many staple and good commodities'. But 'as yet the sixteen years' government now passed had yielded few or none'. This the commissioners blamed on the authorities of the Virginia Company in London. For one thing, the 1606 instructions for government in Virginia itself and in London – the Virginia and London councils nominated by the Crown – had been amended in a more 'popular' direction, 'which caused much contention and confusion'. (It is perfectly correct that the 'Charters' of 1609 and 1612 saw a lessening of royal control in the arrangements of the Company and the colony.) Sandys and the Virginia Company had not submitted their Charters 'to be reformed'. But now 'upon a Quo Warranto brought, and a legal and judicial proceeding therein by due course of law, the said Charters are avoided'.

James died in March 1625. In May 1625 – in the seventh week of his reign – Charles I issued a Proclamation concerning 'the colony of Virginia'.[73] The colony, planted by James 'for the propagation of Christian religion, the increase of trade, and the enlarging of his royal empire' had not 'hitherto prospered so happily as was hoped and desired'. James thought that a 'great occasion' of this was the nature of the Virginia Company: 'incorporated of a multitude of persons of several dispositions, amongst whom the affairs of the greatest moment were and must be ruled by the greater number of votes and voices' – a 'popular government', which James 'did desire to resume', to 'reduce' government of and in Virginia 'into such a right course as might best agree with that form which was held in the rest of his royal monarchy'. James had in mind 'the good of the public'. And Charles takes occassion to declare that 'those territories of Virginia and the Summer Islands, as also that of New England where our colonies are already planted' are

---

[73] Jensen, *American Colonial Documents*, 235-7.

a part of our royal empire, descended upon us and undoubtedly belonging and appertaining unto us; and that we hold ourself as well bound by our regal office to protect, maintain and support the same, and are so resolved to do, as any other part of our dominions. And that our full resolution is, to the end that there may be one uniform course of government in and through our whole monarchy, that the government of the colony of Virginia shall immediately depend upon ourself, and not be committed to any company or corporation, to whom it may be proper to trust matters of trade and commerce, but cannot be fit or safe to communicate the ordering of state affairs, be they of never so mean consequence.

There is to be in London a Council for Virginia, subordinate to the Privy Council, of 'a few persons of understanding and quality, to whom we will give trust for the immediate care of the affairs of that colony'. And in Virginia a Council, subordinate to that of London. All to be paid for by royal finance. This 'course' will 'settle and assure the particular rights and interests of every planter and adventurer'.

It is difficult to imagine a crisper statement of the ideals behind the 'personal monarchy' of James and Charles. Yet a document so revealing for English constitutional history is never considered as relevant: it is, after all, 'colonial' – and, what is worse, 'American'.

The existing Governor in Virginia, Sir Francis Wyatt, was confirmed in office; and thus became the first royal governor in the British colonies in America.

In 1625 there was published in London the massive collection of travel literature edited by the Reverend Samuel Purchas: *Hakluytus Posthumous, or Purchas his Pilgrimes, contayning a History of the World, in Sea Voyages, & lande Travells, by Englishmen and others.* This included a 'Discourse on Virginia' written by Purchas himself: *Virginias Verger: Or a Discourse shewing the benefits which may grow to this Kingdome from American English Plantations, and specially those of Virginia and Summer Ilands.*[74] The essay has a very hectoring tone: Purchas felt that after 1623 English sympathy with the Virginia enterprise could be caught only by shouting. It is highly rhetorical, and Purchas' fustian rhetoric is hardly alluring – 'Look upon Virginia; view her lovely looks (howsoever like a modest virgin she is now veiled with wild coverts and shady woods, expecting rather ravishment than marriage from her native savages)'.[75] It is extremely Biblical, and can best be considered as a sermon, in the line of those sermons discussed in Chapters 17 and 18 above. (Purchas begins with Genesis 1:1.) We are treated to some very angular and knotty Biblical exposition, in a mannered, punning style rather of the school of (but not the quality of) Andrewes or Donne. Very far from the plain style favoured by the puritans; which is odd, because Purchas was a product of St John's College Cambridge in the 1590s. Born in 1577, he entered St John's in 1594, a year before the death of the Master, William Whitaker. (In

---

[74] pp.218-67 of vol.XIX (1906) of the Glasgow edition of *Purchas His Pilgrimes.* Subsequent page references are to this volume.
[75] 242.

1594 Alexander Whitaker was 8.) Purchas took his B.A. in 1597, and his M.A. in 1600. From 1615 until his death in 1626 he was Rector of St Martin's, Ludgate. His own son, Samuel, he sent to St John's in 1622.

In his exhortation 'to plant another England in America, enriched with the best things of Europe', Purchas dwelt on English God-given rights in Virginia:

right natural, right national, right by first discovery, by accepted trade, by possession surrendered voluntarily, continued constantly; right by gift, by birth, by bargain and sale, by cession.[76]

God said: 'Replenish the earth.' Thus men have both a 'divine ordinance' and a 'natural right' so to do. In any country 'not possessed by other men' (such as Bermuda) 'every man by Law of Nature and Humanity hath right of plantation'. They also have that right 'if a country be inhabited in some parts thereof, other parts remaining unpeopled' – 'especially where the people is wild, and holdeth no settled possession in any parts'. Purchas has heard Captain John Smith say of Virginia 'that in near so much as all England they have not above 5,000 men able to bear arms; which manured and civilly planted might well nourish 1,500,000, and many many more'.[77] Moreover, in Virginia there has been 'voluntary subjection of the natives, giving themselves and their lands to the crown of England'.[78] In addition, England has the right of trade. God intended that 'the whole world might be as one body of mankind, each member communicating with other for public good'; thus Solomon sailed over the ocean and negotiated with the 'Ophirians'.[79]

All this is set within an awkward exposition of the contrasting rights to territory of Christians and Heathens.[80] Heathens 'have only a natural right, by the relics of the Law of Nature left in man'. Christians (true Christians, that is: those not merely making 'profession', but 'such as have the grace of the Spirit of Christ') are 'free tenants to our Lord'. Christ compared the position within a household of the servant and the son: 'the servant abideth not in the house for ever: but the son abideth ever' (John 8:35). Purchas quotes the passage, inserting a phrase from St Paul: 'The servant hath his time and abides not in the house for ever: but the son is heir in fee simple (*fide simplici*) for ever.' The Pauline phrase is I Timothy 1:5: 'faith unfained', in the Authorised Version. Purchas' attempt to interpret Pauline theology in terms of the English law of land tenure does not make things easy for the reader. He is more straightforward on Romans Chapter II: 'When the Gentiles, which have not the law, do by nature the things contained in the law, these, having not the law, are a law unto themselves: which shew the work of the law written in their hearts' (verses 14-15, Authorised Version). Purchas prefers 'barbarians' to 'gentiles':[81] the barbarians, 'having not the

[76] 266.   [77] 221-2.   [78] 228.   [79] 223.   [80] 219-20.   [81] 224.

Law, were a law to themselves, practically acknowledging this Law of Nature written by him, which is *natura naturans*, in their hearts' – from which law, Purchas continues, 'if they have since declined, they have lost their own natural, and given us another, national, right'. If there is an Indian 'transgression of the Law of Nature'; if 'they be not worthy of the name of a nation, being wild and savage' – 'barbarians, borderers and outlaws of humanity' – then, in addition to the 'natural right of cohabitation and commerce' the English have a right of 'just invasion and conquest'. We are given the episode of King David sending his ambassadors to Hanun, King of the Ammonites – who slit their beards and their garments in two. Then the Israelites justly 'destroyed the children of Ammon'. We have seen this example from II Samuel 10 used by the Virginia Company in 1610.[82] The Massacre has given it additional relevance. The English have a further right, now, in Virginia, 'by forfeiture, in that late damnable treachery and massacre'.[83] England must hear the 'outcries of so many unnaturally murdered for just vengeance of rooting out the authors and actors of so prodigious injustice'.[84]

In fact, Purchas points out, there have been three massacres:[85] the fifteen or so men left behind on Roanoke by Grenville in 1586; the 'lost colonists'; and the 1622 dead.

Temperance and Justice had before kissed each other, and seemed to bless the co-habitations of English and Indians in Virginia. But when Virginia was violently ravished by her own ruder natives, yea her virgin cheeks dyed with the blood of three colonies (that of Sir Richard Grenville, that of Sir Walter Raleigh, both confessed by themselves; and this last butchery, intended to all, extended to so many hundreds, with so immane, inhumane, devilish treachery) ... Temperance could not temper herself, yea the stupid earth seems distempered with such bloody potions, and cries out that she is ready to spew out her inhabitants. Justice crieth to God for vengeance, and in His name adjureth prudence and fortitude to the execution.

If the 'lost colony' in fact survived, then they continued the right of possession. But

if the savages dealt perfidiously with them (as Powhatan confessed to Captain Smith, that he had been at their slaughter, and had divers utensils of theirs to show) their carcasses, the dispersed bones of their and their countrymen's since murdered carcasses, have taken a mortal immortal possession, and being dead speak, proclaim and cry: This our earth is truly English, and therefore this land is justly ours, O English.

Whatever 'remainders of right the unnatural naturals had' have now been 'confiscated' by 'disloyal treason':

and made both them and their country wholly English: provoking us – if we

[82] Above, p.109.
[83] 266.   [84] 225.   [85] 228-30.

be our own, not base, degenerate, unworthy the name of English, so that we shall not have anything left, like David's ambassadors, which, thus abused, brought their master a just title to Ammon, purchased by their disgraces – to cover our nakedness, till Virginia cover, reward, enrich us with a total subjection at least, if not a fatal revenge.

It is obvious now that the Indians are

bad people, having little of humanity but shape; ignorant of civility, of arts, of religion; more brutish than the beasts they hunt, more wild and unmanly than that unmanned wild country which they range rather than inhabit; captivated also to Satan's tyranny, in foolish pieties, mad impieties, wicked idleness, busy and bloody wickedness.

Thus they are 'fit objects of zeal and pity, to deliver from the power of darkness'. A reference here to Hosea 2:23: 'I will say to them which were not my people, Thou art my people; and they shall say, Thou art my God.' The Christian duty to the Indian remains. Justice must be done, 'in rooting out those murderers'. But the hope survives that 'in judgement (imitating God's dealing with us) we may remember mercy to such as their own innocence shall protect' – those whom 'Hope shall in Charity judge capable of Christian faith'. 'Thus shall we at once overcome both men and devils, and espouse Virginia to one husband, presenting her as a chaste virgin to Christ.'[86] In rescuing the Indians 'if it be possible, as by religion, from the power of Satan to God', in bringing them, 'by humanity and civility' from 'barbarism and savageness to good manners and humane polity', the story of the Good Samaritan must be a guide: 'Humanity and our common nature forbids us to turn our eyes from our own flesh; yea commands us to love our neighbours as ourselves.'[87]

The danger in 1622 arose from 'confidence'. That must never re-occur unless 'a stupid devil possess us'. Also, the colony must pursue a policy of 'extirpation of the more dangerous'. We now have 'just advantage of the savages'. And we can 'make use of their labours'. It is requisite that 'servile natures be servilely used'. The Indians not extirpated may be utilised in 'servileness and serviceableness'.[88]

Virginia may be a hard school. But that can be turned to advantage.[89] The colony could become a 'training place for our youth to endure labour and hardship, and to prepare them like the Jews in Nehemiah's time to use the sword with one hand, and instruments of labour in the other'.

At the Quarter Court of the Virginia Company held on 7 May 1623 an answer had been discussed to a petition of Alderman Robert Johnson. Johnson and his supporters had argued that under the Thomas Smythe regime

---

[86] 231. [87] 237-8. [88] 246. [89] 259.

there was a quiet entertainment of the savage Indians, by which sundry of those infidels, and some of eminent note, were converted to Christian religion; whereas of late there hath been a massacre, and hostility between the natives and our colony of Virginia.

The reply of the Company authorities was this:[90]

It is true that Matoaka, the daughter of Powhatan, being taken prisoner by Captain Argall, and affecting marriage with one Mr Rolfe, became a Christian, and so died at Gravesend. Other matter of note for conversion of those infidels did not happen in those first twelve years; during which time the English were almost also in continual hostility with the infidels, and in the last of those twelve years the Chickahominy by sudden assault murdered ten of our people, which Captain Argall at his coming away left unrevenged. On the other side, what and how chargeable preparations have been made in these last four years for the educating of the infidels' children in Christian religion and Civility, the plantation for the college may sufficiently declare; for which, notwithstanding the late massacre which fell upon them there are yet remaining sixty tenants or thereabouts, and the work, by the assistance of God, shall again in due time proceed. As for the hostility with the infidels: during three of these last four years there hath not been any. Whereof yet we boast not, considering that it lulled the English asleep in too great security, and consequently gave opportunity to the late bloody massacre; which if it had not happened, these opposers must have been mute, having nothing else wherewith to disgrace the plantation.

Late in 1624, Captain Jabez Whitaker died in Virginia at the age of twenty-eight. Jabez had arrived in the autumn of 1619, a Lieutenant in charge of fifty colonists. In July 1621 a resolution was passed in the Quarter Court at London:[91]

as it appeared that Mr Whitaker had obeyed the Company's orders in building a guesthouse for entertainment of sick persons, and for the relief and comfort of such as came weak from sea; and had also begun to plant vines, corn, and such good commodities, and railed in one hundred acres of ground, it was moved that the Court would please to bestow some reward upon him, for his better encouragement in so good a course. Whereupon it was agreed and ordered that he should have two boys sent him, when the Company shall be able; and that the reward of tobacco allowed him by the Governor of Virginia shall be confirmed unto him.

In March 1624 he was promoted to Captain, and elected a member of the General Assembly at Jamestown.

The last appearance of the name Whitaker in the records of the Virginia Company was in February 1625.[92] 'There came into this colony a sister of Mr Whitaker, who made enquiry after the goods of her deceased brother; but found that he left little of value behind him.'

[90] Petition and Reply, Kingsbury, II, 395.
[91] Kingsbury, I, 508.
[92] Kingsbury, IV, 511.

In 1625 it was difficult to countenance an earlier estimate by the English colonists in Virginia:[93] 'that they were the happiest people in the world'.

[93] *ibid.*, 523.

New England Wilderness, 1621-1630

At the end of November 1621 the first reinforcements arrived at Plymouth, in the 'Fortune': there were thirty-five passengers, including John Adams and Philip Delano (de la Noye: a French-speaking Walloon who had joined the Robinson congregation at Leiden). (The thirty-five, Bradford later commented, included too many wild young men: rot was spreading.)[1] Robert Cushman was also on board. He remained at Plymouth for only two weeks, returning on the 'Fortune' on 13 December. During his visit, he preached to the planters. His sermon was printed in London in 1622: *A Sermon preached at Plimmoth in New England, together with a Preface showing the State of the Country and Condition of the Savages*.

Cushman was a layman. But Plymouth Plantation in the 1620s was a lay affair. John Robinson died at Leiden in 1625; the Leiden men at Plymouth had always hoped that 'their Pastor' would join them in New England (in spite of a letter they received from him in 1624: 'our hopes of coming unto you be small, and weaker than ever').[2] The first 'minister' to arrive at Plymouth, sent over by the London Adventurers, was John Lyford, who came in 1624. After a short probation, he was received as a member of the pilgrim congregation. But Lyford objected to the exclusiveness of the pilgrims: the church in Plymouth was, he said, for 'the smallest number in the colony'; who scorned 'honest men not of the Separation'. (The church replied that many such 'they liked well of, and were glad of their company' – they probably thought the same about the Indians.) Lyford preached to 'all in general'; and ministered the sacraments of the Lord's Supper and Baptism 'by his episcopal calling'.[3] There was a crisis, and Lyford and some of his followers left the plantation. He died as an Anglican pastor in Virginia. In 1628 one of the original 'Mayflower' pilgrims brought back from England 'a young man for a minister to the people', a Mr Rogers. But the Plymouth congregation 'perceived upon some trial that he was crazed in his brain'; so he was sent back.[4] Not until 1629, when the Graduate Invasion of Massachusetts began, did the pilgrims find a pastor who appeared (at first, at any rate) to be

[1] Bradford, *Of Plymouth Plantation*, ed. Morison, 1652, p.92. Hereafter cited as *PP*.
[2] *PP* 374. [3] *PP* 147-63. [4] *PP* 210-11.

satisfactory. Ralph Smith, a graduate of Christ's College Cambridge (B.A. 1614) had emigrated 'into the Bay of the Massachusetts' with his wife and family; he was asked to 'exercise his gifts' at Plymouth; and was 'chosen into the ministry' at the end of 1629, nine years after the coming of the 'Mayflower'.[5]

The pilgrims recognised with 'grief' the lack in Plymouth of the two sacraments of Baptism and the Lord's Supper: at Leiden 'we used to have the Lord's Supper every Sabbath, and Baptism as often as there was occasion of children to baptise' – how grievous (1624) that 'our Pastor is kept from us'.[6] There were marriages in Plymouth: rightly 'performed by the magistrate', wrote Bradford, 'as being a civil thing' (following 'the laudable custom of the Low Countries').[7] The first such ceremony was in May 1621 when the widower Edward Winslow was married to the widow Susannah White: their previous partners had died in that first Plymouth winter. The key figure in the spiritual life of Plymouth, until his death in 1643 in his late seventies, was Elder William Brewster. Bradford tells us that 'when the church had no other minister, he taught twice every Sabbath, and that both powerfully and profitably'. He was 'plain and distinct in what he taught'; and 'many were brought to God by his ministry'. He had especially 'a singular good gift in prayer, both public and private, in ripping up the heart and conscience before God in the humble confession of sin'. And he stood for 'good order' in the congregation': to 'preserve purity both in the doctrine and communion of the same', suppressing 'error or contention'.[8] Bradford thought it a pity that Brewster 'would never be persuaded to take higher office'; he had the gifts and learning for the pastorate.[9] Bradford also notes that every Sunday 'some are appointed to visit suspected places, and if any be found idling and neglect the hearing of the word (through idleness or profaneness) they are punished for the same'.[10] The Plymouth settlers, it was reported at the end of 1621 (and quoted by John Smith in 1622) are 'for the most part very religious honest people; the word of God sincerely taught us every Sabbath'.[11]

Brewster had 'spent some small time in Cambridge', Bradford wrote; he knew Latin; and had 'some insight in the Greek'.[12] Brewster left a library of nearly four hundred volumes; Bradford owned about eighty books; and Standish about fifty.[13] (Brewster also left a violet-coloured cloth coat; and Bradford a red waistcoat, silver buttons, a violet cloak and a coloured hat.)[14] There is, unfortunately, Bradford

---

[5] Smith resigned in 1634. John Rayner of Magdalene College Cambridge (BA 1626) was chosen as Teacher: he stayed until 1654. A new Pastor was chosen in 1638: Charles Chauncey, B.D., former Fellow of Trinity College Cambridge (B.A. 1613). Roger Williams of Pembroke College Cambridge (B.A. 1627) was a member of the Plymouth Church in 1631, and assisted Smith; but, being 'singular', he soon left.

[6] *PP* 142. [7] *PP* 86. [8] *PP* 327-8. [9] *PP* 162. [10] *ibid.*

[11] *New Englands Trials.* Everyman Library, *Chronicles of the Pilgrim Fathers*, 254.

[12] *PP* 325. Brewster went up to Peterhouse in 1580.

[13] Andrews, *Colonial Period*, I, 275.

[14] *Dictionary of American Biography*: Morison on Bradford; R.G. Usher on Brewster.

noted in 1624, no 'common school' at Plymouth, for 'want of a fit person', or 'means to maintain one'.[15] Children were educated at home. There was no school at Plymouth until the 1670s.[16] In the period 1673 to 1707, seventeen boys from the 'old colony' (Plymouth and the adjacent settlements) went to Harvard – and over 250 from Massachusetts.[17]

In contrast to the New England settlements from 1629, there was no dominating graduate-clerical leadership in Plymouth. In that respect, early Plymouth was more akin to Virginia than to Massachusetts. It was a community of agricultural workers, and small; 'at least partially literate'.[18] A community very suitable to be harangued in 1621 by Robert Cushman.

Cushman's text was from I Corinthians Chapter 10: verses 23 and 24. In the lucid New English Bible translation they read:

'We are free to do anything', you say. Yes, but is everything good for us? 'We are free to do anything', but does everything help the building of the community? Each of you must regard, not his own interests, but the other man's.

(Authorised Version: 'Let no man seek his own, but every man another's wealth.') One of the great dangers to a plantation is 'idle drones'.[19] The 1620s in America are 'as it were, the dawning of a new world'. Like John Smith in Jamestown in 1609, Cushman reminded the planters of the 'rule' of St Paul: 'If any man would not work, neither should he eat' (II Thessalonians 3:10). Cushman had obviously been reading Smith (and perhaps talking to him). Virginia has its warnings:

It is reported that there are many men gone to that other plantation in Virginia, which, whilst they lived in England, seemed very religious, zealous, and conscionable; and have now lost even the sap of grace, and edge to all goodness; and are become mere worldlings. This testimony I believe to be partly true.

'Mere worldlings': they simply went to church, and left it at that!

The cause of this is Self-Love. Nothing 'more resembles hellish horror, than for every man to shift from himself'. This was a warning from London. The Plymouth planters had been obliged to agree with the London merchant-adventurers that for seven years all property and profits were to be not private, but part of the common stock. Yet

[15] *PP* 143.
[16] Demos, *A Little Commonwealth: Family Life in Plymouth Colony*, 1970, 142-4.
[17] Wright, *Cultural Life of American Colonies*, 117-18.
[18] Demos, *Little Commonwealth*, 142. Literacy in early New England is becoming a fashionable theme: Demos, 22. The latest contribution is by K.A. Lockridge, *Literacy in Colonial New England*, 1974. Dr David Cressy, formerly of Clare College Cambridge, is preparing a book on the topic.
[19] Extracts from the sermon in Everyman *Chronicles*, 235-40.

feeling was growing in Plymouth, after less than one year, that each planter should have a 'particular portion'. Why, asked Cushman: unless you 'thinkest to live better than thy neighbour'? Satan was the founder of 'particularising'. 'Israel was seven years in Canaan before the land was divided into tribes, much longer before it was divided into families.' The planters have given 'names and promises one to another, and are convenanted here to cleave together in the service of God and the King'. So: 'Avoid all factions, frowardness, singularity and withdrawings, and cleave fast to the Lord and one to another continually.'

By doing so, Plymouth will become a 'notable precedent' to the Indians. The English have ventured into 'a wild wilderness'; as 'an instrument to carry the Gospel and humanity among the brutish heathen'. The Indians are 'a helpless and idle people', unable to 'in any comely or comfortable manner help themselves, much less us'. The English must be purged of Self-Love if they are to be an example

to those poor heathens, whose eyes are upon you, and who very brutishly and cruelly do daily eat and consume one another through their emulations, wars and contentions. Be you, therefore, ashamed of it, and win them to peace, both with yourselves and one another, by your peaceable examples; which will preach louder to them than if you could cry in their barbarous language.

But the *vita communis* in Plymouth could not survive economic pressure. There was to be a shortage of corn in 1623. And Governor Bradford, 'after much debate', and 'with the advice of the chiefest among them', ordered that the planters 'should set corn every man for his own particular', trusting to themselves.[20] (In other things, 'to go on in the general way as before'.) Every family received a portion of land; to be allocated yearly by lot (not by 'continuance'). This was very successful, 'for it made all hands very industrious, so as much more corn was planted than otherwise would have been'.

The women now went willingly into the field, and took their little ones with them to set corn; which before would allege weakness and inability; whom to have compelled would have been thought great tyranny.

Bradford later came to see the disadvantages of the 'general employment'; the 'time of the communality'.[21] A 'common course and condition' led to confusion, slowness, and discontent among 'godly and sober men'. Able young men thought themselves working for others without reward; the strong received the same food and clothes as those who did only a quarter of the work; the old thought it an indignity to have the same as the 'meaner and younger sort'. It all diminished 'mutual respects', and 'those relations which God hath set among men'. The desire for the Particular may be due to 'corruption',

---

[20] *PP* 120-1. Good comments by Ziff, *Puritanism in America*, 1973, 37-40.
[21] This phrase, *PP* 133.

thought Bradford: but 'all men have the corruption in them', and a
wise God saw a course 'fitter for them' than that of 'community'. The
Plymouth story, concluded the Governor,

may well evince the vanity of that conceit of Plato's and other ancients,
applauded by some of later times, that the taking away of property, and
bringing in community into a commonwealth would make them happy and
flourishing; as if they wiser than God.

Bradford saw fit not to mention the Acts of the Apostles!

When Cushman's sermon was printed in 1622, he added an Epistle
Dedicatory (written by him?) to 'the adventurers for New England'.[22]
New England: 'so called not only (to avoid novelties) because Captain
Smith hath so entitled it in his Description, but because of the
ressemblance that is in it of England, the native soil of Englishmen'.
The climate is similar. And, 'so far as we can yet find', it is an island,
cut off by the Hudson River from the mainland. And the Plymouth
planters are 'a company of plain Englishmen'. Through them 'a light
may rise up in the dark', bringing the Kingdom of Heaven to 'a people
that shall bring forth the fruit of it'.

Contacts with the 'poor heathens' in 1621 showed that 'God hath
some great work to do towards them'. The Indians were 'wont to be
the most cruel and treacherous people, in all these parts; even like
lions'. But to the men of Plymouth 'they have been like lambs; so kind,
so submissive and trusty, as a man may truly say, many Christians are
not so kind nor sincere.'

The region was found 'empty'; the natives 'all dead and gone away,
and none living by eight or ten miles'. Cushman reckoned that the
plague, and their wars, had left only five per cent surviving: 'and those
that are left have their courage much abated, and their countenance is
dejected, and they seem as a people affrighted.' In the first winter
many of the English were ill, more were dead, and 'there was not six
able persons'. The Indians 'might in one hour have made a dispatch of
us' – they 'came daily to us by hundreds'. Yet 'such a fear was upon
them as that they never offered us the least injury in word or deed'.
Via Squanto, the planters 'have daily commerce with their kings, and
can know what is done or intended towards us'; and the Indians can
be told of the plantation's 'human and religious' purposes. Cushman
mentioned the document of September 1621 swearing obedience to
James. And claimed that the English

through God's grace have with that equity, justice and compassion carried
ourselves towards them, as that they have received much favour, help, and
aid from us; but never the least injury or wrong by us.

The planters help the Indians in winter, supplying them with corn;
they try to maintain peace among the Indians, and aid the chiefs in

[22] Everyman *Chronicles*, 229-35.

dealing with Indian rebels. They have Indians in their houses, 'eating and drinking and warming themselves'. This entertaining of the Indian at Plymouth is 'something a trouble to us': But 'we are content to bear it', because the Indians 'take knowledge of our labours, orders and diligence, both for this life and a better'. And

we find in many of them, especially of the younger sort, such a tractable disposition, both to religion and humanity, as that if we had means to apparel them, and wholly to retain them with us (as their desire is) they would doubtless in time prove serviceable to God and man. And if ever God send us means, we will bring up hundreds of their children to labour and learning.

The 'Fortune' had arrived in London in February 1622, bringing much material from Plymouth for the London printers. The 1622 *Relation* edited by George Morton included a paper by Cushman: 'Reasons and considerations touching the lawfulness of removing out of England into the parts of America.'[23] A central point here was, of course, the emptiness of the territory: 'to them we may go, their land is empty.' It is 'lawful': for

their land is spacious and void, and there are but few, and do but run over the grass, as do also the foxes and wild beasts. They are not industrious, neither have art, science, skill or faculty to use either the land or the commodities of it; but all spoils, rots and is marred for want of manuring, gathering, ordering, etc.

We are referred to Genesis Chapter 13: 'The land was not able to bear them ... Then Lot chose him all the plain of Jordan, and Lot journeyed east' (into the 'cities of the plain', near Sodom). Thus the 'ancient patriarchs' moved 'from straiter places into more roomthy, where the land lay idle and waste, and none used it'. The English possess the 'common land, or unused and undressed country', the 'vast and empty chaos', by 'common consent, composition and agreement'. The agreement is double; Massasoit and other chiefs have acknowledged James as 'Master and Commander', and have promised the English that they can live 'where we will, and bringing as many people as we will'. The English have negotiated with the Indian by 'friendly usage, love, peace, honest and just carriages, good counsel'; not by the sword – 'for our faculty that way is small, and our strength less'. Massasoit 'hath found us just, honest, kind and peaceable, and so loves our company'.

Cushman thus expressed particularly forcibly the assumption that land in America is *vacuus*: empty, virgin, without a valid owner. Alden Vaughan[24] warned us in 1965 not to be misled by the puritans' 'religious rhetoric' in their exposition of this concept – a common

---

[23] 1622 *Relation*, ed. Cheever, 101-8.
[24] *New England Frontier*, 1965, 104-15, 326-7.

concept (held also by the Indian) about the occupation of desolate
land, which, he claimed, was never allowed to over-rule an Indian
claim to title. Francis Jennings, in an important article published in
1971,[25] maintains however that in Massachusetts Bay from 1630 to
1633 there were no 'purchases' of land, the only legal title to land in
America being conceived as deriving from the English: legally,
America *was* vacant. After 1633 it was assumed that an Indian could
be a rightful landlord; but the assumption was merely for
convenience, not a recognition of a right valid in law. Jennings admits
that there was a *show* of legality: but this was a matter of strategem
and pretext, by courts which (until the 1670s) had no Indian
members. The English occupation was thus a 'conquest'. He is
concerned on this point to criticise Vaughan's thesis that in Plymouth
from 1621 and in Massachusetts from 1629 the English 'scrupulously
observed the property rights of the natives' and were 'mindful of
native claims'; and that they observed 'the niceties of purchase'. Land
was acquired by 'conquest', says Vaughan, only at a time of declared
war. (We have seen Edward Waterhouse stating that the 1622
Massacre in Virginia meant that the settlers, by right of war, could
invade Indian villages and cultivated land.)

These approaches are perhaps too technical to be a key to the
policies of the planters of Plymouth in the 1620s.

Neither Vaughan nor Jennings accepts the thesis that Indian land
was tribal, held in common ownership, and therefore not capable of
being sold by an individual. It seems that the tribal sachem had a sort
of domain right over the entire territory, and the final right to sell
land; that subordinate chiefs had hunting and fishing rights; but that
cultivated land was held as common, the sachem annually assigning
the area to be tilled by each family. Any land sale had to be confirmed
by the actual inhabitants of the area. (Jennings is more precise and
detailed than Vaughan.) It is also accepted that the Indians were *eager*
to sell; and, Vaughan says, they always retained hunting, fishing, and,
sometimes, planting rights.

How far the Indians were aware of the implications of all this is
surely doubtful. (Vaughan thinks they were.) And with what did the
English 'purchase' the land? Trinkets, more often than not; or the
promise of friendship.

Of one thing there is no doubt: Plymouth planters engaging in land
deals were closely supervised by the Plymouth General Court. The

[25] 'Virgin Land and Savage People', *American Quarterly*, October 1971 (XIII, 4£,
pp.519-41. See also David Bushnell, 'Treatment of Indians in Plymouth Colony', *New
England Quarterly*, June 1953 (XXVI, 2). W.E. Washburn discusses the land tenure
question down to the 1950s in 'Moral and Legal Justification for Dispossessing the
Indians', being ch.2 of *Seventeenth-Century America*, ed. Smith. 1959. R.H. Pearce's 'The
Indian and the Puritan Mind', *Journal of the History of Ideas*, April 1952 (XIII, 2) is less
satisfactory. Pearce's 1953 book *The Savages of America: A Study of the Indian and the Idea of
Civilisation* is essentially about the place of the Indian in the conscience and imagination
of Americans in the first half of the nineteenth century. See also Nash, *Red, White, and
Black*, 1974.

Court declared in 1643 that 'it hath been the constant custom from our first beginning that no person or persons have or ever did purchase rent or hire any lands, herbage, wood or timber of the natives but by the magistrates' consent'; to do otherwise is 'unlawful and of dangerous consequence'; and any planter negotiating without 'consent and assent of the Court' is to be very heavily fined.[26] The General Court of Massachusetts issued a similar edict in 1634. This was confirmed in the *Laws and Libertyes* printed at Cambridge, Mass., in 1648: 'No person whatsoever shall henceforth buy land of any Indian, without license first had and obtained of the General Court.' We also see in 1648 that Indians with corn fields near the settlements had obtained that land by gift or sale from the English (who were to show them how to fence it). That was the 'ground where they have the right to plant'. The assumption at Boston was that such Indians 'are become subjects to the English; and have engaged themselves to be willing and ready to understand the Law of God'.[27]

Cushman thought that the peace with the Indian will be breached only if 'our security engender in them some unthought of treachery; or our uncivility provoke them to anger'. The English, then, he continued, have the honourable opportunity 'to plant a rude wilderness', and 'to display the efficacy and power of the Gospel', in 'zealous preaching, professing and wise walking under it before the faces of these poor blind infidels'. Naturally we ought to use 'means to convert them' – and not refer only to 'God's extraordinary work from heaven'. We must 'further the knowledge and salvation of the sons of Adam in that New World'.

Old England has its disadvantages. It groans under 'close-fisted and unmerciful men' – compare the 'consumption' at home with 'the easiness, plainess and plentifulness in living in those remote places'. There is 'the bitter contention that hath been about religion, by writing, disputing and inveighing earnestly one against another':

the heat of which zeal, if it were turned against the rude barbarism of the heathens, it might do more good in a day than it hath done here in many years.

If the Indians 'had but a drop of that knowledge which here flieth about the streets', they would be filled with joy; and 'would even pluck the kingdom of heaven by violence, and take it as it were by force'.

At the beginning of 1622 Plymouth Plantation began to be worried about the Indians to the west of Massasoit, the Narragansetts, whose chief was Canonicus (*c.*1565-1647). In January a messenger from Canonicus arrived in Plymouth with a bundle of arrows wrapped in the skin of a rattlesnake. Squanto said that this was a symbol of enmity. Governor Bradford had the skin stuffed with powder and with

[26] Langdon, *Pilgrim Colony*, 1966, 154-5.
[27] D.4.v.-E.1.r. 1929 reprint, ed. M. Farrand, 28-9.

shot, and sent back, as a corresponding gesture of defiance. But the messenger was to tell the Narragansetts that the English 'had done them no wrong'; but they did not fear them, and if the tribe 'had rather have war than peace, they might begin where they would'.[28] According to Edward Winslow, the 'common talk of our neighbour Indians on all sides' was of the warlike preparations of the Narragansetts.[29] Bradford thought that the tribe was taking advantage of the plague deaths (which had not affected them) to attempt a domination of the whole region, and 'conceived the English would be a bar in their way' – as allies of Massasoit and the neighbour chiefs.[30]

The planters realised that Plymouth must be made more secure. In February 1622 the village was enclosed with a 'fence'; there were gates, locked at night; a nightly, and sometimes a daily, watch; and 'a general muster or training'.[31] In the summer, Winslow records, there were 'further thoughts of fortification'. The Indians had been 'giving out how easy it would be ere long to cut us off'. And in June a fort was begun:

Whereas we have a hill called the Mount, enclosed within our pale, under which our town is seated, we resolved to erect a fort thereon; from whence a few might easily secure the town from any assault the Indians can make; ... hoping that this being once finished, and a continual guard there kept, it would utterly discourage the savages from having any hopes of rising against us.[32]

In May news had reached Plymouth of the massacre in Virginia (March 1622).

Of the signers of the Mayflower Compact, Edward Winslow became the most experienced in Indian diplomacy. His *Good News from New England* was published in London in 1624. From the tales Winslow tells, I have chosen as worthy of detailed exposition the account of his visit in March 1623 to the ailing Massasoit.[33]

Word had come to Plymouth that Massasoit was 'like to die'. Winslow knew that it was 'a commendable manner of the Indians, when any, especially of note, are dangerously sick, for all that profess friendship to them to visit them in their extremity'. As 'we had ever professed friendship', so we should ourselves observe 'their laudable custom'.

A trio left Plymouth: Winslow; a London man called John Hamden; and Hobomok, a Wampanoag who had come to live at Plymouth in 1621. They spent their first night fifteen miles south-

---

[28] *PP* 96.
[29] Everyman *Chronicles* 276.
[30] *PP* 97.
[31] *PP* 97. Winslow: Everyman *Chronicles* 279-80.
[32] Everyman *Chronicles* 288-9.
[33] *ibid.*, 303-13.

west, at Namasket (Middleboro, Mass.), and had 'friendly
entertainment'. The next day they entered Corbitant's country. Near
Corbitant's village (Swansea, Mass.) they were told by Indians that
Massasoit was dead. Corbitant was the likely successor: so,

although he were but a hollow-hearted friend toward us, I thought no time so
fit as this to enter into more friendly terms with him, and the rest of the
sachems thereabout; hoping, through the blessing of God, it would be a
means, in that unsettled state, to settle their affections towards us.

So they went on to his village, called Mattapoyat, thirty miles from
Plymouth, and on the way to Massasoit's home. During this journey,
Hobomok broke out into a lament for Massasoit: *Neen womasu sagimus*,
'My loving sachem! Many have I known, but never any like thee'. He
told Winslow that 'whilst I lived, I should never see his like amongst
the Indians': Massasoit

was no liar, he was not bloody and cruel, like other Indians; in anger and
passion he was soon reclaimed; easy to be reconciled towards such as had
offended him; ruled by reason in such measure as he would not scorn the
advice of mean men; and that he governed his men better with few strokes,
than others did with many; truly loving where he loved.

Massasoit had 'oftimes restrained their malice' against the English.
Hobomok feared that now 'we had not a faithful friend left among the
Indians'. All this 'with such signs of lamentation and unfeigned
sorrow, as it would have made the hardest heart relent'. Corbitant
was absent from Mattapoyat; but his wife supplied 'friendly
entertainment'. The Indians there thought Massasoit dead, 'but knew
no certainty'. A messenger was sent the six miles to Sowams. He
returned shortly before sunset. Massasoit 'was not yet dead; though
there was no hope we should find him living'.

The trio set off immediately. It was 'late within night ere we got
hither'. They found Massasoit's house

so full of men, as we could scarce get in, though they used their best diligence
to make way for us. There were they in the midst of their charms for him,
making such a hellish noise, as it distempered us that were well, and
therefore unlike to ease him that was sick.

Massasoit was told 'that his friends the English were come to see him'.
His sight was gone; but he retained his 'understanding'. The Indians
told him 'Winsnow' was here: 'for they cannot pronounce the letter
"l", but ordinarily "n" in the place thereof.' Massasoit 'put forth his
hand to me, which I took'. *Keen Winsnow*: 'Art thou Winslow?' *Ahhe*:
'Yes.' *Matta neen wonckanet namen, Winsnow*: 'O Winslow, I shall never
see thee again.' Winslow, through Hobomok, said that Governor
Bradford was sorry that the sachem was ill; being too busy to travel
himself, he had sent Winslow 'with such things as he thought most

likely to do him good in this hit extremity'.

One of the gifts was 'a confection of many comfortable conserves'. Winslow fed some of this to Massasoit on the end of a knife, 'which I could scarcely get through his teeth'.

When it was dissolved in his mouth, he swallowed the juice of it. Whereat those that were about him much rejoiced, saying he had not swallowed any thing in two days before. Then I desired to see his mouth, which was exceedingly furred, and his tongue swelled in such a manner, as it was not possible for him to eat such meat as they had, his passage being stopped up. Then I washed his mouth, and scraped his tongue, and got abundance of corruption out of the same. After which I gave him more of the confection, which he swallowed with more readiness. Then, he desiring to drink, I dissolved some of it in water, and gave him thereof.

Within half an hour he showed signs of recovery. His sight began to return. Winslow asked the attendants 'how he slept, and when he went to stool'. They said: 'He had not slept in two days before, and had not had a stool in five.' At 2 a.m. two messengers left for Plymouth with a note from Winslow describing the symptoms; they were to bring liquids, chicken for broth, and 'such physic as the surgeon durst administer'.

Shortly before dawn, Massasoit asked Winslow to shoot some fowl and 'make him some English pottage, such as he had eaten at Plymouth'. But he could not wait for this. He wanted some 'pottage' immediately. This presented Winslow with a problem:

being unaccustomed and unacquainted in such businesses, especially having nothing to make it comfortable, my consort being as ignorant as myself. But being we must do somewhat, I caused a woman to bruise some corn, and take the flour from it, and set over the grit, or broken corn, in a pipkin; for they have earthen pots of all sizes. When the day broke we went out, it being now March, to seek herbs; but could not find any but strawberry leaves, of which I gathered a handful and put into the same. And because I had nothing to relish it, I went forth again, and pulled up a sassafras root, and sliced a piece thereof, and boiled it till it had a good relish, and then took it out again. The broth being boiled, I strained it through my hankerchief, and gave him at least a pint, which he drank, and liked it very well.

The patient made progress. His sight continued to improve; he slept a little; and had 'three moderate stools'.

Winslow found himself spending the morning, at Massasoit's request, visiting the sick Indians of the village, washing out their mouths, and administering his amateur soup. 'This pains I took with willingness, though it were much offensive to me, not being accustomed to such poisonous savours.'

In the early afternoon he shot an 'extraordinarily fat' duck; and made some very fatty duck soup. Hobomok advised Massasoit to drain off the fat before drinking. Massasoit ignored the advice, and 'made a gross meal of it, and ate as much as would well have satisfied a man in health'. As a result he was violently sick; and continued to vomit, with nose-bleeds, for four hours. However, he calmed down, and slept until about 10 p.m. When he woke, Winslow 'washed his face, and bathed and suppled his beard and nose with a linen cloth'. Some of the water Massasoit swallowed the wrong way, and the nose-bleeds began again. But for a time only. He was out of danger.

The Indian messengers now returned from Plymouth. They had done the round trip, about eighty miles, in twenty hours. They carried chickens. But Massasoit was not hungry for these, and decided to keep them for breeding. They brought 'physic'. But Winslow decided not to use it, 'because his body was so much altered since our instructions'. Also, it was no longer necessary.

By this time many Indian visitors from the region had arrived: 'some, by their report, from a place not less than an hundred miles.'

To all that came, one of his chief men related the manner of his sickness, how near he was spent, how amongst others his friends the English came to see him, and how suddenly they recovered him to this strength they saw, he being now able to sit upright of himself.

Massasoit could now be adamant: 'Now I see the English are my friends, and love me; and whilst I live, I will never forget this kindness they have showed me' (he lived for another thirty-seven years). This was important; for when he was ill, a sachem had visited Massasoit to tell him

that now he might see how hollow-hearted the English were, saying, if we had been such friends in deed as we were in show, we would have visited him in his sickness; using many arguments to withdraw his affections, and to persuade him to give way to some things against us which were motioned to him not long before.

Massasoit was now immune from that temptation.

On their way home to Plymouth, the trio found Corbitant at home.[34] Winslow had 'much conference with him'; and found him 'a notable politician, yet full of merry jests and squibs, and never better pleased when the like are returned again upon him'. Would medicine be sent from Plymouth if I were ill, asked Corbitant; would Winslow bring it personally? 'To both which I answered, Yea; whereat he gave me many thanks.' Corbitant was surprised that the two Englishmen had 'come so far into the country'. 'I answered, where there was true love, there was no fear. And my heart was so upright towards them, that for mine own part I was fearless to come amongst them.' Next question: why do the Indians see armed guards and musket barrels at Plymouth?

I answered, it was the most honourable and respective entertainment we

[34] *ibid.*, 313-15.

could give them; it being an order amongst us so to receive our best respected friends. And as it was used on the land, so the ships observed it also at sea; which Hobomok knew, and had seen observed.

Corbitant, 'shaking the head', remarked that 'he liked not such salutations'.

The party stayed the night at Mattapoyat: and 'never had better entertainment amongst any of them'. They were even able to indulge in a little missionary activity. Corbitant asked why the Englishmen said grace before food, and gave thanks after it.

I took occasion to tell them of God's works of creation and preservation, of His laws and ordinances; especially of the Ten Commandments. All which they hearkened unto with great attention, and liked well of.

With the exception of the seventh Commandment: 'Thou shalt not commit adultery.' They thought 'there were many inconveniences in it, that a man should be tied to one woman'. About this, 'we reasoned a good time'. Winslow also explained that the English asked blessing on food, and gave thanks, because 'whatsoever good things we had, we received from God, as the author and giver thereof'. This the Indians 'concluded to be very well':

and said, they believed almost all the same things; and that the same power that we called God, they called *Kiehtan*. Much profitable conference was occasioned hereby, which would be too tedious to relate, yet was no less delightful to them, than comfortable to us.

In *Good News from New England*, Winslow devoted a section to 'the manners, customs, religious opinions and ceremonies of the Indians'.[35]

Winslow acknowledged that the Indian language was 'very copious, large and difficult': 'as yet we cannot attain to any great measure thereof.' But it was obvious that the Indians were 'very ingenious and observative'. They are knowledgeable about the stars and the weather. And although they have no records or chronicles, 'many things of great antiquity are fresh in memory', and a visitor is regaled with 'many historical discourses'. In memory of any 'remarkable act' a hole is dug in the ground, one foot wide and one foot deep, kept in good order – and proudly explained.

A 'sachem' exists to protect his people. Their rule is 'successive and not by choice': their land inherited. The sachem grants land, and decides boundaries. He has a 'principal' wife, of equal birth, who is kept for life; lesser wives are discarded at pleasure. In return for protection, his people pay homage: an annual tribute of corn; and, for hunting, the best part of every deer. The sachem punishes offenders. For theft, a rebuke; if repeated, a beating by the sachem; for a third

[35] *ibid.*, 340-52.

offence, the criminal, after a beating, 'hath his nose slit upwards, that thereby all men may know and shun him'. The offender does not attempt to avoid the beating: 'it being a greater disparagement for a man to cry during the time of his correction, than is his offence and punishment.' Murder is punished by death.

The Indians wear 'breeches and stockings in one, like some Irish': a vestment of deer skin – like the shoes and the cloaks. (All worn over a 'a small garment that covereth their secrets'.) The women wear 'strings about their legs'.

The women lead 'a most slavish life'. They

carry all their burdens, set and dress their corn, gather it in, seek out for much of their food, beat and make ready the corn to eat, and have all household care lying upon them.

In disposition, the women vary: 'some as modest, as they will scarce talk with one another in the company of men, being very chaste also'; others 'light, lascivious and wanton'. There are 'common strumpets' – the unmarried, the widowed, and the discarded (for adultery 'the husband will beat his wife, and put her away if he please').

The men 'employ themselves wholly in hunting and other exercises of the bow; except at some times they take some pains in fishing.' The 'younger sort' revere their seniors; and perform 'all mean offices'. 'The men take much tobacco; but for the boys so to do, they account it odious.' What matters is 'courage and resolution': a man is not considered a man until he has proved this in 'some notable act'. There is training in 'great hardness' for 'the most forward and likeliest boys'. Such boys abstain from 'dainty meats'. They drink the juice of bitter plants until they are sick:

which they must disgorge into the platter, and drink again and again; till at length, through extraordinary oppressing of nature, it will seem to be all blood. And this the boys will do with eagerness at the first: and so continue till by reason of faintness they can scarce stand on their legs.

They are beaten about the shins, and made to run through bushes and brambles. All this to make them 'hardy, and acceptable to the Devil, that in time he may appear unto them'. They are trained to be members of the warrior class, 'men of the greatest stature and strength, and such as will endure most hardness'. The Devil reveals himself 'more familiarly' to this class than to others; and 'as we conceive, maketh covenant with them to preserve them from death by wounds'. But men of the warrior class are also 'more discreet, courteous and humane in their carriages than any other among them; scorning theft, lying, and other the like base dealings'.

In 1624 Winslow was concerned to contradict earlier reports by Plymouth planters (including himself) that the Indians were 'without any religion'. Experience among them has taught him that they believe in 'divine powers'. *Kiehtan*, 'made by none', is 'principal, and maker of all the rest'. He created the world; and 'one man and one woman, of whom they and we and all mankind come: but how they became so far dispersed, that know they not' (Indian religious pre-occupations coincide remarkably closely with those of early seventeenth century Europeans!). Kiehtan lives 'far westward in the heavens'. Here all men go when they die. The good men 'see their friends, and have their fill of all things'. The bad men knock at the door; but Kiehtan 'bids them *quatchet*, that is to say, walk abroad, for there is no place for such, so that they wander in restless want and penury'. Kiehtan the Indians 'acknowledge to be good':

and when they would obtain any great matter, meet together and cry unto him; and so likewise for plenty, victory, etc, sing, dance, feast, give thanks and hang up garlands and other things.

Tales of Kiehtan are handed down by the old men.

The other power they worship is *Hobbamock* or *Hobbamoqui*: this, 'so far as we can conceive, is the Devil'. He is invoked to cure injuries and diseases. And appears usually as a snake; though sometimes as a deer, fawn or eagle; and sometimes as a man. The *powahs* are intermediaries with Hobbamock. They have a fixed abode, like the temple of Apollo at Delphi, or of Diana at Ephesus. They promise to offer up gifts of skins, kettles, beads, hatchets and knives to 'the fiend'; 'but whether they perform it, I know not.' All Indians join with the powah in 'the exercise of invocation', and 'sometime break out into a short musical note with him'; but essentially they 'do only consent, or as we term it say Amen, to that he saith'. The powah is 'eager and free in speech, fierce in countenance'. Over the sick and wounded he performs 'many antic and laborious gestures'. He sucks the wounds; or promises to get an eagle or a snake to do it – this is never publicly seen. 'The other practices I have seen, being necessarily called sometimes to be with their sick; and have used the best arguments I could to make them understand against the same.' Winslow was often told that he would see Hobbomock. He never did. And the Indians 'confessed they never saw him when any of us were present'.

When an Indian dies, they 'sow up the corpse in a mat, and so put it in the earth'. A sachem they cover 'with many curious mats, and bury all his riches with him, and enclose the grave with a pale'. When a child dies, the father puts his most valued jewels and ornaments into the earth with the body; and 'will cut his hair, and disfigure himself very much, in token of sorrow'. When the head of a household dies – man or woman – the 'mats' are removed from the house, leaving only the frame; the body is buried nearby; and the household 'either remove their dwelling, or give over housekeeping'. Mourning is lengthy:

Night and day they perform this duty many days after the burial, in a most doleful manner. Inasmuch as, though it be ordinary, and the note musical (which they take one from another, and all together), yet it will draw tears from their eyes; and almost from ours also.

The Narragansetts are the most superstitious tribe. They 'exceed in their blind devotion'. A large dwelling is reserved for 'some few, that are, as we may term them, priests'. The people bring gifts; 'which are cast by the priests into a great fire that they make in the midst of the house, and there consumed to ashes'. The Narragansetts were not affected by the epidemic of 1617. So the Wampanoag Indians regret that they were not addicted to similar ceremonies.

In fact, religion is declining among the Wampanoag. They 'grow more and more cold in their worship to Kiehtan; saying, in their memory he was much more called upon.' It sounds like the Plymouth Old Planters regretting the erosion of the fervour of the Founders: recalling the 'sweet communion' at Leiden, the aging William Bradford noted his sadness 'to find and feel the decay and want thereof (in a great measure) and with grief and sorrow of heart to lament and bewail the same'.[36]

'Many sacrifices the Indians use,' wrote Winslow, 'and in some cases kill children.'

What was Winslow's estimate of the 'hope of convincing the heathen of their evil ways, and converting them to the true knowledge and worship of the living God, and so consequently the salvation of their souls through the merits of Jesus Christ'?

Well, in New England there is 'no less hope than elsewhere'. Elsewhere it is 'much talked on; and lightly or lamely prosecuted'. To the planters of Plymouth, actions spoke louder than words. The Plymouth literature is essentially *practical*. No high-flown academic theories about the Indian for these plain farmers. To appreciate the point, one has only to compare Winslow's *Good News from New England* with Alexander Whitaker's *Good News from Virginia*. And what mattered was to preserve the identity of the Christian community of Plymouth: 'godly', 'honest', of 'upright life and conversation'. Too many 'seeming Christians' have made Christianity 'stink in the nostrils of the poor infidels'. Christianity can be displayed to the 'poor savage heathens' only 'by giving good example'. Missionary activity must, so to say, be inward-looking before it could be outward-going.

Winslow is best known to History for his work in England from 1646, as an agent from New England, in guiding the foundation of the 'Society for Propagation of the Gospel in New England', established by an Act of the House of Commons in July 1649. The fact is that in New England no organised attempts to convert the Indians were made until the mid-1640s. In 1641 a petition was presented to Parliament signed by seventy English clerics (including sixteen D.D.s) complaining that in North America English settlement had been 'as yet been to small purpose' in converting the Indian: either because the English 'have placed themselves but in the skirts of

[36] *PP* 33.

America (as those of New England) or else for want of able and
conscionable ministers (as in Virginia)'.[37] From 1643 a series of tracts
was published in London concerning the spreading of the Gospel in
New England. (From the beginning of the Long Parliament the saints
in New England were slightly on the defensive: had they not
contracted out of the struggle in Old England? To stress the primacy,
and urgency, of missionary work would surely show that they were in
their wilderness with Divine Sanction.)[38] One of these tracts, printed in
1647, was prepared for the press by Winslow, who had brought the
manuscript from Boston: *The Day-breaking if not the Sun-rising of the
Gospel with the Indians in New England* (perhaps written by Thomas
Shepard, a graduate of Emmanuel College Cambridge). In March
1648 the matter of missions to the Indian was discussed in the House
of Commons. A Bill was to be drafted; and Winslow was to help in the
drafting. In May 1649, two months before the Act was finally passed,
Winslow published *The Glorious Progress of the Gospel, amonst the Indians
in New England*: in addition to Winslow's material, this contained
three letters by John Eliot, and a letter by Thomas Mayhew. The
'Society' became in 1662 the 'Company for Propagation of the Gospel
in New England': the New England Company – the oldest English
Protestant missionary society. For its history, the reader is referred to
the book by William Kellaway published in 1961: *The New England
Company 1649-1776: Missionary Society to the American Indians*.[39] In
Chapter 5, 'Missionaries and Indians, 1646-1690', (pp.81-112), Mr
Kellaway discusses the work of John Eliot of Jesus College Cambridge
(B.A. 1622) who went to New England in 1631, Thomas Mayhew,
minister on Martha's Vineyard from 1642, William Leveritch,
missionary in Plymouth Colony (at Sandwich, south of Plymouth);
and the various theories concerning the application of civility and true
religion to the Indian. Chapter 6, 'The Indian Library' (pp.122-65)
has material on Eliot's work of translation into Algonquian: beginning
with his primer or catechism, printed by the press at Harvard in 1653;
and culminating with the complete Bible, 1663, second edition 1685.
Alden Vaughan, in *New England Frontier*, 1965, has seventy pages on
missionary activity from 1620 to 1675: Chapters 9, 10 and 11.[40]

When Massasoit recovered from his illness at Sowams in March
1623, he confided to Hobomok details of an Indian conspiracy against
English settlers in New England.[41] The conspiracy was led by the
Massachusetts tribe and included Indians from Falmouth, Ipswich,

[37] Force, *Tracts*, I, no.13, p.5.

[38] I owe this point, among others, to a 1971 Harvard undergraduate thesis by
William Breitenbach, later of Clare College Cambridge. See also Carroll, *Puritanism and
the Wilderness*, 1969.

[39] The Winslow material in this paragraph is from Kellaway, 11-16.

[40] See below, pp.528-30. This is an appropriate point to note a book about missions,
and ideas of the Indian, in Canada, covering the period 1608-1763. Kennedy, *Jesuit and
Savage in New France*.

[41] Everyman *Chronicles*, 313 (Winslow's *Good News*).

and Martha's Vineyard. They had attempted to gain the support of Massasoit. Winslow's medical success dissuaded Massasoit, who advised Plymouth Plantation 'to kill the men of Massachusett, who were the authors of this intended mischief'.

The conspiracy was primarily directed not against Plymouth, but against a group of English settlers on the Massachusetts coast, twenty-five miles north, at Wessagusett (Weymouth). This settlement, about sixty strong, was a private venture dating from 1622. It was much disapproved of at Plymouth (where the settlers had first landed, and met with a cold reception). Cushman wrote to Bradford in the spring of 1623 advising him to 'signify to Squanto that they are a distinct body from us, and we have nothing to do with them, neither must be blamed for their faults': for one thing, 'these people will hardly deal so well with the savages as they should'.[42] Winslow reported that at Plymouth 'the Indians filled our ears with clamours against them, for stealing their corn, and other abuses'.[43] The Wessagusett colony, wrote Winslow, was 'a stain to Old England that bred them, in respect of their lives and manners amongst the Indians'.[44] The Indians were right to complain. But Plymouth could not countenance Indian use of force against the settlement. So the Indians prepared to move against Plymouth also; and Standish found himself leading a 'preventive massacre' at Massachusetts Bay in 1623.[45]

News of this reached Robinson at Leiden. And in December of 1623 he wrote a letter of rebuke to Bradford.[46]

Concerning the killing of those poor Indians, of which we heard at first by report, and since by more certain relation. Oh how happy a thing it had been, if you had converted some before you had killed any! Besides, where blood is once begun to be shed, it is seldom staunched of a long time after. You will say they deserve it. I grant it; but upon what provocations and invitements by those heathenish Christians?

(That is, the Wessagusett men.) The Plymouth planters were not 'magistrates' over the Indians; the duty of the English was to consider not what the Indians 'deserved', but 'what you were by necessity constrained to inflict'. Robinson could not see the 'necessity' of 'killing so many (and many more, it seems, they would, if they could)'. 'Methinks one or two principals should have been full enough, according to that approved rule: The punishment to a few, and the fear to many.' Robinson feared that the retaliations sprang 'merely from a human spirit'. And

[42] *PP* 108.
[43] Everyman, *Chronicles*, 291.
[44] *ibid.*, 272.
[45] Bushnell, 194 (see note 25).
[46] *PP* 374-5.

there is cause to fear that by occasion, especially of provocation, there may be
wanting that tenderness of the life of man (made after God's image) which is
meet. It is also a thing more glorious in men's eyes, than pleasing in God's or
convenient for Christians, to be a terror to poor barbarous people.

All this seemed less compelling at Plymouth than it did at Leiden to
a former Fellow of Corpus Christi College Cambridge.

The debate about New England's Indian wars became more
trenchant in the 1640s and 1650s; and, like the development of
missionary work among the Indians, it was a product of the fear in
New England that the saints in Old England might consider their
American brethren as lotus-eaters in Canaan, when at home the
struggle with Antichrist was strenuously developing. It was necessary
for New England to stress, first, that a soldier-like spirit was found not
only in the New Model Army; and, secondly, that the Indian was a
dangerous and deceitful foe, inspired by Satan. In 1637
Massachusetts Bay, Connecticut and Plymouth waged war on the
Pequots of Connecticut. The Pequots, it was later said, were strong,
cruel and armed; and they had been the originators of violence, from
1634. Thus to proceed against them was both necessary and just.
Their name was blotted out, just as God had instructed the Israelites
to 'blot out the remembrance of Amalek from under heaven'
(Deuteronomy 25:19). God was at work in New England. And, as
Nathaniel Morton wrote in 1669, 'God hath very evidently made way
for the English by sweeping away the natives by some great
mortalities' – among them that of the Pequots, who fell before 'the
sword of the English'.[47] In his 1689 *Brief Relation of the State of New
England*, Increase Mather declared that when in 1637 'mighty
numbers of the Indians were slain by a few of the Englishmen', a
'terror of God' fell upon the Indians. The 'barbarous heathen' were
docile until 1675, when the English found themselves compelled to
defensive action against Metacom, son of Massasoit. Metacom ('King
Philip') was executed, and 'whole nations of them were destroyed'.
There is an Indian expression, Mather said: 'The Englishmen's God
makes us afraid.'[48] King Philip's War was as traumatic for New
England as the 1622 Massacre had been for Virginia.[49] It originated a
tradition of writing which, as Louis B. Wright has said, 'viewed the
Indians as murderous heathen richly deserving annihilation'. Increase
Mather began the tradition with his *A Brief History of the Wars with the
Indians*, 1676; and continued it with *A Relation of the Troubles which have
Hapned in New-England by reason of the Indians there*, which was published

[47] *New Englands Memoriall*: Everyman Chronicles, 43. For the Pequot War,
Vaughan, *New England Frontier*, Ch.5. The whaling vessel in *Moby Dick* is called
'Pequot' – the vanquished tribe.
[48] Force, *Tracts*, IV, no.11, pp.4-5.
[49] The standard work on King Philip's War is Leach, *Flintlock and Tomahawk*, 1958.
See also Langdon, *Pilgrim Colony*, Chs 12 and 13; and Craven, *Colonies in Transition*,
Ch.4.

in 1677, the same year as a similar work by William Hubbard, *A Narrative of the Troubles with the Indians in New England*. Cotton Mather, son of Increase, published in 1699 an atrocity item about the decade 1688-1698: *Decennium Luctuosum*, to be incorporated into his *Ecclesiastical History of New England from its First Planting*, published in London in 1702 with the Latin title *Magnalia Christi Americana*, 'The Great Achievements of Christ in America'. There were, of course, American authors in the Charles II period who were more sympathetic to the Indian. The layman Daniel Gookin (1612-1687), who lived in Massachusetts from 1644, having originally emigrated to Virginia in the early 1630s, became in the late 1650s 'ruler over the praying Indians', and a leading advocate of Indian education. He wrote in 1677 'An historical Account of the Doings and Sufferings of the Christian Indians of New England'; and also 'Historical Collections of the Indians in New England'. But the latter was not published until 1792, and the former not until 1836.

Wessagusett was not the only settlement of 'strangers' which pained Plymouth in the 1620s. In 1625 a party landed to the north-west of Wessagusett, at Passonagessit (now within the limits of Quincy). The leadership of this little colony soon passed to a product of the Inns of Court who became the most famous (and entertaining) enemy of Plymouth Plantation: Thomas Morton (1575-1646).

Morton decided to name the site 'Mare Mount' (or 'Merry Mount'). The change of name was celebrated on 1 May 1627 (May Day: St Philip and St James): 'in a solemn manner, after the old English custom.' The narrative is from Thomas' *New English Canaan*.[50] Beer was brewed. A maypole was erected 'with the help of the savages, that came thither to see the manner of our revels'.[51] And there was 'merry song':[52]

which (to make their revels more fashionable) was sung with a chorus, every man bearing his part, which they performed in a dance, hand in hand about the maypole, whilst one of the company sang, and filled out the good liquor.

All no more than 'harmless mirth made by young men'.

As reported to Governor Bradford, this seemed like 'feasts of the Roman goddess Flora, or the beastly practices of the mad Baccanalians'.[53] Thomas' men drank and danced around the maypole 'many days together, inviting the Indian women for their consorts, dancing and frisking together like so many fairies rather; and worse practices'. The settlers had fallen to 'great licentiousness, and led a dissolute life, pouring out themselves into all profaneness'. Thomas Morton was a 'Lord of Misrule', maintaining a 'School of Atheism'.

More seriously, Bradford objected to the fact that Thomas had traded arms, powder and shot to the Indians, and taught their use; and employed them as his hunters.[54] The danger of 'covetousness'

[50] Force, *Tracts*, II, no.5. Subsequent page references are to this edition.
[51] 89. [52] 91. [53] *PP* 205-8. [54] *PP* 206.

among English traders was that it made the Indians 'rich and powerful and also proud'.[55] (At Plymouth, 'newcomers' were excluded from the -fur trade.)[56] The English would become like the Dutch and the French, 'gain-thirsty murderers'. And English settlements would live 'at the Indians' mercy' – to be 'overthrown by these barbarous savages thus armed with their own weapons'.[57] Also, the men of Merry Mount had spent their trading profits in 'wine and strong waters in great excess': brandy and aqua vitae.[58] And these also were given to the Indians.

So the English settlements in New England (four at least), prodded by Plymouth, decided to suppress Thomas Morton. Standish went to take the settlement by force; he found only half a dozen settlers, too drunk to resist. Thomas was taken to Plymouth; and then shipped to England in June 1628.[59] In 1628 the maypole was destroyed; much to the anger of the Indians, according to Thomas. The Indians did

reprove these elephants of wit for their humane deed. The Lord above did open their mouths, like Balaam's ass, and made them speak in His behalf sentences of unexpected divinity, besides morality.[60]

Numbers 22:28: 'And the Lord opened the mouth of the ass, and she said unto Balaam, What have I done unto thee, that thou hast smitten me?' The ass reproves Balaam, who is portrayed as both prophet and deceiver. Balaam was Bradford, in Thomas' Biblical gymnastics. And Thomas knew that in the New Testament the name of Balaam is used both as a symbol of avarice (2 Peter 2:15 – Balaam 'loved the wages of unrighteousness') and of instigation to idolatry and fornication (Revelation 2:14). Thomas Morton may have heard the chimes at midnight at Clifford's Inn; but he had also learnt adroitness in manipulating his Biblical texts to vex the pilgrims.

New English Canaan was dedicated to the 'Commissioners for the Government of all His Majesty's Foreign Plantations' (a committee of the Privy Council). It was intended as ammunition in the campaign of the English government, from 1634, led by Laud, to assert the authority of Whitehall over New England. The book was ready by 1633. But it appears not to have been published until 1637; and not in London, but (allegedly) in Amsterdam. Laud had even less sense of humour than Bradford.

'The more I looked, the more I liked it.' Thus Morton on the country of New England. 'And when I had more seriously considered of the beauty of the place, with all her fair endowments, I did not think that in all the known world it could be paralled.'[61] The obvious image was of the land flowing with milk and honey. New England (defined as between Philadelphia and southern Maine) is 'nothing inferior to Canaan of Israel, but a kind of parallel to it in all points'.[62]

[55] *PP* 203-4. [56] *PP* 133. [57] *PP* 207-8. [58] *PP* 205-6. [59] *PP* 210.
[60] *New English Canaan*, ed. Force, 109 (see note 50).
[61] 41. [62] 15.

(And Canaan 'none will deny to be a land far more excellent than Old England'.)[63]

Morton went to New England as a 'good Protestant'.[64] That is, 'a man that endeavoured to advance the dignity of the Church of England';[65] and, as 'a practice of piety', used the Book of Common Prayer 'in a laudable manner' (one can assume the pun was intentional). This incurred the hostility of the 'precise separatists',[66] the 'brethren',[67] 'the Brownists of New Plymouth':[68] this 'sect of cruel schismatics',[69] who 'vilify' the Church of England with 'uncivil terms', 'inveighing against the sacred Book of Common Prayer'.[70]

Morton's coruscating portrait of the 'brethren' is worthy to be set alongside Richard Hooker's brilliant analysis of the sectarian mind (both perceptive and unfair) in 1593;[71] or Ben Jonson's sharp and well-informed puritan caricatures in 'The Alchemist' (1610) and 'Bartholomew Fair' (1614). Indeed, Morton quoted Jonson.[72] The men of Plymouth are 'Ananias and his brethren'.[73] Ananias is the name of the deacon from Amsterdam, haunted by 'ignorant zeal', in 'The Alchemist'; a proletarian tailor. (In the Acts of the Apostles there is an Ananias who is struck dead because of dishonesty, 5:1-5; and 'the high priest Ananias', notorious for his greed, Chapter 24.) In Morton's characterisation, as in Jonson's, the brethren are governed by 'covetousness'.[74] They do worldly things, under the veil of 'spiritual benefit'.[75] They are 'given to envy and malice extremely'.[76] The Plymouth pilgrims had learned in Leiden 'to work all to their own ends, and make a great show of religion, but no humanity'.[77] They believe virtue can spring only from a 'sancified' man (in their definition of the term). Thus they reject help from those 'of the number left without': 'neither will these precise people admit a carnal man into their houses'[78] (and they 'call every good Protestant' a 'carnal man').[79] All the brethren are allowed to exercise spiritual gifts, however 'illiterate' and 'fantastical' they be: grocer, tailor, tapster, cobbler. And 'the unfitness of the person undertaking to be the messenger has brought a blemish upon the message'. This section, Book III, Chapter 27, 'Of the Practice of the Church', is a particularly invigorating piece of Anglican polemic.[80] Morton had no time for the 'leaden capacities' of the English 'commonalty'.[81] All this, of course, has its basis in autobiographical indignation:

The first precept in their politics is to defame the man at whom they aim. And then he is an holy Israelite, in their opinion, who can spread that fame broadest, like butter upon a loaf; no matter how thin it will serve for a veil. And then this man whom they have thus depraved is a spotted unclean leper. He must out, lest he pollute the land and them that are clean. If this be one of their gifts, then Machiavel had as good gifts as they.[82]

[63] 42.   [64] 121.   [65] 93.   [66] 118.   [67] 72.   [68] 19.   [69] 110.   [70] 93.

[71] *Laws of Ecclesiastical Polity*, Preface, Ch.8. Porter, *Puritanism in Tudor England*, part XIII.

[72] 98.   [73] 61.   [74] 103.   [75] 105.   [76] 121.   [77] 96.   [78] 114.   [79] 121.   [80] 115-19.   [81] 39.   [82] 121.

Thomas Morton reminds one also of John Smith. Smith's picture in 1630 of the men of Plymouth is in similar vein. The 'Brownists' had advisors, wrote Smith,

as wise as themselves, but that was best, that liked their own conceits: for indeed they would not be known to have any knowledge of any but themselves, pretending only religion their governor, and frugality their council, when indeed it was only their pride, and singularity, and contempt of authority; because they could not be equals, they would have no superiors. In this fools' paradise they so long used that good husbandry, they have paid soundly in trying their own follies.[83]

Again, personal pique is involved. The colonists of 1620 had used Smith's book on New England, and his map; but they had chosen Miles Standish as their Captain.

Morton's purpose in caricaturing Plymouth Plantation was to emphasise his essential point – that the 'uncivilised people are more just than the civilised';[84] that the Indians, compared with the brethren, are 'more full of humanity, and more friendly'.[85] Plymouth men are adept at 'misapplying the savages' actions'.[86] They consider the Indians 'a dangerous people, subtle, secret and mischievous'.[87] They are not: they are 'poor silly lambs'.[88]

Morton had investigated Indian language and Indian origins. The language shows traces of Greek and Latin: *Pascopan* means 'greedy gut'; from the Latin *pasco*, feed, and the Greek *pan*, all. The Indians (like the British) probably spring from Brutus, a refugee from Troy. 'I am bold to conclude that the original of the natives of New England may be well conjectured to be from the scattered Trojans, after such time as Brutus departed.' Originally, the Indians probably knew the loadstone and the compass; and 'literature' – 'which time hath cancelled and worn out of use'. The Trojan theory is more likely that the opinion of some ('which shall be nameless') that the Indians 'proceed from the race of the Tartars, and came from Tartaria into these parts, over the frozen sea'. The 'sea of ice' theory is unconvincing; a land link is not very likely; and what part of North America 'may be thought to border upon the country of the Tartars, it is yet unknown'.[89]

Indian houses are a circle of poles, covered with mats: 'much like the wild Irish'.[90] Also, when the Indians are attired for hunting, 'they look like Irish'. Indian dress suits them; makes them 'handsomer than when they are in English apparel'. The male who has reached puberty

weareth a belt about his middle, and a broad piece of leather that goeth between his legs and is tucked up, both before and behind, under that belt;

---

[83] Smith, *Advertisements for the unexperienced Planters of New-England, or anywhere. Or, the Path-way to experience to errect a Plantation.* Written October 1630; published 1631; Smith died June 1631. Quotation on p.179 of *Smith's America*, ed. Lankford.
[84] 85. [85] 15. [86] 86. [87] 77. [88] 109. [89] 15-18. [90] 19.

and this they wear to hide their secrets of nature, which by no means will they suffer to be seen, so much modesty they use in that particular.

The women also dress 'in a decent manner'. And this 'is to be noted in people uncivilised, therein they seem to have as much modesty as civilised people, and deserve to be applauded for it'.[91]

They are not 'as some have thought, a dull or slender-witted people; but very ingenious and very subtle'.[92] Their vision and sense of smell are better than ours.[93] Their protocol is admirable. They respect birth, and blood, and the conventions of chivalry.[94] They move their abode with the seasons, 'after the manner of the gentry'.[95] They have a great respect for age. 'It is a thing to be admired, and indeed made a precedent, that a nation yet uncivilised should more respect age than some nations civilised'; consideration of this might induce 'better manners' in our 'irregular young people'.[96] Another sign of their 'humanity' is that if a settler happen to fall asleep in an Indian house, they bring a bowl of food, and when he wakes, say 'if you be hungry, there is meat for you'.[97]

Morton admired the 'solemnity' of Indian mourning. For prominant persons, it is usual to have a 'hearse cloth', 'two great bear skins sowed together at full length, and propped up over the grave'. Once the Plymouth planters removed such a covering from the grave of the mother of a sachem, thinking it 'an act of superstition'. The sachem cried to his god: 'Take revenge of those wild people that hath my monument defaced in despiteful manner, disdaining our ancient antiquities and honorable customs.'[98]

We are given examples of the 'feats and juggling tricks' of the powahs (who have 'some correspondency' with the Devil).[99] One powah claimed he could 'go under water to the further side of a river too broad for any man to undertake without a breath'. He did this by swimming over in the normal way; but 'deluding the company with casting a mist before their eyes: that see him enter in and come out, but no part of the way he has been seen.' Another, on a hot summer day, produced ice from a bowl of clear water, 'which doubtless was done by the agility of Satan, his consort'. An Englishman with a swollen hand was promised a cure by a powah in return for 'a parcel of biscuits':

which being delivered him, he took the party grieved into the woods, aside from company, and with the help of the Devil (as may be conjected) quickly recovered him of that swelling.

In fact, the powahs are but 'weak witches'. The Indians have too much respect for them; it is 'sacrilege' to offend them.

Morton does not agree with Cicero that 'there is no people so barbarous but have some worship or other'.[100] Had Cicero 'been amongst these people as long as I have been, and conversed so much

[91] 22-3. [92] 131. [93] 33. [94] 27. [95] 20. [96] 25. [97] 20. [98] 36, 72-3. [99] 25-6. [100] 21.

with them touching this matter of religion, he would have changed his opinion'. They 'have no worship or religion at all': 'I am more willing to believe that the elephants (which are reported to me the most intelligible of all beasts) do worship the moon.'

What Morton meant was that the Indians have no liturgical or dogmatic system; just as they have no formal code of law, and no sophisticated political organisation. They are Gentiles. And their beliefs are preferable to the worship and faith of Plymouth. To be without *that* sort of worship and religion is admirable.

They are 'not altogether without the knowledge of God'. They have the 'tradition' that 'God made one man and one woman, and bade them live together and beget children, kill deer, beasts, birds, fish and fowl, and what they would, at their pleasure'. The tradition also that the posterity of the first parents was 'full of evil, and made God so angry that He let in the sea upon them, and drowned the greatest part of them, that were naughty men'. These went to the Hell at the centre of the earth, *Sanaconquam*. The survivors of the deluge 'increased the world'; and, so an Indian told Morton, 'when they died, because they were good, went to the house of Kytan (pointing to the setting of the sun) where they eat all manner of dainties'. In the kingdom of Kytan there is corn and fruit; no work; and life 'for ever, void of care'. The Indians assume that 'we that use the Book of Common Prayer' are petitioning Kytan. A married Indian who, in bachelor days, had lodged with Morton, asked him 'that I would let his son be brought up in my house, that he might be taught to read in that Book'. Morton agreed. And the father 'was a very joyful man, to think that his son should thereby (as he said) become an Englishman, and then he would be a good man'.[101]

The Indians are 'to be commended for leading a contented life'.[102] They live 'richly'; for elaborate clothes are 'the badge of sin, and the more variety of fashion is but the greater abuse of the creature'. They need no spices and sauces. 'The rarity of the air begot by the medicinable quality of the sweet herbs of the country always procures good stomachs to the inhabitants.' Their drink is 'of the crystal fountain'. Unlike the English, who are too fond of the 'good ale tap'. Morton denies that he gave liquor to the Indians; although he was told that for trade up north, 'lusty liquors' are essential. He relates that an Indian 'desperately killed himself when he was drunk; a gun being charged, and the cock up, he sets the mouth to his breast, and putting back the trigger with his foot, shot himself dead'. The Indians 'love not to be cumbered with many utensils'. Everyone 'knows his own'. But

all things (so long as they will last) are used in common amongst them. A biscuit cake given to one, that one breaks it equally into so many parts as there be persons in his company, and distributes it. Plato's commonwealth is so much practised by these people.

[101] 33-5.   [102] 38-40.

Their life is 'void of care', and they are 'so loving', that

they make use of those things which they enjoy (the wife only excepted) as common goods; and are therein so compassionate that rather than one should starve for want, they would starve all. Thus do they pass away the time merrily; not regarding our pomp (which they see daily before their faces); but are better content with their own.

In sum: 'According to human reason, guided only by the light of nature, these people leads the more happy and freer life, being void of care, which torments the minds of so many Christians.'

'Thus do they pass away the time merrily.' *Merry*, we recall, was a favourite word in one Tudor book: the Ralph Robinson translation of *Utopia*.

Other English settlers in New England in the 1620s were more attuned than was Thomas Morton to the standards of Plymouth. There were plans for a fishing settlement on the coast of northern Massachusetts; and in 1623 the first fisherman-planters arrived. That scheme of the 1620s was not a success. And in 1627 about thirty men, women and children moved on to Salem, twenty-five miles north of Boston. (The Indian name of this port was Naumkeag, taken to be Hebrew.) In September 1628 forty further settlers landed at Salem, under the leadership of the tough John Endecott. And in June 1629 there arrived at Salem a fleet of five ships, with four hundred colonists. Among them were some clerics, including Francis Higginson, aged forty-two, a graduate of Jesus College Cambridge (B.A. 1610) and Samuel Skelton, aged thirty-five, of Clare College Cambridge (B.A. 1612). Letters were brought for Endecott from Matthew Cradock, Governor of the New England Company (organised in 1628).[103]

Endecott was to be 'not unmindful of the main end of our plantation, by endeavouring to bring the Indians to the knowledge of the Gospel'. This will be impossible unless the settlers 'live unblameable and without reproof, and demean themselves justly and courteous towards the Indians, thereby to draw them to affect our persons, and consequently our religion'. The Company has been 'careful to make plentiful provision of godly ministers': by their 'faithful preaching', 'godly conversation' and 'exemplary life' the Indians may be 'reduced to the obedience of the Gospel', 'in God's appointed time'.[104] (There was also a surgeon, to whom the Indians were to have access.)[105] The Indians were to visit the English only at fixed times and places: the English should be aware of 'the hurt that may follow through overmuch familiarity with the Indians'. No one 'in our precincts' was 'to do any injury (in the least kind) to the heathen people'.[106] Endecott was to 'get some of their children to train up to reading, and consequently to religion, whilst they are young'. And to remember that although the spiritual condition of the Indians

[103] Three letters, here treated as one. *Records of Massachusetts Bay*, ed. Shurtleff, I.
[104] 384-6. [105] 396. [106] 393-4.

may be 'woeful', it is no worse than that, at one time, of the inhabitants of Britain[107] (before the coming of Christianity? before the Reformation?).

Cradock was sensitive to the land question. 'If any of the natives pretend right of inheritance to all or any part of the lands granted in our patent, we pray you endeavour to purchase their title, that we may avoid the least scruple of intrusion.'[108] (Increase Mather was to claim in 1689 that the 1628 'charter' gave 'right to the soil'; 'as of the manor of East Greenwich, and in common socage' – 'notwithstanding they purchased their lands of the Indians, who were the native proprietors'.)[109] The Company has been granted the land: thus any Indian claimants are 'pretenders'. But if such claims are handled in 'discreet' fashion, the Indians 'will be willing to treat and compound with you upon very easy conditions' and 'reasonable composition'.[110]

Down at Plymouth, Bradford rejoiced that the fleet of June 1629 brought to Salem 'many godly persons to begin the churches and plantation of Christ there, and in the Bay of the Massachusetts'. (Some members of the Leiden congregation also came over in 1629.)[111] Endecott decreed that 20 July 1629 should be 'a solemn day of humiliation for the choice of a Pastor and Teacher'. The clerics were questioned 'concerning their callings'. By a 'free voice' of all adult males. Skelton was chosen as Pastor, and Higginson as Teacher. Higginson, 'with three or four of the gravest members of the church', laid hands on Skelton; similarly, Skelton on Higginson. And 6 August was appointed as the day for the choice and ordaining of elders and deacons.[112] Bradford was happy that other settlements besides Plymouth would henceforth be 'a resting place for so many of the Lord's people'.[113] As Endecott had written to Bradford in May:[114]

God's people are all marked with one and the same mark, and sealed with one and the same seal, and have, for the main, one and the same heart, guided by one and the same spirit of truth.

It is hard to resist the assertion of William Kellaway that the New England Way was 'basically antipathetic to evangelical endeavour'.[115]

In 1630 there was published in London *New Englands Plantation*:[116] by Francis Higginson. In Old England he had had 'an extraordinary weakness of my stomach, and abundance of melancholic humours'. But the air of New England, 'extraordinary clear and dry', is 'of a most healing nature to all such as are of a cold, melancholy, phlegmatic, rheumatic temper of body'. He has discarded his cap and thick waistcoats, and wears a light cloak and unlined breeches: 'A sup

[107] 384.
[108] 394. For this (rather mysterious) 'patent', Andrews, *Colonial Period*, I, 354-9.
[109] *Brief Relation of the State of New England*: Force, *Tracts*, IV, no.11, p.4.
[110] 400. [111] *PP* 213. [112] *PP* 223-5. [113] *PP* 213. [114] *PP* 223.
[115] *New England Company*, 5.
[116] Force, *Tracts*, I, no.12.

of New England's air is better than a whole draught of Old England's ale.'[117] The Indians are 'tall', 'strong-limbed', 'tawney', and 'naked' (except of course for deer skins and loin cloths). Their houses are 'homely'. Relations with the colonists are good:

They will come into our houses sometimes by half-a-dozen or half-a-score at a time, when we are at victuals; but will ask or take nothing but what we give them. We purpose to learn their language as soon as we can, which be a means to do them good.

The pestilence 'about twelve years since' means that they 'are not able to make use of the one fourth part of the land'. Moreover, they have no 'settled place, as towns to dwell in, nor any ground they challenge for their own possession, but change their habitation from place to place'. And the men 'for the most part live idly, they do nothing but hunt and fish'. So there is 'abundance of ground that they cannot possess and make use of' – one reason they 'generally profess to like well of our coming and planting here'. Another reason is that

our presence here will be a means both of relief to them when they want, and also a defence from their enemies, wherewith (I say) before this plantation begun, they were often endangered.

On 12 June 1630 the 'Arbella', which had left Southampton on 29 March, entered the harbour of Salem. John Winthrop, Governor of the Massachusetts Bay Company, was on board. Eleven ships left Southampton in March and April, carrying 700 passengers: they all reached New England by the middle of July. Before the end of March a vessel had left Bristol with eighty passengers, and another, with 140 on board, had sailed from Plymouth. In all, seventeen ships crossed to New England in 1630, carrying over 1,000 passengers.[118] The Great Migration had begun. In all, 20,000 people emigrated to New England in the 1630s. They included 96 Cambridge men, thirty-five of them from Emmanuel (among them, Nathaniel Ward, John Harvard and Thomas Shepard; and two former Fellows, John Cotton and Thomas Hooker.)[119] One must remember that also in the 1630s 45,000 English folk went to Virginia and the Caribbean.

In the summer of 1630 some of the new arrivals settled on the peninsula known as Shawmut – Boston.

New England, wrote Increase Mather in 1689, differs from other settlements in America 'in respect of the grounds and motives inducing the first planters to remove into that American desert; other

---

[117] *ibid*, 9-10. Remainder of the paragraph, pp. 12-13.

[118] Andrews, *Colonial Period*, I, 393-5.

[119] Morison, *Founding of Harvard*, 1935, Appendix B, 'English University Men who Migrated to New England'; J.G. Gibson, 'Cambridge: Nurse of a Nation', *Cambridge Journal*, Feb. 1951, IV, 5; Porter, *Reformation and Reaction in Tudor Cambridge*, 1958, 421-2, 253-60.

plantations were built upon wordly interests, New England upon that which is purely religious'.[120] A popular text in Boston was that of the 'city set on a hill', from the Sermon on the Mount. Matthew 5:14-16:

Ye are the light of the world. A city that is set on a hill cannot be hid. Neither do men light a candle and put it under a bushel, but on a candlestick; and it giveth light to all men that are in the house. Let your light so shine before men, that they may see your good works, and glorify your Father.

How far that light shone upon the Indian in New England after 1630 – in Plymouth, Massachusetts, Connecticut, Rhode Island, New Hampshire and New Haven – was, and is, a matter of controversy. The scheme of my book has permitted only a cursory glance at the New England issues. Alden T. Vaughan's book, published in 1965, is an attempt to demonstrate that the New England puritans 'followed a remarkably humane, considerate and just policy in their dealings with the Indians':[121] *New England Frontier: Puritans and Indians 1620-1675.* The thesis was intended to be provocative, to redress an historiographical tradition of hostility to the puritans. It went, so to say, too far in the other direction: perhaps following Thomas Cartwright's puritan rule in the 1570s that 'contraries are cured by their contraries'.[122] Some critics felt not only that the author was too favourable to the New Englanders, but also that evidence had been distorted and withheld.[123] And the lively treatment often relies more on narrative than on analysis. But any reader interested in Indian relations in New England after 1630 will have to reckon with *New England Frontier.* There is relevant material also in a good book by Peter N. Carroll published in 1969: *Puritanism and the Wilderness: The Intellectual Significance of the New England Frontier, 1629-1700.*

Matthew Cradock warned John Endecott in 1629 'not to be too confident of the fidelity of the savages'.[124] 'It is an old proverb, yet as true, The burnt child dreads the fire. Our countrymen have suffered this by their too much confidence in Virginia. Let us by their harms learn to beware.'

It is time to return to Virginia: remembering that Cradock told Endecott to bear in mind the advice of Christ to His disciples when he told them to go forth and preach (Matthew 10:16). 'I send you forth a sheep in the midst of wolves: be ye therefore wise as serpents, and harmless as doves.'

---

[120] *Brief Relation of the State of New England*: Force, *Tracts*, IV, no.11, p.3.

[121] vii.

[122] Quoted by John Whitgift, *Works*, Parker Society, II, 441.

[123] For example T.B. Lewis, *William and Mary Quarterly*, July 1966, XXIII, 3. The 1971 article by Jennings has been discussed (note 25).

[124] *Records of Massachusetts Bay*, ed. Shurtleff, I, 385.

26

Conditions of Peace in Virginia, 1625-1662

By 1632, 22 March had become a Holy Day in Virginia, 'in commemoration of our deliverance from the Indians at the bloody massacre'.[1] The General Assembly at Jamestown in March 1630 had ordered 'that the war begun upon the Indians be effectually followed, and that no peace be concluded with them'.[2] The Indians were held to be – recorded the General Assembly of February 1632 – 'our irreconcilable enemies'.[3]

The Governor of the Colony at the time of the dissolution of the Virginia Company, Sir Francis Wyatt, continued as the first Royal Governor until 1626. The royal 'take-over' was slow. Until 1630 there followed three interim appointments: Yeardley took over in 1626 but died in 1627; Captain Francis West, son of De La Warr (1627-9); and Dr John Pott (1629-30). Charles I appointed Sir John Harvey as Governor in 1628; but he did not arrive in Virginia until 1630. Yeardley, West and Pott took a hard line against the Indian. Shortly before his death, Yeardley organised a massacre by the English. Each 'particular plantation' was to invade an Indian town, kill as many as possible, and seize or destroy the corn. This was not completely successful – the English ran out of ammunition. Pott a medical doctor, had conceived a project in 1624 of exterminating the Indians by poison!

Nancy O.Lurie writes:[4]

Doubtless Opechancanough expected reprisals, but he was totally unprepared for the unprecedented and utter devastation of his lands and the wholesale slaughter of his people. The tribes were scattered, some far beyond the traditional boundaries of their lands, and several of the smaller groups simply ceased to exist as definable entities.

Harvey was Governor for five years.[5] He was thought too lenient to the Indian (and to the – mainly papist – colonists in Maryland from

[1] Hening, *Statutes*, I, 177. [2] *ibid.*, 153. [3] *ibid.*, 176.
[5] For Harvey and his troubles, Washburn, *Virginia under Charles and Cromwell*, 7-9, 20-6; Bailyn, in Smith (ed.), *Seventeenth-Century America*, 96-7.

1634). In 1635 he was deposed by the Jamestown Council. The authority of a Royal Governor was not unlike that of the Head of an Oxford or Cambridge College.

It is clear from the Jamestown legislation of the 1630s that a rigid separation of the English and the Indian was incapable of enforcement. Indians were utilised to kill deer and game, and some settlers (especially 'runaway servants') provided them with guns and ammunition; Indians visited English settlements, and some English went to Indian villages; colonists traded cloth, bays and cotton with the Indian – and indeed, the Jamestown Assembly acknowledged in 1633 that 'trade with the natives is to be cherished for many respects'.[6] All this can be deduced from the attempts of the Assembly to prohibit such practices. In 1632 'all trade with the savages' was banned, 'as well public as private'.[7] In 1633 the sale or barter of guns and ammunition was forbidden, and the trade in cloth (this because the colonists needed the cloth themselves).[8] In 1637 any trade with the Indian was to be a felony; this act was repealed in 1640 – only trade in arms was to be so regarded. The provision about the sale of arms was repeated in 1643: the Indians, 'to the great endangering of the colony, are instructed in the use of our arms' and 'have opportunity given them to store themselves as well with arms as powder and shot'. The 1643 Act has the complaint about runaway servants, 'loitering runaways': a second escape attempt was to incur the branding of 'R' on the cheek.[9] In 1632 it was ordered that

no person or persons shall dare to speak or parley with any Indians, either in the woods or in any plantation, if he can possibly avoid it by any means. But, as soon as he can, to bring them to the commander, or give the commander notice thereof; upon penalty of a month's service for any free man offending, and twenty stripes to any servant.

However, 'the planters of the eastern shore' could observe 'good terms of amity' with the Indian; so long as they 'stand upon their guard', and suffer no Indians 'to make any ordinary resort or abode in their houses'. Any planter visiting an Indian village without permission was to be bound over by the local commander, and brought before the next quarter court.[10]

By 1643 some wished the 'prohibiting of any terms of peace to be entertained with the Indians'.[11] Others looked for 'the settling of peace with friendship with the Indians'.[12] And in general it seemed that the massacre of 1622 had been 'forgiven and forgotten'.[13]

At which point the aged Opechancanough decided to take his revenge.

The second massacre was on 18 April 1644. By that time, according to Robert Beverley, writing in 1705, Opechancanough was

[6] Hening, I, 219.
[7] *ibid.*, 173. [8] *ibid.*, 219. [9] *ibid.*, 255. [10] *ibid.*, 167. [11] *ibid.*, 333. [12] *ibid.*, 237.
[13] *Perfect Description of Virginia*, 1649. Force, *Tracts*, II, no.8, p.11.

grown so decrepit that he was not able to walk alone, but was carried about by his men wherever he had a mind to move. His flesh was all macerated, his sinews slackened, and his eyelids became so heavy that he could not see, but as they were lifted up by his servants.[14]

He was thought to be over 100. Some settlers later stated that he had been 'by some English informed that all was under the sword in England, in their native country, and such divisions in our land, that now was his time, or never, to root out the English'. Lack of supplies from England would kill those who could not be murdered. Beverley said that nearly five hundred settlers were killed (probably an over-estimate). But (from the 1649 account again) the intention of Opechancaough was not fully carried out, because of an Indian failure of nerve.[15] After the initial killings, the Indians were

so affrighted in their own minds, that they had not the heart to follow the councils their king had commanded. But, to admiration of the English, prosecuted not their opportunity, nor were constant to their own principles, but fled away, and retired themselves many miles distant of the colony. Which little space of time gave the English opportunity to gather themselves together, call an Assembly, secure their cattle, and to think upon some way to defend themselves, if need were; and then to offend their enemies.

The campaigns began again. Indians were driven away and killed; villages destroyed; open ground taken over by the English for the sowing of wheat. And in the summer of 1646 Opechancanough was captured and brought to Jamestown by the Governor, Sir William Berkeley. Berkeley, an Oxford M.A. (1629), had come to Virginia as Governor in 1642 aged thirty-four; he was to be dominant in the colony, sometimes as Governor, until his death in 1677.

Beverley tells us that the Indian Emperor, on orders from the Governor, was 'treated with all the respect and tenderness imaginable'. He was in Jamestown for two weeks.

He heard one day a great noise of the treading of people about him, upon which he caused his eyelids to be lifted up. And finding that a crowd of people were let in to see him, he called in high indignation for the Governor. Who, being come, Opechancanough scornfully told him that had it been his fortune to take Sir William Berkeley prisoner, he should not meanly have exposed him as show to the people.

Berkeley intended to have Opechancanough taken to England. But 'one of the soldiers, resenting the calamities the colony had suffered by this prince's means, basely shot him through the back'.[16] He died of the wound. His successor was called Necotowance.

The General Assembly had met in Jamestown in March 1646,

[14] *History and Present State of Virginia*, 62.
[15] *Perfect Description*. See note 13.
[16] *History and Present State of Virginia*, 62.

before the arrival of Opechancanough. There had been nearly two years of war, which had meant 'great and vast expense'. And further revenge upon the Indian seemed impossible: 'they being dispersed and driven from their towns and habitations, lurking up and down the woods in small numbers.' (The success of the massacre, writes Nancy O. Lurie, 'is indicative of the separation that marked the lives of the colonists and the Indians by 1644.')[17] And it was concluded that 'a peace, if honorably obtained, would conduce to the better being and commodity of the country'.[18] The terms of the peace were agreed by the General Assembly of October 1646: Berkeley; the nine members of the Council; the Speaker; and twenty-five burgesses from the then ten 'counties' (Jamestown, Henrico, Charles City, Isle of Wight, Elizabeth, York, Warwick, Northampton, Upper Norfolk and Lower Norfolk).[19]

Indian children of twelve years or under could live with the English, if they 'freely and voluntarily come in' (some of them as 'servants'). Necotowance was to return his English prisoners, 'and all such negroes and guns which are yet remaining either in the possession of himself or any Indians'. The English undertook to protect Necotowance and his Indians 'against any rebels or other enemies'. In return, Necotowance was to 'acknowledge to hold his kingdom from the King's Majesty of England', and pay the Governor yearly tribute of twenty beaver skins (a sign of the growing importance of the fur trade). His successors as Indian King were to be 'appointed or confirmed' by the Governor. In March 1648 Necotowance came to Jamestown with five chiefs, and the beaver skins – to be sent to Charles I – and made a speech:[20]

That the sun and the moon should first lose their glorious lights and shining, before he or his people should ever more hereafter wrong the English in any kind: but they would ever hold love and friendship together. And to give the English better assurance of their faith, he had decreed that if any Indian be seen to come within the limits of the English colony, except they come with some message from him, with such and such tokens, that it shall be lawful to kill them presently. And the English shall be free to pass at all times, and where they please, throughout his dominions.

The importance of the treaty of 1646 was the conception and definition of the limits of English and Indian territory. Necotowance ceded to the English 'that tract of land between York River and James River, from the falls of both the rivers to Kecoughtan'. In that area, no adult Indian was to 'repair or make any abode': any unauthorised Indian seen there could be lawfully killed. If any English colonist entertained, or concealed, any Indian, he should be lawfully

[17] Smith (ed.), *Seventeenth-Century America*, 51.
[18] Hening, I, 318.
[19] *ibid.*, 323-6. See also Craven's *White, Red, and Black*, (1971), 56-67.
[20] *Perfect Description*, 13 (see note 13).

convicted, and executed, 'without benefit of clergy'. Only Indian messengers from Necotawance were allowed within the English reservation; they were to wear a 'token' – a 'coat of striped stuff', which could be collected only at certain stated forts (such as Fort Henry, modern Petersburg). North of the river York was Indian territory: and they were to live and hunt 'without any interruption from the English'. Any colonist found north of the York would be judged a felon, unless he was forced there by 'stress of weather', or went with a warrant from the Governor to fell trees or cut sedge. (The English had until 1 March 1647 to collect cattle and hogs from north of the York.) Wesley Frank Craven has emphasised the importance of the 1646 recognition 'of the Indian's need for a guarantee of his own rights in the land': 'the effort to set aside a reservation in which he could be free of the white man's varied intrusions represents a turn of policy of the first historical significance.'[21] Washburn confirms the point: 'For the first time in Virginia's history, the Indian was considered to have an unquestioned legal right to the land.'[22]

Of course, it was not to work. The English, originally dotted along the James River, were expanding into the whole of Tidewater Virginia. In 1628 the population was 3,000: in 1640 it was 8,000.[23] By 1646, as we shall see, it was 15,000. By 1660 it was probably about 30,000.[24] In 1646 it was recognised that the English might wish to settle in some Indian areas; provision was made for consulting Necotowance. Two years later, in October 1648, the 'felony' provision about English settlement was repealed; and the Assembly noted 'the great and clamorous necessities' of 'a very considerable number' of the settlers, 'brought upon them through the mean produce of their labours upon barren and overwrought grounds, and the apparent decay of their cattle and hogs, for want of sufficient range'.[25] 1646 made no provision for what Professor Craven called 'the relentless advance of the American farmer'.

In April 1648 various letters were sent from Jamestown to England, 'at the request of a gentleman of worthy note, who desired to know the true state of Virginia as it now stands': 'there having been nothing related to the true estate of this plantation these twenty five years.' They were used as the basis for a short book published in London in 1649: *A Perfect Description of Virginia: being a full and true relation of the present state of the plantation.*[26] The running title was 'A new description of Virginia'.

It is this pamphlet which gives the population figure of 15,000. Plus 300 Negroes, 'good servants':[27] that is, 2% of the population: by 1670

[21] W.F. Craven, 'Indian Policy in Early Virginia', *William and Mary Quarterly*, January 1944 (3rd series, vol.1), 76-7.
[22] Washburn, *Virginia under Charles and Cromwell*, 38.
[23] *ibid.*, 2. Andrews, *Colonial Period*, I, 140.
[24] Craven, *Colonies in Transition*, 15-16.
[25] Hening, I, 353-4.
[26] Force, Tracts, II, no.8.
[27] p.3.

the percentage of blacks was 5% (2,000 out of 40,000). (In 1631 the Governor and Council in Jamestown had sentenced a white settler 'to do penance in Church, according to laws of England, for getting a negro woman with child; and the woman whipped'.[28] That at any rate was a step in the right direction. The year before, a colonist had been 'soundly whipped before an assembly of negroes and others for abusing himself to the dishonour of God and shame of Christians by defiling his body in lying with a negro; which fault he is to acknowledge next Sabbath Day.')[29]

The 1649 tract stressed the health of Virginians:[30]

they have health very well, and fewer die in a year there, according to the proportion, than in any place of England; since that men are provided with all necessaries, have plenty of victual, bread, and good beer and housing, all which the Englishman loves full dearly.

What the colony needs is 'thousands' of 'young boys' – 'young youths from sixteen years and upward' (also some 'maidens'). The passage was safe and easy – five to seven weeks there; three to four weeks back. The government is 'after the laws of England'. There are twenty churches, and a minister can count on £100 a year (paid in tobacco and corn by the settlers). Everyone lives 'in peace and love'.[31]

The 'anglicanism' of Virginia had been confirmed in 1643 by a decree of the Jamestown General Assembly expelling 'nonconformists' from the colony.[32] .Three ministers from New England had arrived in 1642 (at the request of some of the settlers in Upper Norfolk County).[33] One of them was John Knowles, who in 1627 had been elected to a Fellowship at St Catharine's College Cambridge, the Master being Richard Sibbes. He had arrived in Boston in 1639. Of the three Bostonian missionaries, two left Virginia in 1643, including Knowles, who later returned to England and in 1672 declined an offer to be President of Harvard.

Wingfield had been conscious in 1606 of the dangers of a 'factious schismatic'; a warning echoed by Benson and Crakanthorpe in 1609, and by Crashaw in 1610.

Our attention in *A Perfect Description* is drawn to the fortunate condition of two 'old planters'. The first, George Pelton, arrived in Virginia shortly after the first massacre, in June 1622, as a 'servant': that summer the 'servants' in Virginia – white servants that is – numbered nineteen: fifteen male and four female.[34] Now, after twenty-five years, Pelton has achieved note as a keeper of bees, which give him a

---

[28] Hening, I, 552.

[29] *ibid.*, 146.

[30] *Perfect Description*, 6-7 (see note 13).

[31] *ibid.*, 7-8.

[32] Brydon, *Virginia's Mother Church*, 444. Brydon prints laws relating to the clergy in Virginia 1632-47 as his Appendix V: 426-51.

[33] Pomfret, *Founding the Colonies*, 91.

[34] Kingsbury, *Records*, III, 618, 674.

profit of £30 a year. He also 'makes excellent good Matheglin; a pleasant and strong drink, and it serves him and his family for good liquor'.[35] The second 'old planter' was Captain Samuel Matthews, Esquire, 'a most deserving Common-wealth's-man'.[36] Matthews had arrived in the autumn of 1619 with Lieutenant Jabez Whitaker, both in charge of tenants for the 'college land'. By 1623 he was on the Jamestown Council. And in 1624 he had been appointed one of the Commissioners to report to the Privy Council on the state of the colony.[37] Now:

He hath a fine house, and all things answerable to it. He sows yearly store of hemp and flax, and causes it to be spun. He keeps weavers; and hath a tan house, causes leather to be dressed, hath eight shoemakers employed in their trade. Hath forty negro servants: brings them up to trades in his house. He yearly sows abundance of wheat, barley, etc; the wheat he sells at four shillings the bushel. Kills store of beavers, and sells them to victual the ships when they come thither. Hath abundance of kine; a brave dairy; swine great store; and poultry. He married the daughter of Sir Thomas Hinton. And, in a word, keeps a good house; lives bravely; and a true lover of Virginia.

These were two of the 'new men' who rose in Virginia in the 1620s and 1630s, a class to which Bernard Bailyn has drawn attention:[38] shrewd hard workers, with 'capacity to survive and flourish in frontier settlements' – and a lack of enthusiasm for public office!

There were, true, dangers from foreigners. The formation of the Swedish West India Company in 1638 had meant fifty Swedish colonists on the Delaware, at Fort Christina (near modern Wilmington): 'within the limits of Virginia', only 'two days' journey by land from our plantations'. Moreover, 'the Hollanders have stolen into a river called Hudson's River, in the limits also of Virginia'. (The Dutch founded New Amsterdam in 1625: it became New York in 1664, by which time 'New Netherland' had 8,000 settlers, who bequeathed to America ice skating, Easter eggs, Santa Claus, and words such as Bowery, Spook, Yacht, Cooky, Boss and Dope.) The Dutch have 'vigilant statesmen': thus 'are the English nosed in all places, and out-traded, by the Dutch'. It is well known, after all, that the English 'despise plantations'.[39]

There is the account of the 1644 massacre, the Indian war, the oration of Necotowance: and the assurance that 'now at this present the colony is in good estate'.[40] Much better than New England, which is to be pitied, the country being like Scotland: 'much cold, frost and snow, and their land so barren' – 'it was great pity all those people,

---

[35] *Perfect Description*, 15 (see note 13).

[36] *ibid.*, 14-15.

[37] Kingsbury, *Records*, III, 227; IV, 70, 465.

[38] Bailyn, 'Politics and Social Structure in Virginia', in Smith (ed.), *Seventeenth-Century America*; 94-6.

[39] *Perfect Description*, 9 (see note 13).

[40] *ibid.*, 11-12.

being now about twenty thousand, did not seat themselves at first to the south of Virginia, in a warm and rich country.' And perhaps more fortunate than Old England: the letters from Jamestown had said that

if God please in mercy now to look upon poor England, that it fall not into a second war, nor relapses, but a happy peace settled in their native country: then they in Virginia shall be as happy a people as any under heaven.

In October 1648 Governor Berkeley had been given an armed guard of ten men, because of possible Indian treachery – Necotowance's messengers had 'frequent resort to him, upon pretence of public negociations'; but also because of 'the many dissaffections to the government from a schismatical party of whose intentions our native country of England hath had, and yet hath, too sad experience'.[41]

In the 1650s, adjustment was made to the terms of Necotowance's title: in 1658 the General Assembly at Jamestown noted that he held his kingdom from the Lord Protector, as confirmed by the Lord Protector's Governor.[42] Berkeley did not relinquish the Governorship until March 1652: and he continued to live in Virginia. On 12 March 1652 articles were

agreed on and concluded at James City in Virginia for the surrendering and settling of that plantation under the obedience and government of the Commonwealth of England by the commissioners of the Council of State, by authority of the Parliament of England, and by the Grand Assembly of the Governor, Council and burgesses of that country.[43]

The 'submission and subscription' was said to be a 'voluntary act'; although the three commissioners had brought a 'fleet and force' to Jamestown 'to reduce that colony under the obedience of the Commonwealth'. The use of the Book of Common Prayer was permitted for one further year, 'provided that those things which relate to the kingship, or that government, be not used publicly'; the Governor and Council were not obliged to take an oath to the Commonwealth for one further year; and for one year neither Governor nor Council were to be 'censured for praying for or speaking well of the King' in private. The inhabitants were to take the 'engagement'; but if they refused, they had a whole year to remove themselves from the colony. In fact Virginia in the 1650s was a haven for exiled royalists, including Lees, Randolphs and Masons (a new oligarchy: Virginia's great eighteenth-century names arrived between 1645 and 1665).[44] The new Governor was one of the commissioners, Richard Bennett.

In 1652 Virginia, writes Professor Frank Craven,[45]

---

[41] Hening, I, 354-5. Unless otherwise indicated, the page references from henceforth are to Hening, I.

[42] 453.   [43] 363-8.

[44] Bailyn, in Smith (ed.), *Seventeenth-Century America*, 98.

[45] *Colonies in Transition*, 10.

became in effect a self-governing commonwealth, and so it remained for eight years, with the power residing in the general assembly. Adaptation to commonwealth practices was not difficult for a people who had learned of necessity to manage their affairs through many years of royal neglect.

In 1658, after a 'diligent review of all the acts formerly in force', and an acknowledgment of the difficulties for the magistrates in Virginia because of the 'multiplicity of alterations and repeals', the General Assembly produced 'one body' of Laws: 130 items, running to sixty pages in the reprint in the early nineteenth-century by William Walter Hening.[46] There was, of course, Indian material therein; though perhaps rather less than one might have expected.

Between 1653 and 1658 the General Assembly had had Indian affairs on every agenda: adjustments, in the main, to the Treaty of 1646. By 1653 there were two new counties. And in July 1653 the J.P.s of the two counties were required 'to proportion the Indians inhabiting in the said counties their several tracts of land', and to 'assign them such places and bounds to hunt in as may be convenient, both for the inhabitants and the Indians'. It was also ordered that colonists who had settled on the land of the Pamunkey tribe and the Chickahominy tribe were to be removed.[47] In the Acts of the Assembly for 1654 we read that the settlers in three counties (two of them new: Lancaster and Westmoreland) had complained of 'injuries and insolencies offered and done by the Rappahannock Indians'. The English feared 'an intended war'. The inhabitants were ordered to raise an armed force, and march with interpreters to the Indian village to demand satisfaction, and to report back to the Governor, who would determine whether it was to be war or peace.[48] We learn also in 1654 that many Indians employed in English territory as 'servants' had been given guns; this was to be illegal, if without permission from the county court.[49] In March 1655 there was an extended provision 'for the better securing the peace both of English and Indians'.[50] No Indian visiting English territory was to be killed, unless 'taken in any acts of mischief'. Indians could be 'entertained' on English territory with permission from two J.P.s of the county. And it was confirmed that Indian children, 'by leave of their parents', could live in English families as 'servants': 'for such a term as shall be agreed on by the said parents and master', and the covenant confirmed before two J.P.s. Such 'servants' were to be 'educated and brought up in the Christian religion'. The Assembly of March 1656 noted that the English had been 'often put into great dangers by the invasions of our neighbouring and bordering Indians'. The human reasons for this were acknowledged: 'our extreme pressures on them; and their wanting of something to hazard and lose beside their lives.'[51] The March 1656 Assembly passed three Acts.[52] First: at public expense, any Indian chief whose people killed eight wolves and brought the heads to the English was to be given a cow: 'This will be a step to civilising them, and to make them Christians.' Secondly:

[46] 432-94. [47] 380-2. [48] 389. [49] 391. [50] 410. [51] 394. [52] 395-6.

If the Indians shall bring in any children, as gages of their good and quiet intentions to us and amity with us, then the parents of such children shall choose the persons to whom the care of such children shall be entrusted; and the country, by us their representatives, do engage that we will not use them as slaves: but do their best to bring them up in Christianity, civility, and the knowledge of necessary trades.

The J.P.s of each county were to report on the families under whose 'tuition' the children were placed: and if they do 'really intend the bettering of the children', they were to receive a fee. Thirdly: no land sale or bargain by the Indians was to be valid unless confirmed by the General Assembly at Jamestown. Otherwise it would

put us to a continual necessity of allotting them new lands and possessions; and they will always be in fear of what they hold, not being able to distinguish between our desires to buy, or enforcements to have – in case their grants and sales be desired.

There was a second session of the 1656 Assembly, in December. In the meantime, there had been an unfortunate episode which occasioned bad consciences in Jamestown. Colonel Edward Hill in the summer of 1656 had gone with one hundred men to parley with Indians who had come down beyond the falls of the James. (It seems that they had come to discuss trade.) Hill had been ordered to attack only in self-defence; he blundered, there was a battle, and five Indians were killed. Hill was suspended.[53] At the December General Assembly[54] it was noted that there existed the Act 'that makes killing of Indians lawful that are taken committing trespass or other harm'; the oath of the killer to be taken as proof of the trespass. That was a bad Act: the oath of one man was hardly evidence; the 'harm' might be too slight to merit death; the wording allowed 'to great a latitude'. Indian blood has been shed for 'small account', and the Assembly viewed with 'sad apprehension' the 'wanton and unnecessary shedding of blood' – an 'injustice': 'whereby we may probably be involved in a war for us and our posterity.' The Act was therefore repealed. No Indian was to be killed unless he commit what in an Englishman would be felony; and this was to be proved by the oaths of two witnesses. For lesser harms, 'viewed and valued by two sufficient men', an Indian could be 'corrected; but not to death or maiming'. It is true that there have been frequent Indian mischiefs. To prevent this, it was enacted that

no Indian come within our fenced plantations without a ticket from some person to be nominated on the head of each river where the Indians live. And it shall be then lawful for all Indians in amity to repair to the house of that party; coming without arms, or having his ticket, they may fowl, fish or

[53] Washburn, *Virginia under Charles and Cromwell*, 54-5.
[54] 415.

gather the wild fruits without hinderance of any, provided it be not within any fenced plantation.

Also, the English could trade with the Indians, within the areas allowed by the 1646 treaty:

It shall be lawful for any freeman to repair to the said houses or Indian marts, and to truck with the said Indians, for any commodities not prohibited by the laws of this country. And of debates arising in their bartering, the first in commission in that place to be judge[55] and to distribute equal justice to them both, and his order in the business to be of force both to the English and Indian.

Such was the position when the Assembly of March 1658 came to revise and codify the Laws, of Virginia. The Laws of Virginia had first been revised in 1632, under Harvey. The 1658 Laws confirmed the annual commemorations of the massacres on 22 March and 18 April.[56] They approved the disposal of Indian children to the English 'for education, or instruction in Christian religion, or for learning the English tongue'; but made clear that such a child was to be 'free' when he or she was twenty five.[57] (Indian 'servants' could be male or female; as were 'negroes imported'.)[58] There had been corruptions in this matter of Indian children. Some had been stolen, or fraudulently acquired; some had been bought from other Englishmen. Such 'perfidious dealing' is 'to the great scandal of Christianity and the English nation': it makes 'religion contemptible, and the name of Englishmen odious'.[59]

No one was to provide the Indians, by sale or barter, with arms or ammunition. Anyone informed upon as doing so was to lose his whole estate, half of which was to go to the informer. Nor was an Indian to be lent arms or ammunition: 'It shall be lawful for any person or persons meeting such Indian so furnished to take away either piece, powder or shot.'[60] Indians could be employed to exterminate wolves: provided they were not armed 'with English arms and guns'.[61]

The provisions about land were the most central. Indians were to have 'liberty of all waste and unfenced land for hunting' (except in the English 'reservation' between the James and the York). No grant of Indian land was to be made to any colonist 'until the Indians be first served with the proportion of fifty acres of land for each bowman'. If any English land patent in the Rappahannock region was to be found to be on Indian land, then the colonist was to give up the land, or purchase it from the Indians.[62] The Assembly had received many complaints

touching wrong done to the Indians in taking away their land, and forcing them into such narrow straits and places that they cannot subsist either by

[55] i.e. the senior JP.
[56] 459.   [57] 455-6.   [58] 454.   [59] 481-2.   [60] 441.   [61] 457.   [62] *ibid*.

planting or hunting; and for that it may be feared they may be justly driven to despair, and to attempt some desperate courses.

Many settlers were entrenching on Indian land: and the Assembly held this

contrary to justice, and the true intent of the English plantation in this country: whereby the Indians might by all just and fair ways be reduced to civility and the true worship of God.

Thus any land which the Indians 'hold' or 'claim' or 'desire' is not to be invaded. Englishmen seated on Indian land with Indian consent are safe; but only by way of the county courts is Indian land to be bought. The English on the north side of the Pamunkey (York) river, near the Pamunkey and Chickahominy tribes, must withdraw. No claim is valid which will 'entrench upon the Indians' land to their discontent'. The Indians are to be sympathetically helped if they desire any land which is 'void or untaken up'.[63]

The question of guns and ammunition seems to have caused most concern. Indians sometimes carried their own guns; and the decrees forbidding the English to lend them guns meant that many colonists suspected the Indians unjustly. In March 1659 the Assembly pointed out that it was 'lawful' for the Indians, in their own territory, to carry their own guns.[64] The 'anti-gun lobby' was fighting a losing battle. The beaver trade was flourishing elsewhere in America because settlers relied on the Indian, and supplied him with arms, 'and do thereby draw from us the trade of beaver, to our great loss and their profit'. So the Assembly legislated that as from 1 April 1660, every Englishman could 'freely trade for guns, powder and shot'.[65]

The General Assembly of March 1660 was the last before the restoration of Charles II (May). One small Indian matter had to be cleared up. It appeared that many Englishmen, governed by 'inordinate covetousness' in their trading with the Indians, had sold them more than the Indians could in fact pay for; and had then seized Indian property, or imprisoned them, 'making use of the benefit of our laws, with which the Indians are utterly unacquainted'. From henceforth trading was to be at the risk of the trader; and he would receive no legal help if he trusted the Indians 'with more truck than they are able to pay for'.[66]

The first session of the Virginia Assembly after the Restoration was in October 1660.[67] There had been skirmishes with the Accomack tribe on the east bank of Chesapeake Bay, who complained 'that they are very straitened for want of land, and that the English seat so near them, that they receive very much damage in their corn'. The Governor was to commission two or three just men, and an impartial surveyor, to go to that territory

---

[63] 467-8. [64] 518. [65] 525. [66] 541.
[67] Hening, II, 13-14.

and lay out such a proportion of the land for the said Indians as shall be sufficient for the maintenance, with hunting and fishing excluded. And that the land so laid out to be so secured to the Indians that they have no power to alienate it, or any part of it, hereafter to the English.

Samuel Matthews, who had died as a Colonel, had bought land from the Wicocomico Indians. There was no record of the purchase or of whether it had been acquired 'justly', by 'voluntary' sale. The Indians were to be offered the land at a value of £50. They could choose to accept or reject the offer 'at their free election'. If they rejected it, the land was to be confirmed by patent to Matthews' heirs (then under the care of guardians). Colonel Fantleroy had similarly acquired Indian land 'not according to Act'. The Assembly decided to tell the Indians of the 'care the Assembly take to protect their rights'; and their case was to be argued before the next Assembly, in March 1661. The 'difference between Colonel Fantleroy and the Indians' was then resolved.[68] The Colonel had given the Indians 'some recompense, though not full satisfaction'. But he had cleared the site, and built on it; so it was confirmed to him and his heirs – on condition that he give to the Indians thirty 'matchcoats', including one for the chief, 'handsomely trimmed with copper lace'.

The Assembly of March 1661 decreed that 29 May, the date of the Restoration, be 'annually celebrated as an holy day'; and that 30 January, the date of the execution of Charles I, 'be annually solemnised with fasting and prayers'. After all, in October 1649 the Assembly had attacked those in Virginia who cast 'blemishes of dishonour upon the late most excellent and now undoubtedly sainted King' – people moved by 'malice, schism and faction, in pursuance of some design of innovation' – and decreed that 'what person soever shall by words or speeches endeavour to insinuate any doubt, scruple or question of or concerning the undoubted inherent right of His Majesty that now is to the colony of Virginia' should be indicted for high treason.[69] The Virginians of 1661 naturally deplored the submission of 1652:

Our late surrender and submission to that execrable power that so bloodily massacred the late King Charles I of ever blessed and glorious memory hath made us, by acknowledging them guilty of their crimes, to show our serious and hearty repentance and detestation of that barbarous act.[70]

Sir William Berkeley, now a thorough Virginian, was sent to England to see the King. He was re-confirmed as Governor, a post which he held until his death in 1677 at the age of seventy.

The Assembly had more pressing local matters to consider:

[68] *ibid.*, 36.
[69] Hening, I, 359-60.
[70] Hening, II, 24. The page references in the next five notes are to Hening II.

The frequent intercourse of divers ill-minded, idle and unskilful people with the Indians filleth the people with rumours, disturbs the people of the country, supplieth the Indians with guns and ammunition, and renders the trade (the chief support of our neighbours) and the government far more dangerous than fruitful.

The skin trade, that is. From henceforth no person without a commission from the Governor (only to be given to men of 'known integrity') was to trade with the Indians for beaver, otter, or other furs.[71] There was a petition to be discussed from the Chickahominy tribe, who had asked for certain land, 743 acres, to be confirmed to them. This was done; with the rider that 'no Englishman shall upon any pretence disturb them', or purchase any of it without consent of the Assembly. On the other hand, the claim of a certain Major General to buy 2,000 acres of Chickahominy land was allowed, if the purchase was with their 'consents' – this provision would testify to the 'honour and reputation' of Virginia.[72] Finally, the Chiskiack tribe were to be allowed to 'quietly hold and enjoy the land they are now seated upon; and have the free use of the guns they now have'. This would 'show other Indians how kind we are to such who are obedient to our laws'. Not too difficult a decision, because the Chiskiack were 'a small inconsiderable nation', with 'few guns', who 'cannot prejudice us'. If 'kindly used' they could be of 'great use and benefit' to the colony.[73]

The next Assembly, of March 1662, took up the theme of 1658 and decided upon a further review of 'the whole body of the laws', 'those that are now in force to be brought into one volume'. The result ran to one hundred pages, comprising 140 Acts, to be in force from 1 August 1662. The Assembly

endeavoured in all things, as near as the capacity and constitution of this country would admit, to adhere to those excellent and often refined laws of England, to which we profess and acknowledge all due obedience and reverence.[74]

Indian affairs were dealt with in Act 138,[75] 'Concerning Indians'. This Act was described as 'Articles of Peace between us and the Indians'. The desire was for 'equitable peace'; in face of 'mutual discontents, complaints, jealousies and fears of English and Indians', 'injuries done on both sides, reports and rumours are spread of the hostile intentions of each to other'. There seemed to loom 'an inevitable and destructive war'. The Indians concerned were of course the 'neighbouring' tribes; those 'within our protection' and 'tributary to the English'. If such Indians were attacked by 'strange Indians', 'foreigners', then the English would help: this 'will make them and us have an equal interest in each other's preservation'.

Certain specific points: no one, without a special warrant from the

71 20.   72 34-5; 39.   73 39.   74 42.   75 138-43.

Governor and two of the Jamestown Council, was to take captive an Indian chief. Such action made the issue of peace and war dependent on the whim of an individual colonist. No one was to trade with the Indians unless he had a license, and was a 'commissioned trader'. No one was to 'buy, take or receive' any 'thing or commodity' from any Indian without such authority. At the moment 'many underhand and unlicensed traders do truck and trade with the Indians' – under the pretence that what they get is a *gift* from the Indian. Such a man was now to pay to the Indian three times the value of the goods. And any dispute between a commissioned trader and an Indian was to be settled by the Governor, or by a referee appointed by him.

With license from the Governor, Indians could be 'entertained' on English territory – brought in, for example, as 'servants'; but they must not be held beyond the legal term, nor could they be sold 'for slaves'. But for an Englishman to 'harbour or entertain' an Indian without licence, or an Indian who was in English territory without permission from his chief, was akin to harbouring a runaway; such an Indian could be taken back to Indian land by any other colonist. Apart from 'servants', no Indian was to enter English territory without a badge, a silver or copper plate engraved with the name of his village. Any Indian with no such badge was to be taken before a J.P. and held to ransom, for 'one hundred arm's length of rohanaoke'. Any Englishman who stole a badge from an Indian was to do two hours in the pillory, with a placard stating his offence, and be fined 5,000 pounds of tobacco.

The crucial question, again, was land. The men of 1662 invoked 'the laws formerly in force for surrendering and acknowledging Indians' lands', 'laws prohibiting the purchase of any Indian's land unless acknowledged at General Courts or Assemblies'. The English continued to behave badly in these matters, by being 'corrupt interpreters' of the Virginia laws, by confusing the Indians, and by 'violent intrusions' into Indian land – 'forcing the Indians by way of revenge to kill the cattle and hogs of the English'. It was now made clear again that there existed 'land now justly claimed, or actually possessed' by the Indian: no Indian could sell this land, and no Englishman could buy it. Any such sale, any such purchase, was 'invalid, void and null', 'any acknowledgement, surrender, law or custom used to the contrary notwithstanding'. If complaints are made of Englishmen on Indian land and they 'make no good proof of their title', the English can be removed by the sheriff and their dwellings 'demolished and burnt'. Of course, many Englishmen occupy Indian land by 'colourable right', given in courts or the Assembly; but they, if they are within three miles of an Indian settlement, are to help the Indians to fence their corn fields. Then there are

the poor Indians whom the seating of the English hath forced from their wonted conveniences of oystering, fishing, and gathering tuckahoe, cortenions, or other wild fruits: by which they were wonted for a great part of the year to subsist.

Such Indians can be licensed by two J.P.s to visit 'that country they desire to oyster or gather wild fruit in' – so long as they carry no weapons, and there is a time limit to their visit. During the visit they will be protected:

If any Englishman shall presume to take from the Indians so coming in any of their goods, or shall kill, wound or maim any Indian, he shall suffer as if he had done the same to an Englishman.

Finally, commissioners were to be sent to 'view the present bounds of the English and Indians', and make annual checks, 'for prevention of future encroachments beyond the bounds once fixed'. Further commissioners, with 'parties of horse', were to be sent out in 1662 to visit every Indian village, fixing the bounds, and informing the Indians of the legislation. And men 'of the most integrity' were to see that such things as the provision for assistance in Indian fencing are in fact carried out. The desire of the Assembly, in sum, was to ensure.

that the Indians proprieties of their goods be hereby assured and confirmed to them. And their persons so secured that whoever shall defraud or take away from them their goods, and do hurt and injury to their persons, shall make such satisfaction, and suffer such punishment, as the laws of England or this country do inflict if the same had been done to an Englishman.

It cannot reasonably be denied that the *intention* of the English administration in Jamestown was thoughtful and humane, an attempt – if no more – to ensure that the 'rights of Englishmen' were not restricted to the English settlers in Virginia.

There were in Virginia no equivalents of the organised communities of Christian Indians in New England. In Massachusetts in the 1650s Indian children lived with English families and servants; and some of them went to the township schools (there were two Indians at Boston Grammar School in 1662). And there was the Indian College at Harvard. Adult Indians could have land, as the Massachusetts General Court noted in 1652, 'among the English, according to the custom of the English'.[76] They could (1648) buy land from the English, and thus 'have right to plant'.[77] The Indian could also claim the protection of the law of New England. In 1660 a case was heard before the Quarterly Court of Essex County Massachusetts, of whether an Indian servant girl could be compelled to return to her former Master. Her advocate argued: 'The law is undeniable that the Indian may have the same distribution of justice with ourselves' – for 'the light of the Gospel is beginning to appear amongst them'. (The argument has been discussed recently because of the advocate's assumption that it is otherwise 'amongst the negroes'.)[78]

---

[76] Vaughan, *New England Frontier*, 208.
[77] *Laws and Liberties of Massachusetts*, 1929 ed., 28-9.
[78] Jordan, *White Over Black*, 92.

But John Eliot had the vision from the mid-1640s of separate Indian villages, under English protection and supervision. The first of these was established in the 1650s at Natick, on the Charles River, eighteen miles west of Boston. In 1651 the General Court granted 2,000 acres for use by Indians: the community was to be allowed to choose its own magistrates, and to hear minor cases, both civil and criminal. But what concerned Eliot was the training of the Indians for Church membership. By 1659 some Indians seemed sufficiently prepared. They joined Eliot's own congregation at Roxbury (of which he had been pastor since 1632). In 1660 an Indian church was founded at Natick. In the 1660s a further five 'Praying Towns' were organised in Massachusetts.[79]

In 1689, in *A Brief Relation of the State of New England*, published in London, Increase Mather drew the attention of an English audience to the 'congregations of the converted Indians'.[80] At Natick, Eliot had 'gathered a church of converted Indians'; they had confessed their faith; received baptism; and were solemnly joined together in a church covenant'. By 1689 they had an Indian minister, one of 24 Indian preachers in New England. As a result of King's Philip's War, 1675 (King Philip was Metacom, son of Massasoit) the Congregational Indians of Massachusetts were regrouped into four communities. Mather wrote that in New England as a whole there were in 1689 six churches of baptised Indians, and eighteen assemblies of Indians undergoing instruction, either by the converted Indians, or by the four English clerics able to preach in Algonquian. It seems that by 1675, of the 15,000 Indians in New England about 2,500 (17%) were members of the separate Christian communities – whether baptised, or catechumens.[81] The number was highest in Massachusetts (over 1,000), and next highest in Plymouth Colony. The Christian Indians supported the colonists in the war against the tribes commanded by 'King Philip'.

Mather described the procedure of the Indian Congregations. All the 'congregations of the converted Indians' (that is, as Mather makes clear, both 'those that are in church order' and those under instruction) meet twice every Sunday. Their Indian minister (chosen by them, ordained by two English clerics) begins with prayer, 'without a form, because from the heart'. This over,

the whole congregation of Indians praise God with singing, in which many of them are excelling. After the psalm, he that preaches reads a piece of scripture and expounds it, gathers doctrine from it, proves them by scripture

[79] Kellaway, *New England Company*, ch. 5; Vaughan, *New England Frontier*, chs 10 and 11. A more recent (and more critical) assessment of Eliot and the Praying Towns is Neal Salisbury 'Red Puritans: The "Praying Indians" of Massachusetts Bay and John Eliot', *William and Mary Quarterly*, January 1974 (series 3, Vol. XXXI, no. 1, pp. 27-54).

[80] Force, *Tracts*, IV, no. 11, pp. 14-17.

[81] Vaughan, *New England Frontier*, 303, 293.

and reasons, and infers use from them, after the manner of the English, of
whom they have been taught.

After the manner, indeed, taught by William Perkins in Cambridge in
the 1590s. One is not surprised to be told that many Indian children
know by heart the catechism of 'that famous divine Mr Will. Perkins';
being translated for them, they can 'in their own mother tongue
answer to all the questions in it'.

After King Philip's War, which was as shattering for New England
as the 1622 Massacre had been to Virginia, the Indian communities
were more carefully supervised; commissioners were appointed, for
example, to have a sort of 'guardian' role. The communities never had
the status of townships: they did not send representatives to the
General Courts. And in time their identity was eroded. The colonists
bought land in them, and went to live there. In *Red Man's Land, White
Man's Law: A Study of the Past and Present Status of the American Indian*
(1971), Dr Wilcomb E. Washburn writes:[82]

Eventually all the Indian towns lost their identity as reservations, although
until late in the nineteenth century, Indian villages continued to exist in
Massachusetts. The vagueness and provisional nature of much of the
Massachusetts legislation concerning Indian reservations suggest that the
authorities did not intend the system to be permanent and that they expected
the eventual assimilation of the Indians into white society.

The news of the 1622 massacre on the James had spurred on the
fortification of Plymouth. Similarly, news of the 1675 Indian war in
New England had its impact in Virginia.

In 1676 Nathaniel Bacon, a gentleman farmer who had been a
Fellow Commoner of St Catharine's College, Cambridge, and crossed
to Virginia in 1674, led a rebellion against Governor Berkeley and his
'cabal' of 'grandees'. His manifesto of 1676[83] named nineteen 'wicked
and pernicious counsellors'; including Robert Beverley and Robert
Lee. (Beverley was to write of Bacon:[84] 'He was young, bold, active, of
an inviting aspect, and powerful elocution. In a word, he was every
way qualified to head a giddy and unthinking multitude.') Bacon,
pleading 'the defence of the frontiers' against the 'barbarous enemy',
claimed that under the Berkeley régime the colonists had been
'betrayed'; and 'in a barbarous and shameful manner exposed to the
incursions and murders of the heathen'. Berkeley had 'unjustly
defended and protected' the Indians 'these many years'; he had
ignored the colonists' complaints; supplied the Indians with arms and
ammunition; and made use of them in commerce – in the beaver

[82] Page 46.
[83] Manifesto in Jensen (ed.), *American Colonial Documents*, 581-5. Craven, *Colonies in
Transition*, ch. 4 ('The Indian Neighbour') discusses Bacon's Rebellion, and King
Philip's War. The standard work on King Philip's War is D.E. Leach, *Flintlock and
Tomahawk*, 1958.
[84] *History and Present State of Virginia*, 78.

trade. When the Indians were in 'open hostility', he withdrew English soldiers, after which the Indians committed 'horrid murders and robberies' and then withdrew to 'obscure and remote places'; thus 'emboldened', they became 'not only a difficult, but a very formidable enemy' – who might earlier have been easily destroyed. Such protection of the Indian was unjust. The Indian was too subtle and elusive to incur redress by legal means: he was 'wholly unqualified for the benefit and protection of the law'. All Indians (including 'neighbour Indians') should be 'outlawed'. Bacon accepted the accusation that the rebels wished 'not only to ruin and extirpate all Indians in general, but all manner of trade and commerce with them'.

The manifesto was concerned largely with the 'invasions, murders and robberies' by the 'protected and darling Indians' – our 'honest, quiet neighbours'! Bacon signed it 'by the consent of the people'. And he ended it with a 'Declaration of the People'.

Thus the frontier farmer was the proud enemy of the 'barbarous outlaws', the 'heathen'. And he so spoke forth in order that government by the people might not perish from Virginia.

27

A Light to Lighten the Gentiles, 1662

In 1662 there was printed in London a seventeen-page pamphlet with the title *Virginia's Cure: or an advisive narrative concerning Virginia. Discovering the true ground of that Churches Unhappiness, and the only true remedy*.[1] The text had been presented to the Bishop of London, Gilbert Sheldon, in September 1661; presumably because the Bishop of London was assumed to have jurisdiction over the American colonies: an assumption apparently dating from Laud's tenure of the see, 1628-1633, but to be made effective only by Henry Compton, Bishop from 1675 to 1713.[2] The author was 'R.G.', Roger Green.[3] He had been among those, he tells us, who went to Virginia 'under the late persecutions' of the 'constitution of the Church of England, in her government and public worship'; which public worship, in that 'pleasant and fruitful land', the inhabitants had

the advantage of liberty to use it constantly among them, after the naval force had reduced that colony under the power (but never to the obedience) of the usurpers. Which liberty we could not have enjoyed, had not the people generally expressed a great love to it.

In 'the late times of our Church's persecution' only the people of Virginia

cheerfully and joyfully embraced, encouraged and maintained the orthodox ministers that went over to them, in their public conformity to the Church of England in her doctrine and stated manner of public worship.[4]

Green had been in Jamestown at the time of the Assembly of March 1656, and formed a poor opinion of the burgesses, with their 'private wordly interest':[5]

[1] Force, *Tracts*, III, no.15.

[2] See the introduction by W.W. Manross (1965) to his Calendar of *The Fulham Papers in the Lambeth Palace Library*.

[3] For the identification, Craven, *Colonies in Transition*, 41. Brydon prints extracts from *Virginia's Cure* in *Virginia's Mother Church*, 492-501. Appendix VI of Brydon (452-81) is a compilation of laws relating to the clergy passed in Virginia 1662-1680.

[4] *Virginia's Cure*, 19. Unless otherwise stated, all the references down to note 32 are to *Virginia's Cure*; paging in Force.

[5] 16.

usually such as went over servants thither, and though by time and industry they may have attained competent estates, yet by reason of their poor and mean education they are unskilful in judging of a good estate either of Church or Commonwealth, or of the means of procuring it.

We also learn that he had spent time 'among divers nations' of the Indians.[6]

The author's theme was 'Virginia's disease and misery'. And in especial, 'the deplorable estate and condition of the poor Church in Virginia, which implores your aid'.[7] The fault was the English 'manner of seating themselves in that wilderness'.[8] That is, 'scattered living' in 'scattered habitations':[9] 'planting themselves after such a manner as may disable them to attend' constantly 'upon sacred public ministrations in the House of God'.[10] (Not to mention 'the great danger that many of the Christians are in, of being destroyed by the heathen'.)[11] The Church is 'forlorn': 'scattered in desolate places of that wilderness'.[12] There are fifty parishes in Virginia, he said (in fact there were slightly less):[13] each

extended many miles in length upon the river's side, and usually not above a mile in breadth backward from the river, which is the common stated breadth of every plantation belonging to each particular proprietor.

Not more than ten parishes 'are supplied with ministers'. Many have no church. And where there is a minister

the people meet together weekly but once, upon the Lord's Day; and sometimes not at all, being hindered by extremities of wind and weather. And divers of the more remote families (being discouraged by the length or tediousness of the way, through extremities of heat in summer, frost and snow in winter, and tempestuous weather in both) do very seldom repair there.[14]

There were 48 parishes in Virginia in 1680, served by 35 ministers; and 51 parishes by 1702, with 37 ministers.[15]

There was only one remedy for 'Virginia's malady' – 'reducing her planters into towns'. Thus will Psalm 92 be vindicated (verse 13): 'Those that be planted in the House of the Lord shall flourish in the courts of our God.'[16]

In less theological vein, Robert Beverley was also to point out that even by 1705 the colonists of Virginia 'have not any place of co-habitation among them that may reasonably bear the name of a

---

[6] 8. [7] 7, 8. [8] 4. [9] 3. [10] 5. [11] 8. [12] 16.

[13] W.H. Seiler, 'The Anglican Parish in Virginia', in Smith (ed.), *Seventeenth-Century America*, 129. Seiler's estimate is between 45 and 48. (The footnote says 58: the text makes clear that this is a misprint.)

[13] 16. [14] 4.

[15] Seiler, 128-30.

[16] 15.

town'. (Williamsburg was still in the construction stage.) Beverley gave some explanation of this:[17] The 'advantages of the many rivers, which afforded a commodious road for shipping at every man's door'; the 'liberty of taking up land' – the tradition of private land and 'particular plantations' since 1616; the aspirations of the settlers – 'the ambition each man had of being lord of a vast, though unimproved territory': 'not minding anything but to be masters of great tracts of land, they planted themselves separately on their several plantations.'

The basic reason for the dispersed manner of settlement was the dominance of tobacco. Louis B. Wright has written:[18]

The cultivation of tobacco, which had proved the one profitable commodity, required fresh and fertile land. Soil on which tobacco had grown for several years became so exhausted that it would produce only weak and spindling stalks. Farmers were obliged, therefore, to have sufficient acreages to ensure new ground for their crops. Since the best sites were on the creeks and rivers, where transportation was easy, planters quickly scattered up and down the numerous waterways until they were strung out over most of the tidewater region. Here and there could be seen a cluster of houses, but no towns dotted the country.

For Robert Green it was a 'stated order of Christ' that Christians should be associated not in 'scattered corners' but in 'visible united societies'. Christians must be 'united in societies in towns'. Cities, towns and villages alone allow of the 'public ministry of God's holy word, sacraments and worship'. This ordinance of Christ was violated by the planters of Virginia, being 'the first that ever planted themselves after such a manner':

as might make their due and constant attendance upon the public worship and service of God impossible to them; and consequently disable them to glorify the name and advance the Kingdom of God in the way God hath ordained and commanded.[19]

Thus the planters of Virginia have committed sacrilege. God has been robbed

of that public worship and service which, as a homage due to His great name, He requires to be constantly paid to Him, at the times appointed for it, in the public congregations of His people in His House of Prayer.

And God imposes His penalty: Haggai, Chapter 1, verse 9:

You looked for much, and, lo, it came to little; and when you brought it home, I did blow upon it. Why, saith the Lord of Hosts? Because of mine house that is waste, and ye run every man unto his own house.

[17] Beverley, *History and Present State of Virginia*, 57.

[18] *Colonial Civilisation of North America*, 37. (This is the English title of *The Atlantic Frontier*.)

[19] 13-14.

God laid His curse upon the Jews: Malachi, Chapter 3, verse 9: 'Ye
are cursed with a curse: for ye have robbed me.' The same curse has
been laid upon the Virginia Colony: 'This sacrilege I judge to be the
prime cause of their long languishing condition; for it puts them under
the curse of God.'[20]

Certain steps can be taken. Obviously, towns must be built in each
county. A collection should be held in the churches of Great Britain to
finance 'sending workmen over for the building towns and schools'.
The planters should reside in their town houses, and *visit* their
plantations. On Saturday afternoon, 'by the custom of Virginia,
servants are freed from their ordinary labour': the servants on the
plantations must then come in to town, and remain for Sunday
worship. There must be a 'continual supply of able ministers'. To help
here, Parliament must endow 'Virginia Fellowships' in the Colleges of
Cambridge and Oxford, to be held by clerics for seven years – on
condition that they thereafter serve for seven years in Virginia.[21] The
custom of hiring Virginia clergy for one year only must be replaced by
the colonial clergy being 'firmly instituted and inducted into livings of
stated value'. The parish should pay the travel expenses; and see that
the tithe of tobacco and corn is of the *best* tobacco and corn. Finally, a
Bishop should be sent over, 'so soon as there shall be a city for his
see'.[22]

In the event, there was never to be a Bishop in Colonial America.
The first American Anglican Bishop was Samuel Seabury, born in
Connecticut in 1729, educated at Yale, ordained in London in 1753,
consecrated Bishop of Connecticut and Rhode Island in 1784 in
Aberdeen, and resident at New London, Connecticut until his death
in 1796.[23]

Until these proposals were implemented, times would continue to
be hard in Virginia.[24] 'We have an English proverb: whilst the grass
grows, the seed starves.' And

many poor Christians there may perish for want of their souls' food; where
there is no vision, the people perish, and that is the case of the far greater part
of that colony.

But once the proposals were in force, the Church in Virginia could
show forth

the glory of the communion of saints, in their united holy societies and
assemblies; the constant beauty of their public worship, of their holy
sacrifices of prayers and praises offered in a comely order in their public
congregations.

Thus 'the poor Church whose plants now grow wild in that

[20] 4-5.   [21] 8-10.   [22] 17-18.
[23] See Carl Bridenbaugh, *Mitre and Sceptre*, 1962.
[24] 17.

wilderness' could become 'like a garden enclosed, like a vineyard fenced, and watched like a flock of sheep with their lambs safely folded by night and fed by day'. And when the Virginians meet death, they would be 'transplanted into the enclosed gardens of God' having become 'fruitful and useful trees of righteousness'. Green hoped for such horticultural transformation in the lifetime of Sheldon. (Sheldon became Archbishop of Canterbury in 1663, and died in 1677, the same year as Governor William Berkeley of Virginia.)

Perhaps more important, England will see 'that Prophecy concerning the calling of the Gentiles fulfilled, in those numerous hordes of heathen in Virginia'; the Prophecy of Isaiah 11:6: 'The wolf also shall dwell with the lamb, and the leopard shall lie down with the kid.'

'God's ordinary way of converting heathen' (as distinct from 'the way of converting them by miracles') is to show to them 'the glory of the Lord shining in the gracious lives of Christians'. This point is buttressed by four quotations from Isaiah.[25] First, 60:2-3: 'The Lord shall arise upon thee, and His glory shall be seen upon thee. And the Gentiles shall come to thy light, and kings to the brightness of thy rising.' Secondly, 62:2: 'And the Gentiles shall see thy righteousness, and all kings thy glory.' Thirdly, 61:9: 'And their seed shall be known among the Gentiles, and their offspring among the people: all that see them shall acknowledge them, that they are the seed which the Lord hath blessed.' (What makes the seed known, Green comments, is 'the righteousness, the holiness, the graces shining in the lives of Christians'.) Fourthly, 49:22-23:

Thus saith the Lord God, Behold, I will lift up mine hand to the Gentiles, and set up my standard to the people: and they shall bring thy sons in their arms, and thy daughters shall be carried upon their shoulders. And kings shall be thy nursing fathers, and their queens their nursing mothers.

(In other words, says Green, the Gentiles will 'bring their sons and daughters to be nursed up at the Church's breast'.)

In Virginia, the Church is in peace – not, that is, under persecution: for 'the Christians have the upper hand of the heathen'. St Paul wrote of the 'infidels' in contact with the Church:

If all prophesy, and there come in one that believeth not, or one unlearned, he is convinced of all, he is judged of all: And thus are the secrets of his heart made manifest; and so, falling down on his face, he will worship God, and report that God is in you, of a truth.

St Paul there writes – in I Corinthians 14:24-5 – of heathens 'of the Athenians' temper', says Green, 'inquisitive after what seems new to them'. So it was to happen in Christian history:[26]

---

[25] 12.   [26] 12-13.

when the Christians in their united societies, having the liberty of their public holy assemblies in the house of God, did constantly attend upon the service of God in them, and the heathen coming in among them them and beholding the comely order and beauty of their holy worship, perceiving their unanimity and uniformity in the same faith and worship of the same God, were so convinced of all and judged of all, that the secrets of their heart were made manifest, and they fell down on their faces and worshipped God, and confessed that God was in them of a Truth.

So it could happen in Virginia. And in history, even the 'rigid heathen', who kept their distance from the Churches, were 'allured' by the light of Christian 'good works',

beholding the comely order of the Christians' government, the amiableness of their conversations, the meekness, humility, charity, their righteousness shining as the light, and their just dealing as the noon day.

The Indians, 'rational heathen', can best be influenced by 'the amiableness of Christian graces and virtues'.[27] Words – especially English words – are 'too barren to express the Christian religion by'. Green tells a story about the 'virtuous heathen Emperor Alexander Severus', who, discovering that two of his servants had been converted by the 'learning' and 'eloquent orations' and 'persuasions' of Origen, said that he himself found that 'the humility and charity of the Christian people, which I do hear of, and daily behold with my eyes, do much more move me to believe their Christ is God'. José de Acosta was of the same opinion.[28] After seventeen years among the American Indians, although 'he was of a Church that pleads much for miracles', he concluded that 'the only miracle necessary to the conversion of the heathen is the gracious lives of Christians, agreeable to that Christian faith they profess'.

The lives of the English in Virginia hinder the conversion of the 'poor heathen' there.[29] A great blemish is the 'almost general want of schools' for English children.[30]

This want of schools, as it renders a very numerous generation of Christians' children born in Virginia (who naturally are of beautiful and comely persons, and generally of more ingenious spirits than these in England) unserviceable for any great employment either in church or state, so likewise it obstructs the hopefullest way they have for the conversion of the heathen, which is, by winning the heathen to bring in their children to be taught and instructed in our schools together with the children of the Christians. For as it is the beauty and glory of Christian graces, shining in the lives of Christians, which must make the heathen, that are men, in love with the Christian religion; so it is that love which can only persuade them to bring in their children to be taught and instructed in it.

The English in Virginia, as they are now planted, are 'for the most

[27] 11. [28] 12. [29] 3. [30] 6.

part destitute of the ordinary means of grace'. So 'it is very unlikely that any rational heathen should be persuaded to commit their children to the teaching and education of such Christians whom they shall perceive to work schools of learning'.

What do the Indians see when they enter – as they do 'frequently' – 'the remote dispersed habitations of the Christians'?[31]

They see their families disordered, their children untaught, the public worship and service of the great God they own, neglected. Neglected upon that very day which they hear called the Lord's Day, and to be by the Christians peculiarly set apart for it. Yea, so far neglected that some of the heathen have complained it was the worst of the seven to them, because the servants of the Christians' plantations nearest to them, being then left at liberty, oft spend that day in visiting their Indian towns; to the disquiet of the heathen, but certainly to the great scandal of the Christian religion. And little hopes have the poor heathen of redress, whilst they see that day so far neglected by the Christians, that in many parishes they see no public holy assemblies of our people, no ministers provided for the holy ministrations of such assemblies, no churches erected and consecrated for such public sacred ministrations – or such in such desolate places, and so remote from many of their habitations, that an ingenuous Christian would blush to tell a heathen that they are the houses of the Christians' great God.

What can all this indicate to 'a sober discreet heathen (and there are many such)'? 'I can truly affirm, by what I have learned among many divers nations of those heathen, that it is a sin which those heathen, by the light of nature, do most detest and abhor.'[32] The Christians rob God: but 'will a heathen do it'? The Indian, the natural man, is held up as a reproving image for the Christian.

The 'idea' of the American Indian was fashionable in literary London in the 1660s. In 1664 *The Indian Queen* was performed.[33] The authors were Sir Robert Howard, and his new brother-in-law John Dryden, a graduate of Trinity College Cambridge (B.A. 1654). (The play is remembered today because of the music written by Henry Purcell for a version performed in 1695.) The piece is set in Peru and Mexico; Montezuma appears, as General to the Inca of Peru – at the end he is revealed as rightful heir to the throne of Mexico. The final Act opens in the Peruvian Temple of the Sun, 'all of gold', where stand 'four priests, in habits of white and red feathers, attending by a bloody altar, as ready for sacrifice'. The play begins as 'the music plays a soft air': 'the curtain rises slowly, and discovers an Indian boy and girl sleeping under two plantain trees.' The exotic, the savage, the innocent; the same combination, really, as had been provided for the Court in 1614 by George Chapman and Inigo Jones, with their *Memorable Mask* of 'Virgineans', enacted by members of the Middle

[31] 7. [32] 8.
[33] In vol.8 of the University of California Press Dryden, 1962.

Temple and Lincoln's Inn.[34] But now the mixture was for the general public.

The Indian Queen was printed in 1665, the year in which a sequel was performed, wholly written by Dryden. This was *The Indian Emperour, or, the Conquest of Mexico by the Spaniards.*[35] The Emperor is Montezuma, and the action passes twenty years after his coronation. By Scene 2 of Act V Montezuma is being tortured on the rack, in the presence of an 'Indian High Priest' and a 'Christian Priest' ('I must by force convert him on the rack'). The priests fall to argument about their religions. Montezuma philosophises:

> In seeking happinesse, you both agree,
> But in the search, the paths soe diff'rent bee,
> That all Religions with each other Fight,
> While only one can lead Us in the right.
> But till that one hath some more certaine marke,
> Poor humane kind must wander in the darke.

The Christian Priest urges him to accept the 'unerring' Pope. Montezuma is scornful: 'The light of Nature should I thus betray.' Cortez (a sympathetic character) enters, releases Montezuma, kneels to him, and weeps. Montezuma stabs himself and dies. All to the chagrin of the villains: the Priests – and Pizarro. Dryden (he pointed out in the 'Dedication')[36] had taken 'all the liberty of a poet' to 'add, alter or diminish, as I thought might best conduce to the beautifying of my work; it being not the business of a poet to represent historical truth, but probability'. But, 'as near as I could', he 'traced the native simplicity and ignorance of the Indians, in relation to European customs'. And he asked his public that when Montezuma

shall relate his sufferings, you will consider him as an *Indian* Prince, and not expect any other eloquence from his simplicity than what his griefs have furnished him withal. His story is, perhaps, the greatest which was ever represented in a poem of this nature; the action of it including the discovery and conquest of a New World.

Montezuma is the absolute, free Hero beloved of Dryden (and of his patron, the later James II). The essential Dryden Hero appeared in 1669, in *The Conquest of Granada*: Almanzor, the Moorish warrior. When published in 1672, the play was dedicated to James. Almanzor, wrote Dryden in the 'Dedication', is 'a hero, I confess, not absolutely perfect, but of an excessive and over-boiling courage', having 'a roughness of character, impatient of injuries, and a confidence of

[34] See above, p.274-5.

[35] In vol.9 of the California Dryden, 1966, edited by John Loftis. There is an article on Dryden's sources, by Dougald MacMillan, in *The Huntington Library Quarterly*, XIII, 4 (August 1950), 353-70; the main sources were *Purchas His Pilgrimes*, and D'Avenant's *The Cruelty of the Spaniards*.

[36] California Dryden, 9, pp.25-7.

himself almost approaching to an arrogance: But these errors are incident only to great spirits'.[37]

In the first scene, Almanzor upbraids the King of Granada, who has accused him of treachery:[38]

> Obeyed as sovereign by thy subjects be,
> But know, that I alone am king of me.
> I am as free as nature first made man,
> Ere the base laws of servitude began,
> When wild in woods the noble savage ran.

The Noble Savage: The first use of the phrase in English.

Oliver Cromwell's capture of Jamaica was confirmed by Charles II; and Restoration interest in the Indians of Spanish America sprang from Cromwell's exploits in the Indies. Cromwell decided in 1654 to attack the Spanish colonies in America; in December thirty-eight ships left Portsmouth, with over 2,000 troops. Edward Winslow was on board: one of the three Civil Commissioners appointed by Cromwell to advise the Commanders (at a salary of £1,000 p.a.).

In April 1655 the English landed on Hispaniola: and were routed. In May they landed on Jamaica. Mismanagement and disease almost ended this rather desperate adventure; Winslow died in May; but reinforcements arrived in January 1655, and Cromwell began his propaganda campaign to attract colonists from the 'wilderness' of Massachusetts to the Promised Land in Jamaica (less than 300 were tempted). The colony, however, survived.

In 1658 the impresario Sir William D'Avenant (1606-1668) presented at his theatre in Drury Lane an entertainment relevant to the 'Western Design':

The cruelty of the Spaniards in Peru; exprest by Instrumentall and vocall Musick, and by Art of Perspective in Scenes, etc. Represented daily at the Cockpit in Drury Lane, at three afternoon punctually.

('Scenes': scenery.) This was the second such piece D'Avenant had presented at the Cockpit. The first had been *The Siege of Rhodes* in the autumn of 1656; with instrumental music by Charles Coleman and George Hudson, and vocal music by Henry Cook, Henry Lawes and Matthew Locke. This was the first English 'opera'. *The Cruelty of the Spaniards* was the second; and *The History of Sir Francis Drake*, in 1659, the third. Dryden explained the necessity for the new medium in a passage about D'Avenant in the preface to *The Conquest of Granada*:

It being forbidden him in the rebellious times to act tragedies and comedies, because they contained some matter of scandal to those good people who

[37] *Works* of Dryden, edited Walter Scott, revised George Saintsbury, Edinburgh, vol.4, 1883, 10.
[38] *ibid.*, p.43.

could more easily dispossess their lawful sovereign than endure a wanton jest, he was forced to turn his thoughts another way; and to introduce the examples of moral virtue writ in verse, and performed in recitative music. The original of this music, and of the scenes which adorned his work, he had from the Italian operas.

The first Italian opera was Monteverdi's *Orfeo*, 1609. D'Avenant never visited Italy; unlike Milton – who had probably met Monteverdi in the late 1630s (some scholars think *Paradise Lost* owes something to the *stile recitativo*). But he had been to Paris, and had been writing plays and masques since 1630 (sometimes in collaboration with Inigo Jones). The music for his three 'operas' has not survived; and the composers of *Drake* and *The Cruelty of the Spaniards* are not known (though one may guess that D'Avenant used the same people as for *The Siege of Rhodes*).[39]

   The Cruelty of the Spaniards in Peru is in six scenes.[40] There is a new décor (a novelty in a public theatre) for each scene; and each scene takes the basic form of an instrumental prelude, a speech by the High Priest (in recitative, presumably) and a chorus. The intention, wrote D'Avenant when the text was printed in 1658, was 'first to represent the happy condition of the people of Peru anciently, when their inclinations were governed by Nature'; then their organisation by the Incas, the dissension under the last Inca, and the arrival of the Spaniards; and 'towards the conclusion it infers the voyages of the English thither, and the amity of the natives towards them' – hoping 'to be freed from the yoke of the Spaniards'. The piece begins with 'instrumental music and a symphony, being a wild air suitable to the region'. The décor for the first scene depicts a landscape of the Indies: distant hills with parched peaks, river banks of shining sand, pine and cocoa trees, with monkeys, apes and parrots on the boughs, distant valleys of sugar cane. Various Indians are discovered; some 'in feathered habits and bonnets, carrying in Indian baskets ingots of gold and wedges of silver', some 'in their natural sports of hunting and fishing'. Enter the High Priest to tell of the golden age before cities and forts. The chorus takes up the theme of the poor, naked, innocent world:

   We danced and we sung,
   And looked ever young,
   And from restraints were free,
   As waves and winds at sea.

Before the second scene an Allemande and a Courante are played.

---

[39] Percy A. Scholes, *The Puritans and Music in England and New England*, 1934, Ch.8, 'Opera in Puritan England'. Also (though there is only a passing mention of *The Cruelty of the Spaniards*) E.J. Dent, *Foundations of English Opera: a Study of Musical Drama in England during the Seventeenth Century*, 1928.

[40] Text, and D'Avenant's comments, in D'Avenant's *Dramatic Works*, IV, Edinburgh, 1873, pp.76-94.

The Priest and Chorus tell of the Incas, in front of scenery showing the approaching Spanish fleet. Scene 3 is introduced by 'a symphony consisting of four tunes': the backcloth is of opposing Indian armies; the Priest laments the end of peace; and after the Chorus there is a martial dance for four Indians, symbolising civil war. The décor for scene four shows a small Spanish force vanquishing the Indian armies; after another symphony of four 'tunes' the Priest and the Chorus explain that the Spaniards were thought to be gods; and two Spaniards dance a Saraband of victory. Scene 5 is doleful. The setting is a prison, the introductory music a Pavane; an Indian Prince is basted on a spit; and Indians and Englishmen are on the rack. The cruelty of the Spaniards is the theme of the Speech and Chorus; and the scene ends with the beating of three Indians with truncheons, to a 'mournful air'. In Scene 6 appear the liberating English, after a symphony. English soldiers enter in red coats; the Priest prophesies the coming of the English. And (after a dance of apes and baboons) the Chorus proclaim that

> ... the English lion now
> Does still victorious grow

– no need to fear 'the Spanish eagle darkly hovering here'. The Indians and English shake hands 'in sign of their future amity'; and there is a concluding dance for one dejected Spaniard, three Indians, and three English redcoats.

D'Avenant explains that

> imaginary English forces may seem improper, because the English had made no discovery of Peru in the time of the Spaniards' first invasion there; but yet in poetical representations of this nature it may pass, as a vision discerned by the Priest of the Sun.

In October 1655 a committee of the Protector's Council had issued a lengthy 'Declaration', in both Latin and English, in defence of war with Spain in the Indies: *A Declaration of His Highness, by the Advice of His Council; setting forth, on the behalf of this Commonwealth, the Justice of their Cause against Spain*. It became traditional to attribute the Latin text (and sometimes the English version also) to Milton. In 1937 it was printed in Volume XIII of the Columbia University Press complete Milton.[41] It now seems more likely that the authors were the committee of the Council. Milton, as Secretary for Foreign Tongues, was among those who prepared Latin letters; but he had assistants (including his nephew, godson and pupil, John Phillips, 1631-1706).

[41] pp.509-63 (Latin and English versions). Subsequent page references are to this edition. The Yale edition of Milton's prose does not accept Milton's authorship, and the 'Declaration' was not printed in the relevant volume, Vol.5, part 2, 1971; the matter is discussed, 711-12.

He may very well have helped with the actual wording of the two texts, no more.

This defence of 'the late expedition and undertaking against the Spaniards in the West Indies'[42] elaborates upon the Necessity, Honour and Justice of the war. The 'transactions between England and Spain' are sketched since 'the Reformation of Religion, and the Discovery of the West Indies; which two great Revolutions (*res maximae*), happening near about the same time, did very much alter the State of Affairs in the World.'[43] The 1588 Armada still rankles. Spanish affronts to the English colonial ventures in America are listed, from 1605; the use of 'the bloody Spanish Inquisition'[44] in America is deplored, and the 'imaginary title' given to America by the Pope undermined![45]

The best title that any can have to what they possess in those parts of America, is plantation and possession, where there were no inhabitants; or where there were any, by their consent, or at least in such waste and desolate parts of their countries as they are not able in any measure to plant and possess. God having made the world for the use of men, and ordained them to replenish the same.

Upon these grounds, the Spaniards have 'little rights' to America. They have proceeded 'contrary to the consents and out of the bowels of the first inhabitants, in whose blood they have founded their Empire (*imperium*)'. They have 'made great islands and whole countries void of inhabitants'; 'rooted out all the natives'. Thus the English have 'a very clear title' to the Spanish plantations; especially to 'divers islands' which are 'unpeopled', either because they never had inhabitants or because the Spaniards exterminated them, and then left. Such deserted islands 'rightfully accrue to the occupiers and possessors thereof': by the Law of Nature and the Law of Nations.

Most important, the English come to the West Indies as 'avengers' of the 'blood and wrongs' of the Indian;[46] to extract 'just revenge' for blood 'so unjustly, so unhumanely, and so cruelly spilt'.[47]

God hath made of one blood all nations of men, for to dwell on all the face of the earth, and hath determined the times before appointed, and the bounds of their habitation. And certainly, at one time or another, by some hand or other, God will have an accompt of the innocent blood of so many millions of Indians so barbarously butchered by the Spaniards, and the wrong and injustice that hath been done unto them.

The 'Declaration' was approved for publication on 26 October 1655. In 1656 there was published in London *The Tears of the Indians: being an historical account of the cruel massacres and slaughters of above 20 millions of innocent people committed by the Spaniards*. This was a translation by John Phillips of Las Casas' *Brevissima relacion de la destruycion de las Indias*.

[42] 563. [43] 517. [44] 559. [45] 555. [46] *ibid*. [47] 517.

Epilogue
Crusoe's Colony, 1659-1686

On 30 September 1659 Robinson Crusoe found himself the sole inhabitant of an island off the gulf of the Orinoco. Aged twenty-eight, he had been for two years a planter in Brazil; but had set sail at the beginning of September in a Portuguese vessel bound for Africa, where he was to be a manager of the slave trade between Guinea and Brazil. The vessel was driven far off course by two hurricanes. And 'Bob' was 'cast on this dreadful place, out of the reach of human kind, out of all hope of relief, or prospect of redemption'.[1] He was 'reduced to a mere state of nature'.[2] It seemed a 'barren island' of 'mere desolation'.[3] He contrived to salvage many things from the wreck; including three English Bibles, two or three 'Popish prayer books',[4] and a 'perspective glass' – through which, on a clear day, he could see what we now know to be the coastlines of Trinidad, Venezuela and Guiana. He did not leave the island until September 1686.

He had no human companionship until 1683, when he rescued an Indian, himself of a cannibal tribe, who had been brought to the island by some of his people to be ceremonially killed and eaten. The Indian 'set my foot upon his head', 'in token of swearing to be my slave for ever'.[5] Crusoe called the Indian 'Friday'.

Crusoe had first come across cannibal remains in 1676. The sight occasioned reflections about 'such a pitch of inhuman, hellish brutality, and the horror of the degeneracy of human nature'.[6] He had thoughts of 'revenge':[7] of shooting cannibals he might encounter in the future on the island – which was 'my own mere property', over which he was 'absolute lord and lawgiver', with 'undouted right of dominion'.[8] But the instinct, he came to feel, was thoughtless:[9] 'fired by the horror I conceived at the unnatural custom of that people' – left by God (in 'His wise disposition of the world') with 'no other guide than that of their own abominable and vitiated passions'. There came 'cooler and calmer thoughts'.

How do I know what God Himself judges in this particular case? It is certain

---

[1] All page references to the World's Classics edition of *Robinson Crusoe*. 113. For Defoe and the 'state of mere Nature', Maximillian E. Novak, 'The Wild Man Comes to Tea', in Dudley and Novak (ed.), *Wild Man Within*, 1972.
[2] 150. [3] 44. [4] 81. [5] 261. [6] 211. [7] 217 [8] 310. [9] 218-20.

these people either do not commit this as a crime; it is not against their own consciences' reproving, or their light reproaching them. They do not know it to be an offence, and then commit it in defiance of Divine justice, as we do in almost all the sins we commit. They think it no more a crime to kill a captive taken in war, than we do to kill an ox; nor to eat human flesh, than we do to eat mutton.

The cannibals are no more murderers than

those Christians were murderers who often put to death the prisoners taken in battle; or, more frequently, upon many occasions, put whole troops of men to the sword, without giving quarter, though they threw down their arms and submitted.

And what authority had Crusoe 'to pretend to be judge and executioner upon these men as criminals, whom Heaven had thought fit, for so many ages, to suffer, unpunished, to go on'? They 'had done me no injury'; they had 'no design upon me'. It could not be 'just' to exterminate them; except in self-defence. To attack them

would justify the conduct of the Spaniards in all their barbarities practised in America, and where they destroyed millions of these people; who, however they were idolaters and barbarians, and had several bloody and barbarous rites in their customs, such as sacrificing human bodies to their idols, were yet, as to the Spaniards, very innocent people; and that the rooting them out of the country is spoken of with the utmost abhorrence and detestation by even the Spaniards themselves at this time, and by all other Christian nations of Europe, as a mere butchery, a bloody and unnatural piece of cruelty, unjustifiable either to God or man.

'These considerations really put me to a pause, and to a kind of full stop.'

Friday talked of white men who 'had killed much mans'. 'I understand he meant the Spaniards, whose cruelties in America had been spread over the whole countries, and were remembered by all the nations from father to son.'[10] That was one bond between Friday and Crusoe, who knew that in New Spain 'an Englishman was certain to be made a sacrifice': 'I had rather be delivered up to the savages, and be devoured alive, than fall into the merciless claws of the priests, and be carried into the Inquisition.'[11] At the very first, Friday had still 'a hankering stomach after some of the flesh, and was still a cannibal in his nature'. He was also 'stark naked'. The cannibal trait withered away; Crusoe clothed him 'tolerably well'; and he became a true servant. No man had

a more faithful, loving, sincere servant than Friday was to me; without passions, sullenness, or designs, perfectly obliged and engaged; his very affections were tied to me, like those of a child to a father.[12]

[10] 277. [11] 314-15. [12] 267-8.

(Friday was twenty-six, Crusoe fifty-two.) They remained together on the island for three years.

I had a singular satisfaction in the fellow himself. His simple, unfeigned honesty appeared to me more and more every day, and I began really to love the creature; and, on his side, I believe he loved me more than it was possible for him ever to love anything before.[13]

The talk between them was such 'as made the three years which we lived there together perfectly and completely happy'.[14]

Friday was 'a comely, handsome fellow, perfectly well made, with straight limbs; not too large, tall, and well shaped'.[15]

He had a very good countenance, not a fierce and surly aspect, but seemed to have something very manly in his face; and yet he had all the sweetness and softness of a European in his countenance too, especially when he smiled. His hair was long and black, not curled like wool; his forehead very high and large; and a great vivacity and sparkling sharpness in his eyes. The colour of his skin was not quite black, but very tawny; and yet not of an ugly, yellow, nauseous tawny, as the Brazilians and Virginians, and other natives of America are, but of a bright kind of a dun olive colour, that had in it something very agreeable, though not easy to describe. His face was round and plump; his nose small, not flat like the negroes; a very good mouth, thin lips, and his fine teeth well set, and white as ivory.

Crusoe knew about negroes, 'merciless savages of human kind';[16] his first two voyages, after he had left York at the age of nineteen to go to sea, had been to Guinea.

Friday was 'merry', 'diligent', and 'the aptest scholar that ever was'. The Biblically pious Crusoe mused on the ways of Providence to the Indians:[17]

He has bestowed upon them the same powers, the same reason, the same affections, the same sentiments of kindness and obligation, the same passions and resentments of wrongs, the same sense of gratitude, sincerity, fidelity, and all the capacities of doing good, and receiving good, that He has given to us; and that when He pleases to offer to them occasions of exerting these, they are as ready, nay, more ready to apply them to the right uses for which they were bestowed than we are.

Such reflections made Crusoe 'very melancholy sometimes'. How 'mean a use' Christians make of these gifts – even though they have

---

[13] 274. [14] 283.

[15] 264. Compare Mrs Aphra Behn's negro hero (a prince) in *Oroonoko*, 1688. Oroonoko's face was not of 'brown rusty black', but of 'perfect ebony, or polished jet'; his nose 'rising and Roman, instead of African and flat'; his finely shaped mouth 'far from those great turn'd lips, which are so natural to the rest of the negroes'. Excepting his colour, 'there could be nothing in nature more beautiful, agreeable and handsome'. Jordan, *White Over Black*, 27-8.

[16] 28. [17] 269-70.

the Spirit and Word of God added to their understanding! Why has it pleased God

to hide the like saving knowledge from so many millions of souls, who, if I might judge by this poor savage, would make a much better use of it than we did?

Such thoughts led Crusoe 'too far to invade the sovereignty of Providence, and as it were arraign the justice of.so arbitrary a disposition of things, that should hide that light from some, and reveal it to others'. But God is 'infinitely holy and just'; if the Indians are 'sentenced to absence from Himself', it is surely

on account of sinning against that light, which, as the Scripture says, was a law to themselves, and by such rules as their consciences would acknowledge to be just.

We are back with Chapter 2 of Paul's Epistle to the Romans.

Crusoe attempted to note details of Friday's native religion.[18] The Creator was 'one old Benamuckee, that lived beyond all'. He is 'very old, much older, he said, than the sea or the land, than the moon or the stars'. Dead Indians 'all went to Benamuckee'. He lives 'but a little way off'. Certain Indians 'went up to the great mountains where he dwelt, to speak to him'. The young men never went:

None went thither but the old men, whom he called their Oowokakee, that is, as I made him explain it to me, their religious, or clergy; and that they went to say O (so he called saying prayers), and then came back, and told them what Benamuckee said.

Thus it was clear to Crusoe that

there is priestcraft even amongst the most blinded, ignorant pagans in the world; and the policy of making a secret religion in order to preserve the veneration of the people to the clergy is not only to be found in the Roman, but perhaps among all religions in the world, even among the most brutish and barbarous savages.

He told Friday that 'their god Benamuckee was a cheat'; and the sayings of the old men 'much more so'. He instructed him in true Protestant knowledge; and Friday

listened with great attention, and received with pleasure the notion of Jesus Christ being sent to redeem us, and of the manner of making our prayers to God, and His being able to hear us, even into heaven. He told me one day that if our God could hear us up beyond the sun, He must needs be a greater God than their Benamuckee.

[18] 278-9.

Crusoe was less successful in explaining the power of the devil. If 'God much strong', said Friday, 'why God no kill the devil, so make him no more do wicked?'[19] However, Friday became a 'Protestant'.[20] On the island they had 'the Word of God to read, and no farther off from His Spirit to instruct than if we had been in England'. The doctrine of salvation is 'plainly' laid down in the Bible; 'bare reading' suffices. The two had no use for 'disputed points in religion'. Thus 'plain instruction' served to enlighten Friday, 'bringing him to be such a Christian, as I have known few equal to him in my life' – 'a good Christian, a much better than I'.

In the autumn of 1686, a group of twenty-one cannibals landed, with three prisoners destined for the cooking pot. (This was shortly before Crusoe was picked up, and returned to Europe; taking 'my man Friday'[21] with him.) This occasioned a further debate about the treatment of cannibals.[22] Crusoe wondered

what occasion, much less what necessity, I was in to go and dip my hands in blood, to attack people who had neither done or intended me any wrong; who, as to me, were innocent, and whose barbarous customs were their own disaster; being in them a token indeed of God's having left them, with the other nations of that part of the world, to such stupidity, and to such inhuman courses; but did not call me to take upon me to be a judge of their actions, much less an excecutioner of His justice.

It might be lawful for Friday to attack: he was 'a declared enemy, and in a state of war with those very particular people'. Crusoe determined merely to 'observe their barbarous feast'; and not to 'meddle' – 'unless something offered that was more a call to me than yet I knew of.'

The call came. One of the prisoners was 'a white man': a Spaniard. The muskets and the fowling-piece were gathered up.[23] ' "Are you ready, Friday?", said I. "Let fly, then", say I, "in the name of God!" '

Crusoe and Friday arrived in England on 11 June 1687. In April 1719 was published *The Life and Strange Adventures of Robinson Crusoe, of York: Mariner. Written by Himself*; but with a brief preface by the 'editor', commending this 'just history of fact'.

[19] 280. [20] 283-5. [21] 387. [22] 299. [23] 301.

BIBLIOGRAPHY

Note: This is not intended to be a comprehensive bibliography of the subject. The aim is merely to give full details of the books cited in the text, in the editions I have used.

1. *Printed Primary Works*

Abbot, George. *Briefe Description of the Whole Worlde*, London, 1599 (Facsimile, Amsterdam and New York, 1970), 1605.

Arber, Edward (ed.). *The first Three English books on America, 1511-55*, Birmingham, 1885.

Augustine, St. *On Christian Doctrine*. In *Works*, ed. M. Dods, IX, (translator J.F. Shaw), Edinburgh, 1873.

Barbour, Philip L. (ed.). *The Jamestown Voyages under the First Charter, 1606-1609*, 2 vols; Hakluyt Society, series 2, nos. 136-7, Cambridge, 1969.

Barlow, Arthur. 'Discourse', written 1585. In Hakluyt, *Principall Navigations*; Quinn, *Roanoke Voyages*; Quinn, *Virginia Voyages*.

Bemiss, Samuel M. (ed.). *The Three Charters of the Virginia Company of London, with Seven Related Documents, 1606-21*, Jamestown Anniversary Booklet, Williamsburg, 1957.

Benson, George. *A Sermon preached at Paules Crosse the Seaventh of May MDCIX*, London, 1609.

Bernard, Richard. *The seaven golden candlestickes*, London, 1621. *Christian see to thy conscience*, London, 1631.

Beverley, Robert. *The History and Present State of Virginia*, 1705; ed. L.B. Wright, Chapel Hill, N.C., 1947.

Bradford, William. *History of Plymouth Plantation*, ed. S.E. Morison, New York, 1952.

Brereton, John. *A Briefe and True Relation of the Discoverie of the North Part of Virginia*, London, 1602. Facsimile, Amsterdam and New York, 1973.

Brerewood, Edward. *Enquiries touching the diversity of languages, and religions*, London, 1614.

Brinsley, John. *A Consolation for our Grammar Schooles*, London, 1622. Facsimile, Amsterdam and New York, 1969. Facsimile, with essay by T.C. Pollock, New York, 1943.

Brown, Alexander (ed.). *The Genesis of the United States. Being a Series of Historical Manuscripts ...*, 2 vols, London, 1890.

Chapman, George. *Eastward Hoe*, 1605; ed. J.H. Harris, New Haven, 1926. *The Memorable Maske ... of 15 of February 1613* (1613/14), London, 1614.

Chronicles of the Pilgrim Fathers. Everyman Library, introduction by John Masefield, London, 1910.

Colet, John. Ed. J.H. Lupton: *Lectures on Romans*, London, 1873; *Lectures on I Corinthians*, London, 1874; *Letters on the Mosaic Account of the Creation ...*, London, 1876.

Columbus, Christopher. *Select Documents illustrating the four voyages of Columbus*, tr. and ed. Cecil Jane. Volume I, Hakluyt Society, series 2, no.81. London, 1930. *The Journal of Christopher Columbus*, tr. Cecil Jane, ed. L.A. Vigneras, London, 1960, 1968. *The Four Voyages of Christopher Columbus*, tr. J.M. Cohen, Penguin Classics, Harmondsworth, 1969.

Constitutions and Canons Ecclesiastical, 1604, ed. J.V. Bullard. London and Milwaukee, 1934.

Copland, Patrick. *Virginias God be Thanked*, London, 1622.

Cortés, Hernando. *Letters from Mexico*, tr. A.R. Pagden. New York, 1971.

Court and Times of James I. Letters, transcribed by Thomas Birch; edited by R.F. Williams, 2 vols, London, 1849.

Crakanthorpe, Richard. *A Sermon at the Solemnizing of the Happie Inauguration of our most gracious and religious Soveraigne ... preached at Paules Crosse, the 24 of March last*, London, 1609. *A Sermon of Predestination, preached at Saint Maries in Oxford*, London, 1620.

Cranmer, Thomas. *Miscellaneous Writings and Letters*, ed. J.E. Cox, Parker Society, Cambridge, 1846.

Crashaw, William. *A New-yeeres Gift to Virginea (A Sermon preached in London before the right honorable the Lord Lawarre ...)* London, 1610.

Crèvecoeur, Hector St. John de. *Letters from an American Farmer*, ed. W.B. Blake, Everyman Library, London, 1912.

Cushman, Robert. *Sermon preached in Plimmoth in New England*, London, 1622.

Daniel, Samuel. *Complete Works*, ed. A.B. Grosart, 5 vols, Blackburn, Lancs., 1885-96; New York, 1963.

Davenant, Sir William. *The cruelty of the Spaniards in Peru*, London, 1658. In his *Dramatic Works*, ed. J. Maidment and W.H. Logan, Vol.IV, Edinburgh, 1873.

Davis, R.B. (ed.). *William Fitzhugh and His Chesapeake World, 1676-1701: the Fitzhugh Letters and other Documents*, Chapel Hill, N.C., 1963.

Dee, John. 'Mathematicall Preface' to *The Elements of Geometrie* by Euclid, tr. Henry Billingsley, London, 1570.

Defoe, Daniel. *Robinson Crusoe*, World's Classics, London.

D'Ewes, Sir Simonds. *The journals of all the parliaments during the reign of Queen Elizabeth*, London, 1693.

Donne, John. *Ignatius His Conclave*, ed. T.S. Healy, Oxford, 1969. *Sermons*, ed. G.R. Potter and E.M. Simpson, Berkeley, Cal., Vol.IV, 1953.

Drake, Francis. *The World Encompassed*, London, 1628. Facsimile, Amsterdam and New York, 1969.

Dryden, John and Sir Robert Howard. *The Indian Queen*, London, 1665. In Dryden, *Works*, Berkeley, Cal., Vol.VIII, ed. J.H. Smith and D. MacMillan, 1962.

Dryden, John. *The Indian Emperour, or, the Conquest of Mexico by the Spaniards*, London, 1667. In *Works*, Berkeley, Cal., Vol.IX, ed. J. Loftis, 1966. *The Conquest of Granada*, London, 1672.

Eburne, Richard. *A Plain Pathway to Plantations*, 1624; ed. L.B. Wright, Ithaca, N.Y., 1962.

Eden, Richard (tr.). *A treatyse of the newe India*, London, 1553. *The Decades of the newe worlde*, London, 1555. Both in Arber (see Arber; see also Martyr, Gómara, Oviedo).

Erasmus, Desiderius. *A playne and godly esposytion or declaration of the commune Creede*, London, 1534. M.M. Phillips, ed. and tr., *The 'Adages' of Erasmus: A Study with Translations*, Cambridge, 1964. *Colloquies*, tr. C.R. Thompson, Chicago, 1965. *The Education of a Christian Prince*, tr. L.K. Born, New York, 1936. *Praise of Folly*, tr. Betty Radice, notes by A.H.T. Levi, Penguin Classics, Harmondsworth, 1971. J.C. Olin, ed., *Christian Humanism and the Reformation: Desiderius Erasmus, Selected Writings*, Harper Torchbook, New York, 1965. H.J. Hillerbrand, ed., *Erasmus and His Age: Selected Letters of Desiderius Erasmus*, Harper Torchbook, New York, 1970.

Fernandéz de Oviedo, Gonzalo. See 'Oviedo'.

Florio, John. *A shorte and briefe narration of the two Navigations and Discoveries to the Northweast partes called Newe Fraunce*, London, 1580. Facsimile reprint in Quinn, *Richard Hakluyt, Editor*, Amsterdam, 1967.

Force, Peter (ed.) *Tracts: and other papers relating principally to the origin, settlement and progress of the colonies in North America from the discovery of the country to 1776*, 4 vols, Washington, D.C., 1836-47. Reprint, New York, 1947.

Foxe, John. *Acts and Monuments*, ed. G. Townshend, 8 vols, London, 1843-9.

Gerard, John. *The herball or generall historie of plantes*, London, 1597.

Gilbert, Sir Humphrey. *A discourse of a Discoverie for a new Passage to Cataia*, London, 1576. Facsimile, Amsterdam and New York, 1968. In Quinn, *Gilbert Voyages*.

Gómara, Francisco de López de. *Historia General de las Indias*, 1552. Partly translated in 1555: see 'Eden'.

Gray, Robert. *A Good Speed to Virginia*, London, 1609. Facsimile, Amsterdam and New York, 1970. Ed. W.F. Craven, New York, 1937.

Green, Roger. *Virginias Cure*, London, 1662. Force, *Tracts*, III, 15.

Hakluyt, Richard. *Divers Voyages touching the discoverie of America*, London, 1582. Facsimile reprint in Quinn, ed., *Richard Hakluyt, Editor*, Amsterdam, 1967. Ed. J.W. Jones, Hakluyt Society, series 1, no.7, London, 1850. *The Principall Navigations*, London, 1589. Facsimile, Hakluyt Society, extra series no.39, introduction by D.B. Quinn and R.A. Skelton, new idex by A.M. Quinn, 2 vols, Cambridge, 1965. *The Principal Navigations*, 3 vols, London, 1599-1600; Everyman Library, 8 vols, London, 1907. *Virginia Voyages from Hakluyt*, ed. D.B. and A.M. Quinn, London, 1973. *The original writings and correspondence of the two Richard Hakluyts*, ed. E.G.R. Taylor, Hakluyt Society, 2 vols, series 2, nos. 76, 77, London, 1935.

Hamor, Ralph. *A true discourse of the present estate of Virginia and the successe of the affaires there till the 18 of June 1614*, first issue, London 1615; facsimile, Amsterdam and New York, 1971. Reprint, Albany, N.Y., 1860. Second issue, London, 1615; facsimile, Richmond, Va., 1957.

Hampden, John (ed.). *Francis Drake, Privateer: contemporary narratives and documents*, London, 1972.

Hariot, Thomas. *A Briefe and True Report of the New Found Land of Virginia*,

London, 1588. Facsimile, Amsterdam and New York, 1971. In Quinn, *Roanoke Voyages*, and Quinn, *Virginia Voyages*. Republished Frankfurt, 1590 (with engravings from John White). Facsimile, New York, 1972.

Harvey, Gabriel. *Pierces Supererogation*, London, 1593.

Hayes, Edward. 'Report' of 1583 Gilbert Expedition. In Hakluyt, *Principall Navigations*; and Quinn, *Gilbert Voyages*.

Hening, William Waller. *The Statutes at Large; being a collection of all the laws of Virginia* (from 1619), 13 vols, New York, 1823.

Herbert, George. *Works*, ed. F.E. Hutchinson, Oxford, 1941.

Higginson, Francis. *New Englands Plantation*, London, 1630. Force, *Tracts*, I, 12.

Hooker, Richard. *Of the Lawes of Ecclesiasticall Politie*, London, 1593, 1597. Everyman Library, 2 vols, 1907.

Jensen, Merrill (ed.) *American Colonial Documents to 1776* (Vol.IX of the series 'English Historical Documents'), London, 1955.

Jewel, John. *Works*, ed. J. Ayre, 4 vols, Parker Society, Cambridge, 1845-50.

Johnson, Robert. *Nova Britannia. Offering most excellent fruites by Planting in Virginia*, London, 1609; facsimile, Amsterdam and New York, 1969. Force, *Tracts*, I, 6. *The New Life of Virginea*, London, 1612; facsimile, Amsterdam and New York, 1971. Force, *Tracts*, I, 7.

Kingsbury, Susan Myra (ed.). *The Records of the Virginia Company of London*, 4 vols, Washington, D.C.; I and II, 1906; III, 1933; IV, 1935.

Knappen, M.M. (ed.). *Two Elizabethan Puritan Diaries*, Chicago, 1935.

Lane, Ralph. 'Discourse', written 1586. In Hakluyt, *Principall Navigations*; and Quinn, *Roanoke Voyages*.

La Peyrère, Isaac de. *Men before Adam*, London, 1656.

Las Casas, Bartolomé de. *Brevissima relacion de la destruycion de las Indias*, 1552; tr. by 'M.M.S.', *The Spanish Colonie, or Briefe Chronicle of the Acts and gestes of the Spaniards in the West Indies*, London, 1583. Tr. by John Phillips, *The Tears of the Indians*, London, 1656.

Latimer, Hugh. *Sermons and Remains*, ed. G.E. Corrie, Parker Society, Cambridge, 1845.

Lawes Divine Morall and Martiall (for *The Colony in Virginia Britannia*), London, 1612; facsimile, Amsterdam and New York, 1972. Force, *Tracts*, III, 2.

L'Estrange, Hamon. *Americans no Jewes*, London, 1652.

Lever, Thomas. *Sermons*, ed. Edward Arber, London, 1871.

López de Gómara, Francisco de. See 'Gómara'.

Manasseh Ben Israel. *The Hope of Israel*, London, 1650. *To His Highnesse the Lord Protector*, London, 1655.

Mandeville, Sir John. *Travels*, ed. Malcolm Letts, Hakluyt Society, 2 vols, series 2, nos 1001-2, Cambridge, 1953.

Martyr, Peter (Pietro Martire d'Anghiera). *De Orbe Novo Decades*: Decades 1 (1511), 2 and 3 (1516) tr. by Richard Eden, *The Decades of the new worlde*, London, 1555 (see 'Arber'). Decades 4-8 (1530) tr. by M. Lok, for the full translation, *De novo orbe, or the historie of the west Indies*, London, 1612.

Massachusetts. *The Book of the General Lawes and Libertyes concerning the Inhabitants of the Massachusets*. Cambridge, Mass., 1648. Ed. Max Farrand, Cambridge, Mass., 1929.

Mather, Increase. *A Brief Relation of the State of New England*, London, 1689. Force, *Tracts*, IV, 11.

Miller, Perry and T.H. Johnson (eds). *The Puritans: A Sourcebook of their Writings*, New York, 1938. Harper Torchbook, 2 vols, New York, 1963.

Milton, John. *The History of Britain*, ed. French R. Fogle (Yale ed. of Milton's prose), New Haven, 1971. *Prose Writings*, introduction by K.M. Burton, Everyman Library, London, 1958.

Montaigne, Michel de. *Essays*, tr. John Florio, 1603; Dent edition, introduction by Desmond MacCarthy, 3 vols, London, 1928.

More, Sir Thomas. *Utopia*, tr. Ralph Robinson, 1551; 1556 (Everyman Library. 1910; modernised spelling 1951). *Utopia*, Yale More edition ed. E. Surtz and J.H. Hexter, New Haven 1965. *Responsio ad Lutherum*, 1523, Vol.V of Yale edition, ed. J.M. Headley, New Haven, 1969. *The second parte of the confutacion of Tyndals answere*, London, 1533. *English Works*, ed. W. Rastell, London, 1557. *Selected Letters*, ed. E.F. Rogers, New Haven, 1961. *The Essential Thomas More*, ed. J.J. Greene and J.P. Dolan, New York, 1967.

Morton, George (ed.). *A Relation or Journall of the beginning and proceedings of the English Plantation setled at Plimoth* ('G. Mourt'), London, 1622; ed. G.B. Cheever, New York, 1848.

Morton, Nathaniel. *New Englands Memorial*, Cambridge, Mass., 1669. In *Chronicles*, Everyman.

Morton, Thomas. *New English Canaan*, Amsterdam (?) 1637; facsimile, Amsterdam and New York, 1969. Force, *Tracts*, II, 5.

New World, The. A Catalogue of an Exhibition of Books, Maps, Manuscripts and Documents held at Lambeth Palace Library between 1 May and 1 December 1957, together with transcripts of five unpublished Documents in the Library relating to the early history of the American Continent, Lambeth, 1957.

Nuttall, Zelia (ed.). *New Light on Drake: a collection of documents*, Hakluyt Society, series 2, no.34, London, 1914.

Oviedo, Gonzalo Fernández de. *Natural hystoria de las Indias*, 1526, used by Eden in 1555: see 'Eden'. Tr. Sterling A. Stoudemire, *Natural History of the West Indies*, Chapel Hill, N.C., 1959.

Pearce, R.H. (ed.). *Colonial American Writing*, New York, 1950, 1956.

Peckham, Sir George. *A true reporte of the late discoveries of the Newfound Landes*, London, 1583; facsimile, Amsterdam and New York, 1971. In Hakluyt, *Principall Navigations*; and Quinn, *Gilbert Voyages*.

Percy, George. 'Discourse of the Plantation of the Southerne Colonie in Virginia', in Purchas, 1625; and Barbour, *Jamestown Voyages*.

Perfect Description of Virginia, London, 1649. Force, *Tracts*, II, 8.

Perkins, William. *Workes*, ed. W. Crashaw et al., 3 vols, Cambridge, 1608-9.

Porter, H.C. (ed.). *Puritanism in Tudor England*, London and Columbia, S.C., 1970.

Price, Daniel. *Sauls Prohibition staide ... With a reproofe of those that traduce the Honourable Plantation of Virginia*, London, 1609.

Purchas, Samuel. *Hakluytus Posthumus, or Purchas his Pilgrimes*, 4 vols, London 1625. 20 vols, Glasgow, 1905-7.

Quinn, D.B. (ed.). *The Voyages and Colonising Enterprises of Sir Humphrey Gilbert*,

2 vols, Hakluyt Society, series 2, nos. 83, 84, London, 1940. *The Roanoke Voyages, 1584-1590: Documents to Illustrate the English Voyages to North America Under the Patent granted to Walter Raleigh in 1584*, 2 vols, Hakluyt Society, series 2, nos 104, 105, Cambridge, 1955. *Richard Hakluyt, Editor* (followed by facsimiles of Hakluyt's 1582 *Divers Voyages* and Florio's 1580 *A shorte and briefe narration*), Amsterdam, 1967. *North American Discovery, c. 1000-1612*, New York, 1971. See also under 'Hakluyt'.

Quinn, D.B. and Paul H. Hulton (eds). *The American Drawings of John White*, 2 vols, London and Chapel Hill, N.C., 1964.

Quinn, D.B. and N.M. Cheshire (eds and trs). *The New Found Land of Stephen Parmenius*, Toronto, 1972.

Raleigh, Sir Walter. *The Discoverie of the Large, Rich and Bewtiful Empyre of Guiana*, London, 1596; facsimile, Amsterdam and New York, 1968. Ed. V.T. Harlow, London, 1928.

Rich, Richard. *News from Virginia*, London, 1610; facsimile, Amsterdam and New York, 1970. Ed. W.F. Craven, New York, 1937.

Robinson, John. *Works*, ed. R. Ashton, 3 vols, London, 1851.

Rolfe, John. 'A True Relation of the State of Virginia', written 1616, printed by H.C. Taylor; New Haven, 1951.

Rosier, James. *A True Relation of the most prosperous voyage made in the discovery of Virginia*, London, 1605.

Sandys, George (tr.). *Ovid's Metamorphosis*, ed. K.K. Hulley and S.T. Vandersall, Lincoln, Nebr., 1970.

Shakespeare, William. *The Tempest*, ed. Frank Kermode, London, 1954.

Shurtleff, Nathaniel Bradstreet (ed.). *Records of the Governor and Company of the Massachusetts Bay*, Vol. I, Boston, 1853. *Records of the Colony of New Plymouth*, vol. I, Boston, 1855.

Smith, Captain John. *A True Relation of such occurences and accidents of noate as hath hapned in Virginia*, London, 1608; in Barbour, *Jamestown Voyages. A Map of Virginia. With a Description of the Countrey, the Commodities, People, Government and Religion*, Oxford, 1612; facsimile, Amsterdam and New York, 1973; in Barbour, *Jamestown Voyages. A Description of New England*, London, 1616. *New Englands Trials*, London, 1620; facsimile, Amsterdam and New York, 1971. *New Englands Trials, and Present Estate*, London, 1622. *The Generall Historie of Virginia, New-England, and the Summer Isles*, London, 1624. *An Accidence for Young Sea-Men, or The Pathway to Experience*, London, 1626. *Advertisements for the unexperienced Planters of New-England, or any where*, London, 1631.

Complete edition by Edward Arber, 1889: *Travels and Works of Captain John Smith*. Reprinted in two volumes (same paging), with introduction by A.G. Bradley, Edinburgh, 1910. This edition now reprinted, New York, no date. Selections in *Captain John Smith's America: Selections from His Writings*, ed. John Lankford, Harper Torchbook, New York, 1967.

Spelman, Henry. 'Relation of Virginia', written 1613; printed by Henry Stevens, London, 1872, and by Arber, *Works of Smith*, ci-cxiv.

Strachey, William. *The Historie of Travell into Virginia Britania* (written 1612), ed. L.B. Wright and V. Freund, Hakluyt Society, series 2, no.103, London, 1953.

Symonds, William. *Virginia: a sermon preached at Whitechapel in the presence of ... the Adventurers and Planters for Virginia, April 25, 1609*, London, 1609;

facsimile, Amsterdam and New York, 1968. *The Proceedings of the English Colonie in Virginia* (Part II of Smith's *Map of Virginia*), Oxford, 1612.

Tacitus. *On Britain and Germany (Agricola* and *Germania*, tr. H. Mattingly), Penguin Classics, Harmondsworth, 1948.

Thorowgood, Thomas. *Jewes in America*, London, 1650.

True Declaration of the estate of the Colonie in Virginia, London, 1610. Force, *Tracts*, III, 1.

True and Sincere Declaration of the purpose and ends of the Plantation begun in Virginia, London, 1610. Brown, *Genesis*, I, pp.337-53.

Tyndale, William. *Doctrinal Treatises*, ed. H. Walter, Parker Society, Cambridge, 1848.

Vespucci, Amerigo. *Letters*, tr. C.R. Markham, Hakluyt Society, series I, no.90, London, 1894. *Americo Vespucci, El Nuevo Mondo* (texts in Italian, Spanish and English; essay by Roberto Levillier), Buenos Aires, 1951.

Washburn, Wilcomb E. (ed.). *The Indian and the White Man* (1492-1961), New York, 1964.

Waterhouse, Edward. *A Declaration of the State of the Colony in Virginia*, London, 1622. Facsimile, Amsterdam and New York, 1970. Kingsbury, *Records*, III, no. CCX.

Whitaker, Alexander. *Good Newes from Virginia*, London, 1613.

Whitaker, William. *Disputation on the Holy Scripture* (1588) tr. William Fitzgerald, Parker Society, Cambridge, 1849.

Whitgift, John. *Works*, ed. J. Ayre, Parker Society, 3 vols, Cambridge, 1851-3.

Williams, C.H. (ed.) *English Historical Documents*, Vol. V, 1485-1558, London, 1967.

Williamson, J.A. (ed.). *The Cabot Voyages and Bristol Discovery under Henry VII*, Hakluyt Society, series 2, no.120, Cambridge, 1962.

Wingfield, Edward Maria. 'Discourse', written 1608; in Barbour, *Jamestown Voyages*.

Winslow, Edward. *Good News from New England*, London, 1624. In *Chronicles*, Everyman.

Winthrop, Robert C. *Life and Letters of John Winthrop*, 2 vols. Second edition, Boston, 1869.

Wright, Louis B. (ed.). *The Elizabethans' America: a collection of early reports by Englishmen on the New World* (1565-1630), London, 1965.

Wright, L.B. and Elaine W. Fowler (eds). *English Colonisation of North America* (1496-1766). In series 'Documents of Modern History', London, 1968.

2. *Secondary Works*

Allen, Don C. *The Legend of Noah: Renaissance Rationalism in Art, Science, and Letters*, Urbana, Ill., 1949.

Andrews, Charles M. *The Colonial Period of American History*, 4 vols, 1934-8, paperback, New Haven, 1964. *Our Earliest Colonial Settlements*, 1933, paperback, Ithaca, N.Y., 1959.

Ashe, Geoffrey T.L. *Land to the West: St Brendan's voyage to America*, London, 1962.

556 *Bibliography*

Ashe, Geoffrey T.L. (ed.). *The Quest for America*, London, 1971.

Atkinson, Geoffroy. *Les Nouveaux Horizons de la renaissance française*, Paris, 1935.

Babcock, William H. *Legendary Islands of the Atlantic: A Study in Medieval Geography*, New York, 1922.

Bainton, Roland H. *Erasmus of Christendom*, New York, 1969; London, 1970.

Barbour, Philip L. *The Three Worlds of John Smith*, London, 1964. *Pocahontas and her World*, London, 1971.

Baudet, H. *Paradise on Earth: some Thoughts on European Images of Non-European Man*, tr. E. Wentholt, New Haven, Conn., 1965.

Bell, Aubrey F.G. *Sepúlveda*, Oxford, 1925.

Bennett, G.V. and J.D. Walsh (eds). *Essays in Modern English Church History: In memory of Norman Sykes*, London, 1966.

Bercovitch, Sacvan (ed.). *The American Puritan Imagination: Essays in Revaluation*, Cambridge, 1974.

Boas, George. *Essays on Primitivism and Related Ideas in the Middle Ages*, Baltimore, 1948.

Bridenbaugh, Carl. *Mitre and Sceptre: transatlantic faiths, ideas, personalities and politics, 1689-1775*, New York and London, 1962.

Brinkworth, Edwin R.C. *Shakespeare and the Bawdy Court of Stratford*, London, 1972.

Brown, John Russell and Bernard Harris (eds). *Later Shakespeare* (Stratford-upon-Avon Studies 8), London, 1966.

Brydon, George M. *Virginia's Mother Church, 1607-1727*, Richmond, Va., 1947.

Carrington, C.E. *The British Overseas: Exploits of a Nation of Shopkeepers*, Cambridge, 1950.

Carroll, Peter N. *Puritanism and the Wilderness: The Intellectual Significance of the New England Frontier, 1629-1700*, New York, 1969.

Cawley, R.R. *Unpathed Waters: studies in the influence of the voyagers on Elizabethan Literature*, Princeton, 1940.

Cell, Gillian T. *British Enterprise in Newfoundland, 1577-1660*, Toronto, 1969.

Chinard, Gilbert. *L'Exotisme américain dans la littérature française au XVIe siècle*, Paris, 1911.

Clarke, Samuel (ed.). *The Lives of Thirty-two English Divines*, London, 1677.

Cook, Sherburne F. and L.B. Simpson. *The Population of Central Mexico in the Sixteenth Century*, Berkeley and Los Angeles, 1948.

Cooper, C.H. *Annals of Cambridge*, I (to 1546), Cambridge, 1842.

Cooper, C.H. and T. *Athenae Cantabrigienses*, 3 vols, Cambridge, 1858, 1861, 1913.

Costello, William T. *The Scholastic Curriculum at Early Seventeenth-Century Cambridge*, Cambridge, Mass., 1958.

Craven, Wesley Frank. *The Dissolution of the Virginia Company: The Failure of a Colonial Experiment*, New York, 1932. Reprint, Gloucester, Mass., 1964. *The Legend of the Founding Fathers*, Ithaca, N.Y., 1956. *The Colonies in Transition, 1660-1713*, New York, 1968. *White, Red, and Black: The Seventeenth-Century Virginian*, Charlottesville, Va., 1971.

Cremin, Lawrence A. *American Education: the colonial experience, 1607-1783*. New York, 1970.

Culliford, S.G. *William Strachey, 1572-1621*, Charlottesville, Va., 1965.

David, Elizabeth. *Mediterranean Food*, Harmondsworth, 1965.

Deacon, Richard. *Madoc and the Discovery of America: some new light on an old controversy*, London, 1967.

Demos, John. *A Little Commonwealth: Family Life in Plymouth Colony*, New York, 1970.

Dickens, A.G. *The English Reformation*, 1964; revised ed., Fontana Library, London, 1967.

Dillingham, William. *Life* of Laurence Chaderton (1700), tr. E.S. Shuckburgh, Cambridge, 1884.

Dudley, Edward and Maximillian E. Novak (eds). *The Wild Man Within: An Image in Western Thought from the Renaissance to Romanticism*, Pittsburgh, 1972.

Duncan, Joseph E. *Milton's Earthly Paradise: A Historical Study of Eden*, Minneapolis, 1972.

Elliott, John H. *Imperial Spain, 1469-1716*, 1963; Mentor Books, New York, 1966. *The Old World and the New, 1492-1650*, Cambridge, 1970. *The Discovery of America and the Discovery of Man* (1972 Raleigh Lecture), London, 1972.

Elton, G.R. *Studies in Tudor and Stuart Politics and Government: papers and reviews, 1946-1972*, 2 vols, Cambridge, 1974.

Emden, Cecil. S. *Oriel Papers*, Oxford, 1948.

Emmison, F.G. *Elizabethan Life*, Chelmsford, 1970.

Fairchild, H.N. *The Noble Savage: A Study in Romantic Naturalism*, New York, 1928.

Frame, Donald M. *Montaigne's Discovery of Man: the humanization of a humanist*, New York, 1955. *Montaigne: a biography*, London, 1965.

Fuller, Thomas. *The History of the University of Cambridge*, 1655; ed. M. Prickett and T. Wright, Cambridge, 1840.

Gonnard, René. *La Légende du bon sauvage: contribution à l'étude des origines du socialisme*, Paris, 1946.

Gookin, W.F. *Bartholomew Gosnold, discoverer and planter*, ed. P.L. Barbour, Hamden, Conn., 1963.

Greenslade, S.L. (ed.). *The Cambridge History of the Bible: the West from the Reformation to the Present Day*, Cambridge, 1963.

Hanke, Lewis. *The Spanish Struggle for Justice in the Conquest of America*, Philadelphia, 1949. *Las Casas: Bookman, Scholar and Propagandist*, Philadelphia, 1952. *Aristotle and the American Indians: A Study of Race Prejudice in the Modern World*, Chicago, 1959.

Hatch, Charles E. *The First Seventeen Years: Virginia 1607-1624* (Jamestown 350th Anniversary Hist. Booklet), Williamsburg, Va., 1957.

Hawke, David. *The Colonial Experience*, New York, 1966.

Haydn, Hiram. *The Counter-Renaissance*, 1950; reprint, Gloucester, Mass., 1966.

Heizer, Robert F. *Francis Drake and the California Indians, 1579*, Berkeley, 1947.

Hexter, J.H. *The Vision of Politics on the Eve of the Reformation: More, Machiavelli, and Seyssel*, London, 1973.

Highfield, J.R.L. (ed.). *Spain in the Fifteenth Century, 1369-1516*, London, 1972.

Hill, Christopher. *Economic Problems of the Church: From Archbishop Whitgift to the Long Parliament*, Oxford, 1956. *Intellectual Origins of the English*

Revolution, Oxford, 1965. *Antichrist in Seventeenth-Century England*, London, 1971.

Hodgen, Margaret T. *Early Anthropology in the Sixteenth and Seventeenth Centuries*, Philadelphia, 1964.

Hoffman, Bernard A. *Cabot to Cartier*, Toronto, 1961.

Holmes, Pauline. *A Tercentenary History of the Boston Public Latin School, 1635-1935*, Cambridge, Mass., 1935.

Huddleston, Lee E. *Origins of the American Indians: European Concepts, 1492-1729*, Austin, Texas, 1967.

Huizinga, Johan. *Erasmus of Rotterdam*, tr. F. Hopman, 1924; London, 1952, with a selection from the letters of Erasmus, tr. Barbara Flower, and a preface by G.N. Clark. American title of this edition, *Erasmus and the Age of Reformation*, Harper Torchbook, New York, 1957.

James, D.G. *The Dream of Prospero*, Oxford, 1967.

Jones, E.D. *The Elizabethan Image of Africa* (Folger Booklet), Charlottesville, Va., 1971.

Jordan, Winthrop D. *White Over Black: American Attitudes Toward the Negro, 1550-1812*, Chapel Hill, N.C., 1968; Pelican Books, Baltimore, 1969.

Kellaway, William. *The New England Company, 1649-1776: Missionary Society to the American Indians*, London, 1961.

Kennedy, J.H. *Jesuit and Savage in New France*, New Haven, 1950.

Lacey, Robert. *Sir Walter Ralegh*, London, 1973.

Langdon, George D. *Pilgrim Colony: A history of New Plymouth, 1620-91*, New Haven, Conn., 1966.

Leach, Douglas E. *Flintlock and Tomahawk: New England in King Philip's War*, New York, 1958.

Levin, Harry. *The Myth of the Golden Age in the Renaissance*. Bloomington, Ind., 1969.

Levy, Babette M. 'Puritanism in the Southern Island Colonies'. *Proceedings American Antiquarian Soc.*, vol.70, pt.1, 1960, pp.69-348.

Little, David. *Religion, Order and Law: A Study in Pre-Revolutionary England*, New York, 1969; Oxford, 1970.

Lovejoy, A.O. and G. Boas. *Primitivism and Related Ideas in Antiquity*, Baltimore, 1935.

McCary, Benjamin C. *Indians in Seventeenth Century Virginia* (Jamestown 350th Anniversary Hist. Booklet), Williamsburg, Va., 1957.

McLean, Antonia. *Humanism and the Rise of Science in Tudor England*, London, 1972.

McKisack, May. *Medieval History in the Tudor Age*, Oxford, 1971.

MacNutt, Francis A. *Bartholomew de Las Casas: His Life, His Apostolate, and His Writings*, New York, 1909.

Madariaga, Salvador de. *Christopher Columbus*, London, 1939.

Maltby, William S. *The Black Legend in England: the development of anti-Spanish sentiment, 1558-1660*, Durham, N.C., 1971.

Miller, Perry. *Errand into the Wilderness*, Cambridge, Mass., 1956.

Morison, Samuel Eliot. *The Founding of Harvard College*, Cambridge, Mass., 1935. *Harvard College in the Seventeenth Century*, 2 vols, Cambridge, Mass., 1936. *Three Centuries of Harvard*, Cambridge, Mass., 1937. *Christopher*

Columbus, Mariner, London, 1956. *The European Discovery of America: The Northern Voyages, A.D. 500-1600*, New York, 1971; *The Southern Voyages, A.D. 1492-1616*, New York, 1974.

Nash, Gary B. *Red, White, and Black: The peoples of early America*, Englewood Cliffs, N.J., 1974.
Nash, Roderick. *Wilderness and the American Mind*, New Haven, Conn., 1967.
Nicolson, Marjorie. *Science and Imagination*, Ithaca, N.Y., 1956.

O'Gorman, Edmundo. *The Invention of America: an inquiry into the historical nature of the New World and the meaning of its history*, Bloomington, Ind., 1961.

Parry, J.H. *The Age of Reconnaissance*, 1963; Mentor, New York, 1964. *The Spanish Seaborne Empire*, London, 1966.
Pearce, Roy H. *The Savages of America: A Study of the Indian and the Idea of Civilisation*, Baltimore, 1953.
Pomfret, John E. with Floyd M. Shumway. *Founding the American Colonies, 1583-1660*, Harper Torchbook, New York, 1971.
Porter, H.C. *Reformation and Reaction in Tudor Cambridge*, Cambridge, 1959; Hamden, Conn., 1972.
Powell, William S. *Paradise Preserved: A History of the Roanoke Island Historical Association*, Chapel Hill, N.C., 1965.
Prowse, Daniel W. *A History of Newfoundland*, London, 1895.

Quinn, D.B. *Raleigh and the British Empire*, 2nd ed., London, 1962. *The Elizabethans and the Irish*, Folger Monograph, Ithaca, N.Y., 1966. *England and the Discovery of America, 1481-1620*, London, 1974.
Quinn, D.G. (ed.) *The Hakluyt Handbook*, 2 vols, Hakluyt Society, series 2, -nos. 144-5, Cambridge, 1974.
Quinn, D.B., W.P. Cumming, and R.A. Skelton. *The Discovery of North America*, London, 1971.

Rabb, Theodore K. *Enterprise and Empire: Merchant and Gentry Investment in the Expansion of England, 1575-1630*, Cambridge, Mass., 1967.
Reed, Arthur W. *Early Tudor Drama: Medwall, the Rastells, Heywood, and the More Circle*, London, 1926.
Rowse, A.L. *The Expansion of Elizabethan England*, London, 1955. *The Elizabethans and America*, London, 1959.
Rutman, Darrett B. *American Puritanism*, 2nd printing, Philadelphia, 1970.

Sanders, Charles R. *The Strachey Family, 1588-1932*, Durham, N.C., 1953.
Sayce, Richard R. *The Essays of Montaigne: A Critical Exploration*, London, 1972.
Shirley, John W. (ed.). *Thomas Harriot: Renaissance Scientist*, Oxford, 1974.
Sibley, John L. *Harvard Graduates (Biographical Sketches of Graduates of Harvard University)*, Vol. I, 1642-1658, Cambridge, Mass., 1873.
Slessarev, Vsevolod. *Prester John: The Letter and the Legend*, Minneapolis, 1959.
Smith, James Morton, (ed.) *Seventeenth-Century America: Essays in Colonial History*, Chapel Hill, N.C., 1959.
Sterry, Wasey. *Annals of the King's College of our Lady of Eton*, London, 1898. *The Eton College Register, 1441-1698*, Eton, 1943.

Stevens, Henry. *Thomas Hariot*, London, 1900.
Sylvester, Richard S. (ed.). *St Thomas More: Action and Contemplation*, New Haven, Conn., 1972.

Thompson, Roger. *Women in Stuart England and America: A Comparative Study*, London, 1974.

Vaughan, Alden, T. *New England Frontier: Puritans and Indians, 1620-1675*, Boston, 1965.
Ver Steeg, Clarence L. *The Formative Years, 1607-1763* ('The Making of America' series), London, 1965.

Wagner, Henry R. *Drake's Voyage round the World*, San Francisco, 1926.
Wagner, Henry R., and H.R. Parish. *The Life and Writings of Bartolomé de las Casas*, Albuquerque, N. Mexico, 1967.
Washburn, Wilcomb E. *Virginia under Charles I and Cromwell, 1625-1660* (Jamestown 350th Anniversary Hist. Booklet), Williamsburg, 1957. *Red Man's Land, White Man's Law: a study of the past and present status of the American Indian*, New York, 1971.
Williams, George H. *Wilderness and Paradise in Christian Thought*, New York, 1962.
Williamson, James A. *The Voyages of the Cabots and the English Discovery of North America under Henry VII and Henry VIII*, London, 1929.
Wright, Louis B. *The First Gentlemen of Virginia: Intellectual Qualities of the Early Colonial Ruling Class*, San Marino, Cal., 1940. *The Colonial Civilisation of North America, 1607-1763*, London, 1949 (American title, *The Atlantic Frontier*, 1947). *The Cultural Life of the Amerian Colonies, 1607-1763*, New York, 1957; Harper Torchbook, New York, 1962.
Wroth, Lawrence C. *The Voyages of Giovanni da Verrazzano, 1524-1528*, New Haven, Conn., 1970.

Yates, Frances A. *John Florio*, Cambridge, 1934.

Ziff, Larzer. *Puritanism in America: New Culture in a New World*, New York and London, 1973.

INDEX

Index

Abbot, Archbishop George. And Emden separatists, 421; Virginia Company, 396, 410, 451, 476. On Atlantis, 44-5; Columbus offer to Henry VII, 214; Drake in California, 187; Virginia in 1599, 254, 259; Spanish atrocities, 173-4; missions, 118; Brownists, 476; negroes and moors, 366-7, 417n; Indians, 129-30

Abraham. 98, 99, 114, 351, 357

Abyssinia, kingdom of. 52-3

Acosta, José de. 332, 333, 537

Acts of the Apostles. On Christian witness, 118, 358. Influence on *Utopia*, 72-3

Adam. 43, 48, 92, 94, 97, 126, 306, 491

Adams, John (1621). 484

Adams, Henry. 293

Adoni-Bezek. 108

Adrian VI, Pope. 88

Adultery, Indian attitude to. 205, 398, 497

Aeschines (Athenian orator). 133

Africa. 1510 *New Lands* on. 38, 39; Gilbert on, 51; Abbot on, 45. Prester John in, 52; evangelism in, 127. Ham and, 93. *See also* blackness, negroes.

Agincourt, battle of. 368

Ahaziah, king of Israel. 178

Ahone, Indian god. 333-4

Ai, Old Testament city. 108

Ailly, Pierre d'. 97

Ainsworth, Henry. 259

Albemarle Sound, N.C. 224

Albion, giant son of Neptune. 189

Alcalá de Henares, Spain. 167, 169, 175

Alexander Severus, emperor. 537

Alexander the Great. 147, 349

Alexander VI, Pope. 157, 180

Alexandria, Egypt. 42, 53, 55

Alfred, Saxon king. 41, 52, 474

Allerton, Remember. 423

Alvey, Henry. 361-2

Amadas, Philip. 224, 231

'Amadis de Gaula'. 49

Amalek (Deuteronomy). 502

Amaziah, king of Judah. 178

Ambrose, St. 43, 135

America. Discovery of, Gómara on, 50. Naming of, 12, 13, 37. As separate continent, 13, 51; New World, 11-12, 13, 35, 44, 45, 47, 48, 49, 52, 78, 116, 146, 154, 309, 486, 539; Azareth (II Esdras), 95; religious asylum, 140-1, 199, 259. *See also* New Found Land, Virginia.

Ames, William. 337n

Amherst Island (Magdalen Islands). 259

Ammon (Ammonites). 109, 357

Anabaptists. 77, 350

Anak (inhabitant of Palestine). 100, 344

Anangula (Aleutian Islands). 96n

Ananias. 505

Andrewes, Bishop Lancelot. 478

Andrews, Charles M. 411

Angera (Anghiera, Angleria). 19, 25

Anne of Denmark, queen of James I. 151, 386, 432

Apocrypha, text and interpretations. II Esdras, 94-6, 97; Wisdom of Solomon, 119-20; Ecclesiasticus, 155

Apollo. 498

Appomattoc, village. 284, 288

Arber, Edward. 13

Arcadia. 45, 194

Archer, Gabriel. St John's Cambridge, 343, 381; 1602 voyage, 265, 266; 1606 voyage, 282; 1609 voyage, 304, 305. Smith on, 298. 'Description of Virginia', 78, 284, 286, 287, 305, 310-11.

Argall, Samuel. Early career, 304. 1609 voyage, 304, 305. Governor in Virginia, 303, 410. Indian policy (1614), 400, 401, 408; (1618), 414. And Spelman, 313, 315; Pocahontas, 406, 408; puritans, 421; Sandys, 477

Aristophanes. 67

Aristotle. 20, 52, 66, 168, 170, 474

'Armenica'. 18, 38, 53

Arrohattoc, village. 287

Arundel, Peter. 468